T0331721

Designs from Linear Codes
Second Edition

Designs from Linear Codes

Second Edition

Cunsheng Ding
The Hong Kong University of Science
and Technology, Hong Kong

Chunming Tang
China West Normal University, China

NEW JERSEY · LONDON · SINGAPORE · BEIJING · SHANGHAI · HONG KONG · TAIPEI · CHENNAI · TOKYO

Published by

World Scientific Publishing Co. Pte. Ltd.

5 Toh Tuck Link, Singapore 596224

USA office: 27 Warren Street, Suite 401-402, Hackensack, NJ 07601

UK office: 57 Shelton Street, Covent Garden, London WC2H 9HE

British Library Cataloguing-in-Publication Data
A catalogue record for this book is available from the British Library.

DESIGNS FROM LINEAR CODES
Second Edition

ISBN 978-981-125-132-0 (hardcover)
ISBN 978-981-125-133-7 (ebook for institutions)
ISBN 978-981-125-134-4 (ebook for individuals)

For any available supplementary material, please visit
https://www.worldscientific.com/worldscibooks/10.1142/12697#t=suppl

Printed in Singapore

Preface

Since the publication of the first edition of this monograph, the following advances on constructing combinatorial t-designs with linear codes have been made:

- A generalization of the Assmus-Mattson theorem for linear codes over finite fields [Tang, Ding and Xiong (2019)].
- The discovery of an infinite family of near MDS codes over finite fields supporting an infinite family of 2-designs [Ding and Tang (2020)].
- The discovery of an infinite family of BCH codes over GF(2^{2m+1}) of length $2^{2m+1} + 1$ supporting an infinite family of 4-designs [Tang and Ding (2021)].

These advances are the main motivation for the second edition of this monograph.

The Assmus-Mattson theorem was developed in 1969, and has been used to construct many infinite families of 2-designs and 3-designs in the past 50 years. However, some infinite families of linear codes do support t-designs, but the t-design property of the incidence structures defined by the linear codes cannot be proved with the Assmus-Mattson theorem and the automorphism group of the codes. In the past 50 years, a strengthening of the Assmus-Mattson theorem for special binary linear codes was documented in Calderbank, Delsarte and Sloane (1991) and several analogues of the Assmus-Mattson theorem in other contexts (for example, certain association schemes [Morales and Tanaka (2018)], codes over $\mathbb{Z}_4$ [Tanabe (2000)], and rank-metric codes [Byrne and Ravagnani (2019)]) were developed. The Assmus-Mattson theorem for matroids developed in Britz, Royle and Shiromoto (2009) does contain the original Assmus-Mattson theorem as a special case, but it becomes the Assmus-Mattson theorem when it is applied to codes. The generalized Assmus-Mattson theorem for linear codes over finite fields developed in Tang, Ding and Xiong (2019) turns out to be useful, and will be the topic of a new chapter in this second edition.

It is well-known that MDS codes support only trivial designs (i.e., complete designs), which are not interesting. The Golay ternary code with parameters $[11,6,5]$ is near MDS and supports a 4-design. It had been a 70-year-old open question whether there is an infinite family of near MDS codes over finite fields supporting an infinite family of 2-designs. Similarly, it was open for 71 years whether there is an infinite family of linear codes supporting an infinite family of 4-designs. The breakthroughs regarding these two open problems will be the main topic of another new chapter in this second edition.

In addition to the breakthroughs mentioned above, other progresses on designs from linear codes have been also made in the past three years. Based on these progresses, some chapters in the first addition were revised and new references were added.

In this second edition, a new appendix (named Appendix C) has been added. Appendix C gives a quick introduction to elementary number theory, groups, rings and finite fields, and provides a lot of exercises on these topics. Postgraduates and advanced undergraduates are advised to read the materials carefully and solve the problems in Appendix C before reading other parts of this book. Another new appendix (named Appendix A) was also added for reporting some new sporadic 4-designs and 5-designs supported by some sporadic linear codes. In this second edition, notes are added at the end of most of the chapters for providing further information on the topics covered in the chapters.

We are very grateful to Dr. Yan Hong Ng, Dr. K. K. Phua and Ms. Kim Tan of World Scientific for helping us with the publication of this second edition. We acknowledge the financial support of the Hong Kong Research Grants Council, under Proj. No. 16300418.

Cunsheng Ding
Chunming Tang
Fall 2021

Preface to the First Edition

Linear codes and t-designs are companions. On one hand, the incidence matrix of a t-design generates a linear code over any finite field GF(q). On the other hand, the supports of codewords of a fixed Hamming weight in a code may form a t-design under certain conditions. Interplay between coding theory and the theory of t-designs has been a very interesting topic for combinatorialists and coding theorists, and has been treated to some extent in a few monographs and textbooks on coding theory and combinatorics. The purpose of this monograph is to give a comprehensive treatment of t-designs from linear codes. A special feature of this monograph is the attention to the determination of the parameters of t-designs held in linear codes.

The determination of the weight distributions of linear codes is an extremely difficult problem in general, and is much more difficult than that of the minimum weights of linear codes. The settlement of the parameters of t-designs held in a linear code over GF(q) is even harder when $q > 2$. A strong motivation of this monograph is the recent advance in the determination of the weight distributions of many families of linear codes. This monograph is a strong demonstration of the usefulness of the weight distributions of linear codes.

One may question the motivation of explicitly constructing designs with small strength. Our interest in explicit designs with small strength comes from the fact that they may yield linear codes with very good parameters, which could be very attractive in both theory and practice, although this monograph deals little with the linear codes of designs.

This monograph studies t-designs mainly from linear codes over finite fields. A few families of nonlinear codes do yield 3-designs. They include Goethals codes, Kerdock codes, and some extended perfect codes. The reader is referred to Tonchev (2007) for further information on designs from these families of nonlinear codes. Several families of t-designs have been constructed from codes over

vii

$\mathbb{Z}_4$. Information about these designs could be found in Helleseth, Rong and Yang (2001). These are the designs missing from this book.

In this monograph, we pay much more attention to infinite families of designs than sporadic designs. Therefore, we will not treat Mathieu groups, which are the automorphism groups of some linear codes and t-designs.

This book is intended to be a reference for postgraduates and researchers in the areas of combinatorics, coding theory and communications engineering. The reader is assumed to have the basic knowledge of linear algebra and finite fields. Nevertheless, some mathematical foundations are recalled and summarized in Chapter 1. In many places, proofs of some results are omitted. In this case, a reference of such result is given, so that the reader could find a proof.

I am indebted to Professor Vladimir D. Tonchev for beneficial discussions on interplay between t-designs and linear codes. I am grateful to my co-authors for collaborations on coding theory, combinatorics and cryptography as well as related topics. I thank Xiran Ai, Dr. Don Mak, Dr. K. K. Phua, and Ning Tu at the Word Scientific for their assistance with the publication of this monograph.

Cunsheng Ding
Hong Kong
Spring 2018

Contents

Chapter 1

Mathematical Foundations

It is impossible to introduce combinatorial designs and linear codes without basic tools in certain mathematical areas. In this chapter, we give a brief introduction to cyclotomy, finite geometry, group actions, group algebra, finite fields, special functions, and sequences, which are the foundations of other chapters. Before reading this chapter, one may study the materials and solve the problems covered in Appendix C, for getting familiar with elementary number theory, group theory, ring theory and finite fields.

1.1 The Rings $\mathbb{Z}_n$

We start with Euler's totient function $\phi(n)$. For every positive integer $n \geq 1$, $\phi(n)$ is defined to be the number of integers a such that $\gcd(a,n) = 1$, where $1 \leq a < n$. This function has the properties summarised in the following theorem.

Theorem 1.1.

(1) For any prime p and positive integer k, $\phi(p^k) = p^{k-1}(p-1)$.

(2) If m, $n \geq 1$ and $\gcd(m,n) = 1$, then $\phi(mn) = \phi(m)\phi(n)$, that is, ϕ is a multiplicative function.

(3) For any integer with the canonical factorization $n = \prod_{i=1}^{t} p_i^{k_i}$, $\phi(n) = \prod_{i=1}^{t} p_i^{k_i-1}(p_i - 1)$, where t and k_i are positive integers, and $p_1, p_2, \cdots, p_t$ are pairwise distinct primes.

An integer g is called a *primitive root* of (or modulo) n if $\mathrm{ord}_n(g) = \phi(n)$, where $\mathrm{ord}_n(g)$ denotes the multiplicative order of g modulo n. If $g \equiv g' \pmod{n}$, then g is a primitive root of n if and only if g' is a primitive root of n.

Throughout this monograph, $\mathbb{Z}_n = \{0, 1, 2, \ldots, n-1\}$, which denotes the ring of integers modulo n, and $\mathbb{Z}_n^*$ consists of all the units of the ring $\mathbb{Z}_n$. Hence, $\mathbb{Z}_n^*$ is a multiplicative group of order $\phi(n)$.

For any subset D of $\mathbb{Z}_n$, the *Hall polynomial* of D is defined by

$$D(x) = \sum_{i \in D} x^i,$$

which can be viewed as a polynomial over any ring or field, depending on the specific application under consideration.

1.2   Finite Fields

In this section, we introduce necessary notation and basic results of finite fields without providing proofs. The reader is referred to Lidl and Niederreiter (1997) for a proof, and Appendix C for mastering the theory of finite fields quickly.

1.2.1   *Introduction to Finite Fields*

A *field* is a set $\mathbb{F}$ associated with two operations: $+$, called addition, and $\cdot$, called multiplication, which satisfy the following axioms. The set $\mathbb{F}$ is an abelian group under $+$ with additive identity called zero and denoted 0; the set $\mathbb{F}^*$ of all nonzero elements of $\mathbb{F}$ is also an abelian group under multiplication with multiplicative identity called one and denoted 1; and multiplication distributes over addition. For convenience, we will usually omit the symbol for multiplication and write ab for the product $a \cdot b$. The field is *finite* if $\mathbb{F}$ has a finite number of elements; the number of elements in $\mathbb{F}$ is called the order of $\mathbb{F}$. We will denote a field with q elements by $GF(q)$. If p is a prime, the integers modulo p form a field, which is then denoted $GF(p)$. These are the simplest examples of finite fields.

Two fields $\mathbb{F}_1$ and $\mathbb{F}_2$ are *isomorphic* if there is a bijection ψ from $\mathbb{F}_1$ to $\mathbb{F}_2$ such that

(1) $\psi(a+b) = \psi(a) + \psi(b)$ for all $a, b \in \mathbb{F}_1$;
(2) $\psi(ab) = \psi(a)\psi(b)$ for all $a, b \in \mathbb{F}_1$; and
(3) $\psi(0) = 0, \psi(1) = 1$.

It is known that all finite fields with the same number of elements are isomorphic [Lidl and Niederreiter (1997)][Theorem 2.5]. Let $GF(q)$ be a finite field with q elements. The following is a list of basic properties of the finite field $GF(q)$ [Lidl and Niederreiter (1997)][Chapters 1 and 2].

- $q = p^m$ for some prime p and some positive integer m, and p is called the *characteristic* of $GF(q)$.
- $GF(q)$ contains $GF(p)$ as a subfield.
- $GF(q)$ is a vector space over $GF(p)$ of dimension m.

- Every subfield of GF(q) has order p^t for some integer t dividing m.
- The multiplicative group GF(q)* of nonzero elements of GF(q) is cyclic. A generator of the multiplicative group GF(q)* is called a *primitive element* of GF(q).

Let GF(q^m) be an extension of GF(q) and let $a \in$ GF(q^m). It is a basic property that $a^{q^m} = a$. The monic polynomial $f(x) \in$ GF(q)$[x]$ such that $f(a) = 0$ with the least degree is called the *minimal polynomial* of a over GF(q) and is denoted by $\mathbb{M}_a(x)$. Clearly, $\mathbb{M}_a(x)$ is a divisor of $x^{q^m} - x$. It is straightforward to prove that the minimal polynomial of a over GF(q) is unique and irreducible over GF(q).

1.2.2 Traces, Norms, and Bases

Let GF(q^m) be an extension of GF(q) and let $a \in$ GF(q^m). The elements $a, a^q, a^{q^2}, \ldots, a^{q^{m-1}}$ are called the *conjugates* of a with respect to GF(q).

The *trace function* from GF(q^m) to GF(q) is defined by

$$\mathrm{Tr}_{q^m/q}(x) = x + x^q + x^{q^2} + \cdots + x^{q^{m-1}}.$$

When q is prime, $\mathrm{Tr}_{q^m/q}(x)$ is called the *absolute trace* of x.

The following theorem summarizes basic properties of the trace function $\mathrm{Tr}_{q^m/q}(x)$.

Theorem 1.2. *The trace function* $\mathrm{Tr}_{q^m/q}(x)$ *has the following properties:*

(a) $\mathrm{Tr}_{q^m/q}(x+y) = \mathrm{Tr}_{q^m/q}(x) + \mathrm{Tr}_{q^m/q}(y)$ *for all* $x, y \in$ GF(q^m).
(b) $\mathrm{Tr}_{q^m/q}(cx) = c\mathrm{Tr}_{q^m/q}(x)$ *for all* $x \in$ GF(q^m) *and all* $c \in$ GF(q).
(c) $\mathrm{Tr}_{q^m/q}$ *is a linear transformation from* GF(q^m) *to* GF(q)*, when both* GF(q^m) *and* GF(q) *are viewed as vector spaces over* GF(q).
(d) *Every linear transformation from* GF(q^m) *to* GF(q) *can be expressed as* $\mathrm{Tr}_{q^m/q}(ax)$ *for some* $a \in$ GF(q^m).
(e) $\mathrm{Tr}_{q^m/q}(a) = ma$ *for all* $a \in$ GF(q).
(f) $\mathrm{Tr}_{q^m/q}(x^q) = \mathrm{Tr}_{q^m/q}(x)$ *for all* $x \in$ GF(q^m).

The *norm* $\mathrm{N}_{q^m/q}(a)$ of an element $a \in$ GF(q^m) is defined by

$$\mathrm{N}_{q^m/q}(a) = a^{(q^m-1)/(q-1)}.$$

It follows that $\mathrm{N}_{q^m/q}(a)$ is always an element of GF(q).

The following theorem summarizes basic properties of the norm function $\mathrm{N}_{q^m/q}(x)$.

Theorem 1.3. *The norm function* $\mathrm{N}_{q^m/q}(x)$ *has the following properties:*

(i) $N_{q^m/q}(xy) = N_{q^m/q}(x)N_{q^m/q}(y)$ *for all* $x, y \in GF(q^m)$.

(ii) $N_{q^m/q}$ *maps* $GF(q^m)$ *onto* $GF(q)$ *and* $GF(q^m)^*$ *onto* $GF(q)^*$.

(iii) $N_{q^m/q}(a) = a^m$ *for all* $a \in GF(q)$.

(iv) $N_{q^m/q}(x^q) = N_{q^m/q}(x)$ *for all* $x \in GF(q^m)$.

Two bases $\{\alpha_1, \ldots, \alpha_m\}$ and $\{\beta_1, \ldots, \beta_m\}$ of $GF(q^m)$ over $GF(q)$ are said to be *dual basis* if for $1 \le i, j \le m$ we have

$$\text{Tr}_{q^m/q}(\alpha_i\beta_j) = \begin{cases} 0 & \text{if } i \ne j, \\ 1 & \text{if } i = j. \end{cases}$$

For any basis $\{\alpha_1, \ldots, \alpha_m\}$ of $GF(q^m)$ over $GF(q)$, it can be easily proved that there exists a dual basis $\{\beta_1, \ldots, \beta_m\}$.

Let α be a primitive element of $GF(q^m)$. Then $\{1, \alpha, \alpha^2, \ldots, \alpha^{m-1}\}$ is called a *polynomial basis* of $GF(q^m)$ over $GF(q)$.

A basis of $GF(q^m)$ over $GF(q)$ of the form $\{\beta, \beta^q, \beta^{q^2}, \ldots, \beta^{q^{m-1}}\}$ is called a *normal basis*. It is known that there exists a normal basis of $GF(q^m)$ over $GF(q)$ [Lidl and Niederreiter (1997)][Theorem 2.35].

1.2.3   *Field Automorphisms*

In field theory, a *field automorphism* is an automorphism of the algebraic structure of a field, that is, a bijective function from the field onto itself which respects the field operations of addition and multiplication.

Let $GF(q^m)$ be an extension of $GF(q)$. By an *automorphism* σ of $GF(q^m)$ over $GF(q)$, we mean an automorphism of $GF(q^m)$ that fixes the elements of $GF(q)$. Thus, in detail, we require that σ be a one-to-one mapping from $GF(q^m)$ to itself with $\sigma(x+y) = \sigma(x) + \sigma(y)$ and $\sigma(xy) = \sigma(x)\sigma(y)$ for all $x, y \in GF(q^m)$ and $\sigma(z) = z$ for all $z \in GF(q)$. The following theorem is well known [Lidl and Niederreiter (1997)][p. 53].

Theorem 1.4. *The distinct automorphisms of* $GF(q^m)$ *over* $GF(q)$ *are the mappings* σ_j *defined by* $\sigma_j(x) = x^{q^j}$, *where* $0 \le j \le m-1$.

1.2.4   *Additive and Multiplicative Characters*

Let A be a finite abelian group (written multiplicatively) of order $|A|$ with identity 1_A. A *character* χ of A is a homomorphism from A into the multiplicative group U of complex numbers of absolute value 1, i.e.,

$$\chi(a_1a_2) = \chi(a_1)\chi(a_2)$$

for all $a_1, a_2 \in A$.

For any finite abelian group A, we have the *trivial* (also called *principal*) character χ_0 defined by $\chi_0(a) = 1$ for all $a \in A$. All other characters of A are *nontrivial* or *nonprincipal*. For each character χ of A, its *conjugate* $\overline{\chi}$ is defined by $\overline{\chi}(a) = \overline{\chi(a)}$. Given any finitely many characters $\chi_1, \ldots, \chi_t$ of A, we define their product character $\chi_1 \cdots \chi_t$ by

$$(\chi_1 \cdots \chi_t)(a) = \chi_1(a) \cdots \chi_t(a)$$

for all $a \in A$. If $\chi_1 = \cdots = \chi_t = \chi$, we write χ^t for $\chi_1 \cdots \chi_t$. It is easily seen that the set $A^\wedge$ of all characters of A form an abelian group under this multiplication of characters. The *order* of a character χ is the least positive integer ℓ such that $\chi^\ell = \chi_0$.

Example 1.5. Let A be a finite cyclic group of order n. Let a be a generator of A. For any fixed integer j with $0 \le j \le n - 1$, define

$$\chi_j(a^k) = e^{2\pi\sqrt{-1}jk/n}, \quad k = 0, 1, \ldots, n - 1.$$

Then χ_j is a character of A. On the other hand, the set $\{\chi_0, \chi_1, \ldots, \chi_{n-1}\}$ contains all characters of A.

Let p be the characteristic of $\mathrm{GF}(q)$. Then the prime field of $\mathrm{GF}(q)$ is $\mathrm{GF}(p)$, which is identified with $\mathbb{Z}_p$. The function χ_1 defined by

$$\chi_1(x) = e^{2\pi\sqrt{-1}\mathrm{Tr}_{q/p}(x)/p} \text{ for all } x \in \mathrm{GF}(q)$$

is a character of the additive group of $\mathrm{GF}(q)$, and is called the *canonical character* of $\mathrm{GF}(q)$. For any $b \in \mathrm{GF}(q)$, the function defined by $\chi_b(x) = \chi_1(bx)$ is a character of $(\mathrm{GF}(q), +)$. On the other hand, every character of $(\mathrm{GF}(q), +)$ can be expressed as $\chi_b(x)$ for some $b \in \mathrm{GF}(q)$. These $\chi_b(x)$ are called *additive characters* of $\mathrm{GF}(q)$.

Since the multiplicative group $\mathrm{GF}(q)^*$ is cyclic, by Example 1.5, all the characters of the multiplicative group $\mathrm{GF}(q)^*$ are given by

$$\psi_j(a^k) = e^{2\pi\sqrt{-1}jk/(q-1)}, \quad k = 0, 1, \ldots, q - 2,$$

where $0 \le j \le q - 2$ and a is a generator of $\mathrm{GF}(q)^*$. These ψ_j are called *multiplicative character* of $\mathrm{GF}(q)$, and form a group of order $q - 1$ with identity element ψ_0. When q is odd, the character $\psi_{(q-1)/2}$ is called the *quadratic character* of $\mathrm{GF}(q)$, and is usually denoted by η. In other words, the quadratic character is defined by

$$\eta(x) = \left(\frac{x}{q}\right),$$

the Legendre symbol from elementary number theory when q is a prime.

1.2.5 *Several Types of Character Sums*

Let ψ be a multiplicative and χ an additive character of $GF(q)$. Then the Gaussian sum is defined by

$$G(\psi, \chi) = \sum_{x \in GF(q)^*} \psi(x)\chi(x).$$

The following theorem will be useful in later chapters and its proof can be found in Lidl and Niederreiter (1997)[Theorem 5.11].

Theorem 1.6. *Let ψ be a multiplicative and χ an additive character of $GF(q)$. The Gaussian sum satisfies*

$$G(\psi, \chi) = \begin{cases} q-1 & \text{if } \psi = \psi_0, \ \chi = \chi_0, \\ -1 & \text{if } \psi = \psi_0, \ \chi \neq \chi_0, \\ 0 & \text{if } \psi \neq \psi_0, \ \chi = \chi_0, \end{cases}$$

where ψ_0 and χ_0 are the trivial multiplicative and additive character of $GF(q)$, respectively.

If $\psi \neq \psi_0$ and $\chi \neq \chi_0$, then

$$|G(\psi, \chi)| = \sqrt{q}.$$

For certain special characters, the associated Gaussian sums can be evaluated explicitly. The following theorem will be needed in subsequent chapters and its proof can be found in Lidl and Niederreiter (1997)[Theorem 5.15].

Theorem 1.7. *Let $q = p^s$, where p is an odd prime and s is a positive integer. Let η be the quadratic character of $GF(q)$, and let χ_1 be the canonical additive character of $GF(q)$. Then*

$$G(\eta, \chi_1) = \begin{cases} (-1)^{s-1}\sqrt{q} & \text{if } p \equiv 1 \pmod 4, \\ (-1)^{s-1}(\sqrt{-1})^s\sqrt{q} & \text{if } p \equiv 3 \pmod 4. \end{cases}$$

Since $G(\psi, \chi_b) = \bar{\psi}(b)G(\psi, \chi_1)$, we just consider $G(\psi, \chi_1)$, briefly denoted as $G(\psi)$, in the sequel. If $\psi \neq \psi_0$, then

$$|G(\psi)| = q^{1/2}. \tag{1.1}$$

Certain types of character sums can be evaluated exactly. The following two theorems describe such cases [Lidl and Niederreiter (1997)][Theorems 5.33 and 5.35].

Theorem 1.8. *Let χ be a nontrivial additive character of $GF(q)$ with q odd, and let $f(x) = a_2 x^2 + a_1 x + a_0 \in GF(q)[x]$ with $a_2 \neq 0$. Then*

$$\sum_{c \in GF(q)} \chi(f(c)) = \chi\left(a_0 - a_1^2 (4a_2)^{-1}\right) \eta(a_2) G(\eta, \chi),$$

where η is the quadratic character of $GF(q)$.

Theorem 1.9. *Let* $\chi_b(x) = \chi_1(bx)$, *where* χ_1 *is the canonical additive character of* GF(q) *with q even and* $b \in$ GF(q)*. *Let* $f(x) = a_2 x^2 + a_1 x + a_0 \in$ GF(q)$[x]$. *Then*

$$\sum_{c \in \mathrm{GF}(q)} \chi_b(f(c)) = \begin{cases} \chi_b(a_0) & \text{if } a_2 = ba_1^2, \\ 0 & \text{otherwise.} \end{cases}$$

In many cases it is difficult to evaluate character sums, and thus necessary to develop tight bounds on the absolute value of the character sums. An example of such bounds is the Weil bound given in the following theorem [Lidl and Niederreiter (1997)][Theorem 5.37].

Theorem 1.10 (Weil bound). *Let* $f \in$ GF(q)$[x]$ *be of degree* $e \geq 1$ *with* $\gcd(e, q) = 1$, *and let* χ *be a nontrivial additive character of* GF(q). *Then*

$$\left| \sum_{x \in \mathrm{GF}(q)} \chi(f(x)) \right| \leq (e - 1)\sqrt{q}.$$

With respect to multiplicative characters, we have the following bound [Lidl and Niederreiter (1997)][Theorem 5.41].

Theorem 1.11. *Let* ψ *be a multiplicative character of* GF(q) *with order* $t > 1$, *and let* $f \in$ GF(q)$[x]$ *be of positive degree that is not a t-th power of a polynomial. Let e be the number of distinct roots of f in its splitting field over* GF(q). *Then for each* $a \in$ GF(q) *we have*

$$\left| \sum_{x \in \mathrm{GF}(q)} \psi(af(x)) \right| \leq (e - 1)\sqrt{q}.$$

Another kind of useful character sums is the *Kloosterman sums*, which are defined by

$$K(\chi; a, b) = \sum_{x \in \mathrm{GF}(q)^*} \chi(ax + bx^{-1}), \tag{1.2}$$

where χ is a nontrivial additive character of GF(q), and $a, b \in$ GF(q).

Kloosterman sums are closely related to many mathematical and engineering problems, and have been extensively studied in the literature. Unfortunately, it is very hard to evaluate Kloosterman sums. Nevertheless, we do have a tight bound on the Kloosterman sums as follows [Lidl and Niederreiter (1997)][Theorem 5.45].

Theorem 1.12. *Let* χ *be a nontrivial additive character of* GF(q), *and let* $a, b \in$ GF(q) *with* $(a, b) \neq (0, 0)$. *Then*

$$|K(\chi; a, b)| \leq 2\sqrt{q}.$$

At the end of this section, we introduce a type of character sums defined by special quadratic functions. Denote by $S_h(a,b)$ the Weil sum given by

$$S_h(a,b) = \sum_{x \in \mathrm{GF}(p^m)} \chi_1(ax^{p^h+1} + bx),$$

where h is a nonnegative integer and χ_1 is the canonical additive character of $\mathrm{GF}(p^m)$. Below we consider the sum $S_h(a,b)$ for $a \neq 0$.

Lemma 1.13 (Coulter (2002)). *Let p be an odd prime and let m/d be odd with $d = \gcd(m,h)$. Suppose that $f(x) = a^{p^h}x^{p^{2h}} + ax$ is a permutation of $\mathrm{GF}(p^m)$. Let x_0 be the unique solution of the equation $f(x) = -b^{p^h}$, $b \neq 0$. Then*

$$S_h(a,b) = \begin{cases} (-1)^{m-1}p^{m/2}\eta(-a)\overline{\chi_1(ax_0^{p^h+1})} & \text{if } p \equiv 1 \pmod 4, \\ \sqrt{-1}^{3m}(-1)^{m-1}p^{m/2}\eta(-a)\overline{\chi_1(ax_0^{p^h+1})} & \text{if } p \equiv 3 \pmod 4, \end{cases}$$

where η denotes the quadratic character of $\mathrm{GF}(p^m)$, and $\overline{y}$ denotes the complex conjugate of the complex number y.

Lemma 1.14 (Coulter (2002)). *Let p be a prime. Define $d = \gcd(m,h)$ and let m/d be even with $m = 2\bar{m}$. Define $f(x) = a^{p^h}x^{p^{2h}} + ax$ and*

$$a_0 = \begin{cases} 1 & \text{if } p = 2, \\ \zeta^{(p^m-1)/2(p^d-1)} & \text{if } p \text{ odd}, \end{cases}$$

where ζ is a primitive element of $\mathrm{GF}(p^m)$. Then $S_h(a,b) = 0$ unless the equation $f(x) = -b^{p^h}$ is solvable. There are two possibilities.

(1) If $a \neq a_0\zeta^{s(p^d+1)}$ for any integer s, then for any choice of $b \in \mathrm{GF}(p^m)$, the equation $f(x) = -b^{p^h}$ has a unique solution x_0 and

$$S_h(a,b) = (-1)^{\bar{m}/d}p^{\bar{m}}\overline{\chi_1(ax_0^{p^h+1})}.$$

(2) If $a = a_0\zeta^{s(p^d+1)}$ for some integer s, then the equation $f(x) = -b^{p^h}$ is solvable if and only if $\mathrm{Tr}_{p^m/p^{2d}}(b\gamma^{-s}) = 0$, where $\gamma \in \mathrm{GF}(p^m)^*$ is the unique element satisfying $\gamma^{(p^h+1)/(p^d+1)} = \zeta$. In such cases,

$$S_h(a,b) = (-1)^{\bar{m}/d}p^{\bar{m}+d}\overline{\chi_1(ax_0^{p^h+1})},$$

where x_0 is any solution to $f(x) = -b^{p^h}$.

The next two lemmas will be useful in subsequent chapters.

Lemma 1.15 (Coulter (2002)). *Let p be an odd prime and let $d = \gcd(m,h)$. Then the equation $a^{p^h}x^{p^{2h}} + ax = 0$ is solvable for $x \in GF(p^m)^*$ if and only if m/d is even with $m = 2\bar{m}$ and*

$$a^{(p^m-1)/(p^d+1)} = (-1)^{\bar{m}/d}.$$

In such cases there are $p^{2d} - 1$ nonzero solutions.

Lemma 1.16 (Draper and Hou (2008)). *Let p be an odd prime, and let m be a positive integer. Let $v_r(m)$ denote the r-adic order of m (that is, $r^{v_r(m)}$ divides m, but $r^{v_r(m)+1}$ does not divide m). Let $a \in GF(p^m)^*$ and let $h \geq 0$ be an integer.*

(1) If $v_2(m) \leq v_2(h)$,

$$S_h(a,0) = \eta(a)(-1)^{m-1}\sqrt{-1}^{m(p-1)^2/4}p^{m/2}.$$

(2) If $v_2(m) = v_2(h) + 1$,

$$S_h(a,0) = \begin{cases} p^{(m+\gcd(2h,m))/2} & \text{if } a^{\frac{(p^h-1)(p^m-1)}{p^{\gcd(2h,m)}-1}} = -1, \\ -p^{m/2} & \text{otherwise.} \end{cases}$$

(3) If $v_2(m) > v_2(h) + 1$,

$$S_h(a,0) = \begin{cases} -p^{(m+\gcd(2h,m))/2} & \text{if } a^{\frac{(p^h-1)(p^m-1)}{p^{\gcd(2h,m)}-1}} = 1, \\ p^{m/2} & \text{otherwise.} \end{cases}$$

1.2.6 Quadratic Forms over $GF(q)$

An n-ary quadratic form (or a quadratic form in n indeterminates) over a field $GF(q)$ is a homogeneous polynomial of degree 2 in n variables with coefficients in $GF(q)$:

$$f(x_1,x_2,\ldots,x_n) = \sum_{i=1}^{n}\sum_{j=1}^{n} a_{ij}x_ix_j, \; a_{ij} \in GF(q).$$

Let $x = (x_1,x_2,\ldots,x_n)^T$ and $A = [a_{ij}]$ be the $n \times n$ matrix whose entries are the coefficients of f. Then the quadratic form f can be expressed as

$$f(x_1,x_2,\ldots,x_n) = x^T A x.$$

We say that f is *nonsingular* or *nondegenerate* if A is nonsingular, and *degenerate* otherwise. The *rank* of f is defined to be the rank of the matrix A.

Two quadratic forms ϕ and ψ over $GF(q)$ are called *equivalent* if there is a nonsingular matrix C such that $\phi(x) = \psi(Cx)$. The following two theorems will be useful [Lidl and Niederreiter (1997)][Section 6.2].

Theorem 1.17. *Let q be odd. Then every n-ary quadratic form $f(x_1, x_2, \ldots, x_n)$ over $\mathrm{GF}(q)$ is equivalent to the following diagonal form*

$$a_1 x_1^2 + a_2 x_2^2 + \cdots + a_s x_s^2, \ a_i \in \mathrm{GF}(q)^*,$$

where $s \leq n$ and s is called the rank *of f. Define*

$$N(f = 0) = |\{(x_1, \ldots, x_n) \in \mathrm{GF}(q)^n : f(x_1, \ldots, x_n) = 0\}|.$$

$$N(f = 0) = \begin{cases} q^{n-1}, & \text{if } s \text{ is odd,} \\ q^{n-1} + \eta(a_1 \ldots a_s)\eta(-1)^{\frac{s}{2}}(q-1)q^{n-\frac{s+2}{2}}, & \text{if } s \text{ is even,} \end{cases} \quad (1.3)$$

where η denotes the quadratic character of $\mathrm{GF}(q)^*$.

Theorem 1.18. *Let q be even, and $f(x_1, x_2, \ldots, x_n)$ be a nondegenerate quadratic form over $\mathrm{GF}(q)$. If n is odd, then f is equivalent to*

$$x_1 x_2 + x_3 x_4 + \cdots + x_{n-2} x_{n-1} + x_n^2.$$

If n is even, then f is equivalent to either

$$x_1 x_2 + x_3 x_4 + \cdots + x_{n-1} x_n$$

or a quadratic form of the type

$$x_1 x_2 + x_3 x_4 + \cdots + x_{n-1} x_n + x_{n-1}^2 + a x_n^2,$$

where $a \in \mathrm{GF}(q)$ satisfies $\mathrm{Tr}_{q/p}(a) = 1$.

1.3   Group Algebra

Let $(G, +)$ be an additive group and $\mathbb{F}$ a field. The *group algebra* $\mathbb{F}[G]$ (or better $(\mathbb{F}[G], +, *)$) is the vector space over $\mathbb{F}$ with elements of G as basis, with addition $+$ and multiplication $*$ defined by

$$\sum_{g \in G} u(g)g + \sum_{g \in G} v(g)g = \sum_{g \in G} (u(g) + v(g))g$$

and

$$\left(\sum_{g \in G} u(g)g \right) * \left(\sum_{h \in G} v(h)h \right) = \sum_{k \in G} \left(\sum_{g+h=k} u(g)v(h) \right) k,$$

where $u(g) \in \mathbb{F}$ and $v(h) \in \mathbb{F}$. In this monograph, we will be mainly concerned with the group algebra when $(G, +) = (\mathrm{GF}(q)^m, +)$ and $\mathbb{F} = \mathbb{C}$ is the field of complex numbers.

Let $\mathbb{F}^G$ denote the set of all functions from G to F. When G is a finite group, the group algebra $\mathbb{F}[G]$ is the same as F^G, as each element $\sum_{g \in G} u(g)g$ corresponds to a function $u(g)$ from G to $\mathbb{F}$.

1.4 Special Types of Polynomials

This section introduces a few types of polynomials over finite fields. The reader is referred to Appendix C for basics of polynomials over fields.

1.4.1 *Permutation Polynomials over Finite Fields*

A polynomial $f \in \mathrm{GF}(r)[x]$ is called a *permutation polynomial* if the associated polynomial function $f : a \mapsto f(a)$ from $\mathrm{GF}(r)$ to $\mathrm{GF}(r)$ is a permutation of $\mathrm{GF}(r)$. Obviously, f is a permutation polynomial of $\mathrm{GF}(r)$ if and only if the equation $f(x) = a$ has exactly one solution $x \in \mathrm{GF}(r)$ for each $a \in \mathrm{GF}(r)$.

Example 1.19. Every linear polynomial ax is a permutation polynomial of $\mathrm{GF}(r)$, where $a \in \mathrm{GF}(r)^*$.

The following is a general criterion for the permutation property of polynomials over $\mathrm{GF}(r)$, but not a very useful one [Lidl and Niederreiter (1997)][Theorem 7.4].

Theorem 1.20 (Hermite's criteria). *Let* $\mathrm{GF}(r)$ *be of characteristic p. Then* $f \in \mathrm{GF}(r)[x]$ *is a permutation polynomial of* $\mathrm{GF}(r)$ *if and only if the following two conditions hold:*

(i) $f(x) = 0$ *has exactly one solution* $x \in \mathrm{GF}(r)$;
(ii) for each integer t with $1 \le t \le r - 2$ *and* $t \not\equiv 0 \pmod{p}$, *the reduction of* $f(x)^t \bmod (x^r - x)$ *has degree at most* $r - 2$.

The Hermite criterion above can be modified into the following [Lidl and Niederreiter (1997)][Theorem 7.6].

Theorem 1.21. *Let* $\mathrm{GF}(r)$ *be of characteristic p. Then* $f \in \mathrm{GF}(r)[x]$ *is a permutation polynomial of* $\mathrm{GF}(r)$ *if and only if the following two conditions hold:*

(i) the reduction of $f(x)^{r-1} \bmod (x^r - x)$ *has degree* $r - 1$;
(ii) for each integer t with $1 \le t \le r - 2$ *and* $t \not\equiv 0 \pmod{p}$, *the reduction of* $f(x)^t \bmod (x^r - x)$ *has degree at most* $r - 2$.

The two criteria above are not very useful as the two conditions in each theorem are not easy to check. For special types of polynomials over $\mathrm{GF}(r)$ there are simple conditions for checking the permutation property.

It is easily seen that the monomial x^n is a permutation polynomial of $\mathrm{GF}(r)$ if and only if $\gcd(n, r - 1) = 1$. For p-polynomials we have the following.

Theorem 1.22. *Let* GF(r) *be of characteristic p. Then the p-polynomial*

$$L(x) = \sum_{i=0}^{m} a_i x^{p^i} \in \text{GF}(r)[x]$$

is a permutation polynomial of GF(r) *if and only if* $L(x)$ *only has the root 0 in* GF(r).

For more information on permutation polynomials, the reader is referred to Lidl and Niederreiter (1997)[Chapter 7].

1.4.2 Dickson Polynomials over Finite Fields

In 1896 Dickson introduced the following family of polynomials over the finite field GF(r) [Dickson (1896)]:

$$D_h(x,a) = \sum_{i=0}^{\lfloor \frac{h}{2} \rfloor} \frac{h}{h-i} \binom{h-i}{i} (-a)^i x^{h-2i}, \tag{1.4}$$

where $a \in \text{GF}(r)$ and $h \geq 0$ is called the *order* of the polynomial. This family is referred to as the *Dickson polynomials of the first kind*.

It is known that Dickson polynomials of the first kind satisfy the following recurrence relation:

$$D_{h+2}(x,a) = xD_{h+1}(x,a) - aD_h(x,a) \tag{1.5}$$

with the initial state $D_0(x,a) = 2$ and $D_1(x,a) = x$.

A proof of the following theorem can be found in Lidl, Mullen and Turnwald (1993)[Theorem 3.2].

Theorem 1.23. $D_h(x,a)$ *is a permutation polynomial over* GF(r) *if and only if* $\gcd(h, r^2 - 1) = 1$.

Dickson polynomials of the second kind over the finite field GF(r) are defined by

$$E_h(x,a) = \sum_{i=0}^{\lfloor \frac{h}{2} \rfloor} \binom{h-i}{i} (-a)^i x^{h-2i}, \tag{1.6}$$

where $a \in \text{GF}(r)$ and $h \geq 0$ is called the *order* of the polynomial. This family is referred to as the *Dickson polynomials of the second kind*.

It is known that Dickson polynomials of the second kind satisfy the following recurrence:

$$E_{h+2}(x,a) = xE_{h+1}(x,a) - aE_h(x,a) \tag{1.7}$$

with the initial state $E_0(x,a) = 1$ and $E_1(x,a) = x$.

Dickson polynomials are an interesting topic of mathematics, and have many applications. For example, the Dickson polynomials $D_5(x,u) = x^5 - ux - u^2 x$ over $GF(3^m)$ were employed to construct a family of planar functions [Ding and Yuan (2006)], and those planar functions give two families of commutative presemi-fields, planes, several classes of linear codes [Carlet, Ding and Yuan (2005)], and two families of skew Hadamard difference sets [Ding and Yuan (2006)]. The reader is referred to Lidl, Mullen and Turnwald (1993) for detailed information about Dickson polynomials.

1.4.3 *Krawtchouk Polynomials*

Let $n \geq 1$ and $k \geq 0$ be integers, and let $q \geq 2$ be an integer. The *Krawtchouk polynomial* $P_k(q,n;x)$ is defined by

$$P_k(q,n;x) = \sum_{i=0}^{k} (-1)^i (q-1)^{k-i} \binom{x}{i} \binom{n-x}{k-i}, \tag{1.8}$$

which can be viewed as a polynomial over the ring of integers, the field of rational numbers, the field of real numbers, and the field of complex numbers. In the definition of the Krawtchouk polynomial,

$$\binom{x}{i} = \frac{x(x-1)\cdots(x-i+1)}{i!}.$$

If x is an integer between 0 and n, $P_k(q,n;x)$ is the coefficient of u^k in the expansion of $(1-u)^x (1+(q-1)u)^{n-x}$.

For example, we have

$$P_0(2,n;x) = 1,$$
$$P_1(2,n;x) = -2x+n,$$
$$P_2(2,n;x) = 2x^2 - 2nx + \binom{n}{2},$$
$$P_3(2,n;x) = -\frac{4}{3}x^3 + 2nx^2 - \left(n^2 - n + \frac{2}{3}\right)x + \binom{n}{3}.$$

An equivalent expression of $P_k(q,n;x)$ is given below.

Lemma 1.24. *Let $n \geq 1$ and $k \geq 0$ be integers, and let $q \geq 2$ be an integer. Then*

$$P_k(q,n;x) = \sum_{i=0}^{k} (-q)^i (q-1)^{k-i} \binom{n-i}{k-i} \binom{x}{i}. \tag{1.9}$$

Proof. Let x be an integer with $0 \le x \le n$. Then

$$\sum_{k=0}^{n} u^k \sum_{i=0}^{k} (-q)^i (q-1)^{k-i} \binom{n-i}{k-i} \binom{x}{i}$$

$$= \sum_{i=0}^{n} (-q)^i \binom{x}{i} u^i \sum_{k=i}^{n} \binom{n-i}{k-i} (q-1)^{k-i} u^{k-i}$$

$$= \sum_{i=0}^{n} (-q)^i \binom{x}{i} u^i (1 + (q-1)u)^{n-i}$$

$$= (1 + (q-1)u)^{n-x} \sum_{i=0}^{n} \binom{x}{i} (-qu)^i (1 + (q-1)u)^{x-i}$$

$$= (1 + (q-1)u)^{n-x} (-qu + 1 + (q-1)u)^x$$

$$= (1 + (q-1)u)^{n-x} (1 - u)^x$$

$$= \sum_{k=0}^{n} P_k(q,n;x) u^k.$$

This means that the two polynomials in u with degree at most n are equal at $n+1$ points. Hence, their coefficients must be equal. This completes the proof. $\square$

One can similarly prove that

$$P_k(q,n;x) = \sum_{i=0}^{k} (-1)^i q^{k-i} \binom{n-k+i}{i} \binom{n-x}{k-i}. \tag{1.10}$$

The following orthogonality relations will be useful in subsequent chapters.

Lemma 1.25. *For integers $0 \le k \le n$ and $0 \le \ell \le n$, we have*

$$\sum_{i=0}^{n} \binom{n}{i} (q-1)^i P_k(q,n;i) P_\ell(q,n;i) = q^n (q-1)^k \binom{n}{k} \delta_{k,\ell}, \tag{1.11}$$

where $\delta_{k,\ell} = 1$ if $k = \ell$, and $\delta_{k,\ell} = 0$ if $k \ne \ell$.

Proof. We have

$$\sum_{k=0}^{n} \sum_{\ell=0}^{n} \sum_{i=0}^{n} \binom{n}{i} (q-1)^i P_k(q,n;i) P_\ell(q,n;i) x^k y^\ell$$

$$= \sum_{i=0}^{n} \binom{n}{i} (q-1)^i (1-x)^i (1+(q-1)x)^{n-i} (1-y)^i (1+(q-1)y)^{n-i}$$

$$= ((q-1)(1-x)(1-y) + (1+(q-1)x)(1+(q-1)y))^n$$

$$= q^n (1 + (q-1)xy)^n$$

$$= q^n \sum_{k=0}^{n} \binom{n}{k} (q-1)^k x^k y^k.$$

The desired result follows immediately after comparing the coefficients of $x^k y^\ell$ on both sides. $\square$

Lemma 1.24 shows that the degree of the polynomial $P_k(q,n;x)$ is k. Then Lemma 1.25 tells us that the polynomials $P_k(q,n;x)$ for $0 \le k \le n$ form a basis in the vector space of polynomials of degree at most n.

Lemma 1.26. *For integers $0 \le k \le n$ and $0 \le \ell \le n$, we have*

$$\binom{n}{\ell}(q-1)^\ell P_k(q,n;\ell) = \binom{n}{k}(q-1)^k P_\ell(q,n;k). \tag{1.12}$$

Proof. We have

$$
\begin{aligned}
\sum_{k=0}^{n}\sum_{\ell=0}^{n} &\binom{n}{\ell}(q-1)^\ell P_k(q,n;\ell)x^k y^\ell \\
&= ((q-1)y(1-x)+(1+(q-1)x))^n \\
&= ((q-1)x(1-y)+(1+(q-1)y))^n \\
&= \sum_{k=0}^{n}\binom{n}{k}(q-1)^k x^k(1-y)^k(1+(q-1)y)^{n-k} \\
&= \sum_{k=0}^{n}\sum_{\ell=0}^{n}\binom{n}{k}(q-1)^k P_\ell(q,n;k)x^k y^\ell.
\end{aligned}
$$

Comparing the coefficients yields the desired result. □

The following is another set of interesting relations.

Lemma 1.27. *For integers $0 \le k \le n$ and $0 \le \ell \le n$, we have*

$$\sum_{i=0}^{n} P_k(q,n;i)P_i(q,n;\ell) = q^n \delta_{k,\ell}. \tag{1.13}$$

Proof. Substituting (1.12) into (1.11) proves the desired conclusion. □

Lemma 1.28. *For integers $0 \le k \le n$, we have*

$$\sum_{\ell=0}^{k} P_\ell(q,n;x) = P_k(q,n-1;x-1). \tag{1.14}$$

Proof. By definition, we have

$$\sum_{\ell=0}^{k} P_\ell(q,n;x) = \sum_{\ell=0}^{k}\sum_{i=0}^{\ell}(-1)^i(q-1)^{\ell-i}\binom{x}{i}\binom{n-x}{\ell-i}$$

$$= \sum_{i=0}^{k}(-1)^i\binom{x}{i}\sum_{\ell=i}^{k}(q-1)^{\ell-i}\binom{n-x}{\ell-i}$$

$$= \sum_{i=0}^{k}(-1)^i\left(\binom{x-1}{i-1}+\binom{x-1}{i}\right)\sum_{\ell=0}^{k-i}(q-1)^\ell\binom{n-x}{\ell}$$

$$= \sum_{i=0}^{k}(-1)^i\binom{x-1}{i}\left[\left(\sum_{\ell=0}^{k-i}-\sum_{\ell=0}^{k-i-1}\right)(q-1)^\ell\binom{n-x}{\ell}\right]$$

$$= \sum_{i=0}^{k}(-1)^i\binom{x-1}{i}(q-1)^{k-i}\binom{n-x}{k-i}$$

$$= P_k(q,n-1;x-1).$$

$\square$

Lemma 1.29. *The Krawtchouk polynomials satisfy the recurrence relation*

$$(k+1)P_{k+1}(q,n;x) = [k+(q-1)(n-k)-qx]P_k(q,n;x) - $$
$$(q-1)(n-k+1)P_{k-1}(q,n;x). \qquad (1.15)$$

Proof. Differentiating the equality

$$\sum_{k} P_k(q,n;x)u^k = (1-u)^x[1+(q-1)u]^{n-x}$$

to u and multiplying the obtained result by $(1-u)(1+(q-1)u)$, we obtain that

$$(1-u)(1+(q-1)u)\sum_{k}kP_k(q,n;x)u^{k-1}$$
$$= (1-u)^x(1+(q-1)u)^{n-x}[-x(1+(q-1)u)+(n-x)(q-1)(1-u)]$$
$$= [n(q-1)-xq-n(q-1)u]\sum_{k}P_k(q,n;x)u^k.$$

The desired recurrence relation follows after comparing the coefficients on both sides. $\square$

The following lemma follows directly from (1.9).

Lemma 1.30.

$$P_k(q,n;0) = (q-1)^k\binom{n}{k}, \qquad (1.16)$$

$$P_k(q,n;n) = (-1)^k \binom{n}{k},\tag{1.17}$$

$$P_k(q,n;1) = (q-1)^{k-1}\left[(q-1)\binom{n}{k} - q\binom{n-1}{k-1}\right].\tag{1.18}$$

The properties of the Krawtchouk polynomials documented in this section will be recalled in subsequent chapters.

1.5 Cyclotomy in GF(r)

1.5.1 *Cyclotomy*

Cyclotomy is to divide the circumference of a given unit circle with its center into n equal parts using only a straightedge (i.e., idealized ruler) and a compass, where the straightedge is only for drawing straight lines and the compass is only for drawing circles. It is equivalent to the problem of constructing the regular n-gon using only a straightedge and a compass.

Greek geometers played this puzzle 2000 years ago. About 300 BC, people in Euclid's School found that the regular n-gon is constructible for any $n \geq 3$ of the form

$$n = 2^a 3^b 5^c, \quad a \geq 0, b \in \{0,1\}, c \in \{0,1\}.$$

For more than 2000 years mathematicians had been unanimous in their view that for any prime p bigger than 5 the p-gon could not be constructed by ruler and compass. The 18-year old Carl Friedrich Gauss proved that the regular 17-gon is constructible [Gauss (1801)]. This achievement of Gauss is one of the most surprising discoveries in mathematics. He asked to have his 17-gon carved on his tombstone! This discovery led him to choose mathematics (rather than philosophy) as his life-time research topic.

Gauss proved that the regular n-gon is constructible when $n = p2^s$, where $p = 2^{2^k} + 1$ is a Fermat prime. In general, we have the following conclusion.

Theorem 1.31. *A regular n-gon in the plane is constructible iff* $n = 2^e p_1 p_2 \cdots p_k$ *for $e \geq 0$ and distinct Fermat primes $p_1, \ldots, p_k$, $k \geq 0$.*

The necessity and sufficiency were proved by Gauss in 1796 and Wanzel in 1836, respectively. A detailed proof of Theorem 1.31 can be found in Pollack (2009)[Chapter 2].

The algebraic criterion for the constructibility of regular n-gon is given in the following theorem [Pollack (2009)][Section 2.2].

Theorem 1.32. *A regular n-gon in the plane is constructible iff all the complex roots of $z^n = 1$ can be found out by solving a chain of linear and quadratic equations.*

To have a better understanding of the algebraic aspect of cyclotomy (a beautiful problem in geometry), we look into the case that $n = 5$.

Let γ_i be the complex roots of $x^4 + x^3 + x^2 + x + 1 = 0$, where $1 \le i \le 4$. Note that 2 is a primitive root modulo 5. Let

$$C_i = \{2^{2s+i} \bmod 5 : s = 0, 1\}, \quad i = 0, 1,$$

which are the *cyclotomic classes* of order 2 modulo 5. It is obvious that $C_0 \cap C_1 = \emptyset$ and $C_0 \cup C_1 = \mathbb{Z}_5 \setminus \{0\}$.

Define $\eta_i = \sum_{j \in C_i} x^j$, where $i = 0, 1$. These η_i are called *Gaussian periods* of order 2. Then we have

$$\eta_0 + \eta_1 + 1 = x^4 + x^3 + x^2 + x + 1 = 0. \tag{1.19}$$

It is easily verified that

$$\eta_0 \eta_1 = \eta_0 + \eta_1. \tag{1.20}$$

Combining (1.19) and (1.20) proves that η_0 and η_1 are solutions of $\eta^2 + \eta - 1 = 0$. Hence

$$\eta_0 = \frac{-1 \pm \sqrt{5}}{2} \text{ and } \eta_1 = \frac{-1 \mp \sqrt{5}}{2}.$$

It is then easy to see that the four roots γ_i are found by solving in chain

$$\eta^2 + \eta - 1 = 0, \quad \gamma^2 - \eta_i \gamma + 1 = 0,$$

where η_0 and η_1 are solutions of $\eta^2 + \eta - 1 = 0$. Hence, the case $n = 5$ is constructible by Theorem 1.32.

It follows from the discussions above that the algebraic aspect of cyclotomy is related to cyclotomic classes and Gaussian periods, which will be the subjects of the next subsection.

1.5.2 *Cyclotomy in* GF(r)

Let r be a power of a prime p. Let $r - 1 = nN$ for two positive integers $n > 1$ and $N > 1$, and let α be a fixed primitive element of GF(r). Define $C_i^{(N,r)} = \alpha^i \langle \alpha^N \rangle$ for $i = 0, 1, ..., N - 1$, where $\langle \alpha^N \rangle$ denotes the subgroup of GF(r)* generated by α^N. The cosets $C_i^{(N,r)}$ are called the *cyclotomic classes* of order N in GF(r). The *cyclotomic numbers* of order N are defined by

$$(i, j)^{(N,r)} = \left| (C_i^{(N,r)} + 1) \cap C_j^{(N,r)} \right|$$

for all $0 \leq i \leq N-1$ and $0 \leq j \leq N-1$.

The following theorem describes elementary facts about cyclotomic numbers, which are not hard to prove [Storer (1967)][Lemma 3].

Theorem 1.33. *Let notation be the same as before. Then the following equations hold.*

(A) $(l,m)^{(N,r)} = (l',m')^{(N,r)}$ *when* $l \equiv l'$ (mod N) *and* $m \equiv m'$ (mod N).

(B) $(l,m)^{(N,r)} = (N-l,m-l)^{(N,r)} = \begin{cases} (m,l)^{(N,r)} \text{ for even } n, \\ (m+N/2,l+N/2)^{(N,r)} \text{ for odd } n. \end{cases}$

(C) $\sum_{m=0}^{N-1}(l,m)^{(N,r)} = n - n_l$, *where*

$$n_l = \begin{cases} 1 & \text{if } l \equiv 0 \pmod{N}, \ n \text{ even,} \\ 1 & \text{if } l \equiv N/2 \pmod{N}, \ n \text{ odd,} \\ 0 & \text{otherwise.} \end{cases}$$

(D) $\sum_{l=0}^{N-1}(l,m)^{(N,r)} = n - k_m$, *where*

$$k_m = \begin{cases} 1 & \text{if } m \equiv 0 \pmod{N}, \\ 0 & \text{otherwise.} \end{cases}$$

(E) $\sum_{l=0}^{N-1}\sum_{m=0}^{N-1}(l,m)^{(N,r)} = Nn - 1 = r - 2$.

(F) $(l,m)^{(N',r)} = (sl,sm)^{(N,r)}$, *where* $(l,m)^{(N',r)}$ *is based on the primitive element* $\alpha' \equiv \alpha^s$ (mod N); *necessarily then s is prime to* $r-1$.

In the sequel we will need the following lemma which was developed in Tze, Chanson, Ding, Helleseth and Parker (2003) and Ding and Yin (2008).

Lemma 1.34. *Let* $r - 1 = nN$ *and let r be a prime power. Then*

$$\sum_{u=0}^{N-1}(u,u+k)^{(N,r)} = \begin{cases} n-1 & \text{if } k = 0, \\ n & \text{if } k \neq 0. \end{cases}$$

In general, it is very hard to determine the cyclotomic numbers $(i,j)^{(N,r)}$. But they are known when N is small or under certain conditions [Storer (1967)]. We will introduce cyclotomic numbers of certain orders in the sequel when we really need them.

The *Gaussian periods* are defined by

$$\eta_i^{(N,r)} = \sum_{x \in C_i^{(N,r)}} \chi(x), \quad i = 0, 1, ..., N-1,$$

where χ is the canonical additive character of GF(r).

The following lemma presents some basic properties of Gaussian periods, and will be employed later.

Lemma 1.35 (Storer (1967)). *Let notation be the same as before. Then we have the following:*

(1) $\sum_{i=0}^{N-1} \eta_i = -1$.

(2) $\sum_{i=0}^{N-1} \eta_i \eta_{i+k} = r\theta_k - n$ *for all* $k \in \{0, 1, \ldots, N-1\}$, *where*

$$\theta_k = \begin{cases} 1 & \textit{if n is even and } k = 0 \\ 1 & \textit{if n is odd and } k = N/2 \\ 0 & \textit{otherwise,} \end{cases}$$

and equivalently $\theta_k = 1$ *if and only if* $-1 \in C_k^{(N,r)}$.

Gaussian periods are closely related to Gaussian sums. From the finite Fourier transform it follows that

$$\eta_i^{(N,r)} = \frac{1}{N} \sum_{j=0}^{N-1} \varepsilon_N^{-ij} G(\psi^j, \chi_1) = \frac{1}{N} \left[-1 + \sum_{j=1}^{N-1} \varepsilon_N^{-ij} G(\psi^j, \chi_1) \right], \tag{1.21}$$

where $\varepsilon_N = e^{2\pi\sqrt{-1}/N}$ and ψ is a primitive multiplicative character of order N over $GF(r)^*$.

From (1.21), one can see that the values of the Gaussian periods in general are also very hard to compute. However, they can be computed in a few cases.

The following lemma follows from Theorems 1.7 and 1.8.

Lemma 1.36. *Let* $r = p^m$. *When* $N = 2$, *the Gaussian periods are given by the following:*

$$\eta_0^{(2,r)} = \begin{cases} \frac{-1+(-1)^{m-1}r^{1/2}}{2} & \textit{if } p \equiv 1 \pmod{4} \\ \frac{-1+(-1)^{m-1}(\sqrt{-1})^m r^{1/2}}{2} & \textit{if } p \equiv 3 \pmod{4} \end{cases}$$

and

$$\eta_1^{(2,r)} = -1 - \eta_0^{(2,r)}.$$

The following result is proved in Myerson (1981).

Lemma 1.37. *If* $r \equiv 1 \pmod{4}$, *we have*

$$(0,0)^{(2,r)} = \frac{r-5}{4}, \ (0,1)^{(2,r)} = (1,0)^{(2,r)} = (1,1)^{(2,r)} = \frac{r-1}{4}.$$

If $r \equiv 3 \pmod{4}$, *we have*

$$(0,1)^{(2,r)} = \frac{r+1}{4}, \ (0,0)^{(2,r)} = (1,0)^{(2,r)} = (1,1)^{(2,r)} = \frac{r-3}{4}.$$

Cyclotomic numbers of small orders were given in Storer (1967)[p. 72, p. 79]. The *period polynomials* $\psi_{(N,r)}(X)$ are defined by

$$\psi_{(N,r)}(X) = \prod_{i=0}^{N-1} \left(X - \eta_i^{(N,r)} \right).$$

It is known that $\psi_{(N,r)}(X)$ is a polynomial with integer coefficients [Myerson (1981)]. The period polynomial $\psi_{(N,r)}(X)$ and its factorization were determined for $N \in \{3,4,5,6,8,12\}$ [Myerson (1981); Gurak (2004); Hoshi (2006)].

The Gaussian periods are also determined in the semiprimitive case and are described in the next theorem.

Theorem 1.38 (Baumert, Mills and Ward (1982)). *Assume that p is a prime, $N \geq 2$ is a positive integer, $r = p^{2j\gamma}$, where $N|(p^j + 1)$ and j is the smallest such positive integer. Then the Guassian periods of order N are given below:*

(a) If $\gamma, p, \frac{p^j+1}{N}$ are all odd, then

$$\eta_{N/2}^{(N,r)} = \sqrt{r} - \frac{\sqrt{r}+1}{N}, \quad \eta_i^{(N,r)} = -\frac{1+\sqrt{r}}{N} \text{ for all } i \neq \frac{N}{2}.$$

(b) In all the other cases,

$$\eta_0^{(N,r)} = -(-1)^\gamma \sqrt{r} + \frac{(-1)^\gamma \sqrt{r}-1}{N}, \quad \eta_i^{(N,r)} = \frac{(-1)^\gamma \sqrt{r}-1}{N} \text{ for all } i \neq 0.$$

1.6 Finite Geometries

In this section, we present the basics of finite geometries, which will be employed in subsequent chapters.

1.6.1 *Projective Spaces* $PG(m, GF(q))$

The points of the *projective space* (also called *projective geometry*) $PG(m, GF(q))$ are all the 1-dimensional subspaces of the vector space $GF(q)^{m+1}$; the lines are the 2-dimensional subspaces of $GF(q)^{m+1}$, the planes are the 3-dimensional subspaces of $GF(q)^{m+1}$, and the hyperplanes are the m-dimensional subspaces of $GF(q)^{m+1}$; and incidence is the set-theoretic inclusion. The elements of the projective space $PG(m, GF(q))$ are the points, lines, planes, ..., and the hyperplanes. But the space $GF(q)^{m+1}$ is not an element of $PG(m, GF(q))$, as it contains every other subspace and thus plays no role. The *projective dimension* of an element in $PG(m, GF(q))$ is one less than that of the corresponding element in the vector space $GF(q)^{m+1}$.

Theorem 1.39. *The number of subspaces of* $\mathrm{GF}(q)^n$ *of dimension* k, *where* $0 \leq k \leq n$, *is equal to*

$$\frac{(q^n - 1)(q^n - q) \cdots (q^n - q^{k-1})}{(q^k - 1)(q^k - q) \cdots (q^k - q^{k-1})}.$$

These numbers are called Gaussian coefficients, *and are denoted by* $\begin{bmatrix} n \\ k \end{bmatrix}_q$.

Proof. The number of k-tuples $(v_1, v_2, \ldots, v_k)$ of k linearly independent vectors v_i in $\mathrm{GF}(q)^n$ is

$$(q^n - 1)(q^n - q) \cdots (q^n - q^{k-1}),$$

as v_{i+1} has $q^n - q^i$ choices after $v_1, v_2, \ldots, v_i$ are chosen for all i. Note that many such k-tuples $(v_1, v_2, \ldots, v_k)$ generate the same subspace. In a similar argument, any k-dimensional subspace of $\mathrm{GF}(q)^n$ has in total $(q^k - 1)(q^k - q) \cdots (q^k - q^{k-1})$ ordered bases. The number of subspaces of dimension k in $\mathrm{GF}(q)^n$ is the number of k-tuples $(v_1, v_2, \ldots, v_k)$ of k linearly independent vectors in $\mathrm{GF}(q)^n$ divided by the number of ordered bases in a k-dimensional subspace. The desired conclusion then follows. $\square$

By definition, the $(m+1)$-tuples $(ax_0, ax_1, \ldots, ax_m)$ with $a \in \mathrm{GF}(q)^*$ define the same point in $\mathrm{PG}(m, \mathrm{GF}(q))$. A k-*flat* of the projective space $\mathrm{PG}(m, \mathrm{GF}(q))$ is the set of all those nonzero points whose coordinates satisfy $m - k$ linearly independent homogeneous linear equations

$$
\begin{aligned}
a_{1,0} \quad x_0 + \cdots + a_{1,m} \quad x_m &= 0 \\
a_{2,0} \quad x_0 + \cdots + a_{2,m} \quad x_m &= 0 \\
\vdots \qquad \vdots \quad \cdots \quad \vdots \qquad \vdots \quad \vdots \\
a_{m-k,0}\, x_0 + \cdots + a_{m-k,m}\, x_m &= 0
\end{aligned}
$$

whose coefficients $a_{i,j} \in \mathrm{GF}(q)$. Hence the number of points in a k-flat in $\mathrm{PG}(m, \mathrm{GF}(q))$ is

$$\begin{bmatrix} k+1 \\ 1 \end{bmatrix}_q = \frac{q^{k+1} - 1}{q - 1}. \tag{1.22}$$

An *automorphism* or *collineation* of $\mathrm{PG}(m, \mathrm{GF}(q))$ is a bijection φ from $\mathrm{PG}(m, \mathrm{GF}(q))$ to itself such that, for U and V in $\mathrm{PG}(m, \mathrm{GF}(q))$, $U \subseteq V$ if and only if $\varphi(U) \subseteq \varphi(V)$. Hence, an automorphism does not change the dimension of an element in $\mathrm{PG}(m, \mathrm{GF}(q))$. The set of all automorphisms of $\mathrm{PG}(m, \mathrm{GF}(q))$ form a group, called the *automorphism group* or *collineation group* of $\mathrm{PG}(m, \mathrm{GF}(q))$. The following result is proved in Artin (1957)[Chapter II], and called the fundamental theorem of $\mathrm{PG}(m, \mathrm{GF}(q))$.

Theorem 1.40. *Let* $m \geq 2$. *Then* $\mathrm{P\Gamma L}_{m+1}(\mathrm{GF}(q))$ *(see Section 1.8.9 for definition) is the automorphism group of* $\mathrm{PG}(m, \mathrm{GF}(q))$.

Our objective of this subsection is to introduce the basic concepts and notation of the projective spaces $\mathrm{PG}(m, \mathrm{GF}(q))$. We refer the reader to Lidl and Niederreiter (1997)[Section 9.3] or Assmus and Key (1992a)[Section 3.2] for geometric properties of $\mathrm{PG}(m, \mathrm{GF}(q))$.

1.6.2 *Affine Spaces* $\mathrm{AG}(m, \mathrm{GF}(q))$

The *affine space* $\mathrm{AG}(m, \mathrm{GF}(q))$ consists of all cosets $\mathbf{x} + U$, of all subspaces U of $\mathrm{GF}(q)^m$ with incidence defined through the natural containment relation. In this case, the dimension is the same as that of the vector space, and if the latter has dimension k, we will call a coset of U a *k-flat*. Thus, the points of $\mathrm{AG}(m, \mathrm{GF}(q))$ are all the vectors in $\mathrm{GF}(q)^m$; the lines are all the 1-dimensional cosets (also called 1-flats); the planes are the 2-dimensional cosets (also called 2-flats); and the hyperplanes are the $(m-1)$-dimensional cosets. Geometric properties of $\mathrm{AG}(m, \mathrm{GF}(q))$ could be found in Assmus and Key (1992a)[Section 3.2].

The next theorem will be useful later.

Theorem 1.41. *The number of k-flats in* $\mathrm{AG}(m, \mathrm{GF}(q))$ *is given by* $q^{m-k} \begin{bmatrix} m \\ k \end{bmatrix}_q$.

Proof. Let E_1 and E_2 be two k-dimensional subspaces of $\mathrm{GF}(q)^m$, and let v_1 and v_2 be two vectors in $\mathrm{GF}(q)^m$. If $E_1 + v_1 = E_2 + v_2$, then $E_1 = E_2 + v_2 - v_1$. This means that both E_2 and $E_2 + v_2 - v_1$ are k-dimensional subspaces. It then follows that $v_2 = v_1$ and $E_1 = E_2$. Therefore, the number of k-flats in $\mathrm{AG}(m, \mathrm{GF}(q))$ is equal to the number of k-dimensional subspaces of $\mathrm{GF}(q)^m$ multiplied by the number of translates (i.e., cosets) of a given k-dimensional subspace. The desired conclusion then follows from Theorem 1.39. $\square$

The *automorphisms* or *collineations* of $\mathrm{AG}(m, \mathrm{GF}(q))$ are the bijections φ from $\mathrm{AG}(m, \mathrm{GF}(q))$ to itself such that, for U and V in $\mathrm{AG}(m, \mathrm{GF}(q))$, $U \subseteq V$ if and only if $\varphi(U) \subseteq \varphi(V)$. Hence, an automorphism does not change the dimension of an element in $\mathrm{AG}(m, \mathrm{GF}(q))$. The set of all automorphisms of $\mathrm{AG}(m, \mathrm{GF}(q))$ form a group, called the *automorphism group* or *collineation group* of $\mathrm{AG}(m, \mathrm{GF}(q))$. Similarly, we have the following fundamental theorem.

Theorem 1.42. *Let* $m \geq 2$. *Then* $\Gamma \mathrm{A}_m(\mathrm{GF}(q))$ *(see Section 1.8.3 for its definition) is the automorphism group of* $\mathrm{AG}(m, \mathrm{GF}(q))$.

1.6.3 *Projective Planes*

A *projective plane* is a triple $\Pi = (\mathcal{P}, \mathcal{L}, \mathcal{R})$, where $\mathcal{P}$ is a set of *points*, $\mathcal{L}$ consists of *lines* (e.g., sets of points), and $\mathcal{R}$ is a *relation* (also called *incidence relation*) between the points and the lines, subject to the following three conditions:

(a) Every pair of distinct lines is incident with a unique point (i.e., to every pair of distinct lines there is one point contained in both lines, called their *intersection*, if $\mathcal{R}$ is the containment relation).

(b) Every pair of distinct points is incident with a unique line (i.e., to every pair of distinct points there is exactly one line which contains both points, if $\mathcal{R}$ is the containment relation).

(c) There exist four points such that no three of them are incident with a single line (i.e., there exist four points such no three of them are on the same line, if $\mathcal{R}$ is the containment relation).

By the definition of projective planes above, each line contains at least three points and through each point there are at least three lines. When the set $\mathcal{P}$ of points is finite, the projective plane is called *finite*. One can prove the following result [Lidl and Niederreiter (1997)][Theorem 9.54].

Theorem 1.43. *Let Π be a finite projective plane. Then*

- *there is an integer $m \geq 2$ such that every point (line) of Π is incident with exactly $m+1$ lines (points) of Π; and*
- *Π contains exactly $m^2 + m + 1$ points (lines).*

The integer m above is called the *order* of the finite projective plane.

Example 1.44. It follows from Theorem 1.43 that the smallest finite plane has order $m = 2$, which has 7 points and 7 lines exactly. Let the set of points be $\mathcal{P} = \{1, 2, 3, 4, 5, 6, 7\}$, the 7 lines be

$$\{1,2,3\}, \{1,4,5\}, \{1,6,7\}, \{2,4,7\}, \{2,5,6\}, \{3,4,6\}, \{3,7,5\}$$

and let the incidence relation be the membership of sets. Then we have the Fano plane depicted in Figure 1.1, where no three points in the set $\{1, 3, 5, 6\}$ are on the same line.

For every prime power q, $\mathrm{PG}(2, \mathrm{GF}(q))$ is a projective plane, where the set membership is the incidence relation. These projective planes will play a special role in some subsequent chapters. We will treat them in the next section.

Given a projective plane $\Pi = (\mathcal{P}, \mathcal{L}, \mathcal{R})$, we define an incidence structure $\Pi^* = (\mathcal{L}, \mathcal{P}, \mathcal{R}^*)$, where $\mathcal{L}$ is the point set, $\mathcal{P}$ is the line set, and $\mathcal{R}^*$ is the *inverse relation*. In the new incidence structure Π^*, a point ℓ is incident with a line P with respect to $\mathcal{R}^*$ if and only if P is incident with ℓ with respect to $\mathcal{R}$. It is easily verified that $\Pi^* = (\mathcal{L}, \mathcal{P}, \mathcal{R}^*)$ is also a projective plane and is called the *dual plane* of Π.

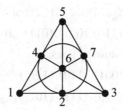

Fig. 1.1   Fano plane

1.6.4 *Desarguesian Projective Planes* $PG(2, GF(q))$

Projective planes were briefly introduced in the previous section. In this section, we treat the projective planes $PG(2, GF(q))$, where q is a prime power.

The projective plane $PG(2, GF(q))$ consists of $v = q^2 + q + 1$ points and the same number of lines. Its *point set* $\mathcal{P}$ is given by

$$\mathcal{P} = \{(x, y, 1) : x, y \in GF(q)\} \cup \{(x, 1, 0) : x \in GF(q)\} \cup \{(1, 0, 0)\}. \quad (1.23)$$

$\mathcal{P}$ is a largest set of points in $GF(q)^3$ such that no two of its elements are linearly dependent over $GF(q)$.

The set L of lines in $PG(2, GF(q))$ is defined by

$$L = \{\ell_{(c,b,a)} : c, b, a \in GF(q)\}, \quad (1.24)$$

where the line

$$\ell_{(c,b,a)} = \{(x, y, z) \in \mathcal{P} : ax + by + cz = 0\}. \quad (1.25)$$

It is easily seen that L consists of the following three types of lines. The first type is composed of the following q^2 lines:

$$\begin{aligned} \ell_{(c,b,1)} &= \{(x, y, z) \in \mathcal{P} : x + by + cz = 0\} \\ &= \{(-by - c, y, 1) : y \in GF(q)\} \cup \{(-b, 1, 0)\}. \end{aligned}$$

The second type has the following q lines:

$$\begin{aligned} \ell_{(c,1,0)} &= \{(x, y, z) \in \mathcal{P} : y + cz = 0\} \\ &= \{(x, -c, 1) : x \in GF(q)\} \cup \{(1, 0, 0)\}. \end{aligned}$$

The third type has only one line, which is given by

$$\begin{aligned} \ell_{(1,0,0)} &= \{(x, y, z) \in \mathcal{P} : z = 0\} \\ &= \{(x, 1, 0) : x \in GF(q)\} \cup \{(1, 0, 0)\}, \end{aligned}$$

and called the *line at infinity*. Clearly, each line has $q + 1$ points.

Example 1.45. The point set $\mathcal{P}$ of $PG(2, GF(2))$ of order 2 is

$$\{(100), (010), (110), (001), (011), (101), (111)\}.$$

The line set $\mathcal{L}$ consist of the following lines:

$$\{(001), (110), (111)\},$$
$$\{(010), (111), (101)\},$$
$$\{(110), (011), (101)\},$$
$$\{(111), (100), (011)\},$$
$$\{(001), (010), (011)\},$$
$$\{(001), (100), (101)\},$$
$$\{(110), (010), (100)\}.$$

This is the Fano plane depicted in Example 1.44.

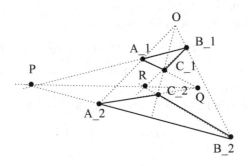

Fig. 1.2   Two triangles are in perspective from a point O

Two triangles $\triangle A_1 B_1 C_1$ and $\triangle A_2 B_2 C_2$ are said to be in *perspective* from a point O if the lines $A_1 A_2$, $B_1 B_2$ and $C_1 C_2$ pass through O. Points on the same lines are said to be *collinear*. For example, the triangles $\triangle A_1 B_1 C_1$ and $\triangle A_2 B_2 C_2$ in Figure 1.2 are in perspective from O.

The projective plane $PG(2, GF(q))$ is special due to the following property.

Theorem 1.46 (Desargues). *If two triangles $\triangle A_1 B_1 C_1$ and $\triangle A_2 B_2 C_2$ in the plane $PG(2, GF(q))$ are in perspective from a point O, then the intersections of the lines $A_1 B_1$ and $A_2 B_2$, $A_1 C_1$ and $A_2 C_2$, and $B_1 C_1$ and $B_2 C_2$ are collinear.*

Proof. The points and lines of $PG(2, GF(q))$ were specifically given before. It is an easy task to verify that the desired property holds using the expressions of the points and lines of $PG(2, GF(q))$. The details are left to the reader.   □

The property of Theorem 1.46 is illustrated by Figure 1.2. A projective plane is said to be *Desarguesian* if the property of Theorem 1.46 holds, and *non-Desarguesian* otherwise. There are non-Desarguesian projective planes. Theorem 1.46 means that the projective planes $PG(2, GF(q))$ are Desarguesian.

1.6.5 *Central Collineations and Homologies of Projective Planes*

Let Π be a projective plane. A *collineation* or *automorphism* φ is a bijection from the point set and line set to themselves that preserves incidence. Thus, it maps point to point and line to line such that a point P is incident with a line ℓ if and only if $\varphi(P)$ is incident with $\varphi(\ell)$. All the collineations of Π form a group under the function composition, which is denoted by $\text{Aut}(\Pi)$, and called the *collineation group* of Π.

Let $g \in \text{Aut}(\Pi)$ for a projective plane Π. We say that g fixes a point P if $g(P) = P$, and fixes a line if it fixes the line setwise. Denote by $\text{Fix}(g)$ the fixed configuration of g, i.e., the union of the set of fixed points and fixed lines. Clearly, $\text{Fix}(g)$ is a closed configuration, i.e., if any two points P and Q are in $\text{Fix}(g)$, so is the line, and dually.

The following result was proved in Hall (1959).

Theorem 1.47. *In a projective plane a collineation fixes the same number of points and lines.*

It then follows from the theorem above that a group generated by a colleation has the number of fixed points equal to the number of fixed lines.

If a collineation g fixes a line ℓ pointwise, i.e., g fixes every point on the line, then we say that g has *axis* ℓ. If g fixes a point P linewise, i.e., g fixes every line with which P is incident, we say that g has *center* P. If $g \neq 1$, then it is known that it has at most one center and one axis, else it will fix the whole plane [Ionin and Shrikhande (2006)][p. 75]. A collineation of a projective plane is called a *central collineation* if it has both an axis and a center. The identity element is a central collineation, with any point permissible as a center and any line permissible as an axis. For any other central collineation, there is a unique center and unique axis.

Let $g \neq 1$ have axis ℓ and center P, i.e., g is a central collineation. Then g is an *elation* if P is incident with ℓ, and a *homology* otherwise. Figure 1.3 gives a pictorial illustration of an elation and homology.

Example 1.48. Consider the following collineation g of $PG(2, GF(q))$ defined by

$$g((x, y, z)) = (x, y, az),$$

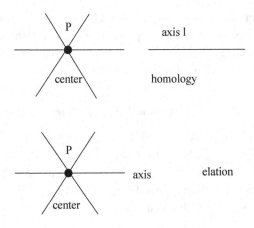

Fig. 1.3   Elation and homology

where $a \in \mathrm{GF}(q) \setminus \{0, 1\}$. Using the point set and line set defined in Section 1.6.4, one can verify that g has the following set of fixed points

$$\{(a, 1, 0) : a \in \mathrm{GF}(q)\} \cup \{(1, 0, 0)\}.$$

The set of fixed lines is

$$\{\ell_{(0,b,1)} : b \in \mathrm{GF}(q)\} \cup \{\ell_{(1,0,0)}\}. \tag{1.26}$$

Note that g fixes every point in the line $\ell_{(1,0,0)}$. Hence, g has axis $\ell_{(1,0,0)}$. Since all the fixed lines in (1.26) do not meet in the same point, g does not have a center.

Example 1.49. Consider the following collineation g of $\mathrm{PG}(2, \mathrm{GF}(q))$ defined by

$$g((x, y, z)) = (x + az, y, z),$$

where $a \in \mathrm{GF}(q) \setminus \{0, 1\}$. Using the point set and line set defined in Section 1.6.4, one can verify that g has the following set of fixed points

$$\ell_{(1,0,0)} = \{(a, 1, 0) : a \in \mathrm{GF}(q)\} \cup \{(1, 0, 0)\}.$$

Hence, g has axis $\ell_{(1,0,0)}$. The set of fixed lines is

$$\{\ell_{(c,1,0)} : b \in \mathrm{GF}(q)\} \cup \{\ell_{(1,0,0)}\}. \tag{1.27}$$

Since $(1, 0, 0)$ is on each of the fixed lines in (1.27), g has center $(1, 0, 0)$. Clearly, the center $(1, 0, 0)$ is on the axis. Notice that $g \neq 1$. We deduce that g is an elation.

A line ℓ is called a *translation line* if for all P incident with ℓ and every pair of distinct points Q and R, where Q, R, P are collinear and Q, R are not on ℓ, there exists an elation g with center P and axis ℓ such that $g(Q) = R$.

If a projective plane Π has a translation line, then Π is called a *translation plane*. The projective plane $\mathrm{PG}(2, \mathrm{GF}(q))$ is a translation plane, where every line is a translation line.

1.6.6 *Affine Planes*

An *affine plane* is a triple $\Pi = (\mathcal{P}, \mathcal{L}, \mathcal{R})$, where $\mathcal{P}$ is a set of *points*, $\mathcal{L}$ consists of *lines* (e.g., sets of points), and $\mathcal{R}$ is an *incidence relation* between the points and the lines such that

(a) every pair of distinct points is incident with a unique line;
(b) every point $p \in \mathcal{P}$ not on a line $L \in \mathcal{L}$ lies on a unique line $M \in \mathcal{L}$ which does not intersect L; and
(c) there exist four points such that no three of them are incident with a single line.

Example 1.50. Let $\mathcal{P} = \text{GF}(q)^2$ be the set of points. For each $(a, b, c) \in \text{GF}(q)^3$ with $(a, b) \neq (0, 0)$, we define a line

$$L_{(a,b,c)} = \{(x, y) : ax + by + c = 0\}.$$

Note that two different triples (a, b, c) may define the same line. Let $\mathcal{L} = \{L_{(a,b,c)} : (a, b, c) \in \text{GF}(q)^3\}$, which does not contain repeated lines. A point $p \in \mathcal{P}$ is incident with a line $L \in \mathcal{L}$ if and only if $p \in L$. Then it is easy to prove that $(\mathcal{P}, \mathcal{L}, \mathcal{R})$ is an affine plane, denoted by $\text{AG}(2, \text{GF}(q))$, and each line of $\text{AG}(2, \text{GF}(q))$ contains exactly q points.

Two lines ℓ and m in an affine plane $\Pi = (\mathcal{P}, \mathcal{B}, \mathcal{R})$ are called *parallel* if $\ell = m$ or no point is incident with both ℓ and m. This relation on the set of lines of Π is called the *parallelism*, and is an equivalence relation. Hence, $\mathcal{B}$ is partitioned into *equivalence classes* under this equivalence relation. Each equivalence class is called a *parallel class*.

The following is a basic result about finite affine planes [Ionin and Shrikhande (2006)][p. 63].

Theorem 1.51. *For any finite affine plane Π, there is an integer $n \geq 2$ such that every line is incident with exactly n points, every point is incident with exactly $n + 1$ lines, and Π has exactly n^2 points, $n^2 + n$ lines, and $n + 1$ parallel classes.*

The integer n in Theorem 1.51 is called the *order* of the affine plane Π.

One can construct a projective plane from an affine plane by adding a line to it. Conversely, one can obtain an affine plane from any projective plane by deleting one line and all the points on it. Points on a line are said to be *collinear*.

Theorem 1.52. *Let $\Pi = (\mathcal{P}, \mathcal{L}, \mathcal{R})$ be a projective plane, where $\mathcal{L} = \{\ell_i : i \in I\}$ and I is an index set, each line is a set of points in $\mathcal{P}$, and $\mathcal{R}$ is the set membership relation. Take any $h \in I$. Define then $\mathcal{P}' = \mathcal{P} \setminus \ell_h$ and $\ell_i' = \ell_i \setminus \ell_h$ for all $i \neq h$. Put*

$L' = \{\ell'_i : i \in I \setminus \{h\}\}$. *Define an incidence relation $\mathcal{R}'$ for the points in $\mathcal{P}'$ and the lines in L' as follows. A point P in $\mathcal{P}'$ is incidence with ℓ'_i with respect to $\mathcal{R}'$ if and only if it is incident with ℓ_i with respect to $\mathcal{R}$ in Π. Then $\Pi' = (\mathcal{P}', L', \mathcal{R}')$ is an affine plane.*

Proof. Let P and Q be two distinct points in $\mathcal{P}'$. If P and Q are incident with both ℓ'_i and ℓ'_j with respect to $\mathcal{R}'$, by definition they are incident with both ℓ_i and ℓ_j with respect to $\mathcal{R}$. It then follows from the second axiom of projective planes that $i = j$. So the first axiom of affine planes holds.

We now consider the second axiom of affine planes. Let ℓ'_i be a line in L' and let $P \in \mathcal{P}'$ be a point not incident with ℓ'_i with respect to $\mathcal{R}'$. Since $P \in \mathcal{P}'$, P is not incident with ℓ_i with respect to $\mathcal{R}$. By definition, $\ell_i = \ell'_i \cup \{Q\}$ for some point $Q \in \ell_h$. By the axioms of projective planes, this point Q is unique. Therefore, P and Q are distinct. It follows from the second axiom of projective planes that $\{P, Q\}$ is incident with a unique line $\ell_j \in L$, which is obviously different from ℓ_i. By the first axiom of projective planes, ℓ_i and ℓ_j are incident with the unique point Q. Consequently,

$$\ell'_i \cap \ell'_j = \emptyset,$$

where $\ell'_j = \ell_j \setminus \{Q\}$ is a line in L'. This means that ℓ'_j is the unique line in L' which contains P and is parallel to ℓ_i. Thus, the second axiom of affine planes holds.

Finally, we verify the third axiom of affine planes. By the third axiom of projective planes, there are four points P, Q, R, S in $\mathcal{P}$ such that no three of them are incident with any line in L. If all of them are not incident with ℓ_h, then they are in $\mathcal{P}'$ such that no three of them are incident with a line in L'. Otherwise, at least one of P, Q, R, S is incident with ℓ_h and at least two of them are not incident with ℓ_h. Without loss of generality, assume that P and Q are not incident with ℓ_h, but R is incident with ℓ_h. Let ℓ_i be the unique line in L that is incident with both P and R, and ℓ_j the unique line in L that is incident with both Q and R. Then $\ell'_i = \ell_i \setminus \{R\}$ and $\ell'_j = \ell_j \setminus \{R\}$ are two distinct lines in L', which are parallel. Take two points in ℓ'_i and two points in ℓ'_j. The four points are the desired ones that fulfil the third axiom of affine planes. $\qquad\square$

The following example illustrates Theorem 1.52 and its proof.

Example 1.53. Consider the Fano plane in Example 1.44. After deleting the last line $\{3, 7, 5\}$ and the points on the line from the point set and all lines in the Fano plane, we obtain an affine plane $(\mathcal{P}', L', \mathcal{R}')$, where $\mathcal{R}'$ is the membership relation, $\mathcal{P}' = \{1, 2, 4, 6\}$ and

$$L' = \{\{1, 2\}, \{1, 4\}, \{1, 6\}, \{2, 4\}, \{2, 6\}, \{4, 6\}\}.$$

These six lines in $\mathcal{L}'$ are divided into the following three parallel classes

$$\{\{1,2\},\{4,6\}\},\{\{1,4\},\{2,6\}\},\{\{1,6\},\{2,4\}\},$$

where the lines in each parallel class are pairwise parallel (i.e., disjoint). Further, each parallel class is a partition of the point set $\mathcal{P}'$.

The following theorem shows how to obtain a projective plane from an affine plane by adding a line.

Theorem 1.54. *Let* $\Pi = (\mathcal{P}, L, \mathcal{R})$ *be an affine plane, where each line is a set of points and $\mathcal{R}$ is the set membership relation. Partition the lines in L into parallel classes as*

$$L = \bigcup_{i \in I} L_i,$$

where I is an index set, and the lines in each L_i are parallel (i.e., disjoint). Then associate each parallel class L_i with a new point $Q_i \notin \mathcal{P}$, where the elements in $\{Q_i : i \in I\}$ are pairwise distinct. Put

$$\overline{\mathcal{P}} = \mathcal{P} \cup \{Q_i : i \in I\},$$

$$\overline{L} = \left(\bigcup_{i \in I} \{\ell \cup \{Q_i\} : \ell \in L_i\} \right) \bigcup \{Q_i : i \in I\}.$$

Then $\overline{\Pi} = (\overline{\mathcal{P}}, \overline{L}, \mathcal{R})$ is a projective plane.

Proof. Note that the new line added to the original affine plane is $q := \{Q_i : i \in I\}$, and the added new points are Q_i.

We first check the first axiom of projective planes. Any line $\ell \cup \{Q_i\}$ meets the new line q at the unique point Q_i. Consider now two distinct lines $\ell \cup \{Q_i\}$ and $\ell' \cup \{Q_{i'}\}$ in $\overline{L}$. If $i = i'$, then ℓ and ℓ' must be in the same parallel class L_i, and are thus disjoint. In this case, $\ell \cup \{Q_i\}$ and $\ell' \cup \{Q_{i'}\}$ meet at the unique point Q_i. If $i \neq i'$, then ℓ and ℓ' must be in two different parallel classes, and meet in a unique point $P \in \mathcal{P}$. Consequently, $\ell \cup \{Q_i\}$ and $\ell' \cup \{Q_{i'}\}$ meet at the unique point P. Hence, the first axiom of projective planes holds.

We then verify the second axiom of projective planes. By definition, any pair of distinct points Q_i and Q_j are only on the new line q. Consider now two old points P and P' in $\mathcal{P}$. By the first axiom of affine planes, they are on a unique line ℓ in L, and are hence on the unique line $\ell \cup \{Q_i\}$ in $\overline{L}$, where $\ell \in L_i$. Consider then a point $P \in \mathcal{P}$ and a point Q_i. Both P and Q_i can be only on some lines in the set

$$\{\ell \cup \{Q_i\} : \ell \in L_i\}.$$

Note that each parallel class is a partition of the point set $\mathcal{P}$. There is exactly one line $\ell \in L$ containing P. Therefore, $\ell \cup \{Q_i\}$ is the unique line in $\overline{L}$ containing P. Thus, the second axiom of projective planes holds.

Finally, we consider the third axiom of projective planes. By the third axiom of affine planes, there are four points P_1, P_2, P_3, P_4 in $\mathcal{P}$ such that no three of them are on the same line in L. If they are on two lines ℓ and ℓ' in L, then each of the two lines contains two of the four points. If ℓ and ℓ' are parallel, then they are on two distinct lines meeting at a point Q_i. Hence, no three of P_1, P_2, P_3, P_4 are on the same line in $\overline{L}$. If ℓ and ℓ' meet at a point P, then $P \notin \{P_1, P_2, P_3, P_4\}$. It is then easy to see that no three of P_1, P_2, P_3, P_4 are on the same line in $\overline{L}$. If P_1, P_2, P_3, P_4 are on at least three lines in L, then it is straightforward that no three of them are the same line in $\overline{L}$. $\qquad\square$

The projective plane $\overline{\Pi}$ obtained from an affine plane Π is called the *projective completion* of the affine plane. The following example explains Theorem 1.54 and its proof.

Example 1.55. Consider the affine plane $(\mathcal{P}', L', \mathcal{R}')$ in Example 1.53, where $\mathcal{R}'$ is the set membership relation, $\mathcal{P}' = \{1, 2, 4, 6\}$ and

$$L' = \{\{1,2\}, \{1,4\}, \{1,6\}, \{2,4\}, \{2,6\}, \{4,6\}\}.$$

We now partition the lines in L' into the following parallel classes $L' = \cup_{i \in I} L'_i$, where the index set $I = \{3, 5, 7\}$ and

$$L'_3 = \{\{1,2\}, \{4,6\}\}, L'_5 = \{\{1,4\}, \{2,6\}\}, L'_7 = \{\{1,6\}, \{2,4\}\}.$$

Finally, associate each parallel class L'_i with the new point i in $Q := \{3, 5, 7\}$. Then the incidence structure $(\overline{\mathcal{P}'}, \overline{L'}, \mathcal{R}')$ becomes the Fano projective plane in Example 1.44.

1.7 Basics of Group Actions

In this monograph, basics of group actions are required. The purpose of this section is to introduce concepts and fundamental results of group actions. Proofs of the results presented in this section can be found in Aschbacher (2000) or Shult and Surowski (2015)[Chapter 4].

In group theory, an *elementary abelian group* is a finite abelian group, where every nonidentity element has order p, where p is a prime. By the classification of finitely generated abelian groups, every elementary abelian group must be of the form $(\mathbb{Z}_p^n, +)$ for n being a nonnegative integer. Here and hereafter $\mathbb{Z}_m$ denotes the *ring of integers modulo m*.

Example 1.56. The elementary abelian group $(\mathbb{Z}_2^2, +)$ has four elements $\{(0,0), (0,1), (1,0), (1,1)\}$. Addition is performed componentwise, taking the result modulo 2. For instance, $(1,0) + (1,1) = (0,1)$.

The *symmetric group* on a finite set S, denoted $\mathrm{Sym}(S)$, is the group whose elements are all permutations on S and whose group operation is that of function composition. When $S = \{1, 2, \ldots, n\}$, the symmetric group on S is denoted by Sym_n or S_n.

An *action* of a group A on a set S is a permutation $\pi_a : S \to S$, for each $a \in A$, such that the following two conditions are met:

(a) (Identity) π_e is the identity, i.e., $\pi_e(s) = s$ for all $s \in S$, where e is the identity of A.
(b) (Compatibility) for every a_1 and a_2 in A, $\pi_{a_1} \circ \pi_{a_2} = \pi_{a_1 a_2}$, where $\circ$ stands for function composition.

Example 1.57. Let Sym_n act on $S = \{1, 2, \ldots, n\}$ in the natural way, i.e., $\pi_\sigma(i) = \sigma(i)$ for all $i \in S$, where $\sigma \in \mathrm{Sym}_n$.

Example 1.58. Any group A acts on itself by left multiplication functions.

A group A may act on a set S in many ways. For simplicity, we get rid of the notation π_a and write $\pi_a(s)$ as $a \cdot s$ or as. With this notation, the two conditions above become the following:

(a) (Identity) For each $s \in S$, $e \cdot s = s$, where e is the identity of A.
(b) (Compatibility) For every a_1 and a_2 in A and $s \in S$, $a_1 \cdot (a_2 \cdot s) = (a_1 a_2) \cdot s$.

Let a group A act on a set S. The *kernel* of the action is the set

$$\ker(A, S) = \{a \in A : a \cdot s = s \text{ for all } s \in S\}.$$

It is easy to prove that $\ker(A, S)$ is a normal subgroup of A.

Group actions can be classified into different types. A group action of A on S is called

- *faithful* if different elements of A act on S in different ways, i.e., when $a_1 \neq a_2$, there is an $s \in S$ such that $a_1 \cdot s \neq a_2 \cdot s$, i.e., $\ker(A, S) = \{e\}$;
- *transitive* if for any s_1, s_2 in S there exists an $a \in A$ such that $a \cdot s_1 = s_2$;
- *free* (or *semiregular*) if, given a_1, a_2 in A, the existence of an $s \in S$ with $a_1 \cdot s = a_2 \cdot s$ implies that $a_1 = a_2$, i.e., only the identity element of A has a fixed point;
- *regular* (or *simply transitive* or *sharply transitive*) if it is both transitive and free, i.e., it is transitive and the only permutation in A having a fixed point is the identity permutation.

Example 1.59. The action of a group A on itself is faithful, as different elements send the identity element e to different elements.

Example 1.60. Let $\mathbb{R}$ denote the set of all real numbers, and let $GL_n(\mathbb{R})$ be the set of all $n \times n$ invertible matrices over $\mathbb{R}$. Then $GL_n(\mathbb{R})$ is a group under the matrix multiplication, and is called the *general linear group* of degree n.

This group acts on the n-dimensional vector space $\mathbb{R}^n$ as follows:

$$A \cdot \mathbf{x} = A\mathbf{x}$$

where $A\mathbf{x}$ means the multiplication of the matrix A with the $n \times 1$ vector $\mathbf{x} \in \mathbb{R}^n$, and $A \in GL_n(\mathbb{R})$. The axioms of a group action are properties of matrix-vector multiplication. It is easily seen that this group action is not transitive, not free, not regular, but faithful.

Let A act on S. The *orbit* of an element $s \in S$ is defined by

$$\mathrm{Orb}_s = \{a \cdot s : a \in A\} \subseteq S$$

and the *stabilizer* of $s \in S$ is

$$\mathrm{Stab}_s = \{a \in A : a \cdot s = s\} \subseteq A.$$

Example 1.61. Let A be a group, and let A act on itself as $a \cdot s = asa^{-1}$ for all a and s in A. Then $\mathrm{Orb}_s = \{asa^{-1} : a \in A\}$, which is called the *conjugate class* of s. The stabilizer $\mathrm{Stab}_s = \{a \in A : as = sa\}$, which is referred to as the *centralizer* of s.

The following theorem is classical and can be easily proved.

Theorem 1.62. *Let A act on S. Then the following statements hold:*

(a) Different orbits are disjoint.

(b) For each $s \in S$, Stab_s is a subgroup of A and $\mathrm{Stab}_{a \cdot s} = a\mathrm{Stab}_s a^{-1}$.

(c) $a \cdot s = a' \cdot s$ if and only if a and a' lie in the same left coset of Stab_s. In particular, the length of the orbit of s is given by

$$|\mathrm{Orb}_s| = [A : \mathrm{Stab}_s] = |A|/|\mathrm{Stab}_s|.$$

As corollaries of Theorem 1.62, we have the following.

Corollary 1.63. *Let A act on S. Then the length of every orbit divides the size of A. In addition, points in a common orbit have conjugate stabilizers, and in particular the size of the stabilizer is the same for all points in an orbit.*

Corollary 1.64. *Let A act on S, where A and S are finite. Let the different orbits of S be represented by $s_1, s_2, \ldots, s_t$. Then*

$$|S| = \sum_{i=1}^{t} |\text{Orb}_{s_i}| = \sum_{i=1}^{t} [A : \text{Stab}_{s_i}].$$

In a group action of A on S, the length of an orbit divides $|A|$, but the number of orbits usually does not divide $|A|$. There is an interesting relation between the number of orbits and the group action as follows.

Lemma 1.65 (Burnside's lemma). *Let a finite group A act on a finite set S with r orbits. Then r is the average number of fixed points of the elements of the group:*

$$r = \frac{1}{|A|} \sum_{a \in A} |\text{Fix}_a(S)|,$$

where $\text{Fix}_a(S) = \{s \in S : a \cdot s = s\}$ is the set of elements of S fixed by a.

Let S be a set and let t be a positive integer. We use $\binom{S}{t}$ to denote the set of t-subsets of S, and S^t to denote the set of ordered t-tuples of S. Let A act on S. Then A acts on both $\binom{S}{t}$ and S^t in the natural way as follows. For any $\{s_1, s_2, \ldots, s_t\} \in \binom{S}{t}$ and $a \in A$, a acts on this subset by

$$a \cdot \{s_1, s_2, \ldots, s_t\} = \{a \cdot s_1, a \cdot s_2, \ldots, a \cdot s_t\}.$$

For any $(s_1, s_2, \ldots, s_t) \in S^t$ and $a \in A$, a acts on this ordered t-tuple by

$$a \cdot (s_1, s_2, \ldots, s_t) = (a \cdot s_1, a \cdot s_2, \ldots, a \cdot s_t).$$

Let $S^{(t)}$ denote the set of all t-tuples of t distinct elements of S. Hence, $S^{(t)}$ is a subset of S^t. Clearly, A acts on $S^{(t)}$ in the same natural way if A acts on S. We say that A is t-*transitive* on S if A acts on $S^{(t)}$ transitively, and A is *sharply t-transitive* on S if the action of A on $S^{(t)}$ is sharply transitive. We say that A is t-*homogeneous* on S if A acts on $\binom{S}{t}$ transitively. If the action of A on S is t-transitive, it must be t-homogeneous, but the converse may not be true. By definition, 1-transitivity means the normal transitivity defined earlier. In the next section, we will deal with specific types of group actions with various transitivity.

Let a finite group A act on a finite set S. It is easily seen that A is isomorphic to a subgroup of $\text{Sym}(S)$. Hence, every group action is a permutation group action. The *order* of A is defined to be $|A|$, and its *degree* is defined to be $|S|$.

The following theorem documents basic properties of the multi-transitivity of group actions.

Theorem 1.66. *Let A be a group acting on S and let $n = |S|$, i.e., the degree of A.*

(a) *If A is t-transitive and t > 1, then A is also (t − 1)-transitive.*
(b) *If A is t-transitive, then |A| divides n(n − 1) ⋯ (n − t + 1).*

Proof. Left to the reader.   □

Theorem 1.67. *The symmetric group* Sym(S) *is t-transitive on S for all positive integer* $t \leq |S|$. *If* $A \leq$ Sym$_n$, *i.e., A is a subgroup of the symmetric group* Sym$_n$, *then A is* $(n − 2)$-*transitive if and only if* $A_n \leq A$, *where* A_n *is the alternating group.*

Proof. Left to the reader.   □

1.8   Permutation Groups and Their Actions

The purpose of this section is to introduce several special permutation groups and their actions. These groups together with their actions will play a vital role in analysing linear codes and constructing certain combinatorial designs in later chapters.

1.8.1   *Semilinear Mappings of* GF(q)^m

Let $q = p^s$, where p is a prime and s is a positive integer. Define $\sigma_i(u) = u^{p^i}$ for all $u \in$ GF(q), where $0 \leq i \leq s − 1$. It is easily seen that σ_i is a one-to-one mapping from GF(q) to GF(q), and satisfies the following:

(1) $\sigma_i(u + v) = \sigma_i(u) + \sigma_i(v)$ for all u and v in GF(q).
(2) $\sigma_i(uv) = \sigma_i(u)\sigma_i(v)$ for all u and v in GF(q).
(3) $\sigma_i(u) = u$ for all $u \in$ GF(p).

These σ_i are all the *automorphisms* of GF(q). σ_1 is referred to as the *Frobenius automorphism*, and generates all others.

Let m be a positive integer. Each vector in GF(q)^m is viewed as an $m \times 1$ column vector. We now define a mapping from GF(q)^m to GF(q)^m by

$$\tau_i((u_1, u_2, \ldots, u_m)^T) = \left(u_1^{p^i}, u_2^{p^i}, \ldots, u_m^{p^i}\right)^T, \tag{1.28}$$

where $u = (u_1, u_2, \ldots, u_m)^T \in$ GF(q)^m, T denotes the transpose of a vector, and $0 \leq i \leq s − 1$. It is straightforward to verify the following:

(a) $\tau_i(u + v) = \tau_i(u) + \tau_i(v)$ for all u and v in GF(q)^m.
(b) $\tau_i(au) = a^{p^i}\tau_i(u)$ for all $u \in$ GF(q)^m and $a \in$ GF(q).

These τ_i are called *semilinear permutations* of $GF(q)^m$. For convenience, we denote $\tau_i(u)$ by u^{p^i}, where $u \in GF(q)^m$. This notation will be used in some subsequent sections and chapters.

In general, a mapping τ from $GF(q)^m$ to itself is called *semilinear* if it satisfies the following:

(a) $\tau(u + v) = \tau(u) + \tau(v)$ for all u and v in $GF(q)^m$.
(b) $\tau(au) = a^{p^i}\tau(u)$ for all $u \in GF(q)^m$ and $a \in GF(q)$ for some i with $0 \leq i \leq s - 1$.

In addition to these τ_i, there are much more semilinear permutations of $GF(q)^m$. For each $m \times m$ invertible matrix A over $GF(q)$, we define

$$\tau_{(i,A)}(u) = Au^{p^i}, \tag{1.29}$$

where $u \in GF(q)^m$ and $0 \leq i \leq s - 1$. Each $\tau_{(i,A)}$ is a semilinear permutation of $GF(q)^m$. All of them form a group under the function composition.

1.8.2 *General Linear Groups* $GL_m(GF(q))$

As before, we view all elements in $GF(q)^m$ as $m \times 1$ (column) vectors. Let $(GF(q)^m)^*$ denote the set $GF(q)^m \setminus \{\mathbf{0}\}$, where $\mathbf{0}$ is the zero vector in $GF(q)^m$. Let $GL_m(GF(q))$ be the set of all permutations

$$\sigma_{(A,0)} : x \mapsto Ax \tag{1.30}$$

of $(GF(q)^m)^*$, where A is an $m \times m$ invertible matrix over $GF(q)$, and x is a vector in $GF(q)^m$. Then $GL_m(GF(q))$ is clearly a permutation group of $(GF(q)^m)^*$ under the function composition, and is called the *general linear group*. The identity of this group is $\sigma_{(I_m,0)}$, where I_m is the $m \times m$ identity matrix over $GF(q)$.

Theorem 1.68. *Let $m \geq 1$ and q be any prime power. Then the order of the group $GL_m(GF(q))$ is*

$$|GL_m(GF(q))| = \prod_{i=0}^{m-1} (q^m - q^i).$$

Proof. We would build an $m \times m$ invertible matrix A over $GF(q)$. The first row of A could be any of the $q^m - 1$ nonzero vectors in $GF(q)^m$. The second row of A must be linearly independent of the first row, and has thus $q^m - q$ choices. In general, the i-th row must be linear independent of the first $i - 1$ rows, and thus has $q^m - q^{i-1}$ choices. Then the desired conclusion follows from the multiplication rule. $\square$

The following conclusion is obvious.

Theorem 1.69. $GL_1(GF(q))$ *is isomorphic to the multiplicative group* $GF(q)^*$ *of the finite field* $GF(q)$.

Theorem 1.70. *The group* $GL_m(GF(q))$ *is transitive on* $(GF(q)^m)^*$.

Proof. Let u and v be any two vectors in $(GF(q)^m)^*$. By definition, both u and v are nonzero. Then u and v can be extended into two invertible matrices U and V, such that the first column of U and V is u and v, respectively. Let $A = VU^{-1}$. Then A is invertible and $Au = v$. Hence, the general linear group $GL_m(GF(q))$ is transitive on $(GF(q)^m)^*$.   □

Theorem 1.71. *Let* $m \geq 2$. *Then the general linear group* $GL_m(GF(2))$ *is doubly transitive on* $(GF(2)^m)^*$.

Proof. Since $m \geq 2$, $(GF(2)^m)^*$ contains at least three elements. Let (u_1, u_2) and (v_1, v_2) be two ordered pairs of distinct elements in $(GF(2)^m)^*$. Since u_1 and u_2 are distinct, they are linearly independent over $GF(2)$. So they can be extended into a basis $\{u_1, u_2, \ldots, u_m\}$ of $GF(2)^m$ over $GF(2)$. Similarly, $\{v_1, v_2\}$ can be extended into a basis $\{v_1, v_2, \ldots, v_m\}$ of $GF(2)^m$ over $GF(2)$. Set

$$U = [u_1, u_2, \ldots, u_m] \text{ and } V = [v_1, v_2, \ldots, v_m].$$

Then U and V are $m \times m$ invertible matrices over $GF(2)$. Define $A = VU^{-1}$. We have then $AU = V$ and hence

$$Au_1 = v_1 \text{ and } Au_2 = v_2.$$

The desired conclusion then follows.   □

1.8.3   *General Semilinear Groups* $\Gamma L_m(GF(q))$

Let $q = p^s$, where p is a prime and s is a positive integer. As before, we view all elements in $GF(q)^m$ as $m \times 1$ (column) vectors. Let $(GF(q)^m)^*$ denote the set $GF(q)^m \setminus \{0\}$, where 0 is the zero vector in $GF(q)^m$. Let $\Gamma L_m(GF(q))$ be the set of all permutations

$$\sigma_{(A,0,i)} : x \mapsto Ax^{p^i} \tag{1.31}$$

of $(GF(q)^m)^*$, where A is an $m \times m$ invertible matrix over $GF(q)$, x is a vector in $GF(q)^m$, and $0 \leq i \leq s - 1$. Then $\Gamma L_m(GF(q))$ is obviously a permutation group of $(GF(q)^m)^*$ under the function composition, and is called the *general semilinear group* of $GF(q)^m$. The identity of this group is $\sigma_{(I_m,0,0)}$, where I_m is the $m \times m$ identity matrix over $GF(q)$.

The following theorem describes basic properties of the group $\Gamma\mathrm{L}_m(\mathrm{GF}(q))$ which are derived from those of the group $\mathrm{GL}_m(\mathrm{GF}(q))$ directly.

Theorem 1.72. *Let $q = p^s$, where p is a prime and s is a positive integer.*

(a) $|\Gamma\mathrm{L}_m(\mathrm{GF}(q))| = s|\mathrm{GL}_m(\mathrm{GF}(q))| = s\prod_{i=0}^{m-1}(q^m - q^i)$.
(b) The group $\Gamma\mathrm{L}_m(\mathrm{GF}(q))$ is transitive on $(\mathrm{GF}(q)^m)^*$.
(c) Let $m \geq 2$. Then $\Gamma\mathrm{L}_m(\mathrm{GF}(2))$ is doubly transitive on $(\mathrm{GF}(2)^m)^*$.

1.8.4 Special Linear Groups $\mathrm{SL}_m(\mathrm{GF}(q))$

Let $\mathrm{SL}_m(\mathrm{GF}(q))$ be the set of all permutations

$$\sigma_{(A,0)} : x \mapsto Ax \tag{1.32}$$

of $(\mathrm{GF}(q)^m)^*$, where A is an $m \times m$ matrix over $\mathrm{GF}(q)$ with determinant $\det(A) = 1$, and x is a vector in $\mathrm{GF}(q)^m$. Then $\mathrm{SL}_m(\mathrm{GF}(q))$ is obviously a permutation group of $(\mathrm{GF}(q)^m)^*$ under the function composition, and is called the *special linear group*. The identity of this group is $\sigma_{(I_m,0)}$, where I_m is the $m \times m$ identity matrix over $\mathrm{GF}(q)$. By definition, $\mathrm{SL}_m(\mathrm{GF}(q))$ is a subgroup of $\mathrm{GL}_m(\mathrm{GF}(q))$.

Theorem 1.73. *The order of $\mathrm{SL}_m(\mathrm{GF}(q))$ is $\left(\prod_{i=0}^{m-1}(q^m - q^i)\right)/(q-1)$.*

Proof. Define a mapping from $\mathrm{GL}_m(\mathrm{GF}(q))$ to $\mathrm{GF}(q)^*$ by

$$\det : \sigma_{(A,0)} \mapsto \det(A).$$

This is a group homomorphism whose kernel is $\mathrm{SL}_m(\mathrm{GF}(q))$. Hence, we have

$$\mathrm{GL}_m(\mathrm{GF}(q))/\mathrm{SL}_m(\mathrm{GF}(q)) \cong \mathrm{GF}(q)^*.$$

The desired conclusion then follows from Theorem 1.68. $\qquad\square$

Theorem 1.74. *Let $m \geq 2$. Then $\mathrm{SL}_m(\mathrm{GF}(q))$ is transitive on $(\mathrm{GF}(q)^m)^*$.*

Proof. Let u and v be two vectors in $(\mathrm{GF}(q)^m)^*$. Then u and v can be extended into two $m \times m$ invertible matrices U and V such that the first columns of U and V are u and v, respectively. Assume that $\det(U) = s$ and $\det(V) = t$. Note that $m \geq 2$. Multiplying the second column of U and V with s^{-1} and t^{-1}, respectively, we obtain two matrices U' and V' whose first columns are still u and v. However, $\det(U') = \det(V') = 1$. Define $A = V'(U')^{-1}$. Then A is an invertible matrix with $\det(A) = 1$ and $AU' = V'$. Therefore, $Au = v$. This completes the proof. $\qquad\square$

It is noted that the condition $m \geq 2$ in Theorem 1.74 is necessary, as $\mathrm{SL}_1(\mathrm{GF}(q))$ consists of only the identity mapping.

Theorem 1.75. *Let $m \geq 2$. Then $\mathrm{SL}_m(\mathrm{GF}(2))$ is doubly transitive on $(\mathrm{GF}(2)^m)^*$.*

Proof. Notice that $\mathrm{SL}_m(\mathrm{GF}(2)) = \mathrm{GL}_m(\mathrm{GF}(2))$. The desired conclusion follows from Theorem 1.71.   □

1.8.5 *General Affine Groups* $\mathrm{GA}_m(\mathrm{GF}(q))$

Let $\mathrm{GA}_m(\mathrm{GF}(q))$ be the set of all permutations

$$\sigma_{(A,b)} : x \mapsto Ax + b \tag{1.33}$$

of $\mathrm{GF}(q)^m$, where A is an $m \times m$ invertible matrix over $\mathrm{GF}(q)$, and b is a vector in $\mathrm{GF}(q)^m$. Then $\mathrm{GA}_m(\mathrm{GF}(q))$ is a permutation group of $\mathrm{GF}(q)^m$ under the function composition, and is referred to as the *general affine group*. The identity of this group is $\sigma_{(I_m,0)}$, where I_m is the $m \times m$ identity matrix over $\mathrm{GF}(q)$. By definition, $\mathrm{GL}_m(\mathrm{GF}(q))$ is a subgroup of $\mathrm{GA}_m(\mathrm{GF}(q))$.

Theorem 1.76. *Let $m \geq 1$ and q be any prime power. Then the order of the group $\mathrm{GA}_m(\mathrm{GF}(q))$ is*

$$|\mathrm{GA}_m(\mathrm{GF}(q))| = q^m \prod_{i=0}^{m-1} (q^m - q^i).$$

Proof. It follows from Theorem 1.68 that

$$|\mathrm{GA}_m(\mathrm{GF}(q))| = q^m |\mathrm{GL}_m(\mathrm{GF}(q))| = q^m \prod_{i=0}^{m-1} (q^m - q^i).$$

□

Theorem 1.77. *The group $\mathrm{GA}_m(\mathrm{GF}(q))$ is doubly transitive on $\mathrm{GF}(q)^m$.*

Proof. Let (u,v) and (s,t) be two ordered pairs of distinct elements in $\mathrm{GF}(q)^m$. We wish to find an $m \times m$ invertible matrix A and a vector $b \in \mathrm{GF}(q)^m$ such that

$$Au + b = s \text{ and } Av + b = t,$$

which has a solution (A,b) if and only if

$$A(u-v) = s-t$$

has a solution A, which is invertible. Note that $u - v \neq 0$ and $s - t \neq 0$. The desired conclusion then follows from Theorem 1.70.   □

Theorem 1.78. *Let $m \geq 2$. Then the group $\mathrm{GA}_m(\mathrm{GF}(2))$ is triply transitive on $\mathrm{GF}(2)^m$.*

Proof. Let (u_1, v_1, w_1) and (u_2, v_2, w_2) be two ordered sets of pairwise distinct vectors in $GF(2)^m$. We would like to find an invertible $m \times m$ matrix A and a vector $b \in GF(2)^m$ such that

$$Au_1 + b = u_2, \ Av_1 + b = v_2, \ Aw_1 + b = w_2.$$

This is equivalent to

$$A(u_1 - v_1) = u_2 - v_2, \ A(u_1 - w_1) = u_2 - w_2, \tag{1.34}$$

where $u_1 - v_1 \neq 0$, $u_2 - v_2 \neq 0$, $u_1 - w_1 \neq 0$, $u_2 - w_2 \neq 0$, $u_1 - v_1 \neq u_1 - w_1$, and $u_2 - v_2 \neq u_2 - w_2$. The existence of an invertible A satisfying (1.34) is ensured by the fact that $GL_m(GF(2))$ is doubly transitive (see Theorem 1.71). Then the desired b is given by $b = Au_1 + u_2$. $\square$

1.8.6 Special Affine Groups $SA_m(GF(q))$

The *special affine group* $SA_m(GF(q))$ consists of all permutations

$$\sigma_{(A,b)} : x \mapsto Ax + b \tag{1.35}$$

of $GF(q)^m$, where A is an $m \times m$ matrix over $GF(q)$ with $\det(A) = 1$, and b is a vector in $GF(q)^m$. It is a permutation group of $GF(q)^m$ under the function composition. The identity of this group is $\sigma_{(I_m,0)}$, where I_m is the $m \times m$ identity matrix over $GF(q)$.

Properties of $SA_m(GF(q))$ are summarised in the following theorem.

Theorem 1.79.

(a) $|SA_m(GF(q))| = q^m \left(\prod_{i=0}^{m-1} (q^m - q^i) \right) / (q - 1)$.

(b) Let $m \geq 2$. Then $SA_m(GF(q))$ is transitive if $q > 2$, and doubly transitive if $q = 2$.

1.8.7 Semilinear Affine Groups $\Gamma A_m(GF(q))$

Let $q = p^s$, where p is a prime and s is a positive integer. The *semilinear affine group* $\Gamma A_m(GF(q))$ is composed of all permutations

$$\sigma_{(A,b,i)} : x \mapsto Ax^{p^i} + b \tag{1.36}$$

of $GF(q)^m$, where A is an $m \times m$ invertible matrix over $GF(q)$, b is a vector in $GF(q)^m$, and $0 \leq i \leq s - 1$. It is a permutation group of $GF(q)^m$ under the function composition. The identity of this group is $\sigma_{(I_m,0,0)}$, where I_m is the $m \times m$ identity matrix over $GF(q)$. Obviously, $GA_m(GF(q))$ is a subgroup of $\Gamma A_m(GF(q))$.

The following theorem describes basic properties of the group $\Gamma A_m(GF(q))$ which are derived from those of the group $GA_m(GF(q))$ directly.

Theorem 1.80. *Let $q = p^s$, where p is a prime and s is a positive integer.*

(a) $|\Gamma A_m(GF(q))| = s|GA_m(GF(q))| = sq^m \prod_{i=0}^{m-1}(q^m - q^i)$.

(b) *The group* $\Gamma A_m(GF(q))$ *is 2-transitive when* $q > 2$, *and 3-transitive when* $q = 2$.

1.8.8 *Projective General Linear Groups* $PGL_m(GF(q))$

Recall the projective space $PG(m-1, GF(q))$ discussed in Section 1.6, which consists of all r-dimensional subspaces of $GF(q)^m$ for $1 \le r \le m-1$. In this section, we view $PG(m-1, GF(q))$ as a set consisting of only its points. Since an invertible linear transformation maps a subspace to another subspace of the same dimension, the general linear group $GL_m(GF(q))$ acts on $PG(m-1, GF(q))$ naturally.

Theorem 1.81. *The kernel of the action of* $GL_m(GF(q))$ *on the set of points of* $PG(m-1, GF(q))$ *is the subgroup*

$$\Sigma_{(m,q)} = \{\sigma_{(cI_m, 0)} : c \in GF(q)^*\} \tag{1.37}$$

of $GL_m(GF(q))$, *where* I_m *is the* $m \times m$ *identity matrix over* $GF(q)$.

Proof. Let $\sigma_{(A,0)}$ be an element in the kernel of this group action. By definition, A fixes every rank 1 subspace of $GF(q)^m$. This means that A maps every nonzero vector x to a scalar multiple cx for some $c \in GF(q)^*$.

Let e_i be the i-th basis vector, with 1 in position i and 0 elsewhere. So $Ae_i = c_i e_i$, so the i-th column of A is $c_i e_i$. This shows that A is a diagonal matrix.

Now for $i \ne j$, we have

$$c_i e_i + c_j e_j = A(e_i + e_j) = c(e_i + e_j)$$

for some $c \in GF(q)^*$. So $c_i = c_j = c$. Thus, A is the diagonal matrix cI_m. $\qquad\square$

The *projective general linear group* is defined to be the group induced on the points of the projective space $PG(m-1, GF(q))$ by $GL_m(GF(q))$. It then follows from Theorem 1.81 that

$$PGL_m(GF(q)) \cong GL_m(GF(q))/\Sigma_{(m,q)},$$

where the normal subgroup $\Sigma_{(m,q)}$ was defined in (1.37) before. So one may use this quotient group to define the projective general linear group directly. In other words, all the permutations

$$\sigma_{(aA,0)}, \ a \in GF(q)^*$$

are viewed as identical and they define only one element in $PGL_m(GF(q))$. As a result, we arrive at the following.

Theorem 1.82. *The order of* $\text{PGL}_m(\text{GF}(q))$ *is*

$$|\text{GL}_m(\text{GF}(q))|/(q-1) = \left(\prod_{i=0}^{m-1}(q^m - q^i)\right)/(q-1).$$

Notice that $\text{PGL}_m(\text{GF}(q))$ and $\text{SL}_m(q)$ have the same order. The following result will be very useful in many applications.

Theorem 1.83. *The projective general linear group* $\text{PGL}_m(\text{GF}(q))$ *is doubly transitive on* $\text{PG}(m-1,\text{GF}(q))$ *for* $m \geq 2$.

Proof. Let (a,b) and (c,d) be two ordered pairs of points in $\text{PG}(m-1,\text{GF}(q))$, where $a \neq b$ and $c \neq d$. Since $a \neq b$, a and b are linearly independent over $\text{GF}(q)$. Hence, a and b can be extended into an invertible $m \times m$ matrix U whose first and second columns are a and b, respectively. For the same reason, c and d can be extended into an invertible $m \times m$ matrix V whose first and second columns are c and d, respectively. Now define $A = VU^{-1}$, which is invertible. We have then

$$\sigma_{(A,0)}(a) = Aa = c \text{ and } \sigma_{(A,0)}(b) = Ab = d.$$

Note that $\sigma_{(uA,0)}$ means the same element in $\text{PGL}_m(\text{GF}(q))$ for all $u \in \text{GF}(q)^*$. This proves the desired conclusion. $\qquad\qquad\square$

It is worthwhile to note that $\text{PG}(m-1,\text{GF}(2))$ and $(\text{GF}(2)^m)^*$ are identical, and $\text{PGL}_m(\text{GF}(2)) = \text{SL}_m(\text{GF}(2)) = \text{GL}_m(\text{GF}(2))$.

Theorem 1.84. *The projective general linear group* $\text{PGL}_2(\text{GF}(q))$ *is triply transitive on* $\text{PG}(1,\text{GF}(q))$.

Proof. Note that $\text{PG}(1,\text{GF}(q))$ has $q+1 \geq 3$ points. Let (u_1,u_2,u_3) be a triple of three pairwise distinct points in $\text{PG}(1,\text{GF}(q))$, where $u_i = (a_i,b_i) \in \text{GF}(q)^2$ for all i. Then u_i and u_j are linearly independent over $\text{GF}(q)$ for $i \neq j$. Since, the vector space $\text{GF}(q)^2$ has dimension 2, there must exist two elements s and t in $\text{GF}(q)^*$ such that $u_3 = su_1 + tu_2$. Let (v_1,v_2,v_3) be a triple of three pairwise distinct points in $\text{PG}(1,\text{GF}(q))$. For the same reason, $v_3 = av_1 + bv_2$ for two elements a and b in $\text{GF}(q)^*$.

Let $U = [u_1,u_2]$ and $V_h = [hv_1,v_2]$, where $h \in \text{GF}(q)^*$. Then U and V_h are invertible matrices over $\text{GF}(q)$. Set $A_h = V_h U^{-1}$. Then $A_h u_1 = hv_1$ and $A_h u_2 = v_2$. We have then

$$A_h u_3 = sA_h u_1 + tA_h u_2 = hsv_1 + tv_2.$$

Note that

$$tb^{-1}v_3 = tab^{-1}v_1 + tv_2.$$

Take $h = tab^{-1}s^{-1}$. We obtain that

$$A_h u_3 = tb^{-1}v_3.$$

Note that in $\mathrm{PG}(1,\mathrm{GF}(q))$, v_1 and hv_1 are the same point, and v_3 and $tb^{-1}v_3$ are the same point. This means that $\sigma_{(A,0)}(u_i) = v_i$ for all $1 \leq i \leq 3$. The desired conclusion then follows. $\square$

Now we work out a different representation of the action of $\mathrm{PGL}_2(\mathrm{GF}(q))$ on $\mathrm{PG}(1,\mathrm{GF}(q))$. Note that the points of $\mathrm{PG}(1,\mathrm{GF}(q))$ can be identified by the elements in the set $\{\infty\} \cup \mathrm{GF}(q)$, where

$$\infty = \begin{pmatrix} 1 \\ 0 \end{pmatrix}, \quad a = \begin{pmatrix} a \\ 1 \end{pmatrix}, \; a \in \mathrm{GF}(q).$$

Let

$$A = \begin{bmatrix} a & c \\ b & d \end{bmatrix}$$

with $ad - bc \neq 0$. We have then

$$\sigma_{(A,0)}\left(\begin{pmatrix} x \\ 1 \end{pmatrix}\right) = \begin{pmatrix} ax+c \\ bx+d \end{pmatrix} = \begin{cases} \begin{pmatrix} \frac{ax+c}{bx+d} \\ 1 \end{pmatrix} & \text{if } bx+d \neq 0, \\ \begin{pmatrix} 1 \\ 0 \end{pmatrix} & \text{otherwise.} \end{cases}$$

Furthermore, we have

$$\sigma_{(A,0)}\left(\begin{pmatrix} 1 \\ 0 \end{pmatrix}\right) = \begin{pmatrix} a \\ b \end{pmatrix} = \begin{cases} \begin{pmatrix} 1 \\ 0 \end{pmatrix} & \text{if } b = 0, \\ \begin{pmatrix} ab^{-1} \\ 1 \end{pmatrix} & \text{if } b \neq 0. \end{cases}$$

Then the transformation induced by $\sigma_{(A,0)}$ can be written as

$$x \mapsto \frac{ax+c}{bx+d} \tag{1.38}$$

provided that we make the following conventions about ∞:

- $\frac{a}{0} = \infty$ for all $a \in \mathrm{GF}(q)^*$.
- $\frac{\infty a+c}{\infty b+d} = \frac{a}{b}$.

Hence, we may redefine $\mathrm{PGL}_2(\mathrm{GF}(q))$ as follows.

Theorem 1.85. *The projective general linear group* $\mathrm{PGL}_2(\mathrm{GF}(q))$ *consists of all the following permutations of the set* $\{\infty\} \cup \mathrm{GF}(q)$:

$$\pi_{(a,b,c,d)}(x) = \frac{ax+c}{bx+d}$$

with $ad - bc \neq 0$, *and the conventions above about* ∞. *The corresponding group action is triply transitive.*

Proof. The 3-transitivity of the group action follows from Theorem 1.84. $\square$

1.8.9 *Projective Semilinear Groups* $\text{P}\Gamma\text{L}_m(\text{GF}(q))$

Let $q = p^s$, where p is a prime and s is a positive integer. We view all elements in $\text{PG}(m-1, \text{GF}(q))$ as $m \times 1$ (column) vectors. The *projective semilinear group* $\text{P}\Gamma\text{L}_m(\text{GF}(q))$ be the set of all permutations

$$\sigma_{(A,0,i)} : x \mapsto Ax^{p^i} \tag{1.39}$$

of $\text{PG}(m-1, \text{GF}(q))$, where A is an $m \times m$ invertible matrix over $\text{GF}(q)$, x is an element in $\text{PG}(m-1, \text{GF}(q))$ and $0 \le i \le s-1$. It is obviously a permutation group of $\text{PG}(m-1, \text{GF}(q))$ under the function composition. The identity of this group is $\sigma_{(I_m,0,0)}$, where I_m is the $m \times m$ identity matrix over $\text{GF}(q)$. Clearly, $\text{PGL}_m(\text{GF}(q))$ is a subgroup of $\text{P}\Gamma\text{L}_m(\text{GF}(q))$.

The following theorem describes basic properties of the group $\text{P}\Gamma\text{L}_m(\text{GF}(q))$ which are derived from those of $\text{PGL}_m(\text{GF}(q))$.

Theorem 1.86. *Let $q = p^s$, where p is a prime and s is a positive integer.*

(a) $|\text{P}\Gamma\text{L}_m(\text{GF}(q))| = s|\text{PGL}_m(\text{GF}(q))| = s\left(\prod_{i=0}^{m-1}(q^m - q^i)\right)/(q-1)$.
(b) *The action of $\text{P}\Gamma\text{L}_m(\text{GF}(q))$ on $\text{PG}(m-1, \text{GF}(q))$ is doubly transitive when $m > 2$, and triply transitive when $m = 2$.*

1.8.10 *Projective Special Linear Groups* $\text{PSL}_m(\text{GF}(q))$

We now define the *projective special linear group*, denoted by $\text{PSL}_m(\text{GF}(q))$, to be the image of $\text{SL}_m(\text{GF}(q))$ under the homomorphism from $\text{GL}_m(\text{GF}(q))$ to $\text{PGL}_m(\text{GF}(q))$, i.e., the group induced on the set $\text{PG}(m-1, \text{GF}(q))$ consisting of only all points in the projective space $\text{PG}(m-1, \text{GF}(q))$ by $\text{SL}_m(\text{GF}(q))$. Thus,

$$\text{PSL}_m(\text{GF}(q)) = \text{SL}_m(\text{GF}(q))/(\text{SL}_m(\text{GF}(q)) \cap \Sigma_{(m,q)}), \tag{1.40}$$

where the subgroup $\Sigma_{(m,q)}$ was defined in (1.37).

In other words, $\text{PSL}_m(\text{GF}(q))$ consists of the maximum number of elements in $\text{SL}_m(\text{GF}(q))$ such that $A \ne uB$ for all $u \in \text{GF}(q)^*$ for any two distinct elements $\sigma_{(A,0)}$ and $\sigma_{(B,0)}$ in $\text{PSL}_m(\text{GF}(q))$. To have a better understanding, we explain the projective special linear group $\text{PSL}_m(\text{GF}(q))$ further below.

Let $\det(A) = 1$, then $\det(uA) = u^m$ and $\sigma_{(A,0)} \in \text{SL}_m(\text{GF}(q))$. All the elements $\sigma_{(uA,0)} \in \text{SL}_m(\text{GF}(q))$ with $u^m = 1$ are clearly $\gcd(m, q-1)$ distinct elements in $\text{SL}_m(\text{GF}(q))$, but they are identical and define the same element in $\text{PSL}_m(\text{GF}(q))$. Hence, the order of $\text{PSL}_m(\text{GF}(q))$ is equal to $|\text{SL}_m(\text{GF}(q))|/\gcd(m, q-1)$. This explanation also proves the following.

Theorem 1.87. $|\mathrm{PSL}_m(\mathrm{GF}(q))| = |\mathrm{SL}_m(\mathrm{GF}(q))|/\gcd(m, q-1)$. *In particular, we have*

$$|\mathrm{PSL}_2(\mathrm{GF}(q))| = \frac{q(q^2-1)}{2}$$

when q is odd.

By definition, the projective special linear group $\mathrm{PSL}_2(\mathrm{GF}(q))$ consists of all the following permutations of the set $\{\infty\} \cup \mathrm{GF}(q)$:

$$\pi_{(a,b,c,d)}(x) = \frac{ax+c}{bx+d}$$

with $ad - bc = 1$ and the conventions above about ∞. This group $\mathrm{PSL}_2(\mathrm{GF}(q))$ will be very useful for us later.

It can be easily verified that

$$\mathrm{PSL}_2(\mathrm{GF}(q)) = \left\{ x \mapsto \frac{ax+c}{bx+d} : ac - bc \text{ is a nonzero square in } \mathrm{GF}(q) \right\}.$$

Theorem 1.88. *Let $q \equiv \pm 1 \pmod{8}$ be an odd prime. Then $\mathrm{PSL}_2(q)$ is generated by the two permutations*

$$S: y \mapsto y+1,$$
$$T: y \mapsto -\frac{1}{y}.$$

Proof. It is left to the reader. $\qquad\square$

We will need the following theorem in subsequent chapters.

Theorem 1.89. *Let $m \geq 2$. Then the group $\mathrm{PSL}_m(\mathrm{GF}(q))$ is doubly transitive on $\mathrm{PG}(m-1, \mathrm{GF}(q))$.*

Proof. Let (u_1, u_2) be an ordered set of two distinct points in $\mathrm{PG}(m-1, \mathrm{GF}(q))$. Then they are linearly independent over $\mathrm{GF}(q)$. Hence, they can be extended into an $m \times m$ invertible matrix $U = [u_1 u_2 \cdots u_m]$. Since, au_1 and u_1 are the same point in $\mathrm{PG}(m-1, \mathrm{GF}(q))$ for each $a \in \mathrm{GF}(q)^*$ and

$$\det([(au_1)u_2 \cdots u_m]) = u\det(U),$$

we can always assume that $\det(U) = 1$.

Let (v_1, v_2) be an ordered set of two distinct points in $\mathrm{PG}(m-1, \mathrm{GF}(q))$. For the same reason, they can be extended into an $m \times m$ invertible matrix $V = [v_1 v_2 \cdots v_m]$ with $\det(V) = 1$. We now put $A = VU^{-1}$. Then $\det(A) = 1$ and $Au_i = v_i$ for all i. Clearly, $\sigma_{(A,0)} \in \mathrm{PSL}_m(\mathrm{GF}(q))$. This completes the proof. $\qquad\square$

Theorem 1.90. *The group* $\mathrm{PSL}_2(\mathrm{GF}(q))$ *is triply transitive on* $\mathrm{PG}(1,\mathrm{GF}(q))$ *if* q *is even.*

Proof. Let q be even. It then follows from Theorem 1.87 that

$$|\mathrm{PSL}_2(\mathrm{GF}(q))| = \frac{|\mathrm{SL}_2(\mathrm{GF}(q))|}{\gcd(2,q-1)} = |\mathrm{SL}_2(\mathrm{GF}(q))| = |\mathrm{PGL}_m(\mathrm{GF}(q))|.$$

This means that $\mathrm{PSL}_2(\mathrm{GF}(q))$ and $\mathrm{PGL}_2(\mathrm{GF}(q))$ become the same group in this case. The desired conclusion then follows from Theorem 1.84. □

1.8.11 *A Summary of the Group Actions on* $\mathrm{GF}(q)^m$ *and* $(\mathrm{GF}(q)^m)^*$

To have a whole picture of the permutation groups covered in previous sections and their actions, we present a summary in Table 1.1, where $\mathrm{PG}(m-1,\mathrm{GF}(q))$ denotes the set of all points in the projective space $\mathrm{PG}(m-1,\mathrm{GF}(q))$. As will be seen later, these permutation groups and their actions will play a significant role in analysing linear codes and combinatorial designs to be dealt with in later chapters.

Table 1.1   A summary of the permutation groups and their actions

Group	Group order	Object set	Transitivity
$\Gamma\mathrm{A}_m(\mathrm{GF}(q))$	$sq^m \prod_{i=0}^{m-1}(q^m - q^i)$	$\mathrm{GF}(q)^m$	$2\ (q = p^s > 2)$
			$3\ (q = 2)$
$\mathrm{GA}_m(\mathrm{GF}(q))$	$q^m \prod_{i=0}^{m-1}(q^m - q^i)$	$\mathrm{GF}(q)^m$	$2\ (q > 2)$
			$3\ (q = 2)$
$\mathrm{SA}_m(\mathrm{GF}(q))$	$q^m(\prod_{i=0}^{m-1}(q^m - q^i))/(q-1)$	$\mathrm{GF}(q)^m$	$1\ (q > 2, m \geq 2)$
			$2\ (q = 2 \text{ and } m \geq 2)$
$\Gamma\mathrm{L}_m(\mathrm{GF}(q))$	$s\prod_{i=0}^{m-1}(q^m - q^i)$	$\mathrm{GF}(q)^m \setminus \{\mathbf{0}\}$	$1\ (q = p^s > 2)$
			$2\ (m \geq 2, q = 2)$
$\mathrm{GL}_m(\mathrm{GF}(q))$	$\prod_{i=0}^{m-1}(q^m - q^i)$	$\mathrm{GF}(q)^m \setminus \{\mathbf{0}\}$	1
			$2\ (m \geq 2, q = 2)$
$\mathrm{SL}_m(\mathrm{GF}(q))$	$\frac{\prod_{i=0}^{m-1}(q^m - q^i)}{q-1}$	$\mathrm{GF}(q)^m \setminus \{\mathbf{0}\}$	$1\ (m > 1, q > 2)$
			$2\ (m > 1, q = 2)$
$\mathrm{P}\Gamma\mathrm{L}_m(\mathrm{GF}(q))$	$s\frac{\prod_{i=0}^{m-1}(q^m - q^i)}{q-1}$	$\mathrm{PG}(m-1,\mathrm{GF}(q))$	$2\ (m \geq 3, q = p^s)$
			$3\ (m = 2, q = p^s)$
$\mathrm{PGL}_m(\mathrm{GF}(q))$	$\frac{\prod_{i=0}^{m-1}(q^m - q^i)}{q-1}$	$\mathrm{PG}(m-1,\mathrm{GF}(q))$	$2\ (m \geq 3)$
			$3\ (m = 2)$
$\mathrm{PSL}_m(\mathrm{GF}(q))$	$\frac{\prod_{i=0}^{m-1}(q^m - q^i)}{(q-1)\gcd(m,q-1)}$	$\mathrm{PG}(m-1,\mathrm{GF}(q))$	$2\ (m \geq 2)$
			$3\ (m = 2, q \text{ even})$

1.8.12 *Permutation Group Actions on* $\mathrm{GF}(q^m)$ *and* $\mathrm{GF}(q^m)^*$

Note that $\mathrm{GF}(q^m)$, as a vector space over $\mathrm{GF}(q)$, is isomorphic to the vector space $\mathrm{GF}(q)^m$. Let $\{\beta_1, \beta_2, \ldots, \beta_m\}$ be a basis of $\mathrm{GF}(q^m)$ over $\mathrm{GF}(q)$. Define

$$\phi : u = \sum_{i=1}^{m} u_i \beta_i \mapsto (u_1, u_2, \ldots, u_m)^T,$$

where T denotes the transpose of a vector and each u_i belongs to $\mathrm{GF}(q)$. This ϕ is the isomorphism mentioned before. Under this mapping, the preimage of each point in $\mathrm{PG}(m-1, \mathrm{GF}(q))$ is subset of $\mathrm{GF}(q^m)^*$ of the form

$$\mathrm{GF}(q)^* u,$$

where $u \in \mathrm{GF}(q^m) \setminus \mathrm{GF}(q)$. Hence, the set $\mathrm{PG}(m-1, \mathrm{GF}(q))$ of points can be represented by the elements in the quotient group $\mathrm{GF}(q^m)^* / \mathrm{GF}(q)^*$.

Let A be an $m \times m$ invertible matrix over $\mathrm{GF}(q)$, and let b be a vector in $\mathrm{GF}(q)^m$. The permutation $\sigma_{(A,b)}(x) = Ax + b$ of $\mathrm{GF}(q)^m$ induces a permutation of $\mathrm{GF}(q^m)$ under a basis $\{\gamma_1, \gamma_2, \ldots, \gamma_m\}$ of $\mathrm{GF}(q^m)$ over $\mathrm{GF}(q)$ as follows:

$$\sigma_{(A,b)}(u) = (\beta_1, \beta_2, \ldots, \beta_m) \cdot \sigma_{(A,b)}(\phi(u)), \ u \in \mathrm{GF}(q^m),$$

which is the dot inner product of the two vectors. The two bases $\{\beta_1, \beta_2, \ldots, \beta_m\}$ and $\{\gamma_1, \gamma_2, \ldots, \gamma_m\}$ may be chosen to be identical or distinct. In this way, we have the following:

(1) $\Gamma\mathrm{A}_m(\mathrm{GF}(q))$ acts on $\mathrm{GF}(q^m)$ as a permutation group.
(2) $\mathrm{GA}_m(\mathrm{GF}(q))$ acts on $\mathrm{GF}(q^m)$ as a permutation group.
(3) $\mathrm{SA}_m(\mathrm{GF}(q))$ acts on $\mathrm{GF}(q^m)$ as a permutation group.
(4) $\Gamma\mathrm{L}_m(\mathrm{GF}(q))$ acts on $\mathrm{GF}(q^m)^*$ as a permutation group.
(5) $\mathrm{GL}_m(\mathrm{GF}(q))$ acts on $\mathrm{GF}(q^m)^*$ as a permutation group.
(6) $\mathrm{SL}_m(\mathrm{GF}(q))$ acts on $\mathrm{GF}(q^m)^*$ as a permutation group.
(7) $\mathrm{PGL}_m(\mathrm{GF}(q))$ acts on $\mathrm{GF}(q^m)^* / \mathrm{GF}(q)^*$ as a permutation group.
(8) $\mathrm{P}\Gamma\mathrm{L}_m(\mathrm{GF}(q))$ acts on $\mathrm{GF}(q^m)^* / \mathrm{GF}(q)^*$ as a permutation group.
(9) $\mathrm{PSL}_m(\mathrm{GF}(q))$ acts on $\mathrm{GF}(q^m)^* / \mathrm{GF}(q)^*$ as a permutation group.

The degrees of transitivity of these group actions are summarized in Table 1.2.

1.8.13 *Highly Transitive Permutation Groups*

The following result was stated in Dixon and Mortimer (1996)[p. 34, p. 218] and Kantor (1972).

Theorem 1.91. *Except for the Mathieu groups listed in Table 1.3 and the alternating group A_n and the symmetric group S_n, no finite permutation groups are more than 3-transitive.*

Table 1.2   A summary of the permutation groups and their actions

Group	Group order	Object set	Transitivity
$\Gamma A_m(\mathrm{GF}(q))$	$sq^m \prod_{i=0}^{m-1}(q^m - q^i)$	$\mathrm{GF}(q^m)$	2 ($q = p^s > 2$) 3 ($q = 2$)
$GA_m(\mathrm{GF}(q))$	$q^m \prod_{i=0}^{m-1}(q^m - q^i)$	$\mathrm{GF}(q^m)$	2 ($q > 2$) 3 ($q = 2$)
$SA_m(\mathrm{GF}(q))$	$q^m(\prod_{i=0}^{m-1}(q^m - q^i))/(q-1)$	$\mathrm{GF}(q^m)$	1 ($q > 2, m \geq 2$) 2 ($q = 2$ and $m \geq 2$)
$\Gamma L_m(\mathrm{GF}(q))$	$s\prod_{i=0}^{m-1}(q^m - q^i)$	$\mathrm{GF}(q^m)^*$	1 ($q = p^s > 2$) 2 ($m \geq 2, q = 2$)
$GL_m(\mathrm{GF}(q))$	$\prod_{i=0}^{m-1}(q^m - q^i)$	$\mathrm{GF}(q^m)^*$	1 2 ($m \geq 2, q = 2$)
$SL_m(\mathrm{GF}(q))$	$\dfrac{\prod_{i=0}^{m-1}(q^m - q^i)}{q-1}$	$\mathrm{GF}(q^m)^*$	1 ($m > 1, q > 2$) 2 ($m > 1, q = 2$)
$P\Gamma L_m(\mathrm{GF}(q))$	$s\dfrac{\prod_{i=0}^{m-1}(q^m - q^i)}{q-1}$	$\mathrm{GF}(q^m)^*/\mathrm{GF}(q)^*$	2 ($m \geq 3, q = p^s$) 3 ($m = 2, q = p^s$)
$PGL_m(\mathrm{GF}(q))$	$\dfrac{\prod_{i=0}^{m-1}(q^m - q^i)}{q-1}$	$\mathrm{GF}(q^m)^*/\mathrm{GF}(q)^*$	2 ($m \geq 3$) 3 ($m = 2$)
$PSL_m(\mathrm{GF}(q))$	$\dfrac{\prod_{i=0}^{m-1}(q^m - q^i)}{(q-1)\gcd(m,q-1)}$	$\mathrm{GF}(q^m)^*/\mathrm{GF}(q)^*$	2 ($m \geq 2$) 3 ($m = 2, q$ even)

For the Mathieu groups in Table 1.3, the reader is referred to Dixon and Mortimer (1996)[Chapter 6] and MacWilliams and Sloane (1977)[Chapter 20] for details.

Table 1.3   The Mathieu groups

Group	Degree	Transitivity	Order
M_{10}	10	3	$2^4 \cdot 3^2 \cdot 5$
M_{11}	11	4	$2^4 \cdot 3^2 \cdot 5 \cdot 11$
M_{12}	12	5	$2^6 \cdot 3^3 \cdot 5 \cdot 11$
M_{22}	22	3	$2^7 \cdot 3^2 \cdot 5 \cdot 7 \cdot 11$
M_{23}	23	4	$2^7 \cdot 3^2 \cdot 5 \cdot 7 \cdot 11 \cdot 23$
M_{24}	24	5	$2^{10} \cdot 3^3 \cdot 5 \cdot 7 \cdot 11 \cdot 23$

1.8.14   *Homogeneous Permutation Groups*

A group A acting in a set S induces an action on the set $\binom{S}{t}$ of t element subsets of S, for all $t \geq 1$. The group A is t-homogeneous if its action on $\binom{S}{t}$ is transitive. Also if A is t-homogeneous of finite degree n, then A is also $(n-t)$-homogeneous.

Clearly any t-transitive group is t-homogeneous. But the converse may not be true. In the finite case, with a small number of well described exceptions, a t-homogeneous group is actually t-transitive. We will summarize such results in the following theorem (see Dixon and Mortimer (1996)[p. 289]).

Theorem 1.92. *Suppose that the group A is t-homogeneous on a finite set S where* $2 \leq t \leq |S|/2$. *Then A is* $(t-1)$-*transitive and, with the following exceptions, A is* *t-transitive:*

(i) $t = 2$, $\mathrm{SA}_1(\mathrm{GF}(q)) \leq A \leq \Gamma\mathrm{A}_1(\mathrm{GF}(q))$, $q \equiv 3 \pmod 4$;
(ii) $t = 3$, $\mathrm{PSL}_2(\mathrm{GF}(q)) \leq A \leq \mathrm{P}\Gamma\mathrm{L}_2(\mathrm{GF}(q))$, $|S| - 1 = q \equiv 3 \pmod 4$;
(iii) $t = 3$, $A = \mathrm{GA}_1(\mathrm{GF}(8))$, $\Gamma\mathrm{A}_1(\mathrm{GF}(8))$, $\Gamma\mathrm{A}_1(\mathrm{GF}(32))$;
(iv) $t = 4$, $A = \mathrm{PGL}_2(\mathrm{GF}(8))$, $\mathrm{P}\Gamma\mathrm{L}_2(\mathrm{GF}(8))$, $\mathrm{P}\Gamma\mathrm{L}_2(\mathrm{GF}(32))$.

1.9 Planar Functions

1.9.1 *Definitions and Properties*

A function f from an abelian group $(A, +)$ to an abelian group $(B, +)$ is called *linear* if $f(x+y) = f(x) + f(y)$ for all $x, y \in A$. Hence, linear functions are group homomorphisms. A function $g : A \to B$ is *affine* if $g = f + b$ for a linear function $f : A \to B$ and a constant $b \in B$.

The *Hamming distance* between two functions f and g from an abelian group A to an abelian group B, denoted by $\mathtt{dist}(f,g)$, is defined to be

$$\mathtt{dist}(f,g) = |\{x \in A | f(x) - g(x) \neq 0\}|.$$

There are different measures of nonlinearity of functions. The first measure of nonlinearity of a function f from $(A, +)$ to $(B, +)$ is defined by

$$N_f = \min_{l \in L} \mathtt{dist}(f,l), \tag{1.41}$$

where L denotes the set of all affine functions from $(A, +)$ to $(B, +)$.

The second measure of nonlinearity of a function f from $(A, +)$ to $(B, +)$ is given by

$$P_f = \max_{0 \neq a \in A} \max_{b \in B} \frac{|\{x \in A : f(x+a) - f(x) = b\}|}{|A|}.$$

It is easily seen that $P_f \geq \frac{1}{|B|}$. If the equality is achieved, f is called a *perfect nonlinear function* (PN function for short).

Example 1.93. The trace function $\mathrm{Tr}_{q^m/q}(x^2)$ from $(\mathrm{GF}(q^m), +)$ to $(\mathrm{GF}(q), +)$ is perfect nonlinear for any odd prime q.

The following result follows from the definition of perfect nonlinear functions.

Theorem 1.94. *Let f be a function from a finite abelian group $(A,+)$ to a finite abelian group $(B,+)$. Then f is perfect if and only if*

$$|\{x \in A : f(x+a) - f(x) = b\}| = \frac{|A|}{|B|} \tag{1.42}$$

for each nonzero element a of A and every $b \in B$.

A perfect nonlinear function from an abelian group $(A,+)$ to an abelian group $(B,+)$ of the same order is called *planar*, i.e., $g_a(x) = f(x+a) - f(x)$ is a one-to-one function from A to B for every nonzero $a \in A$.

Example 1.95. The function x^2 from $(\mathrm{GF}(q),+)$ to itself is planar for any odd q.

Planar functions were introduced by Dembowski and Ostrom for constructing affine and projective planes [Dembowski and Ostrom (1968)]. They have nice applications in cryptography, coding theory [Carlet, Ding and Yuan (2005)], combinatorics, and some engineering areas. We will look into some of their applications in this monograph.

1.9.2 *Some Known Planar Functions*

Polynomials over $\mathrm{GF}(q)$ of the form $\sum_{i,j=0}^{m-1} a_{i,j} x^{p^i + p^j}$ are called *Dembowski-Ostrom polynomials*, where $a_{i,j} \in \mathrm{GF}(q)$ for all i and j.

The following theorem characterizes planar Dembowski-Ostrom polynomials [Chen and Polhill (2011)].

Theorem 1.96. *Let q be odd, and let $f(x)$ be a Dembowski-Ostrom polynomial over $\mathrm{GF}(q)$. Then the following are equivalent:*

- *$f(x)$ is planar;*
- *$f(x)$ is a two-to-one map, $f(0) = 0$ and $f(x) \neq 0$ for $x \neq 0$;*
- *there is a permutation polynomial $g(x)$ over $\mathrm{GF}(q)$ such that $f(x) = g(x^2)$ for all $x \in \mathrm{GF}(q)$. (When $q \equiv 3 \pmod 4$, $g(-x) = -g(x)$.)*

A list of planar monomials over finite fields is documented in the following theorem.

Theorem 1.97. *The function $f(x) = x^s$ from $\mathrm{GF}(p^m)$ to $\mathrm{GF}(p^m)$ is planar when*

- *$s = 2$; or*
- *$s = p^k + 1$, where $m/\gcd(m,k)$ is odd [Dembowski and Ostrom (1968)]; or*
- *$s = (3^k + 1)/2$, where $p = 3$, k is odd, and $\gcd(m,k) = 1$ [Coulter and Matthews (1997)].*

There are planar binomials over finite fields. Below is a class of such planar binomials [Zha, Kyureghyan and Wang (2009)].

Theorem 1.98. *Let* $f(x) = x^{1+p^{k+3\ell}} - u^{p^k-1}x^{p^k+p^{3\ell}}$, *where*

- $m = 3k$ *and* $k \not\equiv 0 \pmod 3$,
- ℓ *is a positive integer,*
- $k/\gcd(k,\ell)$ *is odd, and*
- u *is a generator of* $GF(p^m)^*$.

Then $f(x)$ *is planar.*

The following class of planar functions are based on Dickson polynomials of the first kind.

Theorem 1.99. *The polynomials* $f_u(x) = x^{10} - ux^6 - u^2x^2$ *over* $GF(3^m)$ *are planar for all* $u \in GF(3^m)$, *where m is odd.*

The planar function $x^{10} + x^6 - x^2$ over $GF(3^m)$ was presented in Coulter and Matthews (1997). It was extended into the whole class in Ding and Yuan (2006). More planar monomials can be found in Bierbrauer (2010), Budaghyan and Helleseth (2008) and Zha and Wang (2009).

1.9.3 *Planar Functions from Semifields*

A *semifield* consists of a set K and two binary operations $(+,\times): K \times K \to K$ such that the following axioms hold.

- $(K,+)$ is a group.
- There exists an element 1 of K distinct from zero with $1x = x1 = x$ for each $x \in K$.
- For all $0 \neq a, b \in K$, there is $x \in K$ such that $xa = b$.
- For all $0 \neq a, b \in K$, there is $x \in K$ such that $ax = b$.
- For all $a, b, c \in K$, $(a+b)c = ac + bc$ and $c(a+b) = ca + cb$.

A semifield is a field except that associativity for multiplication may not hold. A semifield is *commutative* if its multiplication is commutative. A *presemifield* is a semifield except that the multiplative identity may not exist.

Example 1.100. Positive real numbers with the usual addition and multiplication form a commutative semifield.

Example 1.101. Rational functions of the form f/g, where f and g are polynomials in one variable with positive coefficients, form a commutative semifield.

An *isotopism* between two semifields $(F, +, *)$ and $(F', +, \circ)$ is a triple (α, β, γ) of additive bijections $F \to F'$ such that

$$(x * y)\gamma = x\alpha \circ y\beta, \quad \forall x, y, z \in F.$$

If there is an isotopisim between two semifields, the two semifields are said *isotopic*. If $\alpha = \beta$ and the above equation holds, the two presemifields are called *strongly isotopic*.

Commutative presemifields can be utilized to construct planar functions, as demonstrated by the next theorem [Kantor (2003)].

Theorem 1.102. *Let $(K, +, \times)$ be a finite presemifield with commutative multiplication. Then the function $f(x) = x \times x$ is a planar function from $(K, +)$ to itself.*

To introduce planar monomials on $\mathrm{GF}(q^2)$ from commutative semifields in the sequel, we do the following preparations.

Let $\{1, \beta\}$ be a basis of $\mathrm{GF}(q^2)$ over $\mathrm{GF}(q)$. Let $x = x_1 + x_2\beta$, where $x_i \in \mathrm{GF}(q)$. It is easily seen that

$$x_1 = \frac{\beta^q x - \beta x^q}{\beta^q - \beta}, \; x_2 = \frac{x^q - x}{\beta^q - \beta},$$

where q is a prime power.

Planar monomials on $\mathrm{GF}(q^2)$ from the Dickson commutative semifields are given in the following theorem, which follows from Theorem 1.102.

Theorem 1.103. *Assume that q is odd. Let k be a nonsquare in $K = \mathrm{GF}(q)$, and let $1 \neq \sigma \in \mathrm{Aut}(K)$. The Dickson semifield $(K^2, +, *)$ has*

$$(a, b) * (c, d) = (ac + jb^\sigma d^\sigma, ad + bc),$$

where j is a nonsquare in K. Different choices of j produce isotopic semifields.

The corresponding planar function from $(K^2, +)$ to $(K^2, +)$ is

$$f(a, b) = (a^2 + j(\sigma(b))^2, 2ab),$$

where $(a, b) \in K^2$.

They can be expressed as

$$x^2 + j\left(\sigma\left(\frac{x^q - x}{\beta^q - \beta}\right)\right)^2 - \beta^2\left(\frac{x^q - x}{\beta^q - \beta}\right),$$

where j is a nonsquare in $\mathrm{GF}(q)$, and $1 \neq \sigma \in \mathrm{Aut}(K)$ and $\mathrm{Aut}(K)$ denotes the automorphism group of K.

Example 1.104. If we choose $\sigma(x) = x^q$ in Theorem 1.103, then we have the planar functions

$$(\beta^q - \beta)^2 x^2 + (j - \beta^2)(x^q - x)^2.$$

Planar monomials from the Ganley commutative semifields are described in the next theorem, which is deduced from Theorem 1.102.

Theorem 1.105. *Assume that* $q = 3^r$, $r \geq 3$ *odd. Let* $K = \mathrm{GF}(q)$. *The Ganley semifield* $(K^2, +, *)$ *has*

$$(a,b) * (c,d) = (ac - b^9 d - bd^9, ad + bc + b^3 d^3).$$

The planar functions on $\mathrm{GF}(q^2)$ *defined by the Ganley commutative semifields are*

$$(\beta^q - \beta)^{10} x^2 - \beta^2 (\beta^q - \beta)^8 (x^q - x)^2 + \beta (\beta^q - \beta)^4 (x^q - x)^6 + (x^q - x)^{10}.$$

Planar monomials from the Ganley-Cohen commutative semifields are presented in the following theorem, which follows from Theorem 1.102.

Theorem 1.106. *Assume that* $q = 3^r$, $r \geq 2$. *Let* $K = \mathrm{GF}(q)$, *and let* $j \in K$ *be a nonsquare. The* Ganley-Cohen *semifield* $(K^2, +, *)$ *has*

$$(a,b) * (c,d) = (ac + jbd + j^3 (bd)^9, ad + bc + j(bd)^3).$$

The planar functions on $\mathrm{GF}(q^2)$ *defined by the Ganley-Cohen commutative semifields are*

$$(\beta^q - \beta)^{18} x^2 - (j - \beta^2)(\beta^q - \beta)^{16} (x^q - x)^2 + \beta j (\beta^q - \beta)^{12} (x^q - x)^6 + j^3 (x^q - x)^{18}.$$

1.9.4 *Affine Planes from Planar Functions*

Planar functions were employed to construct affine planes in the seminal work [Dembowski and Ostrom (1968)]. The following theorem documents the construction.

Theorem 1.107. *Let* $f : (A, +) \to (B, +)$ *be a function. Define* $\mathcal{P} = A \times B$. *The lines are the symbols* $L(a, b)$ *with* $(a, b) \in A \times B$, *together with the symbols* $L(c)$ *with* $c \in A$. *Incidence* $\mathcal{R}$ *is defined by*

- $(x, y) \, \mathcal{R} \, L(a, b)$ *if and only if* $y = f(x - a) + b$; *and*
- $(x, y) \, \mathcal{R} \, L(c)$ *if and only if* $x = c$.

Then f *is planar if and only if* $(\mathcal{P}, L, \mathcal{R})$ *is an affine plane.*

Each affine plane from a planar function can be extended into a projective plane using Theorem 1.54. Consequently, planar functions can produce both affine and projective planes.

1.10 Almost Perfect Nonlinear and Almost Bent Functions

1.10.1 *APN Functions*

Recall that a function f from $GF(q)$ to $GF(q)$ is called perfect nonlinear (i.e., planar), if $g_a(x) = f(x+a) - f(x)$ is a one-to-one function from $GF(q)$ to $GF(q)$ for every nonzero $a \in GF(q)$. Hence, there is no perfect nonlinear function from $GF(2^m)$ to $GF(2^m)$.

A function f from $GF(q)$ to itself is called *almost perfect nonlinear (APN)*, if $f(x+a) - f(x) = b$ has at most 2 solutions $x \in GF(q)$ for every pair $(a,b) \in GF(q)^* \times GF(q)$. APN functions exist on all $GF(q)$, and have many applications in mathematics and engineering.

The monomial x^s on $GF(2^m)$ is APN for the following s:

- $s = 2^i + 1$, where $\gcd(i,m) = 1$ (Gold function, 1968);
- $s = 2^{2i} - 2^i + 1$, where $\gcd(i,m) = 1$ (Kasami function, 1971);
- $s = 2^t + 3$, where $m = 2t + 1$ (Welch function, 1972);
- $s = 2^t + 2^{t/2} - 1$, where $m = 2t + 1$ and t even (Niho function 1972, Hollmann-Xiang 2001);
- $s = 2^t + 2^{(3t+1)/2} - 1$, where $m = 2t + 1$ and t odd (Niho function 1972, Hollmann-Xiang 2001).

More APN functions on $GF(2^m)$ could be found in Pott (2016).

The following is a list of known APN power functions x^d over $GF(p)^m$ where p is an odd prime:

- $d = 3, p > 3$.
- $d = p^m - 2, p > 2$ and $p \equiv 2 \pmod 3$.
- $d = (p^m - 3)/2, p \equiv 3,7 \pmod{20}, p^m > 7, p^m \neq 27$ and m is odd.
- $d = (p^m + 1)/4 + (p^m - 1)/2, p^m \equiv 3 \pmod 8$.
- $d = (p^m + 1)/4, p^m \equiv 7 \pmod 8$.
- $d = (2p^m - 1)/3, p^m \equiv 2 \pmod 3$.
- $d = 3^m - 3, p = 3$ and m is odd.
- $d = p^\ell + 2, p^\ell \equiv 1 \pmod 3$ and $m = 2\ell$.
- $d = (5^\ell + 1)/2, p = 5$ and $\gcd(2m, \ell) = 1$.
-

$$d = \begin{cases} (3^{(m+1)/2} - 1)/2 & \text{if } m \equiv 3 \pmod 4, \\ (3^{(m+1)/2} - 1)/2 + (3^m - 1)/2 & \text{if } m \equiv 1 \pmod 4, \end{cases}$$

where $m \geq 5$ and $p = 3$.

-

$$d = \begin{cases} (3^{m+1} - 1)/8 & \text{if } m \equiv 3 \pmod 4, \\ (3^{m+1} - 1)/8 + (3^m - 1)/2 & \text{if } m \equiv 1 \pmod 4, \end{cases}$$

where $m \geq 5$ and $p = 3$.

- $d = \left(3^{(m+1)/4} - 1\right)\left(3^{(m+1)/2} + 1\right)$, $m \equiv 3 \pmod 4$ and $p = 3$.
- $d = (5^m - 1)/4 + (5^{(m+1)/2} - 1)/2$, $p = 5$ and m is odd.

References about these APN functions could be found in Zha and Wang (2011).

1.10.2   *AB Functions*

For any function F from GF(2^m) to GF(2^m), we define

$$\lambda_F(a,b) = \sum_{x \in \mathrm{GF}(2^m)} (-1)^{\mathrm{Tr}(aF(x)+bx)}, \ a, b \in \mathrm{GF}(2^m).$$

A function F from GF(2^m) to GF(2^m) is called *almost bent* if $\lambda_F(a,b) = 0$, or $\pm 2^{(m+1)/2}$ for every pair (a,b) with $a \neq 0$.

Let m be odd. Known almost bent functions are the following:

- $f_1(x) = x^{2^i+1}$, $\gcd(i,m) = 1$ (Gold function).
- $f_2(x) = x^{2^{2i}-2^i+1}$, $\gcd(i,m) = 1$ (Kasami function).
- $f_3(x) = x^{2^{(m-1)/2}+3}$ (Welch function).
- $f_4(x) = x^{2^{(m-1)/2}+2^{(m-1)/4}-1}$, $m \equiv 1 \pmod 4$ (Niho function).
- $f_5(x) = x^{2^{(m-1)/2}+2^{(3m-1)/4}-1}$, $m \equiv 3 \pmod 4$ (Niho function).

Hence almost bent functions over GF(2^m) exist for every odd m. We will employ almost bent functions to construct linear codes and then combinatorial designs later.

1.11   Periodic Sequences

Both finite and periodic sequences play a very useful role in dealing with codes derived from difference sets and other combinatorial designs. In this section, we briefly introduce periodic sequences.

1.11.1   *The Linear Span*

Let $\lambda^{\infty} = (\lambda_i)_{i=0}^{\infty}$ be a sequence of period n over GF(q). The *linear span* (also called *linear complexity*) of λ^{∞} is defined to be the smallest positive integer ℓ such that there are constants $c_0 \neq 0, c_1, \ldots, c_\ell \in \mathrm{GF}(q)$ satisfying

$$-c_0\lambda_i = c_1\lambda_{i-1} + c_2\lambda_{i-2} + \cdots + c_l\lambda_{i-\ell} \text{ for all } i \geq \ell.$$

The polynomial $c(x) = c_0 + c_1 x + \cdots + c_\ell x^\ell$ is called a *characteristic polynomial* of λ^∞. A characteristic polynomial with the smallest degree is called a *minimal polynomial* of the periodic sequence λ^∞. The degree of a minimal polynomial of λ^∞ is referred to as the *linear span* or *linear complexity* of this sequence. We inform the reader that the minimal polynomial of λ^∞ defined here may be the reciprocal of the minimal polynomial defined in other references.

For periodic sequences, there are a few ways to determine their linear span and minimal polynomials. One of them is given in the following lemma [Ding, Xiao and Shan (1991)][Theorem 2.2].

Lemma 1.108. *Let λ^∞ be a sequence of period n over* GF(q). *The generating polynomial of λ^∞ is defined by $\Lambda^n(x) = \sum_{i=0}^{n-1} \lambda_i x^i \in$* GF$(q)[x]$. *Then a minimal polynomial $m_\lambda(x)$ of λ^∞ is given by*

$$m_\lambda(x) = \frac{x^n - 1}{\gcd(x^n - 1, \Lambda^n(x))};$$

(1.43)

and the linear span $\mathbb{L}_\lambda$ of λ^∞ is given by $n - \deg(\gcd(x^n - 1, \Lambda^n(x)))$.

The other one is given in the following lemma [Antweiler and Bomer (1992)].

Lemma 1.109. *Any sequence λ^∞ over* GF(q) *of period $q^m - 1$ has a unique expansion of the form*

$$\lambda_t = \sum_{i=0}^{q^m - 2} c_i \alpha^{it} \text{ for all } t \geq 0,$$

where $c_i \in$ GF(q^m). *Let the index set be $I = \{i : c_i \neq 0\}$, then the minimal polynomial $\mathbb{M}_\lambda(x)$ of λ^∞ is*

$$\mathbb{M}_\lambda(x) = \prod_{i \in I} (1 - \alpha^i x),$$

and the linear span of λ^∞ is $|I|$.

It should be noticed that in most references the reciprocal of $\mathbb{M}_\lambda(x)$ is called the minimal polynomial of the sequence λ^∞. So Lemma 1.109 is a modified version of the original one in Antweiler and Bomer (1992). We are interested in the linear span of periodic sequences, as they are useful in coding theory.

1.11.2 Correlation Functions

Let χ be an additive character of GF(q), and λ^∞ and γ^∞ be two sequences of period respectively N and M and $P = \text{LCM}\{M, N\}$. Then the *periodic crosscorrelation function* of the two sequences is defined by

$$\text{CC}_{\lambda,\gamma}(l) = \sum_{i=0}^{P-1} \chi(\lambda_i - \gamma_{i+l}) = \sum_{i=0}^{P-1} \chi(\lambda_i)\overline{\chi(\gamma_{i+l})}.$$

(1.44)

If the two sequences are identical, then $P = M = N$ and the crosscorrelation function is the so-called *periodic autocorrelation function* of λ^∞ described by

$$\mathsf{AC}_\lambda(l) = \sum_{i=0}^{N-1} \chi(\lambda_i - \lambda_{i+l}) = \sum_{i=0}^{N-1} \chi(\lambda_i)\overline{\chi(\lambda_{i+l})}. \tag{1.45}$$

If $q = 2$, then $\chi(a) = (-1)^a$ is an additive character of GF(2), here we identify GF(2) with $\mathbb{Z}_2$. Then (1.44) and (1.45) are the usual crosscorrelation and autocorrelation functions of binary sequences.

Let λ^∞ be a binary sequence of period N. It is easy to prove the following.

(1) Let $N \equiv 3 \pmod 4$. Then $\max_{1 \le w \le N-1} |\mathsf{AC}_\lambda(w)| \ge 1$. On the other hand, $\max_{1 \le w \le N-1} |\mathsf{AC}_\lambda(w)| = 1$ iff $\mathsf{AC}_\lambda(w) = -1$ for all $w \not\equiv 0 \pmod N$. In this case, the sequence λ^∞ is said to have *ideal autocorrelation* and *optimal autocorrelation*.

(2) Let $N \equiv 1 \pmod 4$. There is strong evidence that there is no binary sequence of period $N > 13$ with $\max_{1 \le w \le N-1} |\mathsf{AC}_\lambda(w)| = 1$ [Jungnickel and Pott (1999b)]. It is then natural to consider the case $\max_{1 \le w \le N-1} |\mathsf{AC}_\lambda(w)| = 3$. In this case $\mathsf{AC}_\lambda(w) \in \{1, -3\}$ for all $w \not\equiv 0 \pmod N$.

(3) Let $N \equiv 2 \pmod 4$. Then $\max_{1 \le w \le N-1} |\mathsf{AC}_\lambda(w)| \ge 2$. On the other hand, $\max_{1 \le w \le N-1} |\mathsf{AC}_\lambda(w)| = 2$ iff $\mathsf{AC}_\lambda(w) \in \{2, -2\}$ for all $w \not\equiv 0 \pmod N$. In this case, the sequence λ^∞ is said to have *optimal autocorrelation*.

(4) Let $N \equiv 0 \pmod 4$. If $\max_{1 \le w \le N-1} |\mathsf{AC}_\lambda(w)| = 0$, the sequence λ^∞ is called *perfect*. The only known perfect binary sequence up to equivalence is the $(0,0,0,1)$. It is conjectured that there is no perfect binary sequence of period $N \equiv 0 \pmod 4$ greater than 4 [Jungnickel and Pott (1999a)]. This conjecture is true for all $N < 108900$ [Jungnickel and Pott (1999a)]. Hence, it is natural to construct binary sequences of period $N \equiv 0 \pmod 4$ with $\max_{1 \le w \le N-1} |\mathsf{AC}_\lambda(w)| = 4$.

Binary sequences with optimal autocorrelation have close connections with certain combinatorial designs.

1.12   Difference Sets

Difference sets are a classical topic of combinatorics and have many applications in both mathematics and engineering. In this section, we will present basics of difference sets. Specific constructions of difference sets could be found in Ding (2015a) and Beth, Jungnickel and Lenz (1999).

1.12.1 Fundamentals of Difference Sets

In this monograph, we consider only difference sets in finite abelian groups A. We use n to denote the order of abelian groups A that contain a difference set. We also write the operation of an abelian group additively as $+$, and call the identity element of A the zero element.

A subset D of size k in an abelian group $(A, +)$ with order n is called an (n, k, λ) *difference set* in $(A, +)$ if the multiset $\{\{a_1 - a_2 : a_1 \in A, a_2 \in A\}\}$ contains every nonzero element of A exactly λ times.

For convenience later, we define the *difference function* of a subset D of $(A, +)$ as

$$\mathrm{diff}_D(x) = |D \cap (D + x)|, \tag{1.46}$$

where $D + x = \{y + x : y \in D\}$.

In terms of the difference function, a subset D of size k in an abelian group $(A, +)$ with order n is called an (n, k, λ) *difference set* in $(A, +)$ if the difference function $\mathrm{diff}_D(x) = \lambda$ for every nonzero $x \in A$. A difference set D in $(A, +)$ is called *cyclic* if the abelian group A is so. The *order* of an (n, k, λ) difference set is defined to be $k - \lambda$.

By definition, if an (n, k, λ) difference set exists, then

$$k(k - 1) = (n - 1)\lambda. \tag{1.47}$$

If D is an (n, k, λ) difference set in $(A, +)$, its *complement*, $D^c = A \setminus D$, is an $(n, n - k, n - 2k + \lambda)$ difference set in $(A, +)$.

Example 1.110. Let $n = 7$ and let $D = \{1, 2, 4\}$. Then D is a $(7, 3, 1)$ difference set in $(\mathbb{Z}_7, +)$. Its complement, $D^c = \{0, 3, 5, 6\}$, is a $(7, 4, 2)$ difference set in $(\mathbb{Z}_7, +)$.

Let D be an (n, k, λ) difference set in an abelian group $(A, +)$. We associate D with an incidence structure $\mathbb{D}$, called the *development* of D, by defining $\mathbb{D} = (\mathcal{P}, \mathcal{B}, \mathcal{R})$, where $\mathcal{P}$ is the set of the elements in A,

$$\mathcal{B} = \{a + D : a \in A\},$$

and the incidence $\mathcal{R}$ is the membership of sets. Each block $a + D = \{a + x : x \in D\}$ is called a *translate* of D. We say that an element $a \in A$ is incident with a block $B \in \mathcal{B}$, denoted by $a\mathcal{R}B$, if $a \in B$.

Let D be a difference set in an abelian group $(A, +)$ and let $\sigma \in \mathrm{Aut}(A)$, which denotes the automorphism group of A. Then $\sigma(D) = \{\sigma(d) : d \in D\}$ is also a difference set in $(A, +)$. Furthermore, since $\sigma(D + a) = \sigma(D) + \sigma(a)$, the automorphism σ will induce an automorphism of the development of D when

$\sigma(D) = D + a$ for some element $a \in A$. We are now ready to introduce the concept of multipliers of difference sets.

If D is an (n, k, λ) difference set in $(A, +)$ and $\mu \in \text{Aut}(A)$, then μ is a *multiplier* of D if $\mu(D) = D + a$ for some $a \in A$. It is obvious that the set of multipliers of a difference set D in a group A form a subgroup of $\text{Aut}(A)$.

In some applications, we are much more interested in difference sets in $(\mathbb{Z}_n, +)$. The group $(\mathbb{Z}_n^*, \times)$, i.e., the group of invertible integers in $\mathbb{Z}_n$ with the integer multiplication, acts on the group $(\mathbb{Z}_n, +)$ by multiplication. In this case, $\ell \in \mathbb{Z}_n^*$ is a multiplier of a difference set D in $(\mathbb{Z}_n, +)$ if $\ell D = D + a$ for some $a \in A$, where $\ell D = \{\ell d \bmod n : d \in D\}$. Such a multiplier is called a *numerical multiplier*. It is well known that $\text{Aut}((Z_n, +))$ is isomorphic to $(\mathbb{Z}_n^*, \times)$.

Example 1.111. The set $D = \{1, 3, 4, 5, 9\}$ is a $(11, 5, 2)$ difference set in $(\mathbb{Z}_{11}, +)$. Its multiplier group is $(\mathbb{Z}_{11}^*, \times)$.

The following is a result about multipliers [Beth, Jungnickel and Lenz (1999)][Theorem 4.4].

Theorem 1.112. *Let D be an abelian (n, k, λ) difference set, and let p be a prime dividing $k - \lambda$ but not n. If $p > \lambda$, then p is a multiplier of D.*

It is conjectured that Theorem 1.112 holds without the restriction $p > \lambda$, i.e., every prime divisor of $k - \lambda$ is a multiplier.

The following result is due to Bruck-Ryser-Chowla Theorem.

Theorem 1.113. *If $\ell \equiv 1, 2 \pmod 4$, and the square part of ℓ is divisible by a prime $p \equiv 3 \pmod 4$, then no difference set of order ℓ exists.*

Studying the group of numerical multipliers is useful for proving the nonexistence of abelian planar difference sets. McFarland and Rice proved the following [McFarland and Rice (1978)].

Theorem 1.114. *Let D be an abelian (n, k, λ) difference set in $(A, +)$, and let M be the group of numerical multipliers of D. Then there exists a translate of D that is fixed by every element of M.*

A lot of results about multipliers have been developed. The reader is referred to Beth, Jungnickel and Lenz (1999)[Chapter VI] for further information.

Difference sets can also be characterized with group characters. For any character χ of an abelian finite group $(A, +)$, recal that its conjugate $\bar{\chi}$ is defined $\bar{\chi}(a) = \overline{\chi(a)}$. For any subset D of A, we define

$$\chi(D) = \sum_{d \in D} \chi(d).$$

We have then the following result [Beth, Jungnickel and Lenz (1999)][Lemma 3.12].

Theorem 1.115. *A subset D of a finite abelian group $(A, +)$ of order n is an (n, k, λ) difference set if and only if for every nontrival complex character χ of $(A, +)$,*

$$|\chi(D)|^2 = \chi(D)\bar{\chi}(D) = \chi(D)\chi(-D) = k - \lambda.$$

This theorem is important as it can be employed to prove the difference set property in many cases, while other tools and methods may not work easily.

1.12.2 *Divisible and Relative Difference Sets*

Let $(A, +)$ be a group of order mn and $(N, +)$ a subgroup of A of order n. A k-subset D of A is an $(m, n, k, \lambda_1, \lambda_2)$ *divisible difference set* if the multiset $\{\{d_1 - d_2 : d_1, d_2 \in D, d_1 \neq d_2\}\}$ contains every nonidentity element of N exactly λ_1 times and every element of $A \setminus N$ exactly λ_2 times. If $\lambda_1 = 0$, D is called an (m, n, k, λ_2) *relative difference set*, and N is called the *forbidden subgroup*.

Example 1.116. The set $D = \{0, 1, 3\}$ is a $(4, 2, 3, 0, 1)$ divisible difference set in $(\mathbb{Z}_8, +)$, and also a relative difference set in $(\mathbb{Z}_8, +)$ relative to the subgroup $\{0, 4\}$.

There are many references on divisible and relative difference sets. The reader is referred to Beth, Jungnickel and Lenz (1999)[Chapter VI] for information. In this monograph, we will not study divisible and relative difference sets, but will need the concepts later.

1.12.3 *Characteristic Sequence of Difference Sets in $\mathbb{Z}_n$*

Let D be any subset of $(\mathbb{Z}_n, +)$, where $n \geq 2$ and n is a positive integer. The *characteristic sequence* of D, denoted by $s(D)^\infty$, is a binary sequence of period n, where

$$s(D)_i = \begin{cases} 1 & \text{if } i \bmod n \in D, \\ 0 & \text{otherwise.} \end{cases} \tag{1.48}$$

Difference sets in $(\mathbb{Z}_n, +)$ can be characterized with its characteristic sequence $s(D)^\infty$ as follows.

Theorem 1.117. *Let D be any subset of $(\mathbb{Z}_n, +)$ with size k. Then D is an (n, k, λ) difference set in $(\mathbb{Z}_n, +)$ if and only if*

$$\mathrm{AC}_{s(D)}(w) = n - 4(k - \lambda) \tag{1.49}$$

for any nonzero w in $\mathbb{Z}_n$, where $\text{AC}_{s(D)}(w)$ is the autocorrelation function of the periodic binary sequence $s(D)^\infty$ defined in Section 1.11.2.

It is straightforward to prove this theorem. Hence, cyclic difference sets can be defined with the language of sequences.

The following result follows from Theorem 1.117.

Theorem 1.118. *Let $s(D)^\infty$ denote the characteristic sequence of a subset D of $\mathbb{Z}_n$. Let $n \equiv 3 \pmod 4$. Then $\text{AC}_{s(D)}(w) = -1$ for all $w \not\equiv 0 \pmod n$ if and only if D is an $(n, (n+1)/2, (n+1)/4)$ or $(n, (n-1)/2, (n-3)/4)$ difference set in $\mathbb{Z}_n$.*

Theorem 1.118 shows that the characteristic sequence of certain cyclic difference sets has optimal (ideal) autocorrelation.

1.12.4 *Characteristic Functions of Difference Sets*

Let D be any subset of an abelian group $(A, +)$ of order n. The *characteristic function* of D, denoted by ξ_D, is defined by

$$\xi_D(x) = \begin{cases} 1 & \text{if } x \in D, \\ 0 & \text{otherwise.} \end{cases} \tag{1.50}$$

Difference sets in $(A, +)$ can be characterized with its characteristic function ξ_D as follows.

Theorem 1.119. *Let D be any k-subset of an abelian group $(A, +)$ with order n. Then D is an (n, k, λ) difference set in $(A, +)$ if and only if*

$$\text{AC}_{\xi_D}(w) := \sum_{a \in A} (-1)^{\xi_D(a+w) - \xi_D(a)} = n - 4(k - \lambda) \tag{1.51}$$

for any nonzero w in A.

It is also easy to prove this theorem. Thus, difference sets can be defined in terms of the characteristic function ξ_D. In many cases, the characteristic function of a difference set has optimum nonlinearity [Carlet and Ding (2004)].

Chapter 2

Linear Codes over Finite Fields

This chapter introduces the basics of linear codes over finite fields. Fundamental results about linear codes will be summarized. Some of the results presented in this chapter will not be proved. The reader may find out a proof of such theorems and lemmas in Huffman and Pless (2003)[Chapters 1, 2] or work out a proof.

2.1 Linear Codes over GF(q)

As usual, let GF(q)^n denote the vector space of all n-tuples over GF(q). The vectors in GF(q)^n are usually denoted by $(a_1, a_2, \ldots, a_n)$ or $(a_1 a_2 \cdots a_n)$, where $a_i \in$ GF(q). The *Hamming weight* of a vector $\mathbf{a} \in$ GF(q)^n is the number of nonzero coordinates of $\mathbf{a}$, and is denoted by $\mathrm{wt}(\mathbf{a})$. The *Hamming distance* of two vectors $\mathbf{a}$ and $\mathbf{b}$ in GF(q)^n, denoted by $\mathrm{dist}(\mathbf{a}, \mathbf{b})$ is the Hamming weight of the difference vector $\mathbf{a} - \mathbf{b}$. The *inner product* of two vectors $\mathbf{a}$ and $\mathbf{b}$ in GF(q)^n, denoted by $\mathbf{a} \cdot \mathbf{b}$, is defined by

$$\mathbf{a} \cdot \mathbf{b} = \mathbf{a}\mathbf{b}^T = \sum_{i=1}^{n} a_i b_i,$$

where $\mathbf{b}^T$ denotes the transpose of the vector $\mathbf{b}$. The two vectors $\mathbf{a}$ and $\mathbf{b}$ are *orthogonal* if $\mathbf{a} \cdot \mathbf{b} = 0$.

An (n, M, d) *code* $\mathcal{C}$ over GF(q) is a subset of GF(q)^n of cardinality M and minimum Hamming distance d. The vectors in a code $\mathcal{C}$ are called *codewords* in $\mathcal{C}$. An $[n, \kappa]$ *code* over GF(q) is a linear subspace of GF(q)^n with dimension κ. If the minimum Hamming distance of $\mathcal{C}$ is d, we say that $\mathcal{C}$ has parameters $[n, \kappa, d]$. It is easily seen that the minimum Hamming distance of a linear code $\mathcal{C}$ is equal to the minimum nonzero Hamming weight of all codewords in $\mathcal{C}$. By definition, an $[n, \kappa]$ code over GF(q) has q^κ codewords. For convenience, by an $(n, M, d)_q$ (respectively, $[n, \kappa, d]_q$) code we mean an (n, M, d) (respectively, $[n, \kappa, d]$) code over GF(q).

An $[n, \kappa, d]$ code over GF(q) is said to be *dimension-optimal* if there is no $[n, \kappa', d]$ code over GF(q) with $\kappa' > \kappa$, *distance-optimal* if there is no $[n, \kappa, d']$ code over GF(q) with $d' > d$, and *length-optimal* if there is no $[n', \kappa, d]$ code over GF(q) with $n' < n$. A linear code is *optimal* if it is dimension-optimal, or distance-optimal, or length-optimal or meets a bound on linear codes. An $[n, \kappa, d]$ code over GF(q) is said to be *almost optimal* if an $[n, \kappa+1, d]$ or $[n, \kappa, d+1]$ or $[n-1, \kappa, d]$ code over GF(q) is optimal.

Let A_i denote the number of codewords of weight i in an $[n, \kappa]$ code for all i with $0 \le i \le n$. The sequence $(A_0, A_1, \ldots, A_n)$ is called the *weight distribution* of C and the polynomial

$$A_0 + A_1 z + A_2 z^2 + \cdots + A_n z^n$$

is called the *weight enumerator* of C.

The *dual code*, denoted $C^\perp$, of an $[n, \kappa]$ code C over GF(q) is a linear subspace of GF$(q)^n$ with dimension $n - \kappa$ and is defined by

$$C^\perp = \{ \mathbf{u} \in \mathrm{GF}(q)^n : \mathbf{u} \cdot \mathbf{c} = \mathbf{u}\mathbf{c}^T = 0 \text{ for all } \mathbf{c} \in C \}.$$

The code C is said to be *self-orthogonal* if $C \subseteq C^\perp$, and *self-dual* if $C = C^\perp$. If C is self-dual, then the dimension of C is $n/2$.

A *generator matrix* of an $[n, \kappa]$ code over GF(q) is a $\kappa \times n$ matrix G whose rows form a basis for C over GF(q). The generator matrix of the dual code $C^\perp$ is called a *parity-check matrix* of C and is denoted by H. Hence, a linear code C may be described by a generator matrix or a parity-check matrix as follows

$$C = \{ \mathbf{x} \in \mathrm{GF}(q)^n : H\mathbf{x}^T = \mathbf{0} \},$$

where $\mathbf{0}$ denotes the zero vector. Note that the generator matrix and the parity-check matrix of a linear code are not unique.

Example 2.1. Take $q = 2$ and $n = 4$. Then the set

$$C = \{ (0000), (1100), (0011), (1111) \} \subset \mathrm{GF}(2)^4$$

is a $[4, 2, 2]$ binary code with weight enumerator $1 + 2z^2 + z^4$ and weight distribution

$$A_0 = 1, A_1 = 0, A_2 = 2, A_3 = 0, A_4 = 1.$$

A generator matrix of C is

$$G = \begin{bmatrix} 1 & 1 & 0 & 0 \\ 0 & 0 & 1 & 1 \end{bmatrix}.$$

This matrix G is also a parity-check matrix of C. Hence, the code C is self-dual.

A vector $\mathbf{x} = (x_1, x_2, \ldots, x_n)$ in $\mathrm{GF}(q)^n$ is *even-like* provided that $\sum_{i=1}^n x_i = 0$, and is *odd-like* otherwise. The weight of binary even-like vector must be even, and that of binary odd-like vector must be odd. For an $[n, \kappa, d]$ code C over $\mathrm{GF}(q)$, we call the minimum weight of the even-like codewords, respectively the odd-like codewords, the *minimum even-like weight,*, respectively the *minimum odd-like weight,* of the code. Denote the minimum even-like weight by d_e and the minimum odd-like weight by d_o. So $d = \min\{d_e, d_o\}$.

The following theorem can be easily proved.

Theorem 2.2. *Let C be an $[n, \kappa]$ code over $\mathrm{GF}(q)$. Let $C^{(e)}$ be the set of all even-like codewords in C. Then $C^{(e)} = C$ if C does not have odd-like codewords and $C^{(e)}$ is an $[n, \kappa - 1]$ subcode of C otherwise.*

The following theorem characterizes the minimum weight of linear codes and its proof is trivial.

Theorem 2.3. *A linear code has minimum weight d if and only if its parity-check matrix has a set of d linearly independent columns but no set of $d - 1$ linearly independent columns.*

2.2 The MacWilliams Identity and Transform

Let $C^\perp$ be the dual of an $[n, \kappa, d]$ code C over $\mathrm{GF}(q)$. Denote by $A(z)$ and $A^\perp(z)$ the weight enumerators of C and $C^\perp$, respectively. The following theorem, called the *MacWilliams Identity,* shows that $A(z)$ and $A^\perp(z)$ can be derived from each other.

Theorem 2.4. *Let C be an $[n, \kappa, d]$ code over $\mathrm{GF}(q)$ with weight enumerator $A(z) = \sum_{i=0}^n A_i z^i$ and let $A^\perp(z)$ be the weight enumerator of $C^\perp$. Then*

$$A^\perp(z) = q^{-\kappa} \left(1 + (q-1)z \right)^n A\left(\frac{1-z}{1+(q-1)z} \right).$$

Proof. Let χ be a nontrivial additive character of $\mathrm{GF}(q)$. Define a polynomial

$$F(\mathbf{u}) = \sum_{\mathbf{v} \in \mathrm{GF}(q)^n} \chi(\mathbf{u} \cdot \mathbf{v}) z^{\mathrm{wt}(\mathbf{v})},$$

where $\mathbf{u} \cdot \mathbf{v}$ denotes the standard inner product. We have then

$$\sum_{\mathbf{u} \in C} F(\mathbf{u}) = \sum_{\mathbf{u} \in C} \sum_{\mathbf{v} \in \mathrm{GF}(q)^n} \chi(\mathbf{u} \cdot \mathbf{v}) z^{\mathrm{wt}(\mathbf{v})} = \sum_{\mathbf{v} \in \mathrm{GF}(q)^n} z^{\mathrm{wt}(\mathbf{v})} \sum_{\mathbf{u} \in C} \chi(\mathbf{u} \cdot \mathbf{v}).$$

Note that $\mathbf{u} \cdot \mathbf{v}$ is always 0 if $\mathbf{v} \in C^{\perp}$, and takes every element in GF(q) the same number of times when $\mathbf{u}$ ranges over all codewords in C if $\mathbf{v} \notin C^{\perp}$. As a result,

$$\sum_{\mathbf{u} \in C} \chi(\mathbf{u} \cdot \mathbf{v}) = \begin{cases} |C| & \text{if } \mathbf{v} \in C^{\perp}, \\ 0 & \text{if } \mathbf{v} \notin C^{\perp}. \end{cases}$$

Therefore,

$$\sum_{\mathbf{u} \in C} F(\mathbf{u}) = |C| A^{\perp}(z). \tag{2.1}$$

We now extend the weight function to GF(q) by defining $\text{wt}(v) = 0$ if $v = 0$ and $\text{wt}(v) = 1$ otherwise. Denote $\mathbf{u} = (u_1, u_2, \ldots, u_n)$ and $\mathbf{v} = (v_1, v_2, \ldots, v_n)$. It then follows from the definition of $F(\mathbf{u})$ that

$$F(\mathbf{u}) = \sum_{(v_1, v_2, \ldots, v_n) \in \text{GF}(q)^n} z^{\text{wt}(v_1) + \cdots + \text{wt}(v_n)} \chi(u_1 v_1 + \cdots + u_n v_n))$$

$$= \sum_{(v_1, v_2, \ldots, v_n) \in \text{GF}(q)^n} z^{\text{wt}(v_1)} \chi(u_1 v_1) z^{\text{wt}(v_2)} \chi(u_2 v_2) \cdots z^{\text{wt}(v_n)} \chi(u_n v_n)$$

$$= \prod_{i=1}^{n} \sum_{v \in \text{GF}(q)} z^{\text{wt}(v)} \chi(u_i v).$$

Note that

$$1 + z \sum_{b \in \text{GF}(q)^*} \chi(b) = 1 - z.$$

We have then

$$\sum_{v \in \text{GF}(q)} z^{\text{wt}(v)} \chi(u_i v) = \begin{cases} 1 + (q-1)z & \text{if } u_i = 0, \\ 1 - z & \text{if } u_i \neq 0. \end{cases}$$

It then follows that

$$F(\mathbf{u}) = (1-z)^{\text{wt}(\mathbf{u})} (1 + (q-1)z)^{n - wt(\mathbf{u})}. \tag{2.2}$$

Combining (2.1) and (2.2) yields

$$|C| A^{\perp}(z) = \sum_{\mathbf{u} \in C} (1-z)^{\text{wt}(\mathbf{u})} (1 - (q-1)z)^{n - \text{wt}(\mathbf{u})}$$

$$= \sum_{i=0}^{n} A_i (1-z)^i (1 - (q-1)z)^{n-i}$$

$$= \left(1 + (q-1)z\right)^n A\left(\frac{1-z}{1 + (q-1)z}\right).$$

This completes the proof. $\qquad\square$

The weight enumerator of a code C is also given in the following homogeneous form

$$W_C(x,y) = \sum_{\mathbf{c} \in C} x^{n-\text{wt}(\mathbf{c})} y^{\text{wt}(\mathbf{c})}. \tag{2.3}$$

Then the following theorem is a consequence of Theorem 2.4.

Theorem 2.5. *Let C be a linear code. Then*

$$W_{C^\perp}(x,y) = \frac{1}{|C|} W_C(x+y, x-y).$$

The MacWilliams Identity in Theorem 2.4 can be expressed by

$$A_j^\perp = \frac{1}{|C|} \sum_{i=0}^{n} A_i P_j(q,n;i), \tag{2.4}$$

where $P_j(q,n;x)$ is the Krawtchouk polynomial defined in Section 1.4.3. This expression is rarely used.

2.3 The Pless Power Moments

The *Stirling numbers* $S(r,v)$ are defined as follows. If $r < v$, then $S(r,v) = 0$. Define $S(r,r) = 1$. If $r > v$, then define

$$S(r,v) = \frac{1}{v!} \sum_{i=0}^{v} (-1)^{v-i} \binom{v}{i} i^r. \tag{2.5}$$

Let C be an $[n, \kappa, d]$ code over GF(q). Denote by $(A_0, A_1, \ldots, A_n)$ and $(A_0^\perp, A_1^\perp, \ldots, A_n^\perp)$ the weight distributions of C and its dual code $C^\perp$, respectively. The *Pless power moments* are given by

$$\sum_{j=0}^{n} j^r A_j = \sum_{j=0}^{\min\{n,r\}} (-1)^j A_j^\perp \left[\sum_{v=j}^{r} v! S(r,v) q^{\kappa-v} (q-1)^{v-j} \binom{n-j}{n-v} \right] \tag{2.6}$$

for $r \geq 0$.

The first four Pless power moments from (2.6) are the following:

$$\sum_{j=0}^{n} A_j = q^{\kappa},$$

$$\sum_{j=0}^{n} j A_j = q^{\kappa-1}(qn - n - A_1^{\perp}),$$

$$\sum_{j=0}^{n} j^2 A_j = q^{\kappa-2}[(q-1)n(qn - n + 1) - (2qn - q - 2n + 2)A_1^{\perp} + 2A_2^{\perp}],$$

$$\sum_{j=0}^{n} j^3 A_j = q^{\kappa-3}[(q-1)n(q^2 n^2 - 2qn^2 + 3qn - q + n^2 - 3n + 2)$$
$$- (3q^2 n^2 - 3q^2 n - 6qn^2 + 12qn + q^2 - 6q + 3n^2 - 9n + 6)A_1^{\perp}$$
$$+ 6(qn - q - n + 2)A_2^{\perp} - 6A_3^{\perp}].$$

In the binary case these power moments become the following:

$$\sum_{j=0}^{n} A_j = 2^{\kappa},$$

$$\sum_{j=0}^{n} j A_j = 2^{\kappa-1}(n - A_1^{\perp}),$$

$$\sum_{j=0}^{n} j^2 A_j = 2^{\kappa-2}[n(n+1) - 2nA_1^{\perp} + 2A_2^{\perp}],$$

$$\sum_{j=0}^{n} j^3 A_j = 2^{\kappa-3}[n^2(n+3) - (3n^2 + 3n - 2)A_1^{\perp} + 6nA_2^{\perp} - 6A_3^{\perp}].$$

These power moments will be very useful in subsequent chapters. Proofs of these power moments could be found in Huffman and Pless (2003)[Section 7.3].

The Pless power moments in (2.6) can be used to prove the following result [Huffman and Pless (2003)][p. 259].

Theorem 2.6. *Let $S \subseteq \{1, 2, \ldots, n\}$ with $|S| = s$. Then the weight distributions of C and $C^{\perp}$ are uniquely determined by $A_1^{\perp}, A_2^{\perp}, \ldots, A_{s-1}^{\perp}$ and the A_i with $i \notin S$. These values can be found from the first s equations in (2.6).*

2.4   Punctured Codes of a Linear Code

Given an $[n, \kappa, d]$ code C over GF(q), we can puncture it by deleting the coordinate at coordinate position i in each codeword. The resulting code is still linear and has length $n - 1$. We denote the punctured code by $C^{\{i\}}$. If G is a generator matrix for C, then a generator matrix for $C^{\{i\}}$ is obtained from G by deleting the column at position i (and omitting a zero or duplicate row that may occur). This fact can be employed to prove the following theorem.

Theorem 2.7. *Let C be an $[n, \kappa, d]$ code over $GF(q)$, and let $C^{\{i\}}$ denote the code obtained by puncturing C at coordinate position i.*

(i) *When $d > 1$, $C^{\{i\}}$ is an $[n - 1, \kappa, d^{\{i\}}]$ code, where $d^{\{i\}} = d - 1$ if C has a minimum-weight codeword with a nonzero ith coordinate and $d = d^{\{i\}}$ otherwise.*

(ii) *When $d = 1$, $C^{\{i\}}$ is an $[n - 1, \kappa, 1]$ code if C has no codeword of weight 1 whose nonzero entry is in coordinate i; otherwise, if $\kappa > 1$, $C^{\{i\}}$ is an $[n - 1, \kappa - 1, d^{\{i\}}]$ code with $d^{\{i\}} \geq 1$.*

This puncturing technique is useful in obtaining codes with new parameters from old ones. Theorem 2.7 will be employed later.

Let T be a set of coordinate positions in C. We use C^T to denote the code obtained by puncturing C in all the coordinate positions in T. The punctured code C^T has length $n - |T|$, where n is the length of C.

2.5 Shortened Codes of a Linear Code

Let C be an $[n, \kappa, d]$ code over $GF(q)$ and let T be any set of t coordinate positions. Let $C(T)$ be the set of codewords whose coordinates are **0** on T. Then $C(T)$ is a subcode of C. We now puncture $C(T)$ on T, and obtain a linear code over $GF(q)$ with length $n - t$, which is called a *shortened code* of C, and is denoted by C_T.

The following theorem documents properties of the shortened code C_T of C. Its proof could be found in Huffman and Pless (2003)[Theorem 1.5.7]. We will need this theorem in later chapters.

Theorem 2.8. *Let C be an $[n, \kappa, d]$ code over $GF(q)$ and let T be any set of t coordinates. Let C^T denote the punctured code of C in all coordinates in T. Then the following holds.*

(a) *$(C^\perp)_T = (C^T)^\perp$ and $(C^\perp)^T = (C_T)^\perp$.*

(b) *If $t < d$, then C^T and $(C^\perp)_T$ have dimensions κ and $n - t - \kappa$, respectively.*

(c) *If $t = d$ and T is the set of coordinates where a minimum weight codeword is nonzero, then C^T and $(C^\perp)_T$ have dimensions $\kappa - 1$ and $n - t - \kappa + 1$, respectively.*

2.6   Extended Code of a Linear Code

Let C be an $[n, \kappa, d]$ code over $\mathrm{GF}(q)$. The *extended code* $\overline{C}$ of C is defined by

$$\overline{C} = \left\{ (x_1, x_2, \ldots, x_n, x_{n+1}) \in \mathrm{GF}(q)^{n+1} : (x_1, x_2, \ldots, x_n) \in C \text{ with } \sum_{i=1}^{n+1} x_i = 0 \right\}.$$

Let H and $\overline{H}$ denote the parity-check matrix of C and $\overline{C}$, respectively. Then we have the following theorem whose proof is left to the reader.

Theorem 2.9. *Let C be an $[n, \kappa, d]$ code over $\mathrm{GF}(q)$. Then $\overline{C}$ is an $[n+1, \kappa, \overline{d}]$ linear code, where $\overline{d} = d$ or $d + 1$. In the binary case, $\overline{d} = d$ if d is even, and $\overline{d} = d + 1$ otherwise.*

In addition, the parity-check matrix $\overline{H}$ of $\overline{C}$ can be deduced from that of C by

$$\overline{H} = \begin{bmatrix} \mathbf{1} & 1 \\ H & \mathbf{0} \end{bmatrix}, \tag{2.7}$$

where $\mathbf{1} = (1, 1, \ldots, 1)$ and $\mathbf{0} = (0, 0, \ldots, 0)^T$.

In subsequent chapters, we will need the following theorem.

Theorem 2.10. *Let C be an $[n, \kappa, d]$ binary linear code, and let $C^\perp$ denote the dual of C. Denote by $\overline{C^\perp}$ the extended code of $C^\perp$, and let $\overline{C^\perp}^\perp$ denote the dual of $\overline{C^\perp}$. Then we have the following.*

(1) $C^\perp$ has parameters $[n, n - \kappa, d^\perp]$, where $d^\perp$ denotes the minimum distance of $C^\perp$.

(2) $\overline{C^\perp}$ has parameters $[n+1, n - \kappa, \overline{d^\perp}]$, where $\overline{d^\perp}$ denotes the minimum distance of $\overline{C^\perp}$, and is given by

$$\overline{d^\perp} = \begin{cases} d^\perp & \text{if } d^\perp \text{ is even,} \\ d^\perp + 1 & \text{if } d^\perp \text{ is odd.} \end{cases}$$

(3) $\overline{C^\perp}^\perp$ has parameters $[n+1, \kappa + 1, \overline{d^\perp}^\perp]$, where $\overline{d^\perp}^\perp$ denotes the minimum distance of $\overline{C^\perp}^\perp$. Furthermore, $\overline{C^\perp}^\perp$ has only even-weight codewords, and all the nonzero weights in $\overline{C^\perp}^\perp$ are the following:

$$w_1, w_2, \ldots, w_t; n+1 - w_1, n+1 - w_2, \ldots, n+1 - w_t; n+1,$$

where $w_1, w_2, \ldots, w_t$ denote all the nonzero weights of C.

Proof. The conclusions of the first two parts are straightforward. We prove only the conclusions of the third part below.

Since $\overline{C^\perp}$ has length $n + 1$ and dimension $n - \kappa$, the dimension of $\overline{C^\perp}^\perp$ is $\kappa + 1$. By assumption, all codes under consideration are binary. By definition, $\overline{C^\perp}$ has only even-weight codewords. Recall that $\overline{C^\perp}$ is the extended code of $C^\perp$. By Theorem 2.9, the generator matrix of $\overline{C^\perp}^\perp$ is given by

$$\begin{bmatrix} 1 & 1 \\ G & 0 \end{bmatrix},$$

where $\mathbf{1} = (111\cdots1)$ is the all-one vector of length n, $\mathbf{0} = (000\cdots0)^T$, which is a column vector of length κ, and G is the generator matrix of C. Notice again that $\overline{C^\perp}^\perp$ is binary, the desired conclusions on the weights in $\overline{C^\perp}^\perp$ follow from the relation between the two generator matrices of the two codes $\overline{C^\perp}^\perp$ and C. $\qquad\square$

The following result will be employed in subsequent chapters. Its proof is straightforward and left to the reader.

Theorem 2.11. *Let C be an $[n, \kappa, d]$ code over GF(q) with generator matrix G. Let H denote a generator matrix of its dual $C^\perp$ with parameters $[n, n - \kappa, d^\perp]$. Then we have the following:*

- *The code $\overline{C^\perp}^\perp$ has parameters $[n + 1, \kappa + 1]$ and generator matrix*

$$\begin{bmatrix} 1 & 1 \\ G & 0 \end{bmatrix},$$

where $\mathbf{1} = (111\cdots1)$ is the all-one vector of length n, $\mathbf{0} = (000\cdots0)^T$, which is a column vector of length κ.

- *The code $\overline{C}^\perp$ has parameters $[n + 1, n + 1 - \kappa]$ and generator matrix*

$$\begin{bmatrix} 1 & 1 \\ H & 0 \end{bmatrix},$$

where $\mathbf{1} = (111\cdots1)$ is the all-one vector of length n, $\mathbf{0} = (000\cdots0)^T$, which is a column vector of length $n - \kappa$.

- *If $\mathbf{1} \in C$, then $\overline{C^\perp}$ has generator matrix $[H\mathbf{0}]$ and is a subcode of $\overline{C}^\perp$.*

2.7 Augmented Code of a Linear Code

Let C be an $[n, \kappa, d]$ code over GF(q) with generator matrix G. Suppose that the all-1 vector is not a codeword of C. Then the *augmented code*, denoted by $\tilde{C}$, of C is the linear code over GF(q) with generator matrix

$$\begin{bmatrix} G \\ \mathbf{1} \end{bmatrix},$$

where **1** denotes the all-1 vector. The augmented code has length n and dimension $\kappa + 1$. In general, the determination of the minimum distance of the augmented code $\tilde{C}$ may require information of the complete weight distribution of the original code C, and may be a hard problem in general. However, in the binary case (i.e., $q = 2$), it is easily seen that the minimum distance $\tilde{d}$ of $\tilde{C}$ is given by

$$\tilde{d} = \min\{d, n - w_{\max}\},$$

where $w_{\max}$ denotes the maximum weight in C.

2.8 Automorphism Groups and Equivalences of Linear Codes

Two linear codes C_1 and C_2 are *permutation equivalent* if there is a permutation of coordinates which sends C_1 to C_2. This permutation could be described employing a *permutation matrix*, which is a square matrix with exactly one 1 in each row and column and 0s elsewhere. Hence, C_1 and C_2 are permutation equivalent provided there is a permutation matrix P such that G_1 is a generator matrix of C_1 if and only if $G_1 P$ is a generator matrix of C_2. Applying a permutation P to a generator matrix is to rearrange the columns of the generator matrix. If P is a permutation sending C_1 to C_2, we write $C_1 P = C_2$, where

$$C_1 P := \{\mathbf{y} : \mathbf{y} = \mathbf{x}P \ \forall \mathbf{x} \in C_1\}.$$

It is straightforward to prove the following theorem.

Theorem 2.12. *If C_1 and C_2 are permutation equivalent, then*

(1) $C_1^{\perp}$ and $C_2^{\perp}$ are also permutation equivalent, and
(2) C_1 and C_2 have the same dimension and weight distribution.

The set of coordinate permutations that map a code C to itself forms a group, which is referred to as the *permutation automorphism group* of C and denoted by PAut(C). If C is a code of length n, then PAut(C) is a subgroup of the *symmetric group* Sym_n.

A subgroup L of the symmetric group Sym_n is *transitive*, provided that for every ordered pair (i, j), where $1 \leq i, j \leq n$, there is a permutation $\ell \in L$ such that $\ell(i) = j$. When the group PAut($\overline{C}$) is transitive, we have information on the minimum weight of C. A proof of the following theorem can be found in Huffman and Pless (2003)[Theorem 1.6.6].

Theorem 2.13. *Let C be an $[n, k, d]$ code.*

a) Suppose that the group PAut(C) is transitive. Then the n codes obtained from C by puncturing C on a coordinate are permutation equivalent.

b) Suppose that the group $\text{PAut}(\overline{C})$ *is transitive. Then the minimum weight d of C is its minimum odd-like weight* d_o. *Furthermore, every minimum weight codeword of C is odd-like.*

The following theorem will be needed in some subsequent chapters [Huffman and Pless (2003)][p. 22].

Theorem 2.14. *Let* C, C_1 *and* C_2 *be linear codes over* $\text{GF}(q)$. *Then we have the following:*

(1) $\text{PAut}(C) = \text{PAut}(C^{\perp})$.
(2) If $C_1 P = C_2$ *for a permutation matrix P, then* $P^{-1}\text{PAut}(C_1)P = \text{PAut}(C_2)$.

A *monomial matrix* over $\text{GF}(q)$ is a square matrix having exactly one nonzero element of $\text{GF}(q)$ in each row and column. A monomial matrix M can be written either in the form DP or the form PD_1, where D and D_1 are diagonal matrices and P is a permutation matrix.

Let C_1 and C_2 be two linear codes of the same length over $\text{GF}(q)$. Then C_1 and C_2 are *monomially equivalent* if there is a nomomial matrix over $\text{GF}(q)$ such that $C_2 = C_1 M$. Monomial equivalence and permutation equivalence are precisely the same for binary codes. If C_1 and C_2 are monomially equivalent, then they have the same weight distribution.

The set of monomial matrices that map C to itself forms the group $\text{MAut}(C)$, which is called the *monomial automorphism group* of C. Clearly, we have $\text{PAut}(C) \subseteq \text{MAut}(C)$.

Two codes C_1 and C_2 are said to be *equivalent* if there is a monomial matrix M and an automorphism γ such that $C_1 = C_2 M\gamma$. This is the most general notion of equivalence we consider in this monograph. All three are the same if the codes are binary; monomial equivalence and equivalence are the same if the field considered has a prime number of elements.

The *automorphism group* of C, denoted by $\text{Aut}(C)$, is the set of maps of the form $M\gamma$, where M is a monomial matrix and γ is a field automorphism, that map C to itself. In the binary case, $\text{PAut}(C)$, $\text{MAut}(C)$ and $\text{Aut}(C)$ are the same. If q is a prime, $\text{MAut}(C)$ and $\text{Aut}(C)$ are identical. In general, we have

$$\text{PAut}(C) \subseteq \text{MAut}(C) \subseteq \text{Aut}(C).$$

The transitivity of $\text{PAut}(C)$ was defined earlier in this section. To define the transitivity of $\text{MAut}(C)$ and $\text{Aut}(C)$, we introduce the following two sets:

$$\begin{cases} \text{MAutpr}(C) = \{P : DP \in \text{MAut}(C)\}, \\ \text{Autpr}(C) \;\;= \{P : DP\gamma \in \text{Aut}(C)\}, \end{cases} \tag{2.8}$$

where D is a diagonal matrix and P is a permutation matrix.

One can easily prove the following statements.

Theorem 2.15. *Let C be a linear code of length n over* $\mathrm{GF}(q)$. *Then*

1) $\mathrm{MAutpr}(C)$ *and* $\mathrm{Autpr}(C)$ *are subgroups of the symmetric group* Sym_n, *and*
2) $\mathrm{PAut}(C) \subseteq \mathrm{MAutpr}(C) \subseteq \mathrm{Autpr}(C)$.

We say that $\mathrm{MAut}(C)$ ($\mathrm{Aut}(C)$, respectively) is *transitive* if $\mathrm{MAutpr}(C)$ ($\mathrm{Autpr}(C)$, respectively) is transitive. The following theorem will be useful [Huffman and Pless (2003)][Theorem 1.7.13].

Theorem 2.16. *Suppose that the group* $\mathrm{MAut}(\overline{C})$ *is transitive. Then the minimum weight d of C is its minimum odd-like weight d_o. Furthermore, every minimum weight codeword of C is odd-like.*

Theorem 2.17. *Let C be an $[n,k,d]$ code.*

(1) Suppose that $\mathrm{MAut}(C)$ is transitive. Then the n codes obtained from C by puncturing C on a coordinate are monomially equivalent.
(2) Suppose that $\mathrm{Aut}(C)$ is transitive. Then the n codes obtained from C by puncturing C on a coordinate are equivalent.
(3) Suppose that either $\mathrm{MAut}(C)$ or $\mathrm{Aut}(C)$ is transitive. Then the minimum weight d of C is its minimum odd-like weight d_0. Furthermore, every minimum weight codeword of C is odd-like.

The proof of Theorem 2.17 is left to the reader. It will be seen later that the automorphism groups of linear codes will play an important role in some subsequent chapters.

By definition, every element in $\mathrm{Aut}(C)$ is of the form $DP\gamma$, where D is a diagonal matrix, P is a permutation matrix, and γ is an automorphism of $\mathrm{GF}(q)$. The automorphism group $\mathrm{Aut}(C)$ is said to be *t-transitive* if for every pair of t-element ordered sets of coordinates, there is an element $DP\gamma$ of the automorphism group $\mathrm{Aut}(C)$ such that its permutation part P sends the first set to the second set, i.e., there is a permutation P in $\mathrm{Autpr}(C)$ such that P sends the first set to the second set.

2.9 Subfield Subcodes

Let C be an $[n,\kappa]$ code over $\mathrm{GF}(q^t)$. The *subfield subcode* $C|_{\mathrm{GF}(q)}$ of C with respect to $\mathrm{GF}(q)$ is the set of codewords in C each of whose components is in $\mathrm{GF}(q)$. Since C is linear over $\mathrm{GF}(q^t)$, $C|_{\mathrm{GF}(q)}$ is a linear code over $\mathrm{GF}(q)$.

The dimension, denoted κ_q, of the subfield subcode $C|_{\mathrm{GF}(q)}$ may not have an elementary relation with that of the code C. However, we have the following lower and upper bounds on κ_q [Huffman and Pless (2003)][Theorems 3.8.3 and 3.8.4].

Theorem 2.18. *Let C be an $[n, \kappa]$ code over $\mathrm{GF}(q^t)$. Then $C|_{\mathrm{GF}(q)}$ is an $[n, \kappa_q]$ code over $\mathrm{GF}(q)$, where $\kappa \geq \kappa_q \geq n - t(n - \kappa)$. If C has a basis of codewords in $\mathrm{GF}(q)^n$, then this is also a basis of $C|_{\mathrm{GF}(q)}$ and $C|_{\mathrm{GF}(q)}$ has dimension κ.*

Example 2.19. The Hamming code $\mathcal{H}_{2^2,3}$ over $\mathrm{GF}(2^2)$ has parameters $[21, 18, 3]$. The subfield subcode $\mathcal{H}_{2^3,3}|_{\mathrm{GF}(2)}$ is a binary $[21, 16, 3]$ code with parity-check matrix

$$H = \begin{bmatrix} 1 & 0 & 0 & 1 & 1 & 0 & 0 & 1 & 1 & 0 & 0 & 1 & 1 & 1 & 1 & 0 & 0 & 1 & 1 & 0 & 1 \\ 0 & 1 & 0 & 0 & 1 & 0 & 1 & 1 & 0 & 0 & 1 & 1 & 0 & 1 & 0 & 0 & 1 & 1 & 0 & 0 & 1 \\ 0 & 0 & 1 & 1 & 0 & 0 & 1 & 1 & 0 & 0 & 1 & 1 & 0 & 0 & 1 & 1 & 0 & 0 & 1 & 1 & 0 \\ 0 & 0 & 0 & 0 & 0 & 1 & 1 & 1 & 1 & 0 & 0 & 0 & 0 & 0 & 0 & 0 & 0 & 1 & 1 & 1 & 1 \\ 0 & 0 & 0 & 0 & 0 & 0 & 0 & 0 & 1 & 1 & 1 & 1 & 1 & 1 & 1 & 1 & 0 & 0 & 0 & 0 & 0 \end{bmatrix}.$$

In this case, $n = 21$, $\kappa = 18$, and $n - t(n - \kappa) = 15$. Hence $\kappa_q = 16$, which is very close to $n - t(n - \kappa) = 15$.

The *trace* of a vector $\mathbf{c} = (c_1, c_2, \ldots, c_n) \in \mathrm{GF}(q^t)^n$ is defined by

$$\mathrm{Tr}_{q^t/q}(\mathbf{c}) = \left(\mathrm{Tr}_{q^t/q}(c_1), \mathrm{Tr}_{q^t/q}(c_2), \ldots, \mathrm{Tr}_{q^t/q}(c_n) \right).$$

The *trace code* of a linear code C of length n over $\mathrm{GF}(q^t)$ is defined by

$$\mathrm{Tr}_{q^t/q}(C) = \left\{ \mathrm{Tr}_{q^t/q}(\mathbf{c}) : \mathbf{c} \in C \right\}, \tag{2.9}$$

which is a linear code of length n over $\mathrm{GF}(q)$. We have

$$\begin{aligned} \dim_{\mathrm{GF}(q)}(\mathrm{Tr}_{q^t/q}(C)) &= \log_q |\mathrm{Tr}_{q^t/q}(C)| \\ &\leq \log_q(|C|) \\ &= \log_q[(q^t)^{\dim_{q^t}(C)}] \\ &= t \dim_{q^t}(C). \end{aligned}$$

This gives an upper bound on the dimension of the trace code in terms of the dimension of the original code.

The following is called *Delsarte's theorem*, which exhibits a dual relation between subfield subcodes and trace codes. This theorem is very useful in the design and analysis of linear codes. We will frequently get back to it later.

Theorem 2.20 (Delsarte's theorem). *Let C be a linear code of length n over $\mathrm{GF}(q^t)$. Then*

$$(C|_{\mathrm{GF}(q)})^{\perp} = \mathrm{Tr}_{q^t/q}(C^{\perp}).$$

Proof. We first prove that

$$(C|_{\mathrm{GF}(q)})^{\perp} \supseteq \mathrm{Tr}_{q^t/q}(C^{\perp}). \tag{2.10}$$

Let $\mathbf{a} = (a_1, \ldots, a_n) \in C^{\perp}$ and $\mathbf{c} = (c_1, \ldots, c_n) \in C|_{\mathrm{GF}(q)}$. Then

$$\mathbf{c} \cdot \mathrm{Tr}_{q^t/q}(\mathbf{a}) = \sum_{i=1}^{n} c_i \mathrm{Tr}_{q^t/q}(a_i) = \sum_{i=1}^{n} \mathrm{Tr}_{q^t/q}(c_i a_i) = \mathrm{Tr}_{q^t/q}(\mathbf{c} \cdot \mathbf{a}) = 0.$$

This proves (2.10). We then prove

$$(C|_{\mathrm{GF}(q)})^{\perp} \subseteq \mathrm{Tr}_{q^t/q}(C^{\perp}),$$

which is equivalent to

$$C|_{\mathrm{GF}(q)} \supseteq (\mathrm{Tr}_{q^t/q}(C^{\perp}))^{\perp}. \tag{2.11}$$

Note that $bC^{\perp} \subseteq C^{\perp}$ for all $b \in \mathrm{GF}(q^t)$. Let $\mathbf{u} \in (\mathrm{Tr}_{q^t/q}(C^{\perp}))^{\perp}$. Then

$$\mathbf{u} \cdot \mathrm{Tr}_{q^t/q}(\mathbf{v}) = 0 \, \forall \, \mathbf{v} \in C^{\perp}.$$

Consequently,

$$\mathbf{u} \cdot \mathrm{Tr}_{q^t/q}(b\mathbf{v}) = 0 \, \forall \, \mathbf{v} \in C^{\perp} \text{ and } \forall \, b \in \mathrm{GF}(q^t).$$

Write

$$\mathbf{u} = (u_1, \ldots, u_n) \in \mathrm{GF}(q)^n, \, \mathbf{v} = (v_1, \ldots, v_n) \in \mathrm{GF}(q^t)^n.$$

We have then

$$\mathbf{u} \cdot \mathrm{Tr}_{q^t/q}(b\mathbf{v}) = \sum_{i=1}^{n} \mathrm{Tr}_{q^t/q}(bu_i v_i) = \mathrm{Tr}_{q^t/q}\left(b \sum_{i=1}^{n} u_i v_i\right) = \mathrm{Tr}_{q^t/q}(b\mathbf{u} \cdot \mathbf{v}) = 0$$

for all $b \in \mathrm{GF}(q^t)$ and all $\mathbf{v} \in C^{\perp}$. It then follows that

$$\mathbf{u} \cdot \mathbf{v} = 0 \, \forall \, \mathbf{v} \in C^{\perp}.$$

Therefore, $\mathbf{u} \in C$. Hence, $\mathbf{u} \in C|_{\mathrm{GF}(q)}$. This proves (2.11), and thus completes the proof of the theorem. $\square$

Delsarte's theorem says that the trace code can be determined by the subfield subcode of its dual code. It may be combined with Theorem 2.18 to get further information on the trace code.

The following result will be useful in subsequent chapters.

Theorem 2.21. *Let C be an $[n, k, d]$ code over $\mathrm{GF}(q)$, and let $C^{[e]}$ denote the code over $\mathrm{GF}(q^e)$ generated by a generator matrix of C, where e is a positive integer. Then $C^{[e]}$ has parameters $[n, k, d]$.*

Proof. Clearly, the code $C^{[e]}$ is independent of the choice of a generator matrix of C. Note that a generator matrix of C is also a generator matrix of $C^{[e]}$ and the rank of a matrix over $\mathrm{GF}(q)$ is the same as the rank of the matrix over $\mathrm{GF}(q^e)$. Hence,

$$\dim_{\mathrm{GF}(q)}(C) = \dim_{\mathrm{GF}(q^e)}(C^{[e]}).$$

Observe that a parity-check matrix H of C is also a parity-check matrix of $C^{[e]}$. Since d is the largest natural number r such that each $(n-k) \times (r-1)$ submatrix of H has rank $r-1$, the minimum distance of $C^{[e]}$ equals d. $\square$

2.10 Bounds on the Size of Linear Codes

The purpose of this section is to collect bounds on the size of both nonlinear and linear codes together. We will not provide a proof for the bounds, but will refer the reader to a reference where a proof can be found.

Recall that an (n, M, d) code C over $\mathrm{GF}(q)$ is a code of length n with M codewords whose minimum distance is d. The code C could be either linear or nonlinear. If C is linear, it is an $[n, \kappa, d]$ code over $\mathrm{GF}(q)$, where $\kappa = \log_q M$ and d is equal to the minimum weight of C. Let $B_q(n, d)$ (resp. $A_q(n, d)$) denote the largest number of codewords in a linear (resp. arbitrary (linear or nonlinear)) code over $\mathrm{GF}(q)$ of length n and minimum distance at least d. A code C of length n over $\mathrm{GF}(q)$ and minimum distance at least d said to be optimal if it has $A_q(n, d)$ codewords (or $B_q(n, d)$ codewords in the case that C is linear).

The following is a list of targets in the construction of error correcting codes over $\mathrm{GF}(q)$.

(1) Given q, n and d, we want to find a code C over $\mathrm{GF}(q)$ of length n and minimum distance d with the maximum number of codewords.
(2) Given q, n and M, we wish to find a code C over $\mathrm{GF}(q)$ of length n and size M with the largest minimum distance.
(3) Given q, d and M, we wish to find a code C over $\mathrm{GF}(q)$ of minimum distance d and size M with the shortest length n.

However, there are constraints on the parameters n, d, q and M. Such constraints define bounds on the parameters of codes.

By definition, we have obviously that $B_q(n, d) \leq A_q(n, d)$ and $B_q(n, d)$ is a nonnegative power of q. The following theorem summarizes basic properties of $B_q(n, d)$ and $A_q(n, d)$ [Huffman and Pless (2003)][Section 2.1].

Theorem 2.22. *Let $d > 1$. Then we have the following.*

(a) $A_q(n, d) \leq A_q(n - 1, d - 1)$ and $B_q(n, d) \leq B_q(n - 1, d - 1)$.
(b) *If d is even,* $A_2(n, d) = A_2(n - 1, d - 1)$ and $B_2(n, d) = B_2(n - 1, d - 1)$.
(c) *If d is even and $M = A_2(n, d)$, then there exists a binary (n, M, d) code such that all codewords have even weight and the distance between all pairs of codewords is also even.*
(d) $A_q(n, d) \leq q A_q(n - 1, d)$ and $B_q(n, d) \leq q B_q(n - 1, d)$.
(e) *If d is even,* $A_2(2d, d) \leq 4d$.
(f) *If d is odd,* $A_2(2d, d) \leq 2d + 2$.
(g) *If d is odd,* $A_2(2d + 1, d) \leq 4d + 4$.

We are now ready to introduce some bounds on the parameters of codes. The following is the Plotkin bound [Plotkin (1960)], which is useful only when d is close to n.

Theorem 2.23 (Plotkin bound). *Suppose that $rn < d$, where $r = 1 - q^{-1}$. Then*

$$A_q(n,d) \leq \left\lfloor \frac{d}{d - rn} \right\rfloor.$$

In the binary case,

$$A_2(n,d) \leq 2 \left\lfloor \frac{d}{2d - n} \right\rfloor$$

provided that $n < 2d$.

The following theorem describes the Singleton bound [Singleton (1964)], which is simple in format.

Theorem 2.24 (Singleton bound). *Let $d \leq n$. Then*

$$A_q(n,d) \leq q^{n-d+1}.$$

In particular, for any $[n, \kappa, d]$ code over $\mathrm{GF}(q)$, we have $\kappa \leq n - d + 1$.

A code meeting the Singleton bound is called *maximum distance separable* (MDS for short). If C is an MDS linear code, so is $C^\perp$. The weight distribution of MDS codes is given by the following theorem [MacWilliams and Sloane (1977)][p. 321].

Theorem 2.25. *Let C be an $[n, \kappa]$ code over $\mathrm{GF}(q)$ with $d = n - \kappa + 1$, and let the weight enumerator of C be $1 + \sum_{i=d}^{n} A_i z^i$. Then*

$$A_i = \binom{n}{i}(q-1) \sum_{j=0}^{i-d} (-1)^j \binom{i-1}{j} q^{i-j-d} \text{ for all } d \leq i \leq n.$$

For linear codes over finite fields, we have the following Griesmer bound [Griesmer (1960)], which is a generalization of the Singleton bound.

Theorem 2.26 (Griesmer bound). *Let C be an $[n, \kappa, d]$ code over $\mathrm{GF}(q)$ with $\kappa \geq 1$. Then*

$$n \geq \sum_{i=0}^{\kappa-1} \left\lceil \frac{d}{q^i} \right\rceil.$$

For certain parameters n, κ, d and q, there may not exist an $[n, \kappa, d]$ code over $GF(q)$ meeting the Griesmer bound. However, for some other parameters, the Griesmer bound may be achievable. It is quite interesting to construct linear codes meeting the Griesmer bound. There are a lot of references on this problem. It is clear that the Simplex codes meet the Griesmer bound.

Binary linear codes over finite fields meeting the Griesmer bound have the following nice property [Van Tilborg (1980)].

Theorem 2.27. *Let C be an $[n, \kappa, d]$ binary code meeting the Griesmer bound. Then C has a basis of minimum weight codewords.*

The following is the *sphere packing bound*, also called the *Hamming bound*.

Theorem 2.28 (Sphere packing bound).

$$B_q(n, d) \le A_q(n, d) \le \frac{q^n}{\sum\limits_{i=0}^{\lfloor \frac{d-1}{2} \rfloor} \binom{n}{i}(q-1)^i}. \tag{2.12}$$

A code meeting the sphere packing bound is said to be *perfect*. It is straightforward to verify that the Hamming code $\mathcal{H}_{q,m}$ is perfect.

For a code C over $GF(q)$ with minimum dsitance d, we define its *covering radius* by

$$\rho(C) = \max_{x \in GF(q)^n} \min_{\mathbf{c} \in C} \mathrm{dist}(\mathbf{x}, \mathbf{c}).$$

It is easily seen that

$$\left\lfloor \frac{d-1}{2} \right\rfloor \le \rho(C)$$

where the equality holds if and only if C is perfect.

The Gilbert bound is given in the next theorem [Gilbert (1952)].

Theorem 2.29 (Gilbert bound).

$$A_q(n, d) \ge B_q(n, d) \ge \frac{q^n}{\sum\limits_{i=0}^{d-1} \binom{n}{i}(q-1)^i}.$$

The Varshamov bound below is similar to the Gilbert bound [Varshamov (1957)].

Theorem 2.30 (Varshamov bound).

$$A_q(n, d) \ge B_q(n, d) \ge q^{n - \lceil \log_q \left(1 + \sum_{i=0}^{d-2} \binom{n-1}{i}(q-1)^i \right) \rceil}.$$

The next bound is the Elias bound documented in the following theorem.

Theorem 2.31 (Elias bound). *Let $r = 1 - q^{-1}$. Suppose that $w \leq rn$ and $w^2 - 2rnw + rnd > 0$. Then*

$$A_q(n,d) \leq \frac{rnd}{w^2 - 2rnw + rnd} \cdot \frac{q^n}{\sum\limits_{i=0}^{w} \binom{n}{i}(q-1)^i}.$$

In many cases, the linear programming bounds on codes are better than those described before. There are also a number of asymptotic bounds. The reader is referred to Huffman and Pless (2003)[Sections 2.6 and 2.10] for details.

The following Grey-Rankin bound applies only to special binary codes and will be needed in future chapters. A geometric proof of this bound is given in McQuire (1997).

Theorem 2.32 (Grey-Rankin bound). *Let C be a binary (n,M,d) code with $n - \sqrt{n} \leq 2d \leq n$. Suppose that C is self-complementary, i.e., $\mathbf{c} + \mathbf{1} \in C$ for every $\mathbf{c} \in C$. Then*

$$M \leq \frac{8d(n-d)}{n - (n-2d)^2}.$$

2.11   Restrictions on Parameters of Linear Codes

The following theorem was developed in Delsarte (1973a), which will be useful in subsequent chapters.

Theorem 2.33. *Let C be an $[n, \kappa, d]$ code over $\mathrm{GF}(q)$. Assume that C and $C^{\perp}$ have s and $s^{\perp}$ nonzero weights, respectively. Then*

$$q^{n-\kappa} \leq \sum_{i=0}^{s^{\perp}} \binom{n}{i}(q-1)^i$$

and

$$q^{\kappa} \leq \sum_{i=0}^{s} \binom{n}{i}(q-1)^i.$$

The parameter $s^{\perp}$ is called the *external distance* of C. The reader is referred to Delsarte (1973a) for a proof. The two inequalities above could be viewed as duals of each other.

2.12 Bounds on the Size of Constant Weight Codes

A (nonlinear) (n, M, d) code C over $GF(q)$ is a *constant weight code* if every codeword has the same weight. For example, the codewords of a fixed weight w in a linear code form a constant weight code. The following theorem is easily proved.

Theorem 2.34. *If C is a constant weight (n, M, d) code with codewords of weight $w > 1$, then $d \leq 2w$.*

Let $A_q(n, d, w)$ denote the maximum number of codewords in a constant weight (n, M) code over $GF(q)$ of length n and minimum distance at least d whose codewords have weight w. Obviously $A_q(n, d, w) \leq A_q(n, d)$. The following is a list of properties of $A_q(n, d, w)$ collected from the literature:

(a) $A_3(n, 3, 3) = \frac{2n(n-1)}{3}$ for $n \equiv 0, 1 \pmod 3$, $n \geq 4$.

(b) $A_3(n, 3, 3) = \frac{2n(n-1)-4}{3}$ for $n \equiv 2 \pmod 3$, $n \geq 5$.

(c) $A_3(n, 3, 4) \geq \lfloor \frac{n^3 - 5n^2 + 6n}{3} \rfloor$, if $n \geq 4$.

(d) $A_3(n, 3, w) \geq \frac{1}{2n+1} \binom{n}{w} 2^w$.

(e) $A_3(n, 3, w) \geq \frac{1}{2n} \binom{n}{w} 2^w$, if $n \equiv 0, 1 \pmod 4$.

(f) $A_3(2^r - 1, 3, 2^r - 2) = (2^r - 1)2^{2^r - r - 2}$ for $r \geq 2$.

(g) $A_3(2^r - 2, 3, 2^r - 3) = (2^{r-1} - 1)2^{2^r - r - 2}$ for $r \geq 2$.

(h) $A_3(2^r, 3, 2^r - 1) = 2^{2^r - 1}$ for $r \geq 2$.

(i) $A_3\left(q, \frac{q+3}{2}, q-1\right) = q$, where q is a power of odd prime.

(j) $A_3\left(q\frac{q^m - 1}{q - 1}, q^{m-1}\frac{q+3}{2}, q^m - 1\right) = q^m$, where q is a power of odd prime.

(k) $A_3\left(p^m + 1, \frac{p^m + 3}{2}, p^m\right) = 2p^m + 2$, where $p \geq 3$ is a prime.

(l) $A_q(n, 2, w) = \binom{n}{w}(q-1)^w$.

(m) $A_q\left(\frac{q^m - 1}{q - 1}, q^{m-1}, q^{m-1}\right) = q^m - 1$, where q is a prime power.

(n) $A_q\left(q + 1, \frac{q+1}{2}, q\right) \geq 2q + 2$, where $q = p^m$.

(o) $A_q(n, d, w) = 1$ if $d > 2w$ and $0 \leq w \leq n$.

(p) $A_q(n, 2w, w) = \lfloor \frac{n}{w} \rfloor$.

(q) $A_q(n, d, n) = A_{q-1}(n, d)$.

The following is the restricted Johnson bound for $A_q(n, d, w)$ [Huffman and Pless (2003)][Theorem 2.3.4].

Theorem 2.35 (Restricted Johnson bound for $A_q(n, d, w)$).

$$A_q(n, d, w) \leq \left\lfloor \frac{n(q-1)d}{qw^2 - 2(q-1)nw + n(q-1)d} \right\rfloor,$$

provided that $qw^2 - 2(q-1)nw + n(q-1)d > 0$.

This bound is restricted because of the condition $qw^2 - 2(q-1)nw + n(q-1)d > 0$. The following is another bound without such a condition [Huffman and Pless (2003)][Theorem 2.3.6].

Theorem 2.36 (Unrestricted Johnson bound for $A_q(n,d,w)$). *If $2w \geq d$ and $d \in \{2e-1, 2e\}$, then*

$$A_q(n,d,w) \leq \left\lfloor \frac{n\hat{q}}{w} \left\lfloor \frac{(n-1)\hat{q}}{w-1} \left\lfloor \cdots \left\lfloor \frac{(n-w+e)\hat{q}}{e} \right\rfloor \cdots \right\rfloor \right\rfloor \right\rfloor,$$

where $\hat{q} = q - 1$.

2.13 Hamming and Simplex Codes, and One-Weight Codes

A parity-check matrix $H_{(q,m)}$ of the *Hamming code* $\mathcal{H}_{(q,m)}$ over GF(q) is defined by choosing for its columns a nonzero vector from each one-dimensional subspace of GF$(q)^m$. In terms of finite geometry, the columns of $H_{(q,m)}$ are the points of the projective geometry PG$(m-1, \text{GF}(q))$. Hence $\mathcal{H}_{(q,m)}$ has length $n = (q^m - 1)/(q-1)$ and dimension $n - m$. Note that no two columns of $H_{(q,m)}$ are linearly dependent over GF(q). The minimum weight of $\mathcal{H}_{(q,m)}$ is at least 3. Adding two nonzero vectors from two different one-dimensional subspaces gives a nonzero vector from a third one-dimensional space. Therefore, $\mathcal{H}_{(q,m)}$ has minimum weight 3.

Example 2.37. The Hamming code $\mathcal{H}_{(3,3)}$ has parameters $[13, 10, 3]$ and generator matrix

$$G = \begin{bmatrix} 1 & 0 & 0 & 0 & 0 & 0 & 0 & 0 & 0 & 0 & 2 & 1 & 1 \\ 0 & 1 & 0 & 0 & 0 & 0 & 0 & 0 & 0 & 0 & 1 & 1 & 0 \\ 0 & 0 & 1 & 0 & 0 & 0 & 0 & 0 & 0 & 0 & 0 & 1 & 1 \\ 0 & 0 & 0 & 1 & 0 & 0 & 0 & 0 & 0 & 1 & 2 & 0 \\ 0 & 0 & 0 & 0 & 1 & 0 & 0 & 0 & 0 & 0 & 0 & 1 & 2 \\ 0 & 0 & 0 & 0 & 0 & 1 & 0 & 0 & 0 & 2 & 1 & 2 \\ 0 & 0 & 0 & 0 & 0 & 0 & 1 & 0 & 0 & 0 & 2 & 0 & 2 \\ 0 & 0 & 0 & 0 & 0 & 0 & 0 & 1 & 0 & 0 & 2 & 0 & 1 \\ 0 & 0 & 0 & 0 & 0 & 0 & 0 & 0 & 1 & 0 & 1 & 1 & 2 \\ 0 & 0 & 0 & 0 & 0 & 0 & 0 & 0 & 0 & 1 & 2 & 2 & 2 \end{bmatrix}. \tag{2.13}$$

The following theorem is interesting, as it implies that all $[(q^m - 1)/(q-1), (q^m - 1)/(q-1) - m, 3]$ codes over GF(q) have the same weight distribution [Huffman and Pless (2003)][Theorem 1.8.2].

Theorem 2.38. *Any* $[(q^m - 1)/(q-1), (q^m - 1)/(q-1) - m, 3]$ *code over* GF(q) *is monomially equivalent to the Hamming code* $\mathcal{H}_{(q,m)}$.

The duals of the Hamming codes $\mathcal{H}_{(q,m)}$ are called *Simplex codes*, which have parameters $[(q^m - 1)/(q-1), m, q^{m-1}]$. In fact, we have the following conclusion [Huffman and Pless (2003)][Theorem 1.8.3].

Theorem 2.39. *The nonzero codewords of the* $[(q^m - 1)/(q-1), m, q^{m-1}]$ *Simplex codes all have weight* q^{m-1}.

Example 2.40. Let $q = 3$ and $m = 3$. Then the Simplex code has parameters $[13, 3, 9]$ and generator matrix

$$G = \begin{bmatrix} 1 & 0 & 0 & 1 & 2 & 0 & 2 & 0 & 1 & 1 & 1 & 2 & 1 \\ 0 & 1 & 0 & 2 & 2 & 2 & 1 & 2 & 2 & 0 & 0 & 2 & 1 \\ 0 & 0 & 1 & 2 & 0 & 2 & 0 & 1 & 1 & 1 & 2 & 1 & 1 \end{bmatrix}. \tag{2.14}$$

Let $(A_0, A_1, \cdots, A_n)$ be the weight distribution of an $[n, k]$ code over GF(q). Denote by s the Hamming weight of $(A_1, \cdots, A_n)$. Then C is called an s-weight code. A one-weight code C is also called an *equidistant code*, as the Hamming weight between any pair of distinct codewords in C is a constant. All one-weight codes are known because of the following result due to Bonisoli (1984).

Theorem 2.41. *Let* C *be a one-weight code over* GF(q). *Then* C *is monomially-equivalent to a replication of some Simplex code over* GF(q), *possibly with added* 0-*coordinates.*

In this theorem, a replication of a Simplex code means the concatenation of a Simplex code a number of times. A short proof of Theorem 2.41 can be found in Ward (1999).

2.14   A Trace Construction of Linear Codes

Throughout this section, let q be a prime power and let $r = q^m$, where m is a positive integer. Let Tr denote the trace function from GF(r) to GF(q) unless otherwise stated.

Let $D = \{d_1, d_2, \ldots, d_n\} \subseteq$ GF(r). We define a code of length n over GF(q) by

$$C_D = \{(\mathrm{Tr}(xd_1), \mathrm{Tr}(xd_2), \ldots, \mathrm{Tr}(xd_n)) : x \in \mathrm{GF}(r)\}, \tag{2.15}$$

and call D the *defining set* of this code C_D. Since the trace function is linear, the code C_D is linear. By definition, the dimension of the code C_D is at most m.

Different orderings of the elements of D give different linear codes, which are however permutation equivalent. Hence, we do not distinguish these codes obtained by different orderings, and do not consider the ordering of the elements in D. It should be noticed that the defining set D could be a multiset, i.e., some elements in D may be the same.

Define for each $x \in GF(r)$,

$$\mathbf{c}_x = (\mathrm{Tr}(xd_1), \mathrm{Tr}(xd_2), \ldots, \mathrm{Tr}(xd_n)).$$

The Hamming weight $\mathtt{wt}(\mathbf{c}_x)$ of $\mathbf{c}_x$ is $n - N_x(0)$, where

$$N_x(0) = |\{1 \le i \le n : \mathrm{Tr}(xd_i) = 0\}|$$

for each $x \in GF(r)$.

It is easily seen that for any $D = \{d_1, d_2, \ldots, d_n\} \subseteq GF(r)$ we have

$$qN_x(0) = \sum_{i=1}^{n} \sum_{y \in GF(q)} \tilde{\chi}_1(y\mathrm{Tr}(xd_i))$$

$$= \sum_{i=1}^{n} \sum_{y \in GF(q)} \chi_1(yxd_i)$$

$$= n + \sum_{i=1}^{n} \sum_{y \in GF(q)^*} \chi_1(yxd_i)$$

$$= n + \sum_{y \in GF(q)^*} \chi_1(yxD),$$

where χ_1 and $\tilde{\chi}_1$ are the canonical additive characters of $GF(r)$ and $GF(q)$, respectively, aD denotes the set $\{ad : d \in D\}$, and $\chi_1(S) := \sum_{x \in S} \chi_1(x)$ for any subset S of $GF(r)$. Hence,

$$\mathtt{wt}(\mathbf{c}_x) = n - N_x(0) = \frac{(q-1)n - \sum_{y \in GF(q)^*} \chi_1(yxD)}{q}. \qquad (2.16)$$

Thus, the computation of the weight distribution of the code C_D reduces to the determination of the value distribution of the character sum

$$\sum_{y \in GF(q)^*} \sum_{i=1}^{n} \chi_1(yxd_i).$$

This construction technique was employed many years ago for obtaining linear codes with a few weights (see, for example, Wolfmann (1975), Ding and Niederreiter (2007), Ding, Luo and Niederreiter (2008) and Ding (2009)), and is called the *defining-set construction*. Recently, this trace construction of linear codes has attracted a lot of attention, and a huge amount of linear codes with good parameters have been obtained. The following theorem shows that the trace construction is fundamental.

Theorem 2.42. *Every $[n,k]$ code over $\mathrm{GF}(q)$ can be expressed as C_D for some defining set $D \subseteq \mathrm{GF}(q^k)$.*

Proof. Let $(g_{1j}, g_{2j}, \ldots, g_{kj})^T$ denote the jth column of a generator matrix of the code for $1 \leq j \leq n$. Define

$$f_j(x) = (x_1, x_2, \ldots, x_k)(g_{1j}, g_{2j}, \ldots, g_{kj})^T,$$

where $x = (x_1, x_2, \ldots, x_k) \in \mathrm{GF}(q)^k$. By definition, the code is the set

$$\{(f_1(x), f_2(x), \ldots, f_n(x)) : x \in \mathrm{GF}(q)^k\}.$$

Let $\{\alpha_1, \alpha_2, \ldots, \alpha_k\}$ be a basis of $\mathrm{GF}(q^k)$ over $\mathrm{GF}(q)$, and let $\{\beta_1, \beta_2, \ldots, \beta_k\}$ denote its dual basis. For each j with $1 \leq j \leq n$, define

$$d_j = \sum_{i=1}^{k} g_{ij} \beta_i$$

and $D = \{d_1, d_2, \ldots, d_n\} \subseteq \mathrm{GF}(q^k)$. For $x = (x_1, x_2, \ldots, x_k) \in \mathrm{GF}(q)^k$, define

$$x' = \sum_{i=1}^{k} x_i \alpha_i \in \mathrm{GF}(q^k).$$

Clearly, we have

$$\mathrm{Tr}_{q^k/q}(d_j x') = \sum_{i=1}^{k} x_i g_{ij} = f_j(x).$$

Consequently,

$$\begin{aligned}
&\{(f_1(x), \ldots, f_n(x)) : x \in \mathrm{GF}(q)^k\} \\
&= \{\mathrm{Tr}_{q^k/q}(d_1 x'), \ldots, \mathrm{Tr}_{q^k/q}(d_n x') : x' \in \mathrm{GF}(q^k)\} \\
&= C_D.
\end{aligned}$$

This completes the proof. $\qquad\qquad\square$

Theorem 2.42 was implied in Wolfmann (1975) and was presented and proved in a slightly different way in Xiang (2016). Theorem 2.42 and its proof above are refined ones in Heng, Wang and Wang (2021), and show that the defining-set construction is equivalent to the generator-matrix construction. However, the weight formula in (2.16) tells us that an advantage of the former over the latter is that the former can make full use of results about character sums for determining the parameters and weight distributions of linear codes. This advantage has been demonstrated in a lot of recent references on the defining-set construction of linear codes.

2.15   Projective Linear Codes and Projective Geometry

The projective spaces $\mathrm{PG}(k-1,\mathrm{GF}(q))$ were introduced briefly in Section 1.6.1. The objective of this section is to describe a connection between projective linear codes over $\mathrm{GF}(q)$ and projective geometries over $\mathrm{GF}(q)$.

Let C be an $[n,k,d]$ code over $\mathrm{GF}(q)$ with dual distance $d^{\perp} \geq 3$, which is usually called a *projective code*. Let $G = [\mathbf{g}_1, \mathbf{g}_2, \ldots, \mathbf{g}_n]$ be a generator matrix of C. Let

$$\mathbf{g}_j = (g_{1,j}, g_{2,j}, \ldots, g_{k,j})^T,$$

where T stands for the transpose of a vector. Then $S_C := \{\mathbf{g}_1, \mathbf{g}_2, \ldots, \mathbf{g}_n\}$ is a subset of the point set in $\mathrm{PG}(k-1,\mathrm{GF}(q))$.

Consider the ternary Simplex code with parameters $[13,3,9]$ in Example 2.40. The column vectors of the generator matrix G in (2.14) gives the following subset of the point set in $\mathrm{PG}(2,\mathrm{GF}(3))$:

$$\left\{ \begin{bmatrix} 1 \\ 0 \\ 0 \end{bmatrix}, \begin{bmatrix} 0 \\ 1 \\ 0 \end{bmatrix}, \begin{bmatrix} 0 \\ 0 \\ 1 \end{bmatrix}, \begin{bmatrix} 2 \\ 1 \\ 1 \end{bmatrix}, \begin{bmatrix} 1 \\ 1 \\ 0 \end{bmatrix}, \begin{bmatrix} 0 \\ 1 \\ 1 \end{bmatrix}, \begin{bmatrix} 2 \\ 1 \\ 0 \end{bmatrix}, \begin{bmatrix} 0 \\ 2 \\ 1 \end{bmatrix}, \begin{bmatrix} 1 \\ 2 \\ 1 \end{bmatrix}, \begin{bmatrix} 1 \\ 0 \\ 1 \end{bmatrix}, \begin{bmatrix} 2 \\ 0 \\ 1 \end{bmatrix}, \begin{bmatrix} 2 \\ 2 \\ 1 \end{bmatrix}, \begin{bmatrix} 1 \\ 1 \\ 1 \end{bmatrix} \right\}$$

Conversely, given any subset $S := \{\mathbf{g}_1, \mathbf{g}_2, \ldots, \mathbf{g}_n\}$ of the point set in the projective space $\mathrm{PG}(k-1,\mathrm{GF}(q))$, where each $\mathbf{g}_i$ is written as a column vector in $\mathrm{GF}(q)^k$, we define a matrix

$$G = [\mathbf{g}_1 \mathbf{g}_2 \cdots \mathbf{g}_n]. \tag{2.17}$$

Let C_S be the linear code over $\mathrm{GF}(q)$ with generator matrix G. Then we have the following.

Theorem 2.43. *Let the row vectors of the generator matrix G of (2.17) be* $\mathbf{v}_1, \mathbf{v}_2, \ldots, \mathbf{v}_k$, *respectively. Let*

$$\mathbf{c} = a_1 \mathbf{v}_1 + a_2 \mathbf{v}_2 + \cdots + a_k \mathbf{v}_k$$

be a codeword of C_S, where $a_i \in \mathrm{GF}(q)$. Let H_a denote the hyperplane

$$H_a = \left\{ (y_1, y_2, \ldots, y_k)^T \in \mathrm{GF}(q)^k : \sum_{i=1}^{k} y_i a_i = 0 \right\}.$$

Then the Hamming weight $\mathtt{wt}(\mathbf{c})$ of $\mathbf{c}$ is given by

$$\mathtt{wt}(c) = n - |H_a^{(n)} \cap \{\mathbf{g}_1, \mathbf{g}_2, \ldots, \mathbf{g}_n\}|. \tag{2.18}$$

Proof. By definition,

$$\mathbf{c} = \left(\sum_{i=1}^{k} a_i g_{i,1}, \sum_{i=1}^{k} a_i g_{i,2}, \dots \sum_{i=1}^{k} a_i g_{i,n} \right),$$

where $\mathbf{g}_j = (g_{1,j}, g_{2,j}, \dots, g_{k,j})^T$ for each j. The desired conclusion then follows.
$\square$

Although Theorem 2.43 is simple, it is very useful and says that the minimum distance of the code C_S is the least number of points in the set $\{\mathbf{g}_1, \mathbf{g}_2, \dots, \mathbf{g}_n\}$ which are outside every hyperplane H_a for $a \neq 0$. It will be used to determine the weight distributions of several families of projective codes in some subsequent chapters. In addition, it gives a geometric interpretation of the weight distributions of projective linear codes over finite fields.

Note that the code C_S with the generator matrix in (2.17) is projective (i.e., its dual code has minimum distance at least 3). We are usually interested in only projective codes.

Let $q = p^s$ with $s \geq 1$. Recall that the automorphism (collineation) group of the projective space $PG(k-1, GF(q))$ is the projective semilinear group $P\Gamma L_k(GF(q))$ (see Theorem 1.40). A permutation τ of $GF(q)^k$ is called *semilinear* if it satisfies the following:

- $\tau(u+v) = \tau(u) + \tau(v)$ for all u and v in $GF(q)^k$.
- $\tau(au) = a^{p^i} \tau(u)$ for all $u \in GF(q)^k$ and $a \in GF(q)$ for some i with $0 \leq i \leq s-1$.

Projective semilinear permutations of $GF(q)^k$ are of the form

$$\tau_{(i,A)}(x) = Ax^{p^i},$$

where A is a $k \times k$ invertible matrix over $GF(q)$, x is a column vector in $GF(q)^k$, and $0 \leq i \leq s-1$. Two subsets S and S' of the point set in $PG(k-1, GF(q))$ are said to be *equivalent* if there is an automorphism of $PG(k-1, GF(q))$ that sends S to S'.

Let $q = p^s$ with $s \geq 1$. Recall that the automorphisms of $GF(q)$ are defined by

$$\sigma_i(x) = x^{p^i}, \quad 0 \leq i \leq s-1.$$

Let $\mathbf{c} = (c_1, c_2, \dots, c_n) \in GF(q)^n$. Let M be an $n \times n$ monomial matrix over $GF(q)$. Define

$$(M \circ \sigma_i)(\mathbf{c}) = (\sigma_i(c_1), \sigma_i(c_2), \dots, \sigma_i(c_n))M \in GF(q)^n.$$

Two linear codes C and C' of length n over $GF(q)$ are *equivalent* if there exist an automorphism σ of $GF(q)$ and an $n \times n$ monomial matrix M over $GF(q)$ such that $(A \circ \sigma)(C) = C'$.

We are now ready to prove the following result.

Theorem 2.44. *Let* $\{\mathbf{g}_1, \ldots, \mathbf{g}_n\}$ *and* $\{\mathbf{g}_1', \ldots, \mathbf{g}_n'\}$ *be two equivalent n-sets in* $\mathrm{PG}(k-1, \mathrm{GF}(q))$, *where all* $\mathbf{g}_i$ *and* $\mathbf{g}_i'$ *are* $k \times 1$ *vectors. Let* C *and* C' *denote the two linear codes over* $\mathrm{GF}(q)$ *with the generator matrices* $[\mathbf{g}_1, \ldots, \mathbf{g}_n]$ *and* $[\mathbf{g}_1', \ldots, \mathbf{g}_n']$, *respectively. Then* C *and* C' *are equivalent.*

Proof. Assume that the semilinear permutation $f(\mathbf{x}) = A\mathbf{x}^{p^i}$ sends the first set to the second. Then there is a permutation π of $\{1, 2, \ldots, n\}$ such that $\mathbf{g}_j' = A\mathbf{g}_{\pi(j)}^{p^i}$ for all $1 \le j \le n$. Consequently,

$$[\mathbf{g}_1', \ldots, \mathbf{g}_n'] = A[\mathbf{g}_{\pi(1)}^{p^i}, \ldots, \mathbf{g}_{\pi(n)}^{p^i}].$$

Note that $A[\mathbf{g}_{\pi(1)}^{p^i}, \ldots, \mathbf{g}_{\pi(n)}^{p^i}]$ and $[\mathbf{g}_{\pi(1)}^{p^i}, \ldots, \mathbf{g}_{\pi(n)}^{p^i}]$ generate the same code, as A is invertible. Thus, the two codes are equivalent.   □

The next two theorems are straightforward by the equivalence definition of linear codes.

Theorem 2.45. *Let* $G = [g_{ij}]$ *and* $G' = [g_{ij}']$ *be two generator matrices of two projective* $[n, k]$ *codes* C *and* C' *over* $\mathrm{GF}(q)$, *respectively. Then* C *and* C' *are equivalent if and only if there exist an automorphism* σ *of* $\mathrm{GF}(q)$ *and an* $n \times n$ *monomial matrix* M *over* $\mathrm{GF}(q)$ *such that*

$$[\sigma(\mathbf{g}_1), \ldots, \sigma(\mathbf{g}_n)]M = [\mathbf{g}_1', \ldots, \mathbf{g}_n'].$$

Theorem 2.46. *Let* $G = [g_{ij}]$ *and* $G' = [g_{ij}']$ *be two generator matrices of two projective* $[n, k]$ *codes* C *and* C' *over* $\mathrm{GF}(q)$, *respectively. Then* C *and* C' *are equivalent if and only if there exist an integer* j *with* $0 \le j \le s-1$, *a permutation* π *of* $\{1, 2, \ldots, n\}$ *and* $b_1, \ldots, b_n \in \mathrm{GF}(q)^*$ *such that* $\mathbf{g}_i' = b_{\pi(i)}\mathbf{g}_{\pi(i)}^{p^j}$ *for all* i *with* $1 \le i \le n$.

We now prove the converse of Theorem 2.44, which is stated as follows.

Theorem 2.47. *Let* $G = [g_{ij}]$ *and* $G' = [g_{ij}']$ *be two generator matrices of two projective* $[n, k]$ *codes* C *and* C' *over* $\mathrm{GF}(q)$, *respectively. If* C *and* C' *are equivalent, then the two sets* $\{\mathbf{g}_1, \ldots, \mathbf{g}_n\}$ *and* $\{\mathbf{g}_1', \ldots, \mathbf{g}_n'\}$ *are equivalent.*

Proof. Note that $b_{\pi(i)}\mathbf{g}_{\pi(i)}^{p^j}$ and $\mathbf{g}_{\pi(i)}^{p^j}$ are the same point in $\mathrm{PG}(k-1, \mathrm{GF}(q))$. By Theorem 2.46, the semilinear permutation x^{p^j} sends the first set to the second. The desired conclusion then follows.   □

Combining Theorems 2.44 and 2.47, we arrive at the following.

Theorem 2.48. *Let S and S' be two n-subsets of the point set in* $\mathrm{PG}(k-1,\mathrm{GF}(q))$. *Let C_S and $C_{S'}$ be their corresponding linear codes of length n over* $\mathrm{GF}(q)$. *Then C_S and $C_{S'}$ are equivalent if and only if S and S' are equivalent.*

Theorem 2.48 shows a kind of equivalence between projective geometries over finite fields and projective linear codes over finite fields. In some later chapters, we will see specific cases of the equivalence between specific objects in projective geometries and specific projective linear codes.

2.16 Generalised Hamming Weights of Linear Codes

Let C be an $[n,k,d]$ code over $\mathrm{GF}(q)$. Denote by $\mathrm{Suppt}(C)$ the set of coordinate positions, where not all codewords of C are zero, and call it the *support* of C. So $|\mathrm{Suppt}(C)|$ is the number of nonzero columns in a generator matrix for C. The r-th *generalised Hamming weight,* denoted by $d_r(C)$, is defined to be the cardinality of the minimal support of an $[n,r]$ subcode of C, where $1 \le r \le k$, i.e.,

$$d_r(C) = \min\{|\mathrm{Suppt}(C')| : C' \text{ is an } [n,r] \text{ subcode of } C\}. \tag{2.19}$$

Clearly, $d_1(C) = d(C)$, which is the minimum Hamming distance of C. The set $\{d_1(C),\ldots,d_k(C)\}$ is called the *weight hierarchy*. The generalised Hamming weights of linear codes were first defined in Wei (1991).

Below is a list of results regarding the generalised Hamming weights whose proofs can be found in Wei (1991).

Theorem 2.49. *For every $[n,k,d]$ code C over* $\mathrm{GF}(q)$, *we have*

$$0 < d_1(C) < d_2(C) < \cdots < d_k(C) \le n.$$

Theorem 2.50. *Let H be a parity-check matrix of a linear code C. Then $d_r(C) = \delta$ if and only if*

(a) any $\delta - 1$ columns of H have rank greater than or equal to $\delta - r$; and
(b) there exist δ columns in H with rank $\delta - r$.

Theorem 2.51. *Let C be an $[n,k,d]$ code over* $\mathrm{GF}(q)$ *and let $C^\perp$ denote its dual. Then*

$$\{d_r(C) : r = 1,2,\ldots,k\} \cup \{n+1-d_r(C^\perp) : r = 1,2,\ldots,n-k\} = \{1,2,\ldots,n\}.$$

Theorem 2.52 (Generalised Singleton Bound). *Let C be an $[n,k,d]$ code over* $\mathrm{GF}(q)$. *Then*

$$d_r(C) \le n-k+r, \quad r = 1,2,\ldots,k.$$

2.17 Notes

Linear codes over finite fields are of theoretical interest as they are very closely related to several areas of mathematics such as algebra, algebraic function fields, algebraic geometry, association schemes, combinatorics, finite fields, finite geometry, graph theory, and number theory.

Many connections between linear algebra, finite fields, finite geometry and number theory were already shown in this chapter, and further relations will be revealed in Chapter 3, where cyclic codes are treated. Connections between linear codes and algebraic function fields can be found in Stichtenoth (1993). Certain applications of algebraic geometry in coding theory are treated in Niederreiter and Xing (2009). Connections between groups and codes are given in Humphreys and Prest (2004). Interplay between graph theory and coding theory is documented in Cameron and van Lint (1991). Links between codes and association schemes are introduced in MacWilliams and Sloane (1977). Of course this monograph will treat interplay between combinatorics and codes.

Linear codes are of practical importance as some of them are implemented in communication and data storage devices, including mobile phones, laptops and many other consumer devices. Linear codes over finite fields were also used in cryptography. For example, some linear codes were used to construct public-key ciphers [McEliece (1978)], authentication codes ([Ding and Wang (2005)], [Ding, Helleseth, Kløve and Wang (2007)]), and secret sharing schemes ([Carlet, Ding and Yuan (2005)], [Yuan and Ding (2006)]). In addition, some MDS code was employed to construct the Advanced Encryption Standard.

Chapter 3

Cyclic Codes over Finite Fields

A linear code C is called a *cyclic code* if $\mathbf{c} = (c_0, c_1, \ldots, c_{n-1}) \in C$ implies $(c_{n-1}, c_0, c_1, \ldots, c_{n-2}) \in C$. As a subclass of linear codes, cyclic codes have wide applications in consumer electronics, data storage systems, and communication systems as they have some efficient encoding and decoding algorithms. In this chapter, we introduce the basic theory of cyclic codes over finite fields without providing a proof in many cases. We refer the reader to Huffman and Pless (2003)[Chapter 4] for a proof of such result.

3.1 Factorization of $x^n - 1$ over $\mathrm{GF}(q)$

To deal with cyclic codes of length n over $\mathrm{GF}(q)$, we have to study the canonical factorization of $x^n - 1$ over $\mathrm{GF}(q)$. To this end, we need to introduce q-cyclotomic cosets modulo n. Note that $x^n - 1$ has no repeated factors over $\mathrm{GF}(q)$ if and only if $\gcd(n, q) = 1$. Throughout this chapter, we assume that $\gcd(n, q) = 1$.

Recall that $\mathbb{Z}_n$ denotes the set $\{0, 1, 2, \ldots, n-1\}$. Let s be an integer with $0 \leq s < n$. The *q-cyclotomic coset of s modulo n* is defined by

$$C_s = \{s, sq, sq^2, \ldots, sq^{\ell_s - 1}\} \bmod n \subseteq \mathbb{Z}_n,$$

where ℓ_s is the smallest positive integer such that $s \equiv sq^{\ell_s} \pmod{n}$, and is the size of the q-cyclotomic coset. The smallest integer in C_s is called the *coset leader* of C_s. Let $\Gamma_{(n,q)}$ be the set of all the coset leaders. We have then $C_s \cap C_t = \emptyset$ for any two distinct elements s and t in $\Gamma_{(n,q)}$, and

$$\bigcup_{s \in \Gamma_{(n,q)}} C_s = \mathbb{Z}_n. \tag{3.1}$$

Hence, the distinct q-cyclotomic cosets modulo n partition $\mathbb{Z}_n$.

Let $m = \mathrm{ord}_n(q)$, and let α be a generator of $\mathrm{GF}(q^m)^*$. Put $\beta = \alpha^{(q^m - 1)/n}$. Then β is a primitive n-th root of unity in $\mathrm{GF}(q^m)$. In Section 1.2.1, we defined

91

the minimal polynomial $\mathbb{M}_{\beta^s}(x)$ of β^s over $\mathrm{GF}(q)$. It is now straightforward to prove that this polynomial is given by

$$\mathbb{M}_{\beta^s}(x) = \prod_{i \in C_s}(x - \beta^i) \in \mathrm{GF}(q)[x], \tag{3.2}$$

which is irreducible over $\mathrm{GF}(q)$. It then follows from (3.1) that

$$x^n - 1 = \prod_{s \in \Gamma_{(n,q)}} \mathbb{M}_{\beta^s}(x), \tag{3.3}$$

which is the factorization of $x^n - 1$ into irreducible factors over $\mathrm{GF}(q)$. This canonical factorization of $x^n - 1$ over $\mathrm{GF}(q)$ is crucial for the study of cyclic codes.

Example 3.1. Let $q = 3$ and $n = 11$. Then $\mathrm{ord}_{11}(3) = 5$. It is easily checked that $\Gamma_{(11,3)} = \{0, 1, 2\}$ and

$$C_0 = \{0\}, \ C_1 = \{1, 3, 4, 5, 9\}, \ C_2 = \{2, 6, 7, 8, 10\}.$$

Let α be a generator of $\mathrm{GF}(3^{11})^*$ with $\alpha^5 + 2\alpha + 1 = 0$. Then $\beta = \alpha^{22}$ and

$$\mathbb{M}_{\beta^0}(x) = x + 2,$$
$$\mathbb{M}_{\beta^1}(x) = x^5 + x^4 + 2x^3 + x^2 + 2,$$
$$\mathbb{M}_{\beta^2}(x) = x^5 + 2x^3 + x^2 + 2x + 2.$$

The following result will be useful and is not hard to prove [Huffman and Pless (2003)][Theorem 4.1.4].

Theorem 3.2. *The size ℓ_s of each q-cyclotomic coset C_s is a divisor of $\mathrm{ord}_n(q)$, which is the size ℓ_1 of C_1.*

3.2 Generator and Check Polynomials

Recall that a linear code C over $\mathrm{GF}(q)$ is *cyclic* if $\mathbf{c} = (c_0, c_1, \ldots, c_{n-1}) \in C$ implies $(c_{n-1}, c_0, c_1, \ldots, c_{n-2}) \in C$. Put

$$\mathcal{R}_{(n,q)} = \mathrm{GF}(q)[x]/(x^n - 1),$$

which is the residue class ring. By identifying any vector $(c_0, c_1, \ldots, c_{n-1}) \in \mathrm{GF}(q)^n$ with

$$c_0 + c_1 x + c_2 x^2 + \cdots + c_{n-1} x^{n-1} \in \mathcal{R}_{(n,q)},$$

any code C of length n over $\mathrm{GF}(q)$ corresponds to a subset of the residue class ring $\mathcal{R}_{(n,q)}$. One can easily prove that the linear code C is cyclic if and only if the corresponding subset in $\mathcal{R}_{(n,q)}$ is an ideal of the ring $\mathcal{R}_{(n,q)}$. We identify the cyclic code C with the corresponding subset in $\mathcal{R}_{(n,q)}$.

It is well known that $\mathcal{R}_{(n,q)}$ is a principal ideal ring. Hence, for every cyclic code C of length n over GF(q), there is a unique monic polynomial $g(x) \in$ GF$(q)[x]$ of the smallest degree such that $C = \langle g(x) \rangle$. This polynomial $g(x)$ must be a divisor of $x^n - 1$, and is called the *generator polynomial* of C. Therefore, there is a one-to-one correspondence between the set of all cyclic codes of length n over GF(q) and the set of all monic divisors of $x^n - 1$ with degree at least one over GF(q). Hence, the total number of cyclic codes of length n over GF(q) is $2^t - 1$, where t is the total number of distinct q-cyclotomic cosets modulo n, i.e., $t = |\Gamma_{(n,q)}|$. We usually do not consider the zero code $\{\mathbf{0}\}$ of length n over GF(q).

Let C be an $[n, \kappa]$ cyclic code over GF(q) with generator polynomial $g(x)$. By definition, $\kappa = n - \deg(g(x))$ and $\{g(x), xg(x), \ldots, x^{\kappa-1}g(x)\}$ is a basis for C. Let $g(x) = \sum_{i=0}^{n-\kappa} g_i x^i$, where $g_{n-\kappa} = 1$. Then the following is a generator matrix of C:

$$G = \begin{bmatrix} g_0 & g_1 & g_2 & \cdots & g_{n-\kappa} & 0 & \cdots & 0 & 0 \\ 0 & g_0 & g_1 & g_2 & \cdots & g_{n-\kappa} & \cdots & 0 & 0 \\ \vdots & \vdots & \vdots & \vdots & \vdots & & \vdots & \vdots & \vdots \\ 0 & 0 & \cdots & 0 & g_0 & g_1 & g_2 & \cdots & g_{n-\kappa} \end{bmatrix}. \tag{3.4}$$

Let C be an $[n, \kappa]$ cyclic code over GF(q) with generator polynomial $g(x)$. Let $h(x) = (x^n - 1)/g(x) = \sum_{i=0}^{\kappa} h_i x^i$. The polynomial $h(x)$ is called the *check polynomial* of C. It is straightforward to verify that the dual $C^{\perp}$ of C is also cyclic, and has the generator polynomial $g^{\perp}(x) = x^{\kappa} h(x^{-1})/h(0)$. Furthermore, a generator matrix for $C^{\perp}$, and hence a check matrix for C is

$$\begin{bmatrix} h_{\kappa} & h_{\kappa-1} & h_{\kappa-2} & \cdots & h_0 & 0 & \cdots & 0 & 0 \\ 0 & h_{\kappa} & h_{\kappa-1} & h_{\kappa-2} & \cdots & h_0 & \cdots & 0 & 0 \\ \vdots & \vdots & \vdots & \vdots & \vdots & & \vdots & \vdots & \vdots \\ 0 & 0 & \cdots & 0 & h_{\kappa} & h_{\kappa-1} & h_{\kappa-2} & \cdots & h_0 \end{bmatrix}. \tag{3.5}$$

It should be noticed that the cyclic code generated by $h(x)$ is in general different from $C^{\perp}$, but has the same parameters and weight distribution as $C^{\perp}$.

Example 3.3. Let $q = 3$ and $n = 11$. The cyclic code of length n over GF(q) with generator polynomial $g(x) = x^5 + x^4 + 2x^3 + x^2 + 2$ has parameters $[11, 6, 5]$ and check polynomial $h(x) = x^6 + 2x^5 + 2x^4 + 2x^3 + x^2 + 1$. Its dual code has generator polynomial $x^6 + x^4 + 2x^3 + 2x^2 + 2x + 1$.

The conclusions in the following two theorems are straightforward.

Theorem 3.4. *If C is a cyclic code over* GF(q^t)*, then the subfield subcode $C|_{\mathrm{GF}(q)}$ is also cyclic.*

Theorem 3.5. *Let C_1 and C_2 be two cyclic codes with generator polynomials $g_1(x)$ and $g_2(x)$, respectively. Then $C_1 \subseteq C_2$ if and only if g_2 divides $g_1(x)$.*

3.3   Idempotents of Cyclic Codes

An element e in a ring $\mathcal{R}$ is called an *idempotent* if $e^2 = e$. The ring $\mathcal{R}_{(n,q)}$ has in general quite a number of idempotents. Every cyclic code C over GF(q) can be produced with its generator polynomial. In fact, many polynomials can generate C. Let C be a cyclic code over GF(q) with generator polynomial $g(x)$. It can be proved that a polynomial $f(x) \in$ GF$(q)[x]$ generates C if and only if $\gcd(f(x), x^n - 1) = g(x)$.

If an idempotent $e(x) \in \mathcal{R}_{(n,q)}$ generates a cyclic code C, it is then unique in $\mathcal{R}_{(n,q)}$ and called the *generating idempotent*. Given the generator polynomial of a cyclic code, one can compute its generating idempotent with the following theorem [Huffman and Pless (2003)][Theorem 4.3.3].

Theorem 3.6. *Let C be a cyclic code of length n over GF(q) with generator polynomial $g(x)$. Let $h(x) = (x^n - 1)/g(x)$. Then $\gcd(g(x), h(x)) = 1$ due to the assumption $\gcd(n, q) = 1$. Employing the Extended Euclidean Algorithm, one can compute two polynomials $a(x) \in$ GF$(q)[x]$ and $b(x) \in$ GF$(q)[x]$ such that $1 = a(x)g(x) + b(x)h(x)$. Then $e(x) = a(x)g(x) \bmod (x^n - 1)$ is the generating idempotent of C.*

Given the generating idempotent of a cyclic code, one can obtain the generator polynomial of this code as follows [Huffman and Pless (2003)][Theorem 4.3.3].

Theorem 3.7. *Let C be a cyclic code over GF(q) with generating idempotent $e(x)$. Then the generator polynomial of C is given by $g(x) = \gcd(e(x), x^n - 1)$ computed in GF$(q)[x]$.*

Example 3.8. Let $q = 3$ and $n = 11$. The cyclic code C of length n over GF(q) with generator polynomial $g(x) = x^5 + x^4 + 2x^3 + x^2 + 2$ has parameters $[11, 6, 5]$ and check polynomial $h(x) = x^6 + 2x^5 + 2x^4 + 2x^3 + x^2 + 1$.

Let $a(x) = 2x^5 + x^4 + x^2$ and $b(x) = x^4 + x^3 + 1$. It is then easily verified that $1 = a(x)g(x) + b(x)h(x)$. Hence

$$e(x) = a(x)g(x) \bmod (x^n - 1) = 2x^{10} + 2x^8 + 2x^7 + 2x^6 + 2x^2$$

is the generating idempotent of C. On the other hand, we have $g(x) = \gcd(e(x), x^n - 1)$.

A generator matrix of a cyclic code can be derived from its generating idempotent as follows [Huffman and Pless (2003)][Theorem 4.3.6].

Theorem 3.9. *Let C be an $[n, \kappa]$ cyclic code with generating idempotent $e(x) = \sum_{i=0}^{n-1} e_i x^i$. The the following $\kappa \times n$ matrix*

$$\begin{bmatrix} e_0 & e_1 & e_2 & \cdots & e_{n-2} & e_{n-1} \\ e_{n-1} & e_0 & e_1 & \cdots & e_{n-3} & e_{n-2} \\ \vdots & \vdots & \vdots & \ddots & \vdots & \vdots \\ e_{n-\kappa+1} & e_{n-\kappa+2} & e_{n-\kappa+3} & \cdots & e_{n-\kappa-1} & e_{n-\kappa} \end{bmatrix}$$

is a generator matrix of C.

The *sum* of two cyclic codes C_1 and C_2 of length n over $GF(q)$ is denoted by $C_1 + C_2$, and defined by

$$C_1 + C_2 = \{ \mathbf{c}_1 + \mathbf{c}_2 : \mathbf{c}_1 \in C_1, \ \mathbf{c}_2 \in C_2 \}.$$

Both the sum and intersection of two cyclic codes over $GF(q)$ are also cyclic codes. Their generator polynomial and generating idempotent are given in the following theorem [Huffman and Pless (2003)][Theorem 4.3.7].

Theorem 3.10. *Let C_1 and C_2 be two cyclic codes of length n over $GF(q)$ with generator polynomials $g_1(x)$ and $g_2(x)$, and generating idempotents $e_1(x)$ and $e_2(x)$, respectively. Then*

(i) *the intersection code $C_1 \cap C_2$ has generator polynomial $\mathrm{LCM}(g_1(x), g_2(x))$ and generating idempotent $e_1(x)e_2(x)$, and*
(ii) *the sum code $C_1 + C_2$ has generator polynomial $\gcd(g_1(x), g_2(x))$ and generating idempotent $e_1(x) + e_2(x) - e_1(x)e_2(x)$.*

The ring $\mathcal{R}_{(n,q)}$ has a special set of idempotents, called primitive idempotents, which can be used to produce all idempotents in $\mathcal{R}_{(n,q)}$ and therefore all cyclic codes of length n over $GF(q)$. We now introduce them. Before doing this, we recall that an ideal I in a ring $\mathcal{R}$ is a *minimal ideal* if there is no proper ideal between $\{0\}$ and $\mathcal{R}$.

Let $x^n - 1 = f_1(x)f_2(x) \cdots f_t(x)$, where $f_i(x)$ is irreducible over $GF(q)$ for $1 \leq i \leq t$. Since we always assume that $\gcd(n, q) = 1$, all $f_i(x)$'s are distinct. Define

$$\tilde{f}_i(x) = \frac{x^n - 1}{f_i(x)}$$

for all i with $1 \leq i \leq t$. It is known that all the ideals $\langle \tilde{f}_i(x) \rangle$ of $\mathcal{R}_{(n,q)}$ are minimal, and called *minimal cyclic codes* and *irreducible cyclic codes* of length n over $GF(q)$. Let $\tilde{e}_i(x)$ denote the generating idempotent of $\langle \tilde{f}_i(x) \rangle$ for all i. These $\tilde{e}_i(x)$ are the *primitive idempotent* of $\mathcal{R}_{(n,q)}$.

The following theorem lists basic properties of the primitive idempotents [Huffman and Pless (2003)][Theorem 4.3.8].

Theorem 3.11. *Let notation be the same as before. The following statements hold in* $\mathcal{R}_{(n,q)}$.

(a) $\mathcal{R}_{(n,q)}$ *is the vector space direct sum of* $\langle \tilde{f}_i(x) \rangle$ *for* $1 \leq i \leq t$.
(b) *For every pair of distinct i and j, we have* $\tilde{e}_i(x)\tilde{e}_j(x) = 0$ *in* $\mathcal{R}_{(n,q)}$.
(c) $\sum_{i=1}^{t} \tilde{e}_i(x) = 1$ *in* $\mathcal{R}_{(n,q)}$.
(d) *If* $e(x)$ *is a nonzero idempotent in* $\mathcal{R}_{(n,q)}$, *then there is a subset* T *of* $\{1, 2, \ldots, t\}$ *such that*

$$e(x) = \sum_{i \in T} \tilde{e}_i(x) \quad and \quad \langle e(x) \rangle = \sum_{i \in T} \langle \tilde{f}_i(x) \rangle.$$

Part (d) of this theorem says that every nonzero idempotent in $\mathcal{R}_{(n,q)}$ is the sum of some primitive idempotents, and every nonzero cyclic code of length n over GF(q) is the sum of some minimal cyclic codes of length n over GF(q). It is also known that any minimal ideal of $\mathcal{R}_{(n,q)}$ is an extension field of GF(q) [Huffman and Pless (2003)][Theorem 4.3.9].

We will need the following result later [Huffman and Pless (2003)][Corollary 4.3.15].

Theorem 3.12. *Let* C *be a cyclic code of length n over* GF(q) *with generating idempotent* $e(x) = \sum_{i=0}^{n-1} e_i x^i$. *Then*

(i) $e_i = e_j$ *if i and j are in the same q-cyclotomic coset modulo n; and*
(ii) *there is a subset* T *of* $\mathbb{Z}_n$ *such that*

$$e(x) = \sum_{j \in T} a_j \sum_{i \in C_j} x^i,$$

where each $a_i \in$ GF(q)*.
If $q = 2$, *the set* T *is a set of coset leaders and* $a_j = 1$ *for all* $j \in T$.

3.4 Zeros of Cyclic Codes

Let C be a cyclic code of length n over GF(q) with generator polynomial $g(x)$, and let β be a primitive n-th root of unity over GF(q^m), where $m = \text{ord}_n(q)$. It then follows from (3.3) that

$$g(x) = \prod_{t \in T} \mathbb{M}_{\beta^t}(x) = \prod_{t \in T} \prod_{i \in C_t} (x - \beta^i),$$

where T is a set of coset leaders, i.e., $T \subset \Gamma_{(n,q)}$. The set $\cup_{t \in T} \{\beta^i : i \in C_t\}$ is called the *zeros* of C, and the set $\cup_{t \in T} C_t$ is referred to as the *defining set* of C. By definition, $c(x)$ is a codeword of C if and only if $c(\beta^i) = 0$ for all $i \in \cup_{t \in T} C_t$.

If C is a code of length n over $\mathrm{GF}(q)$, then a *complement* of C, is a code C^c such that $C + C^c = \mathrm{GF}(q)^n$ and $C \cap C^c = \{0\}$. If C is cyclic, then C^c is unique and cyclic. We have the following information on the code C^c.

Theorem 3.13. *Let C be a cyclic code of length n over $\mathrm{GF}(q)$ with generator polynomial $g(x)$, generating idempotent $e(x)$, and defining set S. We have then the following conclusions about the complement C^c of C:*

(1) $h(x) = (x^n - 1)/g(x)$ is the generator polynomial and $1 - e(x)$ is its generating idempotent of C^c.

(2) C^c is the sum of the minimal ideals of $\mathcal{R}_{(n,q)}$ not contained in C.

(3) $\mathbb{Z}_n \setminus S$ is the defining set of C^c.

Let $f(x) = \sum_{i=0}^{\ell} f_i x^i$ be a polynomial of degree ℓ. Then its *reciprocal* is defined by

$$f^*(x) = x^\ell f(x^{-1}) = \sum_{i=0}^{\ell} f_{\ell-i} x^\ell.$$

The following result is fundamental and follows from Huffman and Pless (2003)[Theorem 4.4.9].

Theorem 3.14. *Let C be a cyclic code of length n over $\mathrm{GF}(q)$ with generator polynomial $g(x)$. Let $h(x) = (x^n - 1)/g(x)$ be the check polynomial of C. Then the following statements are true:*

(1) $h^*(x)/h(0)$ is the generator polynomial of $C^\perp$.

(2) $C^\perp$ and C^c are permutation equivalent. Hence they have the same dimension and weight distribution.

Self-orthogonal codes are an interesting class of codes. The next theorem gives a characterization of self-orthogonal cyclic codes [Huffman and Pless (2003)][Corollary 4.4.10].

Theorem 3.15. *Let C be a cyclic code of length n over $\mathrm{GF}(q)$ with generator polynomial $g(x)$. Let $h(x) = (x^n - 1)/g(x)$ be the check polynomial of C. Then C is self-orthogonal if and only if $h^*(x) | g(x)$.*

Minimal cyclic codes (also called irreducible cyclic codes) have the following trace representation [Huffman and Pless (2003)][Theorem 4.4.19]. It is a direct consequence of Delsarte's Theorem.

Theorem 3.16 (Trace representation of irreducible cyclic codes). *Let $h(x)$ be an irreducible factor of $x^n - 1$ over* GF(q). *Suppose that $h(x)$ has degree m. Let $\gamma \in$ GF(q^m) be a root of $h(x)$. Then*

$$C(\gamma) = \left\{ \sum_{i=0}^{n-1} \mathrm{Tr}_{q^m/q}(a\gamma^{-i})x^i : a \in \mathrm{GF}(q^m) \right\}$$

is the $[n,m]$ irreducible cyclic code with check polynomial

$$h(x) = \prod_{i=0}^{m-1} \left(x - \gamma^{q^i}\right) \in \mathrm{GF}(q)[x].$$

Put $r = q^m$. Let $N > 1$ be an integer dividing $r - 1$, and put $n = (r-1)/N$. Let α be a primitive element of GF(r) and let $\theta = \alpha^N$. Then the set

$$C(r,N) = \{(\mathrm{Tr}_{r/q}(\beta), \mathrm{Tr}_{r/q}(\beta\theta), ..., \mathrm{Tr}_{r/q}(\beta\theta^{n-1})) : \beta \in \mathrm{GF}(r)\} \qquad (3.6)$$

is an irreducible cyclic $[n,m_0]$ code over GF(q), where m_0 is the multiplicative order of q modulo n and m_0 divides m.

Irreducible cyclic codes have been an interesting subject of study for many years. The celebrated Golay code is an irreducible cyclic code and was used on the Mariner Jupiter-Saturn Mission. They form a special class of cyclic codes and are interesting in theory as they are minimal cyclic codes. The reader is referred to Ding and Yang (2013) for information on irreducible cyclic codes.

3.5   A Trace Construction of Cyclic Codes over Finite Fields

Any cyclic code over any finite field can be generated by a generator matrix, or a generator polynomial, or a generating idempotent. Under certain conditions, cyclic codes over finite fields have a simple trace representation described in the following theorem whose proof is based on Delsarte's Theorem [Wolfmann (1989)].

Theorem 3.17. *Let C be a cyclic code of length n over* GF(q) *with* $\gcd(n,q) = 1$ *and check polynomial $h(x)$. Let β be a primitive n-th root of unity over* GF(q^m), *where $m := \mathrm{ord}_n(q)$ is the order of q modulo n. Let J be a subset of $\mathbb{Z}_n = \{0,1,2,\cdots,n-1\}$ such that*

$$h^*(x) = \prod_{j \in J} \mathbb{M}_{\beta^j}(x),$$

where $\mathbb{M}_{\beta^j}(x)$ denotes the minimal polynomial of β^j over GF(q), *and $h^*(x)$ is the reciprocal of $h(x)$. Then C consists of all the following codewords*

$$c_a(x) = \sum_{i=0}^{n-1} \mathrm{Tr}(f_a(\beta^i))x^i,$$

where Tr *denotes the trace function from* $GF(q^m)$ *to* $GF(q)$, *and*

$$f_a(x) = \sum_{i \in J} a_j x^j, \quad a_j \in GF(q^m).$$

This trace representation of certain subclasses of cyclic codes was known for a long time. For example, the trace representation of irreducible dates back at least to Baumert and McEliece (1972). The trace representation of cyclic codes over finite fields in Theorem 3.17 was presented and proved by Wolfmann in [Wolfmann (1989)] under the restriction that $\gcd(q,n) = 1$. It demonstrates another way of generating many cyclic codes over finite fields. The importance of this trace representation is mostly demonstrated by its application in determining the weight distribution (also called the weight enumerator) of cyclic codes over finite fields. The trace representation allows one to determine the weight distribution of a cyclic code by evaluating certain types of character sums over finite fields, and has led to a lot of recent progress on the weight distribution problem of cyclic codes.

3.6 Lower Bounds on the Minimum Distance

It is usually very difficult to determine the minimum distance of cyclic codes over finite fields. However, due to the cyclicity of cyclic codes, we have some lower bounds on their minimum distance. The first one is described in the following theorem ([Bose and Ray-Chaudhuri (1960)] and [Hocquenghem (1959)]).

Theorem 3.18 (BCH bound). *Let* C *be a cyclic code of length n over* $GF(q)$ *with defining set S and minimum distance d. Assume S contains* $\delta - 1$ *consecutive integers for some integer* δ. *Then* $d \geq \delta$.

Note that the BCH bound depends on the primitive n-th root of unity β. It may yield a very bad lower bound on the minimum distance sometimes. In this case, the lower bound given in the folllowing theorem may be much better. It was discovered in Hartmann and Tzeng (1972). To introduce this bound, we define

$$A + B = \{a + b : a \in A, \ b \in B\},$$

where A and B are two subsets of the ring $\mathbb{Z}_n$, n is a positive integer, and $+$ denotes the integer addition modulo n.

Theorem 3.19 (Hartmann-Tzeng bound). *Let* C *be a cyclic code of length n over* $GF(q)$ *with defining set S and minimum distance d. Let A be a set of* $\delta - 1$ *consecutive elements of S and* $B(b,s) = \{jb \bmod n : 0 \leq j \leq s\}$, *where* $\gcd(b,n) < \delta$. *If* $A + B(b,s) \subseteq S$ *for some b and s, then* $d \geq \delta + s$.

The following theorem is also a generalization of the BCH bound [Huffman and Pless (2003)][Corollary 4.5.11].

Theorem 3.20. *Let C be a cyclic code of length n over* GF(q). *Suppose that $f(x)$ is a codeword such that $f(\beta^b) = f(\beta^{b+1}) = \cdots = f(\beta^{b+w-1}) = 0$ but $f(\beta^{b+w}) \neq 0$, where β is a primitive n-th root of unity in an extension field of* GF(q). *Then* $\mathrm{wt}(f(x)) \geq w + 1$.

When $s = 0$, The Hartmann-Tzeng bound becomes the BCH bound. There are also other bounds. The Roos bounds, which are generalizations of the the Hartmann-Tzeng bound, can be found in Roos (1982a) and Roos (1982b). A number of techniques for finding a lower bound on the minimum distance of cyclic codes are given in Van Lint and Wilson (1986).

3.7 BCH Codes

BCH codes are a subclass of cyclic codes with special properties, and are very important in both theory and practice. The objective of this section is to introduce them and summarize their fundamental results.

3.7.1 *Definition and Basic Properties*

Let δ be an integer with $2 \leq \delta \leq n$ and let b be an integer. A *BCH code* over GF(q) of length n and *designed distance* δ, denoted by $C_{(q,n,\delta,b)}$, is a cyclic code with defining set

$$S(b,\delta) = C_b \cup C_{b+1} \cup \cdots \cup C_{b+\delta-2}, \qquad (3.7)$$

where C_i is the q-cyclotomic coset modulo n containing i. It then follows from Theorem 3.18 that a cyclic code with designed distance δ has minimum weight at least δ. It is possible that the actual minimum distance is equal to the designed distance. Sometimes the actual minimum weight is much larger than the designed distance.

It may happen that $S(b_1,\delta_1) = S(b_2,\delta_2)$ for two distinct pairs (b_1,δ_1) and (b_2,δ_2). The *maximum designed distance* of a BCH code is defined to be the largest δ such that the set $S(b,\delta)$ in (3.7) defines the code for some $b \geq 0$. The maximum designed distance of a BCH code is also called the *Bose distance*.

When $b = 1$, the code $C_{(q,n,\delta,b)}$ with defining set in (3.7) is called a *narrow-sense* BCH code. If $n = q^m - 1$, then $C_{(q,n,\delta,b)}$ is referred to as a *primitive* BCH code.

The dimension of the BCH code $C_{(q,n,\delta,b)}$ with defining set $S(b,\delta)$ in (3.7) depends on the size of the defining set. However, it may not have a clear relation with n, q, b and δ, and thus cannot be given exactly in terms of these parameters. The best we can do in general is to develop tight lower bounds on the dimension of BCH codes. The next theorem introduces such bounds [Huffman and Pless (2003)][Theorem 5.1.7].

Theorem 3.21. *Let C be an $[n, \kappa]$ BCH code over $\mathrm{GF}(q)$ of designed distance δ. Then the following statements hold:*

(i) $\kappa \geq n - \mathrm{ord}_n(q)(\delta - 1)$.
(ii) *If $q = 2$ and C is a narrow-sense BCH code, then δ can be assumed odd; furthermore if $\delta = 2w + 1$, then $\kappa \geq n - \mathrm{ord}_n(q)w$.*

The bounds in Theorem 3.21 may not be improved for the general case, as demonstrated by the following example. However, in some special cases, they could be improved.

Example 3.22. Let $q = 2$ and $n = 15$. Then $m = \mathrm{ord}_{15}(2) = 4$ and the 2-cyclotomic cosets modulo 15 are the following:

$$C_0 = \{0\}, \ C_1 = \{1, 2, 4, 8\}, \ C_3 = \{3, 6, 9, 12\},$$
$$C_5 = \{5, 10\}, \ C_7 = \{7, 11, 13, 14\}.$$

Let α be a generator of $\mathrm{GF}(2^4)^*$ with $\alpha^4 + \alpha + 1 = 0$ and let $\beta = \alpha^{(q^m-1)/n} = \alpha$ be the primitive n-th root of unity.

When $(b, \delta) = (0, 3)$, the defining set $S(b, \delta) = \{0, 1, 2, 4, 8\}$, and the binary cyclic code has parameters $[15, 10, 4]$ and generator polynomial $x^5 + x^4 + x^2 + 1$. In this case, the actual minimum weight is more than the designed distance, and the dimension is larger than the first bound in Theorem 3.21.

When $(b, \delta) = (1, 3)$, the defining set $S(b, \delta) = \{1, 2, 4, 8\}$, and the binary cyclic code has parameters $[15, 11, 3]$ and generator polynomial $x^4 + x + 1$. It is a narrow-sense BCH code. In this case, the actual minimum weight is equal to the designed distance, and the dimension reaches the second bound in Theorem 3.21.

When $(b, \delta) = (2, 3)$, the defining set $S(b, \delta) = \{1, 2, 3, 4, 6, 8, 9, 12\}$, and the binary cyclic code has parameters $[15, 7, 5]$ and generator polynomial $x^8 + x^7 + x^6 + x^4 + 1$. In this case, the actual minimum weight is more than the designed distance, and the dimension achieves the first bound in Theorem 3.21.

When $(b, \delta) = (1, 5)$, the defining set $S(b, \delta) = \{1, 2, 3, 4, 6, 8, 9, 12\}$, and the binary cyclic code has parameters $[15, 7, 5]$ and generator polynomial $x^8 + x^7 + x^6 + x^4 + 1$. In this case, the actual minimum weight is equal to the designed distance, and the dimension is larger than the first bound in Theorem 3.21. Note that the three pairs $(b_1, \delta_1) = (2, 3), (b_2, \delta_2) = (2, 4)$ and $(b_3, \delta_3) = (1, 5)$ define the same binary cyclic code with generator polynomial $x^8 + x^7 + x^6 + x^4 + 1$. Hence the maximum designed distance of this $[15, 7, 5]$ cyclic code is 5.

When $(b, \delta) = (3, 4)$, the defining set $S(b, \delta) = \{1, 2, 3, 4, 5, 6, 8, 9, 10, 12\}$, and the binary cyclic code has parameters $[15, 5, 7]$ and generator polynomial $x^{10} + x^8 + x^5 + x^4 + x^2 + x + 1$. In this case, the actual minimum weight is more than the designed distance, and dimension is larger than the first bound in Theorem 3.21.

Let C be a primitive narrow-sense BCH code of length $n = q^m - 1$ over $\mathrm{GF}(q)$ with designed distance δ. The defining set is then $S(1, \delta) = C_1 \cup C_2 \cup \cdots \cup C_{\delta - 1}$. The following theorem provides useful information on the minimum weight of primitive narrow-sense BCH codes.

Theorem 3.23. *Let C be a primitive narrow-sense BCH code of length $n = q^m - 1$ over $\mathrm{GF}(q)$ with designed distance δ. Then the minimum weight of C is its minimum odd-like weight.*

Proof. By Corollary 6.12, the permutation automorphism group of the extended code $\overline{C}$ is 2-transitive. The desired conclusion then follows from Theorem 2.13. $\square$

We dealt with Hamming codes in Section 2.13, which may not be equivalent to a cyclic code. Now we are ready to tell when they are cyclic codes [Huffman and Pless (2003)][Theorem 5.1.4].

Theorem 3.24. *Let $n = (q^m - 1)/(q - 1)$ with $\gcd(m, q - 1) = 1$. Let C be the narrow-sense BCH code with defining set C_1. Then C is the Hamming code $\mathcal{H}_{q,m}$.*

After introducing BCH codes in general, we are now ready to describe an important subclass of BCH codes, which are referred to as *Reed-Solomon codes* [Reed and Solomon (1960)].

Let $n = q - 1$. Then $\mathrm{ord}_n(q) = 1$, and all the q-cyclotomic cosets modulo n are of size 1. Therefore, the canonical factorization of $x^n - 1$ over $\mathrm{GF}(q)$ is given by

$$x^n - 1 = \prod_{i=0}^{n-1} (x - \alpha^i),$$

where α is a generator of $\mathrm{GF}(q)^*$.

A Reed-Solomon code over $\mathrm{GF}(q)$, denoted $\mathrm{RS}_{(q, \kappa)}$, is of length $n = q - 1$ with designed distance $n - \kappa + 1$. It is straightforward to prove the following theorem [Huffman and Pless (2003)][Theorem 5.2.1].

Theorem 3.25. *Let $n = q - 1$. Then $\mathrm{RS}_{(q, \kappa)}$ has defining set $S(b, n - \kappa + 1)$ for some integer $b \geq 0$ and parameters $[n, \kappa, n - \kappa + 1]$. Furthermore, it is MDS.*

The following theorem gives another way to define the narrow-sense Reed-Solomon code $\mathrm{RS}_{(q,\kappa)}$.

Theorem 3.26. *Let* α *be a generator of* $\mathrm{GF}(q)^*$ *and let* κ *be an integer with* $0 \leq \kappa \leq n = q-1$. *Then*

$$C = \{(f(1), f(\alpha), f(\alpha^2), \ldots, f(\alpha^{n-1})) : f \in \mathcal{P}_{(q,\kappa)}\}$$

is equivalent to the narrow-sense $[n, \kappa, n-\kappa+1]$ *Reed-Solomon code* $\mathrm{RS}_{(q,\kappa)}$, *where* $\mathcal{P}_{(q,\kappa)}$ *denotes all the polynomials of degree less than* κ *over* $\mathrm{GF}(q)$.

3.7.2 Recent Advances in BCH Codes

Determining the parameters of BCH codes is an extremely difficult problem. By now most types of BCH codes have never been touched. For example, there is no reference on BCH codes over $\mathrm{GF}(q)$ of length $(q^\ell + 1)/(q+1)$ for odd ℓ.

Recall that BCH codes $C_{(q,n,\delta,b)}$ with length $n = q^m - 1$ are called primitive. Primitive BCH codes behave better in many senses and have better error-correcting capability. Experimental data shows that they are always the best among all cyclic codes with only a few exceptions (see the experimental data documented in Ding (2015a)[Appendix A]). Recently, a considerable amount of progress on primitive BCH codes has been made in Ding, Du and Zhou (2015), Ding (2015b), Ding, Fan and Zhou (2017), Li, Ding and Li (2017), Liu, Ding and Li (2017), and Li (2017).

BCH codes $C_{(q,n,\delta,b)}$ with length $n = (q^m - 1)/(q - 1)$ are much less studied, compared with primitive BCH codes. Some progress on such BCH codes have been documented in Li, Ding and Li (2017), Li, Ding, Xiong and Ge (2017), and Liu, Ding and Li (2017).

Little about BCH codes $C_{(q,n,\delta,b)}$ with length $n = q^\ell + 1$ has been done. This is because the q-cyclotomic cosets modulo $n = q^\ell + 1$ behave quite irregularly. Some recent progress on this type of BCH codes has been reported in Li, Ding and Li (2017) and Liu, Ding and Li (2017).

3.8 Quadratic Residue Codes

Quadratic residue (QR) codes are a very important class of cyclic codes, which have important applications in engineering and combinatorics. In this section, we introduce these codes and their extended codes, and summarise their properties. Throughout this section, let n be an odd prime, and let q be a different prime. We also require that q is a quadratic residue modulo n.

3.8.1 *Quadratic Residue Codes*

Let γ be a primitive element of $GF(n)$. Recall that the cyclotomic classes of order two with respect to $GF(n)$ are defined by

$$C_i^{(2,n)} = \gamma^i \langle \gamma^2 \rangle,$$

where $i \in \{0,1\}$. The elements in $C_0^{(2,n)}$ and $C_1^{(2,n)}$ are quadratic residues and quadratic nonresidues modulo n, respectively.

Put $m = \text{ord}_n(q)$. Let α be a generator of $GF(q^m)^*$ and let $\beta = \alpha^{(q^m-1)/n}$. Then β is a primitive n-th root of unity in $GF(q^m)$. Define

$$g_0(x) = \prod_{i \in C_0^{(2,n)}} (x - \beta^i) \text{ and } g_1(x) = \prod_{i \in C_1^{(2,n)}} (x - \beta^i).$$

When $q \in C_0^{(2,n)}$, it is straightforward to verify that $g_i(x) \in GF(q)[x]$ for all $i \in \{0,1\}$. In the remainder of this subsection, we always assume that $q \in C_0^{(2,n)}$. Let $QRC_i^{(n,q)}$ and $\underline{QRC}_i^{(n,q)}$ denote the cyclic code over $GF(q)$ of length n with generator polynomial $g_i(x)$ and $(x-1)g_i(x)$, respectively, for each $i \in \{0,1\}$. It then follows that $QRC_i^{(n,q)}$ and $\underline{QRC}_i^{(n,q)}$ have dimension $(n+1)/2$ and $(n-1)/2$, respectively, for each i.

Since $q \in C_0^{(2,n)}$, each $C_i^{(2,n)}$ is the union of some q-cyclotomic cosets modulo n. Therefore, $QRC_i^{(n,q)}$ and $\underline{QRC}_i^{(n,q)}$ are cyclic codes with defining set $C_i^{(2,n)}$ and $\{0\} \cup C_i^{(2,n)}$, respectively. The four codes $QRC_i^{(n,q)}$ and $\underline{QRC}_i^{(n,q)}$ are called *quadratic residue codes*. The two codes $QRC_i^{(n,q)}$ are called odd-like QR codes, and the two codes $\underline{QRC}_i^{(n,q)}$ are even-like QR codes.

Note that the two codes $QRC_0^{(n,q)}$ and $QRC_1^{(n,q)}$ depend on the choice of the primitive n-th root of unity. They have the same parameters and weight distribution. The following theorem provides information on the minimum weight of quadratic residue codes [Huffman and Pless (2003)][Theorem 6.6.22].

Theorem 3.27. *Let d_i and $\underline{d}_i$ denote the minimum weight of $QRC_i^{(n,q)}$ and $\underline{QRC}_i^{(n,q)}$, respectively. Then $d_0 = d_1$ and $\underline{d}_0 = \underline{d}_1$. Furthermore, $d_i = \underline{d}_i - 1$ and $d_i^2 \geq n$. If $n \equiv 3 \pmod 4$, then $d_i^2 - d_i + 1 \geq n$. Additionally, every minimum weight codeword of $QRC_i^{(n,q)}$ is odd-like. If $QRC_i^{(n,q)}$ is binary, d_i is odd; and if in addition, $n \equiv -1 \pmod 8$, then $d_i \equiv 3 \pmod 4$.*

Example 3.28. Let $n = 23$ and $q = 2$. Then $m = \text{ord}_n(q) = 11$. Let α be a generator of $GF(2^{11})^*$ with $\alpha^{11} + \alpha^2 + 1 = 0$, and let $\beta = \alpha^{(q^m-1)/n}$. Then $QRC_0^{(n,q)}$ and $QRC_1^{(n,q)}$ have parameters $[23, 12, 7]$ and generator polynomials

$$g_0(x) = x^{11} + x^9 + x^7 + x^6 + x^5 + x + 1 \text{ and } g_1(x) = x^{11} + x^{10} + x^6 + x^5 + x^4 + x^2 + 1.$$

The two codes $\underline{\text{QRC}}_0^{(n,q)}$ and $\underline{\text{QRC}}_1^{(n,q)}$ have parameters $[23, 11, 8]$ and generator polynomials $(x-1)g_0(x)$ and $(x-1)g_1(x)$.

Example 3.29. Let $n = 13$ and $q = 3$. Then $m = \text{ord}_n(q) = 3$. Let α be a generator of $\text{GF}(3^3)^*$ with $\alpha^3 + 2\alpha + 1 = 0$, and let $\beta = \alpha^{(q^m-1)/n}$. Then $\text{QRC}_0^{(n,q)}$ and $\text{QRC}_1^{(n,q)}$ have parameters $[13, 7, 5]$ and generator polynomials

$$g_0(x) = x^6 + 2x^4 + 2x^3 + 2x^2 + 1 \text{ and } g_1(x) = x^6 + x^5 + 2x^4 + 2x^2 + x + 1.$$

The two codes $\underline{\text{QRC}}_0^{(n,q)}$ and $\underline{\text{QRC}}_1^{(n,q)}$ have parameters $[13, 6, 6]$ and generator polynomials $(x-1)g_0(x)$ and $(x-1)g_1(x)$.

The following theorem demonstrates further relations among the four quadratic residue codes [Assmus and Key (1992a)][Theorem 2.10.1].

Theorem 3.30. If $n \equiv -1 \pmod 4$, then $(\text{QRC}_i^{(n,q)})^\perp = \underline{\text{QRC}}_i^{(n,q)}$. If $n \equiv 1 \pmod 4$, then $(\text{QRC}_0^{(n,q)})^\perp = \underline{\text{QRC}}_1^{(n,q)}$ and $(\text{QRC}_1^{(n,q)})^\perp = \underline{\text{QRC}}_0^{(n,q)}$.

The format of the generating idempotent of QR codes is known and described in the following theorem [Huffman and Pless (2003)][Theorem 6.6.3].

Theorem 3.31. *If C is a quadratic residue code over* $\text{GF}(q)$ *with generating idempotent $e(x)$. Then*

$$e(x) = a_0 + a_1 \sum_{i \in C_0^{(2,n)}} x^i + a_2 \sum_{i \in C_1^{(2,n)}} x^i,$$

for some a_1, a_1, and a_2 in $\text{GF}(q)$.

The following theorem provides more detailed information on the generating idempotents of binary quadratic residue codes [Huffman and Pless (2003)][Theorem 6.6.5].

Theorem 3.32. *Let $n \equiv \pm 1 \pmod 8$ be a prime. Then the following hold.*

(a) The binary codes $\underline{\text{QRC}}_i^{(n,2)}$ *have generating idempotents*

$$\delta + \sum_{i \in C_0^{(2,n)}} x^i \text{ and } \delta + \sum_{i \in C_1^{(2,n)}} x^i,$$

where $\delta = 1$ if $n \equiv -1 \pmod 8$ and $\delta = 0$ if $n \equiv 1 \pmod 8$.

(b) The binary codes $\text{QRC}_i^{(n,2)}$ *have generating idempotents*

$$\varepsilon + \sum_{i \in C_0^{(2,n)}} x^i \text{ and } \varepsilon + \sum_{i \in C_1^{(2,n)}} x^i,$$

where $\varepsilon = 0$ if $n \equiv -1 \pmod 8$ and $\varepsilon = 1$ if $n \equiv 1 \pmod 8$.

For further information about the generating idempotents of quadratic residue codes over other finite fields, the reader is referred to Huffman and Pless (2003)[Section 6.6]. More information on the minimum weight of quadratic residue codes can be found in Newhart (1988).

3.8.2 *Extended Quadratic Residue Codes*

The extended code of a linear code was introduced in Section 2.6. In this section, we extend the QR codes in a slightly different way, and let $\overline{\mathrm{QRC}}_i^{(n,q)}$ denote this extended code of $\mathrm{QRC}_i^{(n,q)}$. QR codes may be extended by adding an overall parity check in such a way that

$$\begin{cases} \overline{\mathrm{QRC}}_i^{(n,q)\perp} = \overline{\mathrm{QRC}}_i^{(n,q)} & \text{if } n \equiv -1 \pmod 4, \\ \overline{\mathrm{QRC}}_0^{(n,q)\perp} = \overline{\mathrm{QRC}}_1^{(n,q)} & \text{if } n \equiv 1 \pmod 4. \end{cases} \tag{3.8}$$

The specific way of adding the parity check is as follows.

We will need the following lemma [Huffman and Pless (2003)][Lemma 6.6.16].

Lemma 3.33. *Let* $n \equiv -1 \pmod 4$ *or* $n \equiv 1 \pmod 4$ *and* $q \equiv -1 \pmod 4$. *Then* $1 + \zeta n^2 = 0$ *has a solution* $\zeta \in \mathrm{GF}(q)$.

If $\mathbf{c} = (c_0, \ldots, c_{n-1})$ is a codeword of $\mathrm{QRC}_i^{(n,q)}$, the extended code is formed by appending

$$c_\infty = -\zeta \sum_{i=0}^{n-1} c_i, \tag{3.9}$$

where $1 + \zeta^2 n = 0$ in $\mathrm{GF}(q)$. When $q \in \{2, 3\}$, ζ may be taken to be 1, and the extended code will be consistent with the conventional one defined in Section 2.6.

Let G_i denote the generator matrix of $\mathrm{QRC}_i^{(n,q)}$. Then the generator matrix $\overline{G}_i$ of $\overline{\mathrm{QRC}}_i^{(n,q)}$ is given by

$$\overline{G}_i = \begin{bmatrix} & & & 0 \\ & & & 0 \\ & G_i & & \vdots \\ & & & 0 \\ 1, 1, & \ldots, & 1, & -\zeta n \end{bmatrix}. \tag{3.10}$$

Clearly, $\overline{\mathrm{QRC}}_i^{(n,q)}$ have parameters $[n+1, (n+1)/2]$. The relations among the two extended codes and their duals are documented in the following theorem [Huffman and Pless (2003)][Theorem 6.6.18].

Theorem 3.34. *Let* $n \equiv -1 \pmod 4$ *or* $n \equiv 1 \pmod 4$ *and* $q \equiv -1 \pmod 4$. *If* $n \equiv -1 \pmod 4$, *both* $\overline{\mathrm{QRC}}_i^{(n,q)}$ *are self-dual* $[n+1, (n+1)/2]$ *codes. If* $n \equiv 1 \pmod 4$, *then* $\left(\overline{\mathrm{QRC}}_0^{(n,q)} \right)^\perp = \overline{\mathrm{QRC}}_1^{(n,q)}$ *and* $\left(\overline{\mathrm{QRC}}_1^{(n,q)} \right)^\perp = \overline{\mathrm{QRC}}_0^{(n,q)}$.

Let $n \equiv \pm 1 \pmod 8$ be a prime. The set of all permutations of $\{0, 1, \ldots, n-1, \infty\}$ of the form

$$y \to \frac{ay+b}{cy+d}, \tag{3.11}$$

where $a, b, c, d \in \mathrm{GF}(n)$ are such that $ad - bc = 1$, form a group, which is called the projective special linear group, and denoted by $\mathrm{PSL}_2(\mathrm{GF}(n))$. This group was treated in Section 1.8.10.

The following result is due to Gleason and Prange.

Theorem 3.35. *If* $n \equiv \pm 1 \pmod 8$, *then the extended code* $\overline{\mathrm{QRC}}_0^{(n,2)}$ *is fixed by* $\mathrm{PSL}_2(\mathrm{GF}(n))$.

Proof. We present here a proof of this theorem developed in Blahut (1991). By Theorem 1.88, it suffices to prove that $\overline{\mathrm{QRC}}_0^{(n,2)}$ is fixed by the coordinate permutation:

$$T : y \to -y^{-1}.$$

Let $m = \mathrm{ord}_n(2)$. Let α be a generator of $\mathrm{GF}(n)^*$, and let $\beta = \alpha^{(2^m - 1)/n}$. Then β is an nth root of unity in $\mathrm{GF}(2^m)$. For any vector $c = (c_0, c_1, \ldots, c_{n-1}) \in \mathrm{GF}(2)^n$, its Fourier transform, denoted by $C = (C_0, C_1, \ldots, C_{n-1}) \in \mathrm{GF}(2^m)^n$, is given by

$$C_j = \sum_{i=0}^{n-1} \beta^{ij} c_i = c(\beta^j),$$

where $c(x) = \sum_{i=0}^{n-1} c_i x^i \in \mathrm{GF}(2)[x]$ and $0 \le j \le n-1$.

By definition, for any codeword $c(x) \in \mathrm{QRC}_0^{(n,q)}$, we have $C_j = c(\beta^j) = 0$ for all nonzero squares j in $\mathrm{GF}(n)$. By definition again, $\overline{\mathrm{QRC}}_0^{(n,q)}$ consists of all the binary vectors

$$c = (c_0, c_1, \ldots, c_{n-1}, c_\infty),$$

where $(c_0, c_1, \ldots, c_{n-1})$ is a codeword in $\mathrm{QRC}_0^{(n,q)}$, and the extended bit indexed by ∞ is defined by

$$c_\infty = \sum_{i=0}^{n-1} c_i.$$

Let π be a generator of $\mathrm{GF}(n)^*$. By a coordinate permutation, the codewords of $\mathrm{QRC}_0^{(n,q)}$ can be represented as

$$c = (c_0, c_{\pi^0}, c_{\pi^1}, \ldots, c_{\pi^{n-2}}).$$

Note that π^{-1} is another generator of $\mathrm{GF}(n)^*$. Similarly, the Fourier transform C of c can be written as

$$C = (C_0, C_{\pi^{-0}}, C_{\pi^{-1}}, \ldots, C_{\pi^{-(n-2)}}).$$

By definition

$$C_0 = \sum_{i=0}^{n-1} c_i \text{ and } C_j = c_0 + \sum_{i=1}^{n-1} \beta^{ij} c_i, \quad j = 1, 2, \ldots, n-1.$$

For $1 \leq i, j \leq n-1$, let $i = \pi^r$ and $j = \pi^{-s}$, where $0 \leq r, s \leq n-2$. Then we have

$$C_{\pi^{-s}} = c_0 + \sum_{r=0}^{n-2} \beta^{\pi^{r-s}} c_{\pi^r}, \quad s = 0, 1, \ldots, n-2. \tag{3.12}$$

We now define $C'_s = C_{\pi^{-s}}$ and $c'_r = c_{\pi^r}$. Then (3.12) becomes

$$C'_s = c_0 + \sum_{r=0}^{n-2} \beta^{\pi^{r-s}} c'_r, \quad s = 0, 1, \ldots, n-2. \tag{3.13}$$

Let

$$u(x) = \sum_{r=0}^{n-2} \beta^{\pi^{-r}} x^r,$$

$$c'(x) = \sum_{r=0}^{n-2} c'_r x^r,$$

$$C'(x) = \sum_{r=0}^{n-2} C'_r x^r.$$

Then all the equations in (3.13) can be expressed into

$$C'(x) = u(x) c'(x) + c_0 \sum_{i=0}^{p-2} x^i \pmod{x^{n-1} - 1}, \tag{3.14}$$

which is a polynomial representation of the equation of the Fourier transform.

Due to Theorem 1.88, it suffices to prove that $\overline{\mathrm{QRC}}_0^{(n,2)}$ is invariant under the permutation $T : y \to -1/y$. For any $c = (c_0, c_1, \ldots, c_{n-1}, c_\infty) \in \overline{\mathrm{QRC}}_0^{(n,2)}$, let $d = (d_0, d_1, \ldots, d_{n-1}, d_\infty)$ be the permuted vector of c. Let C and D be the Fourier transforms of c and d, respectively. We now want to derive a relation between D and C.

The inverse Fourier transform can be written as

$$c_i = C_0 + \sum_{k=1}^{n-1} \beta^{-ik} C_k = c_\infty + \sum_{k=1}^{n-1} \beta^{-ik} C_k.$$

Notice that

$$\sum_{i=0}^{n-1} \beta^{ij} = 0$$

for all j, as β^j is an nth root of unity for all j. Now we have

$$d_i = c_{-1/i} = c_\infty + \sum_{k=1}^{n-1} \beta^{(1/i)k} C_k, \quad i = 1, 2, \ldots, n-1$$

and $d_0 = c_\infty$. Consequently,

$$D_j = d_0 + \sum_{i=1}^{n-1} \beta^{ij} d_i$$

$$= c_\infty + \sum_{i=1}^{n-1} \beta^{ij} \left(c_\infty + \sum_{k=1}^{n-1} \beta^{(1/i)k} C_k \right)$$

$$= \sum_{i=1}^{n-1} \beta^{ij} \sum_{k=1}^{n-1} \beta^{(1/i)k} C_k. \tag{3.15}$$

Now we change indices again as follows:

$$i = \pi^r, \quad k = \pi^t, \quad j = \pi^{-s}.$$

Then (3.15) becomes

$$D_{\pi^{-s}} = \sum_{i=1}^{n-1} \beta^{\pi^{-s+r}} \sum_{k=1}^{n-1} \beta^{\pi^{-r+t}} C_{\pi^t}. \tag{3.16}$$

Consequently, (3.16) can be expressed as

$$D'_{-s} = \sum_{i=1}^{n-1} u_{r-s} \sum_{k=1}^{n-1} u_{t-r} C'_t, \tag{3.17}$$

where $C'_t = C_{\pi^t}$, $D'_{-s} = D_{\pi^{-s}}$ and $u_r = \beta^{\pi^{-r}}$.

Recall that C_i is zero if i is a nonzero square in $GF(n)$. This is the same as $C'_j = 0$ if j is even. In polynomial notation, (3.17) is the same as

$$D'\left(\frac{1}{x}\right) = u(x)^2 C'(x) \pmod{x^{n-1} - 1}. \tag{3.18}$$

But by definition, $C'(x)$ has only odd-indexed coefficients nonzero. The polynomial $u(x)^2$ has clearly only odd-indexed coefficients nonzero, as it is a square of a polynomial over $GF(2)$. As a result, the product $u(x)^2 C'(x) \pmod{x^{n-1} - 1}$ has all even-indexed coefficients equal to zero. Hence, D'_s equals zero if s is even. It means that D_j is zero if j is a nonzero square in $GF(n)$. Therefore, d is a codeword of $\overline{QRC}_0^{(n,2)}$. $\qquad\square$

In fact, the complete automorphism group of $\overline{\text{QRC}}_0^{(n,2)}$ is known and given as follows [Huffman (1998)].

Theorem 3.36. *Let* $n \equiv \pm 1 \pmod 8$ *be a prime. If* $n \notin \{7, 23\}$, *then* $\text{Aut}(\overline{\text{QRC}}_0^{(n,2)}) = \text{PAut}(\overline{\text{QRC}}_0^{(n,2)})$ *is isomorphic to the group of* $\text{PSL}_2(\text{GF}(n))$.

3.9 Duadic Codes

In the previous subsection, we described quadratic residue codes briefly. In this subsection, we introduce a family of cyclic codes that are generalizations of the quadratic residue codes. Binary duadic codes were defined in Leon, Masley and Pless (1984) and were generalized to arbitrary finite fields in Pless (1986, 1993); Rushnan (1986).

As usual, let n be a positive integer and q a prime power with $\gcd(n, q) = 1$. Let S_1 and S_2 be two subsets of $\mathbb{Z}_n$ such that

- $S_1 \cap S_2 = \emptyset$ and $S_1 \cup S_2 = \mathbb{Z}_n \setminus \{0\}$, and
- both S_1 and S_2 are a union of some q-cyclotomic cosets modulo n.

If there is a unit $\mu \in \mathbb{Z}_n$ such that $S_1 \mu = S_2$ and $S_2 \mu = S_1$, then (S_1, S_2, μ) is called a *splitting* of $\mathbb{Z}_n$.

Let $m = \text{ord}_n(q)$ and let β be an nth root of unity in $\text{GF}(q^m)$. Let (S_1, S_2, μ) be a splitting of $\mathbb{Z}_n$, Define

$$g_i(x) = \prod_{i \in S_i} (x - \beta^i) \text{ and } \tilde{g}_i(x) = (x - 1)g_i(x)$$

for $i \in \{1, 2\}$. The pair of cyclic codes C_1 and C_2 of length n over $\text{GF}(q)$ with generator polynomials $g_1(x)$ and $g_2(x)$ are called *odd-like duadic codes*, and the pair of cyclic codes $\tilde{C}_1$ and $\tilde{C}_2$ of length n over $\text{GF}(q)$ with generator polynomials $\tilde{g}_1(x)$ and $\tilde{g}_2(x)$ are called *even-like duadic codes*.

By definition, C_1 and C_2 have parameters $[n, (n+1)/2]$ and $\tilde{C}_1$ and $\tilde{C}_2$ have parameters $[n, (n-1)/2]$. For odd-like duadic codes, we have the following result [Huffman and Pless (2003)][Theorem 6.5.2].

Theorem 3.37 (Square root bound). *Let* C_1 *and* C_2 *be a pair of odd-like duadic codes of length* n *over* $\text{GF}(q)$. *Let* d_o *be their (common) minimum odd-like weight. Then the following hold:*

(a) $d_o^2 \geq n$.

(b) If the splitting defining the duadic codes is given by $\mu = -1$, *then* $d_o^2 - d_o + 1 \geq n$.

(c) *Suppose $d_o^2 - d_o + 1 = n$, where $d_o > 2$, and assume that the splitting defining the duadic codes is given by $\mu = -1$. Then d_o is the minimum weight of both C_1 and C_2.*

It is easily seen that quadratic residue codes are duadic codes. Duadic codes can be defined in terms of their generating idempotents. For further information on the existence, constructions, and properties of duadic codes, the reader is referred to Huffman and Pless (2003)[Chapter 6], Ding, Lam and Xing (1999) and Ding and Pless (1999).

Example 3.38. Let $(n, q) = (49, 2)$. Define

$$S_1 = \{1, 2, 4, 8, 9, 11, 15, 16, 18, 22, 23, 25, 29, 30, 32, 36, 37, 39, 43, 44, 46\}$$
$$\cup \{7, 14, 28\}$$

and

$$S_2 = \{1, 2, \ldots, 48\} \setminus S_1.$$

It is easily seen that $(S_1, S_2, -1)$ is a splitting of $\mathbb{Z}_{48}$. The pair of odd-like duadic codes C_1 and C_2 defined by this splitting have parameters $[49, 25, 4]$ and generator polynomials

$$x^{24} + x^{22} + x^{21} + x^{10} + x^8 + x^7 + x^3 + x + 1$$

and

$$x^{24} + x^{23} + x^{21} + x^{17} + x^{16} + x^{14} + x^3 + x^2 + 1$$

respectively. The minimum weight of the two codes is even.

3.10 A Combinatorial Approach to Cyclic Codes

In this section, we present a combinatorial approach to the construction of cyclic codes over finite fields.

Let D be any nonempty subset of $\mathbb{Z}_n$. The polynomial

$$D(x) := \sum_{i=0}^{n-1} s(D)_i x^i = \sum_{i \in D} x^i \tag{3.19}$$

is called the *Hall polynomial* of the set D, and can be viewed as a polynomial over any finite field.

The cyclic code over $\mathrm{GF}(q)$ with generator polynomial

$$g(x) = \gcd(x^n - 1, D(x)) \tag{3.20}$$

is called the cyclic code of the set D, where $\gcd(x^n - 1, D(x))$ is computed over $\mathrm{GF}(q)$.

It is clear that every cyclic code over a finite field can be produced in this way. The key question about this approach is how to choose a subset D of of $\mathbb{Z}_n$ so that the cyclic code $\mathcal{C}_{\mathrm{GF}(q)}(D)$ has good parameters. Intuitively, if the subset D has good combinatorial structures, its code $\mathcal{C}_{\mathrm{GF}(q)}(D)$ may be optimal. Further information on this combinatorial approach could be found in Ding (2015a).

Note that the correspondence between $s(D)^\infty$ and $D(x)$ is one-to-one. This approach is also a sequence approach to the construction of all cyclic codes over finite fields. The reader is referred to Ding (2018b) for further information on the sequence construction of cyclic codes.

3.11 Notes

Cyclic codes can be treated in other ways. For example, they were treated with q-polynomials over finite fields in Ding and Lin (2013) and with sequences in Ding (2018b), which is closely related to the combinatorial approach introduced in Section 3.10. However, the polynomial approach employed in this chapter seems to be the most effective one.

Although a considerable amount of progress on the study of BCH codes has been made in the past 60 years, little is known about the duals of BCH codes. It is relatively harder to study the duals of BCH codes, as the dual of a BCH code may not be a BCH code. We do not even have an efficient way to test if a given cyclic code is a BCH code.

Let α be a primitive element of $\mathrm{GF}(q^m)$. The following code

$$C(m, q, \alpha) = \{(\mathrm{Tr}_{q^m/q}(a\alpha^0), \mathrm{Tr}_{q^m/q}(a\alpha^1), \cdots, \mathrm{Tr}_{q^m/q}(a\alpha^{q^m-2})) : a \in \mathrm{GF}(q^m)\}$$

is a $[q^m - 1, m, (q-1)q^{m-1}]$ cyclic code with check polynomial $\mathbb{M}_{\alpha^{-1}}(x)$, which is the minimal polynomial of α^{-1} over $\mathrm{GF}(q)$ and is irreducible over $\mathrm{GF}(q)$. The code $C(m, q, \alpha)$ is irreducible. It is easily seen that the weight enumerator of $C(m, q, \alpha)$ is $1 + (q^m - 1)z^{q^m - q^{m-1}}$ [Ding and Yang (2013)]. The following result was proved by Heng and Ding (2019).

Theorem 3.39. *Every linear code of length n over* $\mathrm{GF}(q)$ *with dual distance at least 3 is a punctured code of an irreducible cyclic code* $C(m, q, \alpha)$ *for a positive integer m and primitive element* $\alpha \in \mathrm{GF}(q^m)$.

While cyclic codes form a subclass of linear codes, every linear code with minimum distance at least two can be punctured from a special irreducible cyclic code $C(m,q,\alpha)$. This demonstrates the theoretical importance of the very special subclass of irreducible cyclic codes $C(m,q,\alpha)$ and the puncturing technique.

Due to their nice algebraic structures, cyclic codes have efficient encoding and decoding algorithms. They have been widely used in communication systems, data storage systems and consumer electronics. Reed-Solomon codes are used the most. In addition, cyclic codes have also applications in frequency hopping sequences [Ding, Yang and Tang (2010)].

Chapter 4

Designs and Codes

Designs and codes are companions. On one hand, a design may give many codes. On the other hand, a code may yield many designs. The objective of this chapter is to introduce basic connections between designs and codes, which will lay a foundation for subsequent chapters.

4.1 Fundamentals of t-Designs

4.1.1 *Incidence Structures*

Many combinatorial designs are special incidence structures. The purpose of this section is to give a short introduction to incidence structures.

An *incidence structure* is a triple $\mathbb{D} = (\mathcal{P}, \mathcal{B}, \mathcal{R})$, where $\mathcal{P}$ is a set of elements called *points* and $\mathcal{B}$ is a set of elements called *blocks* (lines), and $\mathcal{R} \subseteq \mathcal{P} \times \mathcal{B}$ is a binary relation, called *incidence relation*. The elements of $\mathcal{R}$ are called *flags*.

We use upper case Latin letters to denote blocks and lower case Latin letters to denote points. If a point p is incident with a block B, we can write either $p\mathcal{R}B$ or $p \in B$ and use geometric languages such as "p lies on B", "B passes through p", and "B contains p".

An incidence structure $\mathbb{D} = (\mathcal{P}, \mathcal{B}, \mathcal{R})$ is called a *finite incidence structure* if both $\mathcal{P}$ and $\mathcal{B}$ are finite sets. In this monograph we consider only finite incidence structures whose blocks have the same cardinality. A finite incidence structure with equally many points and blocks is called a *square*.

Example 4.1. Let $\mathcal{P} = \{1, 2, 3, 4, 5, 6, 7\}$ and put

$$\mathcal{B} = \{\{1, 2, 3\}, \{1, 4, 5\}, \{1, 6, 7\}, \{2, 4, 7\}, \{2, 5, 6\}, \{3, 4, 6\}, \{3, 5, 7\}\}.$$

Let $\mathcal{R}$ be the set membership. Then $(\mathcal{P}, \mathcal{B}, \mathcal{R})$ is an incidence structure obtained from the Fano plane.

115

4.1.2 Incidence Matrices

Let $\mathbb{D} = (\mathcal{P}, \mathcal{B}, \mathcal{R})$ be an incidence structure with $v \geq 1$ points and $b \geq 1$ blocks. The points of $\mathcal{P}$ are usually indexed with $p_1, p_2, \ldots, p_v$, and the blocks of $\mathcal{B}$ are normally denoted by $B_1, B_2, \ldots, B_b$. The *incidence matrix* $M_{\mathbb{D}} = (m_{ij})$ of $\mathbb{D}$ is a $b \times v$ matrix where $m_{ij} = 1$ if p_j is on B_i and $m_{ij} = 0$ otherwise. It is clear that the incidence matrix $M_{\mathbb{D}}$ depends on the labeling of the points and blocks of $\mathbb{D}$, but is unique up to row and column permutations. Conversely, every $(0, 1)$-matrix (entries are 0 or 1) determines an incidence structure. Our definition of the incidence matrix follows Assmus and Key (1992a)[p.12]. In some books, the transpose of the matrix $M_{\mathbb{D}}$ above is defined as the incidence matrix.

Example 4.2. Consider the incidence structure $\mathbb{D} = (\mathcal{P}, \mathcal{B}, \mathcal{R})$ of Example 4.1. Let the labeling of the points and blocks of $\mathbb{D}$ be in the order of their appearance in $\mathcal{P}$ and $\mathcal{B}$. Then the incidence matrix of $\mathbb{D}$ is

$$M_{\mathbb{D}} = \begin{bmatrix} 1 & 1 & 1 & 0 & 0 & 0 & 0 \\ 1 & 0 & 0 & 1 & 1 & 0 & 0 \\ 1 & 0 & 0 & 0 & 0 & 1 & 1 \\ 0 & 1 & 0 & 1 & 0 & 0 & 1 \\ 0 & 1 & 0 & 0 & 1 & 1 & 0 \\ 0 & 0 & 1 & 1 & 0 & 1 & 0 \\ 0 & 0 & 1 & 0 & 1 & 0 & 1 \end{bmatrix}. \tag{4.1}$$

Let q be a prime power. The *q-rank* of an incidence structure $\mathbb{D} = (\mathcal{P}, \mathcal{B}, \mathcal{R})$ is the rank of an incidence matrix over $\mathrm{GF}(q)$, and will be useful later.

4.1.3 Isomorphisms and Automorphisms

An *isomorphism* γ from an incidence structure $\mathbb{D}_1$ onto an incidence structure $\mathbb{D}_2$ is a one-to-one mapping from the points of $\mathbb{D}_1$ onto the points of $\mathbb{D}_2$ and from the blocks of $\mathbb{D}_1$ onto the blocks of $\mathbb{D}_2$ such that p is on B if and only if $\gamma(p)$ is on $\gamma(B)$.

If there is an isomorphism from $\mathbb{D}_1$ to $\mathbb{D}_2$, then we say that the two incidence structures are *isomorphic*. Let M_1 and M_2 be the incidence matrix of $\mathbb{D}_1$ and $\mathbb{D}_2$, respectively. Then $\mathbb{D}_1$ and $\mathbb{D}_2$ are isomorphic if and only if there are permutation matrices P and Q such that

$$PM_1Q = M_2.$$

An *automorphism* of a given incidence structure $\mathbb{D}$ is an isomorphism of $\mathbb{D}$ onto itself. Obviously, the set of automorphisms of $\mathbb{D}$ forms a group, which is called the *full automorphism group* of $\mathbb{D}$ and denoted by $\text{Aut}(\mathbb{D})$. Any subgroup of $\text{Aut}(\mathbb{D})$ will be called an *automorphism group* of $\mathbb{D}$.

4.1.4 Definition and Properties of t-Designs

Let $\mathbb{D} = (\mathcal{P}, \mathcal{B}, \mathcal{R})$ be an incidence structure with $v \geq 1$ points and $b \geq 1$ blocks. Let t and λ be two positive integers. Then the triple $\mathbb{D}$ is said to be t-*balanced* with parameter λ if and only if every subset of t points of $\mathcal{P}$ is incident with exactly λ blocks of $\mathcal{B}$. If every block of $\mathbb{D}$ is also of the same size k, then $\mathbb{D}$ is called a t-(v,k,λ) *design*, or simply t-*design*. The integers t, v, k, λ are referred to as the *parameters* of the design. It is possible for a design to have repeated blocks. Only in Chapter 16 of this monograph, we consider t-designs which may have repeated blocks. But in the rest part of this monograph, we consider only designs without repeated blocks, which are called *simple t-designs*. A t-design is called *symmetric* if $v = b$.

It is clear that t-designs with $k = t$ or $k = v$ always exist. Such t-designs are *trivial*. The family of all k-subsets of $\mathcal{P}$ forms a k-$(v,k,1)$ design and is said to be *complete* or *trivial*. A 1-design is referred to as a *tactical configuration*. A nontrivial 2-design is called a *balanced incomplete block design*. A t-(v,k,λ) design is referred to as a *Steiner system* if $t \geq 2$ and $\lambda = 1$.

Example 4.3. The incidence structure $(\mathcal{P}, \mathcal{B}, \mathcal{R})$ of Example 4.1 is a 2-$(7,3,1)$ design, and also a Steiner system.

The following is a fundamental result about t-designs.

Theorem 4.4. *A t-(v,k,λ_t) design $\mathbb{D}$ is also an s-(v,k,λ_s) design for any $0 \leq s < t$, where*

$$\lambda_s = \lambda_t \frac{\binom{v-s}{t-s}}{\binom{k-s}{t-s}}. \tag{4.2}$$

Proof. We first introduce a useful result. Let U and V be two finite sets, and let $U \times V$ be the Cartesian product of U and V. For any subset $S \subseteq U \times V$, put

$$S(u, \cdot) = \{(u,v) \in S : v \in V\} \text{ and } S(\cdot, v) = \{(u,v) \in S : u \in U\}.$$

Obviously, S is partitioned in the following two ways:

$$S = \bigcup_{u \in U} S(u, \cdot) = \bigcup_{v \in V} S(\cdot, v).$$

Consequently,

$$|S| = \sum_{u \in U} |S(u, \cdot)| = \sum_{v \in V} |S(\cdot, v)|. \tag{4.3}$$

Now let $\mathbb{D} = (\mathcal{P}, \mathcal{B}, \mathcal{R})$ be a t-(v, k, λ_t) design, and let s be an integer with $0 \le s \le t$. We prove the desired conclusion by induction on s. We now assume that the desired conclusion is true for $s = i + 1$, i.e., every set of $i + 1$ points is incident with a fixed number λ_{i+1} blocks of $\mathbb{D}$. Let $\{p_1, \ldots, p_i\}$ be a set of i points in $\mathcal{P}$. Consider now the set

$$S = \{(p, B) \in \mathcal{P} \times \mathcal{B} : p \notin \{p_1, \ldots, p_i\}, \{p_1, \ldots, p_i, p\} \text{ is incident with } B\}.$$

Clearly, $|S(\cdot, B)| = k - i$. By induction hypothesis, $|S(p, \cdot)| = \lambda_{i+1}$. Applying (4.3), we see that the set $\{p_1, \ldots, p_i\}$ of points is incident with

$$\lambda_i = \lambda_{i+1}(v - i)/(k - i)$$

blocks in $\mathcal{B}$, which does not depend on the choice of the points. Hence, the desired conclusion holds also for $s - 1 = i$. This completes the proof. $\qquad\square$

By definition, λ_0 is the number of blocks in $\mathcal{B}$, which is denoted by b in this monograph. λ_1 is the number of blocks that a point is incident with, and is denoted by r traditionally. Hence, λ_0 and λ_1 have special meanings.

As a consequence of (4.2), we have

$$(v - i)\lambda_{i+1} = (k - i)\lambda_i, \ 0 \le i \le t - 1.$$

When $i = 0$, the identity above becomes

$$vr = bk. \tag{4.4}$$

It follows from (4.2) that in a t-(v, k, λ) design we have

$$b = \lambda \frac{\binom{v}{t}}{\binom{k}{t}} \tag{4.5}$$

and every point is incident with (contained in) exactly bk/v blocks. Therefore, the incidence matrix of the t-design $\mathbb{D}$ has a constant column sum r, and a constant row sum k. The *order* of t-(v, k, λ) is defined to be $\lambda_1 - \lambda_2$, i.e., $r - \lambda$ when $t = 2$.

When $t = 2$, combining (4.4) and (4.5) yields

$$r = \lambda(v - 1)/(k - 1) \tag{4.6}$$

and $r > \lambda$ if $k < v$.

The existence of t-(v, k, λ) designs is a basic problem in combinatorial designs. Theorem 4.4 gives necessary conditions for the existence of a t-(v, k, λ) design, i.e., the right-hand side of (4.2) must be an integer for all s with $0 \le s \le t$.

One can easily prove the following necessary and sufficient condition for $\mathbb{D}$ to be a 2-design.

Theorem 4.5. *Let M be an incidence matrix of an incidence structure $\mathbb{D}$. Then $\mathbb{D}$ is a 2-(v, k, λ) design if and only if*

$$M^T M = (r - \lambda)I_v + \lambda J_v, \tag{4.7}$$

where I_v is the $v \times v$ identity matrix and J_v is the all-one $v \times v$ matrix.

Theorem 4.6. *Let M be a v × v matrix with $M^T M$ satisfying (4.7). Then*

$$\det(M^T M) = (r - \lambda)^{v-1}(v\lambda - \lambda + r).$$

If M is an incidence matrix of a 2-(v,k,λ) design with $v > k$, then by (4.6)

$$\det(M^T M) = (r - \lambda)^{v-1} rk \neq 0.$$

Proof. Note that the matrix J_v has the eigenvector $(1,1,\ldots,1)$ with eigenvalue v and the following $v - 1$ eigenvectors

$$(1,-1,0,0,\ldots,0),(1,0,-1,0,\ldots,0),\ldots,(1,0,0,0,\ldots,0,-1)$$

with eigenvalue 0. The matrix $M^T M$ satisfying (4.7) has one eigenvalue $r - \lambda + \lambda v$ and $v - 1$ eigenvalues $r - \lambda$. The desired conclusion of the first part then follows. The conclusion of the second part is a special case of that of the first part. □

As a corollary of Theorem 4.6, we have the following result due to Fisher, which is referred to as the *Fisher inequality*.

Corollary 4.7. *If $\mathbb{D}$ is a nontrivial t-design with $t \geq 2$, then there are at least as many blocks as points, i.e., $b \geq v$.*

Note that the Fisher inequality does not hold for certain 1-designs. A symmetric 2-(v,k,λ) design with $\lambda < k < v - 1$ is simply called a (v,k,λ)-*design*. Summarizing the forgoing discussions, we have the following conclusions about (v,k,λ)-designs.

Theorem 4.8. *Let $\mathbb{D} = (\mathcal{P}, \mathcal{B}, \mathcal{R})$ be a (v,k,λ)-design. Then*

(i) $r = k$ and the order of $\mathbb{D}$ is $k - \lambda$ (it follows from (4.4));
(ii) $\lambda(v - 1) = k(k - 1)$ (this is (4.6)); and
(iii) λ divides $(k - \lambda)(k - \lambda - 1)$ (it follows from the conclusion of the second part).

The development of a (v,k,λ) difference set is a (v,k,λ)-design. There are a huge number of such (v,k,λ)-designs [Ding (2015a)]. The most comprehensive reference on symmetric designs is Ionin and Shrikhande (2006).

The following theorem presents two characterisations of symmetric 2-designs whose proof can be found in Hall (1986) and Beth, Jungnickel and Lenz (1999)[p. 78].

Theorem 4.9. *A 2-(v,k,λ) design $\mathbb{D}$ is symmetric if and only if $r = k$ or $|A \cap B| = \lambda$ for any two distinct blocks A and B in $\mathbb{D}$.*

Symmetric designs are special partially due to the following [Ionin and Shrikhande (2006)][p. 188].

Theorem 4.10. *A t-(v,k,λ) design with $t \geq 3$ and $k \leq v-2$ cannot be a symmetric design.*

4.1.5 Intersection Numbers of t-Designs

Throughout this section, let $\mathbb{D} = (\mathcal{P}, \mathcal{B})$ be a t-(v,k,λ) design, where the incidence relation $\mathcal{R}$ is the set inclusion. Let I and J be two disjoint subsets of $\mathcal{P}$ with $|I| = i$ and $|J| = j$. Denote by $\lambda_{(i,j)}(I,J)$ the number of blocks in $\mathcal{B}$ that contain I and are disjoint from J. These numbers $\lambda_{(i,j)}(I,J)$ are called *intersection numbers*.

Under certain conditions, the intersection numbers $\lambda_{(i,j)}(I,J)$ are independent of the specific choice of the elements in I and J, and depend only on $|I|$ and $|J|$. In this case, we use $\lambda_{(i,j)}$ to denote the intersection numbers. Specifically, we have the following [Huffman and Pless (2003)][p. 295].

Theorem 4.11. *Let i and j be nonnegative integers with $i + j \leq t$. Then $\lambda_{(i,j)}(I,J)$ is independent of the elements in I and J, and for $j \geq 1$,*

$$\lambda_{(i,j)} = \lambda_{(i,j-1)} - \lambda_{(i+1,j-1)}. \tag{4.8}$$

Specifically,

$$\lambda_{(i,j)} = \lambda \frac{\binom{v-i-j}{k-i}}{\binom{v-t}{k-t}}. \tag{4.9}$$

For Steiner designs, the preceding theorem can be extended with the following result [Huffman and Pless (2003)][p. 297].

Theorem 4.12. *Let $\mathbb{D} = (\mathcal{P}, \mathcal{B})$ be a t-$(v,k,1)$ design. Let I and J be two disjoint subsets of $\mathcal{P}$ with $|I| = i$ and $|J| = j$. Assume that $I \cup J$ is a subset of some block in $\mathcal{B}$. If $t < i + j \leq k$, then $\lambda_{(i,j)}(I,J)$ is independent of the elements in I and J, and for $j \geq 1$,*

$$\lambda_{(i,j)} = \lambda_{(i,j-1)} - \lambda_{(i+1,j-1)}. \tag{4.10}$$

Certain of the intersection numbers have specific meaning. For example, we have the following:

(1) $\lambda_{(0,0)} = b$, which is the number of blocks in $\mathcal{B}$.
(2) $\lambda_{(i,0)} = \lambda_i$.
(3) $\lambda_{(0,j)}$ is the number of blocks not intersecting a given set of j points.

The intersection numbers of designs have several applications. We will need them later.

4.1.6 *Related Designs of a t-Design*

Given a t-(v,k,λ) design $\mathbb{D} = (\mathcal{P}, \mathcal{B})$, we can obtain several other designs in a natural way. Below we introduce them briefly.

Let $\mathcal{B}^c$ be the set of the complements of the blocks in $\mathcal{B}$, i.e., $\mathcal{B}^c = \{\mathcal{P} \setminus B : B \in \mathcal{B}\}$. It can be easily proved that $(\mathcal{P}, \mathcal{B}^c)$ is a t-$(v, v - k, \lambda_{(0,t)})$ design, where

$$\lambda_{(0,t)} = \lambda \frac{\binom{v-t}{k}}{\binom{v-t}{k-t}}, \tag{4.11}$$

and is called the *complementary design* of $\mathbb{D}$.

Let $\binom{\mathcal{P}}{k}$ denote the set of all k-subsets of $\mathcal{P}$. Then $(\mathcal{P}, \binom{\mathcal{P}}{k} \setminus \mathcal{B})$ is a t-$(v, k, \binom{v-t}{k-t} - \lambda)$ design, and is called the *supplementary design* of $\mathbb{D}$. Notice that the complementary and supplementary design of a design defined in some references are swapped versions of those defined above.

Let $x \in \mathcal{P}$ be fixed. The *derived design for* $\mathbb{D} = (\mathcal{P}, \mathcal{B})$ *with respect to* x is the design $\mathbb{D}_x$ with point set $\mathcal{P} \setminus \{x\}$ and blocks $\{B \setminus \{x\} : x \in B \in \mathcal{B}\}$ with parameters

$$(t-1)\text{-}(v-1, k-1, \lambda). \tag{4.12}$$

Let $x \in \mathcal{P}$ be fixed. The *residual design for* $(\mathcal{P}, \mathcal{B})$ *with respect to* x is the design with point set $\mathcal{P} \setminus \{x\}$ and blocks $\{B : x \notin B \in \mathcal{B}\}$ with parameters

$$(t-1)\text{-}(v-1, k, \lambda_{t-1} - \lambda). \tag{4.13}$$

Derived and residual designs of a symmetric design $\mathbb{D}$ with respect to a block can also be defined. We will deal with such designs in Chapter 14. The *dual design* of a design $\mathbb{D} = (\mathcal{P}, \mathcal{B}, \mathcal{R})$ is defined by $\mathbb{D}^* = (\mathcal{B}, \mathcal{P}, \mathcal{R}^*)$, where $\mathcal{R}^*$ is the inverse relation of $\mathcal{R}$ in $\mathbb{D}$. By definition, the incidence matrix of the dual design is the transpose of the incidence matrix of the original design. The following statements can be easily verified:

- The dual of a 2-(v,k,λ) design is a 1-$(\lambda v(v-1)/k(k-1), \lambda(v-1)/(k-1), k)$ design.
- The dual design of any 2-design $\mathbb{D}$ cannot be a 2-design if the number of blocks is more than the number of points in $\mathbb{D}$ (due to the Fisher inequality).
- The dual design of a 2-design $\mathbb{D}$ is a 2-design if and only if $\mathbb{D}$ is symmetric.
- The dual of a 1-design may be a t-design for $t \geq 2$.

A design $\mathbb{E}$ is called an *extension* of a design $\mathbb{D}$ if $\mathbb{E}$ has a point p such that the derived design $\mathbb{E}_p$ is isomorphic to $\mathbb{D}$. A design is said to be *extendable* if it has an extension. Since an extension of a t-(v,k,λ) design is a $(t+1)$-$(v+1, k+1, \lambda)$ design, the following theorem then follows from Theorem 4.2.

Theorem 4.13. *If a t-(v,k,λ) design has an extension, then $k+1$ divides $b(v+1)$.*

The following result is quite useful [Alltop (1975)].

Theorem 4.14. *Let* $\mathbb{D} = (\mathcal{P}, \mathcal{B})$ *be a* t-$(2k+1, k, \lambda)$ *design and* ∞ *a new point not in* $\mathcal{P}$.

(1) If t *is even, then* $(\mathcal{P} \cup \{\infty\}, \{B \cup \{\infty\} : B \in \mathcal{B}\} \cup \{\mathcal{P} \setminus B : B \in \mathcal{B}\})$ *is a* $(t+1)$-$(2k+2, k+1, \lambda)$ *design.*

(2) If t *is odd and* $\lambda = \binom{v-t}{k-t}/2$, *then* $(\mathcal{P} \cup \{\infty\}, \{B \cup \{\infty\} : B \in \mathcal{B}\} \cup \{\mathcal{P} \setminus B : B \in \binom{\mathcal{P}}{k} \setminus \mathcal{B}\})$ *is a* $(t+1)$-$(2k+2, k+1, \lambda)$ *design.*

4.2 The Classical Codes of t-Designs

Although the focus of this monograph is constructions and properties of t-designs from linear codes, we would also summarize certain basic results about linear codes from t-designs in this section. We will not prove these basic results, but will give a reference of each result where a proof is available.

4.2.1 *Linear Codes of Incidence Structures*

Let $\mathbb{D} = (\mathcal{P}, \mathcal{B}, \mathcal{R})$ be an incidence structure with $v \geq 1$ points and $b \geq 1$ blocks, and let $M_{\mathbb{D}}$ be its incidence matrix with respect to a labelling of the points and blocks of $\mathbb{D}$. The *linear code* of $\mathbb{D}$ over a field F is the subspace $C_F(\mathbb{D})$ of F^v spanned by the row vectors of the incidence matrix $M_{\mathbb{D}}$. By definition $C_F(\mathbb{D})$ is a linear code over F with length v and dimension at most b.

The linear code $C_F(\mathbb{D})$ depends on the labelling of the points and blocks of the incidence structure $\mathbb{D} = (\mathcal{P}, \mathcal{B}, \mathcal{R})$. Whatever the labelling is, these codes are all equivalent under coordinate permutations.

Example 4.15. Consider the incidence structure of Example 4.1 and the labelling of the points and blocks in Example 4.2. Then the code $C_F(\mathbb{D})$ over GF(2) is the binary Hamming code with parameters $[7, 4, 3]$, and has the generator matrix $M_{\mathbb{D}}$ of (4.1).

The linear code of an incidence structure may have very bad parameters, as an incidence structure may not have good combinatorial properties. However, the linear code of a t-design could be optimal ([Assmus and Key (1992a)] and [Ding (2015a)]).

4.2.2 The Classical Codes of t-Designs

For the codes of 2-designs, we can say much more. The following theorem gives information on the codes of 2-designs [Assmus and Key (1992a)][Theorem 2.4.1].

Theorem 4.16. *Let $\mathbb{D} = (\mathcal{P}, \mathcal{B}, \mathcal{R})$ be a nontrivial 2-(v, k, λ) design with order $r - \lambda$, where r is defined in (4.6). Let p be a prime and let F be a field of characteristic p where p does not divide $r - \lambda$. Then*

$$\mathrm{rank}_p(\mathbb{D}) \geq v - 1$$

with equality if and only if p divides k.

If $\mathrm{rank}_p(\mathbb{D}) = v - 1$, then $(C_F(\mathbb{D}))^{\perp}$ is generated by the all-one vector. If $\mathrm{rank}_p(\mathbb{D}) = v$, then $C_F(\mathbb{D}) = F^v$.

Example 4.17. As a demonstration of Theorem 4.16, we consider the code of the 2-$(7, 3, 1)$ design of Example 4.3. In this case, $r = 3$ and the order of this design $\mathbb{D}$ is $r - \lambda = 2$. We consider now the code $C_{\mathrm{GF}(p)}(\mathbb{D})$ whose generator matrix is given in (4.1).

When $p = 3$, p does not divide $r - \lambda$ and p divides $k = 3$. In this case, we have

$$\mathrm{rank}_3(\mathbb{D}) = v - 1 = 6.$$

Hence, the dimension of the code $C_{\mathrm{GF}(3)}(\mathbb{D})$ is 6. The ternary code $C_{\mathrm{GF}(3)}(\mathbb{D})^{\perp}$ has parameters $[7, 1, 7]$ and generator matrix $[1111111]$.

When $p = 5$, p does not divide $r - \lambda$ and p does not divide $k = 3$. In this case, we have

$$\mathrm{rank}_5(\mathbb{D}) = v = 7.$$

Hence, the dimension of the code $C_{\mathrm{GF}(5)}(\mathbb{D})$ is 7. The code $C_{\mathrm{GF}(5)}(\mathbb{D})$ is $\mathrm{GF}(5)^7$.

For symmetric 2-designs $\mathbb{D}$, we have $r = k$ and the order of $\mathbb{D}$ becomes $r - \lambda = k - \lambda$. In this case, Theorem 4.16 can be refined as follows ([Bridges, Hall and Hayden (1981)], [Huffman and Pless (2003)][Theorem 8.5.2]).

Theorem 4.18. *Let $\mathbb{D} = (\mathcal{P}, \mathcal{B}, \mathcal{R})$ be a symmetric 2-(v, k, λ) design with order $k - \lambda$. Let p be a prime and let F be a field of characteristic p. Then we have the following.*

(a) *If p divides $(k - \lambda)$ and p divides k, then $C_F(\mathbb{D})$ is self-orthogonal and has dimension at most $v/2$.*

(b) *If p does not divide $(k - \lambda)$ but p divides k, then $C_F(\mathbb{D})$ has dimension $v - 1$.*

(c) *If p does not divide $(k - \lambda)$ and p does not divide k, then $C_F(\mathbb{D})$ has dimension v.*

The following theorem is due to Klemm (1986) (see also Assmus and Key (1992a)[Theorem 2.4.2]).

Theorem 4.19. *Let* $\mathbb{D} = (\mathcal{P}, \mathcal{B}, \mathcal{R})$ *be a* 2-(v, k, λ) *design with order* $r - \lambda$, *where* r *is defined in (4.6). Let* p *be a prime dividing* $r - \lambda$. *Then*

$$\mathrm{rank}_p(\mathbb{D}) \le \frac{|\mathcal{B}| + 1}{2};$$

moreover, if p *does not divide* λ *and* p^2 *does not divide* $r - \lambda$, *then*

$$\mathcal{C}_F(\mathbb{D})^\perp \subseteq \mathcal{C}_F(\mathbb{D})$$

and $\mathrm{rank}_p(\mathbb{D}) \ge v/2$, *where* F *is a finite field with characteristic* p.

Example 4.20. As a demonstration of Theorem 4.19, we consider the code of the 2-$(7, 3, 1)$ design of Example 4.3. In this case, $r = 3$ and the order of this design $\mathbb{D}$ is $r - \lambda = 2$. We consider the case that $p = 2$ and the code $\mathcal{C}_{\mathrm{GF}(p)}(\mathbb{D})$. It is clear that p divides $r - \lambda$ and

$$\mathrm{rank}_p(\mathbb{D}) = \frac{|\mathcal{B}| + 1}{2} = 4.$$

Hence, the dimension of the code $\mathcal{C}_{\mathrm{GF}(p)}(\mathbb{D})$ is 4. The binary code $\mathcal{C}_{\mathrm{GF}(p)}(\mathbb{D})$ was treated in Example 4.2, and has parameters $[7, 4, 3]$.

Clearly, p does not divide λ and p^2 does not divide $r - \lambda$. The dual code $\mathcal{C}_{\mathrm{GF}(p)}(\mathbb{D})^\perp$ has the following generator matrix

$$\begin{bmatrix} 1 & 0 & 1 & 0 & 1 & 1 & 0 \\ 0 & 1 & 1 & 0 & 0 & 1 & 1 \\ 0 & 0 & 0 & 1 & 1 & 1 & 1 \end{bmatrix}.$$

Note that the row vectors of this matrix are pairwise orthogonal. In this case, we have indeed

$$\mathcal{C}_{\mathrm{GF}(p)}(\mathbb{D})^\perp \subseteq \mathcal{C}_{\mathrm{GF}(p)}(\mathbb{D}).$$

For symmetric 2-designs, Theorem 4.19 can be refined as follows ([Bridges, Hall and Hayden (1981)], [Huffman and Pless (2003)][Theorem 8.5.3]).

Theorem 4.21. *Let* $\mathbb{D} = (\mathcal{P}, \mathcal{B}, \mathcal{R})$ *be a symmetric* 2-(v, k, λ) *design with order* $k - \lambda$. *Let* p *be the characteristic of a finite field* F. *Assume that* p *divides* $k - \lambda$, *but* p^2 *does not divide* $k - \lambda$. *Then* v *is odd, and we have the following.*

(a) *If* p *divides* k, *then* $\mathcal{C}_F(\mathbb{D})$ *is self-orthogonal and has dimension* $(v - 1)/2$.
(b) *If* p *does not divide* k, *then* $\mathcal{C}_F(\mathbb{D})^\perp \subset \mathcal{C}_F(\mathbb{D})$ *and* $\mathcal{C}_F(\mathbb{D})$ *has dimension* $(v + 1)/2$.

The next result is useful [Assmus and Key (1992a)][p. 54].

Theorem 4.22. *Let* $\mathbb{D} = (\mathcal{P}, \mathcal{B}, \mathcal{R})$ *be a* 2-(v, k, λ) *design with* $k < v$. *If* $C_{\mathrm{GF}(q)}(\mathbb{D}) \neq \mathrm{GF}(q)^v$, *then the minimum weight of* $C_{\mathrm{GF}(q)}(\mathbb{D})^{\perp}$ *is at least*

$$\frac{v-1}{k-1} + 1.$$

4.3 The Support Designs of Linear Codes

So far, we have introduced the classical codes of designs. Conversely, we can obtain t-designs from linear codes. The objective of this section is to introduce the classical construction of t-designs with linear codes and the Assmus-Mattson Theorem.

4.3.1 *The Construction of t-Designs from Linear Codes*

Let C be a linear code of length n. Consider all the codewords of weight w in C. Let $\mathbf{c} = (c_1, c_2, \ldots, c_n)$ be a codeword of weight w in C. The *support* of $\mathbf{c}$ is defined by

$$\mathrm{Suppt}(\mathbf{c}) = \{1 \leq i \leq n : c_i \neq 0\} \subseteq \{1, 2, 3, \ldots, n\}.$$

Two different codewords of weight w may have the same support. Let $\mathcal{P} = \{1, 2, \ldots, n\}$ and $\mathcal{B}$ be the set of the supports of the codewords of weight w in C, where no repeated blocks are allowed. Let the incidence relation $\mathcal{R}$ be the usual containment of sets. Then it is possible that $(\mathcal{P}, \mathcal{B}, \mathcal{R})$ is a t-design for some t. In this case, we say that the codewords of weight w in C hold or support a t-design, which is called a *support design* of C.

Example 4.23. The binary $[7, 4, 3]$ Hamming code has the weight enumerator $1 + 7z^3 + 7z^4 + z^7$. It has 7 codewords of weight 3. The seven codewords are exactly the row vectors of the matrix in (4.1). The supports of the seven codewords form the set $\mathcal{B}$ in Example 4.1. Hence the codewords of weight 3 in the binary $[7, 4, 3]$ Hamming code hold a 2-$(7, 3, 1)$ design, which is the Fano plane.

The Assmus-Mattson theorem below describes t-designs from linear codes [Assmus and Mattson (1969)].

Theorem 4.24 (Assmus-Mattson). *Let C be an $[n, k, d]$ code over* $\mathrm{GF}(q)$. *Let $d^{\perp}$ denote the minimum distance of $C^{\perp}$. Let w be the largest integer satisfying $w \leq n$ and*

$$w - \left\lfloor \frac{w + q - 2}{q - 1} \right\rfloor < d.$$

Define $w^\perp$ analogously using $d^\perp$. Let $(A_i)_{i=0}^n$ and $(A_i^\perp)_{i=0}^n$ denote the weight distribution of C and $C^\perp$, respectively. Fix a positive integer t with $t < d$, and let s be the number of i with $A_i^\perp \neq 0$ for $1 \leq i \leq n - t$. Suppose $s \leq d - t$. Then

(i) *the codewords of weight i in C hold a t-design provided $A_i \neq 0$ and $d \leq i \leq w$, and*

(ii) *the codewords of weight i in $C^\perp$ hold a t-design provided $A_i^\perp \neq 0$ and $d^\perp \leq i \leq \min\{n - t, w^\perp\}$.*

No simple proof of the Assmus-Mattson theorem is known in the literature. The original proof can be found in Assmus and Mattson (1969). We will present a slightly refined proof of this theorem given in Huffman and Pless (2003)[p. 303]. Before doing this, we prove the following lemma.

Lemma 4.25. *Let C be a linear code over $\mathrm{GF}(q)$ with minimum weight d.*

(a) *Let $\mathbf{c}$ and $\mathbf{c}'$ be two codewords of weight d with $\mathrm{Suppt}(\mathbf{c}) = \mathrm{Suppt}(\mathbf{c}')$. Then $\mathbf{c} = a\mathbf{c}'$ for some nonzero $a \in \mathrm{GF}(q)$.*

(b) *Let w be the largest integer with $w \leq n$ satisfying*

$$w - \left\lfloor \frac{w+q-2}{q-1} \right\rfloor < d.$$

Let $\mathbf{c}$ and $\mathbf{c}'$ be two codewords of weight i with $d \leq i \leq w$ and $\mathrm{Suppt}(\mathbf{c}) = \mathrm{Suppt}(\mathbf{c}')$. Then $\mathbf{c} = a\mathbf{c}'$ for some nonzero $a \in \mathrm{GF}(q)$.

Proof. We first prove the conclusion in Part (a). Let i be the smallest integer in $\mathrm{Suppt}(\mathbf{c})$. Then the coordinates c_i of $\mathbf{c}$ and c_i' of $\mathbf{c}'$ are nonzero. Let $a = c_i/c_i' \in \mathrm{GF}(q)^*$. Then $\mathbf{c} - a\mathbf{c}'$ is a codeword in C with weight at most $d - 1$. Thus $\mathbf{c} - a\mathbf{c}'$ must be the zero codeword. The desired conclusion of Part (a) then follows.

We now proceed to prove the conclusion in Part (b). Suppose that $\mathrm{Suppt}(\mathbf{c}) = \{j_1, j_2, \ldots, j_i\}$, where $d \leq i \leq w$. Consider now the multiset

$$\left\{ \left\{ \frac{c_{j_h}}{c_{j_h}'} : 1 \leq h \leq i \right\} \right\}$$

of elements in $\mathrm{GF}(q)^*$. Let a be an element in this multiset with the highest multiplicity, which is at least

$$\left\lfloor \frac{i+q-2}{q-1} \right\rfloor.$$

Then the codeword $\mathbf{c} - a\mathbf{c}'$ has Hamming weight at most

$$i - \left\lfloor \frac{i+q-2}{q-1} \right\rfloor \leq w - \left\lfloor \frac{w+q-2}{q-1} \right\rfloor < d.$$

Consequently, $\mathbf{c} = a\mathbf{c}'$. $\qquad\square$

Let w be defined as in Part (b) of Lemma 4.25. It can be easily shown that w is the largest integer such that a codeword of weight w or less in an $[n,k,d]$ code over $\text{GF}(q)$ is determined uniquely up to scalar multiplication by its support. This can be done by finding two vectors in $\text{GF}(q)^{w+1}$ of weight $w+1$ that generate a $[w+1,2,d]$ code over $\text{GF}(q)$. Lemma 4.25 will be employed to determine the parameters of certain t-designs in later chapters.

Proof of Theorem 4.24. We now proceed to prove the Assmus-Mattson theorem. Let T be any set of t coordinate positions, and let C^T denote the code of length $n-t$ obtained from C by puncturing on T. Let $C^\perp(T)$ be the subcode of $C^\perp$ that is zero on T, and let $(C^\perp)_T$ be the code $C^\perp$ shortened on T. A pictorial illustration of the relations among these codes is below:

$$
\begin{array}{ccc}
[n,k,d],\ A_i & \longleftrightarrow & [n,n-k,d^\perp],A_i^\perp \\
C & & C^\perp \\
\updownarrow & & \updownarrow \\
C^T & & (C^T)^\perp = (C^\perp)_T \\
[n-t,k,d^T],\ A_i' & \longleftrightarrow & [n-t,n-t-k,(d^T)^\perp],\ A_i'^\perp
\end{array}
$$

Since $t < d$, it follows from Theorem 2.8 that C^T is an $[n-t,k,d^T]$ code with $d^T \geq d-t$ and $(C^T)^\perp = (C^\perp)_T$.

Let $A_i' = A_i(C^T)$ and $A_i'^\perp = A_i((C^T)^\perp) = A_i((C^\perp)_T)$, for $0 \leq i \leq n-t$, be the weight distributions of C^T and $(C^T)^\perp$, respectively. Since $s \leq d-t \leq d^T$, we have that $A_i' = 0$ for $1 \leq i \leq s-1$. If $S = \{i : A_i^\perp \neq 0, 0 < i \leq n-t\}$, then the $A_i'^\perp$ are unknown only for $i \in S$, as $A_i'^\perp \leq A_i^\perp$ and $|S| = s$. These facts about A_i' and $A_i'^\perp$ are independent of the choice of the elements in T. By Theorem 2.6, there is a unique solution for all A_i' and $A_i'^\perp$, which must therefore be the same for each set T of size t. The weight distribution of $C^\perp(T)$ is the same as that of $(C^\perp)_T$. Hence, the weight distribution of $C^\perp(T)$ is the same for all T of size t.

Let $\mathcal{B}$ be the set of supports of the codewords of weight d in C. Let T be a set of size t. The codewords of weight d in C, whose support contains T, is in one-to-one correspondence with the codewords of weight $d-t$ in C^T. There are A_{d-t}' such codewords in C^T and hence $A_{d-t}'/(q-1)$ blocks containing T in $\mathcal{B}$ by Lemma 4.25. Thus the codewords of weight d in C hold a t-design.

The rest of Part (i) is then proved by induction as follows. Assume that the codewords of weight x in C with $A_x \neq 0$ and $d \leq x \leq z-1 < w$, for some integer z, hold t-designs. Suppose the intersection numbers of these designs are $\lambda_{(i,j)}(x)$ (see Section 4.1.5 for the definition and properties of intersection numbers). If $d \leq x \leq z-1 < w$ but $A_x = 0$, set $\lambda_{(i,j)}(x) = 0$. By Lemma 4.25, the value w has been chosen to be the largest possible weight so that a codeword of weight w

or less in C is determined uniquely up to scalar multiplication by its support. If $A_z \neq 0$, we show that the codewords of weight z in C hold a t-design. Suppose that there are $N(T)$ codewords of weight z in C whose support contains T. Every codeword of weight z in C whose support contains T is associated with a codeword of weight $z - t$ in C^T. However, every codeword of weight $z - t$ in C^T is associated with a codeword of weight $z - \ell$ in C whose support intersects T in a set of size $t - \ell$ for $0 \le \ell \le z - d$. It then follows from the definition of intersection numbers, the induction hypothesis and Lemma 4.25 that

$$A'_{z-t} = N(T) + (q-1) \sum_{\ell=1}^{z-d} \binom{t}{\ell} \lambda_{(t-\ell, \ell)} (z - \ell).$$

Therefore, $N(T)$ is independent of the elements in T. Hence, the codewords of weight z hold a t-design. Thus, Part (i) holds by induction.

Let $d^\perp \le i \le \min\{n - t, w^\perp\}$. The codewords of weight $w^\perp$ or less in $C^\perp$ are determined uniquely up to scalar multiplication by their supports by Lemma 4.25. Let $\mathcal{B}$ be the set of all supports of the codewords of weight i in $C^\perp$, and let $\mathcal{B}'$ be their complements. Let $\mathcal{B}'_T$ be the set of blocks in $\mathcal{B}'$ that contain T. These blocks are in one-to-one correspondence with the supports of the codewords of weight i which are zero on T, i.e., codewords of weight i in $C^\perp(T)$. The number of blocks in $\mathcal{B}'_T$ is independent of the specific elements in T, as the weight distribution of $C^\perp(T)$ is independent of the elements in T. Therefore, $|\mathcal{B}'_T|$ is independent of the elements of T, and $\mathcal{B}'$ is the set of blocks in a t-design. Hence, $\mathcal{B}$ is the set of blocks in a t-design. This proves Part (ii).   □

A different proof of Theorem 4.24 is given in the proof of Theorem 16.3, which gives a better understanding of the Assmus-Mattson Theorem.

The Assmus-Mattson Theorem applied to C is most useful when $C^\perp$ has only a few nonzero weights. It has been one of the two tools for discovering designs in linear codes. When $q = 2$, Theorem 4.24 becomes the following.

Corollary 4.26 (Assmus-Mattson). *Let C be an $[n, k, d]$ binary code, and let $d^\perp$ denote the minimum distance of $C^\perp$. Let $(A_i)_{i=0}^n$ and $(A_i^\perp)_{i=0}^n$ denote the weight distribution of C and $C^\perp$, respectively. Fix a positive integer t with $t < d$, and let s be the number of i with $A_i^\perp \neq 0$ for $1 \le i \le n - t$. Suppose $s \le d - t$. Then*

- *the codewords of weight i in C hold a t-design provided $A_i \neq 0$ and $d \le i \le n$, and*
- *the codewords of weight i in $C^\perp$ hold a t-design provided $A_i^\perp \neq 0$ and $d^\perp \le i \le n - t$.*

The next theorem will be employed frequently later [MacWilliams and Sloane (1977)][p. 165], and is documented also as Corollary 16.25 with a different proof.

Theorem 4.27. *Let C be an $[n,k,d]$ binary linear code with $k > 1$, such that for each weight $w > 0$ the supports of the codewords of weight w form a t-design, where $t < d$. Then the supports of the codewords of each nonzero weight in $C^{\perp}$ also form a t-design.*

The following theorem may strengthen the Assmus-Mattson Theorem (i.e., Corollary 4.26) [MacWilliams and Sloane (1977)][p. 166]. It is also a special case of Theorem B.8.

Theorem 4.28. *Let C be an $[n,k,d]$ binary code. Let $(A_i)_{i=0}^n$ and $(A_i^{\perp})_{i=0}^n$ be the weight distribution of C and $C^{\perp}$, respectively. Let s and $s^{\perp}$ be the total number of nonzero weights in C and $C^{\perp}$, respectively. Define*

$$\bar{s} = \begin{cases} s & \text{if } A_n = 0, \\ s-1 & \text{if } A_n = 1 \end{cases}$$

and

$$\overline{s^{\perp}} = \begin{cases} s^{\perp} & \text{if } A_n^{\perp} = 0, \\ s^{\perp} - 1 & \text{if } A_n^{\perp} = 1. \end{cases}$$

If either $\bar{s} < d^{\perp}$ or $\overline{s^{\perp}} < d$, then the supports of the codewords of weight w in C form a t-design, where

$$t = \max\{d^{\perp} - \bar{s}, d - \overline{s^{\perp}}\},$$

provided that $t < d$.

The construction of support designs from linear codes goes back at least to Paige (1956), where he obtained two Steiner systems from linear subspaces (i.e., linear codes), though Paige did not use the language of coding theory. Perhaps the first explicit construction of designs from codes was in Bose (1961). In 1996, Assmus and Mattson followed the course Paige started in 1956, and constructed several Steiner systems. These investigations eventually led them to the discovery of the Assmus-Mattson theorem documented in Assmus and Mattson (1969), where Steiner systems were also reported.

4.3.2 *MDS Codes and Complete Designs*

MDS codes can be characterised by designs as follows [Assmus and Mattson (1969)].

Theorem 4.29. *A linear code is MDS if and only if the supports of the minimum weight codewords form a complete design.*

Proof. Let C be a code of length n. The coordinate functions f_i, $0 \le i \le n - 1$, are defined by

$$f_i((c_0, c_1, \ldots, c_{n-1})) = c_i.$$

Suppose that C is an $[n, k, d]$ code over $\mathrm{GF}(q)$ such that the supports of all codewords of weight d form a complete design. Then every d-subset of coordinate places holds a codeword. We wish to prove that $d = n - k + 1$. Consider now the subcode C_1 of C spanned by the minimum weight codewords. Then every subset of d coordinate functions of the dual code $C_1^\perp$ are linearly dependent, but no subset of size $d - 1$ has this property. Therefore, $C_1^\perp$ has dimension $d - 1$. Consequently, C_1 has dimension $n - (d - 1)$. Since C_1 is a subcode of C, $n - (d - 1) \le k$. The reverse inequality follows from the Singleton bound. As a result, $n - (d - 1) = k$. This means that C is MDS.

Conversely, suppose that $d = n - (k - 1)$. Then every k coordinate functions are linearly independent. Given a d-subset of coordinate functions, we consider the $n - d = k - 1$ functions of the complementary subset. The intersection of the kernels of these is non-0. Hence, there is a nonzero codeword with Hamming weight at most d and such that the coordinates are 0 in the complementary subset. Therefore, this codeword must have Hamming weight d and have the given d-subset of coordinates as its support. Consequently, the supports of all codewords of weight d form a complete design. $\qquad\qquad\square$

One can prove that all support designs of MDS codes are complete, which are trivial and not interesting. However, some MDS codes can be used to construct hyperoval designs in a different way (see Chapter 13). Thus, support designs are just one way to obtain designs from linear codes. There are other ways to construct designs with linear codes.

4.3.3 *Constructing Designs from Related Binary Codes*

The objective of this section is to present an idea of constructing t-designs from binary linear codes. Let C be a binary linear code with a few weights. If C holds t-designs, so may $C^\perp$, $\overline{C^\perp}$, and $\overline{C^\perp}^\perp$. The idea goes as follows.

(a) We chose C with only a few weights and known weight distribution.
(b) We derive the weight distribution of $C^\perp$ from that of C with the MacWilliams Identity.
(c) We employ the Assmus-Mattson Theorem to prove that C and $C^\perp$ hold t-designs if C was chosen properly.

(d) We derive the weight distribution of $\overline{C^\perp}^\perp$ from that of C with the help of Theorem 2.10 and the Pless Power Moments.
(e) We derive the weight distribution of $\overline{C^\perp}$ from that of $\overline{C^\perp}^\perp$ with the MacWilliams Identity.
(f) We finally prove that $\overline{C^\perp}$ and $\overline{C^\perp}^\perp$ hold $(t+1)$-designs with the Assmus-Mattson Theorem.

A pictorial description of the process is the following:

$$C^\perp \Longleftarrow C$$
$$\Downarrow$$
$$\overline{C^\perp} \Longleftarrow \overline{C^\perp}^\perp$$

The key to the success of this idea is to find out the right binary linear code C. We will get back to this idea in some subsequent chapters.

4.4   Designs of Codes with Special Automorphism Groups

Recall now the automorphism group $\mathrm{Aut}(C)$ and the permutation group $\mathrm{Autpr}(C)$ defined in Section 2.8. Every element in $\mathrm{Aut}(C)$ is of the form $DP\gamma$, where D is a diagonal matrix, P is a permutation matrix, and γ is a field automorphism. We say that $\mathrm{Aut}(C)$ is *t-homogeneous* (respectively, *t-transitive*) if for every pair of t-element sets of coordinates (respectively, t-element ordered sets of coordinates), there is an element $DP\gamma$ of the automorphism group $\mathrm{Autpr}(C)$ such that its permutation part P sends the first set to the second set, i.e., there is an element P in $\mathrm{Autpr}(C)$ such that P sends the first set to the second set.

Our objective in this section is to introduce and prove the following theorem, which will be employed in some of the subsequent chapters for constructing t-designs from codes.

Theorem 4.30. *Let C be a code of length n over $\mathrm{GF}(q)$ where $\mathrm{Aut}(C)$ is t-homogeneous or t-transitive. Then the codewords of any weight $i \geq t$ of C hold a t-design.*

Proof. Let $\mathcal{P}$ be the set of coordinates of the code and $\mathcal{B}$ the set of supports of the codewords of weight i in C. Consider now all t-subsets of $\mathcal{P}$. Let $T_1 = \{j_1, j_2, \ldots, j_t\} \subseteq \mathcal{P}$ be one that is contained in the maximum number λ of blocks in $\mathcal{B}$. Suppose that these distinct blocks are $B_1, B_2, \ldots, B_\lambda$, which are the supports of the codewords $\mathbf{c}_1, \mathbf{c}_2, \ldots, \mathbf{c}_\lambda$, respectively. Let T_2 be any other t-element subset of $\mathcal{P}$. Then there exists an automorphism g of C whose permutation part maps T_1 to T_2 by definition. The codewords $g(\mathbf{c}_1), g(\mathbf{c}_2), \ldots, g(\mathbf{c}_\lambda)$, have distinct supports, which are blocks of $\mathcal{B}$. Hence, T_2 is contained in these λ blocks. The maximality of λ shows that T_2 is in no more than λ blocks. It then follows that T_2 is contained in exactly λ blocks in $\mathcal{B}$. Hence $(\mathcal{P}, \mathcal{B})$ is a t-(n, i, λ) design.   □

It will be seen in later chapters that determining the parameters of some t-designs could be harder than proving their design property. For instance, one may be able to prove that the automorphism group of a linear code is 2-transitive or 2-homogeneous, and thus have proved that the code holds 2-designs. However, it may be extremely difficult to determine the parameters k and λ in the 2-(v, k, λ) designs.

4.5   Designs from Finite Geometries

Though this monograph is focused on designs from codes, we need to introduce two families of 2-designs from finite geometries, as they are related to designs from codes.

Recall the affine geometry $\mathrm{AG}(m, \mathrm{GF}(q))$, where the points are the vectors in the vector space $\mathrm{GF}(q)^m$, the lines are the cosets of all the one-dimensional subspaces, the planes are the cosets of the two-dimensional subspaces, the i-flats are the cosets of the i-dimensional subspaces, and the hyperplanes are the cosets of the $(m-1)$-dimensional subspaces of $\mathrm{GF}(q)^m$ (see Section 1.6.2). The d-flats of $\mathrm{GF}(q)^m$ can be employed to construct 2-designs.

Theorem 4.31. *Let $\mathcal{B}$ denote the sets of all d-flats in $\mathrm{GF}(q)^m$, and $\mathcal{P}$ the set of all vectors in $\mathrm{GF}(q)^m$, and $\mathcal{R}$ the containment relation. Then the triple $\mathrm{AG}_d(m, \mathrm{GF}(q)) := (\mathcal{P}, \mathcal{B}, \mathcal{R})$ is 2-(v, k, λ) design, where*

$$v = q^m, \ k = q^d, \ \lambda = \begin{bmatrix} m-1 \\ d-1 \end{bmatrix}_q,$$

and the Gaussian coefficients are defined by

$$\begin{bmatrix} n \\ i \end{bmatrix}_q = \frac{(q^n - 1)(q^{n-1} - 1) \cdots (q^{n-i+1} - 1)}{(q^i - 1)(q^{i-1} - 1) \cdots (q - 1)}.$$

In addition, the number of blocks in this design is

$$b = q^{m-d} \begin{bmatrix} m \\ d \end{bmatrix}_q.$$

In particular, $\mathrm{AG}_1(m, \mathrm{GF}(q))$ is a Steiner system $S(2, q, q^m)$. When $d \geq 2$, $\mathrm{AG}_d(m, \mathrm{GF}(2))$ is a 3-design. In particular, $\mathrm{AG}_2(m, \mathrm{GF}(2))$ is a Steiner system $S(3, 4, 2^m)$.

Proof. It is straightforward to see that the group $\mathrm{GA}_m(\mathrm{GF}(q))$ is a subgroup of the automorphism group of the incidence structure $\mathrm{AG}_d(m, \mathrm{GF}(q))$. The desired conclusions on the design property then follow from Theorems 1.77 and 1.78 with an argument similar to the proof of Theorem 4.30. By Theorem 1.41, the number of blocks in the design $\mathrm{AG}_d(m, \mathrm{GF}(q))$ is equal to $q^{m-d} \begin{bmatrix} m \\ d \end{bmatrix}_q$. The desired conclusion on the parameters of the design then follows. $\square$

By adding a new point to $\mathrm{AG}_1(m, \mathrm{GF}(q))$, the Steinter system $\mathrm{AG}_1(m, \mathrm{GF}(q))$ can be extended into a Steiner system $S(3, q+1, q^m+1)$ [Key and Wagner (1986)].

Example 4.32. Consider now the 2-design $\mathrm{AG}_1(2, \mathrm{GF}(q))$. Its point set is $\mathrm{GF}(q)^2$. The blocks are the lines

$$L_{(a,b,c)} = \{(x,y) \in \mathrm{GF}(q)^2 : ax + by + c = 0\},$$

where $(a,b,c) \in \mathrm{GF}(q)^3$ and $(a,b) \neq (0,0)$. These lines are classified into the following two types:

- Those with $a = 0$ and $b \neq 0$ (horizontal lines): There are q such lines defined by

$$L_{(0,b,c)} = \{(x,y) \in \mathrm{GF}(q)^2 : y + c/b = 0\}, \ c/b \in \mathrm{GF}(q).$$

- Those with $a \neq 0$ (slope lines): There are q^2 such lines defined by

$$L_{(1,b/a,c/a)} = \left\{(x,y) \in \mathrm{GF}(q)^2 : x + \frac{b}{a}y + \frac{c}{a} = 0\right\}, \ (b/a, c/a) \in \mathrm{GF}(q)^2.$$

The total number of distinct lines is $q^2 + q$. $\mathrm{AG}_1(2, \mathrm{GF}(q))$ is a Steiner system with parameters 2-$(q^2, q, 1)$.

In particular, let $q = 2$. Then $\mathrm{AG}_1(2, \mathrm{GF}(2))$ has point set

$$\mathcal{P} = \{(00), (01), (10), (11)\}$$

and line set

$$\mathcal{B} = \{\{(10), (00)\}, \{(11), (00)\}, \{(11), (10)\},$$
$$\{(11), (01)\}, \{(01), (10)\}, \{(01), (00)\}\}. \tag{4.14}$$

We now look further into the design $\mathrm{AG}_1(2, \mathrm{GF}(2))$ in Example 4.32. The block set $\mathcal{B}$ in (4.14) can be partitioned into $\{\mathcal{B}_1, \mathcal{B}_2, \mathcal{B}_3\}$, where

$$\mathcal{B}_1 = \{\{(10), (00)\}, \{(11), (01)\}\},$$
$$\mathcal{B}_2 = \{\{(11), (00)\}, \{(01), (10)\}\},$$
$$\mathcal{B}_3 = \{\{(11), (10)\}, \{(01), (00)\}\}.$$

Note that each $\mathcal{B}_i$ (called *parallel class*) is a partition of the point set $\mathcal{P}$, and consists of two blocks. Such design is said to be *resolvable*.

In formal words, a design is *resolvable* if its block set $\mathcal{B}$ could be partitioned into r subsets (called *parallel classes*), each consisting of b/r disjoint blocks and partitioning the point set. Resolvable designs have many applications. However, we will not discuss their applications in this monograph.

The projective space $\mathrm{PG}(m-1,\mathrm{GF}(q))$ and its d-flats were defined in Section 1.6.1. Similarly, the d-flats in the projective geometry $\mathrm{PG}(m-1,\mathrm{GF}(q))$ form a 2-design, which is documented below.

Theorem 4.33. *Let $\mathcal{B}$ denote the set of all d-flats in $\mathrm{PG}(m-1,\mathrm{GF}(q))$, and $\mathcal{P}$ the point set of $\mathrm{PG}(m-1,\mathrm{GF}(q))$, and $\mathcal{R}$ the containment relation. Then the triple $\mathrm{PG}_d(m-1,\mathrm{GF}(q)) := (\mathcal{P},\mathcal{B},\mathcal{R})$ is a 2-(v,k,λ) design, where*

$$v = \frac{q^m-1}{q-1}, \ k = \frac{q^{d+1}-1}{q-1}, \ \lambda = \begin{bmatrix} m-2 \\ d-1 \end{bmatrix}_q.$$

In addition, the number of blocks in this design is

$$b = \begin{bmatrix} m \\ d+1 \end{bmatrix}_q.$$

In particular, $\mathrm{PG}_1(m-1,\mathrm{GF}(q))$ is a Steiner system $S(2,q+1,(q^m-1)/(q-1))$, and $\mathrm{PG}_{m-2}(m-1,\mathrm{GF}(q))$ is a symmetric design with parameters

$$2 - \left(\frac{q^m-1}{q-1}, \ \frac{q^{m-1}-1}{q-1}, \ \frac{q^{m-2}-1}{q-1} \right)$$

for $m \geq 3$.

Proof. Clearly, the group $\mathrm{PGL}_m(\mathrm{GF}(q))$ is a subgroup of the automorphism group of the incidence structure $\mathrm{PG}_d(m-1,\mathrm{GF}(q))$. The design property then follows from Theorem 1.83 with an argument similar to the proof of Theorem 4.30. The desired conclusion on the parameters of the design then follows from Theorem 1.39 and (1.22).   □

The Steiner system $\mathrm{PG}_1(m-1,\mathrm{GF}(4))$ with parameters $S(2,5,(4^m-1)/3)$ can be extended into a Steiner system $S(3,6,(4^m+2)/3)$ for every $m \geq 3$ [Assmus and Key (1986)].

General affine planes were discussed in Section 1.6.6. We have the following result about finite affine planes [Ionin and Shrikhande (2006)][p. 63].

Theorem 4.34. *An affine plane of order n is a 2-$(n^2,n,1)$ design. Conversely, for $n \geq 2$, any 2-$(n^2,n,1)$ design is an affine plane.*

General projective planes were introduced in Section 1.6.3. Similarly, we have the following conclusion about finite projective planes [Ionin and Shrikhande (2006)][p. 73].

Theorem 4.35. *Any projective plane of order n is a 2-$(n^2+n+1, n+1, 1)$ design. Conversely, any 2-$(n^2+n+1, n+1, 1)$ design with $n \geq 2$ is a projective plane.*

The reader may work out a proof for the two theorems above, which should be an easy task.

4.6 The Codes of Geometric Designs

In the preceding section, we treated the designs of the affine geometry $\mathrm{AG}(m, \mathrm{GF}(q))$ and projective geometry $\mathrm{PG}(m-1, \mathrm{GF}(q))$. In this section, we briefly describe the classical codes of the geometric designs. Throughout the whole section, let q be a prime. Notice that every integer i with $0 \leq i \leq q^m - 1$ has the q-adic expression

$$i = i_0 + i_1 q + \cdots + i_{m-1} q^{m-1},$$

where each $i_j \in \{0, 1, \ldots, q-1\}$. The q-weight of i, denoted by $\mathrm{wt}_q(i)$, is defined by

$$\mathrm{wt}_q(i) = i_0 + i_1 + \cdots + i_{m-1}.$$

4.6.1 *The Codes of the Designs of the Affine Geometry*

Recall that q is a prime throughout this section. Let $t \geq 0$ be an integer with $t = a(q-1) + b \leq m(q-1)$, where $0 \leq b \leq q-1$. We define a cyclic code M^t over $\mathrm{GF}(q)$ with length $q^m - 1$ and defining set

$$\{i : 0 \leq i \leq q^m - 1, \mathrm{wt}_q(i) < t\}.$$

Let $\overline{\mathsf{M}^t}$ denote the extended code of M^t. The following theorem was proved in Assmus and Key (1998).

Theorem 4.36. *Let $0 \leq r \leq m$. The code $\overline{\mathsf{M}^t}$ over $\mathrm{GF}(q)$ has length q^m, dimension*

$$|\{i : 0 \leq i \leq q^m - 1, \mathrm{wt}_q(i) \leq m(q-1) - t\}|$$

and minimum weight $(b+1)q^a$, where $t = a(q-1) + b$ and $0 \leq b < q-1$.

The main result of this section is the following whose proof can be found in Assmus and Key (1998).

Theorem 4.37. *Let* $0 \leq r \leq m$. *The code* $C_{\mathrm{GF}(q)}(\mathrm{AG}_r(m, \mathrm{GF}(q)))$ *of the design* $\mathrm{AG}_r(m, \mathrm{GF}(q))$ *of points and r-flats of the affine geometry* $\mathrm{AG}(m, \mathrm{GF}(q))$ *is the code* $\mathsf{M}^{r(q-1)}$ *with minimum weight* q^r *and dimension*

$$|\{i : 0 \leq i \leq q^m - 1, \ \mathtt{wt}_q(i) \leq (m-r)(q-1)\}|.$$

As corollaries of Theorem 4.37, we have the next two results.

Corollary 4.38. *The code* $C_{\mathrm{GF}(q)}(\mathrm{AG}_{m-1}(m, \mathrm{GF}(q)))$ *of the geometric design* $\mathrm{AG}_{m-1}(m, \mathrm{GF}(q))$ *of points and* $(m-1)$-*flats of the affine geometry* $\mathrm{AG}(m, \mathrm{GF}(q))$ *has length* q^m, *minimum weight* q^{m-1} *and dimension* $\binom{m+q-1}{m}$.

Corollary 4.39. *The code* $C_{\mathrm{GF}(q)}(\mathrm{AG}_1(m, \mathrm{GF}(q)))$ *of the geometric design* $\mathrm{AG}_1(m, \mathrm{GF}(q))$ *of points and lines of the affine geometry* $\mathrm{AG}(m, \mathrm{GF}(q))$ *has length* q^m, *minimum weight* q *and dimension* $q^m - \binom{m+q-2}{m}$.

In particular, the code $C_{\mathrm{GF}(3)}(\mathrm{AG}_1(m, \mathrm{GF}(3)))$ *of the Steiner triple system of points and lines of* $\mathrm{AG}(m, \mathrm{GF}(3))$ *has parameters* $[3^m, 3^m - 1 - m, 3]$.

In Chapter 5, we will prove that $C_{\mathrm{GF}(2)}(\mathrm{AG}_r(m, \mathrm{GF}(2)))$ is the binary Reed-Muller code $\mathcal{R}_2(m-r, m)$ of order $m-r$. Below is an example of the case that q is not a prime.

Example 4.40. The binary code $C_{\mathrm{GF}(2)}(\mathrm{AG}_1(2, \mathrm{GF}(4)))$ has parameters $[16, 9, 4]$ and weight enumerator

$$1 + 20z^4 + 160z^6 + 150z^8 + 160z^{10} + 20z^{12} + z^{16}.$$

Its dual has parameters $[16, 7, 6]$ and weight enumerator

$$1 + 48z^6 + 30z^8 + 48z^{10} + z^{16}.$$

4.6.2 The Codes of the Designs of the Projective Geometry

Throughout this section, q is a prime. Let $m \geq 2$. A point of the projective geometry $\mathrm{PG}(m-1, \mathrm{GF}(q))$ is given in homogeneous coordinates by $(x_0, x_1, \ldots, x_{m-1})$ where all x_i are in $\mathrm{GF}(q)$ and are not all zero; each point has $q-1$ coordinate representations, since $(ax_0, ax_1, \ldots, ax_{m-1})$ and $(x_0, x_1, \ldots, x_{m-1})$ yield the same 1-dimensional subspace of $\mathrm{GF}(q)^m$ for any non-zero $a \in \mathrm{GF}(q)$.

For an integer $r \geq 0$, let $\mathrm{PP}(r, m-1, q)$ denote the linear subspace of $\mathrm{GF}(q)[x_0, x_1, \ldots, x_{m-1}]$ that is spanned by all monomial $x_0^{i_0} x_1^{i_1} \cdots x_{m-1}^{i_{m-1}}$ satisfying the following two conditions:

- $\sum_{j=0}^{m-1} i_j \equiv 0 \pmod{q-1}$,
- $0 < \sum_{j=0}^{m-1} i_j \leq r(q-1)$.

Each $a \in \mathrm{GF}(q)$ is viewed as the constant function $f_a(x_0, x_1, \ldots, x_{m-1}) \equiv a$.

Let $\{\mathbf{x}^1, \ldots, \mathbf{x}^N\}$ be the set of projective points in $\mathrm{PG}(m-1, q)$, where $N = \frac{q^m-1}{q-1}$. Then, the *rth order projective generalized Reed-Muller code* $\mathrm{PRM}(r, m-1, q)$ of length $\frac{q^m-1}{q-1}$ is defined by

$$\mathrm{PRM}(r, m-1, q) = \left\{ \left(f(\mathbf{x}^1), \ldots, f(\mathbf{x}^N) \right) : f \in \mathrm{PP}(r, m-1, q) \cup \mathrm{GF}(q) \right\}.$$

When $r > 1$, let $\mathrm{PRM}^*(r, m-1, q)$ be the subcode of $\mathrm{PRM}(r, m-1, q)$ defined by

$$\mathrm{PRM}^*(r, m-1, q) = \left\{ \left(f(\mathbf{x}^1), \ldots, f(\mathbf{x}^N) \right) : f \in \mathrm{PP}(r, m-1, q) \right\}.$$

Thus, $\mathrm{PRM}^*(r, m-1, q)$ is a subcode of $\mathrm{PRM}(r, m-1, q)$. For the minimum weight and the dual of the projective generalized Reed-Muller code, we have the following [Assmus and Key (1998)].

Theorem 4.41. *Let* $0 \leq r \leq m-1$. *Then, the minimal weight of* $\mathrm{PRM}(r, m-1, q)$ *is* $\frac{q^{m-r}-1}{q-1}$ *and*

$$\mathrm{PRM}(r, m-1, q)^{\perp} = \mathrm{PRM}^*(m-1-r, m-1, q).$$

The relation between the codes $C_{\mathrm{GF}(q)}(\mathrm{PG}_{r-1}(m-1, \mathrm{GF}(q)))$ of the designs of projective geometries and the projective generalized Reed-Muller codes is given as follows [Assmus and Key (1998)].

Theorem 4.42. *Let* m *be a positive integer,* q *a prime, and* $0 \leq r \leq m$.

(i) The code $C_{\mathrm{GF}(q)}(\mathrm{PG}_{r-1}(m-1, \mathrm{GF}(q)))$ from the design of points and projective $(r-1)$-dimensional subspaces of the projective geometry $\mathrm{PG}(m-1, \mathrm{GF}(q))$ is the same as $\mathrm{PRM}(m-r, m-1, q)$ up to a permutation of coordinates.

(ii) $C_{\mathrm{GF}(q)}(\mathrm{PG}_{r-1}(m-1, \mathrm{GF}(q)))$ has minimum weight $\frac{q^r-1}{q-1}$ and the minimum-weight vectors are the multiples of the characteristic vectors of the blocks.

(iii) The dual code $C_{\mathrm{GF}(q)}(\mathrm{PG}_{r-1}(m-1, \mathrm{GF}(q)))^{\perp}$ is the same as $\mathrm{PRM}^*(r-1, m-1, q)$ up to a permutation of coordinates and has minimum weight at least $\frac{q^{m-r+1}-1}{q-1} + 1$.

(iv) The dimension of the code $C_{\mathrm{GF}(q)}(\mathrm{PG}_{r-1}(m-1, \mathrm{GF}(q)))$ is

$$\frac{q^m-1}{q-1} - \sum_{i=0}^{r-2} (-1)^i \binom{(r-1-i)(q-1)-1}{i} \binom{m-r+(r-1-i)q}{m-1-i}.$$

In Chapter 5, we will prove that $C_{\mathrm{GF}(2)}(\mathrm{PG}_r(m, \mathrm{GF}(2)))$ is a punctured binary Reed-Muller code. Below is an example of the codes in the case that q is not a prime.

Example 4.43. The binary code $C_{GF(2)}(PG_1(2, GF(4)))$ has parameters $[21, 10, 5]$ and weight enumerator

$$1 + 21z^5 + 210z^8 + 280z^9 + 280z^{12} + 210z^{13} + 21z^{16} + z^{21}.$$

Its dual has parameters $[21, 11, 6]$ and weight enumerator

$$1 + 168z^6 + 210z^8 + 1008z^{10} + 280z^{12} + 360z^{14} + 21z^{16}.$$

4.7 Spherical Geometry Designs

Let q be a power of a prime p, and let m be a positive integer. Recall that the points of $PG(1, GF(q^m))$ are given by

$$\mathcal{P} = \left\{ \begin{pmatrix} a \\ 1 \end{pmatrix} : a \in GF(q^m) \right\} \cup \left\{ \begin{pmatrix} 1 \\ 0 \end{pmatrix} \right\},$$

where $\begin{pmatrix} 1 \\ 0 \end{pmatrix}$ is usually denoted by ∞ and $\begin{pmatrix} a \\ 1 \end{pmatrix}$ is identified by a.

Let

$$A = \begin{bmatrix} a & c \\ b & d \end{bmatrix}$$

with $ad - bc \neq 0$, where $a, b, c, d \in GF(q^m)$. Let $\sigma_{(A,0)} = Ay \in PGL_2(GF(q^m))$ be the permutation defined with A, where $y \in GF(q^m)^2$. Then $\sigma_{(A,0)}$ acts on the point set $\mathcal{P}$ as

$$\sigma_{(A,0)}\left(\begin{pmatrix} x \\ 1 \end{pmatrix} \right) = \begin{cases} \begin{pmatrix} \frac{ax+c}{bx+d} \\ 1 \end{pmatrix} & \text{if } bx + d \neq 0, \\ \begin{pmatrix} 1 \\ 0 \end{pmatrix} & \text{otherwise,} \end{cases}$$

and

$$\sigma_{(A,0)}\left(\begin{pmatrix} 1 \\ 0 \end{pmatrix} \right) = \begin{cases} \begin{pmatrix} 1 \\ 0 \end{pmatrix} & \text{if } b = 0, \\ \begin{pmatrix} ab^{-1} \\ 1 \end{pmatrix} & \text{if } b \neq 0. \end{cases}$$

Put

$$B = \left\{ \begin{pmatrix} a \\ 1 \end{pmatrix} : a \in GF(q) \right\} \cup \left\{ \begin{pmatrix} 1 \\ 0 \end{pmatrix} \right\}$$

and

$$\mathcal{B} = \{ \sigma_{(A,0)}(B) : \sigma_{(A,0)} \in PGL_2(GF(q^m)) \}.$$

Note that B is a subset of $\mathcal{P}$ and $PGL_2(GF(q))$ is a subgroup of $PGL_2(GF(q^m))$.

Define $\mathbb{D} = (\mathcal{P}, \mathcal{B})$. Since $PGL_2(GF(q^m))$ acts 3-transitively on $\mathcal{P}$, $\mathbb{D}$ is a 3-$(q^m + 1, q + 1, \lambda)$ design for some λ. Since $PGL_2(GF(q^m))$ is sharply 3-transitive on $\mathcal{P}$ and $PGL_2(GF(q))$ is sharply 3-transitive on B, $PGL_2(GF(q))$ is the setwise stabiliser of B. Consequently, $\lambda = 1$. This has proved the following theorem.

Theorem 4.44. *Let notation be the same as before. Let $m \geq 2$. Then $\mathbb{D} = (\mathcal{P}, \mathcal{B})$ is a Steiner system $S(3, q + 1, q^m + 1)$.*

The design $\mathbb{D} = (\mathcal{P}, \mathcal{B})$ of Theorem 4.44 was constructed by Witt (1937), and is called a *spherical geometry design*. It is not isomorphic to the design with the same parameters proposed by Key and Wagner (1986). By the definition of the spherical geometry design, the full automorphism group of the design $\mathbb{D} = (\mathcal{P}, \mathcal{B})$ of Theorem 4.44 contains $\mathrm{PGL}_2(\mathrm{GF}(q^m))$. Experimental data indicates that $\mathrm{P\Gamma L}_2(\mathrm{GF}(q^m))$ is the full automorphism group of $\mathbb{D} = (\mathcal{P}, \mathcal{B})$. But a proof of this statement is missing. A coding-theory construction of the spherical geometry design will be presented in Section 15.5, where it will be shown that the p-rank of $\mathbb{D}$ is $q^m + 1$.

Example 4.45. Let $q = 3$ and $m = 2$. Let w be a generator of $\mathrm{GF}(3^2)^*$. Then the design $\mathbb{D} = (\mathcal{P}, \mathcal{B})$ of Theorem 4.44 has point set

$$\mathcal{P} = \{(0,1),(1,1),(w,1),(w^2,1),(w^3,1),(2,1),(w^5,1),(w^6,1),(w^7,1),(1,0)\}$$

here and hereafter the vector (a,b) is used to denote the column vector $\binom{a}{b}$. The block set is

$$
\begin{aligned}
\mathcal{B} = \{ &\{(2,1),(w,1),(w^6,1),(w^5,1)\}, \{(2,1),(w^2,1),(1,0),(w^5,1)\}, \\
&\{(2,1),(0,1),(1,0),(1,1)\}, \{(0,1),(w^2,1),(w^6,1),(1,0)\}, \\
&\{(w^3,1),(w^2,1),(w,1),(w^6,1)\}, \{(2,1),(w^3,1),(0,1),(w^6,1)\}, \\
&\{(w^2,1),(w,1),(1,1),(w^5,1)\}, \{(0,1),(w,1),(1,0),(w^5,1)\}, \\
&\{(w^2,1),(w^7,1),(w,1),(1,0)\}, \{(0,1),(w^7,1),(w,1),(w^6,1)\}, \\
&\{(w^3,1),(w^7,1),(w^6,1),(1,1)\}, \{(w^3,1),(0,1),(w^2,1),(w^5,1)\}, \\
&\{(0,1),(w^2,1),(w^7,1),(1,1)\}, \{(2,1),(w^3,1),(w^2,1),(w^7,1)\}, \\
&\{(w^3,1),(1,0),(w^6,1),(w^5,1)\}, \{(2,1),(w^7,1),(w,1),(1,1)\}, \\
&\{(2,1),(0,1),(w^7,1),(w^5,1)\}, \{(w,1),(w^6,1),(1,0),(1,1)\}, \\
&\{(2,1),(w^3,1),(w,1),(1,0)\}, \{(2,1),(w^7,1),(w^6,1),(1,0)\}, \\
&\{(w^3,1),(w^2,1),(1,0),(1,1)\}, \{(w^2,1),(w^7,1),(w^6,1),(w^5,1)\}, \\
&\{(2,1),(0,1),(w^2,1),(w,1)\}, \{(2,1),(w^3,1),(1,1),(w^5,1)\}, \\
&\{(w^7,1),(1,0),(1,1),(w^5,1)\}, \{(w^3,1),(w^7,1),(w,1),(w^5,1)\}, \\
&\{(w^3,1),(0,1),(w,1),(1,1)\}, \{(w^3,1),(0,1),(w^7,1),(1,0)\}, \\
&\{(2,1),(w^2,1),(w^6,1),(1,1)\}, \{(0,1),(w^6,1),(1,1),(w^5,1)\} \},
\end{aligned}
$$

where the base block is

$$B = \{(2,1),(0,1),(1,0),(1,1)\}.$$

$\mathbb{D} = (\mathcal{P}, \mathcal{B})$ is a Steiner quadruple system $S(3,4,10)$.

4.8 Notes

As mentioned at the beginning of this chapter, the focus of this monograph is the construction of simple t-designs with linear codes. The other direction, i.e., the construction of linear codes with combinatorial designs was gently touched in Sections 4.2.2 and 4.6. The reader is referred to Assmus and Key (1992a) and Assmus and Key (1998) for detailed information on the codes of geometric designs, and Ding (2015a) for information on codes of difference sets. There are many other references on the classical codes of designs.

The conditions in the Assmus-Mattson Theorem make use of only information on the minimum distance $d(C)$ and the weight distribution of $C^{\perp}$. It is not easy to understand why these conditions are sufficient. To have a better understanding of the Assmus-Mattson Theorem, the reader is suggested to read Chapter 16 right after reading this chapter. But one should keep in mind that t-designs in Chapter 16 may have repeated blocks or may be simple, while t-designs in the rest part of this monograph are simple (i.e., they do not have repeated blocks).

Chapter 5

Designs of Binary Reed-Muller Codes

In this chapter, we first treat binary Reed-Muller codes in details and then study their designs. Binary Reed-Muller codes are named after Reed (1954) and Muller (1954). These codes are of special interest, as they hold exponentially many 3-designs.

5.1 Binary Reed-Muller Codes and Their Relatives

We first introduce binary Reed-Muller codes and their punctured versions, and then prove their properties.

We begin with a *decreasing ordering* of the elements in $GF(2)^m$. We will then identify $GF(2)$ with $\{0,1\}$, where 0 and 1 are integers. Then $u = (u_0, u_1, \ldots, u_{m-1}) \in GF(2)^m$ is ordered as the $(2^m - n_u)$-th element in $GF(2)^m$, where

$$n_u = \sum_{i=0}^{m-1} u_i 2^i,$$

and each u_i is viewed as an integer. Thus, $(1,1,\ldots,1)$ and $(0,0,\ldots,0)$ are the first and last elements in $GF(2)^m$.

For example, $GF(2)^3$ is ordered as follows:

$$\begin{array}{c}
P_0\ P_1\ P_2\ P_3\ P_4\ P_5\ P_6\ P_7 \\
\bar{v}_3\ 1\ \ 1\ \ 1\ \ 1\ \ 0\ \ 0\ \ 0\ \ 0 \\
\bar{v}_2\ 1\ \ 1\ \ 0\ \ 0\ \ 1\ \ 1\ \ 0\ \ 0 \\
\bar{v}_1\ 1\ \ 0\ \ 1\ \ 0\ \ 1\ \ 0\ \ 1\ \ 0
\end{array} \qquad (5.1)$$

where $[P_0, P_1, \ldots, P_7]$ are the ordered elements in $GF(2)^3$, and $\bar{v}_i$ denotes the $(4 - i)$th row of the binary 3×8 matrix in (5.1).

In general, we use $P_0, P_1, \ldots, P_{2^m-1}$ to denote the ordered elements in $GF(2)^m$. When viewing P_i as a column vector and arranging them in the form of (5.1) as a binary $m \times 2^m$ matrix, we use $\bar{v}_i$ to denote the $(m-i)$th row of this matrix. We shall fix the notation throughout this section.

A function from $\mathrm{GF}(2)^m$ to $\mathrm{GF}(2)$ is called a *Boolean function*. Every Boolean function, $f(x) = f(x_1, \ldots, x_m)$, defines a vector $(f(x))_{x \in \mathrm{GF}(2)^m} \in \mathrm{GF}(2)^{2^m}$, where x ranges over all elements in $\mathrm{GF}(2)^m$ in the decreasing order. This vector is called the *truth table* of f, and denoted by $\mathbf{f}$.

The support of f, denoted by $\mathrm{Suppt}(f)$, is defined by

$$\mathrm{Suppt}(f) = \{x \in \mathrm{GF}(2)^m : f(x) = 1\} \subseteq \mathrm{GF}(2)^m.$$

By definition,

$$f(x) = \sum_{c \in \mathrm{Suppt}(f)} (x_1 + c_1 + 1)(x + c_2 + 1) \cdots (x + c_m + 1)$$

$$= f_0 + \sum_{t=1}^{m} \sum_{1 \le i_1 < \cdots < i_t \le m} f_{(i_1, \ldots, i_t)} x_{i_1} \cdots x_{i_t}, \tag{5.2}$$

where $c = (c_1, c_2, \ldots, c_m) \in \mathrm{GF}(2)^m$, $x = (x_1, x_2, \ldots, x_m)$, and $f_{(i_1, \ldots, i_t)} \in \mathrm{GF}(2)$. This means that any function f from $\mathrm{GF}(2)^m$ to $\mathrm{GF}(2)$ can be expressed as a linear combination of the following 2^m basis functions:

Basis functions	degree	total number
1	0	$\binom{m}{0}$
$x_i,\ 1 \le i \le m$	1	$\binom{m}{1}$
$x_i x_j,\ 1 \le i < j \le m$	2	$\binom{m}{2}$
$\vdots$	$\vdots$	$\vdots$
$x_{i_1} \cdots x_{i_r},\ 1 \le i_1 < \cdots < i_r \le m$	r	$\binom{m}{r}$
$\vdots$	$\vdots$	$\vdots$
$x_1 x_2 \cdots x_m$	m	$\binom{m}{m}$

The truth tables of these basis functions form a basis of $\mathrm{GF}(2)^{2^m}$ over $\mathrm{GF}(2)$. The expression in (5.2) is called the *algebraic normal form* of the Boolean function f.

The binary Reed-Muller code, denoted by $\mathcal{R}_2(r, m)$, is spanned by the truth tables of all the basis functions with degree at most r, where $0 \le r \le m$. Hence $\mathcal{R}_2(r, m)$ has dimension

$$\kappa = \sum_{i=0}^{r} \binom{m}{i}.$$

To determine the minimum distance of $\mathcal{R}_2(r, m)$, we prove the following.

Theorem 5.1.

$$\mathcal{R}_2(r+1, m+1) = \{(u, u+v) : u \in \mathcal{R}_2(r+1, m), v \in \mathcal{R}_2(r, m)\}.$$

Proof. Let f be a codeword in $\mathcal{R}_2(r+1, m+1)$. By definition, f is a Boolean function with degree at most $r+1$, and can be written as

$$f(x_1, x_2, \ldots, x_{m+1}) = g(x_1, x_2, \ldots, x_m) + x_{m+1}h(x_1, x_2, \ldots, x_m),$$

where g has degree at most $r+1$, and h has degree at most r. Let $\mathbf{g}$ and $\mathbf{h}$ be the vectors of length 2^m corresponding to $g(x_1, x_2, \ldots, x_m)$ and $g(x_1, x_2, \ldots, x_m)$. Clearly, $\mathbf{g} \in \mathcal{R}_2(r+1, m)$ and $\mathbf{h} \in \mathcal{R}_2(r, m)$. We now consider $g(x_1, x_2, \ldots, x_m)$ and $x_{m+1}h(x_1, x_2, \ldots, x_m)$ as polynomials in $x_1, x_2, \ldots, x_{m+1}$. Their corresponding vectors of length 2^{m+1} are $(\mathbf{g}, \mathbf{g})$ and $(\mathbf{0}, \mathbf{h})$. Consequently, $\mathbf{f} = (\mathbf{g}, \mathbf{g}) + (\mathbf{0}, \mathbf{h})$. $\square$

Let $G(r, m)$ be a generator matrix of $\mathcal{R}_2(r, m)$. Then Theorem 5.1 tells us that the generator matrix $G(r+1, m+1)$ of $\mathcal{R}_2(r+1, m+1)$ is given by

$$G(r+1, m+1) = \begin{bmatrix} G(r+1, m) & G(r+1, m) \\ 0 & G(r, m) \end{bmatrix}.$$

Theorem 5.2. $\mathcal{R}_2(r, m)$ *has minimum weight* 2^{m-r}.

Proof. By Theorem 5.1,

$$d(\mathcal{R}_2(r+1, m+1)) = \min\{2d(\mathcal{R}_2(r+1, m)), d(\mathcal{R}_2(r, m))\},$$

where $d(C)$ denotes the minimum distance of C. The desired conclusion then follows by induction on m. $\square$

The following statements on binary Reed-Muller codes are obviously true:

(a) $\mathcal{R}_2(0, m)$ consists of $\mathbf{0}$ and $\mathbf{1}$ only, and is the repetition code.
(b) $\mathcal{R}_2(m-1, m)$ consists of all even weight vectors in $GF(2)^{2^m}$.
(c) $\mathcal{R}_2(m, m) = GF(2)^{2^m}$.
(d) $\mathcal{R}_2(r, m)$ is a subcode of $\mathcal{R}_2(r+1, m)$ for all r with $0 \le r \le m-1$.

The duals of the Reed-Muller codes are related to the original family in the following way.

Theorem 5.3. $\mathcal{R}_2(r, m)^\perp = \mathcal{R}_2(m-r-1, m)$.

Proof. Let $\mathbf{a} \in \mathcal{R}_2(m-r-1, m)$ and $\mathbf{b} \in \mathcal{R}_2(r, m)$. Then $a(x_1, \ldots, x_m)$ is a polynomial of degree at most $m-r-1$, and $b(x_1, \ldots, x_m)$ is a polynomial of degree at most r. It follows that their product ab has degree at most $m-1$. Consequently, $\mathbf{ab} \in \mathcal{R}_2(m-1, m)$. Since all codewords in $\mathcal{R}_2(m-1, m)$ have even weights, $\mathbf{ab}$ has even weight. Consequently, the dot product $\mathbf{a} \cdot \mathbf{b} = 0$. Therefore, $\mathcal{R}_2(m-r-1, m) \subseteq \mathcal{R}_2(r, m)^\perp$. Note that

$$\dim(\mathcal{R}_2(m-r-1, m)) + \dim(\mathcal{R}_2(r, m)) = 2^m.$$

We deduce that $\mathcal{R}_2(m-r-1, m) = \mathcal{R}_2(r, m)^\perp$. $\square$

The error-correcting capability of Reed-Muller codes is not good, compared with binary BCH codes with the same dimensions. But binary Reed-Muller codes can be decoded efficiently with a majority logic decoding technique [MacWilliams and Sloane (1977)][Chapters 14 and 15].

Let $P(\mathrm{GF}(2)^m)$ denote the power set of $\mathrm{GF}(2)^m$. Let $\mathrm{BF}(m)$ denote the set of all Boolean functions with m variables. Then we have the following one-to-one correspondences among $\mathrm{GF}(2)^{2^m}$, $\mathrm{BF}(m)$ and $P(\mathrm{GF}(2)^m)$:

$$
\begin{array}{ccc}
\mathrm{GF}(2)^{2^m} \leftrightarrow & \mathrm{BF}(m) & \leftrightarrow P(\mathrm{GF}(2)^m) \\
\mathbf{f} & \leftrightarrow f(x_1,\ldots,x_m) \leftrightarrow & \mathrm{Suppt}(f),
\end{array}
\tag{5.3}
$$

where $\mathbf{f} \in \mathrm{GF}(2)^{2^m}$ is the truth table of f under the decreasing ordering of $\mathrm{GF}(2)^m$. Thus, every vector $\mathbf{f} \in \mathrm{GF}(2)^{2^m}$ corresponds to a subset $\mathrm{Suppt}(f)$ of $\mathrm{GF}(2)^m$ uniquely. In this case, $\mathbf{f} \in \mathrm{GF}(2)^{2^m}$ is called the *incidence vector* of $\mathrm{Suppt}(f)$ with respect to the ordered set $\mathrm{GF}(2)^m$ of 2^m points. It is obvious that

$$
\mathtt{wt}(\mathbf{f}) = |\mathrm{Suppt}(f)|,
$$

i.e., the Hamming weight of the vector $\mathbf{f}$ is equal to the cardinality of $\mathrm{Suppt}(f)$.

Thus, $\mathcal{R}_2(r,m)$ can be viewed as the set of all Boolean functions with degree at most r, and also a subset of $P(\mathrm{GF}(2)^m)$. This representation allows us to prove more properties of binary Reed-Muller codes with the languages of projective geometry and affine geometry (see Section 1.6).

The *affine geometry* $\mathrm{AG}(m,\mathrm{GF}(2))$ of dimension m employs the elements of $\mathrm{GF}(2)^m$ as its points. Any subset S of the points of $\mathrm{AG}(m,\mathrm{GF}(2))$ is associated with its incidence vector in $\mathrm{GF}(2)^{2^m}$. Recall the vectors $\bar{\mathsf{v}}_1, \bar{\mathsf{v}}_2, \ldots, \bar{\mathsf{v}}_m$ defined earlier. Let v_i denote the complement of $\bar{\mathsf{v}}_i$ for all $1 \leq i \leq m$. One can verify the following statements.

(1) The vectors v_i have Hamming weight 2^{m-1} and their images in $\mathrm{AG}(m,\mathrm{GF}(2))$ are subspaces of dimension $m-1$. Hence, these vectors are the incidence vectors of these hyperplanes which pass through the origin. (There are of course other hyperplanes passing through the origin.)

(2) The vectors $\mathsf{v}_i \mathsf{v}_j$ $(i \neq j)$ has Hamming weight 2^{m-2} and their images in $\mathrm{AG}(m,\mathrm{GF}(2))$ are subspaces of dimension $m-2$. Hence, these vectors are the incidence vectors of these subspaces which pass through the origin. (There are of course other subspaces of dimension $m-2$ passing through the origin.)

Shortly in this section, we will prove that the minimum weight codewords in $\mathcal{R}_2(r,m)$ are the incidence vectors of $(m-r)$-flats in $\mathrm{AG}(m,\mathrm{GF}(2))$, i.e., cosets of subspaces of dimension $m-r$ of $\mathrm{AG}(m,\mathrm{GF}(2))$. Of course, we can state and prove properties of the binary code $\mathcal{R}_2(r,m)$ without using geometric languages.

However, an advantage of using geometric languages is that it may give us a better understanding of some properties.

Lemma 5.4. *The incidence vector of any hyperplane in* $\text{AG}(m, \text{GF}(2))$ *is in* $\mathcal{R}_2(r, m)$ *for all* $1 \leq r \leq m$.

Let $\mathbf{f} \in \mathcal{R}_2(r, m)$ *be the incidence vector of a set* $S \in P(\text{GF}(2)^m)$. *Let* $\mathbf{h}$ *be the incidence vector of a hyperplane* H *in* $\text{AG}(m, \text{GF}(2))$. *Then* $\mathbf{fh} \in \mathcal{R}_2(r+1, m)$ *and is the incidence vector of* $S \cap H$.

Proof. We present two proofs of the conclusion in the first part. Let H be a hyperplane in $\text{AG}(m, \text{GF}(2))$. By definition, $H = H_0 + u$, where H_0 is an $(m-1)$-dimensional subspace of $\text{GF}(2)^m$ and $u \in \text{GF}(2)^m$. Let $h(x_1, \ldots, x_m)$ be the Boolean function with support H. Using the expression in (5.2), one can prove that $h(x_1, \ldots, x_m)$ is a linear combination of $x_1, x_2, \ldots, x_m$ and the constant Boolean function 1. The desired conclusion in the first part then follows from the tact that $\mathcal{R}_2(0, m)$ and $\mathcal{R}_2(1, m)$ are subcodes of $\mathcal{R}_2(r, m)$ for all r with $1 \leq r \leq m$.

The second proof of the conclusion in the first part goes as follows. By definition, any hyperplane H of $\text{AG}(m, \text{GF}(2))$ is the set of solutions $(x_1, x_2, \ldots, x_m) \in \text{GF}(2)^m$ of the equation

$$a_1 x_1 + a_2 x_2 + \cdots + a_m x_m + a_0 = 0,$$

where at least one of these $a_i \in \text{GF}(2)$ is nonzero. Hence, the Boolean function $h(x_1, \ldots, x_m)$ with support H is given by

$$h(x_1, \ldots, x_m) = a_1 x_1 + a_2 x_2 + \cdots + a_m x_m + a_0 + 1.$$

This means that the truth table $\mathbf{h} \in \mathcal{R}_2(1, m) \subset \mathcal{R}_2(r, m)$ for all $1 \leq r \leq m$.

Finally, we prove the conclusion of the second part. Since $\mathbf{f} \in \mathcal{R}_2(r, m)$, the Boolean function f corresponding to $\mathbf{f}$ has degree at most r and support S. Note that $h(x_1, \ldots, x_m)$ has degree 1 and support H. The Boolean function gf has degree at most $r + 1$ and support $S \cap H$. As a result, $\mathbf{fh} \in \mathcal{R}_2(r+1, m)$ and is the incidence vector of $S \cap H$. $\square$

The following lemma will play an important role later [Rothshild and Van Lint (1974)].

Lemma 5.5. *Let* S *be a subset of* $\text{AG}(m, \text{GF}(2))$ *such that* $|S| = 2^{m-r}$, *and* $|S \cap H| = 0, 2^{m-r-1}$ *or* 2^{m-r} *for all hyperplanes* H *in* $\text{AG}(m, \text{GF}(2))$. *Then* S *is an* $(m-r)$*-dimensional flat in* $\text{AG}(m, \text{GF}(2))$.

Proof. The proof is by induction on m. The conclusion is straightforward for $m = 2$.

Case 1: Suppose for some H we have $|S \cap H| = 2^{m-r}$. Then $S \subseteq H$, i.e, $S \subseteq$ AG$(m-1,\mathrm{GF}(2))$. Let X be any hyperplane in H. Then there exists another hyperplane H'' of AG$(m,\mathrm{GF}(2))$ such that $X = H \cap H''$, and $S \cap X = S \cap H''$, i.e., $|S \cap X| = 0$, $2^{m-1-(r-1)-1}$ or $2^{m-1-(r-1)}$. By the induction hypothesis, S is an $((m-1)-(r-1))$-flat in AG$(m-1,\mathrm{GF}(2))$ and hence in AG$(m,\mathrm{GF}(2))$.

Case 2: If for some H, $|S \cap H| = 0$, then replace S with its parallel hyperplane $S' := \mathrm{AG}(m,\mathrm{GF}(2)) \setminus S$. In this way, Case 2 is reduced to Case 1.

Case 3: We finally consider the case when $|S \cap H| = 2^{m-r-1}$ for all hyperplanes H. Let h denote the Boolean function with support H. Consider

$$\sum_{H \subset \mathrm{AG}(m,\mathrm{GF}(2))} |S \cap H|^2 = \sum_{H \subset \mathrm{AG}(m,\mathrm{GF}(2))} \left(\sum_{a \in S} h(a) \right)^2$$
$$= \sum_{a \in S} \sum_{b \in S} \sum_{H \subset \mathrm{AG}(m,\mathrm{GF}(2))} h(a)h(b)$$
$$= |S|(2^m - 1) + |S|(|S| - 1)(2^{m-1} - 1)$$

since there are $2^m - 1$ hyperplanes in AG$(m,\mathrm{GF}(2))$ though a point and $2^{m-1} - 1$ hyperplanes though a line. The left-hand side of the equation above is $2^{2m-2r-1}(2^m - 1)$. Substituting $|S| = 2^{m-r}$ onto the right-hand side leads to a contradiction. $\qquad \square$

We are now ready to prove the following.

Theorem 5.6. *Let $\mathbf{f}$ be a minimum weight codeword of $\mathcal{R}_2(r,m)$, and let S be the support of the Boolean function f corresponding to $\mathbf{f}$ (i.e., the truth table of f is $\mathbf{f}$ under the decreasing order defined earlier, or in other words, $\mathbf{f}$ is the incidence vector of S). Then S is an $(m-r)$-flat in AG$(m,\mathrm{GF}(2))$ (which need not pass through the origin).*

Proof. Let H be any hyperplane in AG$(m,\mathrm{GF}(2))$ and let H' be its parallel hyperplane, so that AG$(m,\mathrm{GF}(2)) = H \cup H'$. By Lemma 5.4, $S \cap H$ and $S \cap H'$ are in $\mathcal{R}_2(r+1,m)$, and so contain 0 or at least 2^{m-r-1} points. Since $|S| = 2^{m-r} = |S \cap H| + |S \cap H'|$, $|S \cap H| = 0$, 2^{m-r-1} or 2^{m-r}. The desired conclusion then follows from Lemma 5.5. $\qquad \square$

The converse of Theorem 5.6 is the following.

Theorem 5.7. *The incidence vector of any $(m-r)$-flat in AG$(m,\mathrm{GF}(2))$ is in $\mathcal{R}_2(r,m)$.*

Proof. We present two proofs here. The first one is a sketch and goes as follows. Let H be an $(m-r)$-flat in AG$(m,\mathrm{GF}(2))$. Then $H = H_0 + u$, where H_0 is an

$(m-r)$-dimensional subspace of $GF(2)^m$ and $u \in GF(2)^m$. Using the expression in (5.2), one can prove that the algebraic normal form of the Boolean function h with support H has degree at most r. It then follows that truth table of h (i.e., the incidence vector of H) is in $\mathcal{R}_2(r, m)$.

It is now time to present the second proof. By definition, any $(m-r)$-flat H in $AG(m, GF(2))$ consists of all points $x = (x_1, \ldots, x_m)$ that satisfy r linear equations over $GF(2)$, say

$$\sum_{j=1}^{m} a_{ij}x_i = b_i, \ i = 1, 2, \ldots, r,$$

or equivalently

$$\sum_{j=1}^{m} a_{ij}x_i + b_i + 1 = 1, \ i = 1, 2, \ldots, r.$$

This can be replaced by the following single equation

$$\prod_{i=1}^{r} \left(\sum_{j=1}^{m} a_{ij}x_i + b_i + 1 \right) = 1.$$

This means that the Boolean function

$$h(x_1, \ldots, x_m) := \prod_{i=1}^{r} \left(\sum_{j=1}^{m} a_{ij}x_i + b_i + 1 \right)$$

has support H and degree at most r. Hence, the truth table of h (i.e., the incidence vector of H) is in $\mathcal{R}_2(r, m)$. $\qquad\square$

Combining Theorems 5.6 and 5.7, we arrive at the following.

Theorem 5.8. *The codewords of minimum weight in $\mathcal{R}_2(r, m)$ are exactly all the incidence vectors of the $(m-r)$-dimensional flats in $AG(m, GF(2))$.*

The next theorem will be useful in determining the parameters of some 3-designs later.

Theorem 5.9. *The number of minimum weight codewords in $\mathcal{R}_2(r, m)$ is*

$$A_{2^{m-r}} = 2^r \prod_{i=0}^{m-r-1} \frac{2^{m-i} - 1}{2^{m-r-i} - 1}.$$

Proof. It follows from Theorems 5.8, 1.39 and 1.41. $\qquad\square$

For $0 \le r \le m-1$, the *punctured binary Reed-Muller code*, denoted by $\mathcal{R}_2(r,m)^*$, is obtained by puncturing (or deleting) the coordinate corresponding to $(x_1, x_2, \ldots, x_m) = \mathbf{0}$ from all the codewords in $\mathcal{R}_2(r,m)$. It then follows from the parameters of $\mathcal{R}_2(r,m)$ that $\mathcal{R}_2(r,m)^*$ has length $2^m - 1$, minimum distance $2^{m-r} - 1$ and dimension $\sum_{i=0}^{r} \binom{m}{i}$.

Minimum weight codewords in $\mathcal{R}_2(r,m)^*$ are obtained from the minimum weight codewords in $\mathcal{R}_2(r,m)$ that have a 1 in coordinate 0 by deleting the 1. The following theorem then follows from Theorem 5.9.

Theorem 5.10. *The number of minimum weight codewords in* $\mathcal{R}_2(r,m)^*$ *is*

$$A_{2^{m-r}-1} = \prod_{i=0}^{m-r-1} \frac{2^{m-i} - 1}{2^{m-r-i} - 1}.$$

Below we present further properties of the punctured Reed-Muller codes $\mathcal{R}_2(r,m)^*$.

Theorem 5.11. *The incidence vectors of all the* $(\mu - 1)$*-flats of* $\mathrm{PG}(m-1, \mathrm{GF}(2))$ *generate* $\mathcal{R}_2(r,m)^*$, *where* $\mu = m - r$.

Proof. Let α be a generator of $\mathrm{GF}(2^m)^*$. Then the points of $\mathrm{PG}(m-1, \mathrm{GF}(2))$ can be taken to be the elements of $\{1, \alpha, \alpha^2, \ldots, \alpha^{2^m-2}\}$. Define $\ell = 2^\mu - 2$.

A subset $T = \{\alpha^{d_0}, \alpha^{d_1}, \ldots, \alpha^{d_u}\}$ of these points will be represented by the polynomial

$$W_T(x) = x^{d_0} + x^{d_1} + \cdots + x^{d_u}.$$

If T is a $(\mu - 1)$-flat in $\mathrm{PG}(m-1, \mathrm{GF}(2))$, then by definition the points of T are all nonzero linear combinations over $\mathrm{GF}(2)$ of μ linearly independent points $\alpha_0, \alpha_1, \ldots, \alpha_{\mu-1}$ of $\mathrm{GF}(2^m)$. In other words, the elements of T are

$$\sum_{j=0}^{\mu-1} a_{i,j} \alpha_j = \alpha^{d_i}, \ i = 0, 1, \ldots, \ell,$$

where $(a_{i,0}, a_{i,1}, \ldots, a_{i,\mu-1})$ runs through all nonzero elements in $\mathrm{GF}(2)^\mu$. Note that $xW_T(x)$ represents the $(\mu - 1)$-flat spanned by $\alpha\alpha_0, \alpha\alpha_1, \ldots, \alpha\alpha_{\mu-1}$. Thus, every cyclic shift of the incidence vector of a $(\mu - 1)$-flat is the incidence vector of another $(\mu - 1)$-flat.

Let $\mathcal{C}$ be the code generated by all $W_T(x)$, where T is any $(\mu - 1)$-flat. It then follows from Theorem 5.7 and the observation above that $\mathcal{C}$ is a cyclic code and is contained in $\mathcal{R}_2(r,m)^*$. Below we prove that $\mathcal{C} = \mathcal{R}_2(r,m)^*$ by showing that

$$\dim(\mathcal{C}) \ge \sum_{i=0}^{r} \binom{m}{i}.$$

The dimension of C is the number of α^s, which are not zeros of C; i.e., the number of α^s such that $W_T(\alpha^s) \neq 0$ for some T. We have now

$$W_T(\alpha^s) = \sum_{i=0}^{\ell} \alpha^{sd_i} = \sum_{i=0}^{\ell} \left(\sum_{j=0}^{\mu-1} a_{i,j}\alpha_j \right)^s = \sum_b (b_0\alpha_0 + \cdots + b_{\mu-1}\alpha_{\mu-1})^s,$$

where the summation extends over all nonzero $b = (b_0, \ldots, b_{\mu-1}) \in \mathrm{GF}(2)^\mu$. Now define

$$F_s(\alpha_0, \ldots, \alpha_{\mu-1}) = \sum_{b \in \mathrm{GF}(2)^\mu \setminus \{0\}} (b_0\alpha_0 + \cdots + b_{\mu-1}\alpha_{\mu-1})^s.$$

Let $\gamma = b_1\alpha_1 + \cdots + b_{\mu-1}\alpha_{\mu-1}$. Then we have

$$\begin{aligned}
F_s(\alpha_0, \ldots, \alpha_{\mu-1}) &= \sum_{b_0, \ldots, b_{\mu-1}} (b_0\alpha_0 + \gamma)^s \\
&= \sum_{b_1, \ldots, b_{\mu-1}} (\gamma^s + (\alpha_0 + \gamma)^s) \\
&= \sum_{b_1, \ldots, b_{\mu-1}} \left(\alpha_0^s + \sum_{j=1}^{s-1} \binom{s}{j} \alpha_0^j \gamma^{s-j} \right) \\
&= \sum_{j=1}^{s-1} \binom{s}{j} \alpha_0^j F_{s-j}(\alpha_1, \ldots, \alpha_{\mu-1}) \\
&= \cdots \\
&= \sum_{\substack{\sum j_i = s \\ j_i \geq 1}} \frac{s!}{j_0! \cdots j_{\mu-1}!} \alpha_0^{j_0} \cdots \alpha_{\mu-1}^{j_{\mu-1}}.
\end{aligned} \tag{5.4}$$

This is a homogeneous polynomial of degree s in $\alpha_0, \ldots, \alpha_{\mu-1}$.

Then the dimension of C is the number of s such that $F_s(\alpha_0, \ldots, \alpha_{\mu-1})$ is not identically zero, when these α_i are linearly independent. In fact, we need to count those $F_s(\alpha_0, \ldots, \alpha_{\mu-1})$ that contain a coefficient, which is nonzero modulo 2. Note that such an F cannot be identically zero and cannot have $\alpha_0, \ldots, \alpha_{\mu-1}$ linearly dependent. By Lucas' Theorem,

$$\frac{s!}{j_0! \cdots j_{\mu-1}!} \equiv 0 \pmod 2$$

if and only if

$$(j_0)_i + (j_1)_i + \cdots + (j_{\mu-1})_i \leq (s)_i \text{ for all } i \text{ with } 0 \leq i \leq m-1,$$

where $(j)_i$ denotes the ith bit in the binary expansion of j.

As a result, (5.4) contains a nonzero coefficient whenever the binary expansion of s contains at least μ 1's. The number of such s in the range $0 \leq s \leq 2^m - 1$ is

$$\sum_{j=\mu}^{m} \binom{m}{j} = \sum_{i=0}^{r} \binom{m}{i}.$$

This completes the proof. $\qquad\square$

Theorem 5.11 explains why $\mathcal{R}_2(r,m)^*$ is called a geometric code and a code of a geometric design. Furthermore, the proof of Theorem 5.11 has actually proved the following fundamental result about $\mathcal{R}_2(r,m)^*$ [Kasami, Lin and Peterson (1968b,c); Kolesnik and Mironchikov (1968)].

Theorem 5.12. *The punctured Reed-Muller code $\mathcal{R}_2(r,m)^*$ is cyclic, and has zeros α^s for all s satisfying*

$$1 \leq \omega_2(s) \leq m - r - 1 \text{ and } 1 \leq s \leq 2^m - 2,$$

where $\omega_2(s)$ is the number of terms in the 2-adic expansion of s.

For $0 \leq r \leq m - 1$, the generator and check polynomials of $\mathcal{R}_2(r,m)$ are

$$g(x) = \prod_{\substack{1 \leq \omega_2(s) \leq m-r-1 \\ 1 \leq s \leq 2^m-2}} \mathbb{M}_{\alpha^s}(x) \tag{5.5}$$

and

$$h(x) = (x-1) \prod_{\substack{m-r \leq \omega_2(s) \leq m-1 \\ 1 \leq s \leq 2^m-2}} \mathbb{M}_{\alpha^s}(x) \tag{5.6}$$

where $\mathbb{M}_{\alpha^s}(x)$ denotes the minimal polynomial of α^s over GF(2). By convention, an empty product is 1.

The following is a consequence of Theorem 5.12.

Corollary 5.13. $\mathcal{R}_2(r,m)^*$ *is a subcode of the narrow-sense primitive BCH code $C_{(2,2^m-1,2^{m-r}-1,1)}$, and $\mathcal{R}_2(r,m)$ is a subcode of the extended BCH code $\overline{C}_{(2,2^m-1,2^{m-r}-1,1)}$.*

The geometric background of the Reed-Muller code $\mathcal{R}_2(r,m)$ is explained by the next theorem.

Theorem 5.14. *The incidence vectors of all the $(m-r)$-flats in $\mathrm{AG}(m,\mathrm{GF}(2))$ generate $\mathcal{R}_2(r,m)$.*

Proof. Recall that $\mathcal{R}_2(r,m)$ can be obtained from $\mathcal{R}_2(r,m)^*$ by adding an overall parity check bit. By Theorem 5.11, the incidence vectors of the $(m-r)$-flats in $\mathrm{AG}(m,\mathrm{GF}(2))$ with a 1 in coordinate 0 generate $\mathcal{R}_2(r,m)$. The desired conclusion then follows.   □

To prove that $\mathcal{R}_2(r,m)$ and $\mathcal{R}_2(r,m)^*$ hold 3-designs and 2-designs, we would determine the automorphism groups of these codes. Before doing this, we recall the general affine group $\mathrm{GA}_m(\mathrm{GF}(2))$ and the general linear group $\mathrm{GL}_m(\mathrm{GF}(2))$ investigated in Sections 1.8.5 and 1.8.8, respectively.

The group $\mathrm{GA}_m(\mathrm{GF}(2))$ consists of all the following permutations of $\mathrm{GF}(2)^m$:

$$\sigma_{(A,b)}(x) = Ax + b \tag{5.7}$$

where $x = (x_1, \ldots, x_m)^T \in \mathrm{GF}(2)^m$ is the transpose of $x = (x_1, \ldots, x_m)$, and A is an $m \times m$ invertible matrix over $\mathrm{GF}(2)$. The group $\mathrm{GL}_m(\mathrm{GF}(2))$ is composed of all the following permutations of $(\mathrm{GF}(2)^m)^*$:

$$\{\sigma_{(A,0)}(x) : A \text{ invertible}\}. \tag{5.8}$$

Recall that $\mathcal{R}_2(r, m)$ consists of the truth tables of all Boolean functions with degree at most r with respect to the decreasing ordering of the elements of $\mathrm{GF}(2)^m$. This means that the coordinates of $\mathcal{R}_2(r, m)$ are indexed by all the elements of $\mathrm{GF}(2)^m$. Since $\mathrm{GA}_m(\mathrm{GF}(2))$ is a permutation group of $\mathrm{GF}(2)^m$, it acts on a Boolean function (hence the corresponding truth table) as follows

$$\sigma_{(A,b)} : f(x_1, \ldots, x_m) \mapsto f\left(\sum a_{1j}x_1 + b_1, \ldots, \sum a_{mj}x_j + b_m\right).$$

Clearly, $\sigma_{(A,b)}$ transforms a Boolean function of degree r to a Boolean function of degree r. This proves the following.

Theorem 5.15. *The group* $\mathrm{GA}_m(\mathrm{GF}(2))$ *is a subgroup of the automorphism group* $\mathrm{Aut}(\mathcal{R}_2(r, m))$.

Note that every $\sigma_{(A,0)}$ fixes the zero vector of $\mathrm{GF}(2)^m$. The following result then follows from Theorem 5.15.

Theorem 5.16. *The group* $\mathrm{GL}_m(\mathrm{GF}(2))$ *is a subgroup of the automorphism group* $\mathrm{Aut}(\mathcal{R}_2(r, m)^*)$.

The next theorem gives the automorphism groups of $\mathcal{R}_2(r, m)$ and $\mathcal{R}_2(r, m)^*$.

Theorem 5.17. *For* $1 \leq r \leq m - 2$,

(a) $\mathrm{Aut}(\mathcal{R}_2(r, m)^*) = \mathrm{GL}_m(\mathrm{GF}(2))$, *and*
(b) $\mathrm{Aut}(\mathcal{R}_2(r, m)) = \mathrm{GA}_m(\mathrm{GF}(2))$.

A proof of Theorem 5.17 can be found in MacWilliams and Sloane (1977)[p. 400]. Theorems 5.15 and 5.16 would be sufficient for studying the designs held in $\mathcal{R}_2(r, m)$ and $\mathcal{R}_2(r, m)^*$.

5.2 Designs from the Binary Reed-Muller Codes

Our task in this section is to investigate the designs held in the binary Reed-Muller code $\mathcal{R}_2(r, m)$. We first justify the following general conclusion.

Theorem 5.18. *Let A_k denote the number of codewords of weight k in $\mathcal{R}_2(r,m)$. If $A_k \neq 0$, then the supports of all codewords with weight k form a 3-$(2^m, k, \lambda)$ design, where*

$$\lambda = \frac{A_k \binom{k}{3}}{\binom{2^m}{3}}.$$

Proof. The desired conclusion on the 3-design property follows from Theorems 5.15, 4.30, and 1.78. The conclusion on the value of λ follows from (4.5). $\qquad\square$

As a consequence of Theorems 5.18 and 5.9, we have the following.

Theorem 5.19. *The supports of all minimum weight codewords in $\mathcal{R}_2(r,m)$ form a 3-$(2^m, 2^{m-r}, \lambda)$ design, where*

$$\lambda = \frac{\binom{2^{m-r}}{3}}{\binom{2^m}{3}} 2^r \prod_{i=0}^{m-r-1} \frac{2^{m-i} - 1}{2^{m-r-i} - 1}.$$

If we would find out the parameters of all the 3-designs held in $\mathcal{R}_2(r,m)$, we have to know the weight distribution of $\mathcal{R}_2(r,m)$. However, this is known only for a few r's. We will determine the parameters of the 3-designs held in $\mathcal{R}_2(r,m)$ for these r.

5.2.1 Designs in $\mathcal{R}_2(1,m)$ and $\mathcal{R}_2(m-2,m)$

The following was proved in Ding and Li (2017).

Lemma 5.20. *The weight distribution of $\mathcal{R}_2(m-2,m)$ is given by*

$$A_{4k} = \frac{1}{2^{m+1}} \left[2\binom{2^m}{4k} + (2^{m+1} - 2)\binom{2^{m-1}}{2k} \right]$$

for $0 \leq k \leq 2^{m-2}$, and by

$$A_{4k+2} = \frac{1}{2^{m+1}} \left[2\binom{2^m}{4k+2} - (2^{m+1} - 2)\binom{2^{m-1}}{2k+1} \right]$$

for $0 \leq k \leq 2^{m-2} - 1$.

Proof. Note that $\mathcal{R}_2(1,m)$ consists of the truth tables of all the following affine Boolean functions

$$f(x_1, \ldots, x_m) = a_1 x_1 + \cdots + a_m x_m + a_0,$$

where all $a_i \in \mathrm{GF}(2)$. Obviously, the weight enumerator of $\mathcal{R}_2(1,m)$ is

$$1 + (2^{m+1} - 2)z^{2^{m-1}} + z^{2^m}.$$

By Theorem 2.4, the weight enumerator of $\mathcal{R}_2(m-2,m)$, which is the dual of $\mathcal{R}_2(1,m)$, is given by

$$
\begin{aligned}
B(z) &= \frac{1}{2^{m+1}}(1+z)^{2^m}\left[1+(2^{m+1}-2)\left(\frac{1-z}{1+z}\right)^{2^{m-1}}+\left(\frac{1-z}{1+z}\right)^{2^m}\right] \\
&= \frac{1}{2^{m+1}}\left[(1+z)^{2^m}+(2^{m+1}-2)(1-z^2)^{2^{m-1}}+(1-z)^{2^m}\right] \\
&= \frac{1}{2^{m+1}}\left[2\sum_{i=0}^{2^{m-1}}\binom{2^m}{2i}z^{2i}+(2^{m+1}-2)\sum_{i=0}^{2^{m-1}}\binom{2^{m-1}}{i}(-1)^i z^{2i}\right] \\
&= \frac{1}{2^{m+1}}\sum_{k=0}^{2^{m-2}}\left[2\binom{2^m}{4k}+(2^{m+1}-2)\binom{2^{m-1}}{2k}\right]z^{4k}+ \\
&\quad \frac{1}{2^{m+1}}\sum_{k=0}^{2^{m-2}-1}\left[2\binom{2^m}{4k+2}-(2^{m+1}-2)\binom{2^{m-1}}{2k+1}\right]z^{4k+2}.
\end{aligned}
$$

The desired conclusion then follows. $\qquad\square$

The following theorem gives parameters of all the 3-designs in both $\mathcal{R}_2(m-2,m)$ and $\mathcal{R}_2(1,m)$.

Theorem 5.21. *Let $m \geq 3$. Then $\mathcal{R}_2(m-2,m)$ has dimension 2^m-m-1 and minimum distance 4. For even positive integer κ with $4 \leq \kappa \leq 2^m-4$, the supports of the codewords with weight κ in $\mathcal{R}_2(m-2,m)$ form a 3-$(2^m,\kappa,\lambda)$ design, where*

$$
\lambda = \begin{cases}
\dfrac{\frac{1}{2^{m+1}}\binom{\kappa}{3}\left(2\binom{2^m}{4k}+(2^{m+1}-2)\binom{2^{m-1}}{2k}\right)}{\binom{2^m}{3}} & \text{if } \kappa = 4k, \\[3ex]
\dfrac{\frac{1}{2^{m+1}}\binom{\kappa}{3}\left(2\binom{2^m}{4k+2}-(2^{m+1}-2)\binom{2^{m-1}}{2k+1}\right)}{\binom{2^m}{3}} & \text{if } \kappa = 4k+2.
\end{cases}
$$

The supports of all codewords of weight 2^{m-1} in $\mathcal{R}_2(1,m)$ form a 3-$(2^m,2^{m-1},2^{m-2}-1)$ design.

Proof. The desired conclusions follow from Lemma 5.20 and Theorem 5.18. $\quad\square$

We remark that Theorem 5.21 can also be proved by the Assmus-Mattson Theorem (i.e., Corollary 4.26) and Lemma 5.20.

As a corollary of Theorem 5.21, we have the following.

Corollary 5.22. *The minimum weight codewords in $\mathcal{R}_2(m-2,m)$ form a 3-$(2^m,4,1)$ design, i.e., a Steiner quadruple system $S(3,4,2^m)$.*

A few infinite families of Steiner systems could be constructed from linear codes. This is the first family. We will introduce other families later.

5.2.2 Designs in $\mathcal{R}_2(2,m)$ and $\mathcal{R}_2(m-3,m)$

In this section, we first introduce the weight distribution of the 2nd-order Reed-Muller code $\mathcal{R}_2(2,m)$ obtained in McEliece (1969) and Slone and Berlekamp (1970), and then describe the parameters of the 3-designs held in $\mathcal{R}_2(2,m)$.

Recall that $\mathcal{R}_2(2,m)$ consists of the truth tables of all Boolean functions $f(x_1,\ldots,x_m)$ of degree at most 2, which is expressed as

$$f(x_1,\ldots,x_m) = \sum_{1 \le i < j \le m} q_{ij}x_ix_j + \sum_{1 \le i \le m} \ell_ix_i + \varepsilon, \tag{5.9}$$

where all q_{ij}, ℓ_i and ε are elements in GF(2).

Let $x = (x_1,\ldots,x_m)$. Define a quadratic and linear form by

$$Q(x) = xQx^T \text{ and } L(x) = Lx^T,$$

where $Q = [q_{ij}]$ is an upper triangular $m \times m$ matrix over GF(2) and $L = (\ell_1,\ldots,\ell_m) \in \mathrm{GF}(2)^m$. Then we have

$$f(x) = Q(x) + L(x) + \varepsilon. \tag{5.10}$$

By definition, $\mathcal{R}_2(1,m)$ is a subspace of the vector space $\mathcal{R}_2(2,m)$. Therefore, $\mathcal{R}_2(2,m)$ is the union of some cosets of $\mathcal{R}_2(1,m)$ in $\mathcal{R}_2(2,m)$. When $Q(x)$ is fixed and $L(x) + \varepsilon$ runs over $\mathcal{R}_2(1,m)$, $f(x) = Q(x) + L(x) + \varepsilon$ runs through a coset of $\mathcal{R}_2(1,m)$ in $\mathcal{R}_2(2,m)$. This coset is defined by the quadratic form $Q(x)$. This quadratic form $Q(x)$ can be characterized by a symmetric matrix $B_Q = Q + Q^T$ whose diagonals are all zero. The correspondence between Q and B_Q is one-to-one. This matrix B_Q defines another form

$$B_Q(x,y) = xB_Qy^T, \tag{5.11}$$

where $y = (y_1,\ldots,y_m)$. By the definitions of $B_Q(x,y)$ and $f(x)$, it is easily checked that

$$B_Q(x,y) = f(x+y) + f(x) + f(y) + \varepsilon. \tag{5.12}$$

One can verify that $B_Q(x,y)$ has the following properties:

(1) $B_Q(x,y)$ is *bilinear*, i.e.,

$$\begin{aligned} B_Q(x+z,y) &= B_Q(x,y) + B_Q(z,y), \\ B_Q(x,y+z) &= B_Q(x,y) + B_Q(x,z). \end{aligned} \tag{5.13}$$

(2) $B_Q(x,y)$ is *alternating*, i.e.,

$$B_Q(x,x) = 0 \text{ and } B_Q(x,y) = B_Q(y,x).$$

A binary form that is both bilinear and alternating is called a *symplectic form*. Similarly, a symmetric matrix with zero diagonal is called a *symplectic matrix*.

Since the correspondence $Q \mapsto B_Q$ is one-to-one, we have the following theorem.

Theorem 5.23. *There is a one-to-one correspondence between symplectic forms and the cosets of $\mathcal{R}_2(1,m)$ in $\mathcal{R}_2(2,m)$. The zero symplectic form corresponds to $\mathcal{R}_2(1,m)$.*

By definition, the total number of symplectic matrices (and thus the number of symplectic forms) is equal to $2^{\binom{m}{2}}$. To determine the weight distribution of $\mathcal{R}_2(2,m)$, we now determine the total number of symplectic forms of each rank, which is the rank of the corresponding symplectic matrix.

We shall need the following lemma.

Lemma 5.24. *Let A be a fixed symplectic $m \times m$ matrix of rank r. Define*

$$B = \begin{bmatrix} A & v^T \\ v & 0 \end{bmatrix}$$

which is a symplectic matrix of size $(m+1) \times (m+1)$ over $GF(2)$ for every $v \in GF(2)^m$. Then among the 2^m different matrices B, $2^m - 2^r$ of them have rank $r+2$, and 2^r of them have rank r.

Proof. The proof is carried out by considering two cases. If the vector v is independent of the rows of A, which happens in $2^m - 2^r$ ways, then $\begin{bmatrix} A \\ v \end{bmatrix}$ has rank $r+1$ and B has thus rank $r+2$. If v is dependent on the rows of A, say $v = uA$, then $\begin{bmatrix} A \\ v \end{bmatrix}$ has rank r. Now $\begin{bmatrix} v^T \\ 0 \end{bmatrix}$ is dependent on the columns of $\begin{bmatrix} A \\ v \end{bmatrix}$ because

$$\begin{bmatrix} A \\ v \end{bmatrix} u^T = \begin{bmatrix} v^T \\ vu^T \end{bmatrix} = \begin{bmatrix} v^T \\ uAu^T \end{bmatrix} = \begin{bmatrix} v^T \\ 0 \end{bmatrix}.$$

Hence, in this case B has rank r. This completes the proof. $\qquad\square$

Theorem 5.25. *Let $N(m,r)$ denote the number of symplectic $m \times m$ matrices of rank r over $GF(2)$. Then we have $N(m, 2h+1) = 0$ for all h with $1 \le 2h+1 \le m$ and*

$$N(m, 2h) = \prod_{i=1}^{h} \frac{2^{2i} - 2}{2^{2i-1} - 1} \times \prod_{i=0}^{2h-1} (2^{m-i} - 1)$$

$$= 2^{h(h-1)} \frac{\prod_{i=0}^{2h-1} (2^{m-i} - 1)}{\prod_{i=1}^{h} (2^{2i} - 1)}$$

for all h with $1 \le 2h \le m$.

Proof. Obviously, $N(1,0) = 1$, $N(1,1) = 0$, $N(2,0) = 1$, $N(2,1) = 0$, and $N(2,2) = 1$. The idea of proof is to derive a recursion formula for $N(m,r)$. It follows from Lemma 5.24 that

$$N(m+1,r) = 2^r N(m,r) + (2^m - 2^{r-2})N(m,r-2).$$

By the initial value $N(1,1) = 0$, we then obtain $N(m,2h+1) = 0$. Using the initial value $N(m,0) = 1$, we arrive at the desired formula for $N(m,2h+1)$ with the recursion formula above.   □

Our next step for determining the weight distribution of $\mathcal{R}_2(r,m)$ is to prove that the weight distribution of the coset defined by the symplectic form $B_Q(x,y)$ depends only on the rank of the matrix B_Q. To do this, we need the following two lemmas due to Dickson.

Lemma 5.26. *Let B be a symplectic $m \times m$ matrix of rank $2h$. Then there exists an invertible binary matrix R such that RBR^T has zeros everywhere except on the two diagonals immediately below and above the main diagonal, and the two diagonals are the same and are $(101010 \cdots 101, 0 \cdots 0)$, where the first part has h 1's, and the second part $0 \cdots 0$ has length $m - 2h$, which does not exist when $h = m/2$.*

Proof. The proof is by induction on m. The conclusion is obviously true for $m = 1$ and $m = 2$. Suppose the statement is true for $m \leq t$ and $h \leq \lfloor t/2 \rfloor$. Then any $(t+1) \times (t+1)$ symplectic matrix B may be written as

$$B = \begin{bmatrix} A & v^T \\ v & 0 \end{bmatrix},$$

where A is a symplectic matrix of size $t \times t$ and the desired form by induction hypothesis.

If $\mathrm{rank}(A) < 2\lfloor t/2 \rfloor$, by elementary row and column operations, we can reduce B to

$$\begin{bmatrix} A' & (v')^T & 0 & \cdots & 0 \\ v' & 0 & 0 & \cdots & 0 \\ 0 & 0 & 0 & \cdots & 0 \\ \vdots & \vdots & & \vdots & \vdots \\ 0 & 0 & 0 & \cdots & 0 \end{bmatrix},$$

where

$$\begin{bmatrix} A' & (v')^T \\ v' & 0 \end{bmatrix} \tag{5.14}$$

is of size at most $t \times t$ and A' is a symplectic matrix of the desired form. By induction hypothesis, the matrix in (5.14) can be reduced into the desired form.

Now suppose that A has rank $2\lfloor t/2 \rfloor$. If $2\lfloor t/2 \rfloor = t$, then B has rank t and

$$B = \begin{bmatrix} 0 & 1 & 0 & \cdots & 0 & 0 & v_1 \\ 1 & 0 & 0 & \cdots & 0 & 0 & v_2 \\ 0 & 0 & 0 & \cdots & 0 & 0 & v_3 \\ \vdots & \vdots & \vdots & \vdots & \vdots & & \vdots & \vdots \\ 0 & 0 & 0 & \cdots & 0 & 1 & v_{t-1} \\ 0 & 0 & 0 & \cdots & 1 & 0 & v_t \\ v_1 & v_2 & v_3 & \cdots & v_{t-1} & v_t & 0 \end{bmatrix},$$

where t must be even, as the rank of a symplectic matrix is always even. In this case, put

$$R = \begin{bmatrix} I & 0 \\ u & 1 \end{bmatrix},$$

where I is the $t \times t$ identity matrix, 0 is the zero column vector, and $u = (v_2 v_1 v_4 v_3 \cdots v_t v_{t-1})$. Obviously, R is invertible. It is easily verified that

$$RBR^T = \begin{bmatrix} 0 & 1 & 0 & \cdots & 0 & 0 & 0 \\ 1 & 0 & 0 & \cdots & 0 & 0 & 0 \\ 0 & 0 & 0 & \cdots & 0 & 0 & 0 \\ \vdots & \vdots & \vdots & & \vdots & \vdots & \vdots \\ 0 & 0 & 0 & \cdots & 0 & 1 & 0 \\ 0 & 0 & 0 & \cdots & 1 & 0 & 0 \\ 0 & 0 & 0 & \cdots & 0 & 0 & 0 \end{bmatrix},$$

which is of the desired form.

If $2\lfloor t/2 \rfloor = t - 1$, then

$$B = \begin{bmatrix} 0 & 1 & 0 & \cdots & 0 & 0 & 0 & v_1 \\ 1 & 0 & 0 & \cdots & 0 & 0 & 0 & v_2 \\ 0 & 0 & 0 & \cdots & 0 & 0 & 0 & v_3 \\ \vdots & \vdots & \vdots & \cdots & \vdots & & \vdots & & \vdots \\ 0 & 0 & 0 & \cdots & 0 & 1 & 0 & v_{t-2} \\ 0 & 0 & 0 & \cdots & 1 & 0 & 0 & v_{t-1} \\ 0 & 0 & 0 & \cdots & 0 & 0 & 0 & \varepsilon \\ v_1 & v_2 & v_3 & \cdots & v_{t-2} & v_{t-1} & \varepsilon & 0 \end{bmatrix},$$

where $\mathrm{rank}(B) = t - 1$ if $\varepsilon = 0$ and $\mathrm{rank}(B) = t + 1$ if $\varepsilon = 1$. In either case, define

$$R = \begin{bmatrix} I & 0 \\ u & 1 \end{bmatrix},$$

where I is the $t \times t$ identity matrix, 0 is the zero column vector, and $u = (v_2 v_1 v_4 v_3 \cdots v_{t-2} v_{t-1} 0)$. Then RBR^T is the desired form. This completes the induction step and thus the proof of the lemma. $\qquad\square$

Lemma 5.27. *Any Boolean function of m variables*

$$f(x) = xQx^T + L(x) + \varepsilon,$$

where Q is an upper triangular matrix and L(x) is an arbitrary linear Boolean function and $\varepsilon \in GF(2)$, becomes

$$g(y) = \sum_{i=1}^{h} y_{2i-1} y_{2i} + L_1(y) + \varepsilon$$

under the transformation of variables $x = Ry$, where R is given in Lemma 5.26, $B = Q + Q^T$, and 2h is the rank of the symplectic matrix B. Moreover, $y_1, \ldots, y_{2h}$ are linearly independent.

If $L_1(y)$ is linearly dependent on $y_1, y_2, \ldots, y_{2h}$, by an affine transformation of variables we may write g(y) as

$$\sum_{i=1}^{h} z_{2i-1} z_{2i} + \varepsilon_1,$$

where $z_1, \ldots, z_{2h}$ are linearly independent, and each z_i is a linear form of $y_1, \ldots, y_{2h}, 1$.

Proof. The conclusions follow from Lemma 5.26. The details of the proof are left to the reader. □

We still need the following two lemmas whose proofs are left to the reader.

Lemma 5.28. *The number of solutions $(x_1, \ldots, x_{2h}) \in GF(2)^{2h}$ of the equation $\sum_{i=1}^{h} x_{2i-1} x_{2i} = 0$ is equal to $2^{2h-1} - 2^{h-1}$.*

Lemma 5.29. *Let $3 \leq 2h + 1 \leq m$. Then the number of solutions $(x_1, \ldots, x_m) \in GF(2)^m$ of the equation*

$$\sum_{i=1}^{h} x_{2i-1} x_{2i} + \sum_{i=2h+1}^{m} a_i x_i = 0,$$

where at least one of these a_i is 1, is equal to 2^{m-1}.

With the preparations above, we are now ready to settle the weight distribution of a coset of $\mathcal{R}_2(1, m)$ in $\mathcal{R}_2(2, m)$. Specifically, we have the following.

Theorem 5.30. *If a symplectic $m \times m$ matrix B has rank 2h, the weight distribution of the coset defined by the symplectic form B(x, y) of $\mathcal{R}_2(1, m)$ in $\mathcal{R}_2(2, m)$ is as follows:*

Weight	Number of vectors
$2^{m-1} - 2^{m-h-1}$	2^{2h}
2^{m-1}	$2^{m+1} - 2^{2h+1}$
$2^{m-1} + 2^{m-h-1}$	2^{2h}

Proof. By Lemma 5.27, the quadratic part of any Boolean function in the coset defined by B can be transformed into

$$Q(x) = \sum_{i=1}^{h} x_{2i-1} x_{2i}.$$

Let $L(x)$ be the linear part. Suppose $L(x)$ is of the form

$$L(x) = \sum_{i=1}^{h} a_i x_i,$$

which can happen in 2^{2h} ways. It then follows from the second part of Lemma 5.27 that $Q(x) + L(x)$ becomes one of

$$\sum_{i=1}^{h} z_{2i-1} z_{2i} \text{ and } \sum_{i=1}^{h} z_{2i-1} z_{2i} + 1,$$

which have weights $2^{m-1} - 2^{m-1-h}$ and $2^{m-1} + 2^{m-1-h}$, respectively, by Lemma 5.28. On the other hand, if $L(x)$ is not dependent on $x_1, \ldots, x_{2h}$, which happens in $2^{m+1} - 2^{2h+1}$ ways, by Lemma 5.29 the codeword has weight 2^{m-1}. This completes the proof. $\qquad\square$

Combining Theorems 5.25 and 5.30, we obtain the following main result of this section due to McEliece (1969) and Slone and Berlekamp (1970).

Theorem 5.31. *Let A_i be the number of codewords of weight i in $\mathcal{R}_2(2,m)$. Then $A_i = 0$ unless $i = 2^{m-1}$ or $i = 2^{m-1} \pm 2^{m-1-h}$ for some h with $0 \leq h \leq \lfloor m/2 \rfloor$. Also $A_0 = A_{2^m} = 1$ and for all h with $1 \leq h \leq \lfloor m/2 \rfloor$ we have*

$$A_{2^{m-1} \pm 2^{m-1-h}} = 2^{h(h-1)} \frac{\prod_{i=0}^{2h-1}(2^{m-i}-1)}{\prod_{i=1}^{h}(2^{2i}-1)}.$$

In addition,

$$A_{2^{m-1}} = 2^{1+m+(m-1)m/2} - \sum_{i \neq 2^{m-1}} A_i.$$

Putting together Theorems 5.18 and 5.31, we deduce the following.

Theorem 5.32. *For each h with $1 \leq h \leq \lfloor m/2 \rfloor$, the code $\mathcal{R}_2(2,m)$ holds a 3-$(2^m, 2^{m-1} \pm 2^{m-1-h}, \lambda)$ design, where*

$$\lambda = \frac{\binom{2^{m-1} \pm 2^{m-1-h}}{3}}{\binom{2^m}{3}} 2^{h(h-1)} \frac{\prod_{i=0}^{2h-1}(2^{m-i}-1)}{\prod_{i=1}^{h}(2^{2i}-1)}.$$

In addition, $\mathcal{R}_2(2,m)$ holds a 3-$(2^m, 2^{m-1}, \lambda)$ design, where

$$\lambda = \frac{\binom{2^{m-1}}{3}}{\binom{2^m}{3}} \left[2^{1+m+m(m-1)/2} - 2 - \sum_{h=1}^{\lfloor m/2 \rfloor} 2^{h(h-1)+1} \frac{\prod_{i=0}^{2h-1}(2^{m-i}-1)}{\prod_{i=1}^{h}(2^{2i}-1)} \right].$$

Recall that $\mathcal{R}_2(m-3,m) = \mathcal{R}_2(2,m)^{\perp}$. In theory, Theorems 5.31 and 2.4 can be employed to give a weight distribution formula and thus a formula for the parameters of the 3-designs held in $\mathcal{R}_2(m-3,m)$. However, these formulas are so complex and hence not readable. We omit them here.

5.2.3 Designs in $\mathcal{R}_2(r,m)$ for $3 \leq r \leq m-4$

Determining the weight distribution of $\mathcal{R}_2(r,m)$ looks infeasible for $3 \leq r \leq m-4$. Therefore, it may be difficult to find out the parameters of all the 3-designs held in $\mathcal{R}_2(r,m)$ for $3 \leq r \leq m-4$. However, some progress was made in Kasami and Tokura (1970). Specifically, we have the following.

Theorem 5.33 (Kasami-Tokura). *Let A_w be the number of codewords of weight w in $\mathcal{R}_2(r,m)$, where $r \geq 2$. Suppose that*

$$d = 2^{m-r} \leq w < 2d.$$

Define $u = \min\{m-r,r\}$ and $v = (m-r+2)/2$.

(1) $A_w = 0$ unless $w = w(\mu) := 2^{m-r-1} - 2^{m-r-\mu}$ for some μ in the range $1 \leq \mu \leq \max\{u,v\}$. The case $\mu = 1$ was covered in Theorem 5.9.

(2) If $\mu = 2$ or $\max\{u,2\} < \mu \leq v$ then

$$A_{w(\mu)} = \frac{2^{r+\mu^2+\mu-2} \prod_{i=0}^{r+2\mu-3}(2^{m-i}-1)}{\prod_{i=0}^{r-3}(2^{r-2-i}-1) \prod_{i=0}^{\mu-1}(4^{i+1}-1)}. \tag{5.15}$$

(3) If $\max\{v,2\} < \mu \leq u$ then

$$A_{w(\mu)} = \frac{2^{r+\mu^2+\mu-1} \prod_{i=0}^{r+\mu-1}(2^{m-i}-1)}{\prod_{i=0}^{r-\mu-1}(2^{r-\mu-i}-1) \prod_{i=0}^{\mu-1}(2^{\mu-i}-1)}. \tag{5.16}$$

(4) If $3 \leq \mu \leq \min\{u,v\}$, then $A_{w(\mu)}$ is equal to the sum of (5.15) and (5.16).

Combining Theorems 5.18 and 5.33, one can write down the parameters of some of the 3-designs held in $\mathcal{R}_2(r,m)$ for $3 \leq r \leq m-4$. This is left to the reader. Theorem 5.33 was extended slightly further in Kasami, Tokura and Azumi (1974). But the technique becomes very complicated. The following problem looks challenging.

Problem 5.34. Determine the weight distribution of $\mathcal{R}_2(r,m)$ for $3 \leq r \leq m-4$, where $m \geq 7$.

5.2.4 *Designs from Binary Codes between $\mathcal{R}_2(r,m)$ and $\mathcal{R}_2(r+1,m)$*

Recall that the automorphism group $\mathrm{Aut}(\mathcal{R}_2(r,m))$ of $\mathcal{R}_2(r,m)$ is the general affine group $\mathrm{GA}_m(\mathrm{GF}(2))$. Since $\mathrm{GA}_m(\mathrm{GF}(2))$ is triply transitive on $\mathrm{GF}(2)^m$, $\mathcal{R}_2(r,m)$ holds 3-designs. For each r with $1 \le r \le m-2$, $\mathcal{R}_2(r,m)$ is a proper subcode of $\mathcal{R}_2(r+1,m)$. There are clearly many binary linear codes C which are a proper subcode of $\mathcal{R}_2(r+1,m)$ and also contain $\mathcal{R}_2(r,m)$ as a proper subcode. We then have the following open problems.

Problem 5.35. Let r be an integer with $1 \le r \le m-2$. Are there binary linear code C of length 2^m such that $\mathcal{R}_2(r,m) \subset C \subset \mathcal{R}_2(r+1,m)$ and C holds nontrivial 3-designs?

Note that $\mathrm{GA}_1(\mathrm{GF}(2^m))$ is a subgroup of the permutation automorphism group of $\mathcal{R}_2(r,m)$, and $\mathrm{GA}_1(\mathrm{GF}(2^m))$ is doubly transitive on $\mathrm{GF}(2^m)$. Some linear codes C between $\mathcal{R}_2(r,m)$ and $\mathcal{R}_2(r+1,m)$ might be affine-invariant. In the case that the answer to Problem 5.35 is negative, we still have the next question.

Problem 5.36. Let r be an integer with $1 \le r \le m-2$. Are there binary linear code C of length 2^m such that $\mathcal{R}_2(r,m) \subset C \subset \mathcal{R}_2(r+1,m)$ and C holds nontrivial 2-designs?

Section 6.2.4 may provide partial answers to the two questions above in the special case $r = 1$. The two problems above do not have any partial answer for $r \ge 2$.

5.3 Designs from the Punctured Binary Reed-Muller Codes

In this section, we investigate designs held in $\mathcal{R}_2(r,m)^*$ and its dual code. We fist state and prove the following general result.

Theorem 5.37. *Let A_k denote the number of codewords of weight k in $\mathcal{R}_2(r,m)^*$. If $A_k \ne 0$, then the supports of all codewords with weight k form a $2\text{-}(2^m-1,k,\lambda)$ design, where*

$$\lambda = \frac{A_k\binom{k}{2}}{\binom{2^m-1}{2}}.$$

Proof. The desired conclusion on the 2-design property follows from Theorems 5.16, 4.30, and 1.71. The conclusion on the value of λ follows from (4.5). $\qquad\square$

As a consequence of Theorems 5.37 and 5.9, we have the following.

Theorem 5.38. *The supports of all minimum weight codewords in $\mathcal{R}_2(r,m)^*$ form a 2-$(2^m - 1, 2^{m-r} - 1, \lambda)$ design, where*

$$\lambda = \frac{\binom{2^{m-r}-1}{2}}{\binom{2^m-1}{2}} \prod_{i=0}^{m-r-1} \frac{2^{m-i} - 1}{2^{m-r-i} - 1}.$$

Theorem 5.39. *Let $A_k^\perp$ denote the number of codewords of weight k in the code $(\mathcal{R}_2(r,m)^*)^\perp$. If $A_k^\perp \neq 0$, then the supports of all codewords with weight k form a 2-$(2^m - 1, k, \lambda)$ design, where*

$$\lambda = \frac{A_k^\perp \binom{k}{2}}{\binom{2^m-1}{2}}.$$

Proof. Since the codes are binary, it follows from Theorems 2.14 and 5.17 that

$$\mathrm{Aut}((\mathcal{R}_2(r,m)^*)^\perp) = \mathrm{PAut}((\mathcal{R}_2(r,m)^*)^\perp) = \mathrm{PAut}(\mathcal{R}_2(r,m)^*) = \mathrm{GL}(m).$$

By Theorem 1.71, $\mathrm{GL}(m)$ is doubly transitive. The 2-design property follows from Theorem 4.30. The conclusion on the value of λ follows from (4.5). $\qquad\square$

To determine the parameters of all the 2-designs held in $\mathcal{R}_2(r,m)^*$ and its dual, we must know the weight distributions of these codes. This is again a very hard problem in general, but can be solved in a few cases.

Recall that $\mathcal{R}_2(1,m)^*$ consists of the punctured versions of the truth tables of all the following affine Boolean functions

$$f(x_1,\ldots,x_m) = a_1 x_1 + \cdots + a_m x_m + a_0,$$

where all $a_i \in \mathrm{GF}(2)$. Obviously, the weight enumerator of $\mathcal{R}_2(1,m)^*$ is

$$A(z) = 1 + (2^m - 1)z^{2^{m-1}-1} + (2^m - 1)z^{2^{m-1}} + z^{2^m-1}. \tag{5.17}$$

Hence, $\mathcal{R}_2(1,m)^*$ holds two nontrivial 2-designs. One of them was described in Theorem 5.38 and has parameters 2-$(2^m - 1, 2^{m-1} - 1, 2^{m-2} - 1)$. The other is documented in the following corollary. Both are the development design of a Singer difference set.

Corollary 5.40. *The supports of all codewords of weight 2^{m-1} in $\mathcal{R}_2(r,m)^*$ form a 2-$(2^m, 2^{m-1}, 2^{m-2})$ design.*

The weight distribution of the code $(\mathcal{R}_2(1,m)^*)^\perp$ is given in the following lemma.

Lemma 5.41. *Let $m \geq 4$. Then the weight distribution of $(\mathcal{R}_2(1,m)^*)^\perp$ is given by $A_0^\perp = 1$ and*

$$A_{2i}^\perp = \frac{\binom{2^m-1}{2i} + (-1)^i (2^m - 1)\binom{2^{m-1}-1}{i}}{2^m} \tag{5.18}$$

for $2 \leq i \leq 2^{m-1} - 2$, and $A_j^{\perp} = 0$ for other j.

In addition, $(\mathcal{R}_2(1,m)^*)^{\perp}$ has parameters $[2^m - 1, 2^m - m - 2, 4]$.

Proof. Since $\mathcal{R}_2(1,m)^*$ contains the all-one codeword $\mathbf{1}$, every weight in $(\mathcal{R}_2(1,m)^*)^{\perp}$ must be even. Recall that $\mathcal{R}_2(1,m)^*$ has parameters $[2^m - 1, m + 1, 2^{m-1} - 1]$ and its weight enumerate $A(z)$ is given in (5.17). By Theorem 2.4, we obtain that

$$2^{m+1}A^{\perp}(z) = (1+z)^{2^m-1}A\left(\frac{1-z}{1+z}\right)$$

$$= (1+z)^{2^m-1} + (1-z)^{2^m-1} + (2^{m+1}-2)(1-z^2)^{2^{m-1}-1}$$

$$= \sum_{i=0}^{2^m-1}\binom{2^m-1}{i}\left(1+(-1)^i\right)z^i +$$

$$(2^{m+1}-2)\sum_{i=0}^{2^{m-1}-1}(-1)^i\binom{2^{m-1}-1}{i}z^{2i}$$

$$= \sum_{i=0}^{2^{m-1}-1}2\binom{2^m-1}{2i}z^{2i} +$$

$$(2^{m+1}-2)\sum_{i=0}^{2^{m-1}-1}(-1)^i\binom{2^{m-1}-1}{i}z^{2i}$$

$$= \sum_{i=0}^{2^{m-1}-1}2\left[\binom{2^m-1}{2i}+(-1)^i(2^m-1)\binom{2^{m-1}-1}{i}\right]z^{2i}.$$

This proves the weight distribution formula in (5.18).

It is easily verified that $A_2^{\perp} = A_{2^m-2}^{\perp} = 0$ and

$$A_4^{\perp} = \frac{\binom{2^m-1}{4}+(2^m-1)\binom{2^{m-1}-1}{2}}{2^m} > 0.$$

Consequently, $(\mathcal{R}_2(1,m)^*)^{\perp}$ has minimum distance 4. $\qquad\square$

The parameters of the 2-designs held in $(\mathcal{R}_2(1,m)^*)^{\perp}$ are presented in the next theorem.

Theorem 5.42. *Let $m \geq 4$. For each $2 \leq k \leq 2^{m-1} - 2$, the supports of the codewords of weight $2k$ in $(\mathcal{R}_2(1,m)^*)^{\perp}$ form a 2-$(2^m - 1, 2k, \lambda)$ design, where*

$$\lambda = \frac{2k(2k-1)\left(\binom{2^m-1}{2k}+(-1)^k(2^m-1)\binom{2^{m-1}-1}{k}\right)}{2^m(2^m-1(2^m-2)}.$$

Proof. With the formula in (5.18), it is straightforward to verify that $A_{2k}^{\perp} > 0$ for all $2 \le k \le 2^{m-1} - 2$. The desired conclusion then follows from Lemma 5.41 and Theorem 5.39.   □

Theorem 5.42 shows that $(\mathcal{R}_2(1,m)^*)^{\perp}$ holds $2^{m-1} - 3$ 2-designs. It can also be proved by the Assmus-Mattson Theorem (i.e., Corollary 4.26) and Lemma 5.41, together with the weight enumerator of $\mathcal{R}_2(1,m)^*$ given in (5.17).

We remark that the code $\mathcal{R}_2(1,m)^*$ contains the Simplex code as a subcode. Hence, the 2-designs held in $\mathcal{R}_2(r,m)^*$ and $(\mathcal{R}_2(r,m)^*)^{\perp}$ are related to those held in the Simplex and Hamming codes (See Section 10.5.4), respectively.

To settle the parameters of the 2-designs held in $\mathcal{R}_2(r,m)^*$ and $(\mathcal{R}_2(r,m)^*)^{\perp}$, we have to solve the following problem.

Problem 5.43. Determine the weight distributions of $\mathcal{R}_2(r,m)^*$ and $(\mathcal{R}_2(r,m)^*)^{\perp}$ for $2 \le r \le m - 2$, where $m \ge 4$.

Given the weight distribution of $\mathcal{R}_2(2,m)$ in Section 5.2.2, one might be able to settle the weight distribution of $\mathcal{R}_2(2,m)^*$.

5.4   Notes

Recall that $\mathcal{R}_2(m,m) = \mathrm{GF}(2)^{2^m}$. Every binary linear code C of length 2^m must be a subcode of $\mathcal{R}_2(r,m)$ for some r with $0 \le r \le m$. The smallest r such that $C \subseteq \mathcal{R}_2(r,m)$ is called the *Reed-Muller cover size*. The existence of the Reed-Muller cover size for any linear code C of length 2^m is clear. If the Reed-Muller cover size of C is r, then the minimum distance $d(C)$ is at least 2^{m-r}. Hence, the following problem is interesting.

Problem 5.44. Work out an efficient method that can determine the Reed-Muller cover size of binary linear codes of length 2^m for positive integers m.

Binary Reed-Muller codes were generalised into two different directions and two families of nonbinary codes were obtained. The two families of generalised codes will be treated separately in Chapter 6, as they support only 2-designs.

Reed–Muller codes are error-correcting codes that are used in wireless communications applications, particularly in deep-space communication in the Mariner 9 Spacecraft. Recently, Reed–Muller codes have become a hot topic due to the fact that they belong to the class of locally testable codes and locally decodable codes, which makes them useful in the design of probabilistically checkable proofs in computational complexity theory.

Chapter 6

Affine Invariant Codes and Their Designs

A cyclic code of length $q^m - 1$ over $GF(q)$ is said to be *primitive*. In this chapter, we treat a special type of primitive cyclic codes and their extended codes over $GF(q)$, which are called *affine-invariant extended cyclic codes*, and describe the support designs of these codes.

6.1 Affine-Invariant Extended Cyclic Codes and Their Designs

In this section, we first give a special representation of primitive cyclic codes and their extended codes, and then define and characterise affine-invariant codes.

Recall that $\mathcal{R}_n$ denotes the quotient ring $GF(q)[x]/(x^n - 1)$. Any cyclic code C of length n over $GF(q)$ is an ideal of $\mathcal{R}_n$, and every codeword of C is a polynomial $c(x) = \sum_{i=0}^{n-1} c_i x^i$, where all $c_i \in GF(q)$.

Let J and J* denote $GF(q^m)$ and $GF(q^m)^*$, respectively. Let α be a primitive element of $GF(q^m)$. The set J will be the index set of the extended cyclic codes of length q^m, and the set J* will be the index set of the cyclic codes of length n. Let X be an indeterminate. Define

$$GF(q)[J] = \left\{ a = \sum_{g \in J} a_g X^g : a_g \in GF(q) \text{ for all } g \in J \right\}. \tag{6.1}$$

The set $GF(q)[J]$ is an algebra under the following operations

$$u \sum_{g \in J} a_g X^g + v \sum_{g \in J} b_g X^g = \sum_{g \in J} (u a_g + v b_g) X^g$$

for all $u, v \in GF(q)$, and

$$\left(\sum_{g \in J} a_g X^g \right) \left(\sum_{g \in J} b_g X^g \right) = \sum_{g \in J} \left(\sum_{h \in J} a_h b_{g-h} \right) X^g. \tag{6.2}$$

The zero and unit of $GF(q)[J]$ are $\sum_{g \in J} 0 X^g$ and X^0, respectively.

165

Similarly, let

$$GF(q)[J^*] = \left\{ a = \sum_{g \in J^*} a_g X^g : a_g \in GF(q) \text{ for all } g \in J^* \right\}. \tag{6.3}$$

The set $GF(q)[J^*]$ is not a subalgebra, but a subspace of $GF(q)[J]$. Obviously, the elements of $GF(q)[J^*]$ are of the form

$$\sum_{i=0}^{n-1} a_{\alpha^i} X^{\alpha^i},$$

and those of $GF(q)[J]$ are of the form

$$a_0 X^0 + \sum_{i=0}^{n-1} a_{\alpha^i} X^{\alpha^i}.$$

Subsets of the subspace $GF(q)[J^*]$ will be used to characterise primitive cyclic codes over $GF(q)$ and those of the algebra $GF(q)[J]$ will be employed to characterise extended primitive cyclic codes over $GF(q)$.

We define a one-to-one correspondence between $\mathcal{R}_n$ and $GF(q)[J^*]$ by

$$\Upsilon : c(x) = \sum_{i=0}^{n-1} c_i x^i \to C(X) = \sum_{i=0}^{n-1} C_{\alpha^i} X^{\alpha^i}, \tag{6.4}$$

where $C_{\alpha^i} = c_i$ for all i.

The following theorem is obviously true.

Theorem 6.1. *$C \subseteq \mathcal{R}_n$ has the circulant cyclic shift property if and only if $\Upsilon(C) \subseteq GF(q)[J^*]$ has the property that*

$$\sum_{i=0}^{n-1} C_{\alpha^i} X^{\alpha^i} = \sum_{g \in J^*} C_g X^g \in \Upsilon(C)$$

if and only if

$$\sum_{i=0}^{n-1} C_{\alpha^i} X^{\alpha \alpha^i} = \sum_{g \in J^*} C_g X^{\alpha g} \in \Upsilon(C).$$

With Theorem 6.1, every primitive cyclic code over $GF(q)$ can be viewed as a special subset of $GF(q)[J^*]$ having the property documented in this theorem. This new representation of primitive cyclic codes over $GF(q)$ will be very useful for determining a subgroup of the automorphism group of certain primitive cyclic codes.

It is now time to extend primitive cyclic codes, which are subsets of $GF(q)[J^*]$. We use the element $0 \in J$ to index the extended coordinate. The extended codeword $\overline{C}(X)$ of a codeword $C(X) = \sum_{g \in J^*} C_g X^g$ in $GF(q)[J^*]$ is defined by

$$\overline{C}(X) = \sum_{g \in J} C_g X^g \tag{6.5}$$

with $\sum_{g \in J} C_g = 0$.

Notice that $X^{\alpha 0} = X^0 = 1$. The following then follows from Theorem 6.1.

Theorem 6.2. *The extended code $\overline{C}$ of a cyclic code $C \subseteq GF(q)[J^*]$ is a subspace of $GF(q)[J]$ such that*

$$\overline{C}(X) = \sum_{g \in J} C_g X^g \in \overline{C} \text{ if and only if } \sum_{g \in J} C_g X^{\alpha g} \in \overline{C} \text{ and } \sum_{g \in J} C_g = 0.$$

If a cyclic code C is viewed as an ideal of $\mathcal{R}_n = GF(q)[x]/(x^n - 1)$, it can be defined by its set of zeros or its defining set (see Section 3.4). When C and $\overline{C}$ are put in the settings $GF(q)[J^*]$ and $GF(q)[J]$, respectively, they can be defined with some counterpart of the defining set. This can be done with the assistance of the following function ϕ_s from $GF(q)[J]$ to J:

$$\phi_s \left(\sum_{g \in J} C_g X^g \right) = \sum_{g \in J} C_g g^s, \qquad (6.6)$$

where $s \in \mathcal{N} = \{i : 0 \leq i \leq n\}$ and by convention $0^0 = 1$ in J.

The following follows from Theorem 6.2 and the definition of ϕ_s directly.

Lemma 6.3. *$\overline{C}(X)$ is the extended codeword of $C(X) \in GF(q)[J^*]$ if and only if $\phi_0(\overline{C}(X)) = 0$. In particular, if $\overline{C}$ is the extended code of a primitive cyclic code $C \subseteq GF(q)[J^*]$, then $\phi_0(\overline{C}(X)) = 0$ for all $\overline{C}(X) \in \overline{C}$.*

Lemma 6.4. *Let C be a primitive cyclic code of length n over $GF(q)$. Let T be the defining set of C with respect to α, when it is viewed as an ideal of $\mathcal{R}_n$. Let $s \in T$ and $1 \leq s \leq n-1$. We have then $\phi_s(\overline{C}(X)) = 0$ for all $\overline{C}(X) \in \overline{C}$.*

Proof. Note that $0^s = 0$ in J, as $s \neq 0$. We have then

$$\phi_s(\overline{C}(X)) = 0^s + \sum_{i=0}^{n-1} C_{\alpha^i}(\alpha^i)^s = \sum_{i=0}^{n-1} c_i(\alpha^s)^i = c(\alpha^s) = 0, \qquad (6.7)$$

where $c(x) \in \mathcal{R}_n$ is the polynomial associated to $C(X) \in GF(q)[J^*]$. $\square$

Lemma 6.5. *Let C be a primitive cyclic code of length n over $GF(q)$. Let T be the defining set of C with respect to α, when it is viewed as an ideal of $\mathcal{R}_n$. Then $0 \in T$ if and only if $\phi_n(\overline{C}(X)) = 0$ for all $\overline{C}(X) \in \overline{C}$.*

Proof. By definition, $\alpha^n = 1$. It then follows from (6.7) that $\phi_n(\overline{C}(X)) = c(1)$, where $c(x) \in \mathcal{R}_n$ is the polynomial associated to $C(X) \in GF(q)[J^*]$. The desired conclusion then follows. $\square$

Combining Lemmas 6.3, 6.4, 6.5 and the discussions above, we can define an extended cyclic code in terms of a defining set as follows.

A code $\overline{C}$ of length q^m is an *extended primitive cyclic code* with defining set $\overline{T}$ provided $\overline{T} \setminus \{n\} \subseteq \overline{\mathcal{N}}$ is a union of q-cyclotomic cosets modulo $n = q^m - 1$ with $0 \in \overline{T}$ and

$$\overline{C} = \{\overline{C}(X) \in \mathrm{GF}(q)[J] : \phi_s(\overline{C}(X)) = 0 \text{ for all } s \in \overline{T}\}. \tag{6.8}$$

The following remarks are helpful for fully understanding the characterisation of extended primitive cyclic codes:

- The condition that $\overline{T} \setminus \{n\} \subseteq \overline{\mathcal{N}}$ is a union of q-cyclotomic cosets modulo $n = q^m - 1$ is to ensure that the code C obtained by puncturing the first coordinate of $\overline{C}$ and ordering the elements of J with $(0, \alpha^n, \alpha^1, \dots, \alpha^{n-1})$ is a primitive cyclic code.
- The additional requirement $0 \in \overline{T}$ and (6.8) are to make sure that $\overline{C}$ is the extended code of C.
- If $n \in \overline{T}$, then C is an even-like code. In this case, the extension is trivial, i.e., the extended coordinate in every codeword of $\overline{C}$ is always equal to 0. If $n \notin \overline{T}$, then $0 \notin T$. Thus, the extension is nontrivial.
- If $\overline{C}$ is the extended code of a primitive cyclic code C, then

$$\overline{T} = \begin{cases} \{0\} \cup T & \text{if } 0 \notin T, \\ \{n\} \cup T & \text{if } 0 \in T, \end{cases}$$

where T and $\overline{T}$ are the defining sets of C and $\overline{C}$, respectively.

A pictorial illustration of the representations of primitive cyclic codes and their extended codes is summarised in Table 6.1.

Table 6.1   A comparison of the representations of primitive cyclic codes and their extensions

Cyclic codes	Cyclic codes	Extended codes
$\mathrm{GF}(q)[x]/(x^n - 1)$	$\mathrm{GF}(q)[J^*]$	$\mathrm{GF}(q)[J]$
C ideal	C subset	$\overline{C}$ subset
$c(x) = \sum_{i=0}^{n-1} c_i x^i$	$C(X) = \sum_{i=0}^{n-1} C_{\alpha^i} X^{\alpha^i}$	$\overline{C}(X) = C_0 + \sum_{i=0}^{n-1} C_{\alpha^i} X^{\alpha^i}$
	$C_{\alpha^i} = c_i,\ 0 \le i \le n-1$	with $C_0 + \sum_{i=0}^{n-1} C_{\alpha^i} = 0$
		C_0 is the extended coordinate
Defining set T		Defining set $\overline{T}$
$\{i \in \mathcal{N} : g(\alpha^i) = 0\}$		$\{s \in \overline{\mathcal{N}} : \phi_s(\overline{C}(X)) = 0\ \forall\ \overline{C}(X) \in \overline{C}\}$
$\mathcal{N} = \{0, 1, \dots, n-1\}$		$\overline{\mathcal{N}} = \{0, 1, \dots, n\}$

Let σ be a permutation on J. This permutation acts on a code $\overline{C} \subseteq \mathrm{GF}(q)[J]$ as follows:

$$\sigma\left(\sum_{g \in J} C_g X^g\right) = \sum_{g \in J} C_g X^{\sigma(g)}. \tag{6.9}$$

Recall that the general affine group $GA_1(GF(q^m))$ consists of the following permutations of $GF(q^m)$:

$$\{\sigma_{(a,b)}(y) = ay + b : a \in J^*, b \in J\}. \tag{6.10}$$

This group was studied in Section 1.8.5. We have the following conclusions about $GA_1(GF(q^m))$:

- $GA_1(GF(q^m))$ is a permutation group on J under the function composition.
- The group action of $GA_1(GF(q^m))$ on $GF(q^m)$ is doubly transitive, i.e., 2-transitive (see Theorem 1.77).
- $GA_1(GF(q^m))$ has order $(n+1)n = q^m(q^m - 1)$ (see Theorem 1.76).
- Obviously, the maps $\sigma_{(a,0)}$ are merely the cyclic shifts on the coordinates $(\alpha^n, \alpha^1, \ldots, \alpha^{n-1})$ each fixing the coordinate 0.

An *affine-invariant code* is an extended primitive cyclic code $\overline{C}$ such that $GA_1(GF(q^m)) \subseteq PAut(\overline{C})$. For certain applications, it is important to know if a given extended primitive cyclic code $\overline{C}$ is affine-invariant or not. This question can be answered by examining the defining set of the code. In order to do this, we introduce a partial ordering $\preceq$ on $\mathcal{N}$. Suppose that $q = p^t$ for some positive integer t. Then by definition $\mathcal{N} = \{0, 1, 2, \ldots, n\}$, where $n = q^m - 1 = p^{mt} - 1$. The p-adic expansion of each $s \in \mathcal{N}$ is given by

$$s = \sum_{i=0}^{mt-1} s_i p^i, \text{ where } 0 \leq s_i < p \text{ for all } 0 \leq i \leq mt - 1.$$

Let the p-adic expansion of $r \in \mathcal{N}$ be

$$r = \sum_{i=0}^{mt-1} r_i p^i.$$

We say that $r \preceq s$ if $r_i \leq s_i$ for all $0 \leq i \leq mt - 1$. By definition, we have $r \leq s$ if $r \preceq s$.

We shall need the following theorem, which is due to Lucas (1878).

Theorem 6.6 (Lucas). *Let $r = \sum_{i=0}^{mt-1} r_i p^i$ and $s = \sum_{i=0}^{mt-1} s_i p^i$ be the p-adic expansions of r and s. Then*

$$\binom{s}{r} \equiv \prod_{i=0}^{mt-1} \binom{s_i}{r_i} \pmod{p}.$$

The following is a characterisation of affine-invariant codes due to Kasami, Lin and Peterson (1968a). The original characterisation of Kasami, Lin and Peterson is combinatorial. The partial order approach presented here comes from Charpin (1990).

Theorem 6.7 (Kasami-Lin-Peterson). *Let $\overline{C}$ be an extended cyclic code of length q^m over $\mathrm{GF}(q)$ with defining set $\overline{T}$. The code $\overline{C}$ is affine-invariant if and only if whenever $s \in \overline{T}$ then $r \in \overline{T}$ for all $r \in \mathcal{N}$ with $r \preceq s$.*

Proof. Let $\overline{C}(X) = \sum_{g \in J} C_g X^g \in \overline{C}$. Let $s \in \mathcal{N}$ and $a, b \in J$ with $a \neq 0$. We have then

$$\sigma_{(a,b)}(\overline{C}(X)) = \sum_{g \in J} C_g X^{ag+b}.$$

Consequently,

$$\phi_s\left(\sigma_{(a,b)}(\overline{C}(X))\right) = \sum_{g \in J} C_g (ag+b)^s = \sum_{g \in J} C_g \sum_{r=0}^{s} \binom{s}{r} (ag)^r b^{s-r}.$$

According to Lucas' Theorem, $\binom{s}{r}$ is nonzero modulo p if and only if $r_i \leq s_i$ for all $0 \leq i \leq mt - 1$, where $r = \sum_{i=0}^{mt-1} r_i p^i$ and $s = \sum_{i=0}^{mt-1} s_i p^i$ are the p-adic expansions of r and s. Hence,

$$\phi_s\left(\sigma_{(a,b)}(\overline{C}(X))\right) = \sum_{g \in J} C_g \sum_{r \preceq s} \binom{s}{r} (ag)^r b^{s-r} = \sum_{r \preceq s} \binom{s}{r} a^r b^{s-r} \sum_{g \in J} C_g g^r.$$

Therefore,

$$\phi_s\left(\sigma_{(a,b)}(\overline{C}(X))\right) = \sum_{r \preceq s} \binom{s}{r} a^r b^{s-r} \phi_r(\overline{C}(X)). \tag{6.11}$$

Let s be any element of $\overline{T}$ and assume that if $r \preceq s$, then $r \in \overline{T}$. By (6.8), $\phi_r(\overline{C}(X)) = 0$ as $r \in \overline{T}$. It then follows from (6.11) that

$$\phi_s\left(\sigma_{(a,b)}(\overline{C}(X))\right) = 0.$$

As s is an arbitrary element of $\overline{T}$, by (6.8), $\overline{C}$ is affine-invariant.

Conversely, assume that $\overline{C}$ is affine-invariant. Let $s \in \overline{T}$ and $r \preceq s$. We would prove that $r \in \overline{T}$, that is $\phi_r(\overline{C}(X)) = 0$ by (6.8). Since $\overline{C}$ is affine-invariant, $\phi_s\left(\sigma_{(a,b)}(\overline{C}(X))\right) = 0$ for all $a \in J^*$ and $b \in J$. In particular, this holds for $a = 1$; putting $a = 1$ in (6.11) gives

$$0 = \sum_{r \preceq s} \binom{s}{r} \phi_r(\overline{C}(X)) b^{s-r}$$

for all $b \in J$. But the right-hand side of this equation is a polynomial in b of degree at most $s < q^m$ with all q^m possible $b \in J$. Hence, this must be the zero polynomial. It follows that $\binom{s}{r} \phi_r(\overline{C}(X)) = 0$ in J for all $r \preceq s$. However, by Lucas' Theorem again, $\binom{s}{r} \not\equiv 0 \pmod{p}$ and thus these binomial coefficients are nonzero in J. As a result, $\phi_r(\overline{C}(X)) = 0$ implies that $r \in \overline{T}$. $\square$

The following corollary will be useful subsequently.

Corollary 6.8. *Let $\overline{C}$ be an extended cyclic code of length q^m over GF(q) with defining set $\overline{T}$. If $\overline{C}$ is affine-invariant and $n = q^m - 1 \in \overline{T}$, then $\overline{C}$ is the zero code.*

Proof. Let $q = p^t$ and $n = q^m - 1 = p^{mt} - 1$. Recall that $\overline{\mathcal{N}} = \{0, 1, \ldots, n\}$. Note that the p-adic expansion of n is $n = \sum_{i=0}^{mt-1}(p-1)p^i$. We have $s \preceq n$ for all $s \in \overline{\mathcal{N}}$. As a result, $\overline{T} = \overline{\mathcal{N}}$. The desired conclusion then follows. $\qquad\square$

Corollary 6.8 implies that the extended code of an even-like primitive cyclic code cannot be affine-invariant.

The following result is fundamental.

Theorem 6.9. *The dual of an affine-invariant code C over GF(q) of length $n = q^m$ is also affine-invariant.*

Proof. Let C be an affine-invariant code over GF(q) with length $n = q^m$. By definition, $\mathrm{GA}_1(\mathrm{GF}(q^m))$ is a subgroup of the permutation automorphism group $\mathrm{PAut}(C)$. It then follows from Theorem 2.14 that $\mathrm{GA}_1(\mathrm{GF}(q^m))$ is also a subgroup of the permutation automorphism group $\mathrm{PAut}(C^\perp)$. The desired conclusion then follows. $\qquad\square$

Affine-invariant codes are very attractive partly due to the following result.

Theorem 6.10. *Let $\overline{A}_i$ denote the number of codewords of weight i in an affine-invariant code $\overline{C}$ of length q^m. Then for each i with $\overline{A}_i \neq 0$, the supports of the codewords of weight i in $\overline{C}$ form a 2-design.*

Proof. By definition, the permutation automorphism group of an affine-invariant code $\overline{C}$ contains $\mathrm{GA}_1(\mathrm{GF}(q^m))$ as a subgroup, and is thus 2-transitive. The desired conclusion then follows from Theorem 4.30. $\qquad\square$

In general, affine-invariant codes of length q^m hold only 2-designs for $q > 2$. However, some binary affine-invariant codes (e.g., binary Reed-Muller codes) hold 3-designs. In the subsequent section, we will introduce several families of affine-invariant codes and investigate their designs. They all hold 2-designs, and some of them hold 3-designs.

6.2 Specific Families of Affine-Invariant Extended Cyclic Codes

In this section, we present several families of affine-invariant extended cyclic codes, and consider the designs of some of these codes. The designs of other affine-invariant codes are dealt with in other chapters.

6.2.1 Extended Narrow-Sense Primitive BCH Codes

BCH codes were briefly introduced in Section 3.7. Recall that the narrow-sense primitive BCH code $C_{(q,q^m-1,\delta,1)}$ has definition set $T = \cup_{i=1}^{\delta-1} C_i$, where C_i is the q-cyclotomic coset modulo $n = q^m - 1$ containing i and $2 \leq \delta \leq n$. By the discussions in Section 6.1, the extended code $\overline{C_{(q,q^m-1,\delta,1)}}$ has defining set $\overline{T} = \{0\} \cup T$, as $0 \notin T$. Note that $n \notin \overline{T}$.

We are now ready to prove the following.

Theorem 6.11. *Let* $2 \leq \delta \leq n$. *Then* $\overline{C_{(q,q^m-1,\delta,1)}}$ *is affine-invariant.*

Proof. As shown above, $\overline{C_{(q,q^m-1,\delta,1)}}$ has defining set $\overline{T} = \{0\} \cup T$, where $T = \cup_{i=1}^{\delta-1} C_i$. Let $s \in \overline{T}$ and $r \in \mathcal{N}$. Assume that $r \preceq s$. We need prove that $r \in \overline{T}$ by Theorem 6.7.

If $s = 0$, then $r = 0$. In this case, we have indeed $r \in \overline{T}$. We now assume that $s > 0$. Since $n = q^m - 1$ and $r \preceq s$, we have $rq^i \bmod n \preceq sq^i \bmod n$ for all nonnegative integer i. Let $sq^i \bmod n$ be the coset leader of C_s for some nonnegative integer i. Then we deduce

$$rq^i \bmod n \leq sq^i \bmod n \leq \delta - 1.$$

Therefore, $rq^i \bmod n \in \overline{T}$. It then follows that

$$r \in C_{rq^i \bmod n} \subseteq \overline{T}.$$

This completes the proof. □

The automorphism group of the code $\overline{C_{(q,q^m-1,\delta,1)}}$ is given in Berger and Charpin (1999). As a corollary of Theorem 6.11, we have the following.

Corollary 6.12. *The automorphism group* $\mathrm{Aut}(\overline{C_{(q,q^m-1,\delta,1)}})$ *is doubly transitive.*

Proof. Recall that the group action of $\mathrm{GA}_1(\mathrm{GF}(q^m))$ on the set $\mathrm{GF}(q^m)$ is doubly transitive. By Theorem 6.11, $\mathrm{GA}_1(\mathrm{GF}(q^m)) \subseteq \mathrm{Aut}(\overline{C_{(q,q^m-1,\delta,1)}})$. Recall that the coordinates of $\overline{C_{(q,q^m-1,\delta,1)}}$ are indexed by the elements in $\mathrm{GF}(q^m)$. The desired conclusion then follows. □

Theorem 6.13. *The supports of the codewords of weight* $i > 0$ *in* $\overline{C_{(q,q^m-1,\delta,1)}}$ *form a 2-design, provided that* $\overline{A}_i \neq 0$.

Proof. The desired conclusion follows from Theorems 6.11 and 6.10. □

We will treat the designs of the codes $\overline{C_{(q,q^m-1,\delta,1)}}$ in Chapters 9 and 8, as narrow-sense primitive BCH codes form a large class of cyclic codes. It is noticed that $\overline{C_{(q,q^m-1,2,1)}}$ is in fact the first-order generalised Reed-Muller code, which will be treated in Section 6.2.2.

6.2.2 Generalised Reed-Muller Codes and Their Designs

Binary Reed-Muller codes were introduced in Section 5.1, and their designs were studied in Section 5.2. In this subsection, we introduce the generalised Reed-Muller codes and describe their designs. Binary Reed-Muller codes were treated in Chapter 5 separately, as they hold 3-designs, while generalised Reed-Muller codes over GF(q) hold only 2-designs for $q > 2$.

We first define the punctured generalised Reed-Muller codes, and will then introduce the generalised Reed-Muller codes. Let q be a prime power as before. For any integer $j = \sum_{i=0}^{m-1} j_i q^i$, where $0 \le j_i \le q-1$ for all $0 \le i \le m-1$ and m is a positive integer, we define

$$\omega_q(j) = \sum_{i=0}^{m-1} j_i, \tag{6.12}$$

where the sum is taken over the ring of integers, and is called the q-weight of j.

Let ℓ be a positive integer with $1 \le \ell < (q-1)m$. The ℓ-th order *punctured generalized Reed-Muller code* $\mathcal{R}_q(\ell, m)^*$ over GF(q) is the cyclic code of length $n = q^m - 1$ with generator polynomial

$$g(x) = \prod_{\substack{1 \le j \le n-1 \\ \omega_q(j) < (q-1)m-\ell}} (x - \alpha^j), \tag{6.13}$$

where α is a generator of GF(q^m)*. Since $\omega_q(j)$ is a constant function on each q-cyclotomic coset modulo $n = q^m - 1$, $g(x)$ is a polynomial over GF(q).

The parameters of the punctured generalized Reed-Muller code $\mathcal{R}_q(\ell, m)^*$ are known and summarized in the next theorem.

Theorem 6.14. *For any ℓ with $0 \le \ell < (q-1)m$, $\mathcal{R}_q(\ell, m)^*$ is a cyclic code over* GF(q) *with length $n = q^m - 1$, dimension*

$$\kappa = \sum_{i=0}^{\ell} \sum_{j=0}^{m} (-1)^j \binom{m}{j} \binom{i - jq + m - 1}{i - jq}$$

and minimum weight $d = (q - \ell_0)q^{m-\ell_1-1} - 1$, where $\ell = \ell_1(q-1) + \ell_0$ and $0 \le \ell_0 < q-1$.

Proof. We first prove the conclusion on the dimension of the code. Notice that the number of ways of picking j objects from a set of m objects with repetitions allowed is equal to $\binom{j+m-1}{j}$. By an inclusion-exclusion argument, one can show that the number of ways of picking i objects from a set of m objects, under the restriction that no objects can be chosen more than $q - 1$ times, is equal to

$$\sum_{j=0}^{m} (-1)^j \binom{m}{j} \binom{i - jq + m - 1}{i - jq}.$$

Summarizing on i gives the desired conclusion on the dimension of this code.

We now deal with the minimum weight d of this code. By definition, we have

$$(q-1)m - \ell = (m - \ell_1 - 1)(q-1) + (q-1-\ell_0).$$

Let h be the smallest integer with $\omega_q(h) = (q-1)m - \ell$. Then

$$h = (q-1-\ell_0)q^{m-\ell_1-1} + \sum_{i=0}^{m-\ell_1-2}(q-1)q^i = (q-\ell_0)q^{m-\ell_1-1} - 1.$$

By the construction of this code, every integer u with $0 < u < h$ satisfies $\omega_q(u) < (q-1)m - \ell$. Hence, the elements $\alpha^1, \alpha^2, \ldots, \alpha^{h-1}$ are all roots of the generator polynomial $g(x)$ of (6.13). It then follows from the BCH bound that

$$d \geq (q - \ell_0)q^{m-\ell_1-1} - 1.$$

It was shown in Assmus and Key (1992a)[Theorem 5.5.3] and Delsarte, Goethals and MacWilliams (1970) that the code has a codeword of Hamming weight $(q - \ell_0)q^{m-\ell_1-1} - 1$. This proves the desired conclusion on the minimum weight. $\square$

Example 6.15. Let $(q, m, \ell) = (3, 3, 3)$, and let α be a generator of $GF(3^3)^*$ with $\alpha^3 + 2\alpha + 1 = 0$. Then $\mathcal{R}_3(3,3)^*$ is a ternary code with parameters $[26, 17, 5]$ and generator polynomial

$$g(x) = x^9 + 2x^8 + x^7 + x^6 + x^5 + 2x^4 + 2x^3 + 2x^2 + x + 1.$$

Example 6.16. Let $(q, m, \ell) = (5, 2, 2)$, and let α be a generator of $GF(5^2)^*$ with $\alpha^2 + 4\alpha + 2 = 0$. Then $\mathcal{R}_5(2,2)^*$ is a cyclic code over $GF(5)$ with parameters $[24, 6, 14]$ and generator polynomial

$$g(x) = x^{18} + 2x^{16} + 3x^{15} + 3x^{13} + x^{11} + 2x^9 + x^8 + 2x^7$$
$$+ 4x^6 + 3x^5 + 2x^4 + 4x^3 + 3x^2 + 4x + 4.$$

The weight distribution of $\mathcal{R}_q(1, m)^*$ is given as follows.

Theorem 6.17. $\mathcal{R}_q(1, m)^*$ *has parameters* $[q^m - 1, m + 1, (q-1)q^{m-1} - 1]$ *and weight enumerator*

$$1 + (q-1)(q^m - 1)z^{(q-1)q^{m-1}-1} + (q^m - 1)z^{(q-1)q^{m-1}} + (q-1)z^{q^m-1}.$$

The dual code $(\mathcal{R}_q(1, m)^*)^\perp$ *has parameters* $[q^m - 1, q^m - m - 2, d^\perp]$, *where* $d^\perp = 4$ *if* $q = 2$, *and* $d^\perp = 3$ *if* $q \geq 3$.

Proof. The proof is left to the reader. $\square$

The weight distribution of $\mathcal{R}_q(2,m)^*$ may be known. However, it looks very challenging to settle the weight distribution of $\mathcal{R}_q(r,m)^*$ for $r \geq 3$.

The dual of the punctured generalized Reed-Muller code is described in the following theorem [Assmus and Key (1992a)][Corollary 5.5.2].

Theorem 6.18. *For $0 \leq \ell < m(q-1)$, the code $(\mathcal{R}_q(\ell,m)^*)^{\perp}$ is the cyclic code with generator polynomial*

$$g^{\perp}(x) = \prod_{\substack{0 \leq j \leq n-1 \\ \omega_q(j) \leq \ell}} (x - \alpha^j), \tag{6.14}$$

where α is a generator of $\mathrm{GF}(q^m)^*$. *In addition,*

$$(\mathcal{R}_q(\ell,m)^*)^{\perp} = (\mathrm{GF}(q)\mathbf{1})^{\perp} \cap \mathcal{R}_q(m(q-1)-1-\ell,m)^*,$$

where $\mathbf{1}$ is the all-one vector in $\mathrm{GF}(q)^n$ *and* $\mathrm{GF}(q)\mathbf{1}$ *denotes the code over* $\mathrm{GF}(q)$ *with length n generated by $\mathbf{1}$.*

The parameters of the dual of the punctured generalized Reed-Muller code are summarized as follows.

Corollary 6.19. *For $0 \leq \ell < m(q-1)$, the code $(\mathcal{R}_q(\ell,m)^*)^{\perp}$ has length $n = q^m - 1$, dimension*

$$\kappa^{\perp} = n - \sum_{i=0}^{\ell} \sum_{j=0}^{m} (-1)^j \binom{m}{j} \binom{i-jq+m-1}{i-jq},$$

and minimum weight

$$d^{\perp} \geq (q - \ell_0')q^{m-\ell_1'-1}, \tag{6.15}$$

where $m(q-1) - 1 - \ell = \ell_1'(q-1) + \ell_0'$ and $0 \leq \ell_0' < q-1$.

Proof. The desired conclusion on the dimension of the cyclic code $(\mathcal{R}_q(\ell,m)^*)^{\perp}$ follows from Theorem 6.14. Note that the generator polynomial $g^{\perp}(x)$ of (6.14) has the extra zero α^0 compared with the generator polynomial of the cyclic code $\mathcal{R}_q(m(q-1)-1-\ell,m)^*$. Then the lower bound of (6.15) follows from the BCH bound and the proof of Theorem 6.14. Another way to prove the lower bound on the minimum distance $d^{\perp}$ goes as follows. By Theorem 6.14, the code $\mathcal{R}_q(m(q-1)-1-\ell,m)^*$ has minimum distance $(q - \ell_0')q^{m-\ell_1'-1} - 1$. Since the extended code of $\mathcal{R}_q(m(q-1)-1-\ell,m)^*$ is affine-invariant, all the minimum weight codewords of $\mathcal{R}_q(m(q-1)-1-\ell,m)^*$ are odd-like. By Theorem 6.18, $(\mathcal{R}_q(\ell,m)^*)^{\perp}$ is the even-like subcode of $\mathcal{R}_q(m(q-1)-1-\ell,m)^*$, the desired lower bound then follows. $\square$

Example 6.20. Let $(q, m, \ell) = (3, 3, 3)$, and let α be a generator of $\mathrm{GF}(3^3)^*$ with $\alpha^3 + 2\alpha + 1 = 0$. Then $(\mathcal{R}_3(3, 3)^*)^\perp$ is a ternary code with parameters $[26, 9, 9]$ and generator polynomial

$$g^\perp(x) = x^{17} + 2x^{16} + 2x^{15} + x^{14} + x^{13} + x^{11} + 2x^{10} + 2x^9 +$$
$$x^8 + 2x^7 + 2x^5 + x^4 + 2x^3 + 2x + 2.$$

The generalized Reed-Muller code $\mathcal{R}_q(\ell, m)$ is defined to be the extended code of $\mathcal{R}_q(\ell, m)^*$, and its parameters are given below.

Theorem 6.21. *Let* $0 \le \ell < q(m-1)$. *Then the generalized Reed-Muller code* $\mathcal{R}_q(\ell, m)$ *has length* $n = q^m$, *dimension*

$$\kappa = \sum_{i=0}^{\ell} \sum_{j=0}^{m} (-1)^j \binom{m}{j} \binom{i - jq + m - 1}{i - jq},$$

and minimum weight

$$d = (q - \ell_0) q^{m - \ell_1 - 1},$$

where $\ell = \ell_1(q-1) + \ell_0$ *and* $0 \le \ell_0 < q - 1$.

Proof. The desired conclusions follow from Theorem 6.14.   □

The following was proved in Delsarte, Goethals and MacWilliams (1970).

Theorem 6.22. *Let* $0 \le \ell < q(m-1)$ *and* $\ell = \ell_1(q-1) + \ell_0$, *where* $0 \le \ell_0 < q-1$. *The total number* $A_{(q-\ell_0)q^{m-\ell_1-1}}$ *of minimum weight codewords in* $\mathcal{R}_q(\ell, m)$ *is given by*

$$A_{(q-\ell_0)q^{m-\ell_1-1}} = (q-1) \frac{q^{\ell_1}(q^m - 1)(q^{m-1} - 1) \cdots (q^{\ell_1+1} - 1)}{(q^{m-\ell_1} - 1)(q^{m-\ell_1-1} - 1) \cdots (q - 1)} N_{\ell_0},$$

where

$$N_{\ell_0} = \begin{cases} 1 & \text{if } \ell_0 = 0, \\ \binom{q}{\ell_0} \frac{q^{m-\ell_1-1}}{q-1} & \text{if } 0 < \ell_0 < q - 1. \end{cases}$$

The generalized Reed-Muller codes $\mathcal{R}_q(\ell, m)$ can also be defined with a multivariate polynomial approach. The reader is referred to Assmus and Key (1992a)[Section 5.4] for details.

As a generalisation of Theorem 5.3, we have the following.

Theorem 6.23. *For* $v < (q-1)m$, *we have*

$$\mathcal{R}_q(v, m)^\perp = \mathcal{R}_q(m(q-1) - 1 - v, m).$$

Proof. A proof can be found in Assmus and Key (1992a)[p. 156]. ☐

One of the major objectives of this section is to prove the following.

Theorem 6.24. *Let ℓ be an integer with $1 \leq \ell < (q-1)m$, and let $q = p^t$ be a prime power for some positive integer t. Then $\mathcal{R}_q(\ell, m)$ is affine-invariant.*

Proof. As before, let $n = q^m - 1$ and let $\overline{T}$ denote the defining set of $\mathcal{R}_q(\ell, m)$. By (6.13), we have
$$\overline{T} = \{0\} \cup \{1 \leq j \leq n-1 : \omega_q(j) < (q-1)m - \ell\}.$$
Put $\overline{\mathcal{N}} = \{0, 1, \ldots, n\}$. Let $s \in \overline{T}$ and $r \in \overline{\mathcal{N}}$. Assume that $r \preceq s$. We need prove that $r \in \overline{T}$ by Theorem 6.7.

Let the q-adic expansions of r and s be
$$r = \sum_{i=0}^{m-1} r_i q^i, \ 0 \leq r_i \leq q-1$$
and
$$s = \sum_{i=0}^{m-1} s_i q^i, \ 0 \leq s_i \leq q-1.$$
Furthermore, let the p-adic expansions of r_i and s_i be
$$r_i = \sum_{j=0}^{t-1} r_{ij} p^j, \ 0 \leq r_{ij} \leq p-1$$
and
$$s_i = \sum_{i=0}^{t-1} s_{ij} p^j, \ 0 \leq s_{ij} \leq p-1.$$
Then the p-adic expansions of r and s are
$$r = \sum_{i=0}^{m-1} \sum_{j=0}^{t-1} r_{ij} p^{j+ti}$$
and
$$s = \sum_{i=0}^{m-1} \sum_{j=0}^{t-1} s_{ij} p^{j+ti}.$$
Since we assumed that $r \preceq s$, it then follows from the definition of the precedence relation that $r_{ij} \leq s_{ij}$ for all i and j. Consequently,
$$r_i = \sum_{j=0}^{t-1} r_{ij} p^j \leq \sum_{i=0}^{t-1} s_{ij} p^j = s_i$$
for all i. We now deduce that
$$\omega_q(r) = \sum_{i=0}^{m-1} r_i \leq \omega_q(s) = \sum_{i=0}^{m-1} s_i < (q-1)m - \ell.$$
This means that $r \in \overline{T}$. ☐

Corollary 6.25. *The automorphism group* $\mathrm{Aut}(\mathcal{R}_q(\ell,m))$ *is doubly transitive.*

Proof. As pointed out earlier, the group action of $\mathrm{GA}_1(\mathrm{GF}(q^m))$ on $\mathrm{GF}(q^m)$ is doubly transitive. By Theorem 6.24, $\mathrm{GA}_1(\mathrm{GF}(q^m)) \subseteq \mathrm{PAut}(\mathcal{R}_q(\ell,m))$. Recall that the coordinates of $\mathcal{R}_q(\ell,m)$ are indexed by the elements in $\mathrm{GF}(q^m)$. The desired conclusion then follows.   □

Theorem 6.26. *Let ℓ be an integer with $1 \leq \ell < (q-1)m$. Then the supports of the codewords of weight $i > 0$ in $\mathcal{R}_q(\ell,m)$ form a 2-design, provided that $A_i \neq 0$.*

Proof. The desired conclusion follows from Theorems 6.24 and 6.10.   □

Combining Theorems 6.22 and 6.26, we deduce the following.

Theorem 6.27. *Let $0 \leq \ell < q(m-1)$ and $\ell = \ell_1(q-1) + \ell_0$, where $0 \leq \ell_0 < q-1$. The supports of the minimum weight codewords in $\mathcal{R}_q(\ell,m)$ form a 2-$(q^m, (q-\ell_0)q^{m-\ell_1-1}, \lambda)$ design, where*

$$\lambda = \frac{A_{(q-\ell_0)q^{m-\ell_1-1}}}{q-1} \frac{\binom{(q-\ell_0)q^{m-\ell_1-1}}{2}}{\binom{q^m}{2}}$$

and $A_{(q-\ell_0)q^{m-\ell_1-1}}$ was given in Theorem 6.22.

Theorem 6.27 is a generalisation of Theorem 5.19. But $\mathcal{R}_q(\ell,m)$ does not hold 3-designs when $q > 2$.

The following result is easy to prove and is left to the reader.

Theorem 6.28. *We have the following equality:*

$$\mathcal{R}_q(1,m) = \overline{\mathcal{C}_{(q,q^m-1,2,1)}}.$$

Theorem 6.29. $\mathcal{R}_q(1,m)$ *has parameters $[q^m, 1+m, (q-1)q^{m-1}]$ and the weight enumerator*

$$1 + q(q^m-1)z^{(q-1)q^{m-1}} + (q-1)z^{q^m}. \tag{6.16}$$

Furthermore, the supports of all minimum weight codewords in $\mathcal{R}_q(1,m)$ form a 2-$(q^m, (q-1)q^{m-1}, (q-1)q^{m-1} - 1)$ design.

Proof. Note that $\mathcal{R}_q((q-1)m-2,m) = \mathcal{R}_q(1,m)^\perp$. The punctured code $\mathcal{R}_q((q-1)m-2,m)^*$ has generator polynomial $\mathbb{M}_\alpha(x)$, where α is a generator of $\mathrm{GF}(q^m)^*$, and is a narrow-sense BCH code with designed distance 2. The parameters and the weight enumerator of $\mathcal{R}_q(1,m)$ are then easily seen. The 2-design property of the supports of all minimum weight codewords in $\mathcal{R}_q(1,m)$ follows from Theorem 6.26. Since $A_{(q-1)q^{m-1}} = q(q^m-1)$ and $(q-1)q^{m-1}$ is the minimum weight of the code, the total number of the supports of all minimum weight codewords is $A_{(q-1)q^{m-1}}/(q-1)$. Hence

$$\lambda = \frac{A_{(q-1)q^{m-1}}}{q-1} \frac{\binom{(q-1)q^{m-1}}{2}}{\binom{q^m}{2}} = (q-1)q^{m-1} - 1.$$

$\square$

Theorem 6.30. *Let $q > 2$. Then the code $\mathcal{R}_q((q-1)m-2,m)$ has parameters $[q^m, q^m - m - 1, 3]$ and weight enumerator*

$$A(z) = \frac{(1+(q-1)z)^{q^m} + (q-1)(1-z)^{q^m}}{q^{m+1}} +$$

$$\frac{q(q^m-1)(1-z)^{(q-1)q^{m-1}}(1+(q-1)z)^{q^{m-1}}}{q^{m+1}}.$$

In particular,

$$A_3 = \frac{q(q^m-1)\left[(q-1)^3\binom{q^{m-1}}{3} - (q-1)^2\binom{q^{m-1}}{2}\binom{(q-1)q^{m-1}}{1}\right]}{q^{m+1}} +$$

$$\frac{q(q^m-1)\left[(q-1)\binom{q^{m-1}}{1}\binom{(q-1)q^{m-1}}{2} - \binom{(q-1)q^{m-1}}{3}\right]}{q^{m+1}} +$$

$$\frac{\binom{q^m}{3}\left[(q-1)^3 - (q-1)\right]}{q^{m+1}}$$

$$= \frac{(q-1)(q-2)(q^m-1)q^m}{6}. \tag{6.17}$$

Proof. Note that $(q-1)m - 2 = (q-1)(m-1) + q - 3$ and $q \geq 3$. It then follows from Theorem 6.21 that $\mathcal{R}_q((q-1)m-2,m)$ has minimum distance 3. By Theorem 6.23, $\mathcal{R}_q((q-1)m-2,m) = \mathcal{R}_q(1,m)^{\perp}$. Hence, the dimension of $\mathcal{R}_q((q-1)m-2,m)$ is $q^m - m - 1$. The desired conclusion on the weight enumerator of $\mathcal{R}_q((q-1)m-2,m)$ follows from Theorem 2.4 and the weight enumerator of $\mathcal{R}_q(1,m)$ given in (6.16). One can verify that the coefficient of z^3 in the weight enumerator $A(z)$ is the A_3 given in (6.17). $\square$

Combining Theorems 6.26 and 6.30, we arrive at the following.

Corollary 6.31. *The supports of all codewords of weight 3 in $\mathcal{R}_q((q-1)m-2,m)$ form a 2-$(q^m, 3, q-2)$ design. In particular, the supports of all minimum codewords in $\mathcal{R}_3(2m-2,m)$ form a 2-$(3^m, 3, 1)$ design, i.e., a Steiner triple system $S(2,3,3^m)$.*

Proof. Combining Theorems 6.26 and 6.30, we have

$$\lambda = \frac{6A_3}{(q-1)(q^m-1)q^m} = q-2.$$

□

It is interesting to obtain an infinite family of Steiner triple systems $S(2,3,3^m)$ from the generalised Reed-Muller ternary codes $\mathcal{R}_3(2m-2,m)$. It was shown in Chapter 5 that the binary Reed-Muller codes $\mathcal{R}_2(m-2,m)$ holds an infinite family of Steiner quadruple systems $S(3,4,2^m)$ (see Corollary 5.22).

Experimental data indicates that $A_i > 0$ for all $4 \leq i \leq q^m$ for the code $\mathcal{R}_q((q-1)m-2,m)$. In theory, one can write down a formula for A_i of all $i \geq 4$ with the weight enumerator given in Theorem 6.30. But this does not mean that one can determine the total number of supports of the codewords with weight i and hence the parameters of the corresponding 2-design.

The weight distribution of the second-order Reed-Muller code $\mathcal{R}_q(2,m)$ for $q > 2$ is documented in Li (2019), which corrects some errors in McEliece (1969). Hence, the parameters of some of the designs held in $\mathcal{R}_q(2,m)$ can be worked out.

Example 6.32. The generalised Reed-Muller code $\mathcal{R}_3(2,3)$ has parameters $[27,10,9]$ and weight enumerator

$$1 + 78z^9 + 1404z^{12} + 14040z^{15} + 27300z^{18} + 15444z^{21} + 702z^{24} + 80z^{27}.$$

It holds 2-$(27,k,\lambda)$ designs with the following pairs (k,λ):

$$(9,4), (12,132), (15,2100), (18,5933), (21,4060), (24,92).$$

As demonstrated in Section 5.2, binary Reed-Muller codes hold 3-designs. However, experimental data indicates that $\mathcal{R}_q(\ell,m)$ does not hold 3-designs in general for $q > 2$. To determine the parameters of the 2-designs held in $\mathcal{R}_q(\ell,m)$, we need to to settle the following problem.

Problem 6.33. Let $3 \leq \ell \leq (q-1)m$. Determine the nonzero weights in $\mathcal{R}_q(\ell,m)$. For each nonzero weight w, determine the number A_w of codewords of weight w and the number of supports of the codewords of weight w.

6.2.3 *Dilix Codes and Their Designs*

In this section, we introduce a type of extended cyclic codes, which are called *Dilix codes* and were developed in Ding, Li and Xia (2018), and prove that they are affine-invariant.

Let m be a positive integer and let $n = q^m - 1$, where $q = p^\rho$, p is a prime and ρ is a positive integer. For any integer a with $0 \le a \le n - 1$, we have the following q-adic expansion

$$a = \sum_{j=0}^{m-1} a_j q^j,$$

where $0 \le a_j \le q - 1$. The Hamming weight of a, denoted by $\mathtt{wt}(a)$, is the Hamming weight of the vector $(a_0, a_1, \ldots, a_{m-1})$.

Let α be a generator of $\mathrm{GF}(q^m)^*$. For any $1 \le h \le m$, we define a polynomial

$$g_{(q,m,h)}(x) = \prod_{\substack{1 \le a \le n-1 \\ 1 \le \mathtt{wt}(a) \le h}} (x - \alpha^a). \tag{6.18}$$

Since $\mathtt{wt}(a)$ is a constant function on each q-cyclotomic coset modulo n, $g_{(q,m,h)}(x)$ is a polynomial over $\mathrm{GF}(q)$. By definition, $g_{(q,m,h)}(x)$ is a divisor of $x^n - 1$.

Let $\Omega(q, m, h)$ denote the cyclic code over $\mathrm{GF}(q)$ with length n and generator polynomial $g_{(m,q,h)}(x)$, which is called the *punctured Dilix code*. To analyse this code, we set

$$I(q, m, h) = \{1 \le a \le n - 1 : 1 \le \mathtt{wt}(a) \le h\}. \tag{6.19}$$

The dimension of the code $\Omega(q, m, h)$ is equal to $n - |I(q, m, h)|$.

Theorem 6.34. *Let $m \ge 2$ and $1 \le h \le m - 1$. Then $\Omega(q, m, h)$ has parameters $[n, k, d \ge (q^{h+1} - 1)/(q - 1)]$, where*

$$k = q^m - \sum_{i=0}^{h} \binom{m}{i} (q - 1)^i.$$

Proof. As shown earlier, $I(q, m, h)$ is the union of some q-cyclotomic cosets modulo n. The total number of elements in $\mathbb{Z}_n$ with Hamming weight i is equal to $\binom{m}{i}(q - 1)^i$. It then follows that

$$|I(q, m, h)| = \sum_{i=1}^{h} \binom{m}{i} (q - 1)^i.$$

Hence, the dimension k of the code is given by

$$k = q^m - 1 - \sum_{i=1}^{h} \binom{m}{i} (q - 1)^i.$$

Note that every integer a with $1 \le a \le (q^{h+1} - 1)/(q - 1) - 1$ has Hamming weight $\mathtt{wt}(a) \le h$. By definition,

$$\left\{ 1, 2, 3, \ldots, (q^{h+1} - 1)/(q - 1) - 1 \right\} \subset I(q, m, h).$$

It then follows from the BCH bound that $d \ge (q^{h+1} - 1)/(q - 1)$. $\qquad\square$

When $q = 2$, $\Omega(q,m,h)$ clearly becomes the classical punctured binary Reed-Muller code $\text{PGRM}_2(m-1-h,m)$. Hence, $\Omega(q,m,h)$ is indeed a generalization of the original punctured binary Reed-Muller code.

Example 6.35. The following is a list of examples of the code $\Omega(q,m,h)$.

- When $(q,m,h) = (3,3,1)$, $\Omega(q,m,h)$ has parameters $[26,20,4]$.
- When $(q,m,h) = (3,4,1)$, $\Omega(q,m,h)$ has parameters $[80,72,4]$.
- When $(q,m,h) = (3,4,2)$, $\Omega(q,m,h)$ has parameters $[80,48,13]$.
- When $(q,m,h) = (3,4,3)$, $\Omega(q,m,h)$ has parameters $[80,16,40]$.
- When $(q,m,h) = (4,3,1)$, $\Omega(q,m,h)$ has parameters $[63,54,5]$.

An interesting fact about the family of newly generalised codes $\Omega(q,m,h)$ is the following.

Corollary 6.36. *Let $m \geq 2$. Then the ternary cyclic code $\Omega(3,m,1)$ has parameters $[3^m - 1, 3^m - 1 - 2m, 4]$ and is distance-optimal.*

Proof. It follows from Theorem 6.34 that the ternary code $\Omega(3,m,1)$ has length $3^m - 1$, dimension $3^m - 1 - 2m$, and minimum distance $d \geq 4$. We now prove that d cannot be 5 or more. Suppose on the contrary that $d \geq 5$. By the sphere-packing bound, we have

$$\sum_{i=0}^{\lfloor (d-1)/2 \rfloor} \binom{n}{i} 2^i \leq 3^{2m} = (n+1)^2,$$

where $n = 3^m - 1$. Since we assume that $d \geq 5$, we have then

$$\sum_{i=0}^{\lfloor (d-1)/2 \rfloor} \binom{n}{i} 2^i \geq \sum_{i=0}^{2} \binom{n}{i} 2^i = 1 + 2n + 4\binom{n}{2} = 2n^2 + 1 > (n+1)^2.$$

This is contrary to the sphere-packing bound. Consequently, $d = 4$, and the ternary code $\Omega(3,m,1)$ is distance-optimal. □

We inform the reader that the dual code $\Omega(3,m,1)^{\perp}$ has three nonzero weights for odd $m \geq 3$ and five nonzero weights for even m. The weight distribution of $\Omega(3,m,1)^{\perp}$ can be worked out. We have also the next special case in which the parameters of the code $\Omega(q,m,h)$ are known.

Theorem 6.37. *Let m be even. Then the cyclic code $\Omega(q,m,1)$ has parameters $[q^m - 1, q^m - 1 - m(q-1), q+1]$.*

Proof. It follows from Theorem 6.34 that $\Omega(q, m, 1)$ has parameters $[q^m - 1, q^m - 1 - m(q-1), d \geq q+1]$. It then suffices to show that $\Omega(q, m, 1)$ has a codeword of weight $q + 1$. Put

$$c(x) = \frac{x^{q^m - 1} - 1}{x^{\frac{q^m - 1}{q+1}} - 1}.$$

Note that every integer a with $1 \leq a \leq n$ and $\text{wt}(a) = 1$ must be of the form $a = iq^j$, where $1 \leq i \leq q-1$ and $0 \leq j \leq m-1$. For every such a, α^a cannot be a solution of $x^{\frac{q^m - 1}{q+1}} - 1 = 0$. As a result, $c(\alpha^a) = 0$. It then follows that the generator polynomial $g_{(q,m,1)}(x)$ of $\Omega(q, m, 1)$ divides $c(x)$. Therefore, $c(x)$ is a codeword of $\Omega(q, m, 1)$. Obviously, $c(x)$ has weight $q + 1$. The desired conclusion then follows. □

The parameters of $\Omega(q, m, h)$ are also known in the following case.

Theorem 6.38. *Let $m \geq 2$. Then the cyclic code $\Omega(q, m, m-1)$ has parameters $[q^m - 1, (q-1)^m, (q^m - 1)/(q-1)]$.*

Proof. Recall that $m \geq 2$. It follows from Theorem 6.34 that $\Omega(q, m, m-1)$ has parameters $[q^m - 1, (q-1)^m, d \geq (q^m - 1)/(q-1)]$. It then suffices to demonstrate that $\Omega(q, m, m-1)$ has a codeword of weight $(q^m - 1)/(q-1)$. To this end, we define $c(x) = (x^{q^m - 1} - 1)/(x^{q-1} - 1)$, which has Hamming weight $(q^m - 1)/(q-1)$. We now prove that $c(x)$ is a codeword of $\Omega(q, m, m-1)$. Notice that

$$\{\alpha^{i(q^m - 1)/(q-1)} : 0 \leq i \leq q-2\}$$

is the set of all roots of $x^{q-1} - 1$ over $\text{GF}(q)$. Obviously, the Hamming weight of $i(q^m - 1)/(q-1)$ is either 0 or m for all $0 \leq i \leq q-2$. We have then

$$\{i(q^m - 1)/(q-1) : 0 \leq i \leq q-2\} \cap I(q, m, m-1) = \emptyset.$$

Consequently, the generator polynomial $g_{(q,m,m-1)}(x)$ of $\Omega(q, m, m-1)$ divides $c(x)$. This proves the desired conclusion. □

In a few special cases above, we were able to settle the minimum distance of the code $\Omega(q, m, h)$. However, the following problem is still open.

Problem 6.39. Is it true that the minimum distance of the code $\Omega(q, m, h)$ is equal to $(q^{h+1} - 1)/(q - 1)$?

When $q = 2$, the dual code $\Omega(q, m, h)^{\perp}$ is the binary Reed-Muller code. Thus, we need to study the dual code $\Omega(q, m, h)^{\perp}$ for the case $q > 2$ only. The following theorem gives information on the parameters of the dual code $\Omega(q, m, h)^{\perp}$.

Theorem 6.40. *Let $m \geq 2$ and $1 \leq h \leq m-1$. The dual code $\Omega(q,m,h)^{\perp}$ has parameters $[n, k^{\perp}, d^{\perp}]$, where*

$$k^{\perp} = \sum_{i=1}^{h} \binom{m}{i}(q-1)^i.$$

The minimum distance $d^{\perp}$ of $\Omega(q,m,h)^{\perp}$ is lower bounded by

$$d^{\perp} \geq q^{m-h} + q - 2.$$

Proof. The desired conclusion on the dimension of $\Omega(q,m,h)^{\perp}$ follows from the dimension of $\Omega(q,m,h)$. What remains to be proved is the lower bound on the minimum distance $d^{\perp}$. Let $\Omega(q,m,h)^c$ denote the complement of $\Omega(q,m,h)$, which is generated by the check polynomial of $\Omega(q,m,h)$. It is well known that $\Omega(q,m,h)^c$ and $\Omega(q,m,h)^{\perp}$ have the same length, dimension and minimum distance.

By definition, the defining set of $\Omega(q,m,h)^c$ is

$$I(q,m,h)^c = \{0\} \cup \{1 \leq b \leq n-1 : \mathtt{wt}(b) \geq h+1\}.$$

Let $b = q^{m-h} + q^{m-h+1} + \cdots + q^{m-1}$. Define

$$A = \{a + b : 1 \leq a \leq q^{m-h} - 1\}$$

and

$$B = \{jb : 0 \leq j \leq q-2\}.$$

It is straightforward to verify that $A + B \subset I(q,m,h)^c$. Note that $n \in A + B$. In this case, we identify n with 0.

Clearly, A is a set of $q^{m-h} - 1$ consecutive elements in the defining set $I(q,m,h)^c$. Note that

$$\gcd(b,n) = \gcd\left(\frac{q^h-1}{q-1}, q^m-1\right) \leq \gcd(q^h-1, q^m-1) = q^{\gcd(h,m)} - 1.$$

By assumption, $1 \leq h \leq m-1$. We then have $\gcd(h,m) \leq m-h$. Consequently,

$$\gcd(b,n) < q^{m-h}.$$

The desired conclusion on $d^{\perp}$ then follows from the Hartmann-Tzeng bound (see Theorem 3.19). □

When $q = 2$, the lower bound on the minimum distance $d^{\perp}$ of $\Omega(q,m,h)^{\perp}$ given in Theorem 6.40 is achieved. The lower bound is not tight when $q > 2$. However, it is open how to improve this lower bound.

Problem 6.41. Determine the minimum distance $d^{\perp}$ of the code $\Omega(q,m,h)^{\perp}$.

To further study the dual code $\Omega(q,m,h)^\perp$, we need to establish some relation between $\text{wt}(a)$ and $\text{wt}(n-a)$ for $a \in \mathbb{Z}_n$. Let $a \in \mathbb{Z}_n$ and let $a = \sum_{j=0}^{m-1} a_j q^j$ be the q-adic expansion of a. We define

$$\gamma(a) = |\{0 \le j \le m-1 : 1 \le a_j < q-1\}| = \text{wt}(a) - |\{0 \le j \le m-1 : a_j = q-1\}|.$$

Then we have the following lemma whose proof is straightforward and omitted.

Lemma 6.42. *For $a \in \mathbb{Z}_n$, we have*

$$\text{wt}(n-a) = m - \text{wt}(a) + \gamma(a) = m - |\{0 \le j \le m-1 : a_j = q-1\}|.$$

For $0 \le i \le m$, define

$$N(i) = \{a \in \mathbb{Z}_n : \text{wt}(a) = i\}$$

and

$$-N(i) = \{n - a : a \in N(i)\}.$$

Clearly, $|N(i)| = \binom{m}{i}(q-1)^i$.

The following lemma will be useful later.

Lemma 6.43. *In the set $-N(i)$, there are exactly $\binom{m}{i}\binom{i}{j}(q-2)^j$ elements with Hamming weight $m - i + j$ for each j with $0 \le j \le i$.*

Proof. Let $a \in N(i)$. By definition, $\text{wt}(a) = i$. It follows from Lemma 6.42 that

$$\text{wt}(n-a) = m - i + \gamma(a).$$

It is easily seen that

$$|\{1 \le a \le n-1 : \text{wt}(a) = i \text{ and } \gamma(a) = j\}| = \binom{m}{i}\binom{i}{j}(q-2)^j.$$

This completes the proof. $\qquad\qquad\square$

Theorem 6.44. *Let $m \ge 2$. Then $\Omega(q,m,h)^\perp$ is a subcode of $\Omega(q,m,m-1-h) \cap \mathbf{1}^\perp$. In particular, $\Omega(2,m,h)^\perp = \Omega(2,m,m-1-h) \cap \mathbf{1}^\perp$.*

Proof. By definition, the defining set of $\Omega(q,m,h)^\perp$ is $-I(q,m,h)^c$, where

$$-I(q,m,h)^c = \{0\} \cup \{n - a : 1 \le a \le n-1 \text{ and } \text{wt}(a) > h\}.$$

We now prove that

$$I(q,m,m-1-h) \cup \{0\} \subseteq -I(q,m,h)^c.$$

Let $a \in I(q,m,m-1-h)$. By definition, $\text{wt}(a) \le m-1-h$. It then follows from Lemma 6.42 that

$$\text{wt}(n-a) = m - \text{wt}(a) + \gamma(a) \ge h+1+\gamma(a) \ge h+1.$$

This means that $n - a \in I(q,m,h)^c$.

Let $b \in -I(q,m,h)^c$ and $b \neq 0$. Then $b = n - a$ for some $a \neq 0$ and $a \in I(q,m,h)^c$. By definition, $\text{wt}(a) \geq h + 1$. It then follows from Lemma 6.42 that

$$\text{wt}(b) = \text{wt}(n - a) = m - \text{wt}(a) + \gamma(a) \leq m - 1 - h + \gamma(a).$$

Notice that $\gamma(a)$ may be positive for $q > 2$. It is likely that $\text{wt}(b) > m - 1 - h$. Consequently, $I(q,m,m-1-h) \cup \{0\}$ may be a proper subset of $-I(q,m,h)^c$ when $q > 3$. However, when $q = 2$ we have always $\gamma(a) = 0$ and thus the identity:

$$\{0\} \cup I(2,m,m-1-h) = -I(2,m,h)^c.$$

This means that $\Omega(2,m,h)^\perp = \Omega(2,m,m-1-h) \cap \mathbf{1}^\perp$.   □

Example 6.45. Let $(q,m,h) = (3,3,1)$. Then

$$I(q,m,m-1-h) \cup \{0\} = \{0,1,2,3,6,9,18\}$$

and

$$-I(q,m,h)^c = \{0,1,2,3,4,5,6,7,9,10,11,12,13,14,15,16,18,19,21,22\}.$$

This means that $\Omega(q,m,h)^\perp$ is indeed a proper subcode of $\Omega(q,m,m-1-h) \cap \mathbf{1}^\perp$ in this case. This shows a fundamental difference between the binary case and the nonbinary case regarding the codes $\Omega(q,m,h)$.

Experimental data shows that one of $I(q,m,m-h) \cup \{0\}$ and $-I(q,m,h)^c$ is not a subset of the other. Consequently, none of $\Omega(q,m,h)^\perp$ and $\Omega(q,m,m-h)$ is a subcode of the other in general.

Example 6.46. The following is a list of examples of the code $\Omega(q,m,h)^\perp$.

- When $(q,m,h) = (2,4,2)$, the code $\Omega(q,m,h)^\perp$ has parameters $[15,10,4]$. In this case, the lower bound on the minimum distance is achieved.
- When $(q,m,h) = (3,3,1)$, the code $\Omega(q,m,h)^\perp$ has parameters $[26,6,15]$. In this case, the lower bound on the minimum distance is 10.
- When $(q,m,h) = (3,3,2)$, the code $\Omega(q,m,h)^\perp$ has parameters $[26,18,6]$. In this case, the lower bound on the minimum distance is 4.

We now consider the extended code $\overline{\Omega(q,m,h)}$ of $\Omega(q,m,h)$, called the *Dilix code*, and have the following result about the permutation automorphism group of the code.

Theorem 6.47. *Let $q = p^\rho$ be a prime power. Then the Dilix code $\overline{\Omega(q,m,h)}$ is affine-invariant.*

Proof. By (6.18), the defining set $\overline{T}$ of $\overline{\Omega(q,m,h)}$ is given by

$$\overline{T} = \{0\} \cup \{1 \le a \le n-1 : 1 \le \mathrm{wt}(a) \le h\}.$$

Put $\overline{\mathcal{N}} = \{0,1,\ldots,n\}$. Let $s \in \overline{T}$ and $r \in \overline{\mathcal{N}}$. Assume that $r \preceq s$. We need prove that $r \in \overline{T}$ by Theorem 6.7.

Let the q-adic expansions of r and s be

$$r = \sum_{i=0}^{m-1} r_i q^i, \ 0 \le r_i \le q-1$$

and

$$s = \sum_{i=0}^{m-1} s_i q^i, \ 0 \le s_i \le q-1.$$

Furthermore, let the p-adic expansions of r_i and s_i be

$$r_i = \sum_{j=0}^{\rho-1} r_{ij} p^j, \ 0 \le r_{ij} \le p-1$$

and

$$s_i = \sum_{i=0}^{\rho-1} s_{ij} p^j, \ 0 \le s_{ij} \le p-1.$$

Then the p-adic expansions of r and s are

$$r = \sum_{i=0}^{m-1}\sum_{j=0}^{\rho-1} r_{ij} p^{j+\rho i}$$

and

$$s = \sum_{i=0}^{m-1}\sum_{j=0}^{\rho-1} s_{ij} p^{j+\rho i}.$$

Since we assumed that $r \preceq s$, it then follows from the definition of the precedence relation that $r_{ij} \le s_{ij}$ for all i and j. Consequently,

$$r_i = \sum_{j=0}^{\rho-1} r_{ij} p^j \le \sum_{i=0}^{\rho-1} s_{ij} p^j = s_i$$

for all i. Hence,

$$\mathrm{wt}(r) \le \mathrm{wt}(s) \le h.$$

This means that $r \in \overline{T}$. The desired conclusion then follows. $\qquad\square$

Corollary 6.48. *The permutation automorphism group* $\mathrm{PAut}\left(\overline{\Omega(q,m,h)}\right)$ *is doubly transitive.*

Proof. Recall that the action of $GA_1(GF(q^m))$ on $GF(q^m)$ is doubly transitive. By Theorem 6.47, $GA_1(GF(q^m)) \subseteq PAut(\overline{\Omega(q,m,h)})$. Recall that the coordinates of $\overline{\Omega(q,m,h)}$ are indexed by the elements in $GF(q^m)$. The desired conclusion then follows. $\square$

Theorem 6.49. *Let $m \geq 2$ and $1 \leq \ell \leq m-1$. Then the supports of the codewords of weight $i > 0$ in the Dilix code $\overline{\Omega(q,m,\ell)}$ form a 2-design, provided that $\overline{A}_i \neq 0$. Further, the same conclusion holds for the dual code $\overline{\Omega(q,m,\ell)}^{\perp}$.*

Proof. The desired conclusion of the first part follows from Theorems 6.47 and 6.10. Note that $\overline{\Omega(q,m,\ell)}^{\perp}$ and $\overline{\Omega(q,m,\ell)}$ have the same permutation automorphism group. The conclusion of the second part follows. $\square$

Example 6.50. The Dilix code $\overline{\Omega(3,3,2)}$ has parameters $[27,8,14]$ and weight enumerator

$$1 + 810z^{14} + 702z^{15} + 1404z^{17} + 780z^{18} + 2106z^{20} + 702z^{21} + 54z^{26} + 2z^{27}.$$

It holds 2-$(27,k,\lambda)$ designs with the following pairs (k,λ):

$$(14,105),\ (15,105),\ (17,272),\ (18,170),\ (20,570),\ (21,210),\ (26,25).$$

Experimental data indicates that the Dilix code $\overline{\Omega(q,m,\ell)}$ does not hold 3-designs in general for $q > 2$. To determine the parameters of the 2-designs held in $\overline{\Omega(q,m,\ell)}$, we need to solve the following problem.

Problem 6.51. *Let $1 \leq \ell \leq m-1$. Determine the nonzero weights in $\overline{\Omega(q,m,\ell)}$. For each nonzero weight w, determine the number $\overline{A}_w$ of codewords of weight w and the number of supports of the codewords of weight w.*

The following theorem provides information on the parameters of the Dilix code $\overline{\Omega(q,m,h)}$.

Theorem 6.52. *Let $m \geq 2$ and $1 \leq h \leq m-1$. Then $\overline{\Omega(q,m,h)}$ has parameters $[q^m, k, d]$, where*

$$k = q^m - \sum_{i=0}^{h} \binom{m}{i} (q-1)^i$$

and

$$\frac{q^{h+1}-1}{q-1} + 1 \leq d \leq 2q^h. \tag{6.20}$$

Proof. The dimension of the code $\overline{\Omega(q,m,h)}$ follows from Theorem 6.34, as $\overline{\Omega(q,m,h)}$ and $\Omega(q,m,h)$ have the same dimension. The upper bound on the minimum distance of $\overline{\Omega(q,m,h)}$ also follows from that of $\Omega(q,m,h)$. The only nontrivial part is the proof of the lower bound on the minimum distance of the code $\overline{\Omega(q,m,h)}$, which goes as follows.

For the convenience of proof, we use $d(C)$ to denote the minimum distance of a linear code C of length n. It is known that every minimum weight codeword of C must be odd-like if the permutation automorphism group of the extended code $\overline{C}$ is transitive (see Theorem 2.13). It then follows that

$$d(\overline{C}) = d(C) + 1$$

if the permutation automorphism group of the extended code $\overline{C}$ is transitive.

By the proof of Theorem 6.47, the permutation automorphism group of $\overline{\Omega(q,m,h)}$ is transitive. It then follows from the discussion above that

$$d(\overline{\Omega(q,m,h)}) = d(\Omega(q,m,h)) + 1. \tag{6.21}$$

The desired lower bound on the minimum distance of $\overline{\Omega(q,m,h)}$ then follows from the lower bound on the minimum distance of the code $\Omega(q,m,h)$ given in Theorem 6.34. $\square$

In the following special cases, we are able to determine the parameters of the code $\overline{\Omega(q,m,h)}$. The following theorem follows from (6.21) and Corollary 6.36

Theorem 6.53. *Let $m \geq 2$. Then the ternary code $\overline{\Omega(3,m,1)}$ has parameters $[3^m, 3^m - 1 - 2m, 5]$ and is dimension-optimal.*

The ternary code $\overline{\Omega(3,m,1)}$ is said to be dimension-optimal, as there is no ternary code with parameters $[3^m, 3^m - 2m, 5]$. This can be proved with the sphere-packing bound. The next theorem follows from (6.21) and Theorem 6.37.

Theorem 6.54. *Let m be even. Then the Dilix code $\overline{\Omega(q,m,1)}$ has parameters $[q^m, q^m - 1 - m(q-1), q+2]$.*

The following theorem follows from (6.21) and Theorem 6.38.

Theorem 6.55. *Let $m \geq 2$. Then the Dilix code $\overline{\Omega(q,m,m-1)}$ has parameters*

$$\left[q^m, (q-1)^m, \frac{q^m + q - 2}{q - 1} \right].$$

6.2.4   Extended Binary Cyclic Codes with Zeros of the Forms α and α^{1+2^e} and Their Designs

In this section, we deal with only binary codes and their support designs, and we define $n = 2^m - 1$ and $\bar{n} = 2^m$. The materials of this section comes from Ding (2018a).

Let $m \geq 2$ be a positive integer. Define $\overline{m} = \lfloor m/2 \rfloor$ and $M = \{1, 2, \ldots, \overline{m}\}$. Let E be any nonempty subset of M. Let

$$g_E(x) = \mathbb{M}_\alpha(x)\text{LCM}\{\mathbb{M}_{\alpha^{1+2^e}}(x) : e \in E\}, \tag{6.22}$$

where α is a generator of $\text{GF}(2^m)^*$, $\mathbb{M}_{\alpha^i}(x)$ denotes the minimal polynomial of α^i over $\text{GF}(2)$, and LCM denotes the least common multiple of a set of polynomials. Note that every $e \in E$ satisfies $e \leq \overline{m}$, and the 2-cyclotomic cosets C_1 and C_e are disjoint. Consequently, the two irreducible polynomials $\mathbb{M}_\alpha(x)$ and $\mathbb{M}_{\alpha^{1+2^e}}(x)$ are relatively prime. It then follows that $g_E(x)$ divides $x^n - 1$. Let C_E denote the binary cyclic code of length n with generator polynomial $g_E(x)$.

Theorem 6.56. *Let $m \geq 3$. Then the generator polynomial of C_E is given by*

$$g_E(x) = \mathbb{M}_\alpha(x) \prod_{e \in E} \mathbb{M}_{\alpha^{1+2^e}}(x).$$

Furthermore, C_E has dimension

$$\dim(C_E) = \begin{cases} 2^m - 1 - (2|E| + 1)m/2 & \text{if } m \text{ is even and } m/2 \in E, \\ 2^m - 1 - (|E| + 1)m & \text{otherwise.} \end{cases} \tag{6.23}$$

Proof. The following list of properties was proved in Dianwu and Zhengming (1996):

- For each $e \in E$, $1 + 2^e$ is a coset leader.
- For each $e \in E$, $|C_e| = m$, except that m is even and $e = m/2$, in which case $|C_{m/2}| = m/2$.

Note that 1 is the coset leader of the 2-cyclotomic coset C_1 with $|C_1| = m$. Then the desired conclusions on the generator polynomial and dimension follow. $\square$

Theorem 6.57. *The extended code $\overline{C_E}$ is affine invariant.*

Proof. We prove the desired conclusion with Theorem 6.7 and follow the notation employed in the proof of Theorem 6.7. Let $\overline{\mathcal{N}} = \{0, 1, 2, \ldots, n\}$, where $n = 2^m - 1$. The defining set T of the cyclic code C_E is $T = C_1 \cup (\cup_{e \in E} C_e)$. Since $0 \notin T$, the defining set $\overline{T}$ of $\overline{C_E}$ is given by

$$\overline{T} = C_1 \cup (\cup_{e \in E} C_e) \cup \{0\}.$$

Let $s \in \overline{T}$ and $r \in \overline{\mathcal{N}}$. Assume that $r \preceq s$. We need prove that $r \in \overline{T}$ by Theorem 6.7.

If $r = 0$, then obviously $r \in \overline{T}$. Consider now the case $r > 0$. In this case $s \geq r \geq 1$. If $s \in C_1$, then the Hamming weight $\mathtt{wt}(s) = 1$. As $r \preceq s$, $r = s$. Consequently, $r \in C_1 \subset \overline{T}$. If $s \in C_e$, then the Hamming weight $\mathtt{wt}(s) = 2$. As $r \preceq s$, either $\mathtt{wt}(r) = 1$ or $r = s$. In bother cases, $r \in \overline{T}$. The desired conclusion then follows from Theorem 6.7. $\qquad\square$

Combining Theorems 6.57, 6.10 and 4.27, we arrive at the following.

Theorem 6.58. *Let $m \geq 3$. The supports of the codewords of every weight k in $\overline{C_E}$ (respectively, $\overline{C_E}^{\perp}$) form a 2-design, provided that $\overline{A}_k \neq 0$ (respectively, $\overline{A}_k^{\perp} \neq 0$).*

Theorem 6.58 includes a class of $2^{\lfloor m/2 \rfloor} - 1$ affine invariant binary codes $\overline{C_E}$ and their duals. They give exponentially many infinite families of $2\text{-}(2^m, k, \lambda)$ designs. To determine the parameters $(2^m, k, \lambda)$ of the 2-designs, we need to settle the weight distributions of these codes. The weight distributions of these codes are related to quadratic form, bilinear forms, and alternating bilinear forms, and are open in general. Note that the code C_E may be a BCH code in some cases, but is not a BCH code in most cases.

We would construct an infinite family of Steiner systems $S(2, 4, 2^m)$. To this end, we consider the code C_E and its extended code $\overline{C_E}$ for the special case $E = \{1 + 2^e\}$, where $1 \leq e \leq \overline{m} = \lfloor m/2 \rfloor$. For simplicity, we denote this code by C_e.

Table 6.2	Weight distribution I
Weight w	No. of codewords A_w
0	1
$2^{m-1} - 2^{m-1-h}$	$(2^m - 1)(2^h + 1)2^{h-1}$
2^{m-1}	$(2^m - 1)(2^m - 2^{2h} + 1)$
$2^{m-1} + 2^{m-1-h}$	$(2^m - 1)(2^h - 1)2^{h-1}$

Table 6.3	Weight distribution II
Weight w	No. of codewords A_w
0	1
$2^{m-1} - 2^{(m-2)/2}$	$(2^{m/2} - 1)(2^{m-1} + 2^{(m-2)/2})$
2^{m-1}	$2^m - 1$
$2^{m-1} + 2^{(m-2)/2}$	$(2^{m/2} - 1)(2^{m-1} - 2^{(m-2)/2})$

The following theorem provides information on the parameters of C_e and its dual $C_e^{\perp}$ [Kasami (1969)].

Table 6.4   Weight distribution III

Weight w	No. of codewords A_w
0	1
$2^{m-1} - 2^{(m+\ell-2)/2}$	$2^{(m-\ell-2)/2}(2^{(m-\ell)/2}+1)(2^m-1)/(2^{\ell/2}+1)$
$2^{m-1} - 2^{(m-2)/2}$	$2^{(m+\ell-2)/2}(2^{m/2}+1)(2^m-1)/(2^{\ell/2}+1)$
2^{m-1}	$((2^{\ell/2}-1)2^{m-\ell}+1)(2^m-1)$
$2^{m-1} + 2^{(m-2)/2}$	$2^{(m+\ell-2)/2}(2^{m/2}-1)(2^m-1)/(2^{\ell/2}+1)$
$2^{m-1} + 2^{(m+\ell-2)/2}$	$2^{(m-\ell-2)/2}(2^{(m-\ell)/2}-1)(2^m-1)/(2^{\ell/2}+1)$

Theorem 6.59. *Let $m \geq 4$ and $1 \leq e \leq m/2$. Then $C_e^{\perp}$ is a three-weight code if and only if either $m/\gcd(m,e)$ is odd or m is even and $e = m/2$, where $n = 2^m - 1$.*

When $m/\gcd(m,e)$ is odd, define $h = (m - \gcd(m,e))/2$. Then the dimension of $C_e^{\perp}$ is $2m$, and the weight distribution of $C_e^{\perp}$ is given in Table 6.2. The code C_e has parameters $[n, n - 2m, d]$, where

$$d = \begin{cases} 3 & \text{if } \gcd(e,m) > 1; \\ 5 & \text{if } \gcd(e,m) = 1. \end{cases}$$

When m is even and $e = m/2$, $C_e^{\perp}$ has dimension $3m/2$ and the weight distribution of Table 6.3. The code C_e has parameters $[n, n - 3m/2, 3]$.

When $m/\gcd(m,e)$ is even and $1 \leq e < m/2$, $C_e^{\perp}$ has dimension $2m$ and the weight distribution in Table 6.4, where $\ell = 2\gcd(m,e)$, and C_e has parameters $[n, n - 2m, d]$, where

$$d = \begin{cases} 3 & \text{if } \gcd(e,m) > 1; \\ 5 & \text{if } \gcd(e,m) = 1. \end{cases}$$

The weight distributions of the code $C_e^{\perp}$ documented in Theorem 6.59 were indeed proved in Kasami (1969). However, the conclusions on the minimum distance d of C_e were stated in Kasami (1969) without proof. We inform the reader that they can be proved with the proved weight distribution of $C_e^{\perp}$ and Theorem 2.4, though the details of proof are tedious in some cases.

We would find the parameters of the 2-designs held in the codes $\overline{C_e}$ and $\overline{C_e}^{\perp}$, and need to know the weight distributions of these two codes, which could be derived from those of the code $C_e^{\perp}$ described in Theorem 6.59. We first determine the weight distribution of $\overline{C_e}^{\perp}$.

The following theorem provides information on the parameters of $\overline{C_e}$ and its dual $\overline{C_e}^{\perp}$.

Theorem 6.60. *Let $m \geq 4$ and $1 \leq e \leq m/2$. When $m/\gcd(m,e)$ is odd, define $h = (m - \gcd(m,e))/2$. Then $\overline{C_e}^{\perp}$ has parameters $[2^m, 2m+1, 2^{m-1} - 2^{m-1-h}]$, and the*

Table 6.5   Weight distribution IV

Weight w	No. of codewords A_w
0	1
$2^{m-1} - 2^{m-1-h}$	$(2^m - 1)2^{2h}$
2^{m-1}	$(2^m - 1)(2^{m+1} - 2^{2h+1} + 2)$
$2^{m-1} + 2^{m-1-h}$	$(2^m - 1)2^{2h}$
2^m	1

Table 6.6   Weight distribution V

Weight w	No. of codewords A_w
0	1
$2^{m-1} - 2^{(m-2)/2}$	$(2^{m/2} - 1)2^m$
2^{m-1}	$2^{m+1} - 2$
$2^{m-1} + 2^{(m-2)/2}$	$(2^{m/2} - 1)2^m$
2^m	1

Table 6.7   Weight distribution VI

Weight w	No. of codewords A_w
0	1
$2^{m-1} - 2^{(m+\ell-2)/2}$	$2^{m-\ell}(2^m - 1)/(2^{\ell/2} + 1)$
$2^{m-1} - 2^{(m-2)/2}$	$2^{(2m+\ell)/2}(2^m - 1)/(2^{\ell/2} + 1)$
2^{m-1}	$2((2^{\ell/2} - 1)2^{m-\ell} + 1)(2^m - 1)$
$2^{m-1} + 2^{(m-2)/2}$	$2^{(2m+\ell)/2}(2^m - 1)/(2^{\ell/2} + 1)$
$2^{m-1} + 2^{(m+\ell-2)/2}$	$2^{m-\ell}(2^m - 1)/(2^{\ell/2} + 1)$
2^m	1

weight distribution in Table 6.5. The parameters of $\overline{C_e}$ are $[2^m, 2^m - 1 - 2m, \overline{d}]$, where

$$\overline{d} = \begin{cases} 4 & \text{if } \gcd(e,m) > 1; \\ 6 & \text{if } \gcd(e,m) = 1. \end{cases}$$

When m is even and $e = m/2$, $\overline{C_e}^{\perp}$ has parameters $[2^m, 1 + 3m/2, 2^{m-1} - 2^{(m-2)/2}]$ and the weight distribution in Table 6.6. The code $\overline{C_e}$ has parameters $[2^m, 2^m - 1 - 3m/2, 4]$.

When $m/\gcd(m,e)$ is even and $1 \le e < m/2$, $\overline{C_e}^{\perp}$ has parameters

$$[2^m, 2m+1, 2^{m-1} - 2^{(m+\ell-2)/2}]$$

and the weight distribution in Table 6.7, where $\ell = 2\gcd(m,e)$, and $\overline{C_e}$ has parameters $[2^m, 2^m - 1 - 2m, \overline{d}]$, where

$$\overline{d} = \begin{cases} 4 & \text{if } \gcd(e,m) > 1; \\ 6 & \text{if } \gcd(e,m) = 1. \end{cases}$$

Proof. We prove only the conclusions of the first part. The conclusions of the other parts can be proved similarly.

Consider now the case that $m/\gcd(m,e)$ is odd. Since the minimum weight of C_e is odd, the minimum distance of $\overline{C_e}$ is one more than that of C_e. This proves the conclusion on the minimum distance of $\overline{C_e}$. By definition, $\dim(C_e) = \dim(\overline{C_e})$, and the length of $\overline{C_e}$ is $\bar{n} = n+1 = 2^m$.

The dimension of $\overline{C_e}^{\perp}$ follows from that of $\overline{C_e}$. It remains to prove the weight distribution of $\overline{C_e}^{\perp}$. By definition, $\overline{C_e}$ has only even weights. It then follows that the all-one vector is a codeword of $\overline{C_e}^{\perp}$. Then by Theorems 2.10 and 6.59, $\overline{C_e}^{\perp}$ has all the following weights

$$2^{m-1} \pm 2^{m-1-h},\ 2^{m-1} \pm 2^{(m-2)/2},\ 2^{m-1},\ 2^m.$$

Due to symmetry of weights and the existence of the all-one vector in $\overline{C_e}^{\perp}$,

$$A_{2^{m-1}+2^{m-1-h}} = A_{2^{m-1}-2^{m-1-h}},\ A_{2^{m-1}+2^{(m-2)/2}} = A_{2^{m-1}-2^{(m-2)/2}}.$$

Note that the minimum distance of $\overline{C_e}$ is 4 or 6. Solving the first four Pless power moments yields the frequencies of all the weights.

$\square$

Combining Theorem 6.58 and (9.1), we deduce the following.

Theorem 6.61. *Let $m \geq 4$ and $1 \leq e \leq m/2$. When $m/\gcd(m,e)$ is odd, define $h = (m - \gcd(m,e))/2$. Then $\overline{C_e}^{\perp}$ holds a 2-$(2^m, k, \lambda)$ design for the following pairs (k, λ):*

- $(k, \lambda) = \left(2^{m-1} \pm 2^{m-1-h},\ (2^{2h-1} \pm 2^{h-1})(2^{m-1} \pm 2^{m-1-h} - 1)\right),$
- $(k, \lambda) = \left(2^{m-1},\ (2^{m-1} - 1)(2^m - 2^{2h} + 1)\right).$

When m is even and $e = m/2$, $\overline{C_e}^{\perp}$ holds a 2-$(2^m, k, \lambda)$ design for the following pairs (k, λ):

- $(k, \lambda) = \left(2^{m-1} \pm 2^{(m-2)/2},\ 2^{(m-2)/2}(2^{m/2} - 1)(2^{(m-2)/2} \pm 1)\right),$
- $(k, \lambda) = \left(2^{m-1},\ 2^{m-1} - 1\right).$

When $m/\gcd(m,e)$ is even and $1 \leq e < m/2$, $\overline{C_e}^{\perp}$ holds a 2-$(2^m, k, \lambda)$ design for the following pairs (k, λ):

- $(k, \lambda) = \left(2^{m-1} \pm 2^{(m+\ell-2)/2},\ \dfrac{(2^{m-1} \pm 2^{(m+\ell-2)/2})(2^{m-1} \pm 2^{(m+\ell-2)/2} - 1)}{2^{\ell}(2^{\ell/2} + 1)}\right),$
- $(k, \lambda) = \left(2^{m-1} \pm 2^{(m-2)/2},\ \dfrac{2^{(m+\ell-2)/2}(2^{m/2} \pm 1)(2^{m-1} \pm 2^{(m-2)/2} - 1)}{2^{\ell/2} + 1}\right),$
- $(k, \lambda) = \left(2^{m-1},\ ((2^{\ell/2} - 1)2^{m-\ell} + 1)(2^{m-1} - 1)\right),$

where $\ell = 2\gcd(m,e)$.

To determine the parameters of the 2-designs held in the extended code $\overline{C_e}$, we need to find out the weight distribution of $\overline{C_e}$. In theory, the weight distribution of $\overline{C_e}$ can be settled using the weight enumerator of $\overline{C_e}^{\perp}$ given in Tables 6.5, 6.6, and 6.7. However, it is practically hard to find a simple expression of the weight distribution of $\overline{C_e}$.

In the rest of this section, we consider only the weight distribution of $\overline{C_e}$ in a special case, in order to construct an infinite family of Steiner systems $S(2,4,2^m)$ for all $m \equiv 2 \pmod 4$.

As a special case of Theorem 6.60, we have the following.

Corollary 6.62. *Let $m \equiv 2 \pmod 4$ and $2 \le e \le \lfloor m/2 \rfloor$. If $\gcd(m,e) = 2$, then $\overline{C_e}^{\perp}$ has parameters $[2^m, 2m+1, 2^{m-1} - 2^{m/2}]$ and weight enumerator*

$$\overline{A}^{\perp}(z) = 1 + uz^{2^{m-1}-2^{m/2}} + vz^{2^{m-1}} + uz^{2^{m-1}+2^{m/2}} + z^{2^m}, \tag{6.24}$$

where

$$u = (2^m - 1)2^{m-2}, \quad v = (2^m - 1)(2^{m+1} - 2^{m-1} + 2). \tag{6.25}$$

Theorem 6.63. *Let $m \equiv 2 \pmod 4$ and $2 \le e \le \lfloor m/2 \rfloor$. If $\gcd(m,e) = 2$, then $\overline{C_e}$ has parameters $[2^m, 2^m - 1 - 2m, 4]$ and weight distribution*

$$2^{2m+1}\overline{A}_k = (1 + (-1)^k)\binom{2^m}{k} + \frac{1 + (-1)^k}{2}(-1)^{\lfloor k/2 \rfloor}\binom{2^{m-1}}{\lfloor k/2 \rfloor}v +$$

$$u \sum_{\substack{0 \le i \le 2^{m-1} - 2^{\frac{m}{2}} \\ 0 \le j \le 2^{m-1} + 2^{\frac{m}{2}} \\ i+j=k}} [(-1)^i + (-1)^j]\binom{2^{m-1} - 2^{m/2}}{i}\binom{2^{m-1} + 2^{m/2}}{j}$$

for $0 \le k \le 2^m$, where u and v are given in (6.25).

Proof. The parameters of $\overline{C_e}$ were proved in Theorem 6.60. The weight distribution formula for $\overline{C_e}$ follows from the weight enumerator $\overline{A}^{\perp}(z)$ of $\overline{C_e}^{\perp}$ in (6.24) and Theorem 2.4. $\square$

We are now ready to prove the main result of this section.

Theorem 6.64. *Let $m \equiv 2 \pmod 4$, $2 \le e \le \lfloor m/2 \rfloor$, and $\gcd(m,e) = 2$. Then the supports of the codewords of weight 4 in $\overline{C_e}$ form a 2-$(2^m, 4, 1)$ design, i.e., a Steiner system $S(2,4,2^m)$.*

Proof. Employing the weight distribution formula $\overline{A}_k$ given in Theorem 6.63, we obtain

$$\overline{A}_4 = \frac{2^{m-1}(2^m - 1)}{6}.$$

It then follows that

$$\lambda = \overline{A}_4 \frac{\binom{4}{2}}{\binom{2^m}{2}} = 1.$$

This completes the proof. □

For every $m \equiv 2 \pmod 4$ and $m \geq 6$, we can choose $e = 2e_1$ with $\gcd(m/2, e_1) = 1$ and $e_1 \leq \lfloor m \rfloor /2$. Such e will satisfy the conditions in Theorem 6.64. At least we can choose $e = 2$. This means that for every $m \equiv 2 \pmod 4$ with $m \geq 6$, Theorem 6.64 gives at least one Steiner system $S(2, 4, 2^m)$. In fact, it constructs more than one Steiner system $S(2, 4, 2^m)$. For example, when $m = 14$, we can choose e to be any element of $\{2, 4, 6\}$. Therefore, Theorem 6.64 gives an infinite family of Steiner system $S(2, 4, 2^m)$.

In addition to the infinite family of Steiner systems $S(2, 4, 2^m)$, Theorem 6.64 gives many other 2-designs. Below we present two more examples.

Theorem 6.65. *Let* $m \equiv 2 \pmod 4$, $2 \leq e \leq \lfloor m/2 \rfloor$, *and* $\gcd(m, e) = 2$. *Then the supports of the codewords of weight 6 in* $\overline{C_e}$ *form a* 2-$(2^m, 6, \lambda)$ *design, where*

$$\lambda = \frac{(2^m - 4)(2^m - 24)}{24}.$$

Proof. Using the weight distribution formula $\overline{A}_k$ in Theorem 6.63, we obtain

$$\overline{A}_6 = \frac{2^m(2^m - 1)(2^m - 4)(2^m - 24)}{720}.$$

It then follows that

$$\lambda = \overline{A}_6 \frac{\binom{6}{2}}{\binom{2^m}{2}} = \frac{(2^m - 4)(2^m - 24)}{24}.$$

This completes the proof. □

Theorem 6.66. *Let* $m \equiv 2 \pmod 4$, $2 \leq e \leq \lfloor m/2 \rfloor$, *and* $\gcd(m, e) = 2$. *Then the supports of the codewords of weight 8 in* $\overline{C_e}$ *form a* 2-$(2^m, 8, \lambda)$ *design, where*

$$\lambda = \frac{(2^m - 4)(2^{3m} - 23 \times 2^{2m} + 344 \times 2^m - 1612)}{720}.$$

Proof. Using the weight distribution formula $\overline{A}_k$ in Theorem 6.63, we obtain

$$\overline{A}_8 = \frac{2^m(2^m-1)(2^m-4)(2^{3m}-23\times 2^{2m}+344\times 2^m-1612)}{2\times 20160}.$$

It then follows that

$$\lambda = \overline{A}_8 \frac{\binom{8}{2}}{\binom{2^m}{2}} = \frac{(2^m-4)(2^{3m}-23\times 2^{2m}+344\times 2^m-1612)}{720}.$$

This completes the proof. □

We point out that Theorems 6.64, 6.65 and 6.66 cannot be proved with the Assmus-Mattson Theorem due to the weight distribution of $\overline{C_e}^{\perp}$ and the low minimum distance of $\overline{C_e}$. Results similar to Theorems 6.64 and 6.65 for the case $m \equiv 0$ (mod 4) were recently developed in Wang (2019).

When m is odd and $\gcd(m,e)=1$, the code C_e and their relatives are also very interesting due to the following:

- The code C_e and its dual $C_e^{\perp}$ hold many infinite families of 2-designs.
- The extended code $\overline{C_e}$ and its dual $\overline{C_e}^{\perp}$ hold many infinite families of 3-designs.

These results were proved by the Assmus-Mattson Theorem, and the designs of those codes will be treated in Section 9.2.

When $m/\gcd(m,e)$ is even and $1 \le e \le \overline{m}$, one can find an algebraic expression of the weight distribution of the code $\overline{C_e}$ with the weight distribution of $\overline{C_e}^{\perp}$ depicted in Table 6.7 and Theorem 2.4, and then determine the parameters of some of the two designs held in $\overline{C_e}$.

We now provide information on the support designs from other codes C_E and their relatives. When $m \ge 5$ is odd and $E = \{(m-3)/2, (m-1)/2\}$ or $E = \{1,2\}$, C_E has parameters $[2^m-1, 2^m-1-3m, 7]$ and $\overline{C_E}$ has parameters $[2^m, 2^m-1-3m, 8]$. $\overline{C_E}^{\perp}$ has dimension $3m+1$ and has six weights. In this case, C_E and $C_E^{\perp}$ hold many infinite families of 2-designs, while the codes $\overline{C_E}$ and $\overline{C_E}^{\perp}$ hold many infinite families of 3-designs. These designed will be treated in Sections 8.3 and 8.4.

When $m \ge 4$ is even and $E = \{1,2\}$, C_E does not hold 2-designs. But $\overline{C_E}$ and $\overline{C_E}^{\perp}$ hold 2-designs. The parameters of these 2-designs are determined in Section 9.4.

When $m \ge 4$ is even and $E = \{(m-2)/2, m/2\}$, C_E has parameters $[2^m-1, 2^m-1-3m/2, 5]$, $\overline{C_E}$ has parameters $[2^m, 2^m-1-3m/2, 6]$, and the weight distribution of $\overline{C_E}^{\perp}$ is known [Kasami (1969)]. The parameters of the 2-designs held in $\overline{C_E}$ and $\overline{C_E}^{\perp}$ are the same as those of the 2-designs held in some codes in Section 9.4.

When $m \geq 7$ is odd and $E = \{(m-5)/2, (m-3)/2, (m-1)/2\}$, the code $C_E^{\perp}$ has dimension $4m$ and has 7 weights [Kasami (1969)]. Its weight distribution is given below.

Theorem 6.67. *Let $m \geq 7$ be odd and $E = \{(m-5)/2, (m-3)/2, (m-1)/2\}$. Then $C_{(1,v,2,m)}$ has parameters $[n, n-4m, d]$ and $\overline{C_E}$ has parameters $[2^m, 2^m - 1 - 4m, d+1]$, where $d \geq 7$. The code $C_E^{\perp}$ has dimension $4m$ and its weight distribution is given by*

$$A_{2^{m-1} \pm 2^{\frac{m+3}{2}}} = (2^{m-6} \mp 2^{(m-7)/2})(2^{m-3} - 1)(2^{m-1} - 1)(2^m - 1)/45,$$

$$A_{2^{m-1} \pm 2^{\frac{m+1}{2}}} = (2^{m-2} \mp 2^{(m-1)/2})(23 \cdot 2^{m-5} + 1)(2^{m-1} - 1)(2^m - 1)/9,$$

$$A_{2^{m-1} \pm 2^{\frac{m-1}{2}}} = (2^{m-1} \mp 2^{(m-1)/2})(151 \cdot 2^{2m-3} + 25 \cdot 2^m + 2^5)(2^m - 1)/45,$$

$$A_{2^{m-1}} = 2^{4m} - 1 - A_{2^{m-1} + 2^{\frac{m+3}{2}}} - A_{2^{m-1} - 2^{\frac{m+3}{2}}} - A_{2^{m-1} + 2^{\frac{m+1}{2}}} -$$
$$A_{2^{m-1} - 2^{\frac{m+1}{2}}} - A_{2^{m-1} + 2^{\frac{m-1}{2}}} - A_{2^{m-1} - 2^{\frac{m-1}{2}}},$$

and $A_i = 0$ for all other i.

It can be proved that C_E has parameters $[2^m - 1, 2^m - 1 - 4m, 7]$. The weight distribution of $\overline{C_E}^{\perp}$ can be determined. Hence, the parameters of the 2-designs held in $\overline{C_E}^{\perp}$ and some of the 2-designs held in $\overline{C_E}$ can be worked out.

The cyclic codes C_E treated in this section are closely related to the punctured binary Reed-Muller codes $\mathcal{R}_2(2, m)^*$. To introduce the connection, we need the following result from Kasami (1969).

Theorem 6.68. *Let C be a binary linear code of length $2^m - 1$ whose generator polynomial $g(x)$ satisfies $g(1) = 0$. Then C is a subcode of $\mathcal{R}_2(r, m)^*$ if and only if*

$$g(x) = \frac{x^{2^m - 1} - 1}{h_1(x) \cdots h_t(x)},$$

where $h_1(x), \ldots, h_t(x)$ are pairwise distinct irreducible polynomials over GF(2) and there are integers μ_i such that

$$0 \leq \mu_1 < \mu_2 < \cdots \mu_t \leq m/2, \; h_i\left(\alpha^{-(2^{\mu_i} + 1)}\right) = 0 \text{ for all } i,$$

and α is a generator of $GF(2^m)^*$.

It follows from Theorem 6.68 that the code C_E is the dual code of a subcode of $\mathcal{R}_2(2, m)^*$.

6.3   Another Family of Affine-Invariant Codes and Their Designs

In this section, we introduce a family of affine-invariant linear codes which are also extended cyclic codes [Ding and Tang (2020)]. We order the elements of $\mathrm{GF}(q^m)$ and $\mathrm{GF}(q^m)^*$ as

$$\{1, \alpha, \alpha^2, \ldots, \alpha^{q^m-2}, 0\}$$

and

$$\{1, \alpha, \alpha^2, \ldots, \alpha^{q^m-2}\},$$

respectively, where α is a primitive element of $\mathrm{GF}(q^m)$. Throughout this section, let $\mathrm{Tr}(x)$ be the trace function from $\mathrm{GF}(q^m)$ to $\mathrm{GF}(q)$.

Let t be a positive integer, and let f_i be a polynomial over $\mathrm{GF}(q^m)$ with $f_i(0) = 0$ and $1 \leq \deg(f_i) \leq q^m - 2$ for $1 \leq i \leq t$. We define two related linear codes over $\mathrm{GF}(q)$ by

$$C_f = \left\{ \left(\mathrm{Tr}\left(\sum_{i=1}^{t} a_i f_i(x) \right) + h \right)_{x \in \mathrm{GF}(q^m)} : a_i \in \mathrm{GF}(q^m),\ h \in \mathrm{GF}(q) \right\} \quad (6.26)$$

and

$$C_f^* = \left\{ \left(\mathrm{Tr}\left(\sum_{i=1}^{t} a_i f_i(x) \right) \right)_{x \in \mathrm{GF}(q^m)^*} : a_i \in \mathrm{GF}(q^m) \right\}. \quad (6.27)$$

By definition, C_f and C_f^* are a linear code over $\mathrm{GF}(q)$ with length q^m and $q^m - 1$, respectively. Their dimensions satisfy $\dim(C_f) \leq tm + 1$ and $\dim(C_f^*) \leq tm$. The two codes C_f and C_f^* are related in the following way.

Theorem 6.69. *Let notation be the same as before. Then* $C_f = \overline{(C_f^*)^{\perp}}^{\perp}$. *Further,* $\dim(C_f) = \dim(\overline{C_f^*}) + 1$, *and* $\overline{C_f^*}$ *is a subcode of* C_f.

Proof. Define

$$G = \begin{bmatrix} \mathrm{Tr}(\alpha^0 f_1(\alpha^0)) & \mathrm{Tr}(\alpha^0 f_1(\alpha^1)) & \cdots & \mathrm{Tr}(\alpha^0 f_1(\alpha^{q^m-2})) \\ \mathrm{Tr}(\alpha^1 f_1(\alpha^0)) & \mathrm{Tr}(\alpha^1 f_1(\alpha^1)) & \cdots & \mathrm{Tr}(\alpha^1 f_1(\alpha^{q^m-2})) \\ \vdots & \vdots & \vdots & \vdots \\ \mathrm{Tr}(\alpha^{m-1} f_1(\alpha^0)) & \mathrm{Tr}(\alpha^{m-1} f_1(\alpha^1)) & \cdots & \mathrm{Tr}(\alpha^{m-1} f_1(\alpha^{q^m-2})) \\ \vdots & \vdots & \vdots & \vdots \\ \mathrm{Tr}(\alpha^0 f_t(\alpha^0)) & \mathrm{Tr}(\alpha^0 f_t(\alpha^1)) & \cdots & \mathrm{Tr}(\alpha^0 f_t(\alpha^{q^m-2})) \\ \mathrm{Tr}(\alpha^1 f_t(\alpha^0)) & \mathrm{Tr}(\alpha^1 f_t(\alpha^1)) & \cdots & \mathrm{Tr}(\alpha^1 f_t(\alpha^{q^m-2})) \\ \vdots & \vdots & \vdots & \vdots \\ \mathrm{Tr}(\alpha^{m-1} f_t(\alpha^0)) & \mathrm{Tr}(\alpha^{m-1} f_t(\alpha^1)) & \cdots & \mathrm{Tr}(\alpha^{m-1} f_t(\alpha^{q^m-2})) \end{bmatrix}.$$

Then G is a generator matrix of C_f^*, though the rank of G could be less than tm.

Notice that $f(0) = 0$. By the ordering of the elements in $\mathrm{GF}(q^m)$ and $\mathrm{GF}(q^m)^*$ and the definition of the two codes C_f^* and C_f in (6.26) and (6.27), C_f has the following generator matrix

$$\begin{bmatrix} 1 & 1 \\ G & \mathbf{0} \end{bmatrix},$$

where $\mathbf{1} = (111 \cdots 1)$ is the all-one vector of length $q^m - 1$, $\mathbf{0} = (000 \cdots 0)^T$, which is a column vector of length tm. It follows from Theorem 2.11 that $C_f = \overline{(C_f^*)^\perp}^\perp$ and $\dim(C_f) = \dim(\overline{C_f^*}) + 1$.

Finally, we are in a position to prove the last conclusion. We first prove that $\sum_{x \in \mathrm{GF}(q^m)^*} x^j = 0$ for each j with $1 \le j \le q^m - 2$. Let $i = \gcd(j, q^m - 1)$. Set $\beta = \alpha^i$. Then $\beta^{(q^m - 1)/i} = 1$. Consequently,

$$\sum_{x \in \mathrm{GF}(q^m)^*} x^j = \sum_{x \in \mathrm{GF}(q^m)^*} x^i = \sum_{\ell=0}^{q^m - 2} \alpha^{ij} = i \sum_{\ell=0}^{\frac{q^m-1}{i}-1} \beta^\ell = 0.$$

It then follows from $f_i(0) = 0$ that

$$\sum_{x \in \mathrm{GF}(q^m)^*} f_i(x) = 0.$$

As a result, $\overline{C_f^*}$ has the generator matrix

$$\begin{bmatrix} G & \mathbf{0} \end{bmatrix}.$$

The last desired conclusion then follows. Notice that $\overline{C_f^*}$ is a trivial extension. $\square$

When each f_i is a monomial, the codes C_f^* and $(C_f^*)^\perp$ are cyclic, and C_f is the dual of an extended cyclic code by Theorem 6.69. In general, C_f^* and $(C_f^*)^\perp$ may not be cyclic, and C_f is not an extended cyclic code. The code C_f is obtained from C_f^* in the following order:

$$C_f^* \longrightarrow (C_f^*)^\perp \longrightarrow \overline{(C_f^*)^\perp} \longrightarrow \overline{(C_f^*)^\perp}^\perp = C_f.$$

Let the coordinates of the code C_f be indexed by the elements in the ordered set $\mathrm{GF}(q^m)$. Any $\sigma_{(u,v)}(y) = uy + v \in \mathrm{GA}_1(\mathrm{GF}(q^m))$ maps C_f into the following code

$$\left\{ \left(\mathrm{Tr}\left(\sum_{i=1}^t a_i f_i(ux + v) \right) + h \right)_{x \in \mathrm{GF}(q^m)} : a_i \in \mathrm{GF}(q^m), h \in \mathrm{GF}(q) \right\}.$$

In general, the code C_f may not be affine-invariant. In some special cases, C_f is affine-invariant.

Let $t \geq 2$ be an integer. For any set of integers $\{i_2, \cdots, i_t\}$ with $0 \leq i_2 < \cdots < i_t \leq \lfloor m/2 \rfloor$, we consider the following code

$$C(1, i_2, \cdots, i_t) = \{\mathbf{c}_{(h, a_1, \ldots, a_t)} : h \in \mathrm{GF}(q),\, a_i \in \mathrm{GF}(q^m)\} \tag{6.28}$$

where

$$\mathbf{c}_{(h, a_1, \ldots, a_t)} = \left(h + \mathrm{Tr}\left(a_1 x + \sum_{\ell=2}^{t} a_\ell x^{1+q^{i_\ell}} \right) \right)_{x \in \mathrm{GF}(q^m)}. \tag{6.29}$$

We now prove that $C(1, i_2, \cdots, i_t)$ and its dual are affine-invariant and hold support 2-designs.

Theorem 6.70. *The code $C(1, i_2, \cdots, i_t)$ defined in (6.28) is affine-invariant and the supports of all codewords of any fixed weight in the code form a 2-design. The same conclusions hold for the dual code $C(1, i_2, \cdots, i_t)^\perp$.*

Proof. Define

$$f(x) = h + \mathrm{Tr}\left(a_1 x + \sum_{\ell=2}^{t} a_\ell x^{1+q^{i_\ell}} \right).$$

For $u \in \mathrm{GF}(q^m)^*$ and $v \in \mathrm{GF}(q^m)$, we have

$$f(ux+v) = h + \mathrm{Tr}\left(a_1(ux+v) + \sum_{\ell=2}^{t} a_\ell (ux+v)^{1+q^{i_\ell}} \right)$$

$$= g(h) + \mathrm{Tr}\left(u\left(a_1 + \sum_{\ell=2}^{t} \left[a_\ell v^{q^{i_\ell}} + (a_\ell v)^{q^{m-i_\ell}} \right] \right) x \right) +$$

$$\mathrm{Tr}\left(\sum_{\ell=2}^{t} a_\ell u^{1+q^{i_\ell}} x^{1+q^{i_\ell}} \right). \tag{6.30}$$

Let $\sigma_{(u,v)}(x) = ux + v$, where $u \in \mathrm{GF}(q^m)^*$ and $v \in \mathrm{GF}(q^m)$. It then follows from (6.30) that

$$\sigma_{(u,v)}(\mathbf{c}_{(h, a_1, \ldots, a_t)}) = \mathbf{c}_{(h', a_1', \ldots, a_t')} \in C(1, i_2, \cdots, i_t),$$

where

$$h' = f(v),$$

$$a_1' = u\left(a_1 + \sum_{\ell=2}^{t} \left[a_\ell v^{q^{i_\ell}} + (a_\ell v)^{q^{m-i_\ell}} \right] \right),$$

$$a_\ell' = a_\ell u^{1+q^{1+q^{i_\ell}}} \quad \text{for } 2 \leq \ell \leq t.$$

Hence, $C(1, i_2, \ldots, i_t)$ is affine-invariant. Since the group $\mathrm{GA}_1(\mathrm{GF}(q^m))$ acts on $\mathrm{GF}(q^m)$ doubly transitively, the conclusion on the support designs of $C(1, i_2, \ldots, i_t)$ holds.

It is well known that the permutation automorphism groups of any code C and its dual are the same. The desired conclusions on $C(1, i_2, \ldots, i_t)^{\perp}$ follow from those of $C(1, i_2, \ldots, i_t)$. $\qquad\qquad\square$

It is easily seen that $C(1, i_2, \ldots, i_t)$ is an extended cyclic code, as the permutation $\sigma(x) = \alpha x$ fixes the code. In fact, it is the extended code of the cyclic code over $\mathrm{GF}(q)$ with length $q^m - 1$ and check polynomial

$$\mathbb{M}_{\alpha^{-1}}(x) \prod_{\ell=2}^{t} \mathbb{M}_{\alpha^{-(1+q^{i_\ell})}}(x),$$

where α is a generator of $\mathrm{GF}(q^m)$ and $\mathbb{M}_{\alpha^{\ell}}(x)$ denotes the minimal polynomial of α^{ℓ} over $\mathrm{GF}(q)$. The dimension of the code $C(1, i_2, \ldots, i_t)$ in Theorem 6.70 depends on the rank of the quadratic functions $\mathrm{Tr}(f(x))$. The weight distribution of the code $C(1, i_2, \ldots, i_t)$ is known in some special cases. The determination of the parameters of the support designs of the codes $C(1, i_2, \ldots, i_t)$ and $C(1, i_2, \ldots, i_t)^{\perp}$ is difficult in general, but can be done in some special cases.

Theorem 6.70 says that the code $C(1, i_2, \ldots, i_t)$ and its dual hold 2-designs. It will be pointed out below that the two codes hold 3-designs in some special cases.

6.3.1 *The Special Case $q = 2$*

When $q = 2$, the codes $C(1, i_2, \ldots, i_t)$ and $C(1, i_2, \ldots, i_t)^{\perp}$ become the affine-invariant binary codes treated in Section 6.2.4, where a class of Steiner systems $S(2, 4, 2^m)$ was obtained.

6.3.2 *Several Special Cases of 3-Designs*

Let $m \geq 5$ be an odd integer and $(i_2, i_3) = (1, 2)$ or $(i_2, i_3) = (1, (m+1)/2)$. Let $\mathcal{P} = \{0, 1, 2, \cdots, 2^m - 1\}$, and let $\mathcal{B}_k$ be the set of the supports of the codewords of $C(1, i_2, i_3)$ with weight k, where $A_k \neq 0$. Then $(\mathcal{P}, \mathcal{B}_k)$ is a 3-$(2^m, k, \lambda)$ design. The dual code $C(1, i_2, i_3)$ holds also 3-designs. Details of these 3-designs will be treated in Section 8.3.3.

6.4 Notes

Let p be a prime and let r, e and m be positive integers such that $r | e$ and $e | m$. Extended cyclic codes of length p^m over $\mathrm{GF}(p^r)$, which are invariant under the group $\mathrm{GA}_{m/e}(\mathrm{GF}(p^e))$, can be characterised under a partial order $\preceq_e$ in the set

$$\{0, 1, \ldots, p^m - 1\}.$$

The characterisation is a generalisation of Theorem 6.7. For information on this characterisation and such codes, the reader is referred to Berger and Charpin (1996), Berger and Charpin (1999), Delsarte (1970), and Hou (2005).

Recently, a lot of progress on the study of affine-invariant codes and their designs has been made. For details, the reader is referred to Ding and Tang (2020); Du, Wang and Fan (2020); Du, Wang, Tang and Wang (2020a); Du, Wang, Tang and Wang (2020b); Wang, Du and Fan (2021); Wang, Du, Fan and Niu (2021); and Wang (2019).

Chapter 7

Weights in Some BCH Codes over GF(q)

BCH codes are an important class of cyclic codes and were treated in Section 3.7. In this chapter, we introduce several families of BCH codes whose weight distributions are known. Some of these codes will be employed to construct t-designs in subsequent chapters.

7.1 A Recall of BCH Codes

Throughout this chapter, let q be a prime power, and let n be a positive integer such that $\gcd(q,n) = 1$. Let $m = \mathrm{ord}_n(q)$. Put $\beta = \alpha^{(q^m-1)/n}$, where α is a primitive element of GF(q^m). Then β is an n-th primitive root of unity in GF(q^m).

Let δ be an integer with $2 \le \delta \le n$ and let b be an integer. Recall that the *BCH code* over GF(q) of length n and *designed distance* δ, denoted by $C_{(q,n,\delta,b)}$, is the cyclic code with generator polynomial

$$g_{(q,n,\delta,b)}(x) = \mathrm{LCM}(\mathbb{M}_{\beta^b}(x), \mathbb{M}_{\beta^{b+1}}(x), \dots, \mathbb{M}_{\beta^{b+\delta-2}}(x)), \qquad (7.1)$$

where $\mathbb{M}_{\beta^s}(x)$ is the minimal polynomial of β^s over GF(q) and is given by

$$\mathbb{M}_{\beta^s}(x) = \sum_{j \in C_s} (x - \beta^j)$$

and C_s is the q-cyclotomic coset modulo n containing s. Recall that $C_{(q,n,\delta,b)}$ is primitive if $n = q^m - 1$, and narrow-sense if $b = 1$.

7.2 The Parameters of the Codes $C_{(q,q^m-1,\delta_1,1)}$ and $C_{(q,q^m-1,\delta_1+1,0)}$, where $\delta_1 = (q-1)q^{m-1} - 1$

The following two lemmas are fundamental, and were proved in Ding (2015b).

Lemma 7.1. *The largest q-cyclotomic coset leader modulo $n = q^m - 1$ is given by* $\delta_1 = (q-1)q^{m-1} - 1$. *Furthermore,* $|C_{\delta_1}| = m$.

Theorem 7.2. *The code $C_{(q,q^m-1,\delta_1+1,0)}$ has parameters $[n, m, \delta_1 + 1]$, and meets the Griesmer bound, where $n = q^m - 1$ and $\delta_1 = (q-1)q^{m-1} - 1$. The code $C_{(q,q^m-1,\delta_1,1)}$ has parameters $[n, m+1, \delta_1]$, and meets the Griesmer bound.*

7.3 The Parameters of the Codes $C_{(q,q^m-1,\delta_2,1)}$ and $C_{(q,q^m-1,\delta_2+1,0)}$, where $\delta_2 = (q-1)q^{m-1} - 1 - q^{\lfloor(m-1)/2\rfloor}$

In this section, we determine the parameters of the codes $C_{(q,q^m-1,\delta_2,1)}$ and $C_{(q,q^m-1,\delta_2+1,0)}$, where $\delta_2 = (q-1)q^{m-1} - 1 - q^{\lfloor(m-1)/2\rfloor}$. The results presented in this section are mainly taken from Ding, Fan and Zhou (2017). We will need the following lemma shortly.

Lemma 7.3. *The second largest q-cyclotomic coset leader modulo n is given by $\delta_2 = (q-1)q^{m-1} - 1 - q^{\lfloor(m-1)/2\rfloor}$. Furthermore,*

$$|C_{\delta_2}| = \begin{cases} m & \text{if } m \text{ is odd,} \\ \frac{m}{2} & \text{if } m \text{ is even.} \end{cases}$$

Proof. The proof is divided into the following two cases according to the parity of m.

Case I, i.e., m is odd:

In this case, we have

$$\delta_2 = (q-1)q^{m-1} - 1 - q^{(m-1)/2} = n - \left(q^{(m-1)/2} + 1\right)q^{(m-1)/2}.$$

It is easily seen that

$$q\delta_2 \bmod n = n - (q^{(m+1)/2} + 1).$$

One can then verify that

$$C_{\delta_2} = \left\{n - \left(q^{(m+1)/2} + 1\right)q^i : i = 0,1,\ldots,\frac{m-3}{2}\right\} \cup$$
$$\left\{n - \left(q^{(m-1)/2} + 1\right)q^i : i = 0,1,\ldots,\frac{m-1}{2}\right\}.$$

Therefore, δ_2 is the smallest integer in C_{δ_2} and is thus the coset leader. Clearly, we have $|C_{\delta_2}| = m$.

Let $t = (m-3)/2$, $1 \leq i \leq q^{(m-1)/2} - 1$ and let $J_i = (q-1)q^{m-1} - 1 - i$. Notice that

$$q^{(m-1)/2} - 1 = (q-1)q^t + (q-1)q^{t-1} + \cdots + (q-1)q + q - 1.$$

The q-adic expansion of i must be of the form

$$i = i_t q^t + i_{t-1} q^{t-1} + \cdots + i_1 q + i_0,$$

where each i_j satisfies $0 \le i_j \le q-1$, but at least one of the i_j's is nonzero. It then follows that the q-adic expansion of J_i is given by

$$J_i = (q-2)q^{m-1} + (q-1)q^{m-2} + (q-1)q^{m-3} + \cdots + (q-1)q^{t+1} +$$
$$(q-1-i_t)q^t + (q-1-i_{t-1})q^{t-1} + \cdots + (q-1-i_1)q + q - 1 - i_0.$$

Subcase I.1, i.e., $q = 2$:

In this subcase, we have

$$J_i = 2^{m-2} + 2^{m-3} + \cdots + 2^{t+1} + (1-i_t)2^t +$$
$$(1-i_{t-1})2^{t-1} + \cdots + (1-i_1)2 + 1 - i_0.$$

If $i_0 = 1$, then $J_i/2$ and J_i are in the same 2-cyclotomic coset modulo n. Hence, J_i cannot be a coset leader.

We now assume that $i_0 = 0$. Since $i \ne 0$, one of the i_ℓ's must be nonzero. Let ℓ denote the largest one such that $i_\ell = 1$. One can then verify that

$$J_i 2^{m-1-\ell} \bmod n < J_i.$$

Whence, J_i cannot be a coset leader.

Subcase I.2, i.e., $q > 2$:

If $i_\ell > 1$ for some ℓ with $0 \le \ell \le t$, then $J_i q^{m-1-\ell} \bmod n < J_i$. In this case, J_i cannot be a coset leader.

We now assume that all $i_\ell \in \{0, 1\}$. Since $i \ge 1$, at least one of the i_ℓ's must be 1. Let ℓ denote the largest one such that $i_\ell = 1$. One can then verify that

$$J_i q^{m-1-\ell} \bmod n < J_i.$$

Whence, J_i cannot be a coset leader.

Summarizing all the conclusions above, we conclude that δ_2 is the second largest coset leader for the case that m is odd.

Case II, i.e., m is even:

In this case, we have

$$\delta_2 = (q-1)q^{m-1} - 1 - q^{(m-2)/2} = n - \left(q^{m/2} + 1 \right) q^{(m-2)/2}.$$

It is easily seen that

$$C_{\delta_2} = \left\{ n - \left(q^{m/2} + 1 \right) q^i : i = 0, 1, \ldots, \frac{m-2}{2} \right\}.$$

Therefore, δ_2 is the smallest integer in C_{δ_2} and is the coset leader. Obviously, $|C_{\delta_2}| = m/2$.

When $m = 2$, $\delta_2 = \delta_1 + 1$, where δ_1 was defined in Lemma 7.1. There does not exist any coset leader between δ_1 and δ_2. Therefore, we now assume that $m \geq 4$.

Let $t = (m-4)/2$, $1 \leq i \leq q^{(m-2)/2} - 1$ and let $J_i = (q-1)q^{m-1} - 1 - i$. Notice that

$$q^{(m-2)/2} - 1 = (q-1)q^t + (q-1)q^{t-1} + \cdots + (q-1)q + q - 1.$$

The q-adic expansion of i must be of the form

$$i = i_t q^t + i_{t-1} q^{t-1} + \cdots + i_1 q + i_0,$$

where each i_j satisfies $0 \leq i_j \leq q - 1$, but at least one of the i_j's is nonzero. It then follows that the q-adic expansion of J_i is given by

$$J_i = (q-2)q^{m-1} + (q-1)q^{m-2} + (q-1)q^{m-3} + \cdots + (q-1)q^{t+1} +$$
$$(q-1-i_t)q^t + (q-1-i_{t-1})q^{t-1} + \cdots + (q-1-i_1)q + q - 1 - i_0.$$

Subcase II.1, i.e., $q = 2$:

In this subcase, we have

$$J_i = 2^{m-2} + 2^{m-3} + \cdots + 2^{t+1} + (1 - i_t)2^t +$$
$$(1 - i_{t-1})2^{t-1} + \cdots + (1 - i_1)2 + 1 - i_0.$$

If $i_0 = 1$, then $J_i/2 < J_i$. But $J_i/2$ and J_i are in the same 2-cyclotomic coset modulo n. Hence, J_i cannot be a coset leader.

We now assume that $i_0 = 0$. Since $i \neq 0$, one of the i_ℓ's must be nonzero. Let ℓ denote the largest one such that $i_\ell = 1$. One can then verify that

$$J_i 2^{m-1-\ell} \bmod n < J_i.$$

Whence, J_i cannot be a coset leader.

Subcase II.2, i.e., $q > 2$:

If $i_\ell > 1$ for some ℓ with $0 \leq \ell \leq t$, then $J_i q^{m-1-\ell} \bmod n < J_i$. In this case, J_i cannot be a coset leader.

We now assume that all $i_\ell \in \{0, 1\}$. Since $i \geq 1$, at least one of the i_ℓ's must be 1. Let ℓ denote the largest one such that $i_\ell = 1$. One can then verify that

$$J_i q^{m-1-\ell} \bmod n < J_i.$$

Table 7.1 Weight distribution of $C_{(2,2^m-1,\delta_2+1,0)}$ for odd m

Weight w	No. of codewords A_w
0	1
$2^{m-1} - 2^{(m-1)/2}$	$(2^m - 1)(2^{(m-1)/2} + 1)2^{(m-3)/2}$
2^{m-1}	$(2^m - 1)(2^{m-1} + 1)$
$2^{m-1} + 2^{(m-1)/2}$	$(2^m - 1)(2^{(m-1)/2} - 1)2^{(m-3)/2}$

Table 7.2 Weight distribution of $C_{(2,2^m-1,\delta_2+1,0)}$ for even m

Weight w	No. of codewords A_w
0	1
$2^{m-1} - 2^{(m-2)/2}$	$(2^{m/2} - 1)(2^{m-1} + 2^{(m-2)/2})$
2^{m-1}	$2^m - 1$
$2^{m-1} + 2^{(m-2)/2}$	$(2^{m/2} - 1)(2^{m-1} - 2^{(m-2)/2})$

Table 7.3 Weight distribution of $C_{(q,q^m-1,\delta_2+1,0)}$ for odd m

Weight w	No. of codewords A_w
0	1
$(q-1)q^{m-1} - q^{(m-1)/2}$	$(q-1)(q^m-1)(q^{m-1} + q^{(m-1)/2})/2$
$(q-1)q^{m-1}$	$(q^m-1)(q^{m-1}+1)$
$(q-1)q^{m-1} + q^{(m-1)/2}$	$(q-1)(q^m-1)(q^{m-1} - q^{(m-1)/2})/2$

Table 7.4 Weight distribution of $C_{(q,q^m-1,\delta_2+1,0)}$ for even m

Weight w	No. of codewords A_w
0	1
$(q-1)q^{m-1} - q^{(m-2)/2}$	$(q-1)(q^{(3m-2)/2} - q^{(m-2)/2})$
$(q-1)q^{m-1}$	$q^m - 1$
$(q-1)(q^{m-1} + q^{(m-2)/2})$	$q^{(m-2)/2}(q^m - q^{(m+2)/2} + q - 1)$

Whence, J_i cannot be a coset leader.

Summarizing all the conclusions above, we deduce that δ_2 is the second largest coset leader for the case that m is even. $\qquad\square$

Theorem 7.4. *The code $C_{(q,q^m-1,\delta_2+1,0)}$ has parameters $[n, \tilde{k}, \tilde{d}]$, where $n = q^m - 1$, $\delta_2 = (q-1)q^{m-1} - 1 - q^{\lfloor(m-1)/2\rfloor}$, $\tilde{d} \geq \delta_2 + 1$ and*

$$\tilde{k} = \begin{cases} 2m & \text{for odd } m, \\ \frac{3m}{2} & \text{for even } m. \end{cases} \qquad (7.2)$$

In particular,

- *when $q = 2$ and m is odd, $\tilde{d} = \delta_2 + 1$ and the weight distribution of the code is given in Table 7.1;*

- *when $q = 2$ and m is even, $\tilde{d} = \delta_2 + 1$ and the weight distribution of the code is given in Table 7.2; and*
- *when q is an odd prime, $\tilde{d} = \delta_2 + 1$ and $C_{(q,q^m-1,\delta_2+1,0)}$ is a three-weight code with the weight distribution of Table 7.3 for odd m and Table 7.4 for even m.*

Proof. The conclusions on the dimension $\tilde{k}$ follow from Lemmas 7.1 and 7.3. By the BCH bound, the minimum distance $\tilde{d} \geq \delta_2 + 1$.

When $q = 2$, $\tilde{d} = \delta_2 + 1$ and the weight distribution of the code $C_{(q,q^m-1,\delta_2+1,0)}$ was determined in Goethals (1979); Gold (1968); Kasami (1969).

We now treat the weight distribution of $C_{(q,q^m-1,\delta_2+1,0)}$ for the case that q is an odd prime. From now on, we assume that q is an odd prime. Let η' and η denote the quadratic characters of $\mathrm{GF}(q^m)$ and $\mathrm{GF}(q)$, respectively. Let χ_1' and χ_1 denote the canonical additive characters of $\mathrm{GF}(q^m)$ and $\mathrm{GF}(q)$, respectively. We will need the following results regarding Gauss sums [Lidl and Niederreiter (1997)][Section 5.2]:

$$G(\eta, \chi_1) = \sum_{y \in \mathrm{GF}(q)^*} \eta(y)\chi_1(y) = \begin{cases} \sqrt{q} & \text{if } q \equiv 1 \pmod 4 \\ \imath\sqrt{q} & \text{if } q \equiv 3 \pmod 4 \end{cases} \tag{7.3}$$

where $\imath = \sqrt{-1}$ and

$$G(\eta, \chi_a) = \eta(a)G(\eta, \chi_1) \tag{7.4}$$

for all $a \in \mathrm{GF}(q)^*$, where $\chi_a(x) = \chi_1(ax)$ for all $x \in \mathrm{GF}(q)$.

It follows from the definition of $C_{(q,q^m-1,\delta_2+1,0)}$ and Lemmas 7.1 and 7.3 that the check polynomial of this code is $\mathbb{M}_{\beta^{\delta_1}}(x)\mathbb{M}_{\beta^{\delta_2}}(x)$. Notice that $\delta_1 = n - q^{m-1}$ and

$$\delta_2 = (q-1)q^{m-1} - 1 - q^{\lfloor (m-1)/2 \rfloor} = n - (q^{m-1} + q^{\lfloor (m-1)/2 \rfloor}).$$

From Delsarte's Theorem (see Theorem 2.20 for detail), we then deduce that $C_{(q,q^m-1,\delta_2+1,0)}$ is equivalent to the following code (up to coordinate permutation)

$$\tilde{C}_{\delta_2} = \left\{ \left(\mathrm{Tr}\left(ax^{1+q^{\lfloor (m-1)/2 \rfloor+1}} + bx \right) \right)_{x \in \mathrm{GF}(q^m)^*} : a, b \in \mathrm{GF}(q^m) \right\}, \tag{7.5}$$

herein and hereafter Tr denotes the trace function from $\mathrm{GF}(q^m)$ to $\mathrm{GF}(q)$. In the definition of the code $\tilde{C}_{\delta_2}$, we do not specify the order in which the elements of $\mathrm{GF}(q^m)$ are arranged when the codewords are defined, due to the fact that the codes resulted from different orderings of the elements of $\mathrm{GF}(q^m)^*$ are equivalent, and thus have the same weight distribution.

Define $h = \lfloor (m-1)/2 \rfloor + 1$. For $a \in \mathrm{GF}(q^m)$ and $b \in \mathrm{GF}(q^m)$, let

$$f(x) = \mathrm{Tr}\left(ax^{1+q^h} + bx \right).$$

We now consider the Hamming weight of the codeword

$$\mathbf{c}_{(a,b)} = (f(x))_{x \in \mathrm{GF}(q^m)^*}$$

where $a \in \mathrm{GF}(q^m)$ and $b \in \mathrm{GF}(q^m)$. It is straightforward to deduce that

$$\mathrm{wt}(\mathbf{c}_{(a,b)}) = (q-1)q^{m-1} - \frac{1}{q} \sum_{z \in \mathrm{GF}(q)^*} \sum_{x \in \mathrm{GF}(q^m)} \chi_1'(zf(x))$$

$$= (q-1)q^{m-1} - \frac{1}{q} \sum_{z \in \mathrm{GF}(q)^*} \sum_{x \in \mathrm{GF}(q^m)} \chi_1'(zax^{1+q^h} + zbx). \quad (7.6)$$

We treat the weight distribution of $\tilde{\mathcal{C}}_{\delta_2}$ according to the parity of m as follows.

Case 1: q is an odd prime and $m \geq 3$ is odd

In this case, we have the following basic facts that will be employed later:

(a) $h = (m+1)/2$.
(b) $\gcd(h, m) = 1$.
(c) $\eta'(z) = \eta(z)$ for all $z \in \mathrm{GF}(q)^*$ (due to the fact that $(q^m - 1)/(q-1)$ is odd).
(d) $\chi_1'(x) = \chi_1(\mathrm{Tr}(x))$ for all $x \in \mathrm{GF}(q^m)$.
(e) $F(x) := a^{q^h}x^{q^{2h}} + ax = a^{q^h}x^q + ax$ is a permutation polynomial on $\mathrm{GF}(q^m)$ for each $a \in \mathrm{GF}(q^m)^*$, as x^{1+q^h} is a planar monomial over $\mathrm{GF}(q^m)$.

Case 1.1: Let $a \neq 0$ and $b \neq 0$

Recall that $F(x) = a^{q^h}x^q + ax$ is a permutation polynomial over $\mathrm{GF}(q^m)$ for any $a \in \mathrm{GF}(q^m)^*$. Let x_0 be the unique solution of $F(x) = a^{q^h}x^q + ax = -b^{q^h}$ for any $a \in \mathrm{GF}(q^m)^*$ and $b \in \mathrm{GF}(q^m)$. Put

$$u = \mathrm{Tr}\left(ax_0^{1+q^h}\right).$$

In this subcase, it follows from Lemma 1.13 that

$$\sum_{x \in \mathrm{GF}(q^m)} \chi_1'(af(x)) = \begin{cases} q^{m/2}\overline{\eta'(-za)}\chi_1'(zax_0^{1+q^h}), & \text{if } q \equiv 1 \pmod 4 \\ \iota^{3m}q^{m/2}\overline{\eta'(-za)}\chi_1'(zax_0^{1+q^h}), & \text{if } q \equiv 3 \pmod 4 \end{cases}$$

$$= \begin{cases} q^{m/2}\eta'(-a)\overline{\eta(z)}\chi_1(zu), & \text{if } q \equiv 1 \pmod 4, \\ \iota^{3m}\eta'(-a)q^{m/2}\eta(z)\chi_1(zu), & \text{if } q \equiv 3 \pmod 4, \end{cases}$$

where $\overline{\ell}$ denotes the complex conjugate of the complex number ℓ.

When $u = 0$, we have

$$\sum_{z \in \mathrm{GF}(q)^*} \sum_{x \in \mathrm{GF}(q^m)} \chi'_1(af(x))$$

$$= \begin{cases} \sum_{z \in \mathrm{GF}(q)^*} q^{m/2} \eta'(-a) \eta(z), & \text{if } q \equiv 1 \pmod 4 \\ \sum_{z \in \mathrm{GF}(q)^*} \iota^{3m} \eta'(-a) q^{m/2} \eta(z), & \text{if } q \equiv 3 \pmod 4 \end{cases}$$

$$= 0.$$

Consequently, $\mathtt{wt}(\mathbf{c}_{(a,b)}) = (q-1)q^{m-1}$.

When $u \neq 0$, we have

$$\sum_{z \in \mathrm{GF}(q)^*} \sum_{x \in \mathrm{GF}(q^m)} \chi'_1(af(x))$$

$$= \begin{cases} q^{m/2} \eta'(-a) \overline{G(\eta, \chi_u)}, & \text{if } q \equiv 1 \pmod 4 \\ \iota^{3m} \eta'(-a) q^{m/2} \overline{G(\eta, \chi_u)}, & \text{if } q \equiv 3 \pmod 4 \end{cases}$$

$$= \begin{cases} q^{(m+1)/2} \eta'(-a) \eta(u), & \text{if } q \equiv 1 \pmod 4, \\ q^{(m+1)/2} \iota^{3m+1} \eta'(-a) \eta(u), & \text{if } q \equiv 3 \pmod 4. \end{cases}$$

Consequently, $\mathtt{wt}(\mathbf{c}_{(a,b)}) = (q-1)q^{m-1} \pm q^{(m-1)/2}$.

Case 1.2: Let $a \neq 0$ and $b = 0$

In this case, it follows from Lemma 1.16 that

$$\sum_{x \in \mathrm{GF}(q^m)} \chi'_1(af(x)) = \sum_{x \in \mathrm{GF}(q^m)} \chi'_1(azx^{1+q^h})$$

$$= \begin{cases} q^{m/2} \eta'(za), & \text{if } q \equiv 1 \pmod 4 \\ \iota^m q^{m/2} \eta'(za), & \text{if } q \equiv 3 \pmod 4 \end{cases}$$

$$= \begin{cases} q^{m/2} \eta'(a) \eta(z), & \text{if } q \equiv 1 \pmod 4, \\ \iota^m q^{m/2} \eta'(a) \eta(z), & \text{if } q \equiv 3 \pmod 4. \end{cases}$$

As a result, we obtain

$$\sum_{z \in \mathrm{GF}(q)^*} \sum_{x \in \mathrm{GF}(q^m)} \chi'_1(af(x)) = 0.$$

Hence, $\mathtt{wt}(\mathbf{c}_{(a,b)}) = (q-1)q^{m-1}$.

Case 1.3: Let $a = 0$ and $b \neq 0$

In this case, $f(x) = \mathrm{Tr}(bx)$. Obviously, $\mathtt{wt}(\mathbf{c}_{(0,b)}) = (q-1)q^{m-1}$.

Summarizing the conclusions of Cases 1.1, 1.2, and 1.3, we see that the code $\tilde{C}_{\delta_2}$ has the following three nonzero weights:

$$w_1 = (q-1)q^{m-1} - q^{(m-1)/2},$$
$$w_2 = (q-1)q^{m-1},$$
$$w_3 = (q-1)q^{m-1} + q^{(m-1)/2}.$$

Let A_{w_i} be the total number of codewords with Hamming weight w_i in $\tilde{C}_{\delta_2}$. It is straightforward to see that the minimum distance of the dual of $\tilde{C}_{\delta_2}$ is at least 3. Then the first three Pless power moments described in Section 2.3 yield the following set of equations:

$$\begin{cases} \sum_{i=1}^{3} A_{w_i} = q^{2m} - 1, \\ \sum_{i=1}^{3} w_i A_{w_i} = q^{2m-1}(q-1)(q^m - 1), \\ \sum_{i=1}^{3} w_i^2 A_{w_i} = q^{2m-2}(q-1)(q^{m+1} - q^m - q + 2). \end{cases} \tag{7.7}$$

Solving this system of equations gives the A_{w_i}'s in Table 7.3.

Case 2: q is an odd prime and $m \geq 4$ is even

In this case, we have the following basic facts that will be used subsequently:

(a) $h = \lfloor (m-1)/2 \rfloor + 1 = m/2$.

(b) $\gcd(h,m) = h = m/2$.

(c) $\eta'(z) = 1$ for all $z \in GF(q)^*$ (due to the fact that $(q^m - 1)/(q-1)$ is even).

(d) $\chi_1'(x) = \chi_1(\mathrm{Tr}(x))$ for all $x \in GF(q^m)$.

(e) The equation $y^{q^h} + y = 0$ has q^h solutions y in $GF(q^m)$ (it follows from Lemma 1.15).

(f) $F(x) := a^{q^h} x^{q^{2h}} + ax = (a^{q^h} + a)x$ is a permutation polynomial on $GF(q^m)$ for $q^m - q^{m/2} - 1$ nonzero $a \in GF(q^m)$, and is not a permutation polynomial on $GF(q^m)$ for $q^{m/2} - 1$ nonzero elements $a \in GF(q^m)$.

We now consider the Hamming weight $\mathrm{wt}(\mathbf{c}_{(a,b)})$ of the codeword $\mathbf{c}_{(a,b)}$ case by case for Case 2.

Case 2.1: Let $a \neq 0$, $a^{q^h} + a \neq 0$ and $b \neq 0$

In this subcase, let $x_0 = -b^{q^h}/(a^{q^h} + a)$. Then we have

$$ax_0^{1+q^h} = \frac{ab^{1+q^h}}{(a^{q^h} + a)^2}.$$

Put

$$u = \mathrm{Tr}\left(ax_0^{1+q^h}\right) = \mathrm{Tr}\left(\frac{ab^{1+q^h}}{(a^{q^h} + a)^2}\right).$$

It then follows from Theorem 1.13 that

$$\sum_{x \in \mathrm{GF}(q^m)} \chi_1'(af(x)) = -q^{m/2}\overline{\chi_1'\left(azx_0^{1+q^h}\right)} = -q^{m/2}\overline{\chi_1(zu)}.$$

We obtain then

$$\sum_{z \in \mathrm{GF}(q)^*} \sum_{x \in \mathrm{GF}(q^m)} \chi_1'(af(x)) = \begin{cases} -(q-1)q^{m/2}, & \text{if } u = 0, \\ q^{m/2}, & \text{if } u \neq 0. \end{cases}$$

Consequently,

$$\mathrm{wt}(\mathbf{c}_{(a,b)}) = \begin{cases} (q-1)\left(q^{m-1}+q^{(m-2)/2}\right), & \text{if } u = 0, \\ (q-1)q^{m-1}-q^{(m-2)/2}, & \text{if } u \neq 0. \end{cases}$$

Case 2.2: *Let* $a \neq 0$, $a^{q^h} + a = 0$ *and* $b \neq 0$

In this subcase $F(x) = -b^{q^h}$ has no solution $x \in \mathrm{GF}(q^m)$. It then follows from Theorem 1.14 that

$$\sum_{x \in \mathrm{GF}(q^m)} \chi_1'(af(x)) = 0.$$

As a result, we have

$$\sum_{z \in \mathrm{GF}(q)^*} \sum_{x \in \mathrm{GF}(q^m)} \chi_1'(af(x)) = 0.$$

It then follows from (7.6) that $\mathrm{wt}(\mathbf{c}_{(a,b)}) = (q-1)q^{m-1}$.

Case 2.3: *Let* $a \neq 0$ *and* $b = 0$

In this case, it follows from Theorem 1.16 that

$$\sum_{x \in \mathrm{GF}(q^m)} \chi_1'(af(x)) = \begin{cases} -q^{m/2} & \text{if } a^{q^h} + a \neq 0, \\ q^m & \text{if } a^{q^h} + a = 0. \end{cases}$$

Hence,

$$\sum_{z \in \mathrm{GF}(q)^*} \sum_{x \in \mathrm{GF}(q^m)} \chi_1'(af(x)) = \begin{cases} -(q-1)q^{m/2} & \text{if } a^{q^h} + a \neq 0, \\ (q-1)q^m & \text{if } a^{q^h} + a = 0. \end{cases}$$

We then deduce that

$$\mathrm{wt}(\mathbf{c}_{(a,b)}) = \begin{cases} (q-1)\left(q^{m-1}+q^{m/2}\right) & \text{if } a^{q^h} + a \neq 0, \\ 0 & \text{if } a^{q^h} + a = 0. \end{cases}$$

Case 2.4: Let $a = 0$ and $b \neq 0$

In this subcase, we have $f(x) = \text{Tr}(bx)$. Obviously, $\text{wt}(\mathbf{c}_{(a,b)}) = (q-1)q^{m-1}$.

Summarizing the conclusions of Cases 2.1, 2.2, 2.3, and 2.4, we conclude that $\tilde{C}_{\delta_2}$ has the following three nonzero weights:

$$w_1 = (q-1)q^{m-1} - q^{(m-2)/2},$$
$$w_2 = (q-1)q^{m-1},$$
$$w_3 = (q-1)\left(q^{m-1} + q^{(m-2)/2}\right).$$

Let A_{w_i} be the total number of codewords with Hamming weight w_i in $\tilde{C}_{\delta_2}$. It is straightforward to see that the minimum distance of the dual of $\tilde{C}_{\delta_2}$ is at least 3. Then the first three Pless power moments documented in Section 2.3 yield the following set of equations:

$$\begin{cases} \sum_{i=1}^{3} A_{w_i} = q^{3m/2} - 1, \\ \sum_{i=1}^{3} w_i A_{w_i} = q^{(3m-2)/2}(q-1)(q^m - 1), \\ \sum_{i=1}^{3} w_i^2 A_{w_i} = q^{(3m-4)/2}(q-1)(q^m - 1)(q^{m+1} - q^m - q + 2). \end{cases} \tag{7.8}$$

Solving this system of equations gives the A_{w_i}'s in Table 7.4. This completes the proof of this theorem. □

Note that the proof of Theorem 7.4 actually characterizes all the codewords in $\tilde{C}_{\delta_2}$ with the minimum Hamming weight. Specifically, we have the following.

Theorem 7.5. *Let q be an odd prime, and let $m \geq 4$. When m is odd, all the codewords of $\tilde{C}_{\delta_2}$ with minimum weight $\tilde{d} = \delta_2 + 1$ are those $\mathbf{c}_{(a,b)}$ such that*

- *$ab \neq 0$ and $\eta'(-a)\eta\left(\text{Tr}\left(ax_0^{1+q^{(m+1)/2}}\right)\right) = 1$ if $q \equiv 1 \pmod 4$, where x_0 is the unique solution of $a^{q^{(m+1)/2}}x^q + ax + b^{q^{(m+1)/2}} = 0$; and*
- *$ab \neq 0$ and $\iota^{3m+1}\eta'(-a)\eta\left(\text{Tr}\left(ax_0^{1+q^{(m+1)/2}}\right)\right) = 1$ if $q \equiv 3 \pmod 4$, where x_0 is the unique solution of $a^{q^{(m+1)/2}}x^q + ax + b^{q^{(m+1)/2}} = 0$.*

When m is even, all the codewords of $\tilde{C}_{\delta_2}$ with minimum weight $\tilde{d} = \delta_2 + 1$ are those $\mathbf{c}_{(a,b)}$ such that $a^{q^{m/2}} + a \neq 0$, $b \neq 0$ and

$$\text{Tr}\left(\frac{ab^{1+q^{m/2}}}{(a^{q^{m/2}} + a)^2}\right) \neq 0.$$

Examples of the code $C_{(q,q^m-1,\delta_2+1,0)}$ are summarized in Table 7.5. They either are optimal, or have the same parameters as the best linear codes known.

The following theorem is proved in Gold (1968); Kasami (1969).

Table 7.5 Examples of $C_{(q,q^m-1,\delta_2+1,0)}$ of Theorem 7.4

n	k	$d = \delta_2 + 1$	m	q	Optimality
15	6	6	4	2	Optimal
31	10	12	5	2	Optimal
63	9	28	6	2	Optimal
127	14	56	7	2	Optimal
256	12	120	8	2	Best known
26	6	15	3	3	Optimal
80	6	51	4	3	Optimal
242	10	153	5	3	Best known

Theorem 7.6. *The minimum distance $\tilde{d}^{\perp}$ of the dual of $C_{(2,2^m-1,\delta_2+1,0)}$ is equal to 5 when $m \geq 5$ is odd, and 3 when $m \geq 4$ is even.*

Theorem 7.7. *The code $C_{(q,q^m-1,\delta_2,1)}$ has parameters $[n, k, d]$, where $n = q^m - 1$, $\delta_2 = (q-1)q^{m-1} - 1 - q^{\lfloor (m-1)/2 \rfloor}$, $d \geq \delta_2$ and*

$$k = \begin{cases} 2m+1 & \text{for odd } m, \\ \frac{3m}{2} + 1 & \text{for even } m. \end{cases} \tag{7.9}$$

Furthermore, $d = \delta_2$ if q is a prime.

Proof. The conclusions on the dimension k follow from Lemmas 7.1 and 7.3. By the BCH bound, the minimum distance $d \geq \delta_2$.

It follows from the definition of $C_{(q,q^m-1,\delta_2,1)}$ and Lemmas 7.1 and 7.3 that the check polynomial of this code is $(x-1)\mathbb{M}_{\beta^{\delta_1}}(x)\mathbb{M}_{\beta^{\delta_2}}(x)$. Notice that $\delta_1 = n - q^{m-1}$ and

$$\delta_2 = (q-1)q^{m-1} - 1 - q^{\lfloor (m-1)/2 \rfloor} = n - (q^{m-1} + q^{\lfloor (m-1)/2 \rfloor}).$$

From Delsarte's Theorem (i.e., Theorem 2.20), we deduce that $C_{(q,q^m-1,\delta_2,1)}$ is equivalent to the following code

$$C_{\delta_2} = \left\{ \left(\mathrm{Tr}\left(ax + bx^{1+q^{\lfloor (m-1)/2 \rfloor + 1}} \right) + c \right)_{x \in \mathrm{GF}(q^m)^*} : \begin{array}{l} a \in \mathrm{GF}(q^m) \\ b \in \mathrm{GF}(q^m) \\ c \in \mathrm{GF}(q) \end{array} \right\}.$$

$$\tag{7.10}$$

To prove that $d = \delta_2$ for the case that q is a prime, one can refine the proof of Theorem 7.4 with the quadratic expression of (7.10) to obtain the weight distribution of the code. We leave the details to the reader. $\qquad\square$

Examples of the code $C_{(q,q^m-1,\delta_2,1)}$ are summarized in Table 7.6. They are sometimes optimal, and sometimes have the same parameters as the best linear

Table 7.6   Examples of $C_{(q,q^m-1,\delta_2,1)}$ of Theorem 7.7

n	k	$d = \delta_2$	m	q	Optimality
15	7	5	4	2	Yes
31	11	11	5	2	Yes
63	10	27	6	2	Best known
127	15	55	7	2	Best known
255	13	119	8	2	Best known
26	7	14	3	3	Optimal
80	7	50	4	3	Optimal
242	11	152	5	3	Best known

codes known. When $(q,m) = (2,6)$, $C_{(q,q^m-1,\delta_2,1)}$ has parameters $[63,10,27]$, which are the best possible parameters according to Ding (2015a)[p. 258]. When $(q,m) = (3,3)$, $C_{(q,q^m-1,\delta_2,1)}$ has parameters $[26,7,14]$, which are the best possible parameters according to Ding (2015a)[p. 300].

Table 7.7   Weight distribution of $C_{(2,2^m-1,\delta_2,1)}$ for odd m

Weight w	No. of codewords A_w
0	1
$2^{m-1} - 2^{(m-1)/2} - 1$	$(2^m - 1)(2^{(m-1)/2} - 1)2^{(m-3)/2}$
$2^{m-1} - 2^{(m-1)/2}$	$(2^m - 1)(2^{(m-1)/2} + 1)2^{(m-3)/2}$
$2^{m-1} - 1$	$(2^m - 1)(2^{m-1} + 1)$
2^{m-1}	$(2^m - 1)(2^{m-1} + 1)$
$2^{m-1} + 2^{(m-1)/2} - 1$	$(2^m - 1)(2^{(m-1)/2} + 1)2^{(m-3)/2}$
$2^{m-1} + 2^{(m-1)/2}$	$(2^m - 1)(2^{(m-1)/2} - 1)2^{(m-3)/2}$
$2^m - 1$	1

Table 7.8   Weight distribution of $C_{(2,2^m-1,\delta_2,1)}$ for even m

Weight w	No. of codewords A_w
0	1
$2^{m-1} - 2^{(m-2)/2} - 1$	$(2^{m/2} - 1)(2^{m-1} - 2^{(m-2)/2})$
$2^{m-1} - 2^{(m-2)/2}$	$(2^{m/2} - 1)(2^{m-1} + 2^{(m-2)/2})$
$2^{m-1} - 1$	$2^m - 1$
2^{m-1}	$2^m - 1$
$2^{m-1} + 2^{(m-2)/2} - 1$	$(2^{m/2} - 1)(2^{m-1} + 2^{(m-2)/2})$
$2^{m-1} + 2^{(m-2)/2}$	$(2^{m/2} - 1)(2^{m-1} - 2^{(m-2)/2})$
$2^m - 1$	1

Theorem 7.8. *The binary code* $C_{(2,2^m-1,\delta_2,1)}$ *has parameters* $[n, k, d]$, *where* $n = 2^m - 1$, $\delta_2 = 2^{m-1} - 1 - 2^{\lfloor (m-1)/2 \rfloor}$, $d = \delta_2$ *and*

$$k = \begin{cases} 2m+1 & \textit{for odd } m, \\ \frac{3m}{2} + 1 & \textit{for even } m. \end{cases} \tag{7.11}$$

Table 7.9   Weight distribution of $C_{(q,q^m-1,\delta_2,1)}$ for odd m

Weight w	Frequency A_w
0	1
$(q-1)q^{m-1}-1-q^{(m-1)/2}$	$(q-1)(q^m-1)(q^m-q^{m-1}-q^{(m-1)/2})/2$
$(q-1)q^{m-1}-q^{(m-1)/2}$	$(q-1)(q^m-1)(q^{m-1}+q^{(m-1)/2})/2$
$(q-1)q^{m-1}-1$	$(q-1)(q^m-1)(q^{m-1}+1)$
$(q-1)q^{m-1}$	$(q^m-1)(q^{m-1}+1)$
$(q-1)q^{m-1}-1+q^{(m-1)/2}$	$(q-1)(q^m-1)(q^m-q^{m-1}+q^{(m-1)/2})/2$
$(q-1)q^{m-1}+q^{(m-1)/2}$	$(q-1)(q^m-1)(q^{m-1}-q^{(m-1)/2})/2$
q^m-1	$q-1$

Table 7.10   Weight distribution of $C_{(q,q^m-1,\delta_2,1)}$ for even m

Weight w	Frequency A_w
0	1
$(q-1)q^{m-1}-1-q^{\frac{m}{2}-1}$	$q^{\frac{m}{2}-1}(q^{m+2}-2q^{m+1}+q^m-q^{\frac{m}{2}+2}+q^{\frac{m}{2}+1}+q-1)$
$(q-1)q^{m-1}-q^{\frac{m}{2}-1}$	$(q-1)(q^{\frac{3m}{2}-1}-q^{\frac{m}{2}-1})$
$(q-1)q^{m-1}-1$	$(q-1)(q^m-1)$
$(q-1)q^{m-1}$	q^m-1
$(q-1)(q^{m-1}+q^{\frac{m}{2}-1})-1$	$(q-1)(q^{\frac{3m}{2}-1}-q^{\frac{m}{2}-1})$
$(q-1)(q^{m-1}+q^{\frac{m}{2}-1})$	$q^{\frac{m}{2}-1}(q^m-q^{\frac{m}{2}+1}+q-1)$
q^m-1	$q-1$

Furthermore, the weight distribution of this code is given in Table 7.7 for odd m, and in Table 7.8 for even m.

Proof. It follows from Theorem 7.4 directly. □

Theorem 7.9 (Li, Wu, Liu (2019)). *Let q be an odd prime and $m \geq 3$ an odd integer. Then $C_{(q,q^m-1,\delta_2,1)}$ is a $[q^m-1, 2m+1, q^m-q^{m-1}-1-q^{(m-1)/2}]$ seven-weight code with the weight distribution of Table 7.9.*

Theorem 7.10 (Li, Wu, Liu (2019)). *Let q be an odd prime and $m \geq 4$ an even integer. Then $C_{(q,q^m-1,\delta_2,1)}$ is a $[q^m-1, \frac{3m}{2}+1, q^m-q^{m-1}-1-q^{\frac{m}{2}-1}]$ seven-weight code with the weight distribution of Table 7.10.*

The weight distribution of the extended code of $C_{(q,q^m-1,\delta_2,1)}$ was also settled in Li, Wu, Liu (2019).

7.4   The Parameters of the Codes $C_{(q,q^m-1,\delta_3,1)}$ and $C_{(q,q^m-1,\delta_3+1,0)}$, where $\delta_3 = (q-1)q^{m-1} - 1 - q^{\lfloor (m+1)/2 \rfloor}$

In this section, we determine the parameters of the codes $C_{(q,q^m-1,\delta_3,1)}$ and $C_{(q,q^m-1,\delta_3+1,0)}$, where $\delta_3 = (q-1)q^{m-1} - 1 - q^{\lfloor (m+1)/2 \rfloor}$. The results presented in this section are taken from Ding, Fan and Zhou (2017). To determine the parameters of the two codes, we need the following lemma.

Lemma 7.11. *Let $m \geq 4$. Then the third largest q-cyclotomic coset leader modulo n is $\delta_3 = (q-1)q^{m-1} - 1 - q^{\lfloor (m+1)/2 \rfloor}$. In addition, $|C_{\delta_3}| = m$.*

Proof. The proof is divided into the following two cases according to the parity of m.

Case I, i.e., m is odd:

In this case, we have

$$\delta_3 = (q-1)q^{m-1} - 1 - q^{(m+1)/2} = n - \left(q^{(m-3)/2} + 1 \right) q^{(m+1)/2}.$$

It can be verified that

$$C_{\delta_3} = \left\{ n - \left(q^{(m+3)/2} + 1 \right) q^i : i = 0,1,\ldots, \frac{m-5}{2} \right\} \cup$$
$$\left\{ n - \left(q^{(m-3)/2} + 1 \right) q^i : i = 0,1,\ldots, \frac{m+1}{2} \right\}.$$

Therefore, δ_3 is the smallest integer in C_{δ_3} and is thus the coset leader. Clearly, we have $|C_{\delta_3}| = m$.

Let $t = (m-1)/2$. By definition,

$$\delta_2 = (q-1)q^{m-1} - 1 - q^{(m-1)/2}$$
$$= (q-2)q^{m-1} + (q-1)q^{m-2} + (q-1)q^{m-3} + \cdots + (q-1)q^{t+1} +$$
$$(q-2)q^t + (q-1)q^{t-1} + (q-1)q^{t-2} + \cdots + (q-1)q + (q-1).$$

Observe that $\delta_2 - \delta_3 = (q-1)q^t$. We need to prove that $J_i := \delta_2 - i$ is not a coset leader for all i with $1 \leq i \leq (q-1)q^t - 1$.

Notice that

$$(q-1)q^t - 1 = (q-2)q^t + (q-1)q^{t-1} + (q-1)q^{t-2} + \cdots + (q-1)q + q - 1.$$

The q-adic expansion of i must be of the form

$$i = i_t q^t + i_{t-1} q^{t-1} + \cdots + i_1 q + i_0,$$

where i_ℓ satisfies $0 \le i_\ell \le q-1$ for all $0 \le \ell \le t-1$ and $0 \le i_t \le q-2$, but at least one of the i_ℓ's is nonzero. It then follows that the q-adic expansion of J_i is given by

$$J_i = (q-2)q^{m-1} + (q-1)q^{m-2} + (q-1)q^{m-3} + \cdots + (q-1)q^{t+1} +$$
$$(q-2-i_t)q^t + (q-1-i_{t-1})q^{t-1} + (q-1-i_{t-2})q^{t-2} + \cdots +$$
$$(q-1-i_1)q + q-1-i_0.$$

Subcase I.1, i.e., $q = 2$:

In this subcase, we have $i_t = 0$ and

$$J_i = 2^{m-2} + 2^{m-3} + \cdots + 2^{t+1} + (1-i_{t-1})2^{t-1} + \cdots + (1-i_1)2 + 1 - i_0.$$

If $i_0 = 1$, then $J_i/2 < J_i$. But $J_i/2$ and J_i are in the same 2-cyclotomic coset modulo n. Hence, J_i cannot be a coset leader.

We now assume that $i_0 = 0$. Since $i \ne 0$, one of the i_ℓ's must be nonzero. Let ℓ denote the largest one such that $i_\ell = 1$. One can then verify that

$$J_i 2^{m-1-\ell} \bmod n < J_i.$$

Whence, J_i cannot be a coset leader.

Subcase I.2, i.e., $q > 2$:

If $i_t \ge 1$, then $J_i q^{m-1-t} \bmod n < J_i$. In this case, J_i cannot be a coset leader.

If $i_\ell \ge 2$ for some ℓ with $0 \le \ell \le t-1$, then $J_i q^{m-1-\ell} \bmod n < J_i$. In this case, J_i cannot be a coset leader.

We now assume that all $i_\ell \in \{0, 1\}$ for all $0 \le \ell \le t-1$ and $i_t = 0$. Since $i \ge 1$, at least one of the i_ℓ's must be 1. Let ℓ denote the largest one such that $i_\ell = 1$. One can then verify that

$$J_i q^{m-1-\ell} \bmod n < J_i.$$

Whence, J_i cannot be a coset leader.

Summarizing all the conclusions above, we deduce that δ_3 is the third largest coset leader for the case that m is odd.

Case II, i.e., m is even

In this case, we have

$$\delta_3 = (q-1)q^{m-1} - 1 - q^{(m+2)/2} = n - \left(q^{(m-4)/2} + 1 \right) q^{(m+2)/2}.$$

It is easily seen that

$$C_{\delta_3} = \left\{ n - \left(q^{(m-4)/2} + 1 \right) q^i : i = 0, 1, \ldots, \frac{m+2}{2} \right\} \cup$$
$$\left\{ n - \left(q^{(m+4)/2} + 1 \right) q^i : i = 0, 1, \ldots, \frac{m-6}{2} \right\}.$$

Therefore, δ_3 is the smallest integer in C_{δ_3} and is the coset leader. Obviously, $|C_{\delta_3}| = m$.

Similarly as in the case that m is odd, one can prove that δ_3 is the third largest coset leader for the case that m is even. Details are omitted here. $\square$

Table 7.11   The weight distribution of $C_{(2,2^m-1,\delta_3+1,0)}$ for odd m

Weight w	No. of codewords A_w
0	1
$2^{m-1} - 2^{(m+1)/2}$	$(2^m - 1) \cdot 2^{(m-5)/2} \cdot (2^{(m-3)/2} + 1) \cdot (2^{m-1} - 1)/3$
$2^{m-1} - 2^{(m-1)/2}$	$(2^m - 1) \cdot 2^{(m-3)/2} \cdot (2^{(m-1)/2} + 1) \cdot (5 \cdot 2^{m-1} + 4)/3$
2^{m-1}	$(2^m - 1) \cdot (9 \cdot 2^{2m-4} + 3 \cdot 2^{m-3} + 1)$
$2^{m-1} + 2^{(m-1)/2}$	$(2^m - 1) \cdot 2^{(m-3)/2} \cdot (2^{(m-1)/2} - 1) \cdot (5 \cdot 2^{m-1} + 4)/3$
$2^{m-1} + 2^{(m+1)/2}$	$(2^m - 1) \cdot 2^{(m-5)/2} \cdot (2^{(m-3)/2} - 1) \cdot (2^{m-1} - 1)/3$

Table 7.12   The weight distribution of $C_{(2,2^m-1,\delta_3+1,0)}$ for even m

Weight w	No. of codewords A_w
0	1
$2^{m-1} - 2^{m/2}$	$(2^{m/2} - 1)(2^{m-3} + 2^{(m-4)/2})(2^{m+1} + 2^{m/2} - 1)/3$
$2^{m-1} - 2^{(m-2)/2}$	$(2^{m/2} - 1)(2^{m-1} + 2^{(m-2)/2})(2^m + 2^{(m+2)/2} + 4)/3$
2^{m-1}	$(2^{m/2} - 1)(2^{2m-1} + 2^{(3m-4)/2} - 2^{m-2} + 2^{m/2} + 1)$
$2^{m-1} + 2^{(m-2)/2}$	$(2^{m/2} - 1)(2^{m-1} - 2^{(m-2)/2})(2^m + 2^{(m+2)/2} + 4)/3$
$2^{m-1} + 2^{m/2}$	$(2^{m/2} - 1)(2^{m-3} - 2^{(m-4)/2})(2^{m+1} + 2^{m/2} - 1)/3$

Theorem 7.12. *Let* $m \geq 4$. *The code* $C_{(q,q^m-1,\delta_3+1,0)}$ *has parameters* $[n, \tilde{k}, \tilde{d}]$, *where* $n = q^m - 1$, $\delta_3 = (q-1)q^{m-1} - 1 - q^{\lfloor (m+1)/2 \rfloor}$, $\tilde{d} \geq \delta_3 + 1 = (q-1)q^{m-1} - q^{\lfloor (m+1)/2 \rfloor}$ *and*

$$\tilde{k} = \begin{cases} 3m & \text{for odd } m, \\ \frac{5m}{2} & \text{for even } m. \end{cases} \tag{7.12}$$

Furthermore,

- *when* $q = 2$ *and* m *is odd, the binary code* $C_{(q,q^m-1,\delta_3+1,0)}$ *has minimum distance* $\tilde{d} = \delta_3 + 1$ *and its weight distribution is given in Table 7.11;*
- *when* $q = 2$ *and* m *is even, the binary code* $C_{(q,q^m-1,\delta_3+1,0)}$ *has minimum distance* $\tilde{d} = \delta_3 + 1$ *and its weight distribution is given in Table 7.12;*

- *when q is an odd prime and $m \geq 4$ is even, the code $C_{(q,q^m-1,\delta_3+1,0)}$ has minimum distance $\tilde{d} = \delta_3 + 1$ and its weight distribution is given in Table 7.13; and*
- *when q is an odd prime and $m \geq 5$ is odd, the code $C_{(q,q^m-1,\delta_3+1,0)}$ has minimum distance $\tilde{d} = \delta_3 + 1$ and its weight distribution is given in Table 7.14.*

Proof. The conclusions on the dimension $\tilde{k}$ follow from Lemmas 7.1, 7.3 and 7.11. By the BCH bound, the minimum distance $\tilde{d} \geq \delta_3 + 1$.

It follows from the definition of $C_{(q,q^m-1,\delta_3+1,0)}$ and Lemmas 7.1, 7.3 and 7.11 that the check polynomial of this code is $\mathbb{M}_{\beta^{\delta_1}}(x)\mathbb{M}_{\beta^{\delta_2}}(x)\mathbb{M}_{\beta^{\delta_3}}(x)$. Notice that

$$\delta_3 = (q-1)q^{m-1} - 1 - q^{\lfloor (m+1)/2 \rfloor} = n - (q^{m-1} + q^{\lfloor (m+1)/2 \rfloor}).$$

From Delsarte's Theorem (i.e., Theorem 2.20), we deduce that $C_{(q,q^m-1,\delta_3+1,0)}$ is equivalent to the following code

$$\tilde{C}_{\delta_3} = \left\{ \left(\mathrm{Tr}\left(ax + bx^{1+q^h} + cx^{1+q^{h+1}} \right) \right)_{x \in \mathrm{GF}(q^m)^*} : \begin{array}{l} a \in \mathrm{GF}(q^m) \\ b \in \mathrm{GF}(q^m) \\ c \in \mathrm{GF}(q^m) \end{array} \right\},$$

where $h = \lfloor (m-1)/2 \rfloor + 1$.

When $q = 2$, the binary code $\tilde{C}_{\delta_3}$ has minimum distance $\tilde{d} = \delta_3 + 1$ and its weight distribution was settled in Kasami (1969).

When q is an odd prime and $m \geq 4$ is even, the code $\tilde{C}_{\delta_3}$ has minimum distance $\tilde{d} = \delta_3 + 1$ and its weight distribution in Table 7.13 is a special case of Table 2 in Zeng, Li and Hu (2008).

When q is an odd prime and $m \geq 5$ is odd, we have $h = (m+1)/2$ and $h+1 = (m+3)/2$. It is easy to see that $\gcd(m,h) = 1$ and

$$1 + q^{3h} \equiv 1 + q^{h+1} \pmod{n}.$$

It then follows that

$$\tilde{C}_{\delta_3} = \left\{ \left(\mathrm{Tr}\left(ax + bx^{1+q^h} + cx^{1+q^{3h}} \right) \right)_{x \in \mathrm{GF}(q^m)^*} : \begin{array}{l} a \in \mathrm{GF}(q^m) \\ b \in \mathrm{GF}(q^m) \\ c \in \mathrm{GF}(q^m) \end{array} \right\}.$$

In this case, the weight distribution of $\tilde{C}_{\delta_3}$ is a special case of Theorem 2 in Zeng, Hu, Jiang, Yue and Cao (2010). $\qquad\square$

The following theorem is proved in Kasami (1969).

Theorem 7.13. *The minimum distance $\tilde{d}^{\perp}$ of the dual of $C_{(2,2^m-1,\delta_3+1,0)}$ is equal to 7 when $m \geq 5$ is odd, and 5 when $m \geq 6$ is even.*

Table 7.13   The weight distribution of $C_{(q,\,q^m-1,\,\delta_3+1,0)}$ for even m and odd q

Weight w	No. of codewords A_w
0	1
$(q-1)q^{m-1}-q^{\frac{m}{2}}$	$\frac{(q^m-1)((q^2-1)(q^{\frac{3m-6}{2}}+q^{m-2})+2(q^{\frac{m-2}{2}}-1)(q^{m-3}+q^{\frac{m-4}{2}}))}{2(q+1)}$
$(q-1)(q^{m-1}-q^{\frac{m-2}{2}})$	$\frac{q(q^{\frac{m}{2}}+1)(q^m-1)(q^{m-1}+(q-1)q^{\frac{m-2}{2}})}{2(q+1)}$
$(q-1)q^{m-1}-q^{\frac{m-2}{2}}$	$\frac{(q^{m+1}-2q^m+q)(q^{\frac{m}{2}}-1)(q^{m-1}+q^{\frac{m-2}{2}})}{2}$
$(q-1)q^{m-1}$	$(q^m-1)(1+q^{\frac{3m-2}{2}}-q^{\frac{3m-4}{2}}+2q^{\frac{3m-6}{2}}-q^{m-2})$
$(q-1)q^{m-1}+q^{\frac{m-2}{2}}$	$\frac{q(q^{\frac{m}{2}}+1)(q^m-1)(q-1)(q^{m-1}-q^{\frac{m-2}{2}})}{2(q+1)}$
$(q-1)(q^{m-1}+q^{\frac{m-2}{2}})$	$\frac{(q^{m+1}-2q^m+q)(q^{\frac{m}{2}}-1)(q^{m-1}-(q-1)q^{\frac{m-2}{2}})}{2(q-1)}$
$(q-1)q^{m-1}+q^{\frac{m}{2}}$	$\frac{q^{\frac{m-2}{2}}(q^m-1)(q-1)(q^{m-2}-q^{\frac{m-2}{2}})}{2}$
$(q-1)(q^{m-1}+q^{\frac{m}{2}})$	$\frac{(q^{\frac{m-2}{2}}-1)(q^m-1)(q^{m-3}-(q-1)q^{\frac{m-4}{2}})}{(q^2-1)}$

Table 7.14   The weight distribution of $C_{(q,\,q^m-1,\,\delta_3+1,0)}$ for odd m and odd q

Weight w	No. of codewords A_w
0	1
$(q-1)q^{m-1}-q^{\frac{m+1}{2}}$	$\frac{(q^m-1)(q^{m-3}+q^{(m-3)/2})(q^{m-1}-1)}{2(q+1)}$
$(q-1)(q^{m-1}-q^{\frac{m+1}{2}})$	$\frac{(q^m-1)(q^{m-1}+q^{(m-1)/2})(q^{m-2}+(q-1)q^{(m-3)/2})}{2}$
$(q-1)q^{m-1}-q^{\frac{m+1}{2}}$	$\frac{(q^m-1)(q^{m-2}+q^{\frac{m-3}{2}})(q^{m+3}-q^{m+2}-q^{m-1}-q^{\frac{m+3}{2}}+q^{\frac{m-1}{2}}+q^3)}{2(q+1)}$
$(q-1)q^{m-1}$	$(q^m-1)(1+(q^2-q+1)q^{m-3}+(q-1)q^{2m-4})+$ $(q^m-1)((q-2)q^{2m-2}+q^{2m-1})$
$(q-1)q^{m-1}+q^{\frac{m+1}{2}}$	$\frac{(q^m-1)(q^{m-2}-q^{\frac{m-3}{2}})(q^{m+3}-q^{m+2}-q^{m-1}+q^{\frac{m+3}{2}}-q^{\frac{m-1}{2}}+q^3)}{2(q+1)}$
$(q-1)(q^{m-1}+q^{\frac{m+1}{2}})$	$\frac{(q^m-1)(q^{m-1}-q^{\frac{m-1}{2}})(q^{m-2}-(q-1)q^{\frac{m-3}{2}})}{2}$
$(q-1)q^{m-1}+q^{\frac{m+1}{2}}$	$\frac{(q^m-1)(q^{m-3}-q^{\frac{m-3}{2}})(q^{m-1}-1)}{2(q+1)}$

Example 7.14. Let $(q,m)=(2,4)$. Then $\delta_3=3$, and $C_{(2,15,4,0)}$ has parameters $[15,10,4]$ and weight enumerator $1+105z^4+280z^6+435z^8+168z^{10}+35z^{12}$.

Example 7.15. Let $(q,m)=(2,5)$. Then $\delta_3=7$, and $C_{(2,31,8,0)}$ has parameters $[31,15,8]$ and weight enumerator $1+465z^8+8680z^{12}+18259z^{16}+5208z^{20}+155z^{24}$.

Example 7.16. Let $(q,m)=(3,4)$. Then $\delta_3=44$, and the ternary code $C_{(3,80,45,0)}$ has parameters $[80,10,45]$ and weight enumerator

$$1+3040z^{45}+9900z^{48}+10080z^{51}+16640z^{54}+$$
$$14400z^{57}+3528z^{60}+1440z^{63}+20z^{72}.$$

Example 7.17. Let $(q,m)=(3,5)$. Then $\delta_3=134$, and the ternary code

Table 7.15   Examples of $C_{(q,q^m-1,\delta_3+1,0)}$ of Theorem 7.12

n	k	$d = \delta_3 + 1$	m	q	Optimality
15	10	4	4	2	Yes
31	15	8	5	2	Yes
63	15	24	6	2	Yes
127	21	48	7	2	Best known
255	20	112	8	2	Best known
26	10	9	3	3	No
80	10	45	4	3	Best known
242	15	135	5	3	No

$C_{(3,242,135,0)}$ has parameters $[242, 15, 135]$ and weight enumerator

$$1 + 29040z^{135} + 359370z^{144} + 3855060z^{153} + 6719372z^{162} +$$
$$3188592z^{171} + 182952z^{180} + 14520z^{189}.$$

The optimality of the code $C_{(q,q^m-1,\delta_3+1,0)}$ is indicated in Table 7.15, where further examples of the code is documented. As shown in this table, the code $C_{(q,q^m-1,\delta_3+1,0)}$ is sometimes optimal, and sometimes has the same parameters as the best linear code known.

Theorem 7.18. *Let $m \geq 4$. The code $C_{(q,q^m-1,\delta_3,1)}$ has parameters $[n, k, \delta_3]$, where $n = q^m - 1$, $\delta_3 = (q-1)q^{m-1} - 1 - q^{\lfloor(m+1)/2\rfloor}$ and*

$$k = \begin{cases} 3m + 1 & \text{for odd } m, \\ \frac{5m}{2} + 1 & \text{for even } m. \end{cases} \tag{7.13}$$

Proof. The conclusions on the dimension k follow from Lemmas 7.1, 7.3 and 7.11. By the BCH bound, the minimum distance $d \geq \delta_3$.

It follows from the definition of $C_{(q,q^m-1,\delta_3,1)}$ and Lemmas 7.1, 7.3 and 7.11 that the check polynomial of this code is $(x-1)\mathbb{M}_{\beta^{\delta_1}}(x)\mathbb{M}_{\beta^{\delta_2}}(x)\mathbb{M}_{\beta^{\delta_3}}(x)$. Notice that

$$\delta_3 = (q-1)q^{m-1} - 1 - q^{\lfloor(m+1)/2\rfloor} = n - (q^{m-1} + q^{\lfloor(m+1)/2\rfloor}).$$

From Delsarte's Theorem (i.e., Theorem 2.20), we then deduce that $C_{(q,q^m-1,\delta_3,1)}$ is equal to the following code

$$C_{\delta_3} = \left\{ \left(\text{Tr}\left(ax + bx^{1+q^{\lfloor(m-1)/2\rfloor+1}} + cx^{1+q^{\lfloor(m+1)/2\rfloor+1}} \right) + e \right)_{x \in \text{GF}(q^m)^*} : \atop a \in \text{GF}(q^m), b \in \text{GF}(q^m), c \in \text{GF}(q^m), e \in \text{GF}(q) \right\}.$$

Similarly, the weights and their frequencies of the codewords in $C_{(q,q^m-1,\delta_3,1)}$ are determined by the affine and quadratic functions

$$\text{Tr}\left(ax + bx^{1+q^{\lfloor(m-1)/2\rfloor+1}} + cx^{1+q^{\lfloor(m+1)/2\rfloor+1}} \right) + e.$$

One can refine the proofs in Kasami (1969), Zeng, Li and Hu (2008), Zeng, Hu, Jiang, Yue and Cao (2010) and Zhou and Tang (2011), to prove that $d = \delta_3$. We omit the lengthy details here. □

Table 7.16   Examples of $C_{(q,q^m-1,\delta_3,1)}$ of Theorem 7.18

n	k	$d = \delta_3$	m	q	Optimality
15	11	3	4	2	Yes
31	16	7	5	2	No (optimal $d = 8$)
63	16	23	6	2	Best known
127	22	47	7	2	Best known
255	21	111	8	2	Best known
26	11	8	3	3	No (best $d = 9$)
81	11	44	4	3	No (best $d = 45$)
242	16	134	5	3	No (best $d = 135$)

Examples of the code $C_{(q,q^m-1,\delta_3,1)}$ are listed in Table 7.16. Some of them are optimal, and some have the same parameters as the best codes known. When $(q,m) = (3,3)$, the code $C_{(q,q^m-1,\delta_3,1)}$ has parameters $[26,11,8]$, which are the best possible according to Ding (2015a)[p. 300].

Theorem 7.19. *Let* $q > 2$. *Then* $C_{(q,q^3-1,q^3-q^2-q-1,0)}$ *and* $C_{(q,q^3-1,q^3-q^2-q-2,1)}$ *have parameters*

$$[q^3 - 1, 7, \tilde{d} \geq q^3 - q^2 - q - 1] \text{ and } [q^3 - 1, 8, d \geq q^3 - q^2 - q - 2],$$

respectively.

Proof. When $m = 3$, one can similarly prove that the third largest coset leader $\delta_3 = \delta_2 - 1 = q^3 - q^2 - q - 2$ and $|C_{\delta_3}| = 1$. The conclusions on the dimensions of $C_{(q,q^3-1,q^3-q^2-q-1,0)}$ and $C_{(q,q^3-1,q^3-q^2-q-2,1)}$ follow from Lemmas 7.1 and 7.3. The conclusions on the minimum distances follow from the BCH bound. □

The following theorem follows from Theorem 7.13, as $C^{\perp}_{(2,2^m-1,\delta_3+1,0)}$ is the even-weight subcode of $C^{\perp}_{(2,2^m-1,\delta_3,1)}$.

Theorem 7.20. *The minimum distance* $d^{\perp}$ *of the dual of* $C_{(2,2^m-1,\delta_3+1,0)}$ *is equal to 8 when* $m \geq 5$ *is odd, and 6 when* $m \geq 6$ *is even.*

Theorem 7.21. *Let* $m \geq 4$. *The binary code* $C_{(2,2^m-1,\delta_3,1)}$ *has parameters* $[n, k, \delta_3]$, *where* $n = 2^m - 1$, $\delta_3 = 2^{m-1} - 1 - 2^{\lfloor (m+1)/2 \rfloor}$ *and*

$$k = \begin{cases} 3m + 1 & \text{for odd } m, \\ \frac{5m}{2} + 1 & \text{for even } m. \end{cases} \tag{7.14}$$

Table 7.17   The weight distribution of $C_{(2,2^m-1,\delta_3,1)}$ for odd m

Weight w	No. of codewords A_w
0	1
$2^{m-1}-2^{(m+1)/2}-1$	$(2^m-1)\cdot 2^{(m-5)/2}\cdot(2^{(m-3)/2}-1)\cdot(2^{m-1}-1)/3$
$2^{m-1}-2^{(m+1)/2}$	$(2^m-1)\cdot 2^{(m-5)/2}\cdot(2^{(m-3)/2}+1)\cdot(2^{m-1}-1)/3$
$2^{m-1}-2^{(m-1)/2}-1$	$(2^m-1)\cdot 2^{(m-3)/2}\cdot(2^{(m-1)/2}-1)\cdot(5\cdot2^{m-1}+4)/3$
$2^{m-1}-2^{(m-1)/2}$	$(2^m-1)\cdot 2^{(m-3)/2}\cdot(2^{(m-1)/2}+1)\cdot(5\cdot2^{m-1}+4)/3$
$2^{m-1}-1$	$(2^m-1)\cdot(9\cdot2^{2m-4}+3\cdot2^{m-3}+1)$
2^{m-1}	$(2^m-1)\cdot(9\cdot2^{2m-4}+3\cdot2^{m-3}+1)$
$2^{m-1}+2^{(m-1)/2}-1$	$(2^m-1)\cdot 2^{(m-3)/2}\cdot(2^{(m-1)/2}+1)\cdot(5\cdot2^{m-1}+4)/3$
$2^{m-1}+2^{(m-1)/2}$	$(2^m-1)\cdot 2^{(m-3)/2}\cdot(2^{(m-1)/2}-1)\cdot(5\cdot2^{m-1}+4)/3$
$2^{m-1}+2^{(m+1)/2}-1$	$(2^m-1)\cdot 2^{(m-5)/2}\cdot(2^{(m-3)/2}+1)\cdot(2^{m-1}-1)/3$
$2^{m-1}+2^{(m+1)/2}$	$(2^m-1)\cdot 2^{(m-5)/2}\cdot(2^{(m-3)/2}-1)\cdot(2^{m-1}-1)/3$
2^m-1	1

Table 7.18   The weight distribution of $C_{(2,2^m-1,\delta_3,1)}$ for even m

Weight w	No. of codewords A_w
0	1
$2^{m-1}-2^{m/2}-1$	$(2^{m/2}-1)(2^{m-3}-2^{(m-4)/2})(2^{m+1}+2^{m/2}-1)/3$
$2^{m-1}-2^{m/2}$	$(2^{m/2}-1)(2^{m-3}+2^{(m-4)/2})(2^{m+1}+2^{m/2}-1)/3$
$2^{m-1}-2^{(m-2)/2}-1$	$(2^{m/2}-1)(2^{m-1}-2^{(m-2)/2})(2^m+2^{(m+2)/2}+4)/3$
$2^{m-1}-2^{(m-2)/2}$	$(2^{m/2}-1)(2^{m-1}+2^{(m-2)/2})(2^m+2^{(m+2)/2}+4)/3$
$2^{m-1}-1$	$(2^{m/2}-1)(2^{2m-1}+2^{(3m-4)/2}-2^{m-2}+2^{m/2}+1)$
2^{m-1}	$(2^{m/2}-1)(2^{2m-1}+2^{(3m-4)/2}-2^{m-2}+2^{m/2}+1)$
$2^{m-1}+2^{(m-2)/2}-1$	$(2^{m/2}-1)(2^{m-1}+2^{(m-2)/2})(2^m+2^{(m+2)/2}+4)/3$
$2^{m-1}+2^{(m-2)/2}$	$(2^{m/2}-1)(2^{m-1}-2^{(m-2)/2})(2^m+2^{(m+2)/2}+4)/3$
$2^{m-1}+2^{m/2}-1$	$(2^{m/2}-1)(2^{m-3}+2^{(m-4)/2})(2^{m+1}+2^{m/2}-1)/3$
$2^{m-1}+2^{m/2}$	$(2^{m/2}-1)(2^{m-3}-2^{(m-4)/2})(2^{m+1}+2^{m/2}-1)/3$
2^m-1	1

Furthermore, the weight distribution of this code is given in Table 7.17 for odd m, and Table 7.18 for even m.

Proof. It follows from Theorem 7.12 directly.   □

Theorem 7.22 (Li, Wu, Liu (2019)). *Let q be an odd prime and $m \geq 5$ an odd integer. Then $C_{(q,q^m-1,\delta_3,1)}$ is a $[q^m-1, 3m+1, q^m-q^{m-1}-1-q^{(m+1)/2}]$ fifteen-weight code with the weight distribution of Table 7.19.*

Theorem 7.23 (Li, Wu, Liu (2019)). *Let q be an odd prime and $m \geq 4$ an even integer. Then $C_{(q,q^m-1,\delta_3,1)}$ is a $[q^m-1, \frac{5m}{2}+1, q^m-q^{m-1}-1-q^{\frac{m}{2}}]$ seventeen-weight code with the weight distribution of Table 7.20.*

The weight distribution of the extended code of $C_{(q,q^m-1,\delta_3,1)}$ was also settled

Table 7.19   Weight distribution of $C_{(q,q^m-1,\delta_3,1)}$ for odd m

Weight w; Frequency A_w
0; 1
$(q-1)q^{m-1}-1-q^{(m+1)/2}$; $(q^{m-1}-1)(q^m-1)((q-1)q^{m-3}-q^{(m-3)/2})/2(q+1)$
$(q-1)q^{m-1}-q^{(m+1)/2}$; $(q^{m-1}-1)(q^m-1)(q^{m-3}+q^{(m-3)/2})/2(q+1)$
$(q-1)(q^{m-1}-q^{(m-1)/2})-1$; $(q-1)(q^m-1)(q^{m-1}+q^{(m-1)/2})(q^{m-2}-q^{(m-3)/2})/2$
$(q-1)(q^{m-1}-q^{(m-1)/2})$; $(q^m-1)(q^{m-1}+q^{(m-1)/2})(q^{m-2}+(q-1)q^{(m-3)/2})/2$
$(q-1)q^{m-1}-1-q^{(m-1)/2}$; $\dfrac{(q^m-1)((q-1)q^{m-2}-q^{\frac{m-3}{2}})(q^{m+3}-q^{m+2}-q^{m-1}-q^{\frac{m+3}{2}}+q^{\frac{m-1}{2}}+q^3)}{2(q+1)}$
$(q-1)q^{m-1}-q^{(m-1)/2}$; $\dfrac{(q^m-1)(q^{m-2}+q^{\frac{m-3}{2}})(q^{m+3}-q^{m+2}-q^{m-1}-q^{\frac{m+3}{2}}+q^{\frac{m-1}{2}}+q^3)}{2(q+1)}$
$(q-1)q^{m-1}-1$; $(q-1)(q^m-1)((q-1)(2q^{2m-2}+q^{2m-4}+q^{m-2})+q^{m-3}+1)$
$(q-1)q^{m-1}$; $(q^m-1)((q-1)(2q^{2m-2}+q^{2m-4}+q^{m-2})+q^{m-3}+1)$
$(q-1)q^{m-1}-1+q^{(m-1)/2}$; $\dfrac{(q^m-1)((q-1)q^{m-2}+q^{\frac{m-3}{2}})(q^{m+3}-q^{m+2}-q^{m-1}+q^{\frac{m+3}{2}}-q^{\frac{m-1}{2}}+q^3)}{2(q+1)}$
$(q-1)q^{m-1}+q^{(m-1)/2}$; $\dfrac{(q^m-1)(q^{m-2}-q^{\frac{m-3}{2}})(q^{m+3}-q^{m+2}-q^{m-1}+q^{\frac{m+3}{2}}-q^{\frac{m-1}{2}}+q^3)}{2(q+1)}$
$(q-1)(q^{m-1}+q^{(m-1)/2})-1$; $(q-1)(q^m-1)(q^{m-1}-q^{(m-1)/2})(q^{m-2}+q^{(m-3)/2})/2$
$(q-1)(q^{m-1}+q^{(m-1)/2})$; $(q^m-1)(q^{m-1}-q^{(m-1)/2})(q^{m-2}-(q-1)q^{(m-3)/2})/2$
$(q-1)q^{m-1}-1+q^{(m+1)/2}$; $(q^{m-1}-1)(q^m-1)((q-1)q^{m-3}+q^{(m-3)/2})/2(q+1)$
$(q-1)q^{m-1}+q^{(m+1)/2}$; $(q^{m-1}-1)(q^m-1)(q^{m-3}-q^{(m-3)/2})/2(q+1)$
q^m-1; $q-1$

in Li, Wu, Liu (2019).

7.5   Weights in $C_{(2,2^m-1,\delta,1)}$ and Its Dual for $\delta \in \{3,5,7\}$

$C_{(2,2^m-1,3,1)}^{\perp}$ is the Simplex code, which is a one-weight code. $C_{(2,2^m-1,3,1)}$ is the binary Hamming code whose weight distribution formula is given in Section 10.5.4.

Theorem 7.24. *The code* $C_{(2,2^m-1,5,1)}^{\perp}$ *has dimension 2m, and the weight distribution of Tables 7.1 and 7.21 for even and odd m, respectively.*

Proof. A proof can be found in Kasami (1969) and Schoof (1995).   □

The automorphism of the double-error correcting code $C_{(2,2^m-1,5,1)}$ and its dual is the semi-linear group

$$\Gamma L_1(GF(2^m)) = \{ax^{2^i} : a \in GF(2^m), i \in \{0,1,\ldots,m-1\}\},$$

which is proved in Berger (1994).

Theorem 7.25. *Let* $m \geq 5$. *When m is odd,* $C_{(2,2^m-1,7,1)}^{\perp}$ *has dimension 3m, and the weight distribution of Table 7.11.*

Proof. A proof can be found in Kasami (1969).   □

Table 7.20   Weight distribution of $C_{(q,q^m-1,\delta_3,1)}$ for even m

Weight w; Frequency A_w
$0;\ 1$
$(q-1)q^{m-1}-1-q^{\frac{m}{2}};\ \frac{q^{\frac{m}{2}-2}(q^m-1)(q^{\frac{m}{2}}-q^{\frac{m}{2}-1}-1)[q^{\frac{m}{2}}(q^2-1)+2(q^{\frac{m}{2}-1}-1)]}{2(q+1)}$
$(q-1)q^{m-1}-q^{\frac{m}{2}};\ \frac{(q^m-1)[q^{\frac{m}{2}-1}(q^2-1)(q^{m-2}+q^{\frac{m}{2}-1})+2(q^{\frac{m}{2}-1}-1)(q^{m-3}+q^{\frac{m}{2}-2})]}{2(q+1)}$
$(q-1)(q^{m-1}-q^{\frac{m}{2}-1})-1;\ \frac{q(q-1)(q^{\frac{m}{2}}+1)(q^m-1)(q^{m-1}-q^{\frac{m}{2}-1})}{2(q+1)}$
$(q-1)(q^{m-1}-q^{\frac{m}{2}-1});\ \frac{q(q^{\frac{m}{2}}+1)(q^m-1)(q^{m-1}+(q-1)q^{\frac{m}{2}-1})}{2(q+1)}$
$(q-1)q^{m-1}-q^{\frac{m}{2}-1}-1;\ (q^{m+1}-2q^m+q)(q^{\frac{m}{2}}-1)(q^m-q^{m-1}-q^{\frac{m}{2}-1})/2$
$(q-1)q^{m-1}-q^{\frac{m}{2}-1};\ (q^{m+1}-2q^m+q)(q^{\frac{m}{2}}-1)(q^{m-1}+q^{\frac{m}{2}-1})/2$
$(q-1)q^{m-1}-1;\ (q-1)(q^m-1)(1+q^{\frac{3m}{2}-1}-q^{\frac{3m}{2}-2}+2q^{\frac{3m}{2}-3}-q^{m-2})$
$(q-1)q^{m-1};\ (q^m-1)(1+q^{\frac{3m}{2}-1}-q^{\frac{3m}{2}-2}+2q^{\frac{3m}{2}-3}-q^{m-2})$
$(q-1)q^{m-1}+q^{\frac{m}{2}-1}-1;\ \frac{q(q-1)(q^{\frac{m}{2}}+1)(q^m-1)(q^m-q^{m-1}+q^{\frac{m}{2}-1})}{2(q+1)}$
$(q-1)q^{m-1}+q^{\frac{m}{2}-1};\ \frac{q(q-1)(q^{\frac{m}{2}}+1)(q^m-1)(q^{m-1}-q^{\frac{m}{2}-1})}{2(q+1)}$
$(q-1)(q^{m-1}+q^{\frac{m}{2}-1})-1;\ (q^{m+1}-2q^m+q)(q^{\frac{m}{2}}-1)(q^{m-1}+q^{\frac{m}{2}-1})/2$
$(q-1)(q^{m-1}+q^{\frac{m}{2}-1});\ \frac{(q^{m+1}-2q^m+q)(q^{\frac{m}{2}}-1)(q^{m-1}-(q-1)q^{\frac{m}{2}-1})}{2(q-1)}$
$(q-1)q^{m-1}-1+q^{\frac{m}{2}};\ q^{m-2}(q-1)(q^m-1)(q^{\frac{m}{2}}-q^{\frac{m}{2}-1}+1)/2$
$(q-1)q^{m-1}+q^{\frac{m}{2}};\ q^{\frac{m}{2}-1}(q-1)(q^m-1)(q^{m-2}-q^{\frac{m}{2}-1})/2$
$(q-1)(q^{m-1}+q^{\frac{m}{2}})-1;\ \frac{(q-1)(q^{\frac{m}{2}-1}-1)(q^m-1)(q^{m-3}+q^{\frac{m}{2}-2})}{q^2-1}$
$(q-1)(q^{m-1}+q^{\frac{m}{2}});\ \frac{(q^{\frac{m}{2}-1}-1)(q^m-1)(q^{m-3}-(q-1)q^{\frac{m}{2}-2})}{q^2-1}$
$q^m-1;\ q-1$

Table 7.21   The weight distribution of $C_{(2,2^m-1,5,1)}^{\perp}$ for even m

Weight w	No. of codewords A_w
0	1
$2^{m-1}-2^{m/2}$	$(2^m-1)(2^{m-3}+2^{(m-4)/2})/3$
$2^{m-1}-2^{(m-2)/2}$	$(2^m-1)(2^m+2^{m/2})/3$
2^{m-1}	$(2^m-1)(2^{m-2}+1)$
$2^{m-1}+2^{(m-2)/2}$	$(2^m-1)(2^m-2^{m/2})/3$
$2^{m-1}+2^{m/2}$	$(2^m-1)(2^{m-3}-2^{(m-4)/2})/3$

7.6   Notes

Recently, the weight distribution of the narrow-sense primitive BCH code $C_{(q,q^m-1,\delta_2,1)}$ for general q and even m was settled in Heng, Wang and Ding (2020) in a different way and some 2-designs were obtained there. Some related work was done in Li (2017).

Chapter 8

Designs from Four Types of Linear Codes

In this chapter, we will present many infinite families of 2-designs and 3-designs, which are derived from three types of binary codes and a type of ternary codes whose weight distributions are of special forms. We do not need the description of the codes, but only their weight distributions. In this case, we have to make full use of the Assmus-Mattson Theorem (i.e., Theorem 4.24 and Corollary 4.26), as the automorphism groups of such codes could not be determined with only the knowledge of the weight distribution. The materials presented in this chapter are from Ding (2018c) and Ding and Li (2017).

8.1 Designs from a Type of Binary Codes with Three Weights

In this section, we construct many infinite families of 2-designs and 3-designs with a type of binary linear codes with the weight distribution in Table 8.1 and their related codes. The existence of such codes will be demonstrated at the end of this section.

Table 8.1 Weight distribution for odd m

Weight w	Number of codewords A_w in the code
0	1
$2^{m-1} - 2^{\frac{m-1}{2}}$	$(2^m - 1)(2^{\frac{m-1}{2}} + 1)2^{\frac{m-3}{2}}$
2^{m-1}	$(2^m - 1)(2^{m-1} + 1)$
$2^{m-1} + 2^{\frac{m-1}{2}}$	$(2^m - 1)(2^{\frac{m-1}{2}} - 1)2^{\frac{m-3}{2}}$

Lemma 8.1. *Let $m \geq 5$ be odd. Let C_m be a binary linear code of length $2^m - 1$ such that its dual code $C_m^\perp$ has the weight distribution of Table 8.1. Then the*

weight distribution of C_m is given by

$$22^m A_k = \sum_{\substack{0 \le i \le 2^{m-1}-2^{\frac{m-1}{2}} \\ 0 \le j \le 2^{m-1}+2^{\frac{m-1}{2}}-1 \\ i+j=k}} (-1)^i a \binom{2^{m-1}-2^{\frac{m-1}{2}}}{i} \binom{2^{m-1}+2^{\frac{m-1}{2}}-1}{j}$$

$$+ \binom{2^m-1}{k} + \sum_{\substack{0 \le i \le 2^{m-1} \\ 0 \le j \le 2^{m-1}-1 \\ i+j=k}} (-1)^i b \binom{2^{m-1}}{i} \binom{2^{m-1}-1}{j} +$$

$$\sum_{\substack{0 \le i \le 2^{m-1}+2^{\frac{m-1}{2}} \\ 0 \le j \le 2^{m-1}-2^{\frac{m-1}{2}}-1 \\ i+j=k}} (-1)^i c \binom{2^{m-1}+2^{\frac{m-1}{2}}}{i} \binom{2^{m-1}-2^{\frac{m-1}{2}}-1}{j}$$

for $0 \le k \le 2^m - 1$, where

$$a = (2^m-1)(2^{\frac{m-1}{2}}+1)2^{\frac{m-3}{2}},$$
$$b = (2^m-1)(2^{m-1}+1),$$
$$c = (2^m-1)(2^{\frac{m-1}{2}}-1)2^{\frac{m-3}{2}}.$$

In addition, C_m has parameters $[2^m-1, 2^m-1-2m, 5]$.

Proof. By assumption, the weight enumerator of $C_m^{\perp}$ is given by

$$A^{\perp}(z) = 1 + az^{2^{m-1}-2^{\frac{m-1}{2}}} + bz^{2^{m-1}} + cz^{2^{m-1}+2^{\frac{m-1}{2}}}.$$

It then follows from Theorem 2.4 that the weight enumerator of C_m is given by

$$A(z) = \frac{1}{2^{2m}}(1+z)^{2^m-1}\left[1 + a\left(\frac{1-z}{1+z}\right)^{2^{m-1}-2^{\frac{m-1}{2}}}\right] +$$

$$\frac{1}{2^{2m}}(1+z)^{2^m-1}\left[b\left(\frac{1-z}{1+z}\right)^{2^{m-1}} + c\left(\frac{1-z}{1+z}\right)^{2^{m-1}+2^{\frac{m-1}{2}}}\right]$$

$$= \frac{1}{2^{2m}}\left[(1+z)^{2^m-1} + a(1-z)^{2^{m-1}-2^{\frac{m-1}{2}}}(1+z)^{2^{m-1}+2^{\frac{m-1}{2}}-1} +\right.$$

$$b(1-z)^{2^{m-1}}(1+z)^{2^{m-1}-1} +$$

$$\left. c(1-z)^{2^{m-1}+2^{\frac{m-1}{2}}}(1+z)^{2^{m-1}-2^{\frac{m-1}{2}}-1}\right].$$

Obviously, we have

$$(1+z)^{2^m-1} = \sum_{k=0}^{2^m-1} \binom{2^m-1}{k} z^k.$$

It is easily seen that

$$(1-z)^{2^{m-1}-2^{\frac{m-1}{2}}} (1+z)^{2^{m-1}+2^{\frac{m-1}{2}}-1}$$

$$= \sum_{k=0}^{2^m-1} \left[\sum_{\substack{0 \le i \le 2^{m-1}-2^{\frac{m-1}{2}} \\ 0 \le j \le 2^{m-1}+2^{\frac{m-1}{2}}-1 \\ i+j=k}} (-1)^i \binom{2^{m-1}-2^{\frac{m-1}{2}}}{i} \binom{2^{m-1}+2^{\frac{m-1}{2}}-1}{j} \right] z^k$$

and

$$(1-z)^{2^{m-1}+2^{\frac{m-1}{2}}} (1+z)^{2^{m-1}-2^{\frac{m-1}{2}}-1}$$

$$= \sum_{k=0}^{2^m-1} \left[\sum_{\substack{0 \le i \le 2^{m-1}+2^{\frac{m-1}{2}} \\ 0 \le j \le 2^{m-1}-2^{\frac{m-1}{2}}-1 \\ i+j=k}} (-1)^i \binom{2^{m-1}+2^{\frac{m-1}{2}}}{i} \binom{2^{m-1}-2^{\frac{m-1}{2}}-1}{j} \right] z^k.$$

Similarly, we have

$$(1-z)^{2^{m-1}}(1+z)^{2^{m-1}-1} = \sum_{k=0}^{2^m-1} \left[\sum_{\substack{0 \le i \le 2^{m-1} \\ 0 \le j \le 2^{m-1}-1 \\ i+j=k}} (-1)^i \binom{2^{m-1}}{i} \binom{2^{m-1}-1}{j} \right] z^k.$$

Combining these formulas above yields the weight distribution formula for A_k.

The weight distribution in Table 8.1 tells us that the dimension of $C_m^\perp$ is $2m$. Therefore, the dimension of C_m is equal to $2^m - 1 - 2m$. Finally, we prove that the minimum distance d of C_m equals 5.

After tedious computations with the formula of A_k given in Lemma 8.1, one can verify that $A_1 = A_2 = A_3 = A_4 = 0$ and

$$A_5 = \frac{4 \times 2^{3m-5} - 22 \times 2^{2m-4} + 26 \times 2^{m-3} - 2}{15}. \tag{8.1}$$

When $m \ge 5$, we have

$$4 \times 2^{3m-5} = 4 \times 2^{m-1}2^{2m-4} \ge 64 \times 2^{2m-4} > 22 \times 2^{2m-4}$$

and

$$26 \times 2^{m-3} - 2 > 0.$$

Consequently, $A_5 > 0$ for all odd m. This proves that $d = 5$. $\qquad\square$

Theorem 8.2. *Let $m \geq 5$ be odd. Let C_m be a binary linear code of length $2^m - 1$ such that its dual code $C_m^{\perp}$ has the weight distribution of Table 8.1. Let $\mathcal{P} = \{0, 1, 2, \ldots, 2^m - 2\}$, and let $\mathcal{B}$ be the set of the supports of the codewords of C_m with weight k, where $A_k \neq 0$. Then $(\mathcal{P}, \mathcal{B})$ is a $2\text{-}(2^m - 1, k, \lambda)$ design, where*

$$\lambda = \frac{k(k-1)A_k}{(2^m-1)(2^m-2)},$$

and A_k is given in Lemma 8.1.

Let $\mathcal{P} = \{0, 1, 2, \ldots, 2^m - 2\}$, and let $\mathcal{B}^{\perp}$ be the set of the supports of the codewords of $C_m^{\perp}$ with weight k and $A_k^{\perp} \neq 0$. Then $(\mathcal{P}, \mathcal{B}^{\perp})$ is a $2\text{-}(2^m - 1, k, \lambda)$ design, where

$$\lambda = \frac{k(k-1)A_k^{\perp}}{(2^m-1)(2^m-2)},$$

and $A_k^{\perp}$ is given in Lemma 8.1.

Proof. The weight distribution of C_m is given in Lemma 8.1 and that of $C_m^{\perp}$ is given in Table 8.1. By Lemma 8.1, the minimum distance d of C_m is equal to 5. Put $t = 2$. The number of i with $A_i^{\perp} \neq 0$ and $1 \leq i \leq 2^m - 1 - t$ is $s = 3$. Hence, $s = d - t$. The desired conclusions then follow from Corollary 4.26 and the fact that two binary vectors have the same support if and only if they are equal. $\qquad\square$

Corollary 8.3. *Let $m \geq 5$ be odd. Then $C_m^{\perp}$ gives three 2-designs with the following parameters:*

- $(v, k, \lambda) = \left(2^m - 1, \ 2^{m-1} - 2^{\frac{m-1}{2}}, \ 2^{m-3}(2^{m-1} - 2^{\frac{m-1}{2}} - 1)\right).$
- $(v, k, \lambda) = \left(2^m - 1, \ 2^{m-1} + 2^{\frac{m-1}{2}}, \ 2^{m-3}(2^{m-1} + 2^{\frac{m-1}{2}} - 1)\right).$
- $(v, k, \lambda) = \left(2^m - 1, \ 2^{m-1}, \ (2^m - 1)(2^{m-1} + 1)\right).$

Corollary 8.4. *Let $m \geq 5$ be odd. Then the supports of all codewords of weight 5 in C_m give a $2\text{-}(2^m - 1, 5, (2^{m-1} - 4)/3)$ design.*

Proof. By Lemma 8.1,

$$A_5 = \frac{(2^{m-1} - 1)(2^{m-1} - 4)(2^m - 1)}{30}.$$

The desired value for λ then follows from Theorem 8.2. $\qquad\square$

Corollary 8.5. *Let* $m \geq 5$ *be odd. Then the supports of all codewords of weight 6 in* C_m *give a* 2-$(2^m - 1, 6, \lambda)$ *design, where*

$$\lambda = \frac{(2^{m-2} - 2)(2^{m-1} - 3)}{3}.$$

Proof. By Lemma 8.1,

$$A_6 = \frac{(2^{m-1} - 1)(2^{m-1} - 4)(2^{m-1} - 3)(2^m - 1)}{90}.$$

The desired value for λ then follows from Theorem 8.2. □

Corollary 8.6. *Let* $m \geq 5$ *be odd. Then the supports of all codewords of weight 7 in* C_m *give a* 2-$(2^m - 1, 7, \lambda)$ *design, where*

$$\lambda = \frac{2 \times 2^{3(m-1)} - 25 \times 2^{2(m-1)} + 123 \times 2^{m-1} - 190}{30}.$$

Proof. By Lemma 8.1,

$$A_7 = \frac{(2^{m-1} - 1)(2^m - 1)(2 \times 2^{3(m-1)} - 25 \times 2^{2(m-1)} + 123 \times 2^{m-1} - 190)}{630}.$$

The desired value for λ then follows from Theorem 8.2. □

Corollary 8.7. *Let* $m \geq 5$ *be odd. Then the supports of all codewords of weight 8 in* C_m *give a* 2-$(2^m - 1, 8, \lambda)$ *design, where*

$$\lambda = \frac{(2^{m-2} - 2)(2 \times 2^{3(m-1)} - 25 \times 2^{2(m-1)} + 123 \times 2^{m-1} - 190)}{45}.$$

Proof. By Lemma 8.1,

$$A_8 = \frac{(2^h - 1)(2^h - 4)(2^m - 1)(2 \times 2^{3(m-1)} - 25 \times 2^{2h} + 123 \times 2^h - 190)}{8 \times 315},$$

where $h = m - 1$. The desired value for λ then follows from Theorem 8.2. □

Lemma 8.8. *Let* $m \geq 5$ *be odd. Let* C_m *be a linear code of length* $2^m - 1$ *such that its dual code* $C_m^\perp$ *has the weight distribution of Table 8.1. Denote by* $\overline{C}_m$ *the extended code of* C_m *and let* $\overline{C}_m^\perp$ *denote the dual of* $\overline{C}_m$*. Then the weight distribution of* $\overline{C}_m$ *is given by*

$$2^{2m+1}\overline{A}_k = (1 + (-1)^k)\binom{2^m}{k} + \frac{1 + (-1)^k}{2}(-1)^{\lfloor k/2 \rfloor}\binom{2^{m-1}}{\lfloor k/2 \rfloor}v +$$

$$u \sum_{\substack{0 \leq i \leq 2^{m-1} - 2^{\frac{m-1}{2}} \\ 0 \leq j \leq 2^{m-1} + 2^{\frac{m-1}{2}} \\ i+j=k}} [(-1)^i + (-1)^j]\binom{2^{m-1} - 2^{\frac{m-1}{2}}}{i}\binom{2^{m-1} + 2^{\frac{m-1}{2}}}{j}$$

for $0 \leq k \leq 2^m$, where

$$u = 2^{2m-1} - 2^{m-1} \text{ and } v = 2^{2m} + 2^m - 2.$$

In addition, $\overline{C}_m$ has parameters $[2^m, 2^m - 1 - 2m, 6]$.
   The code $\overline{C}_m^{\perp}$ has weight enumerator

$$\overline{A}^{\perp}(z) = 1 + uz^{2^{m-1} - 2^{\frac{m-1}{2}}} + vz^{2^{m-1}} + uz^{2^{m-1} + 2^{\frac{m-1}{2}}} + z^{2^m}, \tag{8.2}$$

and parameters $[2^m,\ 2m+1,\ 2^{m-1} - 2^{\frac{m-1}{2}}]$.

Proof. It was proved in Lemma 8.1 that C_m has parameters $[2^m - 1, 2^m - 1 - 2m, 5]$. By definition, the extended code $\overline{C}_m$ has parameters $[2^m, 2^m - 1 - 2m, 6]$. By Table 8.1, all weights of $C_m^{\perp}$ are even. Note that $C_m^{\perp}$ has length $2^m - 1$ and dimension $2m$, while $\overline{C}_m^{\perp}$ has length 2^m and dimension $2m + 1$. By definition, $\overline{C}_m^{\perp}$ has only even weights. Therefore, the all-one vector must be a codeword in $\overline{C}_m^{\perp}$. It can be shown that the weights in $\overline{C}_m^{\perp}$ are the following:

$$0,\ w_1,\ w_2,\ w_3,\ 2^m - w_1,\ 2^m - w_2,\ 2^m - w_3,\ 2^m,$$

where w_1, w_2 and w_3 are the three nonzero weights in $C_m^{\perp}$. Consequently, $\overline{C}_m^{\perp}$ has the following four weights

$$2^{m-1} - 2^{\frac{m-1}{2}},\ 2^{m-1},\ 2^{m-1} + 2^{\frac{m-1}{2}},\ 2^m.$$

Recall that $\overline{C}_m$ has minimum distance 6. Employing the first few Pless Moments, one can prove that the weight enumerator of $\overline{C}_m^{\perp}$ is the one given in (8.2).
   By Theorem 2.4, the weight enumerator of $\overline{C}_m$ is given by

$$2^{2m+1}\overline{A}(z) = (1+z)^{2^m} \left[1 + u\left(\frac{1-z}{1+z}\right)^{2^{m-1} - 2^{\frac{m-1}{2}}} + v\left(\frac{1-z}{1+z}\right)^{2^{m-1}} \right] +$$

$$(1+z)^{2^m} \left[u\left(\frac{1-z}{1+z}\right)^{2^{m-1} + 2^{\frac{m-1}{2}}} + \left(\frac{1-z}{1+z}\right)^{2^m} \right]$$

$$= (1+z)^{2^m} + (1-z)^{2^m} + v(1-z^2)^{2^{m-1}} +$$

$$u(1-z)^{2^{m-1} - 2^{\frac{m-1}{2}}}(1+z)^{2^{m-1} + 2^{\frac{m-1}{2}}} +$$

$$u(1-z)^{2^{m-1} + 2^{\frac{m-1}{2}}}(1+z)^{2^{m-1} - 2^{\frac{m-1}{2}}}. \tag{8.3}$$

We now treat the terms in (8.3) one by one. We first have

$$(1+z)^{2^m} + (1-z)^{2^m} = \sum_{k=0}^{2^m} \left(1 + (-1)^k\right) \binom{2^m}{k}. \tag{8.4}$$

One can easily see that

$$(1-z^2)^{2^{m-1}} = \sum_{k=0}^{2^m} \frac{1+(-1)^k}{2} (-1)^{\lfloor k/2 \rfloor} \binom{2^{m-1}}{\lfloor k/2 \rfloor} z^k. \tag{8.5}$$

Notice that

$$(1-z)^{2^{m-1}-2^{\frac{m-1}{2}}} = \sum_{i=0}^{2^{m-1}-2^{\frac{m-1}{2}}} \binom{2^{m-1}-2^{\frac{m-1}{2}}}{i} (-1)^i z^i$$

and

$$(1+z)^{2^{m-1}+2^{\frac{m-1}{2}}} = \sum_{i=0}^{2^{m-1}+2^{\frac{m-1}{2}}} \binom{2^{m-1}+2^{\frac{m-1}{2}}}{i} z^i.$$

We have then

$$(1-z)^{2^{m-1}-2^{\frac{m-1}{2}}} (1+z)^{2^{m-1}+2^{\frac{m-1}{2}}} =$$

$$\sum_{k=0}^{2^m} \left[\sum_{\substack{0 \leq i \leq 2^{m-1}-2^{\frac{m-1}{2}} \\ 0 \leq j \leq 2^{m-1}+2^{\frac{m-1}{2}} \\ i+j=k}} (-1)^i \binom{2^{m-1}-2^{\frac{m-1}{2}}}{i} \binom{2^{m-1}+2^{\frac{m-1}{2}}}{j} \right] z^k. \tag{8.6}$$

Similarly, we have

$$(1-z)^{2^{m-1}+2^{\frac{m-1}{2}}} (1+z)^{2^{m-1}-2^{\frac{m-1}{2}}} =$$

$$\sum_{k=0}^{2^m} \left[\sum_{\substack{0 \leq i \leq 2^{m-1}+2^{\frac{m-1}{2}} \\ 0 \leq j \leq 2^{m-1}-2^{\frac{m-1}{2}} \\ i+j=k}} (-1)^i \binom{2^{m-1}+2^{\frac{m-1}{2}}}{i} \binom{2^{m-1}-2^{\frac{m-1}{2}}}{j} \right] z^k. \tag{8.7}$$

Plugging (8.4), (8.5), (8.6), and (8.7) into (8.3) proves the desired conclusion of this lemma. $\square$

Theorem 8.9. *Let $m \geq 5$ be odd. Let C_m be a linear code of length $2^m - 1$ such that its dual code $C_m^{\perp}$ has the weight distribution of Table 8.1. Denote by $\overline{C}_m$ the extended code of C_m and let $\overline{C}_m^{\perp}$ denote the dual of $\overline{C}_m$. Let $\mathcal{P} = \{0,1,2,\ldots,2^m - 1\}$, and let $\overline{\mathcal{B}}$ be the set of the supports of the codewords of $\overline{C}_m$ with weight k, where $\overline{A}_k \neq 0$. Then $(\mathcal{P}, \overline{\mathcal{B}})$ is a 3-$(2^m, k, \lambda)$ design, where*

$$\lambda = \frac{\overline{A}_k \binom{k}{3}}{\binom{2^m}{3}},$$

and $\overline{A}_k$ is given in Lemma 8.8.

Let $\mathcal{P} = \{0, 1, 2, \ldots, 2^m - 1\}$, and let $\overline{\mathcal{B}}^\perp$ be the set of the supports of the codewords of $\overline{C}_m^\perp$ with weight k and $\overline{A}_k^\perp \neq 0$. Then $(\mathcal{P}, \overline{\mathcal{B}}^\perp)$ is a 3-$(2^m, k, \lambda)$ design, where

$$\lambda = \frac{\overline{A}_k^\perp \binom{k}{3}}{\binom{2^m}{3}},$$

and $\overline{A}_k^\perp$ is given in Lemma 8.8.

Proof. The weight distributions of $\overline{C}_m$ and $\overline{C}_m^\perp$ were described in Lemma 8.8. Notice that the minimum distance d of $\overline{C}_m$ is equal to 6. Put $t = 3$. The number of i with $\overline{A}_i^\perp \neq 0$ and $1 \leq i \leq 2^m - t$ is $s = 3$. Hence, $s = d - t$. The desired conclusions then follow from Corollary 4.26 and the fact that two binary vectors have the same support if and only if they are identical.   □

Corollary 8.10. *Let $m \geq 5$ be odd. Then the code $\overline{C}_m^\perp$ holds three 3-designs with the following parameters:*

- $(v, k, \lambda) = \left(2^m, \ 2^{m-1} - 2^{\frac{m-1}{2}}, \ (2^{m-3} - 2^{\frac{m-3}{2}})(2^{m-1} - 2^{\frac{m-1}{2}} - 1)\right).$
- $(v, k, \lambda) = \left(2^m, \ 2^{m-1} + 2^{\frac{m-1}{2}}, \ (2^{m-3} + 2^{\frac{m-3}{2}})(2^{m-1} - 2^{\frac{m-1}{2}} - 1)\right).$
- $(v, k, \lambda) = \left(2^m, \ 2^{m-1}, \ (2^{m-1} + 1)(2^{m-2} - 1)\right).$

Corollary 8.11. *Let $m \geq 5$ be odd. Then the supports of all codewords of weight 6 in $\overline{C}_m$ give a 3-$(2^m, 6, \lambda)$ design, where*

$$\lambda = \frac{2^{m-1} - 4}{3}.$$

Proof. By Lemma 8.8,

$$\overline{A}_6 = \frac{2^{m-1}(2^{m-1} - 1)(2^{m-1} - 4)(2^m - 1)}{90}.$$

The desired value for λ then follows from Theorem 8.9.   □

Corollary 8.12. *Let $m \geq 5$ be odd. Then the supports of all codewords of weight 8 in $\overline{C}_m$ give a 3-$(2^m, 8, \lambda)$ design, where*

$$\lambda = \frac{2 \times 2^{3(m-1)} - 25 \times 2^{2(m-1)} + 123 \times 2^{m-1} - 190}{30}.$$

Proof. By Lemma 8.8,

$$\overline{A}_8 = \frac{2^h(2^h - 1)(2^{h+1} - 1)(2 \times 2^{3h} - 25 \times 2^{2h} + 123 \times 2^h - 190)}{8 \times 315},$$

where $h = m - 1$. The desired value for λ then follows from Theorem 8.9.   □

Corollary 8.13. *Let* $m \geq 5$ *be odd. Then the supports of all codewords of weight* 10 *in* $\overline{C}_m$ *give a* 3-$(2^m, 10, \lambda)$ *design, where*

$$\lambda = \frac{(2^h - 4)(2 \times 2^{4h} - 34 \times 2^{3h} + 235 \times 2^{2h} - 931 \times 2^h + 1358)}{315},$$

and $h = m - 1$.

Proof. By Lemma 8.8,

$$\overline{A}_{10} = \frac{2^h(2^h - 1)(2^h - 4)(2 \times 2^{4h} - 34 \times 2^{3h} + 235 \times 2^{2h} - 931 \times 2^h + 1358)}{4 \times 14175},$$

where $h = m - 1$. The desired value for λ then follows from Theorem 8.9. $\qquad \square$

To show the existence of the 2-designs and 3-designs presented in Theorems 8.2 and 8.9, respectively, we describe a list of binary codes that have the weight distribution of Table 8.1 below.

Let α be a generator of GF$(2^m)^*$. Let $g_s(x) = \mathbb{M}_\alpha(x)\mathbb{M}_{\alpha^s}(x)$, where $\mathbb{M}_{\alpha^i}(x)$ is the minimal polynomial of α^i over GF(2). Let C_m denote the cyclic code of length $v = 2^m - 1$ over GF(2) with generator polynomial $g_s(x)$. It is known that $C_m^{\perp}$ has dimension $2m$ and the weight distribution of Table 8.1 when m is odd and s takes on the following values [Ding, Li, Li and Zhou (2016)]:

- $s = 2^h + 1$, where $\gcd(h, m) = 1$ and h is a positive integer.
- $s = 2^{2h} - 2^h + 1$, where h is a positive integer.
- $s = 2^{\frac{m-1}{2}} + 3$.
- $s = 2^{\frac{m-1}{2}} + 2^{\frac{m-1}{4}} - 1$, where $m \equiv 1 \pmod 4$.
- $s = 2^{\frac{m-1}{2}} + 2^{\frac{3m-1}{4}} - 1$, where $m \equiv 3 \pmod 4$.

In all these cases, C_m has parameters $[2^m - 1, 2^m - 1 - 2m, 5]$ and is optimal.

It was shown in Theorem 7.4 the binary narrow-sense primitive BCH code with designed distance $2^{m-1} - 2^{(m-1)/2}$ has also the weight distribution of Table 8.1.

These codes and their extended codes give 2-designs and 3-designs when they are plugged into Theorems 8.2 and 8.9.

It is known that C_m has parameters $[2^m - 1, 2^m - 1 - 2m, 5]$ if and only if x^e is an APN monomial over GF(2^m). However, even if x^e is APN, the dual code $C_m^{\perp}$ may have many weights, and thus the code C_m and its dual $C_m^{\perp}$ may not give 2-designs. One of such examples is the inverse APN monomial.

8.2 An Extended Construction from Almost Bent Functions

In the preceding section, we employed almost bent functions to construct cyclic codes whose extended codes and their duals hold 3-designs. In this section, we give a trace representation of these codes and extend the construction of the preceding section.

For a function g from $\mathrm{GF}(2^m)$ to $\mathrm{GF}(2^m)$, we define

$$\lambda_g(a,b) = \sum_{x \in \mathrm{GF}(2^m)} (-1)^{\mathrm{Tr}_{2^m/2}(ag(x)+bx)}, \ a, b \in \mathrm{GF}(2^m).$$

A function g from $\mathrm{GF}(2^m)$ to $\mathrm{GF}(2^m)$ is called *almost bent* if $\lambda_g(a,b) = 0$, or $\pm 2^{(m+1)/2}$ for every pair (a,b) with $a \neq 0$. By definition, almost bent functions over $\mathrm{GF}(2^m)$ exist only for odd m.

For any given function g from $\mathrm{GF}(2^m)$ to $\mathrm{GF}(2^m)$ with $g(0) = 0$, we define the following linear code

$$C_g = \{ \left(\mathrm{Tr}_{2^m/2}(ag(x)+bx)+h \right)_{x \in \mathrm{GF}(2^m)}, \ a, b \in \mathrm{GF}(2^m), h \in \mathrm{GF}(2) \}. \quad (8.8)$$

Let $m \geq 5$. It follows from the definition of almost bent function that the code C_g of (8.8) has parameters $[2^m, 2m+1, 2^{m-1} - 2^{(m-1)/2}]$ and the weight enumerator of (8.2). Hence, C_g and its dual hold 3-designs. Note that the construction of this section works for all almost bent functions, including almost bent monomials. There are almost bent functions which are not monomials.

8.3 Designs from a Type of Binary Codes with Five Weights

In this section, we present many infinite families of 2-designs and 3-designs, which are derived from a type of binary linear codes with five weights and their related codes. The constructions of such designs are quite general, as they depend only on the weight distribution of the underlying binary linear code.

8.3.1 *The Codes with Five Weights and Their Related Codes*

We first assume the existence of a binary linear code C_m of length $n = 2^m - 1$ with the weight distribution of Table 8.2, and then analyze its dual code $C_m^\perp$, the extended code $\overline{C_m^\perp}$, and the dual $\overline{C_m^\perp}^\perp$. Such codes will be employed to construct t-designs in Sections 8.3.2 and 8.3.3. Examples of such codes will be given in Section 8.3.4.

Theorem 8.14. *Let $m \geq 5$ be an odd integer and let C_m be a binary code with the weight distribution of Table 8.2. Then the dual code $C_m^\perp$ has parameters $[2^m -$*

Table 8.2   The weight distribution for odd m

Weight w	Number of codewords A_w in the code
0	1
$2^{m-1}-2^{\frac{m+1}{2}}$	$(2^m-1)\cdot 2^{\frac{m-5}{2}}\cdot(2^{\frac{m-3}{2}}+1)\cdot(2^{m-1}-1)/3$
$2^{m-1}-2^{\frac{m-1}{2}}$	$(2^m-1)\cdot 2^{\frac{m-3}{2}}\cdot(2^{\frac{m-1}{2}}+1)\cdot(5\cdot 2^{m-1}+4)/3$
2^{m-1}	$(2^m-1)\cdot(9\cdot 2^{2m-4}+3\cdot 2^{m-3}+1)$
$2^{m-1}+2^{\frac{m-1}{2}}$	$(2^m-1)\cdot 2^{\frac{m-3}{2}}\cdot(2^{\frac{m-1}{2}}-1)\cdot(5\cdot 2^{m-1}+4)/3$
$2^{m-1}+2^{\frac{m+1}{2}}$	$(2^m-1)\cdot 2^{\frac{m-5}{2}}\cdot(2^{\frac{m-3}{2}}-1)\cdot(2^{m-1}-1)/3$

$1, 2^m - 1 - 3m, 7]$, *and its weight distribution is given by*

$$2^{3m}A_k^{\perp} = \binom{2^m-1}{k} + aU_a(k) + bU_b(k) + cU_c(k) + dU_d(k) + eU_e(k),$$

where $0 \le k \le 2^m - 1$,

$$a = (2^m-1)2^{\frac{m-5}{2}}(2^{\frac{m-3}{2}}+1)(2^{m-1}-1)/3,$$
$$b = (2^m-1)2^{\frac{m-3}{2}}(2^{\frac{m-1}{2}}+1)(5\times 2^{m-1}+4)/3,$$
$$c = (2^m-1)(9\times 2^{2m-4}+3\times 2^{m-3}+1),$$
$$d = (2^m-1)2^{\frac{m-3}{2}}(2^{\frac{m-1}{2}}-1)(5\times 2^{m-1}+4)/3,$$
$$e = (2^m-1)2^{\frac{m-5}{2}}(2^{\frac{m-3}{2}}-1)(2^{m-1}-1)/3,$$

and

$$U_a(k) = \sum_{\substack{0\le i\le 2^{m-1}-2^{\frac{m+1}{2}} \\ 0\le j\le 2^{m-1}+2^{\frac{m+1}{2}}-1 \\ i+j=k}} (-1)^i \binom{2^{m-1}-2^{\frac{m+1}{2}}}{i}\binom{2^{m-1}+2^{\frac{m+1}{2}}-1}{j},$$

$$U_b(k) = \sum_{\substack{0\le i\le 2^{m-1}-2^{\frac{m-1}{2}} \\ 0\le j\le 2^{m-1}+2^{\frac{m-1}{2}}-1 \\ i+j=k}} (-1)^i \binom{2^{m-1}-2^{\frac{m-1}{2}}}{i}\binom{2^{m-1}+2^{\frac{m-1}{2}}-1}{j},$$

$$U_c(k) = \sum_{\substack{0\le i\le 2^{m-1} \\ 0\le j\le 2^{m-1}-1 \\ i+j=k}} (-1)^i \binom{2^{m-1}}{i}\binom{2^{m-1}-1}{j},$$

$$U_d(k) = \sum_{\substack{0\le i\le 2^{m-1}+2^{\frac{m-1}{2}} \\ 0\le j\le 2^{m-1}-2^{\frac{m-1}{2}}-1 \\ i+j=k}} (-1)^i \binom{2^{m-1}+2^{\frac{m-1}{2}}}{i}\binom{2^{m-1}-2^{\frac{m-1}{2}}-1}{j},$$

$$U_e(k) = \sum_{\substack{0 \le i \le 2^{m-1}+2^{\frac{m+1}{2}} \\ 0 \le j \le 2^{m-1}-2^{\frac{m+1}{2}}-1 \\ i+j=k}} (-1)^i \binom{2^{m-1}+2^{\frac{m+1}{2}}}{i}\binom{2^{m-1}-2^{\frac{m+1}{2}}-1}{j}.$$

Proof. By assumption, the weight enumerator of $\mathcal{C}_m$ is given by

$$A(z) = 1 + az^{2^{m-1}-2^{\frac{m+1}{2}}} + bz^{2^{m-1}-2^{\frac{m-1}{2}}} + cz^{2^{m-1}} + dz^{2^{m-1}+2^{\frac{m-1}{2}}} + ez^{2^{m-1}+2^{\frac{m+1}{2}}}.$$

It then follows from Theorem 2.4 that the weight enumerator of $\mathcal{C}_m^\perp$ is given by

$$2^{3m}A^\perp(z) =$$

$$(1+z)^{2^m-1}\left[a\left(\frac{1-z}{1+z}\right)^{2^{m-1}-2^{\frac{m+1}{2}}} + b\left(\frac{1-z}{1+z}\right)^{2^{m-1}-2^{\frac{m-1}{2}}}\right] +$$

$$(1+z)^{2^m-1}\left[c\left(\frac{1-z}{1+z}\right)^{2^{m-1}} + d\left(\frac{1-z}{1+z}\right)^{2^{m-1}+2^{\frac{m-1}{2}}}\right] +$$

$$(1+z)^{2^m-1}\left[e\left(\frac{1-z}{1+z}\right)^{2^{m-1}+2^{\frac{m+1}{2}}} + 1\right].$$

Hence, we have

$$2^{3m}A^\perp(z) = (1+z)^{2^m-1} +$$
$$a(1-z)^{2^{m-1}-2^{\frac{m+1}{2}}}(1+z)^{2^{m-1}+2^{\frac{m+1}{2}}-1} +$$
$$b(1-z)^{2^{m-1}-2^{\frac{m-1}{2}}}(1+z)^{2^{m-1}+2^{\frac{m-1}{2}}-1} +$$
$$c(1-z)^{2^{m-1}}(1+z)^{2^{m-1}-1} +$$
$$d(1-z)^{2^{m-1}+2^{\frac{m-1}{2}}}(1+z)^{2^{m-1}-2^{\frac{m-1}{2}}-1} +$$
$$e(1-z)^{2^{m-1}+2^{\frac{m+1}{2}}}(1+z)^{2^{m-1}-2^{\frac{m+1}{2}}-1}.$$

Obviously, we have

$$(1+z)^{2^m-1} = \sum_{k=0}^{2^m-1}\binom{2^m-1}{k}z^k.$$

It is easily seen that

$$(1-z)^{2^{m-1}-2^{\frac{m+1}{2}}}(1+z)^{2^{m-1}+2^{\frac{m+1}{2}}-1} = \sum_{k=0}^{2^m-1}U_a(k)z^k$$

and

$$(1-z)^{2^{m-1}-2^{\frac{m-1}{2}}}(1+z)^{2^{m-1}+2^{\frac{m-1}{2}}-1} = \sum_{k=0}^{2^m-1} U_b(k)z^k.$$

Similarly,

$$(1-z)^{2^{m-1}+2^{\frac{m-1}{2}}}(1+z)^{2^{m-1}-2^{\frac{m-1}{2}}-1} = \sum_{k=0}^{2^m-1} U_d(k)z^k$$

and

$$(1-z)^{2^{m-1}+2^{\frac{m+1}{2}}}(1+z)^{2^{m-1}-2^{\frac{m+1}{2}}-1} = \sum_{k=0}^{2^m-1} U_e(k)z^k.$$

Finally, we have

$$(1-z)^{2^{m-1}}(1+z)^{2^{m-1}-1} = \sum_{k=0}^{2^m-1} U_c(k)z^k.$$

Combining these formulas above yields the weight distribution formula for $A_k^\perp$.

The weight distribution in Table 8.2 tells us that the dimension of C_m is $3m$. Therefore, the dimension of $C_m^\perp$ is equal to $2^m - 1 - 3m$. Finally, we prove that the minimum distance of $C_m^\perp$ equals 7.

We now prove that $A_k^\perp = 0$ for all k with $1 \le k \le 6$. Let $x = 2^{(m-1)/2}$. With the weight distribution formula for $C_m^\perp$ obtained before, we have

$$\binom{2^m-1}{1} = 2x^2 - 1,$$

$$aU_a(1) = \frac{1}{3}x^7 + \frac{7}{12}x^6 - \frac{2}{3}x^5 - \frac{7}{8}x^4 + \frac{5}{12}x^3 + \frac{7}{24}x^2 - \frac{1}{12}x,$$

$$bU_b(1) = \frac{10}{3}x^7 + \frac{5}{3}x^6 - \frac{2}{3}x^5 + \frac{1}{2}x^4 - \frac{11}{6}x^3 - \frac{2}{3}x^2 + \frac{2}{3}x,$$

$$cU_c(1) = -\frac{9}{2}x^6 + \frac{3}{4}x^4 - \frac{5}{4}x^2 + 1,$$

$$dU_d(1) = -\frac{10}{3}x^7 + \frac{5}{3}x^6 + \frac{2}{3}x^5 + \frac{1}{2}x^4 + \frac{11}{6}x^3 - \frac{2}{3}x^2 - \frac{2}{3}x,$$

$$eU_e(1) = -\frac{1}{3}x^7 + \frac{7}{12}x^6 + \frac{2}{3}x^5 - \frac{7}{8}x^4 - \frac{5}{12}x^3 + \frac{7}{24}x^2 + \frac{1}{12}x.$$

Consequently,

$$2^{3m}A_1^\perp = \binom{2^m-1}{1} + aU_a(1) + bU_b(1) + cU_c(1) + dU_d(1) + eU_e(1) = 0.$$

Plugging $k = 2$ into the weight distribution formula above for $C_m^{\perp}$, we get that

$$\binom{2^m - 1}{2} = 2x^4 - 3x^2 + 1,$$

$$aU_a(2) = \frac{7}{12}x^8 + \frac{5}{6}x^7 - \frac{35}{24}x^6 - \frac{13}{12}x^5 + \frac{7}{6}x^4 + \frac{1}{6}x^3 - \frac{7}{24}x^2 + \frac{1}{12}x,$$

$$bU_b(2) = \frac{5}{3}x^8 - \frac{5}{3}x^7 - \frac{7}{6}x^6 + \frac{7}{6}x^5 - \frac{7}{6}x^4 + \frac{7}{6}x^3 + \frac{2}{3}x^2 - \frac{2}{3}x,$$

$$cU_c(2) = -\frac{9}{2}x^8 + \frac{21}{4}x^6 - 2x^4 + \frac{9}{4}x^2 - 1,$$

$$dU_d(2) = \frac{5}{3}x^8 + \frac{5}{3}x^7 - \frac{7}{6}x^6 - \frac{7}{6}x^5 - \frac{7}{6}x^4 - \frac{7}{6}x^3 + \frac{2}{3}x^2 + \frac{2}{3}x,$$

$$eU_e(2) = \frac{7}{12}x^8 - \frac{5}{6}x^7 - \frac{35}{24}x^6 + \frac{13}{12}x^5 + \frac{7}{6}x^4 - \frac{1}{6}x^3 - \frac{7}{24}x^2 - \frac{1}{12}x.$$

As a result,

$$2^{3m}A_2^{\perp} = \binom{2^m - 1}{2} + aU_a(2) + bU_b(2) + cU_c(2) + dU_d(2) + eU_e(2) = 0.$$

Putting $k = 3$ into the weight distribution formula above for $C_m^{\perp}$, we obtain that

$$\binom{2^m - 1}{3} = \frac{4}{3}x^6 - 4x^4 + \frac{11}{3}x^2 - 1,$$

$$aU_a(3) = \frac{5}{9}x^9 + \frac{19}{36}x^8 - \frac{14}{9}x^7 + \frac{1}{72}x^6 + \frac{43}{36}x^5 - \frac{17}{18}x^4 - \frac{1}{9}x^3 + \frac{29}{72}x^2 - \frac{1}{12}x,$$

$$bU_b(3) = -\frac{10}{9}x^9 - \frac{25}{9}x^8 + \frac{22}{9}x^7 + \frac{35}{18}x^6 - \frac{7}{18}x^5 + \frac{35}{18}x^4 - \frac{29}{18}x^3 - \frac{10}{9}x^2 + \frac{2}{3}x,$$

$$cU_c(3) = \frac{9}{2}x^8 - \frac{21}{4}x^6 + 2x^4 - \frac{9}{4}x^2 + 1,$$

$$dU_d(3) = \frac{10}{9}x^9 - \frac{25}{9}x^8 - \frac{22}{9}x^7 + \frac{35}{18}x^6 + \frac{7}{18}x^5 + \frac{35}{18}x^4 + \frac{29}{18}x^3 - \frac{10}{9}x^2 - \frac{2}{3}x,$$

$$eU_e(3) = -\frac{5}{9}x^9 + \frac{19}{36}x^8 + \frac{14}{9}x^7 + \frac{1}{72}x^6 - \frac{43}{36}x^5 - \frac{17}{18}x^4 + \frac{1}{9}x^3 + \frac{29}{72}x^2 + \frac{1}{12}x.$$

Hence,

$$2^{3m}A_3^{\perp} = \binom{2^m - 1}{3} + aU_a(3) + bU_b(3) + cU_c(3) + dU_d(3) + eU_e(3) = 0.$$

Plugging $k = 4$ into the weight distribution formula above for $C_m^{\perp}$, we get that

$$\binom{2^m - 1}{4} = \frac{2}{3}x^8 - \frac{10}{3}x^6 + \frac{35}{6}x^4 - \frac{25}{6}x^2 + 1,$$

$$aU_a(4) = \frac{19}{72}x^{10} - \frac{1}{36}x^9 - \frac{25}{48}x^8 + \frac{113}{72}x^7 - \frac{35}{72}x^6 - \frac{77}{36}x^5 + \frac{55}{48}x^4 + \frac{37}{72}x^3 - \frac{29}{72}x^2 + \frac{1}{12}x,$$

$$bU_b(4) = -\frac{25}{18}x^{10} - \frac{5}{18}x^9 + \frac{15}{4}x^8 - \frac{53}{36}x^7 - \frac{35}{36}x^6 + \frac{49}{36}x^5 - \frac{5}{2}x^4 + \frac{19}{18}x^3 + \frac{10}{9}x^2 - \frac{2}{3}x,$$

$$cU_c(4) = \frac{9}{4}x^{10} - \frac{57}{8}x^8 + \frac{25}{4}x^6 - \frac{25}{8}x^4 + \frac{11}{4}x^2 - 1,$$

$$dU_d(4) = -\frac{25}{18}x^{10} + \frac{5}{18}x^9 + \frac{15}{4}x^8 + \frac{53}{36}x^7 - \frac{35}{36}x^6 - \frac{49}{36}x^5 - \frac{5}{2}x^4 - \frac{19}{18}x^3 + \frac{10}{9}x^2 + \frac{2}{3}x,$$

$$eU_e(4) = \frac{19}{72}x^{10} + \frac{1}{36}x^9 - \frac{25}{48}x^8 - \frac{113}{72}x^7 - \frac{35}{72}x^6 + \frac{77}{36}x^5 + \frac{55}{48}x^4 - \frac{37}{72}x^3 - \frac{29}{72}x^2 - \frac{1}{12}x.$$

Consequently,

$$2^{3m}A_4^{\perp} = \binom{2^m - 1}{4} + aU_a(4) + bU_b(4) + cU_c(4) + dU_d(4) + eU_e(4) = 0.$$

Putting $k = 5$ into the weight distribution formula above for $\mathcal{C}_m^{\perp}$, we obtain that

$$\binom{2^m - 1}{5} = \frac{4}{15}x^{10} - 2x^8 + \frac{17}{3}x^6 - \frac{15}{2}x^4 + \frac{137}{30}x^2 - 1,$$

$$aU_a(5) = -\frac{1}{90}x^{11} - \frac{103}{360}x^{10} + \frac{59}{90}x^9 + \frac{1279}{720}x^8 - \frac{97}{40}x^7 - \frac{49}{40}x^6 + \frac{211}{90}x^5 - \frac{529}{720}x^4 - \frac{173}{360}x^3 + \frac{169}{360}x^2 - \frac{1}{12}x,$$

$$bU_b(5) = -\frac{1}{9}x^{11} + \frac{23}{18}x^{10} - \frac{14}{45}x^9 - \frac{781}{180}x^8 + \frac{121}{60}x^7 + \frac{91}{60}x^6 - \frac{169}{180}x^5 + \frac{263}{90}x^4 - \frac{119}{90}x^3 - \frac{62}{45}x^2 + \frac{2}{3}x,$$

$$cU_c(5) = -\frac{9}{4}x^{10} + \frac{57}{8}x^8 - \frac{25}{4}x^6 + \frac{25}{8}x^4 - \frac{11}{4}x^2 + 1,$$

$$dU_d(5) = \frac{1}{9}x^{11} + \frac{23}{18}x^{10} + \frac{14}{45}x^9 - \frac{781}{180}x^8 - \frac{121}{60}x^7 + \frac{91}{60}x^6 +$$
$$\frac{169}{180}x^5 + \frac{263}{90}x^4 + \frac{119}{90}x^3 - \frac{62}{45}x^2 - \frac{2}{3}x,$$

$$eU_e(5) = \frac{1}{90}x^{11} - \frac{103}{360}x^{10} - \frac{59}{90}x^9 + \frac{1279}{720}x^8 + \frac{97}{40}x^7 - \frac{49}{40}x^6 -$$
$$\frac{211}{90}x^5 - \frac{529}{720}x^4 + \frac{173}{360}x^3 + \frac{169}{360}x^2 + \frac{1}{12}x.$$

Consequently,

$$2^{3m}A_5^{\perp} = \binom{2^m - 1}{5} + aU_a(5) + bU_b(5) + cU_c(5) + dU_d(5) + eU_e(5) = 0.$$

Plugging $k = 6$ into the weight distribution formula above for $C_m^{\perp}$, we arrive at that

$$\binom{2^m - 1}{6} = \frac{4}{45}x^{12} - \frac{14}{15}x^{10} + \frac{35}{9}x^8 - \frac{49}{6}x^6 + \frac{406}{45}x^4 - \frac{49}{10}x^2 + 1,$$

$$aU_a(6) = -\frac{103}{1080}x^{12} - \frac{97}{540}x^{11} + \frac{1897}{2160}x^{10} + \frac{571}{1080}x^9 - \frac{1573}{720}x^8 + \frac{193}{120}x^7 +$$
$$\frac{2117}{2160}x^6 - \frac{3061}{1080}x^5 + \frac{385}{432}x^4 + \frac{857}{1080}x^3 - \frac{169}{360}x^2 + \frac{1}{12}x,$$

$$bU_b(6) = \frac{23}{54}x^{12} + \frac{29}{54}x^{11} - \frac{1471}{540}x^{10} - \frac{613}{540}x^9 + \frac{218}{45}x^8 - \frac{68}{45}x^7 -$$
$$\frac{293}{540}x^6 + \frac{1033}{540}x^5 - \frac{913}{270}x^4 + \frac{233}{270}x^3 + \frac{62}{45}x^2 - \frac{2}{3}x,$$

$$cU_c(6) = -\frac{3}{4}x^{12} + \frac{37}{8}x^{10} - \frac{221}{24}x^8 + \frac{175}{24}x^6 - \frac{97}{24}x^4 + \frac{37}{12}x^2 - 1,$$

$$dU_d(6) = \frac{23}{54}x^{12} - \frac{29}{54}x^{11} - \frac{1471}{540}x^{10} + \frac{613}{540}x^9 + \frac{218}{45}x^8 + \frac{68}{45}x^7 -$$
$$\frac{293}{540}x^6 - \frac{1033}{540}x^5 - \frac{913}{270}x^4 - \frac{233}{270}x^3 + \frac{62}{45}x^2 + \frac{2}{3}x,$$

$$eU_e(6) = -\frac{103}{1080}x^{12} + \frac{97}{540}x^{11} + \frac{1897}{2160}x^{10} - \frac{571}{1080}x^9 - \frac{1573}{720}x^8 - \frac{193}{120}x^7 +$$
$$\frac{2117}{2160}x^6 + \frac{3061}{1080}x^5 + \frac{385}{432}x^4 - \frac{857}{1080}x^3 - \frac{169}{360}x^2 - \frac{1}{12}x.$$

As a result,

$$2^{3m}A_6^{\perp} = \binom{2^m - 1}{6} + aU_a(6) + bU_b(6) + cU_c(6) + dU_d(6) + eU_e(6) = 0.$$

Plugging $k = 7$ into the weight distribution formula above for $C_m^\perp$, we obtain

$$\binom{2^m - 1}{7} = \frac{8}{315}x^{14} - \frac{16}{45}x^{12} + \frac{92}{45}x^{10} - \frac{56}{9}x^8 + \frac{967}{90}x^6 - \frac{469}{45}x^4 + \frac{363}{70}x^2 - 1$$

and

$$aU_a(7) = -\frac{97}{1890}x^{13} - \frac{11}{1512}x^{12} + \frac{125}{378}x^{11} - \frac{8711}{15120}x^{10} - \frac{523}{7560}x^9 + \frac{15643}{5040}x^8 - \frac{18281}{7560}x^7 - \frac{39307}{15120}x^6 + \frac{23141}{7560}x^5 - \frac{6619}{15120}x^4 - \frac{5818}{7560}x^3 + \frac{1303}{2520}x^2 - \frac{1}{12}x,$$

$$bU_b(7) = \frac{29}{189}x^{13} - \frac{103}{378}x^{12} - \frac{814}{945}x^{11} + \frac{9071}{3780}x^{10} + \frac{2659}{3780}x^9 - \frac{554}{105}x^8 + \frac{3889}{1890}x^7 + \frac{4117}{3780}x^6 - \frac{6299}{3780}x^5 + \frac{6857}{1890}x^4 - \frac{1991}{1890}x^3 - \frac{494}{315}x^2 + \frac{2}{3}x,$$

$$cU_c(7) = \frac{3}{4}x^{12} - \frac{37}{8}x^{10} + \frac{221}{24}x^8 - \frac{175}{24}x^6 + \frac{97}{24}x^4 - \frac{37}{12}x^2 + 1,$$

$$dU_d(7) = -\frac{29}{189}x^{13} - \frac{103}{378}x^{12} + \frac{814}{945}x^{11} + \frac{9071}{3780}x^{10} - \frac{2659}{3780}x^9 - \frac{554}{105}x^8 - \frac{3889}{1890}x^7 + \frac{4117}{3780}x^6 + \frac{6299}{3780}x^5 + \frac{6857}{1890}x^4 + \frac{1991}{1890}x^3 - \frac{494}{315}x^2 - \frac{2}{3}x,$$

$$eU_e(7) = \frac{97}{1890}x^{13} - \frac{11}{1512}x^{12} - \frac{125}{378}x^{11} - \frac{8711}{15120}x^{10} + \frac{523}{7560}x^9 + \frac{15643}{5040}x^8 + \frac{18281}{7560}x^7 - \frac{39307}{15120}x^6 - \frac{23141}{7560}x^5 - \frac{6619}{15120}x^4 + \frac{5819}{7560}x^3 + \frac{1303}{2520}x^2 + \frac{1}{12}x.$$

It then follows that

$$A_7^\perp = 2^{-3m}\left(\binom{2^m - 1}{7} + aU_a(7) + bU_b(7) + cU_c(7) + dU_d(7) + eU_e(7)\right)$$

$$= \frac{(x^2 - 1)(2x^2 - 1)(x^4 - 5x^2 + 34)}{630}.$$

Notice that $x^4 - 5x^2 + 34 = (x^2 - 5/2)^2 + 34 - 25/4 > 0$. We have $A_7^\perp > 0$ for all odd $m \geq 5$. This proves the desired conclusion on the minimum distance of $C_m^\perp$. $\qquad\square$

Theorem 8.15. *Let $m \geq 5$ be an odd integer and let C_m be a binary code with the weight distribution of Table 8.2. The code $\overline{C_m^\perp}^\perp$ has parameters*

$$\left[2^m, 3m + 1, 2^{m-1} - 2^{\frac{m+1}{2}}\right],$$

and its weight enumerator is given by

$$\overline{A^{\perp}}^{\perp}(z) = 1 + uz^{2^{m-1}-2^{\frac{m+1}{2}}} + vz^{2^{m-1}-2^{\frac{m-1}{2}}} +$$
$$wz^{2^{m-1}} + vz^{2^{m-1}+2^{\frac{m-1}{2}}} + uz^{2^{m-1}+2^{\frac{m+1}{2}}} + z^{2^m}, \qquad (8.9)$$

where

$$u = \frac{2^{3m-4} - 3 \times 2^{2m-4} + 2^{m-3}}{3},$$

$$v = \frac{5 \times 2^{3m-2} + 3 \times 2^{2m-2} - 2^{m+1}}{3},$$

$$w = 2(2^m - 1)(9 \times 2^{2m-4} + 3 \times 2^{m-3} + 1).$$

Proof. It follows from Theorem 2.10 that the code has all the weights given in (8.9). It remains to determine the frequencies of these weights. The weight distribution of the code C_m given in Table 8.2 and the generator matrix of the code $\overline{C_m^{\perp}}^{\perp}$ documented in the proof of Theorem 2.10 show that

$$\overline{A^{\perp}}^{\perp}_{2^{m-1}} = 2c = w,$$

where c was defined in Theorem 8.14.

We now determine u and v. Recall that $C_m^{\perp}$ has minimum distance 7. It then follows from Theorem 2.10 that $\overline{C_m^{\perp}}$ has minimum distance 8. The first and third Pless power moments say that

$$\begin{cases} \sum_{i=0}^{2^m} \overline{A^{\perp}}_i = 2^{3m+1}, \\ \sum_{i=0}^{2^m} i^2 \overline{A^{\perp}}_i = 2^{3m-1}2^m(2^m + 1). \end{cases}$$

These two equations become

$$1 + u + v + c = 2^{3m},$$
$$(2^{2m-2} + 2^{m+1})u + (2^{2m-2} + 2^{m-1})v + 2^{2m-2}c + 2^{2m-1} = 2^{4m-2}(2^m + 1).$$

Solving this system of two equations proves the desired conclusion on the weight enumerator of this code. $\qquad\square$

Finally, we settle the weight distribution of the code $\overline{C_m^{\perp}}$.

Theorem 8.16. *Let $m \geq 5$ be an odd integer and let C_m be a binary code with the weight distribution of Table 8.2. The code $\overline{C_m^{\perp}}$ has parameters $[2^m, 2^m - 1 - 3m, 8]$, and its weight distribution is given by*

$$2^{3m+1}\overline{A^{\perp}}_k = \left(1 + (-1)^k\right)\binom{2^m}{k} + wE_0(k) + uE_1(k) + vE_2(k), \qquad (8.10)$$

where w, u, v are defined in Theorem 8.15, and

$$E_0(k) = \frac{1+(-1)^k}{2}(-1)^{\lfloor k/2 \rfloor}\binom{2^{m-1}}{\lfloor k/2 \rfloor},$$

$$E_1(k) = \sum_{\substack{0 \le i \le 2^{m-1}-2^{\frac{m+1}{2}} \\ 0 \le j \le 2^{m-1}+2^{\frac{m+1}{2}} \\ i+j=k}} [(-1)^i + (-1)^j]\binom{2^{m-1}-2^{\frac{m+1}{2}}}{i}\binom{2^{m-1}+2^{\frac{m+1}{2}}}{j},$$

$$E_2(k) = \sum_{\substack{0 \le i \le 2^{m-1}-2^{\frac{m-1}{2}} \\ 0 \le j \le 2^{m-1}+2^{\frac{m-1}{2}} \\ i+j=k}} [(-1)^i + (-1)^j]\binom{2^{m-1}-2^{\frac{m-1}{2}}}{i}\binom{2^{m-1}+2^{\frac{m-1}{2}}}{j},$$

and $0 \le k \le 2^m$.

Proof. By definition,

$$\dim\left(\overline{C_m^\perp}\right) = \dim\left(C_m^\perp\right) = 2^m - 1 - 3m.$$

It has been showed in the proof of Theorem 8.14 that the minimum distance of $\overline{C_m^\perp}$ is equal to 8. We now prove the conclusion on the weight distribution of this code.

By Theorems 2.4 and 8.15, the weight enumerator of $\overline{C_m^\perp}$ is given by

$$2^{3m+1}\overline{A^\perp}(z)$$
$$= (1+z)^{2^m}\left[1 + \left(\frac{1-z}{1+z}\right)^{2^m} + w\left(\frac{1-z}{1+z}\right)^{2^{m-1}}\right] +$$
$$(1+z)^{2^m}\left[u\left(\frac{1-z}{1+z}\right)^{2^{m-1}-2^{\frac{m+1}{2}}} + v\left(\frac{1-z}{1+z}\right)^{2^{m-1}-2^{\frac{m-1}{2}}}\right] +$$
$$(1+z)^{2^m}\left[v\left(\frac{1-z}{1+z}\right)^{2^{m-1}+2^{\frac{m-1}{2}}} + u\left(\frac{1-z}{1+z}\right)^{2^{m-1}+2^{\frac{m+1}{2}}}\right]. \quad (8.11)$$

Consequently, we have

$$2^{3m+1}\overline{A^\perp}(z) = (1+z)^{2^m} + (1-z)^{2^m} + w(1-z^2)^{2^{m-1}} +$$
$$u(1-z)^{2^{m-1}-2^{\frac{m+1}{2}}}(1+z)^{2^{m-1}+2^{\frac{m+1}{2}}} +$$
$$v(1-z)^{2^{m-1}-2^{\frac{m-1}{2}}}(1+z)^{2^{m-1}+2^{\frac{m-1}{2}}} +$$
$$v(1-z)^{2^{m-1}+2^{\frac{m-1}{2}}}(1+z)^{2^{m-1}-2^{\frac{m-1}{2}}} +$$
$$u(1-z)^{2^{m-1}+2^{\frac{m+1}{2}}}(1+z)^{2^{m-1}-2^{\frac{m+1}{2}}}. \quad (8.12)$$

We now treat the terms in (8.12) one by one. We first have

$$(1+z)^{2^m} + (1-z)^{2^m} = \sum_{k=0}^{2^m} \left(1+(-1)^k\right) \binom{2^m}{k}. \tag{8.13}$$

One can easily see that

$$(1-z^2)^{2^{m-1}} = \sum_{i=0}^{2^{m-1}} (-1)^i \binom{2^{m-1}}{i} z^{2i}$$

$$= \sum_{k=0}^{2^m} \frac{1+(-1)^k}{2} (-1)^{\lfloor k/2 \rfloor} \binom{2^{m-1}}{\lfloor k/2 \rfloor} z^k. \tag{8.14}$$

Notice that

$$(1-z)^{2^{m-1}-2^{\frac{m+1}{2}}} = \sum_{i=0}^{2^{m-1}-2^{\frac{m+1}{2}}} \binom{2^{m-1}-2^{\frac{m+1}{2}}}{i} (-1)^i z^i$$

and

$$(1+z)^{2^{m-1}+2^{\frac{m+1}{2}}} = \sum_{i=0}^{2^{m-1}+2^{\frac{m+1}{2}}} \binom{2^{m-1}+2^{\frac{m+1}{2}}}{i} z^i.$$

We have then

$$(1-z)^{2^{m-1}-2^{\frac{m+1}{2}}} (1+z)^{2^{m-1}+2^{\frac{m+1}{2}}} = \sum_{k=0}^{2^m} E_1(k) z^k. \tag{8.15}$$

Similarly, we have

$$(1-z)^{2^{m-1}-2^{\frac{m-1}{2}}} (1+z)^{2^{m-1}+2^{\frac{m-1}{2}}} = \sum_{k=0}^{2^m} E_2(k) z^k, \tag{8.16}$$

$$(1-z)^{2^{m-1}+2^{\frac{m-1}{2}}} (1+z)^{2^{m-1}-2^{\frac{m-1}{2}}} = \sum_{k=0}^{2^m} E_3(k) z^k, \tag{8.17}$$

$$(1-z)^{2^{m-1}+2^{\frac{m+1}{2}}} (1+z)^{2^{m-1}-2^{\frac{m+1}{2}}} = \sum_{k=0}^{2^m} E_4(k) z^k. \tag{8.18}$$

Plugging (8.13), (8.14), (8.15), (8.16), (8.17), and (8.18) into (8.12) proves the desired conclusion.

$\square$

8.3.2 *Infinite Families of 2-Designs from* $C_m^\perp$ *and* C_m

Theorem 8.17. *Let $m \geq 5$ be an odd integer and let C_m be a binary code with the weight distribution of Table 8.2. Let $\mathcal{P} = \{0, 1, 2, \ldots, 2^m - 2\}$, and let $\mathcal{B}$ be the set of the supports of the codewords of C_m with weight k, where $A_k \neq 0$. Then $(\mathcal{P}, \mathcal{B})$ is a 2-$(2^m - 1, k, \lambda)$ design, where*

$$\lambda = \frac{k(k-1)A_k}{(2^m - 1)(2^m - 2)},$$

and A_k is given in Table 8.2.

Let $\mathcal{P} = \{0, 1, 2, \ldots, 2^m - 2\}$, and let $\mathcal{B}^\perp$ be the set of the supports of the codewords of $C_m^\perp$ with weight k and $A_k^\perp \neq 0$. Then $(\mathcal{P}, \mathcal{B}^\perp)$ is a 2-$(2^m - 1, k, \lambda)$ design, where

$$\lambda = \frac{k(k-1)A_k^\perp}{(2^m - 1)(2^m - 2)},$$

where $A_k^\perp$ is given in Theorem 8.14.

Proof. The weight distribution of $C_m^\perp$ is given in Theorem 8.14 and that of C_m is given in Table 8.2. By Theorem 8.14, the minimum distance $d^\perp$ of $C_m^\perp$ is equal to 7. Put $t = 2$. The number of i with $A_i \neq 0$ and $1 \leq i \leq 2^m - 1 - t$ is $s = 5$. Hence, $s = d^\perp - t$. The desired conclusions then follow from Corollary 4.26 and the fact that two binary vectors have the same support if and only if they are equal. $\square$

Corollary 8.18. *Let $m \geq 5$ be an odd integer and let C_m be a binary code with the weight distribution of Table 8.2. Then the BCH code C_m holds five 2-$(2^m - 1, k, \lambda)$ designs with the following pairs (k, λ):*

- $\left(2^{m-1} - 2^{\frac{m+1}{2}}, \dfrac{2^{\frac{m-5}{2}}\left(2^{\frac{m-3}{2}}+1\right)\left(2^{m-1}-2^{\frac{m+1}{2}}\right)\left(2^{m-1}-2^{\frac{m+1}{2}}-1\right)}{6} \right).$

- $\left(2^{m-1} - 2^{\frac{m-1}{2}}, \dfrac{2^{m-2}\left(2^{m-1}-2^{\frac{m-1}{2}}-1\right)\left(5 \times 2^{m-1}+4\right)}{6} \right).$

- $\left(2^{m-1}, \ 2^{m-2}(9 \times 2^{2m-4} + 3 \times 2^{m-3} + 1) \right).$

- $\left(2^{m-1} + 2^{\frac{m-1}{2}}, \dfrac{2^{m-2}\left(2^{m-1}+2^{\frac{m-1}{2}}-1\right)\left(5 \times 2^{m-1}+4\right)}{6} \right).$

- $\left(2^{m-1} + 2^{\frac{m+1}{2}}, \dfrac{2^{\frac{m-5}{2}}\left(2^{\frac{m-3}{2}}-1\right)\left(2^{m-1}+2^{\frac{m+1}{2}}\right)\left(2^{m-1}+2^{\frac{m+1}{2}}-1\right)}{6} \right).$

Corollary 8.19. *Let $m \geq 5$ be an odd integer and let C_m be a binary code with the weight distribution of Table 8.2. Then the supports of all codewords of weight 7 in $C_m^\perp$ give a 2-$(2^m - 1, 7, \lambda)$ design, where*

$$\lambda = \frac{2^{2(m-1)} - 5 \times 2^{m-1} + 34}{30}.$$

Proof. By Theorem 8.14, we have

$$A_7^\perp = \frac{(2^{m-1} - 1)(2^m - 1)(2^{2(m-1)} - 5 \times 2^{m-1} + 34)}{630}.$$

The desired conclusion on λ follows from Theorem 8.17. $\qquad\square$

Corollary 8.20. *Let $m \geq 5$ be an odd integer and let C_m be a binary code with the weight distribution of Table 8.2. Then the supports of all codewords of weight 8 in $C_m^\perp$ give a 2-$(2^m - 1, 8, \lambda)$ design, where*

$$\lambda = \frac{(2^{m-1} - 4)(2^{2(m-1)} - 5 \times 2^{m-1} + 34)}{90}.$$

Proof. By Theorem 8.14, we have

$$A_8^\perp = \frac{(2^{m-1} - 1)(2^{m-1} - 4)(2^m - 1)(2^{2(m-1)} - 5 \times 2^{m-1} + 34)}{2520}.$$

The desired conclusion on λ follows from Theorem 8.17. $\qquad\square$

Corollary 8.21. *Let $m \geq 7$ be an odd integer and let C_m be a binary code with the weight distribution of Table 8.2. Then the supports of all codewords of weight 9 in $C_m^\perp$ give a 2-$(2^m - 1, 9, \lambda)$ design, where*

$$\lambda = \frac{(2^{m-1} - 4)(2^{m-1} - 16)(2^{2(m-1)} - 2^{m-1} + 28)}{315}.$$

Proof. By Theorem 8.14, we have

$$A_9^\perp = \frac{(2^{m-1} - 1)(2^{m-1} - 4)(2^{m-1} - 16)(2^m - 1)(2^{2(m-1)} - 2^{m-1} + 28)}{11340}.$$

The desired conclusion on λ follows from Theorem 8.17. $\qquad\square$

8.3.3 Infinite Families of 3-Designs from $\overline{C_m^\perp}$ and $\overline{C_m^\perp}^\perp$

Theorem 8.22. *Let $m \geq 5$ be an odd integer and let C_m be a binary code with the weight distribution of Table 8.2. Let $\mathcal{P} = \{0, 1, 2, \ldots, 2^m - 1\}$, and let $\overline{\mathcal{B}^\perp}^\perp$ be the* *set of the supports of the codewords of $\overline{C_m^{\perp}}^{\perp}$ with weight k, where $\overline{A^{\perp}}_k^{\perp} \neq 0$. Then $(\mathcal{P}, \overline{\mathcal{B}^{\perp}}^{\perp})$ is a 3-$(2^m, k, \lambda)$ design, where*

$$\lambda = \frac{\overline{A^{\perp}}_k^{\perp} \binom{k}{3}}{\binom{2^m}{3}},$$

and $\overline{A^{\perp}}_k^{\perp}$ is given in Theorem 8.15.

Let $\mathcal{P} = \{0, 1, 2, \ldots, 2^m - 1\}$, *and let $\overline{\mathcal{B}^{\perp}}$ be the set of the supports of the codewords of $\overline{C_m^{\perp}}$ with weight k and $\overline{A^{\perp}}_k \neq 0$. Then $(\mathcal{P}, \overline{\mathcal{B}^{\perp}})$ is a 3-$(2^m, k, \lambda)$ design, where*

$$\lambda = \frac{\overline{A^{\perp}}_k \binom{k}{3}}{\binom{2^m}{3}},$$

and $\overline{A^{\perp}}_k$ is given in Theorem 8.16.

Proof. The weight distributions of $\overline{C_m^{\perp}}^{\perp}$ and $\overline{C_m^{\perp}}$ are described in Theorems 8.15 and 8.16. Notice that the minimum distance $\overline{d^{\perp}}$ of $\overline{C_m^{\perp}}$ is equal to 8. Put $t = 3$. The number of i with $\overline{A^{\perp}}_i \neq 0$ and $1 \leq i \leq 2^m - t$ is $s = 5$. Hence, $s = \overline{d^{\perp}} - t$. Clearly, two binary vectors have the same support if and only if they are equal. The desired conclusions then follow from Corollary 4.26. $\qquad \square$

Corollary 8.23. *Let $m \geq 5$ be an odd integer and let C_m be a binary code with the weight distribution of Table 8.2. Then $\overline{C_m^{\perp}}^{\perp}$ holds five 3-$(2^m, k, \lambda)$ designs with the following pairs (k, λ):*

- $\left(2^{m-1} - 2^{\frac{m+1}{2}}, \dfrac{\left(2^{m-1} - 2^{\frac{m+1}{2}}\right)\left(2^{m-1} - 2^{\frac{m+1}{2}} - 1\right)\left(2^{m-1} - 2^{\frac{m+1}{2}} - 2\right)}{48} \right).$

- $\left(2^{m-1} - 2^{\frac{m-1}{2}}, \dfrac{2^{\frac{m-1}{2}}\left(2^{m-1} - 2^{\frac{m-1}{2}} - 1\right)\left(2^{\frac{m-1}{2}} - 2\right)\left(5 \times 2^{m-3} + 1\right)}{3} \right).$

- $\left(2^{m-1}, \, (2^{m-2} - 1)(9 \times 2^{2m-4} + 3 \times 2^{m-3} + 1) \right).$

- $\left(2^{m-1} + 2^{\frac{m-1}{2}}, \dfrac{2^{\frac{m-1}{2}}\left(2^{m-1} + 2^{\frac{m-1}{2}} - 1\right)\left(2^{\frac{m-1}{2}} + 2\right)\left(5 \times 2^{m-3} + 1\right)}{3} \right).$

- $\left(2^{m-1} + 2^{\frac{m+1}{2}}, \dfrac{\left(2^{m-1} + 2^{\frac{m+1}{2}}\right)\left(2^{m-1} + 2^{\frac{m+1}{2}} - 1\right)\left(2^{m-1} + 2^{\frac{m+1}{2}} - 2\right)}{48} \right).$

Corollary 8.24. *Let* $m \geq 5$ *be an odd integer and let* C_m *be a binary code with the weight distribution of Table 8.2. Then the supports of all codewords of weight 8 in* $\overline{C_m^{\perp}}$ *give a* 3-$(2^m, 8, \lambda)$ *design, where*

$$\lambda = \frac{2^{2(m-1)} - 5 \times 2^{m-1} + 34}{30}.$$

Proof. By Theorem 8.16, we have

$$\overline{A^{\perp}}_8 = \frac{2^m (2^{m-1} - 1)(2^m - 1)(2^{2(m-1)} - 5 \times 2^{m-1} + 34)}{315}.$$

The desired value of λ follows from Theorem 8.22. $\qquad\square$

Corollary 8.25. *Let* $m \geq 7$ *be an odd integer and let* C_m *be a binary code with the weight distribution of Table 8.2. Then the supports of all codewords of weight 10 in* $\overline{C_m^{\perp}}$ *give a* 3-$(2^m, 10, \lambda)$ *design, where*

$$\lambda = \frac{(2^{m-1} - 4)(2^{m-1} - 16)(2^{2(m-1)} - 2^{m-1} + 28)}{315}.$$

Proof. By Theorem 8.16, we have

$$\overline{A^{\perp}}_{10} = \frac{2^{m-1}(2^{m-1} - 1)(2^m - 1)(2^{m-1} - 4)(2^{m-1} - 16)(2^{2(m-1)} - 2^{m-1} + 28)}{4 \times 14175}.$$

The desired value of λ follows from Theorem 8.22. $\qquad\square$

Corollary 8.26. *Let* $m \geq 5$ *be an odd integer and let* C_m *be a binary code with the weight distribution of Table 8.2. Then the supports of all codewords of weight 12 in* $\overline{C_m^{\perp}}$ *give a* 3-$(2^m, 12, \lambda)$ *design, where*

$$\lambda = \frac{(2^{h-2} - 1)(2 \times 2^{5h} - 55 \times 2^{4h} + 647 \times 2^{3h} - 2727 \times 2^{2h} + 11541 \times 2^h - 47208)}{2835}$$

and $h = m - 1$.

Proof. By Theorem 8.16, we have

$$\overline{A^{\perp}}_{12} = \frac{\varepsilon^2(\varepsilon^2 - 1)(\varepsilon^2 - 4)(2\varepsilon^2 - 1)(2\varepsilon^{10} - 55\varepsilon^8 + 647\varepsilon^6 - 2727\varepsilon^4 + 11541\varepsilon^2 - 47208)}{8 \times 467775},$$

where $\varepsilon = 2^{(m-1)/2}$. The desired value of λ follows from Theorem 8.22. $\qquad\square$

8.3.4 Two Families of Binary Cyclic Codes with the Weight Distribution of Table 8.2

To justify the existence of the 2-designs in Section 8.3.2 and the 3-designs in Section 8.3.3, we present two families of binary codes of length $2^m - 1$ with the weight distribution of Table 8.2.

Let $m \geq 5$ be an odd integer and let $\delta = 2^{m-1} - 1 - 2^{(m+1)/2}$. Then the BCH code $C_{(2,2^m-1,\delta,0)}$ has length $n = 2^m - 1$, dimension $3m$, and the weight distribution in Table 8.2 (see Section 7.4).

Let $m \geq 5$ be an odd integer. Let C_m be the dual of the narrow-sense primitive BCH code $C_{(2,2^m-1,7,1)}$. Then C_m has the weight distribution of Table 8.2 [Kasami (1969)].

There are more families of binary cyclic codes with the weight distribution of Table 8.2. The reader is referred to Herbert and Sarkar (2011) for detailed information.

8.4 Infinite Families of Designs from a Type of Ternary Codes

In this section, we present infinite families of 2-designs with a type of primitive ternary cyclic codes.

Table 8.3   Weight distribution of some ternary linear codes

Weight w	Number of codewords A_w in the code
0	1
$2 \times 3^{m-1} - 3^{(m-1)/2}$	$(3^m - 1)(3^{m-1} + 3^{(m-1)/2})$
$2 \times 3^{m-1}$	$(3^m - 1)(3^{m-1} + 1)$
$2 \times 3^{m-1} + 3^{(m-1)/2}$	$(3^m - 1)(3^{m-1} - 3^{(m-1)/2})$

Table 8.4   Weight distribution of some ternary linear codes

Weight w	Number of codewords A_w in the code
0	1
$2 \times 3^{m-1} - 3^{(m-1)/2}$	$3^{2m} - 3^m$
$2 \times 3^{m-1}$	$(3^m + 3)(3^m - 1)$
$2 \times 3^{m-1} + 3^{(m-1)/2}$	$3^{2m} - 3^m$
3^m	2

Lemma 8.27. *Let $m \geq 3$ be odd. Assume that C_m is a ternary linear code of length $3^m - 1$. Denote by $\overline{C}_m$ the extended code of C_m and let $\overline{C}_m^{\perp}$ denote the dual of $\overline{C}_m$. Assume that $\overline{C}_m^{\perp}$ has the weight distribution in Table 8.4. Then we have the following conclusions.*

- *The code $\overline{C}_m^{\perp}$ has parameters $[3^m, 2m+1, 2 \times 3^{m-1} - 3^{(m-1)/2}]$.*
- *The code $\overline{C}_m$ has parameters $[3^m, 3^m - 1 - 2m, 5]$, and its weight distribution is given by*

$$32^{m+1}\overline{A}_k = \left(2^k + (-1)^k 2\right)\binom{3^m}{k} + v \sum_{\substack{0 \le i \le 2 \times 3^{m-1} \\ 0 \le j \le 3^{m-1} \\ i+j=k}} (-1)^i \binom{2 \times 3^{m-1}}{i} 2^j \binom{3^{m-1}}{j} +$$

$$u \sum_{\substack{0 \le i \le 2 \times 3^{m-1} - 3^{\frac{m-1}{2}} \\ 0 \le j \le 3^{m-1} + 3^{\frac{m-1}{2}} \\ i+j=k}} (-1)^i \binom{2 \times 3^{m-1} - 3^{\frac{m-1}{2}}}{i} 2^j \binom{3^{m-1} + 3^{\frac{m-1}{2}}}{j} +$$

$$u \sum_{\substack{0 \le i \le 2 \times 3^{m-1} + 3^{\frac{m-1}{2}} \\ 0 \le j \le 3^{m-1} - 3^{\frac{m-1}{2}} \\ i+j=k}} (-1)^i \binom{2 \times 3^{m-1} + 3^{\frac{m-1}{2}}}{i} 2^j \binom{3^{m-1} - 3^{\frac{m-1}{2}}}{j}$$

for $0 \le k \le 3^m$, where

$$u = 3^{2m} - 3^m \text{ and } v = (3^m + 3)(3^m - 1).$$

Proof. The proof is similar to that of Lemma 8.8 and is omitted here. □

Theorem 8.28. *Let $m \ge 3$ be odd. Let C_m be a linear code of length $3^m - 1$. Denote by $\overline{C}_m$ the extended code of C_m and let $\overline{C}_m^{\perp}$ denote the dual of $\overline{C}_m$. Assume that $\overline{C}_m^{\perp}$ has the weight distribution in Table 8.4. Let $\mathcal{P} = \{0, 1, 2, \ldots, 3^m - 1\}$, and let $\overline{\mathcal{B}}$ be the set of the supports of the codewords of $\overline{C}_m$ with weight k, where $5 \le k \le 10$ and $\overline{A}_k \ne 0$. Then $(\mathcal{P}, \overline{\mathcal{B}})$ is a 2-$(3^m, k, \lambda)$ design for some λ.*

Let $\mathcal{P} = \{0, 1, 2, \ldots, 3^m - 1\}$, and let $\overline{\mathcal{B}}^{\perp}$ be the set of the supports of the codewords of $\overline{C}_m^{\perp}$ with weight k and $\overline{A}_k^{\perp} \ne 0$. Then $(\mathcal{P}, \overline{\mathcal{B}}^{\perp})$ is a 2-$(3^m, k, \lambda)$ design for some λ.

Proof. The weight distributions of the codes $\overline{C}_m$ and $\overline{C}_m^{\perp}$ are described in Lemma 8.27. Notice that the minimum distance d of $\overline{C}_m$ is equal to 5. Put $t = 2$. The number of i with $\overline{A}_i^{\perp} \ne 0$ and $1 \le i \le 3^m - t$ is $s = 3$. Hence, $s = d - t$. The desired conclusions then follow from Theorem 4.24. □

Corollary 8.29. *Let $m \ge 3$ be odd. Let C_m be a linear code of length $3^m - 1$. Denote by $\overline{C}_m$ the extended code of C_m and let $\overline{C}_m^{\perp}$ denote the dual of $\overline{C}_m$. Assume that $\overline{C}_m^{\perp}$ has the weight distribution in Table 8.4. Let $\mathcal{P} = \{0, 1, 2, \ldots, 3^m - 1\}$, and* let $\overline{\mathcal{B}}^{\perp}$ be the set of the supports of the codewords of $\overline{C}_m^{\perp}$ with weight $2 \times 3^{m-1} - 3^{(m-1)/2}$. Then $(\mathcal{P}, \overline{\mathcal{B}}^{\perp})$ is a 2-$(3^m, 2 \times 3^{m-1} - 3^{(m-1)/2}, \lambda)$ design, where

$$\lambda = \frac{(2 \times 3^{m-1} - 3^{(m-1)/2})(2 \times 3^{m-1} - 3^{(m-1)/2} - 1)}{2}.$$

Proof. It follows from Theorem 8.28 that $(\mathcal{P}, \overline{\mathcal{B}}^{\perp})$ is a 2-design. We now determine the value of λ. Note that $\overline{C}_m^{\perp}$ has minimum weight $2 \times 3^{m-1} - 3^{(m-1)/2}$. Any two codewords of minimum weight $2 \times 3^{m-1} - 3^{(m-1)/2}$ have the same support if and only if one is a scalar multiple of the other. Consequently,

$$\left| \overline{\mathcal{B}}^{\perp} \right| = \frac{3^{2m} - 3^m}{2}.$$

It then follows that

$$\lambda = \frac{3^{2m} - 3^m}{2} \frac{\binom{2 \times 3^{m-1} - 3^{(m-1)/2}}{2}}{\binom{3^m}{2}}$$

$$= \frac{(2 \times 3^{m-1} - 3^{(m-1)/2})(2 \times 3^{m-1} - 3^{(m-1)/2} - 1)}{2}.$$

$\square$

Corollary 8.30. *Let $m \geq 3$ be odd. Let C_m be a linear code of length $3^m - 1$. Denote by $\overline{C}_m$ the extended code of C_m and let $\overline{C}_m^{\perp}$ denote the dual of $\overline{C}_m$. Assume that $\overline{C}_m^{\perp}$ has the weight distribution in Table 8.4. Let $\mathcal{P} = \{0, 1, 2, \ldots, 3^m - 1\}$, and let $\mathcal{B}$ be the set of the supports of the codewords of $\overline{C}_m$ with weight 5. Then $(\mathcal{P}, \mathcal{B})$ is a 2-$(3^m, 5, \lambda)$ design, where*

$$\lambda = \frac{5(3^{m-1} - 1)}{2}.$$

Proof. It follows from Theorem 8.28 that $(\mathcal{P}, \overline{\mathcal{B}})$ is a 2-design. We now determine the value of λ. Using the weight distribution formula in Lemma 8.27, we obtain that

$$\overline{A}_5 = \frac{3^{3m-1} - 4 \times 3^{2m-1} + 3^m}{4}.$$

Recall that $\overline{C}_m$ has minimum weight 5. Any two codewords of minimum weight 5 have the same support if and only if one is a scalar multiple of the other. As a result,

$$\left| \overline{\mathcal{B}}^{\perp} \right| = \frac{\overline{A}_5}{2}.$$

It then follows that

$$\lambda = \frac{\overline{A}_5}{2} \frac{\binom{5}{2}}{\binom{3^m}{2}} = \frac{5(3^{m-1} - 1)}{2}.$$

$\square$

Theorem 8.28 gives more 2-designs. However, determining the corresponding value λ may be hard, as the number of blocks in the design may be difficult to derive from $\overline{A}_k$ or $\overline{A}_k^\perp$.

It would be interesting to settle the following open problems.

Problem 8.31. Determine the value of λ of the 2-$(3^m, k, \lambda)$ design for $6 \leq k \leq 10$, which are described in Theorem 8.28.

Problem 8.32. Determine the values of λ of the 2-$(3^m, 3^{m-1}, \lambda)$ design and the 2-$(3^m, 2 \times 3^{m-1} - 3^{(m-1)/2}, \lambda)$ design, which are described in Theorem 8.28.

To demonstrate the existence of the 2-designs presented in Theorem 8.28, we present the following lemma.

Lemma 8.33. *Let $m \geq 3$ be an odd integer and $n = 3^m - 1$. Let α be a generator of* $\mathrm{GF}(3^m)^*$. *Define $g_s(x) = \mathbb{M}_{\alpha^{n-1}}(x)\mathbb{M}_{\alpha^{n-(3^s+1)}}(x)$, where $\mathbb{M}_{\alpha^i}(x)$ is the minimal polynomial of α^i over* $\mathrm{GF}(3)$ *and $s \geq 0$ is an integer. Let $C(m,n,s)$ denote the cyclic code of length $n = 3^m - 1$ over* $\mathrm{GF}(3)$ *with generator polynomial $g_s(x)$. Then $\overline{C(m,n,s)}^\perp$ has the weight distribution of Table 8.4.*

Proof. It is known that $C(m,n,s)^\perp$ has dimension $2m$ and the weight distribution of Table 8.3 [Yuan, Carlet and Ding (2006)]. With the help of Theorem 2.11, one can similarly prove that $\overline{C(m,n,s)}^\perp$ has the weight distribution of Table 8.4. $\qquad\square$

More classes of such ternary codes may be found in Ding, Li, Li and Zhou (2016). They give also 2-designs via Theorem 8.28.

8.5 Infinite Families of Designs from Another Type of Ternary Codes

8.5.1 *Conjectured Infinite Families of 2-Designs*

Let $m \geq 3$ be an odd integer and let α be a primitive element of $\mathrm{GF}(3^m)$. Put $n = (3^m - 1)/2$. Let C_1 and C_2 be linear codes defined by

$$C_1 = \left\{ \left(\mathrm{Tr}_{3^m/3}\left(a\alpha^{4i} + b\alpha^{2i} \right) \right)_{i=0}^{\frac{3^m-1}{2}-1} : a, b \in \mathrm{GF}(3^m) \right\}, \qquad (8.19)$$

and

$$C_2 = \left\{ \left(\mathrm{Tr}_{3^m/3}\left(a\alpha^{\left(3^{\frac{m-3}{2}}+1\right)i} + b\alpha^{\left(3^{\frac{m-1}{2}}+1\right)i} \right) \right)_{i=0}^{\frac{3^m-1}{2}-1} : a, b \in \mathrm{GF}(3^m) \right\},$$

$$(8.20)$$

where $\mathrm{Tr}_{3^m/3}(\cdot)$ is the trace function from $\mathrm{GF}(3^m)$ to $\mathrm{GF}(3)$. Then the codes C_i $(i = 1, 2)$ have parameters $[n, 2m, 3^{m-1} - 3^{\frac{m-1}{2}}]$, and their weight distributions are given in Table 8.5 [Li, Ding, Xiong and Ge (2017); Ding and Li (2017)]. Moreover, the dual codes $C_i^{\perp}$ of C_i $(i = 1, 2)$ have parameters $[n, n - 2m, 4]$.

Table 8.5 The weight distribution of C_1 and C_2

Weight	Frequency
0	1
$3^{m-1} - 3^{\frac{m-1}{2}}$	$\frac{1}{2} \cdot \left(3^{m-1} + 3^{\frac{m-1}{2}}\right)(3^m - 1)$
3^{m-1}	$(2 \cdot 3^{m-1} + 1)(3^m - 1)$
$3^{m-1} + 3^{\frac{m-1}{2}}$	$\frac{1}{2} \cdot \left(3^{m-1} - 3^{\frac{m-1}{2}}\right)(3^m - 1)$

Let $(A_k(C_i))_{k=0}^n$ and $(A_k(C_i^{\perp}))_{k=0}^n$ denote the weight distributions of C_i and $C_i^{\perp}$, respectively. Denote by $\mathcal{B}_k(C_i)$ the set of supports of the codewords of weight k in C_i. Let $\mathcal{P}(C_i)$ denote the set of the coordinates of the codewords in C_i. The following conjectures about 2-designs from the two linear codes C_i were made by Ding and Li (2017).

Conjecture 8.34. *Let C_i be the ternary code in (8.19) or (8.20). Let k be an integer satisfying $A_k(C_i) > 1$. Then $(\mathcal{P}(C_i), \mathcal{B}_k(C_i))$ is a 2-design.*

Conjecture 8.35. *Let C_i be the ternary code in (8.19) or (8.20). Then $(\mathcal{P}(C_i^{\perp}), \mathcal{B}_4(C_i^{\perp}))$ is a Steiner system $S(2, 4, \frac{3^m - 1}{2})$.*

Conjecture 8.36. *Let C_i be the ternary code in (8.19) or (8.20). Let k be an integer satisfying $A_k(C_i^{\perp}) > 1$. Then $(\mathcal{P}(C_i^{\perp}), \mathcal{B}_k(C_i^{\perp}))$ is a 2-design.*

It will be shown that the minimum distance of the dual code $C_i^{\perp}$ is only 4. Hence, the Assmus-Mattson theorem guarantees only 1-designs supported by C_i. When $m = 5$ and 7, Magma experimental results showed that C_i is not 2-transitive or 2-homogeneous. Thus, in general, C_i is not 2-transitive or 2-homogeneous. Consequently, the degree of transitivity or homogeneity of their automorphism groups cannot be employed to prove that the two codes C_i support 2-designs.

Conjectures 8.34, 8.35 were confirmed and Conjecture 8.36 was settled for $k \in \{4, 5, 6, 7\}$ by Tang, Ding and Xiong (2019). Furthermore, a large class of ternary cyclic codes containing the codes C_1 and C_2 was constructed and proved to support 2-designs by Tang, Ding and Xiong (2019). The objective of Section 8.5 is to introduce the work of Tang, Ding and Xiong (2019).

8.5.2 *A Class of Ternary Cyclic Codes of Length* $\frac{3^m-1}{2}$

In this section, we introduce a class of ternary cyclic codes of length $\frac{3^m-1}{2}$, and determine the parameters of these codes and their dual codes.

Let m be a positive integer, α be a generator of $GF(3^m)^*$ and $\beta = \alpha^2$. Then β is a primitive $\frac{3^m-1}{2}$-th root of unity in $GF(3^m)$. Let l be a positive integer and $E = \{k_i : 0 \le i \le l\}$ a set of integers with $0 \le k_0 < k_1 < \cdots < k_l \le \frac{m}{2}$. A *ternary cyclic code* $C(E)$ of length $n = \frac{3^m-1}{2}$ is defined by

$$C(E) = \{\mathbf{c}(\underline{a}) : \underline{a} = (a_0, \ldots, a_l) \in GF(3^m)^{l+1}\}, \tag{8.21}$$

where $\mathbf{c}(\underline{a}) = \left(\mathrm{Tr}_{3^m/3} \left(\sum_{j=0}^l a_j \alpha^{(3^{k_j}+1)i} \right) \right)_{i=0}^{n-1}$. We also write $C(k_0, k_1, \ldots, k_l)$ for $C(E)$. By Delsarte's theorem, the dual code $C(E)^\perp$ of $C(E)$ can be given by

$$C(E)^\perp = \left\{ (w_0, \ldots, w_{n-1}) \in GF(3)^n : \sum_{i=0}^{n-1} w_i \mathbf{u}_i = 0 \right\},$$

where $\mathbf{u}_i = \left(\alpha^{i(3^{k_j}+1)} \right)_{j=0}^l \in GF(3^m)^{l+1}$. Note that for the linear codes defined in (8.19) and (8.20), $C_1 = C(0, 1)$ and $C_2 = C(\frac{m-3}{2}, \frac{m-1}{2})$.

To determine the parameters of $C(E)$ and its dual, we need some results on irreducible polynomials. For an integer e, let $\mathbb{M}_{\alpha^{-e}}(x) \in GF(3)[x]$ be the minimal polynomial of α^{-e} over $GF(3)$. We have the following lemma on $\mathbb{M}_{\alpha^{-e}}(x)$.

Lemma 8.37. *Let k and k' be two integers such that $0 \le k, k' \le \frac{m}{2}$. Then*

(i) $\deg \left(\mathbb{M}_{\alpha^{-(3^k+1)}}(x) \right) = \begin{cases} m, & \text{if } k < \frac{m}{2}, \\ \frac{m}{2}, & \text{if } m \text{ is even and } k = \frac{m}{2}. \end{cases}$

(ii) $\mathbb{M}_{\alpha^{-(3^k+1)}}(x) = \mathbb{M}_{\alpha^{-(3^{k'}+1)}}(x)$ *if and only if $k = k'$.*

Proof. (i) Note that $\deg \left(\mathbb{M}_{\alpha^{-(3^k+1)}}(x) \right)$ is the least positive integer $d \le m$ such that

$$(3^k+1)3^d \equiv (3^k+1) \pmod{3^m-1}. \tag{8.22}$$

It suffices to prove that Equation (8.22) holds if and only if $d = k = \frac{m}{2}$ or $d = m$. If $d = k = \frac{m}{2}$ or $d = m$, we can easily verify that Equation (8.22) holds. Conversely, suppose that $(3^k+1)3^d \equiv (3^k+1) \pmod{3^m-1}$ and $d < m$. If $k+d < m$, then $3^{k+d}+3^d = 3^k+1$ and $d = 0$, which leads to a contradiction with $d > 0$. If $k+d \ge m$, then $(3^k+1)3^d \equiv 3^{k+d-m}+3^d \pmod{3^m-1}$. From $0 \le k+d-m \le \frac{m}{2}$, we have $3^{k+d-m}+3^d = 3^k+1$, i.e., $d = k$, $k+d-m = 0$, and $d = k = \frac{m}{2}$. Part (i) follows.

(ii) Suppose $\mathbb{M}_{\alpha^{-(3^k+1)}}(x) = \mathbb{M}_{\alpha^{-(3^{k'}+1)}}(x)$. This holds if and only if there exists a positive integer $d \le m$ such that $(3^k+1)3^d \equiv 3^{k'}+1 \pmod{3^m-1}$. If $d = m$, then $k = k'$. If $d < m$ and $k+d < m$, then we have $3^{k+d}+3^d = 3^{k'}+1$, which contradicts the fact that $d \ge 1$. If $d < m$ and $k+d \ge m$, then we get $3^{k+d-m}+3^d \equiv 3^{k'}+1 \pmod{3^m-1}$. Hence $k' = d$ and $k = m-d$. From $k, k' \le \frac{m}{2}$, one obtains $k' = k = d = \frac{m}{2}$. Part (ii) follows. $\square$

As a consequence of Lemma 8.37, we have the following proposition on some parameters of $\mathcal{C}(E)$.

Proposition 8.38. *The linear code $\mathcal{C}(E)$ defined by (8.21) is a ternary cyclic code of length $\frac{3^m-1}{2}$ and dimension*

$$\dim(\mathcal{C}(E)) = \begin{cases} (l+1)m, & \text{if } k_l < \frac{m}{2}, \\ \frac{2l+1}{2}m, & \text{if } m \text{ is even and } k_l = \frac{m}{2}. \end{cases}$$

In particular, the linear code $C\left(0,1,2,\ldots,\left\lfloor\frac{m}{2}\right\rfloor\right)$ is a cyclic code with dimension $\frac{m(m+1)}{2}$, where $\left\lfloor\frac{m}{2}\right\rfloor$ is the greatest integer less than or equal to $\frac{m}{2}$.

In the following, we will determine the parameters of the codes $C\left(0,1,2,\ldots,\left\lfloor\frac{m}{2}\right\rfloor\right)$ and $C\left(0,1,\ldots,\left\lfloor\frac{m}{2}\right\rfloor\right)^{\perp}$.

Let $\{\alpha_0,\ldots,\alpha_{m-1}\}$ be a basis of $\mathrm{GF}(3^m)$ over $\mathrm{GF}(3)$. Let ρ be the linear transformation from $\mathrm{GF}(3^m)$ to $\mathrm{GF}(3)^m$ defined by

$$\rho(x) = (x_0, x_1, \ldots, x_{m-1}) \in \mathrm{GF}(3)^m,$$

where $x = \sum_{i=0}^{m-1} x_i\alpha_i \in \mathrm{GF}(3^m)$. From this isomorphism ρ, a function $f : \mathrm{GF}(3^m) \to \mathrm{GF}(3)$ induces a function $F : \mathrm{GF}(3)^m \to \mathrm{GF}(3)$. In particular, the function

$$f_{a_0,\ldots,a_{\lfloor\frac{m}{2}\rfloor}}(x) = \mathrm{Tr}_{3^m/3}\left(\sum_{i=0}^{\lfloor\frac{m}{2}\rfloor} a_i x^{3^i+1}\right)$$

with $a_i \in \mathrm{GF}(3^m)$ induces a quadratic form

$$\begin{aligned}
&F_{a_0,\ldots,a_{\lfloor\frac{m}{2}\rfloor}}(x_0,\ldots,x_{m-1}) \\
&= \mathrm{Tr}_{3^m/3}\left(\sum_{t=0}^{\lfloor\frac{m}{2}\rfloor} a_t \left(\sum_{i=0}^{m-1} x_i\alpha_i\right)^{3^t+1}\right) \\
&= \mathrm{Tr}_{3^m/3}\left(\sum_{t=0}^{\lfloor\frac{m}{2}\rfloor} a_t \left(\sum_{i=0}^{m-1} x_i\alpha_i^{3^t}\right)\left(\sum_{j=0}^{m-1} x_j\alpha_j\right)\right) \\
&= \sum_{i,j=0}^{m-1} \mathrm{Tr}_{3^m/3}\left(\sum_{t=0}^{\lfloor\frac{m}{2}\rfloor} a_t\alpha_i^{3^t}\alpha_j\right) x_i x_j \in \mathrm{PP}(1,m-1,3),
\end{aligned} \tag{8.23}$$

where $\mathrm{PP}(1, m-1, 3)$ was defined in Section 4.6.2. From the definition of $F_{a_0,\ldots,a_{\lfloor \frac{m}{2}\rfloor}}$, we have $F_{a_0,\ldots,a_{\lfloor \frac{m}{2}\rfloor}}(\rho(x)) = f_{a_0,\ldots,a_{\lfloor \frac{m}{2}\rfloor}}(x)$ for any $x \in \mathrm{GF}(3^m)$.

Note that the set of all projective points of $\mathrm{PG}(m-1, \mathrm{GF}(3))$ is

$$\left\{ \rho\left(\alpha^i\right) : i = 0, \ldots, \frac{3^m-1}{2} - 1 \right\},$$

where α is a generator of $\mathrm{GF}(3^m)^*$. Hence, we can choose $\mathbf{x}^i = \rho\left(\alpha^i\right)$ in the definition of $\mathrm{PRM}(1, m-1, 3)$ and $\mathrm{PRM}^*(1, m-1, 3)$ (see Section 4.6.2). A map π from $C\left(0, 1, \ldots, \lfloor\frac{m}{2}\rfloor\right)$ to $\mathrm{PRM}^*(1, m-1, 3)$ can be defined by

$$\pi : C\left(0, 1, \ldots, \lfloor\frac{m}{2}\rfloor\right) \longrightarrow \mathrm{PRM}^*(1, m-1, 3)$$

$$\left(f_{a_0,\ldots,a_{\lfloor \frac{m}{2}\rfloor}}\left(\alpha^i\right) \right)_{i=0}^{\frac{3^m-1}{2}-1} \longmapsto \left(F_{a_0,\ldots,a_{\lfloor \frac{m}{2}\rfloor}}\left(\rho(\alpha^i)\right) \right)_{i=0}^{\frac{3^m-1}{2}-1},$$

where $f_{a_0,\ldots,a_{\lfloor \frac{m}{2}\rfloor}}(x) = \mathrm{Tr}_{3^m/3}\left(\sum_{i=0}^{\lfloor \frac{m}{2}\rfloor} a_i x^{3^i+1} \right)$ with $a_i \in \mathrm{GF}(3^m)$ and $F_{a_0,\ldots,a_{\lfloor \frac{m}{2}\rfloor}}$ was defined in (8.23). Since $F_{a_0,\ldots,a_{\lfloor \frac{m}{2}\rfloor}}(\rho(\alpha^i)) = f_{a_0,\ldots,a_{\lfloor \frac{m}{2}\rfloor}}(\alpha^i)$ and π is an inclusion map, we have

$$C\left(0, 1, \ldots, \lfloor\frac{m}{2}\rfloor\right) \subseteq \mathrm{PRM}^*(1, m-1, 3).$$

On the other hand, from Theorem 4.42 and Proposition 8.38, we deduce that

$$\dim\left(C\left(0, 1, \ldots, \lfloor\frac{m}{2}\rfloor\right) \right) = \dim\left(\mathrm{PRM}^*(1, m-1, 3)\right) = \frac{m(m+1)}{2}.$$

Using Theorem 4.42 again, we have

$$C\left(0, 1, \ldots, \lfloor\frac{m}{2}\rfloor\right) = C_{\mathrm{GF}(3)}\left(\mathrm{PG}_1(m-1, \mathrm{GF}(3))\right)^{\perp} = \mathrm{PRM}^*(1, m-1, 3).$$

Note that $\mathrm{PG}_1(m-1, \mathrm{GF}(3))$ is a Steiner system $S(2, 4, \frac{3^m-1}{2})$ with $\frac{(3^m-1)(3^{m-1}-1)}{16}$ blocks. From the previous discussion and Theorem 4.42, we have the following theorem.

Theorem 8.39. *Let $m \geq 3$ be an integer.*

(i) $C\left(0, 1, \ldots, \lfloor\frac{m}{2}\rfloor\right) = \mathrm{PRM}^*(1, m-1, 3)$, that is, $C\left(0, 1, \ldots, \lfloor\frac{m}{2}\rfloor\right)$ is the even-like subcode of the first order projective generalized Reed-Muller code $\mathrm{PRM}(1, m-1, 3)$.

(ii) $C\left(0, 1, \ldots, \lfloor\frac{m}{2}\rfloor\right)^{\perp}$ is the code $C_{\mathrm{GF}(3)}\left(\mathrm{PG}_1(m-1, \mathrm{GF}(3))\right)$ of the Steiner system $\mathrm{PG}_1(m-1, \mathrm{GF}(3))$.

(iii) $C\left(0, 1, \ldots, \lfloor\frac{m}{2}\rfloor\right)^{\perp}$ has minimum distance 4 and the minimum-weight codewords are the multiples of the characteristic vectors of the blocks of the 2-design $\mathrm{PG}_1(m-1, \mathrm{GF}(3))$.

(iv) The number $A_4^{\perp}$ of codewords with Hamming weight 4 in the code $C\left(0, 1, \ldots, \lfloor\frac{m}{2}\rfloor\right)^{\perp}$ is $\frac{(3^m-1)(3^{m-1}-1)}{8}$.

By definition, the Steiner system $PG_1(m-1, GF(3))$ is also equivalent to the Steiner system $(\mathcal{P}, \mathcal{B})$, where

$$\mathcal{P} = \{a^2 : a \in GF(3^m)^*\}$$

and

$$\mathcal{B} = \{\{a^2, b^2, (a+b)^2, (a-b)^2\} : a, b \in GF(3^m)^* \text{ and } a \neq \pm b\}.$$

The minimum distance of the code $C(0, 1, \ldots, \lfloor \frac{m}{2} \rfloor)$ is described in the next theorem.

Theorem 8.40. *Let m be an integer with $m \geq 3$. Then the set $C(0, 1, \ldots, \lfloor \frac{m}{2} \rfloor)$ is a $[\frac{3^m-1}{2}, \frac{m(m+1)}{2}, 2 \cdot 3^{m-2}]$ cyclic code.*

Proof. By Part (i) of Theorem 8.39, for any nonzero codeword $\mathbf{c} = (c_0, \ldots, c_{n-1})$, there is a unique quadratic form $F \in PP(1, m-1, 3)$ such that $c_i = F(\rho(\alpha^i))$, where $n = \frac{3^m-1}{2}$. Then,

$$\mathrm{wt}(\mathbf{c}) = \frac{3^m - N(F = 0)}{2},$$

where F was defined in (1.3) and $\mathrm{wt}(\mathbf{c})$ is the Hamming weight of $\mathbf{c}$. Suppose that F is equivalent to the diagonal form $a_0 x_0^2 + \cdots + a_{s-2} x_{s-2}^2 + a_{s-1} x_{s-1}^2$ with $a_i \in GF(3)^*$. Using (1.3), one gets

$$\mathrm{wt}(\mathbf{c}) = \begin{cases} 3^{m-1}, & \text{if } s \equiv 1 \pmod 2, \\ 3^{m-1} \pm 3^{m-1-\frac{s}{2}}, & \text{if } s \equiv 0 \pmod 2. \end{cases}$$

Since $F \neq 0$, then $s \geq 1$. Thus, $\mathrm{wt}(\mathbf{c}) \geq 3^{m-1} - 3^{m-1-1} = 2 \cdot 3^{m-2}$. In addition, choose $F = x_0^2 - x_1^2$ and $\mathbf{c} = (F(\rho(\alpha^i)))_{i=0}^{n-1}$. Then, $\mathrm{wt}(\mathbf{c}) = 2 \cdot 3^{m-2}$. Hence, the minimum weight of $C(0, 1, \ldots, \lfloor \frac{m}{2} \rfloor)$ is $2 \cdot 3^{m-2}$. From Proposition 8.38, this theorem follows. $\qquad\square$

8.5.3 Shortened Codes and Punctured Codes from $C(E)$

In this subsection, we present some ternary codes by shortening and puncturing some subcodes of $C(0, 1, \ldots, \lfloor \frac{m}{2} \rfloor)$ with the weight distribution in Table 8.5, and determine their weight distributions.

Let C be an $[n, k, d]$ code and T a set of t coordinate positions in C. We use C^T to denote the code obtained by puncturing C on T, which is called the *punctured code* of C on T. Let $C(T)$ be the subcode of C, which is the set of codewords which are $\mathbf{0}$ on T. We now puncture $C(T)$ on T, and obtain a linear code C_T, which is called the *shortened code* of C on T. We have the following result on the punctured code and shortened code of a code C (see Theorem 2.8):

$$(C_T)^\perp = \left(C^\perp\right)^T. \tag{8.24}$$

To determine the weight distributions of shortened codes from $C(E)$, we will need the following lemma.

Lemma 8.41. *Let C be an $[n,k,d]$ code over $\mathrm{GF}(q)$ and $d^\perp$ the minimum distance of $C^\perp$. Let $i_1,\ldots,i_s$ be s positive integers and T a set of t coordinate positions of C, where $i_1 < \cdots < i_s \le n$ and $t < d^\perp$. Suppose that $A_i(C) = 0$ for any $i \notin \{0, i_1,\ldots,i_s\}$ and $A_1\left(\left(C^\perp\right)^T\right), \ldots, A_{s-1}\left(\left(C^\perp\right)^T\right)$ are independent of the elements of T. Then, the code C_T has dimension $k-t$. Furthermore, the weight distributions of C_T and $\left(C^\perp\right)^T$ are independent of the elements of T and can be determined from the first s equations in (2.6).*

Proof. By Theorem 2.8, C_T has dimension $k-t$, and $(C_T)^\perp = \left(C^\perp\right)^T$. Then the desired conclusions of this lemma follow from Theorem 2.6. □

The next lemma will be useful in the sequel.

Lemma 8.42. *Let $m \ge 3$ be odd. Let C be a subcode of $C\left(0,1,\ldots,\lfloor\frac{m}{2}\rfloor\right)$ with the weight distribution in Table 8.5. Then, the weight distribution $A_1^\perp,\ldots,A_{(3^m-1)/2}^\perp$ of $C^\perp$ is given by*

$$
\begin{aligned}
3^{2m} A_k^\perp =& \sum_{i=0}^{k}(-1)^i 2^{k-i} a \binom{3^{m-1}-3^{(m-1)/2}}{i}\binom{\frac{3^{m-1}+2\cdot3^{(m-1)/2}-1}{2}}{k-i} \\
&+ \binom{\frac{3^m-1}{2}}{k} 2^k + \sum_{i=0}^{k}(-1)^i 2^{k-i} b \binom{3^{m-1}}{i}\binom{\frac{3^{m-1}-1}{2}}{k-i} \\
&+ \sum_{i=0}^{k}(-1)^i 2^{k-i} c \binom{3^{m-1}+3^{(m-1)/2}}{i}\binom{\frac{3^{m-1}-2\cdot3^{(m-1)/2}-1}{2}}{k-i}
\end{aligned}
$$

for $0 \le k \le \frac{3^m-1}{2}$, where

$$
\begin{aligned}
a =& \frac{1}{2}\cdot\left(3^{m-1}+3^{\frac{m-1}{2}}\right)(3^m-1), \\
b =&(3^m-3^{m-1}+1)(3^m-1), \\
c =& \frac{1}{2}\cdot\left(3^{m-1}-3^{\frac{m-1}{2}}\right)(3^m-1).
\end{aligned}
$$

In addition, $C^\perp$ has parameters $\left[\frac{3^m-1}{2}, \frac{3^m-1}{2}-2m, 4\right]$ and $A_4^\perp = \frac{(3^m-1)(3^{m-1}-1)}{8}$.

Proof. Note that the weight enumerator of $C_m^{\perp}$ is

$$1 + az^{3^{m-1}-3^{(m-1)/2}} + bz^{3^{m-1}} + cz^{3^{m-1}+3^{(m-1)/2}}.$$

The proof of this theorem is similar to that of Lemma 8.1 and is omitted. $\square$

Let $W_i(C)$ denote the set of codewords of weight i in a code C.

Lemma 8.43. *Let* $m \geq 3$ *be odd and* C *be a subcode of* $C\left(0,1,\ldots,\lfloor\frac{m}{2}\rfloor\right)$ *with the weight distribution in Table 8.5. Let* T *be a set of* t *coordinate positions in* C.

(i) If $t = 1$, then $A_1\left(\left(C^{\perp}\right)^T\right) = A_2\left(\left(C^{\perp}\right)^T\right) = 0$.

(ii) If $t = 2$, then $A_1\left(\left(C^{\perp}\right)^T\right) = 0$ and $A_2\left(\left(C^{\perp}\right)^T\right) = 2$.

(iii) $W_4\left(C^{\perp}\right) = W_4\left(C\left(0,1,\ldots,\lfloor\frac{m}{2}\rfloor\right)^{\perp}\right)$.

Proof. By Lemma 8.42, the minimum weight of $C^{\perp}$ is 4. Thus, $A_1\left(\left(C^{\perp}\right)^T\right) = A_2\left(\left(C^{\perp}\right)^T\right) = 0$ for $t = 1$ and $A_1\left(\left(C^{\perp}\right)^T\right) = 0$ for $t = 2$.

Notice that $C \subseteq C\left(0,1,\ldots,\lfloor\frac{m}{2}\rfloor\right)$. We have $C\left(0,1,\ldots,\lfloor\frac{m}{2}\rfloor\right)^{\perp} \subseteq C^{\perp}$ and $W_4\left(C\left(0,1,\ldots,\lfloor\frac{m}{2}\rfloor\right)^{\perp}\right) \subseteq W_4\left(C^{\perp}\right)$. Combining Part (iv) of Theorem 8.39 and Lemma 8.42, one obtains $\left|W_4\left(C\left(0,1,\ldots,\lfloor\frac{m}{2}\rfloor\right)^{\perp}\right)\right| = \left|W_4\left(C^{\perp}\right)\right|$. As a result,

$$W_4\left(C\left(0,1,\ldots,\lfloor\frac{m}{2}\rfloor\right)^{\perp}\right) = W_4\left(C^{\perp}\right).$$

By Part (iii) of Theorem 8.39, $W_4\left(C^{\perp}\right)$ is the set of the multiples of the characteristic vectors of the blocks of $\mathrm{PG}_1(m-1,\mathrm{GF}(3))$. Since $\mathrm{PG}_1(m-1,\mathrm{GF}(3))$ is a Steiner system $S(2,4,\frac{3^{m}-1}{2})$, $A_2\left(\left(C^{\perp}\right)^T\right) = 2$. This completes the proof. $\square$

For $T = \{t\}$ and $T = \{t_1,t_2\}$, we determine the weight distribution of the shortened code C_T of some subcodes of $C\left(0,1,\ldots,\lfloor\frac{m}{2}\rfloor\right)$.

Theorem 8.44. *Let* t *be an integer and* $m \geq 3$ *odd, where* $0 \leq t \leq \frac{3^{m}-1}{2} - 1$. *Let* C *be a subcode of* $C\left(0,1,\ldots,\lfloor\frac{m}{2}\rfloor\right)$ *with the weight distribution in Table 8.5. Then, the shortened code* $C_{\{t\}}$ *is a ternary linear code of length* $\frac{3^{m}-1}{2} - 1$ *and dimension* $2m - 1$, *and has the weight distribution in Table 8.6.*

Proof. It follows from Lemma 8.42 that $d(C^{\perp}) = 4$. By Lemma 8.41, $C_{\{t\}}$ has length $n = \frac{3^{m}-1}{2} - 1$ and dimension $k = 2m - 1$. Note that $A_i = A_i\left(C_{\{t\}}\right) = 0$ for $i \notin \{0,i_1,i_2,i_3\}$, where $i_1 = 3^{m-1} - 3^{\frac{m-1}{2}}$, $i_2 = 3^{m-1}$ and $i_3 = 3^{m-1} + 3^{\frac{m-1}{2}}$. It follows from (8.24) and Lemma 8.43 that

$$A_1((C_{\{t\}})^{\perp}) = A_2((C_{\{t\}})^{\perp}) = 0.$$

Table 8.6 The weight distribution of the shortened code $C_{\{t\}}$

Weight	Frequency
0	1
$3^{m-1} - 3^{\frac{m-1}{2}}$	$\frac{1}{2} \cdot \left(3^{m-1} + 2 \cdot 3^{\frac{m-1}{2}} - 1\right)\left(3^{m-1} + 3^{\frac{m-1}{2}}\right)$
3^{m-1}	$\left(2 \cdot 3^{m-1} + 1\right)\left(3^{m-1} - 1\right)$
$3^{m-1} + 3^{\frac{m-1}{2}}$	$\frac{1}{2} \cdot \left(3^{m-1} - 2 \cdot 3^{\frac{m-1}{2}} - 1\right)\left(3^{m-1} - 3^{\frac{m-1}{2}}\right)$

The first three Pless power moments in (2.6) give

$$\begin{cases} A_{i_1} + A_{i_2} + A_{i_3} = 3^{2m-1} - 1, \\ i_1 A_{i_1} + i_2 A_{i_2} + i_3 A_{i_3} = 2 \cdot 3^{2m-1-1} n, \\ i_1^2 A_{i_1} + i_2^2 A_{i_2} + i_3^2 A_{i_3} = 2 \cdot 3^{2m-1-2} n(2n+1). \end{cases}$$

Solving this system of equations yields the weight distribution in Table 8.6. □

Example 8.45. Let $m = 5$, $E = \{0,1\}$, $0 \le t \le \frac{3^m-1}{2} - 1$ and $C = C(E)$. Then C has the weight distribution in Table 8.5. Furthermore, the shortened code $C_{\{t\}}$ has parameters $[120, 9, 72]$ and weight enumerator $1 + 4410z^{72} + 13040z^{81} + 2232z^{90}$. This code has the same parameters as the best ternary linear code known in the database maintained by Markus Grassl.

Magma experiments showed that all the shortened codes $C_{\{t\}}$ have the same weight distribution and are pairwise equivalent.

Theorem 8.46. *Let t_1 and t_2 be two integers and $m \ge 3$ odd, where $0 \le t_1 < t_2 \le \frac{3^m-1}{2} - 1$. Let C be a subcode of $C\left(0,1,\ldots,\lfloor\frac{m}{2}\rfloor\right)$ with the weight distribution in Table 8.5. Then, the shortened code $C_{\{t_1,t_2\}}$ is a ternary linear code of length $\frac{3^m-1}{2} - 2$ and dimension $2m-2$, and has the weight distribution in Table 8.7.*

Table 8.7 The weight distribution of the shortened code $C_{\{t_1,t_2\}}$

Weight	Frequency
0	1
$3^{m-1} - 3^{\frac{m-1}{2}}$	$\frac{1}{6} \cdot \left(3^{m-1} + 2 \cdot 3^{\frac{m-1}{2}} - 1\right)\left(3^{m-1} + 3^{\frac{m+1}{2}}\right)$
3^{m-1}	$\left(2 \cdot 3^{m-1} + 1\right)\left(3^{m-2} - 1\right)$
$3^{m-1} + 3^{\frac{m-1}{2}}$	$\frac{1}{6} \cdot \left(3^{m-1} - 2 \cdot 3^{\frac{m-1}{2}} - 1\right)\left(3^{m-1} - 3^{\frac{m+1}{2}}\right)$

Proof. By Lemma 8.42, $d(C^\perp) = 4$. It follows from Lemma 8.41 that $C_{\{t_1,t_2\}}$ has length $n = \frac{3^m-1}{2} - 2$ and dimension $k = 2m-2$. Note that $A_i = A_i\left(C_{\{t_1,t_2\}}\right) = 0$ for $i \notin \{0, i_1, i_2, i_3\}$, where $i_1 = 3^{m-1} - 3^{\frac{m-1}{2}}$, $i_2 = 3^{m-1}$ and $i_3 = 3^{m-1} + 3^{\frac{m-1}{2}}$. Combining (8.24) and Lemma 8.43, we deduce that $A_1\left(\left(C_{\{t_1,t_2\}}\right)^\perp\right) = 0$ and

$A_2((C_{\{t_1,t_2\}})^\perp) = 2$. The first three Pless power moments in (2.6) give

$$\begin{cases} A_{i_1} + A_{i_2} + A_{i_3} = 3^{2m-2} - 1, \\ i_1 A_{i_1} + i_2 A_{i_2} + i_3 A_{i_3} = 2 \cdot 3^{2m-2-1} n, \\ i_1^2 A_{i_1} + i_2^2 A_{i_2} + i_3^2 A_{i_3} = 3^{2m-2-2}[n(4n+2)+4]. \end{cases}$$

Solving this system of equations, we get the weight distribution in Table 8.7. $\square$

Example 8.47. Let $m = 5$, $E = \{0,1\}$, $0 \le t_1 < t_2 \le \frac{3^m-1}{2} - 1$ and $C = C(E)$. Then C has the weight distribution in Table 8.5. Furthermore, the shortened code $C_{\{t_1,t_2\}}$ has parameters $[119,8,72]$ and weight enumerator $1 + 1764z^{72} + 4238z^{81} + 558z^{90}$. This code has the same parameters as the best ternary linear code known in the database maintained by Markus Grassl.

Magma experiments showed that all the shortened codes $C_{\{t_1,t_2\}}$ have the same weight distribution. However, for many pairs of (t_1,t_2) and (t_1',t_2'), the codes $C_{\{t_1,t_2\}}$ and $C_{\{t_1',t_2'\}}$ are not equivalent. Therefore, the automorphism group of the code C is in general not 2-homogeneous and 2-transitive.

To determine the weight distributions of some punctured codes from $C(E)$, we need the next lemma.

Lemma 8.48. *Let C be an $[n,k,d]$ code over $GF(q)$ and let $d^\perp$ denote the minimum distance of $C^\perp$. Let t be a positive integer and T a subset of the coordinate positions of C, where $t < d^\perp$ and $|T| \le t$. Suppose that $A_i(C_T)$ is independent of the elements of T and depends only on the size of T. Define*

$$W_i(C,T) = \{\mathbf{c} = (c_0,\ldots,c_{n-1}) \in C : \mathrm{wt}(\mathbf{c}) = i, c_j \ne 0 \text{ for all } j \in T\}.$$

Then, $|W_i(C,T)|$ is independent of the elements of T and depends only on the size of T. Moreover,

$$|W_i(C,T)| = A_i(C) - \sum_{j=1}^{|T|} (-1)^{j-1} \binom{|T|}{j} A_i(C_{\{0,1,\ldots,j-1\}}).$$

Proof. By the inclusion-exclusion principle, one has

$$|W_i(C,T)| = A_i(C) - \sum_{j=1}^{|T|} (-1)^{j-1} \sum_{J \subseteq T, |J|=j} A_i(C(J)).$$

By assumption, $A_i(C(J)) = A_i(C_J) = A_i(C_{\{0,1,\ldots,|J|-1\}})$. The desired conclusions then follow. $\square$

For $T = \{t\}$ and $T = \{t_1, t_2\}$, we determine the weight distribution of the punctured code C^T from some subcodes of $C\left(0, 1, \ldots, \lfloor \frac{m}{2} \rfloor\right)$.

Theorem 8.49. *Let t be an integer and $m \geq 3$ odd, where $0 \leq t \leq \frac{3^m - 1}{2} - 1$. Let C be a subcode of $C\left(0, 1, \ldots, \lfloor \frac{m}{2} \rfloor\right)$ with the weight distribution in Table 8.5. Then, the punctured code $C^{\{t\}}$ is a ternary linear code of length $\frac{3^m - 1}{2} - 1$ and dimension $2m$, and has the weight distribution in Table 8.8.*

Table 8.8 The weight distribution of the punctured code $C^{\{t\}}$

Weight	Frequency
0	1
$3^{m-1} - 3^{\frac{m-1}{2}}$	$\frac{1}{2} \cdot \left(3^{m-1} + 2 \cdot 3^{\frac{m-1}{2}} - 1\right)\left(3^{m-1} + 3^{\frac{m-1}{2}}\right)$
$3^{m-1} - 3^{\frac{m-1}{2}} - 1$	$3^{m-1}(3^{m-1} - 1)$
3^{m-1}	$\left(2 \cdot 3^{m-1} + 1\right)\left(3^{m-1} - 1\right)$
$3^{m-1} - 1$	$2 \cdot 3^{m-1}\left(2 \cdot 3^{m-1} + 1\right)$
$3^{m-1} + 3^{\frac{m-1}{2}}$	$\frac{1}{2} \cdot \left(3^{m-1} - 2 \cdot 3^{\frac{m-1}{2}} - 1\right)\left(3^{m-1} - 3^{\frac{m-1}{2}}\right)$
$3^{m-1} + 3^{\frac{m-1}{2}} - 1$	$3^{m-1}(3^{m-1} - 1)$

Proof. It follows from Lemma 8.42 that $d(C^\perp) = 4$. According to Theorem 2.8, $C^{\{t\}}$ has length $n = \frac{3^m - 1}{2} - 1$ and dimension $k = 2m$. For $i \in \{3^{m-1} - 3^{\frac{m-1}{2}}, 3^{m-1}, 3^{m-1} + 3^{\frac{m-1}{2}}\}$, by the definition of $C^{\{t\}}$, we have

$$A_i(C^{\{t\}}) = A_i(C_{\{t\}})$$

and

$$A_{i-1}(C^{\{t\}}) = A_i(C) - A_i(C_{\{t\}}).$$

The desired conclusions then follow from Theorem 8.44. □

Example 8.50. Let $m = 5$, $E = \{0, 1\}$, $0 \leq t \leq \frac{3^m - 1}{2} - 1$ and $C = C(E)$. Then the punctured code $C^{\{t\}}$ has parameters $[120, 10, 71]$ and weight enumerator $1 + 6480z^{71} + 4410z^{72} + 26406z^{80} + 13040z^{81} + 6480z^{89} + 2232z^{90}$. This code has the same parameters as the best ternary linear code known in the database maintained by Markus Grassl.

All the punctured codes $C^{\{t\}}$ are equivalent, as the automorphism group of the code C is transitive.

Theorem 8.51. *Let t_1 and t_2 be two integers and $m \geq 3$ be odd, where $0 \leq t_1 < t_2 \leq \frac{3^m - 1}{2} - 1$. Let C be a subcode of $C\left(0, 1, \ldots, \lfloor \frac{m}{2} \rfloor\right)$ with the weight distribution in Table 8.5. Then, the punctured code $C^{\{t_1, t_2\}}$ is a ternary linear code of length $\frac{3^m - 1}{2} - 2$ and dimension $2m$, and has the weight distribution in Table 8.9.*

Table 8.9 The weight distribution of the punctured code $C^{\{t_1,t_2\}}$

Weight	Frequency
0	1
$3^{m-1}-3^{\frac{m-1}{2}}$	$\frac{1}{6}\cdot\left(3^{m-1}+2\cdot3^{\frac{m-1}{2}}-1\right)\left(3^{m-1}+3^{\frac{m+1}{2}}\right)$
$3^{m-1}-3^{\frac{m-1}{2}}-1$	$2\cdot3^{m-2}\left(3^{m-1}+2\cdot3^{\frac{m-1}{2}}-1\right)$
$3^{m-1}-3^{\frac{m-1}{2}}-2$	$2\cdot3^{m-2}\left(3^{m-1}-3^{\frac{m-1}{2}}-1\right)$
3^{m-1}	$\left(2\cdot3^{m-1}+1\right)\left(3^{m-2}-1\right)$
$3^{m-1}-1$	$4\cdot3^{m-2}\left(2\cdot3^{m-1}+1\right)$
$3^{m-1}-2$	$4\cdot3^{m-2}\left(2\cdot3^{m-1}+1\right)$
$3^{m-1}+3^{\frac{m-1}{2}}$	$\frac{1}{6}\cdot\left(3^{m-1}-2\cdot3^{\frac{m-1}{2}}-1\right)\left(3^{m-1}-3^{\frac{m+1}{2}}\right)$
$3^{m-1}+3^{\frac{m-1}{2}}-1$	$2\cdot3^{m-2}\left(3^{m-1}-2\cdot3^{\frac{m-1}{2}}-1\right)$
$3^{m-1}+3^{\frac{m-1}{2}}-2$	$2\cdot3^{m-2}\left(3^{m-1}+3^{\frac{m-1}{2}}-1\right)$

Proof. By Lemma 8.42, $d(C^{\perp})=4$. According to Theorem 2.8, $C^{\{t_1,t_2\}}$ has length $n=\frac{3^m-1}{2}-2$ and dimension $k=2m$. For $i\in\{3^{m-1}-3^{\frac{m-1}{2}},3^{m-1},3^{m-1}+3^{\frac{m-1}{2}}\}$, using the definition of $C^{\{t_1,t_2\}}$, we deduce that

$$\begin{cases} A_i(C^{\{t_1,t_2\}})=A_i(C_{\{t_1,t_2\}}), \\ A_{i-1}(C^{\{t_1,t_2\}})=A_i(C)-A_i(C_{\{t_1,t_2\}})-|W_i(C,\{t_1,t_2\})|, \\ A_{i-2}(C^{\{t_1,t_2\}})=|W_i(C,\{t_1,t_2\})|. \end{cases}$$

It then follows from Lemma 8.48 that

$$|W_i(C,\{t_1,t_2\})|=A_i(C)-2A_i(C_{\{0\}})+A_i(C_{\{0,1\}}).$$

The desired conclusions then follow from Theorems 8.44 and 8.46. $\qquad\square$

Example 8.52. Let $m=5$, $E=\{0,1\}$, $0\le t_1<t_2\le\frac{3^m-1}{2}-1$ and $C=C(E)$. Then the punctured code $C^{\{t_1,t_2\}}$ has parameters $[119,10,70]$ and weight enumerator $1+3834z^{70}+5292z^{71}+1764z^{72}+17604z^{79}+17604z^{80}+4238z^{81}+4806z^{88}+3348z^{89}+558z^{90}$. This code has the same parameters as the best ternary linear code known in the database maintained by Markus Grassl.

Our Magma experiments showed that for many different pairs of $\{t_1,t_2\}$ and $\{t_1',t_2'\}$, the punctured codes $C^{\{t_1,t_2\}}$ and $C^{\{t_1',t_2'\}}$ are not equivalent. Therefore, the automorphism group of the code C is in general not 2-homogeneous and 2-transitive.

8.5.4 *Steiner Systems and 2-Designs from $C(E)$*

In this section, we confirm Conjectures 1 and 2, and Conjecture 3 for $k\in\{4,5,6,7\}$. In addition, we construct more 2-designs from subcodes of $C\left(0,1,\ldots,\lfloor\frac{m}{2}\rfloor\right)$.

Let C be an $[n,k,d]$ linear code. Define

$$W_i(C) = \{\mathbf{c} \in C : \text{wt}(\mathbf{c}) = i\}, \quad 0 \leq i \leq n.$$

Theorem 8.53. *Let $m \geq 3$ be a positive integer and C a subcode of $C\left(0,1,\ldots,\lfloor\frac{m}{2}\rfloor\right)$ such that $A_4(C^{\perp}) = \frac{(3^m-1)(3^{m-1}-1)}{8}$. Then $(\mathcal{P}(C^{\perp}),\mathcal{B}_4(C^{\perp}))$ is the Steiner system $\text{PG}_1(m-1,\text{GF}(3))$ with parameters $S(2,4,\frac{3^m-1}{2})$.*

Proof. It is easily seen that $C\left(0,1,\ldots,\lfloor\frac{m}{2}\rfloor\right)^{\perp} \subseteq C^{\perp}$. Hence,

$$W_4\left(C\left(0,1,\ldots,\lfloor\frac{m}{2}\rfloor\right)^{\perp}\right) \subseteq W_4\left(C^{\perp}\right).$$

From Part (iv) of Theorem 8.39 and $A_4(C^{\perp}) = \frac{(3^m-1)(3^{m-1}-1)}{8}$, we have $W_4\left(C\left(0,1,\ldots,\lfloor\frac{m}{2}\rfloor\right)^{\perp}\right) = W_4\left(C^{\perp}\right)$ and $\mathcal{B}_4\left(C^{\perp}\right) = \mathcal{B}_4\left(C\left(0,1,\ldots,\lfloor\frac{m}{2}\rfloor\right)^{\perp}\right)$. The conclusions of this theorem finally follow from Part (iii) of Theorem 8.39. $\square$

Corollary 8.54. *Let $m \geq 3$ be an odd integer and C a subcode of $C\left(0,1,\ldots,\lfloor\frac{m}{2}\rfloor\right)$ with the weight distribution in Table 8.5. If C' is a linear code such that $C \subseteq C' \subseteq C\left(0,1,\ldots,\lfloor\frac{m}{2}\rfloor\right)$, then $(\mathcal{P}(C'^{\perp}),\mathcal{B}_4(C'^{\perp}))$ is the Steiner system $\text{PG}_1(m-1,\text{GF}(3))$ with parameters $S(2,4,\frac{3^m-1}{2})$.*

Proof. Note that $W_4\left(C\left(0,1,\ldots,\lfloor\frac{m}{2}\rfloor\right)^{\perp}\right) \subseteq W_4\left(C'^{\perp}\right) \subseteq W_4\left(C^{\perp}\right)$. From Part (iv) of Theorem 8.39 and Lemma 8.42, we then deduce that $A_4(C'^{\perp}) = \frac{(3^m-1)(3^{m-1}-1)}{8}$. From Theorem 8.53, this corollary follows. $\square$

Corollary 8.54 confirmed Conjecture 8.35, and proved that the Steiner system $\text{PG}_1(m-1,\text{GF}(3))$ is supported by many ternary linear codes. It is an interesting problem to find a linear code that supports a given design [Assmus (1995); Jung-nickel, Magliveras, Tonchev and Wassermann (2017); Jungnickel and Tonchev (2018, 2019)]. This is in general a hard problem. In addition, Corollary 8.54 says that the duals of many subcodes of $C\left(0,1,\ldots,\lfloor\frac{m}{2}\rfloor\right)$ do not support a new Steiner system, but the geometric Steiner system $\text{PG}_1(m-1,\text{GF}(3))$ It is known that an $S(2,4,v)$ exists if and only if $v \equiv 1,4 \pmod{12}$ [Hanani (1975)]. It is open if the geometric Steiner system $\text{PG}_1(m-1,\text{GF}(3))$ was discovered before the work of Hanani (1975).

Let $\mathbb{D}$ be a t-(v,k,λ) design. For a majority decoding of the code $C_q(\mathbb{D})^{\perp}$, Tonchev introduced the *dimension* of $\mathbb{D}$ over $\text{GF}(q)$, which is defined to be the minimum dimension of all linear codes of length v over $\text{GF}(q)$ that contain the blocks of $\mathbb{D}$ as the supports of codewords of weight k [Tonchecv (1999)]. When $q = 2$, the dimension of $\mathbb{D}$ over $\text{GF}(q)$ is the same as the rank of $\mathbb{D}$ over $\text{GF}(q)$.

When $q > 2$, the rank of $\mathbb{D}$ over GF(q) is an upper bound of the dimension of $\mathbb{D}$ over GF(q). Since $C\left(0,1,\ldots,\lfloor\frac{m}{2}\rfloor\right)$ has dimension $m(m+1)/2$, its dual has dimension $(3^m - 1 - m(m+1))/2$. As a result, the dimension of PG$_1(m-1,\text{GF}(3))$ over GF(3) is upper bounded by $(3^m - 1 - m(m+1))/2$. Then the following open problem arises.

Problem 8.55. Is the dimension of the Steiner system PG$_1(m-1,\text{GF}(3))$ over GF(3) equal to $(3^m - 1 - m(m+1))/2$.

The p-rank of the design PG$_1(m-1,\text{GF}(p))$ was computed in Hamada (1973), and was also given in Theorem 4.42. In particular, the 3-rank of the Steiner system PG$_1(m-1,\text{GF}(3))$ is $(3^m - 3)/2$. Hence, the upper bound $(3^m - 1 - m(m+1))/2$ on the dimension of PG$_1(m-1,\text{GF}(3))$ over GF(3) is much better than the upper bound from the 3-rank of PG$_1(m-1,\text{GF}(3))$. This shows another interesting aspect of Theorem 8.53 and Corollary 8.54.

To determine the parameters of some t-designs, we will need the following lemma which is a special case of Lemma 4.25.

Lemma 8.56. *Let C be a linear code over* GF(3) *with minimum weight d. Let $\mathbf{c}$ and $\mathbf{c}'$ be two codewords of weight i and* Supp($\mathbf{c}$) = Supp($\mathbf{c}'$), *where $d \leq i \leq 2d - 1$. Then $\mathbf{c}' = \mathbf{c}$ or $\mathbf{c}' = -\mathbf{c}$.*

Theorem 8.57. *Let $m \geq 5$ be an odd integer and let C be a subcode of $C\left(0,1,\ldots,\lfloor\frac{m}{2}\rfloor\right)$ with the weight distribution in Table 8.5. Let k be an element of the set $\left\{3^{m-1} - 3^{\frac{m-1}{2}}, 3^{m-1}, 3^{m-1} + 3^{\frac{m-1}{2}}\right\}$. Then $(\mathcal{P}(C), \mathcal{B}_k(C))$ is a 2-$\left(\frac{3^m-1}{2}, k, \lambda\right)$ design, where*

$$\lambda = \frac{A_k(C) + A_k\left(C_{\{0,1\}}\right)}{2} - A_k\left(C_{\{0\}}\right).$$

Proof. Let $k \in \left\{3^{m-1} - 3^{\frac{m-1}{2}}, 3^{m-1}, 3^{m-1} + 3^{\frac{m-1}{2}}\right\}$ and assume that $0 \leq i < j \leq \frac{3^m-1}{2} - 1$. Define

$$\mathcal{B}_k(C, \{i,j\}) = \{\text{Supp}(\mathbf{c}) : \mathbf{c} \in W_k(C, \{i,j\})\},$$

where $W_k(C, \{i,j\})$ was defined in Lemma 8.48. Since $m \geq 5$, we have $k \leq 2 \cdot \left(3^{m-1} - 3^{\frac{m-1}{2}}\right) - 1$. From Lemma 8.56, we get

$$|\mathcal{B}_k(C, \{i,j\})| = \frac{1}{2}|W_k(C, \{i,j\})|.$$

Using Theorems 8.44, 8.46 and Lemma 8.48, we obtain

$$|\mathcal{B}_k(C, \{i,j\})| = \frac{A_k(C) + A_k\left(C_{\{0,1\}}\right)}{2} - A_k\left(C_{\{0\}}\right).$$

Therefore, $|\mathcal{B}_k(C,\{i,j\})|$ is independent of i and j. Consequently, the codewords of weight k hold a 2-design. This completes the proof. $\qquad\square$

Corollary 8.58. *Let $m \geq 5$ be an odd integer and C a subcode of $C\left(0,1,\ldots,\lfloor\frac{m}{2}\rfloor\right)$ with the weight distribution in Table 8.5. Then C holds three 2-$(\frac{3^m-1}{2},k,\lambda)$ designs with the following pairs (k,λ):*

- $\left(3^{m-1} - 3^{\frac{m-1}{2}}, 3^{m-2}\left(3^{m-1} - 3^{\frac{m-1}{2}} - 1\right)\right)$.
- $\left(3^{m-1}, 2 \cdot 3^{m-2}\left(2 \cdot 3^{m-1} + 1\right)\right)$.
- $\left(3^{m-1} + 3^{\frac{m-1}{2}}, 3^{m-2}\left(3^{m-1} + 3^{\frac{m-1}{2}} - 1\right)\right)$.

Proof. From Theorems 8.44 , 8.46, and 8.57, this corollary follows. Alternatively, the conclusions of this corollary follow from Theorem 8.57 and Lemma 8.56. $\quad\square$

Remark 8.59. Theorem 8.57 confirmed Conjecture 8.34, and extends Conjecture 8.34 if more subcodes of $C\left(0,1,\ldots,\lfloor\frac{m}{2}\rfloor\right)$ with the weight distribution in Table 8.5 exist.

Lemma 8.60. *Let $m \geq 3$ be an odd integer and C a subcode of $C\left(0,1,\ldots,\lfloor\frac{m}{2}\rfloor\right)$ with the weight distribution in Table 8.5. Let $A = (3^m - 1)(3^m - 3)$ and $\lambda_k^{\perp} = \frac{2k(k-1)A_k(C^{\perp})}{(3^m-1)(3^m-3)}$ with $0 \leq k \leq \frac{3^m-1}{2} - 1$. Then, $\left(A_k(C^{\perp}),\lambda_k^{\perp}\right)$ is given in Table 8.10, where $k \in \{4,5,6,7\}$.*

Table 8.10 $A_k(C^{\perp})$ and $\lambda_k^{\perp}$ for $4 \leq k \leq 7$

k	$\lambda_k^{\perp}$	$A_k(C^{\perp})$
4	1	$\frac{1}{8}A$
5	$3^{m-1} - 9$	$\frac{1}{40}A\lambda_5^{\perp}$
6	$\frac{3}{4}\left(3^{2m-2} - 38 \cdot 3^{m-2} + 53\right)$	$\frac{1}{60}A\lambda_6^{\perp}$
7	$\frac{1}{20}\left(3^{3m-2} - 5 \cdot 3^{2m} + 1006 \cdot 3^{m-2} - 1000\right)$	$\frac{1}{84}A\lambda_7^{\perp}$

Proof. The desired conclusions follow from Lemma 8.42. $\qquad\square$

Theorem 8.61. *Let $m \geq 5$ be an odd integer and C a subcode of $C\left(0,1,\ldots,\lfloor\frac{m}{2}\rfloor\right)$ with the weight distribution in Table 8.5. Let $k \in \{4,5,6,7\}$. Then the incidence structure $\left(\mathcal{P}(C^{\perp}),\mathcal{B}_k(C^{\perp})\right)$ is a 2-$(\frac{3^m-1}{2},k,\lambda_k^{\perp})$ design, where $\lambda_k^{\perp}$ is given in Table 8.10.*

Proof. Let $4 \leq k \leq 7$ and $0 \leq i < j \leq \frac{3^m-1}{2} - 1$. Define

$$\mathcal{B}_k\left(C^{\perp},\{i,j\}\right) = \left\{\mathrm{Supp}(\mathbf{c}) : \mathbf{c} \in W_k\left(C^{\perp},\{i,j\}\right)\right\},$$

where $W_k \left(C^\perp, \{i, j\} \right)$ was defined in Lemma 8.48. It follows from Lemma 8.42 that $d(C^\perp) = 4$ and $k \leq 2d(C^\perp) - 1$. From Lemma 8.56, we get

$$\left| \mathcal{B}_k \left(C^\perp, \{i, j\} \right) \right| = \frac{1}{2} \left| W_k \left(C^\perp, \{i, j\} \right) \right|.$$

Using the inclusion-exclusion principle, one has

$$\left| W_k \left(C^\perp, \{i, j\} \right) \right|$$

$$= A_k \left(C^\perp \right) - A_k \left(\left(C^\perp \right)_{\{i\}} \right) - A_k \left(\left(C^\perp \right)_{\{j\}} \right) + A_k \left(\left(C^\perp \right)_{\{i, j\}} \right). \quad (8.25)$$

From Theorems 8.49 and 8.51, for any $0 \leq i \leq \frac{3^m - 1}{2} - 1$, one has

$$A_i \left(C^{\{j_0\}} \right) = A_i \left(C^{\{0\}} \right), \ A_i \left(C^{\{j_0, j_1\}} \right) = A_i \left(C^{\{0, 1\}} \right).$$

Using the MacWilliams Identity, one gets

$$A_i \left(\left(C^{\{j_0\}} \right)^\perp \right) = A_i \left(\left(C^{\{0\}} \right)^\perp \right), \ A_i \left(\left(C^{\{j_0, j_1\}} \right)^\perp \right) = A_i \left(\left(C^{\{0, 1\}} \right)^\perp \right),$$

where $0 \leq i \leq \frac{3^m - 1}{2} - 1$. From (8.24), $(C^\perp)_{\{T\}} = (C^T)^\perp$ for any $T \subseteq \{0, 1, \ldots, \frac{3^m - 1}{2} - 1\}$. Thus,

$$A_i \left(\left(C^\perp \right)_{\{j_0\}} \right) = A_i \left(\left(C^\perp \right)_{\{0\}} \right), \ A_i \left(\left(C^\perp \right)_{\{j_0, j_1\}} \right) = A_i \left(\left(C^\perp \right)_{\{0, 1\}} \right),$$

where $0 \leq i \leq \frac{3^m - 1}{2} - 1$. From (8.25), one obtains

$$\left| W_k \left(C^\perp, \{i, j\} \right) \right| = A_k \left(C^\perp \right) - 2 A_k \left(\left(C^\perp \right)_{\{0\}} \right) + A_k \left(\left(C^\perp \right)_{\{0, 1\}} \right).$$

Then,

$$\left| \mathcal{B}_k \left(C^\perp, \{j_0, j_1\} \right) \right| = \frac{A_k \left(C^\perp \right) + A_k \left(\left(C^\perp \right)_{\{0, 1\}} \right)}{2} - A_k \left(\left(C^\perp \right)_{\{0\}} \right).$$

Therefore, $\left| \mathcal{B}_k \left(C^\perp, \{j_0, j_1\} \right) \right|$ is independent of j_0 and j_1. Hence, the codewords of weight k hold a 2-$(\frac{2^m - 1}{3}, k, \lambda_k^\perp)$ design with $A_k \left(C^\perp \right)$ blocks. Thus,

$$\lambda_k^\perp = \frac{2k(k - 1) A_k \left(C^\perp \right)}{(3^m - 1)(3^m - 3)}.$$

The desired conclusions finally follow from Lemma 8.60. $\qquad \square$

Remark 8.62. Theorem 8.61 confirmed Conjecture 8.36 for $k = 4, 5, 6$ and 7.

8.6 Notes

All the results of Section 8.5 come from Tang, Ding and Xiong (2019), and are one of the major motivations of the development of a generalized Assmus-Mattson theorem documented in Theorem 16.28 of Chapter 16. The ideas and tools of this section are useful for understanding the theory in Chapter 16. Recent works related to some topics in this chapter were reported in Ding and Tang (2020).

Chapter 9

Designs from BCH Codes

In this chapter, we first introduce a general theorem about 2-designs from narrow-sense primitive BCH codes and then determine the parameters of 2-designs from some classes of binary primitive BCH codes. It should be noted that the Assmus-Mattson Theorem does not apply to most of the codes in this chapter. We have to use the automorphism groups of these BCH codes, in order to prove that they hold designs. In the last section of this chapter, we present several families of conjectured designs from extended narrow-sense BCH codes. Most of the materials presented in this chapter are from Ding and Zhou (2017).

9.1 A General Theorem on Designs from Primitive BCH Codes

Let b denote the number of blocks in a t-(v,k,λ) design. Recall that

$$b = \lambda \frac{\binom{v}{t}}{\binom{k}{t}}. \tag{9.1}$$

Let C be a $[v, \kappa, d]$ code over $\mathrm{GF}(q)$. For each integer k with $A_k \neq 0$, let $\mathcal{B}_k$ denote the set of the supports of all codewords with Hamming weight k in C, where the coordinates of a codeword are indexed by $(0, 1, 2, \ldots, v - 1)$. Let $\mathcal{P} = \{0, 1, 2, \ldots, v - 1\}$. The pair $(\mathcal{P}, \mathcal{B}_k)$ may be a t-(v,k,λ) design for some positive integer λ. Such a design is called a support t-design of the code C. In this case, we say that C holds a t-(v,k,λ) design.

Recall the binary primitive BCH code $C_{(2,n,\delta,h)}$ defined in Section 7.1, where $n = 2^m - 1$, $2 \leq \delta \leq n$ and h could be any integer. We first develop some general results on the automorphism group of the binary primitive BCH code $C_{(2,n,\delta,h)}$. Since the code is binary, we have

$$\mathrm{PAut}(C_{(2,n,\delta,h)}) = \mathrm{MAut}(C_{(2,n,\delta,h)}) = \mathrm{Aut}(C_{(2,n,\delta,h)}).$$

Theorem 9.1. Let $q^m - 1 \geq \delta \geq 2$. The supports of all codewords of each weight in the extended narrow-sense primitive BCH code $\overline{C_{(q,q^m-1,\delta,1)}}$ form a 2-design.

Proof. The desired conclusion follows from Corollary 6.12 and Theorem 4.30.

$\square$

Theorem 9.2. *Let* $\delta \geq 2$. *The supports of all codewords of each weight in the dual code* $\overline{C_{(2,2^m-1,\delta,1)}}^{\perp}$ *form a 2-design.*

Proof. It follows from Corollary 6.12 and Theorem 2.14 that the permutation automorphism group $\mathrm{PAut}(\overline{C_{(2,2^m-1,\delta,1)}}^{\perp})$ is doubly transitive. The desired conclusion then follows from Theorem 4.30.

$\square$

9.2   Designs from the Primitive BCH Codes $C_{(2,2^m-1,\delta_2,1)}$

With the help of Theorem 9.1, we now describe several families of 2-designs from the narrow-sense primitive binary codes $C_{(2,2^m-1,\delta_2,1)}$, where $\delta_2 = 2^{m-1} - 1 - 2^{\lfloor (m-1)/2 \rfloor}$.

Table 9.1   The weight distribution of the code $\overline{C_{(2,2^m-1,\delta_2,1)}}$ for odd m

Weight w	No. of codewords A_w
0	1
$2^{m-1} - 2^{(m-1)/2}$	$(2^m - 1)2^{m-1}$
2^{m-1}	$2(2^m - 1)(2^{m-1} + 1)$
$2^{m-1} + 2^{(m-1)/2}$	$(2^m - 1)2^{m-1}$
2^m	1

Table 9.2   The weight distribution of the code $\overline{C_{(2,2^m-1,\delta_2,1)}}$ for even m

Weight w	No. of codewords A_w
0	1
$2^{m-1} - 2^{(m-2)/2}$	$(2^{m/2} - 1)2^m$
2^{m-1}	$2(2^m - 1)$
$2^{m-1} + 2^{(m-2)/2}$	$(2^{m/2} - 1)2^m$
2^m	1

Theorem 9.3. *Let* $m \geq 3$ *be an integer. Let* $\overline{C_{(2,2^m-1,\delta_2,1)}}$ *denote the extended code of* $C_{(2,2^m-1,\delta_2,1)}$. *Then for odd* m, $\overline{C_{(2,2^m-1,\delta_2,1)}}$ *holds* 2-$(2^m, k, \lambda)$ *designs with the following pairs of* (k, λ):

- $(k, \lambda) = \left(2^{m-1} - 2^{(m-1)/2}, (2^{m-2} - 2^{(m-3)/2})(2^{m-1} - 2^{(m-1)/2} - 1) \right)$.
- $(k, \lambda) = \left(2^{m-1}, 2^{2(m-1)} - 1 \right)$.

- $(k,\lambda) = \left(2^{m-1}+2^{(m-1)/2}, (2^{m-2}+2^{(m-3)/2})(2^{m-1}+2^{(m-1)/2}-1)\right)$.

For even m, it holds $2\text{-}(2^m,k,\lambda)$ *designs with the following pairs of* (k,λ):

- $(k,\lambda) = \left(2^{m-1}-2^{(m-2)/2}, (2^{m-1}-2^{(m-2)/2})(2^{(m-2)/2}-1)\right)$.
- $(k,\lambda) = \left(2^{m-1}, 2^{m-1}-1\right)$.
- $(k,\lambda) = \left(2^{m-1}+2^{(m-2)/2}, 2^{(m-2)/2}(2^{m-1}+2^{(m-2)/2}-1)\right)$.

Proof. Recall that the weight distribution of $C_{(2,2^m-1,\delta_2,1)}$ is given in Tables 7.6 and 7.7 for odd and even m, respectively. We first determine the parameters of the code $\overline{C_{(2,2^m-1,\delta_2,1)}}$. It follows from the definition of the extended code and Theorem 7.8 that the length of the code is 2^m, the dimension $\overline{k}$ is given by

$$\overline{k} = \begin{cases} 2m+1 & \text{for odd } m, \\ \frac{3m}{2}+1 & \text{for even } m, \end{cases} \tag{9.2}$$

and the weight distribution is given in Tables 9.1 and 9.2 for odd m and even m, respectively. The desired conclusions then follow from the weight distribution of the code, Theorem 9.1 and (9.1). $\qquad\square$

Theorem 9.2 tells us that the code $\overline{C_{(2,2^m-1,\delta_2,1)}}^{\perp}$ holds also 2-designs for both even and odd m. We will prove that the support designs of the code $\overline{C_{(2,2^m-1,\delta_2,1)}}^{\perp}$ are in fact 3-designs.

Theorem 9.4. *Let* $m \geq 5$ *be an odd integer. Then* $\overline{C_{(2,2^m-1,\delta_2,1)}}^{\perp}$ *has parameters* $[2^m, 2^m-2m-1,6]$. *Let* $\overline{A}_i^{\perp}$ *denote the number of codewords with weight i in* $\overline{C_{(2,2^m-1,\delta_2,1)}}^{\perp}$ *for all* $0 \leq i \leq 2^m$. *Then for every i with* $\overline{A}_i^{\perp} \neq 0$, *the supports of the codewords with weight i in this code form a* $3\text{-}(2^m,i,\lambda)$ *design with*

$$\lambda = \frac{\overline{A}_i^{\perp}\binom{i}{3}}{\binom{2^m}{3}},$$

where these $\overline{A}_i^{\perp}$ *are given in Lemma 8.8.*

Proof. Let $\overline{d}^{\perp}$ denote the minimum weight in $\overline{C_{(2,2^m-1,\delta_2,1)}}^{\perp}$. It then follows from Lemma 8.8 that $\overline{d}^{\perp}=6$. Then the desired conclusions follow from Corollary 4.26 (i.e., the Assmus-Mattson Theorem), Table 9.1 and (9.1). $\qquad\square$

Notice that the parameters of examples of the 3-designs documented in Theorem 9.4 are given in Section 8.1.

To determine the parameters of some of the 2-designs held in $\overline{C_{(2,2^m-1,\delta_2,1)}}^{\perp}$ for even m, we need to determine the weight distribution of the code for even m.

Lemma 9.5. *Let $m \geq 4$ be even. Then the weight distribution of $\overline{C_{(2,2^m-1,\delta_2,1)}}^{\perp}$ is given by*

$$2^{(3m+2)/2}\overline{A}_k^{\perp} =$$

$$(1+(-1)^k)\binom{2^m}{k} + \frac{1+(-1)^k}{2}(-1)^{\lfloor k/2 \rfloor}\binom{2^{m-1}}{\lfloor k/2 \rfloor}v +$$

$$u \sum_{\substack{0 \leq i < 2^{m-1}-2^{(m-2)/2} \\ 0 \leq j < 2^{m-1}+2^{(m-2)/2} \\ i+j=k}} ((-1)^i+(-1)^j)\binom{2^{m-1}-2^{\frac{m-2}{2}}}{i}\binom{2^{m-1}+2^{\frac{m-2}{2}}}{j}$$

for $0 \leq k \leq 2^m$, where

$$u = (2^{m/2}-1)2^m \text{ and } v = 2^{m+1}-2.$$

In addition, $\overline{C_{(2,2^m-1,\delta_2,1)}}^{\perp}$ has parameters $[2^m, 2^m-1-3m/2, 4]$.

Proof. With the weight distribution of $\overline{C_{(2,2^m-1,\delta_2,1)}}$ given in Table 9.2, one can prove the desired conclusions by slightly modifying the proof of Lemma 8.8. The details are left to the reader. $\qquad\square$

Theorem 9.6. *Let $m \geq 4$ be an even integer. Let $\overline{A}_i^{\perp}$ denote the number of codewords with weight i in $\overline{C_{(2,2^m-1,\delta_2,1)}}^{\perp}$ for all $0 \leq i \leq 2^m$. Then for every i with $\overline{A}_i^{\perp} \neq 0$, the supports of the codewords with weight i in this code form a $2\text{-}(2^m, i, \lambda)$ design with*

$$\lambda = \frac{\overline{A}_i^{\perp}\binom{i}{2}}{\binom{2^m}{2}},$$

where these $\overline{A}_i^{\perp}$ are given in Lemma 9.5.

Proof. The desired conclusions follow from Theorem 9.2 and (9.1). $\qquad\square$

Corollary 9.7. *Let $m \geq 4$ be an even integer. Then the supports of all codewords of weight 4 in $\overline{C_{(2,2^m-1,\delta_2,1)}}^{\perp}$ give a $2\text{-}(2^m, 4, 2^{(m-2)/2}-1)$ design.*

Proof. By Lemma 9.5, we have

$$\overline{A}_4^{\perp} = \frac{2^{m-2}(2^{(m-2)/2}-1)(2^m-1)}{3}.$$

The desired conclusions then follow from Theorem 9.6. $\qquad\square$

Corollary 9.8. *Let $m \geq 4$ be an even integer. Then the supports of all codewords of weight 6 in $\overline{C_{(2,2^m-1,\delta_2,1)}}^{\perp}$ give a 2-$(2^m, 6, \lambda)$ design, where*

$$\lambda = \frac{(2^{m-1}-2)(2^{(3m-4)/2} - 5 \times 2^{(m-2)/2} + 4)}{3}.$$

Proof. By Lemma 9.5, we have

$$\overline{A}_6^{\perp} = \frac{2^m(2^m-1)(2^{m-2}-1)(2^{(3m-4)/2} - 5 \times 2^{(m-2)/2} + 4)}{45}.$$

The desired conclusions then follow from Theorem 9.6. □

Corollary 9.9. *Let $m \geq 4$ be an even integer. Then the supports of all codewords of weight 8 in $\overline{C_{(2,2^m-1,\delta_2,1)}}^{\perp}$ give a 2-$(2^m, 8, \lambda)$ design, where*

$$\lambda = \frac{(h^2-1)(32h^7 - 184h^5 + 406h^3 - 132h^2 - 308h + 213)}{45}$$

and $h = 2^{(m-2)/2}$.

Proof. By Lemma 9.5, we have

$$\overline{A}_8^{\perp} = \frac{h^2(h^2-1)(4h^2-1)(32h^7 - 184h^5 + 406h^3 - 132h^2 - 308h + 213)}{630},$$

where $h = 2^{(m-2)/2}$. The desired conclusions follow from Theorem 9.6. □

It would be interesting to settle the following problem.

Problem 9.10. Determine the weight distribution of the code $\overline{C_{(q,q^m-1,\delta_2,1)}}$ and the parameters of the 2-designs held in this code, where $q = 2^s$ with $s \geq 2$.

9.3 Designs from the Primitive BCH Codes $C_{(q,q^m-1,\delta_2,1)}$ for Odd Prime q

With the help of Theorem 9.1, we now describe several families of 2-designs from the narrow-sense primitive nonbinary codes $C_{(q,q^m-1,\delta_2,1)}$, where $\delta_2 = (q-1)q^{m-1} - 1 - q^{\lfloor (m-1)/2 \rfloor}$ and q is an odd prime.

Theorem 9.11. *Let $m \geq 2$ be an integer and let q be an odd prime. Let $\overline{C_{(q,q^m-1,\delta_2,1)}}$ denote the extended code of $C_{(q,q^m-1,\delta_2,1)}$. Then for odd m, $\overline{C_{(q,q^m-1,\delta_2,1)}}$ holds 2-(q^m, k, λ) designs with the following pairs of (k,λ):*

- $(k,\lambda) = \left((q-1)q^{m-1} - q^{\frac{m-1}{2}}, \frac{((q-1)q^{m-1} - q^{\frac{m-1}{2}})((q-1)q^{m-1} - q^{\frac{m-1}{2}} - 1)}{2}\right)$.
- $(k,\lambda) = \left((q-1)q^{m-1}, (q^{m-1}+1)((q-1)q^{m-1} - 1)\right)$.

Table 9.3   Weight distribution of $\overline{C_{(q,q^m-1,\delta_2,1)}}$ for odd $m \geq 3$ and odd q

Weight w	No. of codewords A_w
0	1
$(q-1)q^{m-1} - q^{(m-1)/2}$	$(q-1)q^m(q^m-1)/2$
$(q-1)q^{m-1}$	$(q^m+q)(q^m-1)$
$(q-1)q^{m-1} + q^{(m-1)/2}$	$(q-1)q^m(q^m-1)/2$
q^m	$q-1$

Table 9.4   Weight distribution of $\overline{C_{(q,q^m-1,\delta_2,1)}}$ for even $m \geq 2$ and odd q

Weight w	No. of codewords A_w
0	1
$(q-1)q^{m-1} - q^{(m-2)/2}$	$(q-1)(q^{3m/2} - q^m)$
$(q-1)q^{m-1}$	$q^{m+1} - q$
$(q-1)q^{m-1} + (q-1)q^{(m-2)/2}$	$q^{3m/2} - q^m$
q^m	$q-1$

- $(k,\lambda) = \left((q-1)q^{m-1} + q^{\frac{m-1}{2}}, \frac{((q-1)q^{m-1}+q^{\frac{m-1}{2}})((q-1)q^{m-1}+q^{\frac{m-1}{2}}-1)}{2} \right).$

For even $m \geq 2$, it holds 2-(q^m,k,λ) designs with the following pairs of (k,λ):

- $(k,\lambda) = \left((q-1)q^{m-1} - q^{\frac{m-2}{2}}, ((q-1)q^{m-1} - q^{\frac{m-2}{2}})(q^{\frac{m}{2}} - q^{\frac{m-2}{2}} - 1) \right).$
- $(k,\lambda) = \left((q-1)q^{m-1}, (q-1)q^{m-1} - 1 \right).$
- $(k,\lambda) = \left((q-1)(q^{m-1} + q^{\frac{m-2}{2}}), q^{\frac{m-2}{2}}\left((q-1)(q^{m-1} + q^{\frac{m-2}{2}}) - 1 \right) \right).$

Proof. We sketch a proof below. The details of the proof are left to the reader. By refining the analysis in Section 7.3, one can determine the weight distribution of the code $C_{(q,q^m-1,\delta_2,1)}$, which contains $C_{(q,q^m-1,\delta_2+1,0)}$ as a subcode. With the derived weight distribution of $C_{(q,q^m-1,\delta_2,1)}$, one can prove that the code $\overline{C_{(q,q^m-1,\delta_2,1)}}$ has the weight distribution in Tables 9.3 and 9.4 for odd and even m, respectively.

With the help of Lemma 4.25, one can then prove that in the code $\overline{C_{(q,q^m-1,\delta_2,1)}}$ the number of supports of all codewords with weight $k \neq 0$ is equal to $\overline{A}_k/(q-1)$ for each k, where $\overline{A}_k$ denotes the total number of codewords with weight k in $\overline{C_{(q,q^m-1,\delta_2,1)}}$. Then the desired conclusions follow from the weight distribution of the code, Theorem 9.1 and (9.1). □

Experimental data indicates that the code $\overline{C_{(q,q^m-1,\delta_2,1)}}^{\perp}$ holds also 2-designs for both even and odd m. However, the Assmus-Mattson Theorem may not give a proof of the 2-design property, as $\overline{C_{(q,q^m-1,\delta_2,1)}}^{\perp}$ has minimum distance 4 in some cases. To settle this problem in general, we need find out the automorphism group of the code $\overline{C_{(q,q^m-1,\delta_2,1)}}^{\perp}$.

Problem 9.12. Determine the automorphism group $\mathrm{Aut}(\overline{C_{(q,q^m-1,\delta_2,1)}}^{\perp})$. Prove or disprove that $\mathrm{Aut}(\overline{C_{(q,q^m-1,\delta_2,1)}}^{\perp})$ is doubly transitive.

9.4 Designs from the Primitive BCH Codes $C_{(2,2^m-1,\delta_3,1)}$

With the help of Theorem 9.1, we now describe several families of 2-designs from the narrow-sense primitive binary code $C_{(2,2^m-1,\delta_3,1)}$, where $\delta_3 = 2^{m-1} - 1 - 2^{\lfloor (m+1)/2 \rfloor}$.

Table 9.5　The weight distribution of $\overline{C_{(2,2^m-1,\delta_3,1)}}$ for odd m

Weight w	No. of codewords A_w
0	1
$2^{m-1} - 2^{(m+1)/2}$	$(2^m-1)2^{m-3}(2^{m-1}-1)/3$
$2^{m-1} - 2^{(m-1)/2}$	$(2^m-1)2^{m-1}(5 \cdot 2^{m-1}+4)/3$
2^{m-1}	$2(2^m-1)(9 \cdot 2^{2m-4}+3 \cdot 2^{m-3}+1)$
$2^{m-1} + 2^{(m-1)/2}$	$(2^m-1)2^{m-1}(5 \cdot 2^{m-1}+4)/3$
$2^{m-1} + 2^{(m+1)/2}$	$(2^m-1)2^{m-3}(2^{m-1}-1)/3$
2^m	1

Table 9.6　The weight distribution of $\overline{C_{(2,2^m-1,\delta_3,1)}}$ for even m

Weight w	No. of codewords A_w
0	1
$2^{m-1} - 2^{m/2}$	$(2^{m/2}-1)2^{m-2}(2^{m+1}+2^{m/2}-1)/3$
$2^{m-1} - 2^{(m-2)/2}$	$(2^{m/2}-1)2^m(2^m+2^{(m+2)/2}+4)/3$
2^{m-1}	$2(2^{m/2}-1)(2^{2m-1}+2^{(3m-4)/2}-2^{m-2}+2^{m/2}+1)$
$2^{m-1} + 2^{(m-2)/2}$	$(2^{m/2}-1)2^m(2^m+2^{(m+2)/2}+4)/3$
$2^{m-1} + 2^{m/2}$	$(2^{m/2}-1)2^{m-2}(2^{m+1}+2^{m/2}-1)/3$
2^m	1

Theorem 9.13. *Let $m \geq 4$ be an integer. Let $\overline{C_{(2,2^m-1,\delta_3,1)}}$ denote the extended code of $C_{(2,2^m-1,\delta_3,1)}$. Then for odd m, $\overline{C_{(2,2^m-1,\delta_3,1)}}$ holds 2-$(2^m,k,\lambda)$ designs with the following pairs of (k,λ):*

- $\left(2^{m-1}-2^{\frac{m+1}{2}}, (2^{m-1}-1)(2^{m-4}-2^{\frac{m-5}{2}})(2^{m-1}-2^{\frac{m+1}{2}}-1)/3\right)$.
- $\left(2^{m-1}-2^{\frac{m-1}{2}}, (5 \cdot 2^{m-1}+4)(2^{m-2}-2^{\frac{m-3}{2}})(2^{m-1}-2^{\frac{m-1}{2}}-1)/3\right)$.
- $\left(2^{m-1}, (2^{m-1}-1)(9 \cdot 2^{2m-4}+3 \cdot 2^{m-3}+1)\right)$.

- $\left(2^{m-1}+2^{\frac{m-1}{2}}, (5\cdot 2^{m-1}+4)(2^{m-2}+2^{\frac{m-3}{2}})(2^{m-1}+2^{\frac{m-1}{2}}-1)/3\right).$
- $\left(2^{m-1}+2^{\frac{m+1}{2}}, (2^{m-1}-1)(2^{m-4}+2^{\frac{m-5}{2}})(2^{m-1}+2^{\frac{m+1}{2}}-1)/3\right).$

For even m, it holds 2-$(2^m, k, \lambda)$ designs with the following pairs of (k, λ):

- $\left(2^{m-1}-2^{\frac{m}{2}}, (2^{\frac{m+2}{2}}-1)(2^{m-3}-2^{\frac{m-4}{2}})(2^{m-1}-2^{\frac{m}{2}}-1)/3\right).$
- $\left(2^{m-1}-2^{\frac{m-2}{2}}, (2^m+2^{\frac{m+2}{2}}+4)(2^{m-1}-2^{\frac{m-2}{2}})(2^{\frac{m-2}{2}}-1)/3\right).$
- $\left(2^{m-1}, ((2^{\frac{m+2}{2}}-1)2^{m-2}+1)(2^{m-1}-1)\right).$
- $\left(2^{m-1}+2^{\frac{m-2}{2}}, (2^m+2^{\frac{m+2}{2}}+4)(2^{m-1}+2^{\frac{m-2}{2}}-1)2^{\frac{m-2}{2}}/3\right).$
- $\left(2^{m-1}+2^{\frac{m}{2}}, (2^{\frac{m+2}{2}}-1)(2^{m-3}+2^{\frac{m-4}{2}})(2^{m-1}+2^{\frac{m}{2}}-1)/3\right).$

Proof. We first determine the parameters of the code $\overline{C_{(2,2^m-1,\delta_3,1)}}$. It follows from the definition of the extended code and Theorem 7.21 that the length of the code is 2^m, the dimension $\overline{k}$ is given by

$$\overline{k} = \begin{cases} 3m+1 & \text{for odd } m, \\ \frac{5m}{2}+1 & \text{for even } m, \end{cases} \tag{9.3}$$

and the weight distribution is given in Tables 9.5 and 9.6 for odd m and even m, respectively. The desired conclusions then follow from the weight distribution of the code, Theorem 9.1 and (9.1). $\qquad\square$

If m is odd, $\overline{C_{(2,2^m-1,\delta_3,1)}}^{\perp}$ has the same parameters and weight distribution as the code $\overline{C_m^{\perp}}$ in Theorem 8.16. Hence, $\overline{C_{(2,2^m-1,\delta_3,1)}}^{\perp}$ and $\overline{C_m^{\perp}}$ hold the same 3-designs, which are documented in Theorem 8.9.

If m is even, $\overline{C_{(2,2^m-1,\delta_3,1)}}^{\perp}$ does not hold 3-designs. Below we determine the parameters of some of the 2-designs held in $\overline{C_{(2,2^m-1,\delta_3,1)}}^{\perp}$. To this end, we need the following lemma.

Lemma 9.14. *Let $m \geq 6$ be even. Then the weight distribution of $\overline{C_{(2,2^m-1,\delta_3,1)}}^{\perp}$ is given by*

$$2^{(5m+2)/2}\overline{A_k^{\perp}} = \left(1+(-1)^k\right)\binom{2^m}{k} + wE_0(k) + uE_1(k) + vE_2(k),$$

where

$$u = (2^{m/2}-1)2^{m-2}(2^{m+1}+2^{m/2}-1)/3,$$
$$v = (2^{m/2}-1)2^m(2^m+2^{(m+2)/2}+4)/3,$$
$$w = 2(2^{m/2}-1)(2^{2m-1}+2^{(3m-4)/2}-2^{m-2}+2^{m/2}+1),$$

and

$$E_0(k) = \frac{1+(-1)^k}{2}(-1)^{\lfloor k/2 \rfloor}\binom{2^{m-1}}{\lfloor k/2 \rfloor},$$

$$E_1(k) = \sum_{\substack{0 \le i \le 2^{m-1}-2^{m/2} \\ 0 \le j \le 2^{m-1}+2^{m/2} \\ i+j=k}} [(-1)^i+(-1)^j]\binom{2^{m-1}-2^{m/2}}{i}\binom{2^{m-1}+2^{m/2}}{j},$$

$$E_2(k) = \sum_{\substack{0 \le i \le 2^{m-1}-2^{\frac{m-2}{2}} \\ 0 \le j \le 2^{m-1}+2^{\frac{m-2}{2}} \\ i+j=k}} [(-1)^i+(-1)^j]\binom{2^{m-1}-2^{\frac{m-2}{2}}}{i}\binom{2^{m-1}+2^{\frac{m-2}{2}}}{j},$$

and $0 \le k \le 2^m$.

In addition, $\overline{C_{(2,2^m-1,\delta_3,1)}}^{\perp}$ has parameters $[2^m, 2^m - 1 - 5m/2, 6]$.

Proof. With the weight distribution of $\overline{C_{(2,2^m-1,\delta_3,1)}}$ given in Table 9.6, one can prove the desired conclusions by slightly modifying the proof of Theorem 8.16. □

Theorem 9.15. *Let $m \ge 4$ be an even integer. Let $\overline{A_i}^{\perp}$ denote the number of codewords with weight i in $\overline{C_{(2,2^m-1,\delta_3,1)}}^{\perp}$ for all $0 \le i \le 2^m$. Then for every i with $\overline{A_i}^{\perp} \ne 0$, the supports of the codewords with weight i in this code form a $2\text{-}(2^m, i, \lambda)$ design with*

$$\lambda = \frac{\overline{A_i}^{\perp}\binom{i}{2}}{\binom{2^m}{2}},$$

where these $\overline{A_i}^{\perp}$ are given in Lemma 9.14.

Proof. The desired conclusions follow from Theorem 9.2 and (9.1). □

Corollary 9.16. *Let $m \ge 4$ be an even integer. Then the supports of all codewords of weight 6 in $\overline{C_{(2,2^m-1,\delta_3,1)}}^{\perp}$ give a $2\text{-}(2^m, 6, \lambda)$ design, where*

$$\lambda = \frac{(2^{(m-2)/2}-2)(2^{m-2}-1)}{3}.$$

Proof. By Lemma 9.14, we have

$$\overline{A_6}^{\perp} = \frac{2^{m-1}(2^{(m-2)/2}-2)(2^{m-2}-1)(2^m-1)}{45}.$$

The desired conclusions then follow from Theorem 9.15. □

Corollary 9.17. *Let $m \geq 4$ be an even integer. Then the supports of all codewords of weight 8 in $\overline{C_{(2,2^m-1,\delta_3,1)}}^{\perp}$ give a 2-$(2^m, 8, \lambda)$ design, where*

$$\lambda = \frac{(h^2-1)(8h^5-46h^3+50h^2+56h-95)}{45}$$

and $h = 2^{(m-2)/2}$.

Proof. By Lemma 9.14, we have

$$\overline{A}_8^{\perp} = \frac{h^2(h^2-1)(4h^2-1)(8h^5-46h^3+50h^2+56h-95)}{630},$$

where $h = 2^{(m-2)/2}$. The desired conclusions then follow from Theorem 9.15. $\square$

9.5 Designs from the Primitive BCH Codes $C_{(q,q^m-1,\delta_3,1)}$ for Odd q

In order to determine the parameters of of the 2-designs held in $\overline{C_{(q,q^m-1,\delta_3,1)}}$, we need settle the following problem.

Problem 9.18. Determine the weight distribution of the code $\overline{C_{(q,q^m-1,\delta_3,1)}}$ and the parameters of the 2-designs held in this case, for $q > 2$.

This problem could be settled, as the weight distribution of $C_{(q,q^m-1,\delta_3+1,0)}$ was settled in Section 7.4. By defining and extending the analysis of Section 7.4, one may be able to find the weight distributions of $C_{(q,q^m-1,\delta_3,1)}$ and $\overline{C_{(q,q^m-1,\delta_3,1)}}$ for $m \geq 4$.

However, the case $m = 3$ is special, as in this case the third largest coset leader $\delta_3 \neq (q-1)q^{m-1} - q^{(m+1)/2}$. In this case, $\delta_3 = q^3 - q^2 - q - 2$. The weight distribution of $C_{(q,q^3-1,\delta_3,1)}$ was conjectured in Yan (2018). Table 9.7 describes the conjectured weight distribution of $\overline{C_{(q,q^m-1,\delta_3,1)}}$.

Table 9.7   The conjectured weight distribution
of $\overline{C_{(q,q^3-1,\delta_3,1)}}$, where q is an odd prime

Weight w	No. of codewords A_w
0	1
q^3-q^2-q-1	$q^4(q-1)^2(q^2-q-1)/2$
q^3-q^2-q	$q^3(q-1)(q^3-1)/2$
q^3-q^2-1	$q^3(q-1)(q^3-1)$
q^3-q^2	$q(q^2+1)(q^3-1)$
q^3-q^2+q-1	$q^4(q-1)(q^3-1)/2$
q^3-q^2+q	$q^3(q-1)(q^3-1)/2$
q^3-1	$q^3(q-1)$
q^m	$q-1$

The following conjecture is based on the conjectured weight distribution of $\overline{C_{(q,q^3-1,q^3-q^2-q-2,1)}}$ given in Table 9.7.

Conjecture 9.19. *Let q be an odd prime. Then the code $\overline{C_{(q,q^3-1,q^3-q^2-q-2,1)}}$ holds 2-(q^3,k,λ) designs for the following pairs:*

- $(k,\lambda) = \left(q^3 - q^2 - q - 1, q(q-2)(q^2 - q - 1)(q^3 - q^2 - q - 1)/2\right)$.
- $(k,\lambda) = \left(q^3 - q^2 - q, (q^3 - q^2 - q)(q^3 - q^2 - q - 1)/2\right)$.
- $(k,\lambda) = \left(q^3 - q^2 - 1, (q^3 - q^2 - 1)(q^3 - q^2 - 2)\right)$.
- $(k,\lambda) = \left(q^3 - q^2, (q^2 + 1)(q^3 - q^2 - 1)\right)$.
- $(k,\lambda) = \left(q^3 - q^2 + q - 1, q(q^3 - q^2 + q - 1)(q^3 - q^2 + q - 2)/2\right)$.
- $(k,\lambda) = \left(q^3 - q^2 + q, (q^3 - q^2 + q)(q^3 - q^2 + q - 1)/2\right)$.

It would be good if this conjecture could be settled. The reader is warmly invited to attack this conjecture.

9.6 Designs from $\overline{C_{(2,2^m-1,5,1)}}$ and $\overline{C_{(2,2^m-1,5,1)}}^{\perp}$ for Even $m \geq 4$

In this section, we will determine the parameters of some of the 2-designs held in both $\overline{C_{(2,2^m-1,5,1)}}$ and $\overline{C_{(2,2^m-1,5,1)}}^{\perp}$ for even $m \geq 4$. Before doing this, we need to settle the weight distribution of of the two codes.

Table 9.8 The weight distribution of the code $\overline{C_{(2,2^m-1,5,1)}}^{\perp}$ for even $m \geq 4$

Weight w	No. of codewords $\overline{A}_w^{\perp}$
0	1
$2^{m-1} - 2^{m/2}$	$(2^m - 1)2^{m-2}/3$
$2^{m-1} - 2^{(m-2)/2}$	$(2^m - 1)2^{m+1}/3$
2^{m-1}	$(2^m - 1)(2^{m-1} + 2)$
$2^{m-1} + 2^{(m-2)/2}$	$(2^m - 1)2^{m+1}/3$
$2^{m-1} + 2^{m/2}$	$(2^m - 1)2^{m-2}/3$
2^m	1

Lemma 9.20. *Let $m \geq 4$ be even. The code $\overline{C_{(2,2^m-1,5,1)}}^{\perp}$ has length 2^m, dimension $2m + 1$ and the weight distribution in Table 9.8.*

Proof. The conclusion on the dimension of the code follows from Theorem 7.21. The desired conclusion on the weight distribution of $\overline{C_{(2,2^m-1,5,1)}}^{\perp}$ follows from Theorem 2.10 and the weight distribution of $C_{(2,2^m-1,5,1)}^{\perp}$ in Table 7.21. □

Theorem 9.21. *Let $m \geq 4$ be an integer. Then $\overline{C_{(2,2^m-1,5,1)}}^{\perp}$ holds $2\text{-}(2^m, k, \lambda)$ designs with the following pairs of (k, λ):*

- $\left(2^{m-1} - 2^{\frac{m}{2}}, (2^{m-3} - 2^{(m-4)/2})(2^{m-1} - 2^{m/2} - 1)/3\right)$.
- $\left(2^{m-1} - 2^{\frac{m-2}{2}}, (2^m - 2^{m/2})(2^{m-1} - 2^{(m-2)/2} - 1)/3\right)$.
- $\left(2^{m-1}, (2^{m-2} + 1)(2^{m-1} - 1)\right)$.
- $\left(2^{m-1} + 2^{\frac{m-2}{2}}, (2^m + 2^{m/2})(2^{m-1} + 2^{(m-2)/2} - 1)/3\right)$.
- $\left(2^{m-1} + 2^{\frac{m}{2}}, (2^{m-3} + 2^{(m-4)/2})(2^{m-1} + 2^{m/2} - 1)\right)/3$.

Proof. The desired conclusions then follow from the weight distribution of the code in Table 9.8, Theorem 9.1 and (9.1). $\qquad\square$

Lemma 9.22. *Let $m \geq 4$ be even. Then the weight distribution of $\overline{C_{(2,2^m-1,5,1)}}$ is given by*

$$2^{2m+1}\overline{A}_k = \left(1 + (-1)^k\right)\binom{2^m}{k} + wE_0(k) + uE_1(k) + vE_2(k),$$

where

$$u = (2^m - 1)2^{m-2}/3,$$
$$v = (2^m - 1)2^{m+1}/3,$$
$$w = (2^m - 1)(2^{m-1} + 2),$$

and

$$E_0(k) = \frac{1 + (-1)^k}{2}(-1)^{\lfloor k/2 \rfloor}\binom{2^{m-1}}{\lfloor k/2 \rfloor},$$

$$E_1(k) = \sum_{\substack{0 \leq i \leq 2^{m-1} - 2^{m/2} \\ 0 \leq j \leq 2^{m-1} + 2^{m/2} \\ i+j=k}} [(-1)^i + (-1)^j]\binom{2^{m-1} - 2^{m/2}}{i}\binom{2^{m-1} + 2^{m/2}}{j},$$

$$E_2(k) = \sum_{\substack{0 \leq i \leq 2^{m-1} - 2^{\frac{m-2}{2}} \\ 0 \leq j \leq 2^{m-1} + 2^{\frac{m-2}{2}} \\ i+j=k}} [(-1)^i + (-1)^j]\binom{2^{m-1} - 2^{\frac{m-2}{2}}}{i}\binom{2^{m-1} + 2^{\frac{m-2}{2}}}{j},$$

and $0 \leq k \leq 2^m$.

In addition, $\overline{C_{(2,2^m-1,5,1)}}$ has parameters $[2^m, 2^m - 1 - 2m, 6]$.

Proof. With the weight distribution of $\overline{C_{(2,2^m-1,5,1)}}^{\perp}$ given in Table 9.8, one can prove the desired conclusions by slightly modifying the proof of Theorem 8.16. □

Theorem 9.23. *Let $m \geq 4$ be an even integer. Let $\overline{A}_i$ denote the number of codewords with weight i in $\overline{C_{(2,2^m-1,5,1)}}$ for all $0 \leq i \leq 2^m$. Then for every i with $\overline{A}_i \neq 0$, the supports of the codewords with weight i in this code form a $2\text{-}(2^m, i, \lambda)$ design with*

$$\lambda = \frac{\overline{A}_i \binom{i}{2}}{\binom{2^m}{2}},$$

where these $\overline{A}_i$ are given in Lemma 9.22.

Proof. The desired conclusions follow from Theorem 9.2 and (9.1). □

Corollary 9.24. *Let $m \geq 4$ be an even integer. Then the supports of all codewords of weight 6 in $\overline{C_{(2,2^m-1,5,1)}}$ give a $2\text{-}(2^m, 6, \lambda)$ design, where*

$$\lambda = \frac{2 \times (2^{m-2} - 1)^2}{3}.$$

Proof. By Lemma 9.22, we have

$$\overline{A}_6 = \frac{2^m(2^m - 1)(2^{m-2} - 1)^2}{45}.$$

The desired conclusions then follow from Theorem 9.23. □

Corollary 9.25. *Let $m \geq 4$ be an even integer. Then the supports of all codewords of weight 8 in $\overline{C_{(2,2^m-1,5,1)}}$ give a $2\text{-}(2^m, 8, \lambda)$ design, where*

$$\lambda = \frac{(h^2 - 1)(16h^6 - 92h^4 + 162h^2 - 95)}{630},$$

where $h = 2^{(m-2)/2}$.

Proof. By Lemma 9.22, we have

$$\overline{A}_8 = \frac{h^2(h^2 - 1)(4h^2 - 1)(16h^6 - 92h^4 + 162h^2 - 95)}{630}.$$

The desired conclusions then follow from Theorem 9.23. □

Corollary 9.26. *Let $m \geq 4$ be an even integer. Then the supports of all codewords of weight 10 in $\overline{C_{(2,2^m-1,5,1)}}$ give a $2\text{-}(2^m, 10, \lambda)$ design, where*

$$\lambda = \frac{2(h^2 - 1)(16h^{10} - 160h^8 + 666h^6 - 1401h^4 + 1498h^2 - 679)}{315},$$

where $h = 2^{(m-2)/2}$.

Proof. By Lemma 9.22, we have

$$\overline{A}_{10} = \frac{4h^2(4h^2-1)(h^2-1)(16h^{10}-160h^8+666h^6-1401h^4+1498h^2-679)}{14175}.$$

The desired conclusions then follow from Theorem 9.23. $\qquad\square$

At the end of this section, we point out that the following code

$$C = \{(\mathrm{Tr}_{2^m/2}(a(x^6+x^4+x^2)+bx)+h)_{x\in\mathrm{GF}(2^m)} : a, b \in \mathrm{GF}(2^m),\ h \in \mathrm{GF}(2)\}$$

is permutation-equivalent to $\overline{C_{(2,2^m-1,5,1)}}^{\perp}$, which is a consequence of the identity:

$$\mathrm{Tr}_{2^m/2}\left(a(x^6+x^4+x^2)+bx\right) = \mathrm{Tr}_{2^m/2}\left(a^{2^{m-1}}x^3+(a^{2^{m-2}}+a^{2^{m-1}}+b)x\right).$$

Therefore, C holds the same 3-designs for odd m and 2-designs for even m as $\overline{C_{(2,2^m-1,5,1)}}^{\perp}$.

9.7 Designs from the Primitive BCH Codes $C_{(q,q^m-1,3,1)}$ for $q \geq 3$

Let $q \geq 3$. The weight distribution of the code $\overline{C_{(q,q^m-1,3,1)}}^{\perp}$ can be worked out easily. The weight distribution of $\overline{C_{(q,q^m-1,3,1)}}$ can then be given with the help of the MacWilliams Identity. We will outline the procedure below and leave the details to the reader.

According to the Delsarte Theorem, the code $\overline{C_{(q,q^m-1,3,1)}}^{\perp}$ is equivalent to the following linear code

$$C_{(q,m)} := \{(\mathrm{Tr}_{q^m/q}(ax^2+bx)+c)_{x\in\mathrm{GF}(q^m)} : a,\ b \in \mathrm{GF}(q^m),\ c \in \mathrm{GF}(q)\}.$$

One can employ Theorems 1.8 and 1.9 to determine the weight distribution of $C_{(q,m)}$, and then the parameters of the 2-designs held in $\overline{C_{(q,q^m-1,3,1)}}^{\perp}$. We have the following conclusions.

Theorem 9.27. *If q is odd, then $\overline{C_{(q,q^m-1,3,1)}}$ has parameters $[q^m, q^m-1-2m, 4]$, and $\overline{C_{(q,q^m-1,3,1)}}^{\perp}$ is a four-weight code for odd m, and six-weight code for even m.*

Theorem 9.28. *Let $q \geq 4$ be even. Then $\overline{C_{(q,q^m-1,3,1)}}^{\perp}$ has parameters $[q^m, 2m+1, (q-2)q^{m-1}]$ and weight enumerator*

$$1 + \frac{(q-1)(q^{m+1}-q)}{2}z^{(q-2)q^{m-1}} + (q^{2m+1}-(q-1)q^{m+1}+(q-2)q)z^{(q-1)q^{m-1}} +$$
$$\frac{(q-1)(q^{m+1}-q+2)}{2}z^{q^m}.$$

Its dual distance is 4. The supports of all codewords of weight $(q-2) \times q^{m-1}$ in $\overline{C_{(q,q^m-1,3,1)}}^{\perp}$ *form a design with parameters*

$$2\text{-}\left(q^m,\ (q-2)q^{m-1},\ \frac{(q-2)((q-2)q^{m-1}-1)}{2}\right).$$

Theorem 9.29. *[Xiang (2021)] Both* $\overline{C_{(4,4^m-1,3,1)}}$ *and* $\overline{C_{(4,4^m-1,3,1)}}^{\perp}$ *hold 3-designs for all $m \geq 2$.*

Experimental data indicates that $\overline{C_{(q,q^m-1,3,1)}}$ and $\overline{C_{(q,q^m-1,3,1)}}^{\perp}$ do not hold 3-designs except that $q = 4$ and $q = 2$. Clearly, $\overline{C_{(2,2^m-1,3,1)}}^{\perp}$ is the first-order Reed-Muller code, and hence holds 3-designs. The case $q = 4$ treated in Theorem 9.29 is very special. For the parameters of some of the 3-designs held in $\overline{C_{(4,4^m-1,3,1)}}$ and $\overline{C_{(4,4^m-1,3,1)}}^{\perp}$, the reader is referred to Xiang (2021).

9.8 Designs from Nonprimitive BCH Codes

In the preceding sections of this chapter, we dealt with designs from narrow-sense primitive BCH codes or their extended codes. In this section, we present a family of designs from the extended codes of nonprimitive BCH codes. The purpose of this section is to show that the extended code of a nonprimitive BCH code may give a design.

Theorem 9.30. *Let $m \geq 2$ be a positive integer. The code* $\overline{C_{(2^m,2^{m+1}-1,3,1)}}$ *over* $\mathrm{GF}(2^m)$ *has parameters* $[2^{m+1}, 2^{m+1} - m - 2, 4]$. *The dual code* $\overline{C_{(2^m,2^{m+1}-1,3,1)}}^{\perp}$ *over $\mathrm{GF}(2^m)$ has parameters* $[2^{m+1}, m+2, 2^m]$. *Furthermore, the minimum weight codewords in* $\overline{C_{(2^m,2^{m+1}-1,3,1)}}$ *support a Steiner quadruple system $S(3,4,2^{m+1})$, and the minimum weight codewords in the dual code* $\overline{C_{(2^m,2^{m+1}-1,3,1)}}^{\perp}$ *support a* $3\text{-}(2^{m+1}, 2^m, 2^{m-1} - 1)$ *design.*

Note that the code $C_{(2^m,2^{m+1}-1,3,1)}$ is over $\mathrm{GF}(q)$, where $q = 2^m$. But its length is $2q - 1$. Therefore, by definition it is not a primitive BCH code over $\mathrm{GF}(q)$.

Theorem 9.30 may be proved as follows. Using the trace expression of $\overline{C_{(2^m,2^{m+1}-1,3,1)}}^{\perp}$, one can prove that the subfield subcode $\overline{C_{(2^m,2^{m+1}-1,3,1)}}^{\perp}|_{\mathrm{GF}(2)}$ is the first-order Reed-Muller code $\mathcal{R}_2(1,m+1)$ and the code $\overline{C_{(2^m,2^{m+1}-1,3,1)}}^{\perp}$ over $\mathrm{GF}(2^m)$ is actually generated by a generator matrix of $\mathcal{R}_2(1,m+1)$. Thus, the $3\text{-}(2^{m+1}, 2^m, 2^{m-1} - 1)$ design held in $\overline{C_{(2^m,2^{m+1}-1,3,1)}}^{\perp}$ is the same as the 3-design held in $\mathcal{R}_2(1,m+1)$. Similarly, one can prove that the subfield subcode $\overline{C_{(2^m,2^{m+1}-1,3,1)}}|_{\mathrm{GF}(2)}$ is the Reed-Muller code $\mathcal{R}_2(m-1,m+1)$ and the code $\overline{C_{(2^m,2^{m+1}-1,3,1)}}$ over $\mathrm{GF}(2^m)$ is actually generated by a generator matrix of $\mathcal{R}_2(m-1,m+1)$. Consequently, the Steiner quadruple system $S(3,4,2^{m+1})$ held in $\overline{C_{(2^m,2^{m+1}-1,3,1)}}$ is the same as the one held in the binary Reed-Muller code $\mathcal{R}_2(m-1,m+1)$.

We point out that Theorem 9.30 can be modified for the code $\overline{C_{(p^m,p^{m+1}-1,3,1)}}$ over $\mathrm{GF}(p^m)$, where p is an odd prime. Note that the minimum distance of $\overline{C_{(p^m,p^{m+1}-1,3,1)}}$ is 3 when p is odd. For example, the code $\overline{C_{(3^m,3^{m+1}-1,3,1)}}$ has parameters $[3^{m+1},3^{m+1}-m-2,3]$ and the minimum weight codewords in $\overline{C_{(3^m,3^{m+1}-1,3,1)}}$ support a Steiner triple system $S(2,3,3^{m+1})$, which is very likely isomorphic to the design $\mathrm{AG}_1(m+1,\mathrm{GF}(3))$.

9.9   Notes

This chapter documented a number of infinite families of 2-designs and 3-designs supported by primitive BCH codes over small fields and their extended codes. Chapter 15 will treat some families of BCH codes of length $q+1$ over $\mathrm{GF}(q)$ and the 3-designs and 4-designs supported by these codes. This shows that BCH codes are very attractive. BCH codes may lead to more interesting results in combinatorial t-designs.

Chapter 10

Designs from Codes with Regularity

In this chapter, we will introduce several types of codes with regularity and deal with their support designs. These codes include perfect codes, quasi-perfect codes, uniformly packed codes, and t-regular codes. The codes dealt with in this chapter may be linear or nonlinear. The materials in Sections 10.2, 10.3 and 10.6 come from Goethals and Van Tilborg (1975).

10.1   Packing and Covering Radii

An (n,M,d) code over $GF(q)$ is a nonempty subset of $GF(q)^n$ with cardinality $M \geq 2$ and minimum Hamming distance d. Let C be an (n,M,d) code over $GF(q)$. Due to the Sphere-Packing Bound, the packing radius of C, denoted by $e(C)$, is defined to be

$$e(C) = \left\lfloor \frac{d-1}{2} \right\rfloor. \tag{10.1}$$

Recall that C is called an $e(C)$-error correcting code. The covering radius, denoted by $\rho(C)$, is the smallest r such that

$$|C| \sum_{i=0}^{r} \binom{n}{i} (q-1)^i \geq q^n. \tag{10.2}$$

By definition, we have

$$\rho(C) = \max_{\mathbf{x} \in GF(q)^n} \min_{\mathbf{c} \in C} \mathrm{dist}(\mathbf{x},\mathbf{c}). \tag{10.3}$$

The covering radius of codes is an interesting and challenging topic. The reader is referred to Cohen, Honkala, Litsyn and Lobstein (1997) for detailed information.

289

10.2   The Characteristic Polynomial of a Code

The *distance enumerator* of a code C is the formal polynomial

$$A_C(z) = \frac{1}{|C|} \sum_{u,v \in C} z^{\text{dist}(u,v)}.$$

Thus, the coefficient A_i of z^i in its expansion $A_C(z) = \sum A_i z^i$, is the average over all codewords of the number of codewords at distance i from a given codeword. Note that the A_i are rational numbers with $A_0 = 1$, and $\sum A_i = |C|$. A code C is *distance-invariant* if, for any given codeword u, the number $A_i(u)$ of codewords at distance i from u is a constant not depending on u for every i with $0 \le i \le n$. Every linear code is obviously distance-invariant. In this chapter, the weight enumerator of a code C is defined to be the formal polynomial

$$W_C(z) = \sum_{u \in C} z^{\text{wt}(u)},$$

where $\text{wt}(u)$ denotes the Hamming weight of u. For any distance-invariant code C containing the zero vector, its distance enumerator and weight enumerator are identical.

Group algebras were defined in Section 1.3. Consider now the group algebra $\mathbb{C}[\text{GF}(q)^n]$, which is a vector space of dimension q^n over the complex field $\mathbb{C}$. To each element $u \in \text{GF}(q)^n$, we associate a basis element $e(u)$ of $\mathbb{C}[\text{GF}(q)^n]$. Then every element of $\mathbb{C}[\text{GF}(q)^n]$ is a linear combination $\sum c(u)e(u)$ of these q^m basis elements, where the coefficients $c(u) \in \mathbb{C}$. We then define

$$e(u) * e(v) = e(u+v),$$

which is the product for any two basis elements $e(u)$ and $e(v)$. This induces the following multiplication $*$ for the elements in $\mathbb{C}[\text{GF}(q)^m]$:

$$\left(\sum_u b(u)e(u) \right) * \left(\sum_v c(v)e(v) \right) = \sum_y \left(\sum_{u+v=y} b(u)c(v) \right) e(y). \tag{10.4}$$

To each subset $S \subset \text{GF}(q)^n$, we associate the element

$$\sum_{u \in S} e(u) \in \mathbb{C}[\text{GF}(q)^n].$$

Without confusion, we use S to denote $\sum_{u \in S} e(u)$. The following mapping

$$S \mapsto \sum_{u \in S} e(u)$$

from the power set $P(\text{GF}(q)^n)$ to $\mathbb{C}[\text{GF}(q)^n]$ is one-to-one. Hence, $P(\text{GF}(q)^n)$ can be viewed as a subset of $\mathbb{C}[\text{GF}(q)^n]$. In this way, a code $C \subset \text{GF}(q)^n$ can be viewed as an element of $\mathbb{C}[\text{GF}(q)^n]$, i.e.,

$$C \subseteq \text{GF}(q)^n \iff \sum_{c \in C} e(c) \in \mathbb{C}[\text{GF}(q)^n].$$

Define

$$Y_i = \{u \in \mathrm{GF}(q)^n : \mathrm{wt}(u) = i\}, \quad i = 0, 1, \ldots, n.$$

When these Y_i are considered as elements in $\mathbb{C}[\mathrm{GF}(q)^n]$, they form the basis of an $(n+1)$-dimensional subalgebra. For any code $C \subset \mathrm{GF}(q)^n$,

$$Y_i * C = \left(\sum_{y \in Y_i} e(y)\right) \left(\sum_{c \in C} e(c)\right)$$

$$= \sum_u \left(\sum_{\substack{y+c=u \\ y \in Y_i, c \in C}} 1\right) e(u)$$

$$= \sum_u f_i(u) e(u), \tag{10.5}$$

where $f_i(u)$ is the number of codewords at distance i from u.

Now view Y_i as elements in $\mathbb{C}[\mathrm{GF}(q)^n]$, and define

$$S_j = \sum_{i=0}^{j} Y_i, \quad 0 \leq j \leq n.$$

Then

$$S_j * C = \sum_u g_j(u) e(u), \tag{10.6}$$

where

$$g_j(u) = \sum_{i=0}^{j} f_i(u)$$

is the number of codewords at distance at most j from u. For any j with $2j < d(C)$, where $d(C)$ denotes the minimum distance of C, we have $g_j(u) = 0$ or 1 in (10.6), as any two codewords are at least at distance $d(C)$ from each other.

Let χ be any nonprincipal character of $(\mathrm{GF}(q), +)$. For each $u \in \mathrm{GF}(q)^n$, we define a character $\chi_u : \mathrm{GF}(q)^n \to \mathbb{C}$ by

$$\chi_u(v) = \chi((u, v)), \quad \text{for all } v \in \mathrm{GF}(q)^n,$$

where (u, v) is the inner product in $\mathrm{GF}(q)^n$. Each character χ_u induces a linear function from $\mathbb{C}[\mathrm{GF}(q)^n]$ to $\mathbb{C}$ by

$$\chi_u\left(\sum_v a(v) e(v)\right) = \sum_v a(v) \chi_u(v).$$

These linear functions have the following properties whose proof can be found in Van Lint (1971)[Chapter 5].

Lemma 10.1. *Let notation be the same as before. Then we have the following.*

(a) *For any A and B in* $\mathbb{C}[\mathrm{GF}(q)^n]$, $\chi_u(A * B) = \chi_u(A)\chi_u(B)$.

(b) *For any* $u \in \mathrm{GF}(q)^n$ *with* $\mathrm{wt}(u) = j$, $\chi_u(Y_i) = P_i(q,n;j)$, *where* $P_i(q,n;x)$ *is the Krawtchouk polynomial defined in Section 1.4.3.*

(c) $S_n = \sum_{i=0}^n Y_i$ *is the unique element of* $\mathbb{C}[\mathrm{GF}(q)^n]$ *satisfying*

$$\chi_0(S_n) = q^n, \quad \chi_u(S_n) = 0 \text{ for all } u \neq 0.$$

For a code $C \subset \mathrm{GF}(q)^n$, we define

$$B_j = \frac{1}{|C|^2} \sum_{u \in Y_j} |\chi_u(C)|^2 \tag{10.7}$$

for all j with $0 \leq j \leq n$. These numbers B_i are called *characteristic numbers* of C. When C is a linear code, (B_i) will become the weight distribution of the dual code $C^\perp$ (this will be proved later).

We further define the set

$$N(C) = \{j : 1 \leq j \leq n, \ B_j \neq 0\}. \tag{10.8}$$

Let $F_C(x)$ be the polynomial

$$F_C(x) = \frac{q^n}{|C|} \prod_{j \in N(C)} \left(1 - \frac{x}{j}\right), \tag{10.9}$$

which is called the *characteristic polynomial* of C. Since the Krawtchouk polynomials form a basis of the set of polynomials of degree at most n (see Section 1.4.3), $F_C(x)$ is uniquely expressed as

$$F_C(x) = \sum_{i=0}^n \alpha_i P_i(q,n;x), \tag{10.10}$$

which is referred to as the Krawtchouk expansion of the characteristic polynomial $F_C(x)$.

The following result is due to Delsarte (1973a) (see also Goethals and Van Tilborg (1975)).

Theorem 10.2. *Let* $\alpha_0, \alpha_1, \ldots, \alpha_n$ *be the coefficients of the Krawtchouk expansion of the characteristic polynomial* $F_C(x)$ *of a code* $C \subseteq \mathrm{GF}(q)^n$. *Then, as an element of* $\mathbb{C}[\mathrm{GF}(q)^n]$, *the code* C *satisfies*

$$\sum_{i=0}^n \alpha_i Y_i * C = S_n. \tag{10.11}$$

Proof. By Lemma 10.1 (a), we have

$$\chi_u \left(\sum_{i=0}^n \alpha_i Y_i * C \right) = \chi_u \left(\sum_{i=0}^n \alpha_i Y_i \right) \chi_u(C). \tag{10.12}$$

Let u have weight j. Then by Lemma 10.1 (b), we have

$$\chi_u \left(\sum_{i=0}^{n} \alpha_i Y_i \right) = \sum \alpha_i P_i(q, n; j) = F_C(j),$$

and from (10.7), (10.8) and (10.9), it follows that, for any $u \neq 0$, if $\chi(C) \neq 0$, then $F_C(j) = 0$. Now, for $u = 0$ we have $\chi_u(C) = |C|$, and $F_C(0) = q^n/|C|$, from which it follows that the value of (10.12) is zero for any $u \neq 0$, and q^n for $u = 0$. The desired conclusion then follows from Lemma 10.1 (c). $\qquad \Box$

Corollary 10.3. *Let* $\alpha_0, \alpha_1, \ldots, \alpha_n$ *be the coefficients of the Krawtchouk expansion of the characteristic polynomial* $F_C(x)$ *of a code* $C \subseteq \mathrm{GF}(q)^n$, *and let* $f_i(u)$ *denote, for any* $u \in \mathrm{GF}(q)^n$, *the number of codewords at distance i from u. Then,*

$$\sum_{i=0}^{n} \alpha_i f_i(u) = 1 \text{ for all } u \in \mathrm{GF}(q)^n. \tag{10.13}$$

Proof. As an element of $\mathbb{C}[\mathrm{GF}(q)^n]$,

$$S_n = \sum_{u \in \mathrm{GF}(q)^n} e(u).$$

By (10.5),

$$\sum_{i=0}^{n} \alpha_i Y_i * C = \sum_{i=0}^{n} \alpha_i \sum_{u \in \mathrm{GF}(q)^n} f_i(u) e(u) = \sum_{u \in \mathrm{GF}(q)^n} \left(\sum_{i=0}^{n} \alpha_i f_i(u) \right) e(u).$$

The desired conclusion then follows from (10.11). $\qquad \Box$

Delsarte called $F_C(x)$ the *minimal polynomial*, and its degree the *external distance* of C due to the following result [Delsarte (1973a)].

Corollary 10.4. *Let* s *be the degree of* $F_C(x)$ *of a code* C *and let* $\rho(C)$ *be its covering radius. Then* $\rho(C) \leq s$.

Proof. By Corollary 10.3, for all $u \in \mathrm{GF}(q)^n$ we have

$$\sum_{i=0}^{s} \alpha_i f_i(u) = 1.$$

Now suppose $\rho(C) > s$. Then there exits $u \in \mathrm{GF}(q)^n$ such that $\mathrm{dist}(u, v) > s$ for all $v \in C$. Whence $f_i(u) = 0$ for all i with $0 \leq i \leq s$, and

$$\sum_{i=0}^{s} \alpha_i f_i(u) = 0,$$

which contradicts Corollary 10.3. $\qquad \Box$

When C is linear, we have the following result.

Theorem 10.5. *When C is linear, the B_i defined in (10.7) equals the number of codewords with weight i in $C^{\perp}$. That is, (B_i) is the weight distribution of $C^{\perp}$. Hence, the distance enumerator of the code $C^{\perp}$ is the polynomial*

$$B_C(z) = \sum_j B_j z^j.$$

Proof. By definition, we have

$$\chi_u(C) = \begin{cases} |C| & \text{if } u \in C^{\perp}, \\ 0 & \text{otherwise.} \end{cases} \tag{10.14}$$

The desired conclusion of the first part then follows from (10.7). The conclusion of the second part is obvious. $\qquad\square$

The following theorem is a generalization of a result on the weight enumerator of a code obtained in MacWilliams, Sloane and Goethals (1972), and can be proved in the same line (see also Van Tilborg (1976)). It is equivalent to Theorem 2.4.

Theorem 10.6. *The distance enumerator $A_C(z)$ of a linear code C, and B_C of its dual, are related by (the MacWilliams Identity)*

$$A_C(z) = \frac{|C|}{q^n} \sum_{j=0}^{n} B_j(1-z)^j (1 + (q-1)z)^{n-j},$$

where the number of distinct nonzero B_i is equal to $s+1$, and s is the degree of $F_C(x)$.

The following result was developed in MacWilliams, Sloane and Goethals (1972), and will be employed later.

Theorem 10.7. *For a code $C \subseteq \mathrm{GF}(q)^n$, let the $n+1$ real numbers H_j, $j = 0, 1, \ldots, n$, be defined by*

$$H_j = \frac{1}{|C|} \sum_{u \in Y_j} \chi_u(C). \tag{10.15}$$

Then, the weight enumerator $W_C(z)$ of C is given by (the Macwilliams Identify)

$$W_C(z) = \frac{|C|}{q^n} \sum_{j=0}^{n} H_j(1-z)^j (1 + (q-1)z)^{n-j}. \tag{10.16}$$

Regarding Theorem 10.7, we have the following remarks:

(1) If the characteristic number B_j defined in (10.7) is zero, we have $\chi_u(C) = 0$ for all $u \in Y_j$, whence $H_j = 0$. Hence, the number of distinct nonzero H_j is at most $s + 1$.

(2) Note that

$$H_j = \frac{1}{|C|} \sum_{v \in C} \chi_v(Y_j).$$

We know that these H_j are real numbers.

(3) If C is linear, it follows from (10.14) that $H_j = B_j$, which equals the number of codewords of weight j in $C^{\perp}$.

10.3 Regular Codes and Their Designs

The objective of this section is to introduce the so-called *t-regular codes* and their designs.

Let $C \subseteq \mathrm{GF}(q)^n$ be a code with minimum distance d. The packing radius $e(C) = \lfloor (d-1)/2 \rfloor$. By Corollary 10.4, we have

$$\frac{d-1}{2} \le \rho(C) \le s,$$

where s is the external distance of C. In this section, we will study codes C with $d \ge s$, as they have certain regularity. The following theorem documents a regularity aspect of such codes.

Theorem 10.8. *Let the external distance s and the minimum distance d of a code C satisfy $d \ge s$. Then C is distance-invariant.*

Proof. See Delsarte (1973a) for a proof. $\square$

Given a code $C \subseteq \mathrm{GF}(q)^n$ and a vector $v \in \mathrm{GF}(q)^n$, we define the code
$$D_C(v) = C - v = \{u - v : u \in C\}, \tag{10.17}$$
which is a translate of C. We have the following conclusions:

- Clearly, all $D_C(v)$ have the same distance enumerator and the same characteristic numbers.
- The weight enumerators of these codes $D_C(v)$ are, in general, different.

A very interesting question is whether $D_C(u)$ and $D_C(v)$ have the same weight enumerator for distinct u and v in $\mathrm{GF}(q)^n$. The following theorem will be helpful in answering this question [Delsarte (1973a)].

Theorem 10.9. *Let s be the external distance of a code $C \subseteq \mathrm{GF}(q)^n$. The weight enumerator $W_C(z) = \sum_{i=0}^{n} w_i z^i$ of C is uniquely determined from its first s components $w_0, w_1, \ldots, w_{s-1}$.*

Proof. Let $F_C(x)$ be the characteristic polynomial of C and let $s = \deg(F_C(x))$ be the external distance of C. Let $N(C)$ be the set of distinct zeros of $F_C(x)$ defined in (10.8). By Theorem 10.7, the weight enumerator $W_C(z)$ is uniquely determined from the real numbers H_i defined in (10.15), where $H_0 = 1$, and for any $j \neq 0$, $H_j \neq 0$ only if $j \in N(C)$. By the definition of the Krawtchouk polynomials,

$$\sum_i P_i(q,n;x)z^i = (1 + (q-1)z)^{n-x}(1-z)^x.$$

It then follows from (10.16) that the coefficients of the expression $W_C(z) = \sum_{i=0}^n w_i z^i$ are given by

$$w_i = \frac{1}{q^n} |C| \sum_j H_j P_i(q,n;j), \quad i = 0, 1, \ldots, n.$$

We have then

$$\sum_{j \in N(C)} H_j P_i(q,n;j) = q^n |C|^{-1} w_i - P_i(q,n;0) \qquad (10.18)$$

for all $i \in \{0, 1, \ldots, s-1\}$. We would now show that this system of s linear equations with s unknowns H_j ($j \in N(C)$) has a unique solution. Let k be any given element of $N(C)$, and let $F_k(x)$ be the unique polynomial of degree $s-1$ with $F_k(k) = 1$ and $F_k(j) = 0$, for any $j \neq k$, $j \in N(C)$. If $F_k(x)$ has the Krawtchouk expansion

$$F_k(x) = \sum_{i=0}^{s-1} \beta_i P_i(q,n;x),$$

it then follows from (10.18) that

$$H_k = \frac{q^n}{|C|} \sum_{i=0}^{s-1} \beta_i w_i - F_k(0).$$

Consequently, the nonzero H_i are uniquely determined from the first s coefficients of the weight enumerator. The desired conclusion then follows from Theorem 10.7. $\qquad\square$

We now consider the weight enumerator of $D_C(v)$ for any $v \in \mathrm{GF}(q)^n$. $D_C(v)$ has the same external distance s with C. In the weight enumerate

$$W(z) = \sum_i f_i(v)z^i$$

of $D_C(v)$, the coefficient $f_i(v)$ is the number of codewords $u \in C$ at distance i from v. Then according to Theorem 10.9, $W(z)$ is uniquely determined from the s components $f_i(v)$, $i = 0, 1, \ldots, s-1$. Let w be the minimum weight of $D_C(v)$, i.e., the smallest w such that $f_w(v) \neq 0$ and $f_i(v) = 0$ for $i = 0, 1, \ldots, w - 1$, in the weight enumerator of $D_C(v)$. Note that we must have $w \leq s$.

We are now ready to define t-regular codes. Let C be a code with external distance s. Let t be an integer with $0 \leq t \leq s$. We say that C is *t-regular* if for every $v \in GF(q)^n$ such that $D_C(v)$ has minimum weight $w \leq t$, the weight enumerator of $D_C(v)$ depends only on w. An s-regular code with external distance s is said to be *completely regular*. By definition, a zero-regular code is distance-invariant.

The following theorem was developed in Delsarte (1973a) (see also Goethals and Van Tilborg (1975)), and will be useful for constructing designs.

Theorem 10.10.

(a) *If the minimum distance d and the external distance s of a code C satisfy $s \leq d < 2s - 1$, then C is $(d - s)$-regular.*

(b) *If $d \geq 2s - 1$, then C is completely regular.*

Proof. Let $v \in GF(q)^n$ be any vector such that $D_C(v) = D - v$ has minimum weight $w \leq d - s$, and let $x \in D_C(v)$ with weight w. Since the minimum distance of $D_C(v)$ is d, any other vector $y \in D_C(v)$ has weight at least equal $d - w \geq s$. It follows that the first s components $f_i(v)$, $i = 0, 1, \ldots, s - 1$, of the weight enumerator of $D_C(v)$ all equal zero, except that $f_w(v) \geq 1$. Hence, by Theorem 10.9, the weight enumerator is uniquely determined from these s components, which clearly depend only on w. This proves the first part of this theorem.

We now prove the second part of this theorem. Assume now that $d \geq 2s - 1$, i.e., $d - s \geq s - 1$. Then from the discussions above it is clear that C is $(s - 1)$-regular. For any $D_C(v)$ with minimum weight $w = s$, we have, by definition, $f_i(v) = 0$ for $i = 0, 1, \ldots, s - 1$, and by Theorem 10.9, the same conclusion holds on its weight enumerator. Thus, in this case, C is completely regular. $\square$

The following theorem shows that certain t-regular codes hold t-designs. It is a variation of Theorem 5.7 in Delsarte (1973a). Its proof is very similar and omitted here (a proof could be found in Van Tilborg (1976)).

Theorem 10.11. *Let C be a t-regular binary code of length n, containing the zero vector, and let its minimum distance d satisfy $d \geq 2t$. Then for each weight k, the supports of all codewords of weight k form a t-design.*

Example 10.12. Regarding the extended binary Hamming code $\overline{C_{(2,3)}}$, we have the following conclusions:

(a) It has parameters $[8, 4, 4]$ and weight enumerator $1 + 14z^4 + z^8$, and is self-dual.

(b) The external distance of the code is 2 as its dual code (in this case, the code is self-dual) has two nonzero weights. Hence, it is 2-regular and completely regular by Theorem 10.10.

(c) It holds 2-designs by Theorem 10.11.

10.4 Perfect Codes

Recall the packing radius $e(C)$ and covering radius $\rho(C)$ of a code C defined in Section 10.1. By definition, $e(C) \leq \rho(C)$. A code C is said to be *perfect* if $e(C) = \rho(C)$. By definition, an e-error correcting code is perfect if, for every $v \in \mathrm{GF}(q)^n$, there exists exactly one codeword at distance e or less from v.

Perfect codes can be characterized as follows [Goethals and Van Tilborg (1975)].

Theorem 10.13. *An e-error correcting code C is perfect if and only if, as an element in $\mathbb{C}[\mathrm{GF}(q)^n]$, it satisfies $S_e * C = S_n$.*

Proof. Equation (10.6) says that

$$S_e * C = \sum_{v \in \mathrm{GF}(q)^n} g_e(v)e(v),$$

where the coefficient $g_e(v)$ is equal to the number of codewords at distance e or less from v. Hence, an e-error correcting code is perfect if and only if $g_e(v) = 1$ for all $v \in \mathrm{GF}(q)^n$. This completes the proof. □

As corollaries of Theorem 10.13, we have the following whose proofs can be found in Van Lint (1971).

Corollary 10.14. *The characteristic polynomial of a perfect e-error correcting code $C \subset \mathrm{GF}(q)^n$ is given by*

$$L_e(x) = \sum_{i=0}^{e} P_i(q,n;x),$$

which has degree e.

The following is a consequence of Theorem 10.10.

Corollary 10.15. *A perfect code is completely regular.*

The next theorem documents a lower bound on the covering radius of linear codes and is due to Delsarte (1973a), and follows from Corollary 10.4 and Theorem 10.5.

Theorem 10.16. *Let C be an $[n, \kappa, d]$ code over* GF(q)*. Assume that $C^{\perp}$ has $s^{\perp}$ nonzero weights. Then*

$$|C| \sum_{i=0}^{s^{\perp}} \binom{n}{i} (q-1)^i \geq q^n. \tag{10.19}$$

Consequently, $\rho(C) \leq s^{\perp}$. In addition, C is perfect if and only if the equality of (10.19) holds.

The following theorem then follows from the definition of perfect codes, the Sphere-Packing Bound and Theorem 10.16.

Theorem 10.17. *Let C be an $[n, \kappa, d]$ code over* GF(q)*. Then the following three statements are equivalent.*

- *C is perfect.*
- *The equality of the Sphere-Packing Bound holds.*
- *$s^{\perp} = \lfloor \frac{d-1}{2} \rfloor$.*

The weight enumerator of perfect codes is given in the next theorem [Van Lint (1975)].

Theorem 10.18. *If C is a perfect single-error-correction code of length n over an alphabet of q symbols (q not necessarily a prime power), then*

$$A(z) = \frac{[1 + (q-1)z]^n + n(q-1)[1 + (q-1)z]^{\frac{n-1}{q}} (1-z)^{\frac{n(q-1)+1}{q}}}{n(q-1)+1}.$$

Perfect codes are very rare. The following are the only perfect linear codes over finite fields [Cohen, Honkala, Litsyn and Lobstein (1997); Van Lint (1975)].

(1) $[n, n, 1]$ codes over GF(q) with covering radius 0 for each $n \geq 1$.
(2) $[2s + 1, 1, 2s + 1]$ repetition codes over GF(q) with covering radius s for each $s \geq 1$.
(3) Codes of length n containing only one codeword.
(4) q-ary codes with the parameters of Hamming codes.
(5) The binary Golay code with parameters $[23, 12, 7]$.
(6) The ternary Golay code with parameters $[11, 6, 5]$.

We will treat the designs from some of these perfect codes in the next section.

10.5 Designs in Perfect Codes

Perfect codes are fascinating partially because they hold designs. Some extended perfect codes contain also designs. In this section, we first prove several general theorems about designs held in perfect codes, and then document designs from specific perfect codes.

10.5.1 *Theory of Designs in Perfect Codes*

The following is a characterisation of perfect linear codes with t-design, and was developed in Assmus and Mattson (1974).

Theorem 10.19. *A linear code C over* $GF(q)$ *with length n and minimum distance $d = 2e + 1$ is perfect if and only if the supports of the codewords of weight d form an $(e+1)$-$(n, 2e+1, (q-1)^e)$ design.*

Proof. Let C be a perfect linear code over $GF(q)$ with length n and minimum distance $d = 2e + 1$. Let T be an arbitrary $(e+1)$-subset of the point set $\mathcal{P} = \{0, 1, \ldots, n-1\}$. Any vector $u \in GF(q)^n$ with Hamming weight $e + 1$ and support $\text{Suppt}(u) = T$ is at distance e from exactly one codeword $c \in C$, and the weight of c is equal to $d = 2e + 1$. The number of all vectors in $GF(q)^n$ with T as the support is $(q-1)^{e+1}$, and each two such vectors are at distance e from distinct codewords. Hence, not counting scalar multiples, T is contained in exactly $(q-1)^e$ supports of the codewords of weight $d = 2e + 1$. As a result, the set of supports of the codewords with minimum weight d is an $(e+1)$-$(n, 2e+1, (q-1)^e)$ design.

Assume now that the supports of all codewords of minimum weight $d = 2e + 1$ in a linear code C over $GF(q)$ with length n form an $(e+1)$-$(n, 2e+1, (q-1)^e)$ design. Any vector x in $GF(q)^n$ with weight not exceeding e is at distance at most e from the zero codeword. Suppose, on the contrary, that the spheres of radius e around all codewords of C do not contain all vectors in $GF(q)^n$, and let y be a vector of smallest weight among all vectors that are at distance no less than $e + 1$ from every codeword. Hence, the weight of y (i.e., the distance of y from the zero codeword) is at least $e + 1$. Let $y_{i_1}, y_{i_2}, \ldots, y_{i_{e+1}}$ be the set of $e + 1$ nonzero coordinates of y. The set of indices $T = \{i_1, i_2, \ldots, i_{e+1}\}$ is contained in $(q-1)^e$ supports of the codewords of minimum weight. The number of codewords of minimum weight whose supports contain T is equal to $(q-1)^{e+1}$, and any two such codewords differ in at least one position from T. Therefore, there is a codeword z of minimum weight which coincides with y in all positions from T, i.e., $z_{i_j} = y_{i_j}$ for all $1 \leq j \leq e + 1$. As a result, the vector $u = z - y$ is of weight smaller than the weight of y, and is at distance at least $e + 1$ from all codewords.

This is contrary to the choice of y. ◻

Corollary 10.20. *In a perfect linear code C over GF(q) with length n and minimum distance $d = 2e + 1$, the number of minimum weight codewords is*

$$A_d = (q-1)^{e+1} \frac{\binom{n}{e+1}}{\binom{2e+1}{e+1}}.$$

Proof. Note that C is linear. Any two codewords of minimum weight d have the same support if and only if one is the scaler multiple of the other. It then follows from Theorem 10.19 that

$$A_d = (q-1)b = (q-1) \times (q-1)^e \frac{\binom{n}{e+1}}{\binom{2e+1}{e+1}},$$

where b is the number of blocks in the $(e+1)$-$(n, 2e+1, (q-1)^e)$ design formed by the supports of the codewords of minimum weight. ◻

Perfect codes are attractive, as their extended codes sometimes hold t-designs also. The next theorem gives the details and was proved in Assmus and Mattson (1974).

Theorem 10.21. *If C is a perfect binary code of length n and minimum weight $d = 2e + 1$ and contains the zero vector, the supports of the codewords of weight $2e + 2$ in the extended code $\overline{C}$ form an $(e+2)$-$(n+1, 2e+2, 1)$ design.*

Theorem 10.21 is not really useful, as the only nontrivial binary perfect codes are the Hamming codes and the binary Golay code with parameters $[23, 12, 7]$. Hence, we omit its proof and refer the reader to Assmus and Mattson (1974) for a proof.

10.5.2 *Designs in the* $[23, 12, 7]$ *Golay Binary Code*

The binary quadratic residue code $\text{QRC}_0^{(23,2)}$ is perfect. It has parameters $[23, 12, 7]$ and generator polynomial

$$g(x) = x^{11} + x^9 + x^7 + x^6 + x^5 + x + 1,$$

which is irreducible over GF(2). Its weight enumerator is

$$1 + 253z^7 + 506z^8 + 1288z^{11} + 1288z^{12} + 506z^{15} + 253z^{16} + z^{23}.$$

The weight enumerator of $(\text{QRC}_0^{(23,2)})^{\perp}$ is given by

$$1 + 506z^8 + 1288z^{12} + 253z^{16}.$$

The 4-designs held by $\mathrm{QRC}_0^{(23,2)}$ have the following parameters (v,k,λ):

$$(23,7,1), \ (23,8,4), \ (23,11,48), \ (23,12,72), \ (23,15,78), \ (23,16,52).$$

The 4-designs held by $(\mathrm{QRC}_0^{(23,2)})^\perp$ have the following parameters (v,k,λ):

$$(23,8,4), \ (23,12,72), \ (23,16,52).$$

By Theorem 10.19, the minimum weight codewords hold a 4-design. One can apply for the Assmus-Mattson Theorem to prove that the supports of the codewords of every fixed weight form a 4-design. The parameters of the designs are computed with Magma. They can also be computed from Theorem 10.18. The automorphism group of the code is the Mathieu group M_{23}, which is 4-transitive. Some of the designs above are complete and are not interesting. Further information about Golay codes can be found in MacWilliams and Sloane (1977)[Chapter 20].

10.5.3 *Designs in the* $[11,6,5]$ *Golay Ternary Code*

The ternary quadratic residue code $\mathrm{QRC}_0^{(11,3)}$ is perfect. It has parameters $[11,6,5]$ and generator polynomial

$$g(x) = x^5 + x^4 + 2x^3 + x^2 + 2,$$

which is irreducible over $\mathrm{GF}(3)$. Its weight enumerator

$$1 + 132z^5 + 132z^6 + 330z^8 + 110z^9 + 24z^{11}.$$

The code $(\mathrm{QRC}_0^{(11,3)})^\perp$ has parameters $[11,5,6]$ and weight enumerator

$$1 + 132z^6 + 110z^9.$$

The 4-designs held by $\mathrm{QRC}_0^{(11,3)}$ have the following parameters (v,k,λ):

$$(11,5,1), \ (11,6,3), (11,8,35), \ (11,9,21).$$

The 4-designs held by $(\mathrm{QRC}_0^{(11,3)})^\perp$ have the following parameters:

$$(11,6,3), \ (11,9,21).$$

By Theorem 10.19, the minimum weight codewords hold a 4-design. By the Assmus-Mattson Theorem, the supports of the codewords of every fixed weight form a 4-design. The parameters of the designs are computed with Magma. They can also be computed from Theorem 10.18. The automorphism group of the code is 4-transitive [MacWilliams and Sloane (1977)][Section 7]. Some of the designs above are complete and not interesting.

10.5.4 *Designs in the Hamming and Simplex Codes*

Hamming codes and Simplex codes are duals of each other. Hamming codes are widely employed in communication systems, data storage systems, and consumer electronics. They also hold many infinite families of designs. In this section, we will investigate the designs derived from these codes. This section is mainly based on Ding and Li (2017).

Hamming and Simplex codes were introduced in Section 2.13. Hamming codes are not cyclic in general. However, they are equivalent to cyclic codes under certain conditions.

Let α be a generator of $GF(q^m)^*$. Set $\beta = \alpha^{q-1}$. Let $g(x)$ be the minimal polynomial of β over $GF(q)$. Let $C_{(q,m)}$ denote the cyclic code of length $v = (q^m - 1)/(q - 1)$ over $GF(q)$ with generator polynomial $g(x)$. Then $C_{(q,m)}$ has parameters $[(q^m - 1)/(q - 1), (q^m - 1)/(q - 1) - m, d]$, where $d \in \{2, 3\}$. When $\gcd(q - 1, m) = 1$, $C_{(q,m)}$ has minimum weight 3 and is equivalent to the Hamming code. In this section, we use $C_{(q,m)}$ to denote the $[(q^m - 1)/(q - 1), (q^m - 1)/(q - 1) - m, 3]$ Hamming code over $GF(q)$, which may be cyclic or non-cyclic.

Lemma 10.22. *The weight distribution of* $C_{(q,m)}$ *is given by*

$$q^m A_k = \sum_{\substack{0 \le i \le \frac{q^{m-1}-1}{q-1} \\ 0 \le j \le q^{m-1} \\ i+j=k}} \left[\binom{\frac{q^{m-1}-1}{q-1}}{i} \binom{q^{m-1}}{j} \left((q-1)^k + (-1)^j (q-1)^i (q^m - 1) \right) \right]$$

for $0 \le k \le (q^m - 1)/(q - 1)$.

Proof. $C_{(q,m)}^\perp$ is the Simplex code and has weight enumerator is $1 + (q^m - 1)z^{q^{m-1}}$. By Theorem 2.4, the weight enumerator of $C_{(q,m)}$ is given by

$$q^m A(z) = (1 + (q-1)z)^v \left[1 + (q^m - 1) \left(\frac{1-z}{1 + (q-1)z} \right)^{q^{m-1}} \right]$$

$$= \left[(1 + (q-1)z)^v + (q^m - 1)(1-z)^{q^{m-1}} (1 + (q-1)z)^{\frac{q^{m-1}-1}{q-1}} \right]$$

$$= (1 + (q-1)z)^{\frac{q^{m-1}-1}{q-1}} \left[(1 + (q-1)z)^{q^{m-1}} + (q^m - 1)(1-z)^{q^{m-1}} \right].$$

The desired conclusion then follows. $\qquad\qquad\square$

It is known that the Hamming code over $GF(q)$ is perfect, and the codewords of weight 3 hold a 2-design by Theorem 10.19. The 2-designs documented in the following theorem may be viewed as an extension of this result.

Theorem 10.23. *Let $m \geq 3$ and $q = 2$ or $m \geq 2$ and $q > 2$, and let $\gcd(q-1,m) = 1$. Let $\mathcal{P} = \{0,1,2,\ldots,(q^m-q)/(q-1)\}$, and let $\mathcal{B}$ be the set of the supports of the codewords of Hamming weight k with $A_k \neq 0$ in $C_{(q,m)}$, where $3 \leq k \leq w$ and w is the largest such that $w - \lfloor(w+q-2)/(q-1)\rfloor < 3$. Then $(\mathcal{P},\mathcal{B})$ is a $2\text{-}((q^m-1)/(q-1),k,\lambda)$ design. In particular, the supports of the codewords of weight 3 in $C_{(q,m)}$ form a $2\text{-}((q^m-1)/(q-1),3,q-1)$ design.*

The supports of all codewords of weight q^{m-1} in $C_{(q,m)}^{\perp}$ form a $2\text{-}((q^m-1)/(q-1),q^{m-1},(q-1)q^{m-2})$ design. In particular, the complementary design of the design formed by the supports of all codewords of weight q^2 in $C_{(q,3)}^{\perp}$ is a Steiner system with parameters $2\text{-}(q^2+q+1,q+1,1)$.

Proof. $C_{(q,m)}^{\perp}$ is the Simplex code, and has weight enumerator $1 + (q^m-1)z^{q^{m-1}}$. Recall now Theorem 4.24 and the definition of w for $C_{(q,m)}$ and $w^{\perp}$ for $C_{(q,m)}^{\perp}$. Since $C_{(q,m)}$ has minimum weight 3. Given that the weight enumerator of $C_{(q,m)}^{\perp}$ is $1 + (q^m-1)z^{q^{m-1}}$, we deduce that $w^{\perp} = q^{m-1}$. Put $t = 2$. It then follows that $s = 1 = d - t$. The desired conclusion on the 2-design property then follows from Theorem 4.24 and Lemma 10.22.

We now prove that the supports of codewords of weight 3 in $C_{(q,m)}$ form a $2\text{-}((q^m-1)/(q-1),3,q-1)$ design. We have already proved that these supports form a $2\text{-}((q^m-1)/(q-1),3,\lambda)$ design. To determine the value λ for this design, we need to compute the total number b of blocks in this design. To this end, we first compute the total number of codewords of weight 3 in $C_{(q,m)}$. It follows from Lemma 10.22 that

$$
\begin{aligned}
q^m A_3 &= \binom{\frac{q^{m-1}-1}{q-1}}{0}\binom{q^{m-1}}{3}[(q-1)^3 - (q-1)^0(q^m-1)] + \\
&\quad \binom{\frac{q^{m-1}-1}{q-1}}{1}\binom{q^{m-1}}{1}[(q-1)^3 - (q-1)^1(q^m-1)] + \\
&\quad \binom{\frac{q^{m-1}-1}{q-1}}{2}\binom{q^{m-1}}{1}[(q-1)^3 - (q-1)^2(q^m-1)] + \\
&\quad \binom{\frac{q^{m-1}-1}{q-1}}{3}\binom{q^{m-1}}{0}[(q-1)^3 - (q-1)^3(q^m-1)] \\
&= q^m(q^m-1)(q^m-q).
\end{aligned}
$$

We obtain then

$$
A_3 = \frac{(q^m-1)(q^m-q)}{6},
$$

which also follows directly from Theorem 10.19. Since 3 is the minimum nonzero weight in $C_{(q,m)}$, it is easy to see that two codewords of weight 3 in $C_{(q,m)}$ have the same support if and only one is a scalar multiple of another. Thus, the total number b of blocks is given by

$$b := \frac{A_3}{q-1} = \frac{(q^m-1)(q^m-q)}{6(q-1)}.$$

It then follows that

$$\lambda = \frac{b\binom{3}{2}}{\binom{\frac{q^m-1}{q-1}}{2}} = q-1.$$

Since $C_{(q,m)}^\perp$ has weight enumerator $1+(q^m-1)z^{q^{m-1}}$, the total number $b^\perp$ of blocks in the design held in $C_{(q,m)}^\perp$ is given by

$$b^\perp = \frac{q^m-1}{q-1}.$$

Consequently,

$$\lambda^\perp = \frac{\frac{q^m-1}{q-1}\binom{q^{m-1}}{2}}{\binom{\frac{q^{m-1}-1}{q-1}}{2}} = (q-1)q^{m-2}.$$

Thus, the supports of all codewords of weight q^{m-1} in $C_{(q,m)}^\perp$ form a 2-design with parameters

$$\left((q^m-1)/(q-1),\, q^{m-1},\, (q-1)q^{m-2}\right).$$

$\square$

The Steiner system with the parameters 2-$(q^2+q+1,q+1,1)$ in Theorem 10.23 may be isomorphic to the projective plane $PG_1(2,q)$. Theorem 10.23 tells us that for some $k \geq 3$ with $A_k \neq 0$, the supports of the codewords with weight k in $C_{(q,m)}$ form 2-$((q^m-1)/(q-1),k,\lambda)$ design. However, it looks complicated to determine the parameter λ corresponding to $k \geq 4$. We propose the following problem.

Problem 10.24. Let $q \geq 3$ and $m \geq 2$. For $k \geq 4$ with $A_k \neq 0$, determine the value λ in the 2-$((q^m-1)/(q-1),k,\lambda)$ design formed by the supports of the codewords with weight k in $C_{(q,m)}$.

Notice that two binary codewords have the same support if and only if they are equal. When $q=2$, Theorem 10.23 becomes the following.

Corollary 10.25. Let $m \geq 3$. Let $\mathcal{P} = \{0,1,2,\ldots,2^m-2\}$, and let $\mathcal{B}$ be the set of the supports of the codewords with Hamming weight k in $C_{(2,m)}$, where $3 \leq k \leq 2^m-3$. Then $(\mathcal{P},\mathcal{B})$ is a 2-$(2^m-1,k,\lambda)$ design, where

$$\lambda = \frac{(k-1)kA_k}{(2^m-1)(2^m-2)}$$

and A_k is given in Lemma 10.22.

The supports of all codewords of weight 2^{m-1} in $C_{(2,m)}^{\perp}$ form a 2-$(2^m - 1, 2^{m-1}, 2^{m-2})$ design.

Corollary 10.25 says that each binary Hamming code $C_{(2,m)}$ and its dual code give a total number $2^m - 4$ of 2-designs with various block sizes.

The following are examples of the 2-designs held in the binary Hamming code.

Corollary 10.26. *Let $m \geq 4$. Let $\mathcal{P} = \{0, 1, 2, \ldots, 2^m - 2\}$, and let $\mathcal{B}$ be the set of the supports of the codewords with Hamming weight 3 in $C_{(2,m)}$. Then $(\mathcal{P}, \mathcal{B})$ is a 2-$(2^m - 1, 3, 1)$ design, i.e., a Steiner triple system $S(2, 3, 2^m - 1)$.*

Proof. By Lemma 10.22, we have

$$A_3 = \frac{(2^{m-1} - 1)(2^m - 1)}{3}.$$

The desired value for λ then follows from Corollary 10.25. $\square$

Corollary 10.26 presents another infinite family of Steiner systems. Two other families were described in Corollaries 6.31 and 5.22. Theorem 6.64 documents an infinite family of Steiner systems $S(2, 4, 2^m)$ for $m \equiv 2 \pmod 4$.

Corollary 10.27. *Let $m \geq 4$. Let $\mathcal{P} = \{0, 1, 2, \ldots, 2^m - 2\}$, and let $\mathcal{B}$ be the set of the supports of the codewords with Hamming weight 4 in $C_{(2,m)}$. Then $(\mathcal{P}, \mathcal{B})$ is a 2-$(2^m - 1, 4, 2^{m-1} - 2)$ design.*

Proof. By Lemma 10.22, we have

$$A_4 = \frac{(2^{m-1} - 1)(2^{m-1} - 2)(2^m - 1)}{6}.$$

The desired value for λ then follows from Corollary 10.25. $\square$

Corollary 10.28. *Let $m \geq 4$. Let $\mathcal{P} = \{0, 1, 2, \ldots, 2^m - 2\}$, and let $\mathcal{B}$ be the set of the supports of the codewords with Hamming weight 5 in $C_{(2,m)}$. Then $(\mathcal{P}, \mathcal{B})$ is a 2-$(2^m - 1, 5, \lambda)$ design, where*

$$\lambda = \frac{2(2^{m-1} - 2)(2^{m-1} - 4)}{3}.$$

Proof. By Lemma 10.22, we have

$$A_5 = \frac{(2^{m-1} - 1)(2^{m-1} - 2)(2^{m-1} - 4)(2^m - 1)}{15}.$$

The desired value for λ then follows from Corollary 10.25. $\square$

Corollary 10.29. *Let $m \geq 4$. Let $\mathcal{P} = \{0, 1, 2, \ldots, 2^m - 2\}$, and let $\mathcal{B}$ be the set of the supports of the codewords with Hamming weight 6 in $C_{(2,m)}$. Then $(\mathcal{P}, \mathcal{B})$ is a $2\text{-}(2^m - 1, 6, \lambda)$ design, where*

$$\lambda = \frac{(2^{m-1} - 2)(2^{m-1} - 3)(2^{m-1} - 4)}{3}.$$

Proof. By Lemma 10.22, we have

$$A_6 = \frac{(2^{m-1} - 1)(2^{m-1} - 2)(2^{m-1} - 3)(2^{m-1} - 4)(2^m - 1)}{45}.$$

The desired value for λ then follows from Corollary 10.25. $\qquad\square$

Corollary 10.30. *Let $m \geq 4$. Let $\mathcal{P} = \{0, 1, 2, \ldots, 2^m - 2\}$, and let $\mathcal{B}$ be the set of the supports of the codewords with Hamming weight 7 in $C_{(2,m)}$. Then $(\mathcal{P}, \mathcal{B})$ is a $2\text{-}(2^m - 1, 7, \lambda)$ design, where*

$$\lambda = \frac{(2^{m-1} - 2)(2^{m-1} - 3)(4 \times 2^{2(m-1)} - 30 \times 2^{m-1} + 71)}{30}.$$

Proof. By Lemma 10.22, we have

$$A_7 = (2^{m-1} - 1)(2^{m-1} - 2)(2^{m-1} - 3)(2^m - 1) \times$$
$$\frac{4 \times 2^{2(m-1)} - 30 \times 2^{m-1} + 71}{630}.$$

The desired value for λ then follows from Corollary 10.25. $\qquad\square$

10.6 Designs in Uniformly Packed Codes

Quasi-perfect codes are an interesting class of codes, and uniformly packed codes are a subclass of quasi-perfect codes. The purpose of this section is to treat these codes and their designs.

10.6.1 *Definitions, Properties and General Results*

Recall that a code C is perfect if its covering radius equals its packing radius, i.e., $\rho(C) = e(C)$. In view that there is only one infinite family of perfect linear codes, it would be very interesting to consider codes C such that $\rho(C) = e(C) + 1$.

A code C over $\mathrm{GF}(q)$ with minimum distance d is *quasi perfect* if

$$\rho(C) = e(C) + 1 = \left\lfloor \frac{d-1}{2} \right\rfloor + 1.$$

By definition, in a quasi-perfect code every vector in $\mathrm{GF}(q)^n$ is at distance $e + 1$ or less from at least one codeword, here and hereafter e means $e(C)$.

Let C be a quasi-perfect e-error correcting code. Then the minimum distance $d(C) = 2e + 2$ or $d(C) = 2e + 1$. Let $v \in \mathrm{GF}(q)^n$ be at distance $e + 1$ from some codeword $c \in C$. If $d(C) = 2e + 2$, then v is at distance $e + 1$ or more from every codeword in C. But, if $d(C) = 2e + 1$, v can be at distance e from some other codeword, or be at distance $e + 1$ or more from every codeword. In general, the number of codewords at distance $e + 1$ from v depends on v.

We say that an e-error correcting code C is a *uniformly packed code* with parameters λ and μ if,

- it is quasi-perfect (i.e., $\rho(C) = e + 1$); and
- for every vector $v \in \mathrm{GF}(q)^n$ at distance e from some codeword, the number of codewords at distance $e + 1$ from v is a constant λ; and
- for every vector $v \in \mathrm{GF}(q)^n$ at distance $e + 1$ or more from every codeword, the number of codewords at distance $e + 1$ from v is a constant μ.

Note that $\lambda = 0$ if $d(C) = 2e + 2$.

The following two theorems give a characterisation of uniformly packed codes [Goethals and Van Tilborg (1975)].

Theorem 10.31. *A quasi-perfect e-error correcting code C is uniformly packed with parameters λ and μ if and only if, as an element in $\mathbb{C}[\mathrm{GF}(q)^n]$, it satisfies*
$$(\mu S_e - \lambda Y_e + Y_{e+1}) * C = \mu S_n.$$

Theorem 10.32. *An e-error correcting code $C \subseteq \mathrm{GF}(q)^n$ is a uniformly packed code with parameters λ and μ if and only if it is quasi-perfect and its characteristic polynomial is the polynomial of degree $e + 1$ defined by the Krawtchouk expansion $\sum \alpha_i P_i(q, n; x)$ with coefficients*
$$\alpha_{e+1} = \frac{1}{\mu}, \ \alpha_e = 1 - \frac{\lambda}{\mu} \ \text{and} \ \alpha_i = 1 \ \text{for} \ 0 \le i \le e - 1. \tag{10.20}$$

Corollary 10.33. *Any uniformly packed e-error correcting code C is completely regular.*

Proof. By Theorem 10.32, the external distance s of C is $e + 1$. By definition, $d \ge 2e + 1$. The desired conclusion then follows from Theorem 10.10. $\quad\square$

The following is a very interesting result [Goethals and Van Tilborg (1975)].

Corollary 10.34. *In a uniformly packed e-error correcting binary code containing the zero vector, the supports of all codewords with any nonzero weight k form a t-design, where*
$$t = \begin{cases} e & \text{if } d = 2e + 1, \\ e + 1 & \text{if } d = 2e + 2. \end{cases}$$

Proof. The desired conclusion of corollary follows from Theorem 10.11 and Corollary 10.33. □

Corollary 10.34 tells us that uniformly packed e-error correcting binary codes hold t-designs. However, we do not have results on possible t-designs held in uniformly packed e-error correcting codes over $GF(q)$ for $q > 2$. The reader should be informed that uniformly packed codes over $GF(q)$ do hold "q-ary t-designs", which are different from classical t-designs for $q > 2$ [Goethals and Van Tilborg (1975)].

Uniformly packed binary codes with $\lambda + 1 = \mu$ were introduced in [Semakov, Zinovjev and Zaitzev (1973)]. Such codes are said to be *strongly uniformly packed*. We have the following result for these codes [Van Tilborg (1976)].

Theorem 10.35. *Let C be a uniformly packed e-error correcting binary code containing the zero vector and satisfying $\mu - \lambda = 1$ and $d = 2e + 1$. Then in the extended code $\overline{C}$, the supports of codewords of any fixed weight form an $(e+1)$-design.*

Since the main objective of this monograph is to give a well-rounded treatment of designs from linear codes, the following theorem will be very useful to us [Van Tilborg (1976)].

Theorem 10.36. *Let C be an e-error correcting linear code. Then C is uniformly packed if and only if the dual code $C^{\perp}$ contains exactly $e + 1$ nonzero weights.*

The following is a corollary of Theorem 10.32 [Goethals and Van Tilborg (1975)].

Corollary 10.37. *A linear single-error-correcting code is uniformly packed if and only if its dual is a two-weight code.*

Example 10.38. For the extended binary Hamming code $\overline{C_{(2,3)}}$ with parameters $[8, 4, 4]$, we have the following:

(a) It is quasi perfect, as its packing and covering radii are 1 and 2, respectively.
(b) It is a uniformly packed code with parameters $(\lambda, \mu) = (0, 4)$, as the code is self-dual and has two nonzero weight 4 and 8 (by Corollary 10.37).

10.6.2 *Designs in Uniformly Packed Binary Codes*

We are much interested in uniformly packed e-error correcting codes, as they hold designs. Such codes with a large e are desired. However, we have the following result due to Van Tilborg (1976).

Theorem 10.39. *There is no uniformly packed e-error correcting code for $e \geq 4$.*

No infinite family of uniformly packed 3-error correcting codes is known in the literature. There are only a small number of sporadic uniformly packed 3-error correcting codes. Only a few finite families of uniformly packed 2-error correcting codes are known.

The parameters of known infinite families of uniformly packed single-error correcting codes are summarized in Tables 10.1, 10.2, and 10.3, where k is the dimension of the codes. Three more families of uniformly packed single-error correcting binary codes were introduced in Van Tilborg (1976). These codes are obtained from two-weight projective codes. When $q = 2$, some of these codes hold either 1-designs or 2-designs. The extended codes of some of them may hold 2-designs. For detailed descriptions of these codes, the reader should consult Goethals and Van Tilborg (1975) and Van Tilborg (1976). We are not interested in 1-designs, and thus will not work out parameters of these designs.

Table 10.1　Parameters of uniformly packed 1-error correcting codes (I)

Number	1	2	3	4
q	q	q	2^m	2^m
n	$r\frac{q^m-1}{q-1}$	$r\frac{q^m+1}{q-1}$	2^m+2	$2^{2m}-1$
k	$2m$	$2m$	3	3
λ	$\binom{r-1}{2}+\frac{q^m-q}{2}$	$\binom{r+2}{2}-\frac{q^m+q}{2}$	0	$2^{3m-1}-2^{2m}-2^m+3$
μ	$\binom{r}{2}$	$\binom{r+1}{2}$	$2^{m-1}+1$	$(2^{m-1}-1)(2^{2m}-1)$

Table 10.2　Parameters of uniformly packed 1-error correcting codes (II)

Number	5	6
q	2^m	2^m
n	$2^{m-1}(2^m-1)$	$(2^{m-1}+1)(2^m+1)$
k	3	3
λ	$(2^{m-2}-1)(2^{m-1}-1)(2^m+1)$	$2^{m-2}(2^{m-1}+3)(2^m-1)$
μ	$2^{m-2}(2^{m-1}-1)(2^m-1)$	$2^{m-2}(2^{m-1}+1)(2^m+1)$

Table 10.3　Parameters of uniformly packed 1-error correcting codes (III)

Number	7	8
q	2	q
n	$(2^m-1)(2^{2m}-1)$	$(q^m-q)/(q-1)$
k	$3m$	m
λ	$2^{3m-1}-2^{2m}-2^{m-1}+2$	$(n-2)(q-1)/2$
μ	$(2^{m-1}-1)(2^{2m}-1)$	$n(q-1)/2$

Parameters of known uniformly packed e-error correcting codes for $e \in \{2,3\}$ are summarised in Table 10.4. The parameters in the first row are from the Preparata codes, which are nonlinear. The narrow-sense primitive BCH binary code with length $2^{2\ell+1} - 1$ and designed distance 5 is uniformly packed, and has the parameters of the second row [Gorenstein, Peterson and Zieler (1960)]. Its dual code has the weight distribution of Table 8.1.

Table 10.4 Parameters of uniformly packed e-error correcting codes for $e \geq 2$

No.	q	e	n	λ	μ
1	2	2	$2^{2\ell} - 1$	$\frac{2^{2\ell}-4}{3}$	$\frac{2^{2\ell}-1}{3}$
2	2	2	$2^{2\ell+1} - 1$	$\frac{2^{2\ell}-1}{3}$	$\frac{2^{2\ell}-1}{3}$
3	2	2	11	2	3
4	2	2	21	1	4
5	2	2	22	0	2
6	2	3	24	0	6
7	3	1	9	4	9
8	3	1	10	0	3
9	3	2	12	0	4

Now we present a general construction of other families of linear codes that are uniformly packed and have also the parameters of the second row. Let f be a function from $\mathrm{GF}(2^m)$ to itself with $f(0) = 0$. Let α be a generator of $\mathrm{GF}(2^m)$. Define a matrix

$$H_f = \begin{bmatrix} 1 & \alpha & \alpha^2 & \cdots & \alpha^{2^m-2} \\ f(1) & f(\alpha) & f(\alpha^2) & \cdots & f(\alpha^{2^m-2}) \end{bmatrix}, \tag{10.21}$$

where each entry b means the column vector $(b_1, b_2, \ldots, b_m)^T$ in $\mathrm{GF}(2)^m$, where

$$b = \sum_{i=1}^{m} b_i \beta_i$$

and $\{\beta_1, \beta_2, \ldots, \beta_m\}$ is a basis of $\mathrm{GF}(2^m)$ over $\mathrm{GF}(2)$. Thus, H_f is a $2m \times (2^m - 1)$ matrix over $\mathrm{GF}(2)$. Let C_f denote the linear code over $\mathrm{GF}(2)$ with parity-check matrix H_f. When $f(x) = x^e$, the code is the cyclic code over $\mathrm{GF}(2)$ with generator polynomial $g(x) = \mathrm{LCM}(\mathbb{M}_\alpha(x), \mathbb{M}_{\alpha^e}(x))$.

The following result was proved in Carlet, Charpin and Zinoviev (1998).

Theorem 10.40. *Let m be odd. Let f be a mapping from $\mathrm{GF}(2^m)$ to itself with $f(0) = 0$. Then, f is almost bent if and only if C_f is a uniformly packed code with minimum distance 5 and covering radius 3.*

If f is almost bent, then the dual code $C_f^{\perp}$ has the weight distribution in Table 8.1, and the code C_f has the parameters of the second column in Table 10.4.

Several families of known almost bent functions were introduced in Section 1.10. Plugging them into Theorem 10.40, one obtains several families of cyclic codes which are uniformly packed and double-error correcting. These codes and the narrow-sense primitive BCH code with designed distance 5 all hold 2-designs. The parameters of the 2-designs were determined in Section 8.1. Uniformly packed codes were also investigated in Calderbank (1982), Tonchev (1996) and Rifà and Zinoviev (2010).

Uniformly packed codes over $GF(q)$ hold t-designs in many cases for $q \geq 3$. But it is open when they hold t-designs in general. Some quasi-perfect codes may not be uniformly packed, but may still hold t-designs. For example, a class of quasi-perfect ternary codes in Danev and Dodunekov (2008) hold 1-designs.

Chapter 11

Designs from QR and Self-Dual Codes

Self-dual codes are fascinating in both theory and application. The objective of this chapter is to present a summary of results about self-dual codes and extended quadratic residue codes as well as their designs. We restrict ourselves to only theories of these codes that are related to t-designs, as self-dual codes form a huge topic with hundreds of references.

11.1 Self-Dual Codes and Their Designs

11.1.1 *Definition and Existence*

So far in this monograph, we have only associated to the ambient space $\mathrm{GF}(q)^n$ the following standard (Euclidean) inner product

$$\langle x, y \rangle = \sum_{i=1}^{n} x_i y_i, \tag{11.1}$$

where $x = (x_1, \ldots, x_n) \in \mathrm{GF}(q)^n$ and $y = (y_1, \ldots, y_n) \in \mathrm{GF}(q)^n$. If $q = r^2$, the *Hermitian inner product* is defined by

$$\langle u, v \rangle = \sum_{i=1}^{n} u_i v_i^r, \tag{11.2}$$

where $u = (u_1, \ldots, u_n) \in \mathrm{GF}(q)^n$ and $v = (v_1, \ldots, v_n) \in \mathrm{GF}(q)^n$. The map $x \mapsto x^r$, $x \in \mathrm{GF}(r^2)$, is called the *global conjugation*.

Recall that the (Hermitian) dual of a linear code C over $\mathrm{GF}(q)$ is defined to be

$$C^{\perp} = \{x \in \mathrm{GF}(q)^n : \langle x, y \rangle = 0 \text{ for all } y \in C\}.$$

A code C is *self-orthogonal* if $C \subseteq C^{\perp}$, and C is *self-dual* if $C = C^{\perp}$. By definition, the length n of a self-dual code must be even, and the dimension of a self-dual code is equal to half of the length. A code C is *formally self-dual* if C and $C^{\perp}$ have the same weight distribution. By definition, formally self-dual codes contain self-dual codes as a subclass.

In this section, we consider linear codes over $\mathrm{GF}(q)$, where $q \in \{2,3,4\}$. Whenever we talk about the orthogonality and dual of a linear code over $\mathrm{GF}(4)$, we mean the orthogonality and dual with respect to the Hermitian inner product, unless otherwise stated.

Let C be an $[n, n/2, d]$ self-dual code over $\mathrm{GF}(q)$, where $q \in \{2,3,4\}$. By definition, we have $\langle c, c \rangle = 0$ for all $c \in C$. When $q \in \{2,3\}$,

$$0 = \langle c, c \rangle = \sum_{i=0}^{n-1} c_i^2 = \mathtt{wt}(c) \bmod q.$$

When $q = 4$,

$$0 = \langle c, c \rangle = \sum_{i=0}^{n-1} c_i^3 = \mathtt{wt}(c) \bmod 2.$$

Thus, for self-dual codes over $\mathrm{GF}(2)$, $\mathrm{GF}(3)$, and $\mathrm{GF}(4)$ all weights are divisible by 2, 3, and 2, respectively.

A linear code C is said to be *divisible* if there is an integer $\Delta > 1$ such that every weight in C is divisible by Δ. The largest integer Δ, for which a code C is divisible, is called the *divisor* of C.

The following is a fundamental theorem about self-dual codes over small fields ([Ward (1981, 1998)], [Huffman and Pless (2003)][p. 339]), and is called the Gleason-Pierce-Ward Theorem.

Theorem 11.1. *Let C be an $[n, n/2]$ divisible code of length n over $\mathrm{GF}(q)$ with divisor Δ. Then one (or more) of the following holds:*

(I) $(q, \Delta) = (2, 2)$.

(II) $(q, \Delta) = (2, 4)$ *and* C *is self-dual.*

(III) $(q, \Delta) = (3, 3)$ *and* C *is self-dual.*

(IV) $(q, \Delta) = (4, 2)$ *and* C *is Hermitian self-dual.*

(V) $\Delta = 2$ *and* C *is equivalent to the code over* $\mathrm{GF}(q)$ *with generator matrix* $[I_{n/2} I_{n/2}]$.

The code in the last case in Theorem 11.1 is not interesting from the viewpoint of design theory. Self-dual codes over small fields are classified into the following types according to Theorem 11.1. A self-dual code C over $\mathrm{GF}(q)$ is said to be of

- Type I if $(q, \Delta) = (2, 2)$ and there is a codeword with weight $w \equiv 2 \pmod 4$;
- Type II if $(q, \Delta) = (2, 4)$;
- Type III if $(q, \Delta) = (3, 3)$; and

- Type IV if $(q, \Delta) = (4, 2)$ and C is Hermitian self-dual.

Binary divisible codes with $\Delta = 4$ are said to be *doubly-even*. Codes with $\Delta = 2$ and at least one codeword of weight 2 mod 4 are said to be *singly-even*.

A basic question regarding self-dual codes is their existence. The theorem below answers this question [Pless (1968)].

Theorem 11.2. *There exists a self-dual code over* $\mathrm{GF}(q)$ *of even length n if and only if* $(-1)^{n/2}$ *is a square in* $\mathrm{GF}(q)$. *Furthermore, if n is even and* $(-1)^{n/2}$ *is not a square in* $\mathrm{GF}(q)$, *then the dimension of a maximal self-orthogonal code of length n is* $(n-2)/2$. *If n is odd, then the dimension of a maximal self-orthogonal code of length n is* $(n-1)/2$.

The following follows from Theorem 11.2.

Corollary 11.3. *Self-dual doubly-even binary codes of length n exist if and only if* $8|n$; *self-dual ternary codes of length n exist if and only if* $4|n$; *and Hermitian self-dual codes over* $\mathrm{GF}(4)$ *of length n exist if and only if n is even.*

Example 11.4. Define

$$G = \begin{bmatrix} 1 & 0 & 0 & 0 & 1 & 0 & 1 & 1 \\ 0 & 1 & 0 & 0 & 1 & 1 & 1 & 0 \\ 0 & 0 & 1 & 0 & 1 & 1 & 0 & 1 \\ 0 & 0 & 0 & 1 & 0 & 1 & 1 & 1 \end{bmatrix}.$$

The binary code generated by G is a self-dual code of Type II and has parameters $[8, 4, 4]$. Its weight enumerator is $1 + 14z^4 + z^8$.

11.1.2 Weight Enumerators of Self-Dual Codes

The weight enumerator of a code C of length n has the univariate polynomial form

$$A_C(z) = \sum_{i=0}^{n} A_i z^i.$$

It can also be expressed with the following bivariate polynomial

$$W_C(x, y) = \sum_{i=0}^{n} A_i x^i y^{n-i}.$$

In this section, we use the later.

The weight enumerator of a self-dual code over $\mathrm{GF}(q)$ differs from code to code in general, but can be expressed as a combination of special polynomials that are the weight enumerators of specific codes of small length, when $q \in \{2, 3, 4\}$. The following theorem gives such expression ([Huffman and Pless (2003)][p. 341], [Gleason (1971)], [MacWilliams, Mallows and Sloane (1972)]).

Theorem 11.5 (Gleason). *Let C be a self-dual code of length n over* GF(q) *with* $q \leq 4$ *and let*

$$g_1(x,y) = x^2 + y^2,$$
$$g_2(x,y) = x^8 + 14x^4y^4 + y^8,$$
$$g_3(x,y) = x^{24} + 759x^{16}y^8 + 2576x^{12}y^{12} + 759x^8y^{16} + y^{24},$$
$$g_4(x,y) = y^4 + 8x^3y,$$
$$g_5(x,y) = y^{12} + 264x^6y^6 + 440x^9y^3 + 24x^{12},$$
$$g_6(x,y) = y^2 + 3x^2,$$
$$g_7(x,y) = y^6 + 45x^4y^2 + 18x^6.$$

Then we have the following:

(i) If $q = 2$ and C is formally self-dual and even,

$$W_C(x,y) = \sum_{i=0}^{\lfloor \frac{n}{8} \rfloor} a_i g_1(x,y)^{\frac{n}{2}-4i} g_2(x,y)^i.$$

(ii) If $q = 2$ and C is self-dual and doubly-even,

$$W_C(x,y) = \sum_{i=0}^{\lfloor \frac{n}{24} \rfloor} a_i g_2(x,y)^{\frac{n}{8}-3i} g_3(x,y)^i.$$

(iii) If $q = 3$ and C is self-dual,

$$W_C(x,y) = \sum_{i=0}^{\lfloor \frac{n}{12} \rfloor} a_i g_4(x,y)^{\frac{n}{4}-3i} g_5(x,y)^i.$$

(iv) If $q = 4$ and C is Hermitian self-dual,

$$W_C(x,y) = \sum_{i=0}^{\lfloor \frac{n}{6} \rfloor} a_i g_6(x,y)^{\frac{n}{6}-3i} g_7(x,y)^i.$$

In all cases, all a_i are rational and $\sum_i a_i = 1$.

An immediate corollary of Theorem 11.5 is the restriction on the length of a self-dual code.

Corollary 11.6. *Let C be a self-dual code of length n over* GF(q) *with* $q \leq 4$. *Then*

- $2 \mid n$ *if C is of Type I or Type IV,*
- $4 \mid n$ *if C is of Type III, and*
- $8 \mid n$ *if C is of Type II.*

The polynomials g_i in Theorem 11.5 are weight enumerators of certain codes with small length. For instances, $g_1(x,y)$ is the weight enumerator of the binary repetition code of length 2, and $g_2(x,y)$ is the weight enumerator of the binary code of Example 11.4.

With the help of Theorem 11.5, it could be easier to determine the weight enumerator of some self-dual codes theoretically and experimentally. In addition, Theorem 11.5 could be employed to develop upper bounds on the minimum weight of self-dual codes (see the following subsection for further information).

11.1.3 *Extremal Self-Dual Codes and Their Designs*

Theorem 11.5 was employed to develop the following upper bounds on the minimum distance of seld-dual codes ([MacWilliams, Odlyzko, Sloane and Ward (1978)], [Mallows and Sloane (1973)], [Rains (1998)]).

Theorem 11.7. *Let C be a self-dual divisible $[n, n/2, d]$ code over* GF(q). *Then*

$$d \leq 4\lfloor \tfrac{n}{24} \rfloor + 4, \quad \text{if } C \text{ is of Type II or Type I and } n \not\equiv 22 \pmod{24},$$
$$d \leq 4\lfloor \tfrac{n}{24} \rfloor + 6, \quad \text{if } C \text{ is of Type I and } n \equiv 22 \pmod{24},$$
$$d \leq 3\lfloor \tfrac{n}{12} \rfloor + 3, \quad \text{if } C \text{ is of Type III},$$
$$d \leq 2\lfloor \tfrac{n}{6} \rfloor + 2, \quad \text{if } C \text{ is of Type IV}.$$

Self-dual codes that achieve the corresponding bound in Theorem 11.7 are said to be *extremal*. Extremal self-dual codes are interesting to us as they hold t-designs as a consequence of the Assmus-Mattson Theorem.

Theorem 11.8. *The following results on t-designs hold in extremal codes of Types II, III, and IV.*

(a) *Let C be a $[24m + 8\mu, 12m + 4\mu, 4m + 4]$ extremal Type II code for $\mu \in \{0, 1, 2\}$. Then codewords of any fixed weight except 0 hold t-designs for the following parameters:*

    (1) $t = 5$ if $\mu = 0$ and $m \geq 1$,
    (2) $t = 3$ if $\mu = 1$ and $m \geq 0$, and
    (3) $t = 1$ if $\mu = 2$ and $m \geq 0$.

(b) *Let C be a $[12m + 4\mu, 6m + 2\mu, 3m + 3]$ extremal Type III code for $\mu \in \{0, 1, 2\}$. Then codewords of any fixed weight i with $3m + 3 \leq i \leq 6m + 3$ hold t-designs for the following parameters:*

    (1) $t = 5$ if $\mu = 0$ and $m \geq 1$,
    (2) $t = 3$ if $\mu = 1$ and $m \geq 0$, and
    (3) $t = 1$ if $\mu = 2$ and $m \geq 0$.

(c) *Let C be a $[6m+2\mu, 3m+\mu, 2m+2]$ extremal Type IV code for $\mu \in \{0,1,2\}$. Then codewords of any fixed weight i with $2m+2 \le i \le 3m+2$ hold t-designs for the following parameters:*

  (1) $t = 5$ if $\mu = 0$ and $m \ge 2$,
  (2) $t = 3$ if $\mu = 1$ and $m \ge 1$, and
  (3) $t = 1$ if $\mu = 2$ and $m \ge 0$.

The conclusions of Theorem 11.8 can be proved with the Assmus-Mattson Theorem (see Huffman and Pless (2003)[p. 349]). Part (a) of Theorem 11.8 has been generalised as follows [Janusz (2000)].

Theorem 11.9. *Let C be a $[24m+8\mu, 12m+4\mu, 4m+4]$ extremal Type II code for $\mu \in \{0,1,2\}$, where $m \ge 1$ if $\mu = 0$. Then*

  (i) either the codewords of any fixed weight $i \ne 0$ hold t-designs for $t = 7 - 2\mu$, or

  (ii) the codewords of any fixed weight $i \ne 0$ hold t-designs for $t = 5 - 2\mu$ and there is no i with $0 < i < 24m+8\mu$ such that codewords of weight i hold a $(6-2\mu)$-design.

Below is an example of self-dual codes and their designs.

Example 11.10. Let C be the binary cyclic code of length 31 generated by

$$g(x) = x^{15} + x^{13} + x^{12} + x^{11} + x^9 + x^7 + x^5 + x^4 + x^3 + x + 1.$$

Then C has parameters $[31, 16, 7]$. The extended code $\overline{C}$ has parameters $[32, 16, 8]$ and weight enumerator

$$y^{32} + 620x^8y^{24} + 13888x^{12}y^{30} + 36518x^{16}y^{16} + 13888x^{20}y^{12} + 620x^{24}y^8 + x^{32}.$$

$\overline{C}$ is doubly-even and self-dual. By Theorem 11.7, it holds 3-designs with the following parameters:

$$(32,8,7), \ (32,12,616), \ (32,16,4123), \ (32,20,3193), \ (32,24,253).$$

The existence and construction of extremal self-dual codes are important for the theory of t-designs. Unfortunately, we have the following negative results regarding the existence question [Zhang (1999)].

Theorem 11.11. *Let C be an extremal self-dual code of length n and of Type II or IV. Assume that n is divisible by 8 or 2, respectively. Then we have the following:*

  (a) Type II: $i < 154$ if $n = 24i$, $i < 159$ if $n = 24i+8$ and $i < 164$ if $n = 24i+16$. In particular C cannot exist for $n > 3928$.

(b) *Type IV:* $i < 17$ *if* $n = 6i$, $i < 20$ *if* $n = 6i + 2$ *and* $i < 22$ *if* $n = 6i + 4$. *In particular* C *cannot exist for* $n > 130$.

Theorem 11.12. *Let* C *be an extremal self-dual code of Type III and length* n. *Then* $n < 144$ *and, moreover,* $n \neq 72, 96, 120$.

There is no explicit bound on the length of an extremal Type I code. In this case only an asymptotic bound is known [Rains (2003)]. Anyway, Type I extremal self-dual codes are not interesting to us, as they may not hold t-designs. In view there are only finitely many extremal self-dual codes, extremal self-dual codes are of limited interest to us. There are many references on the constructions and classification of extremal self-dual codes of length within the ranges defined by Theorems 11.11 and 11.12. The reader is referred to Malevich (2012) for details.

11.2 Designs from Extended Quadratic Residue Codes

Let n be an odd prime and q be a prime power with $\gcd(n, q) = 1$. Assume that q is a quadratic residue modulo n. Recall the quadratic residue code $\mathrm{QRC}_0^{(n,q)}$ and its extended code $\overline{\mathrm{QRC}}_0^{(n,q)}$ treated in Section 3.8.

11.2.1 *Infinite Families of 2-Designs and 3-Designs*

Theorem 11.13. *For every nonzero weight* k *in* $\overline{\mathrm{QRC}}_0^{(n,q)}$, *the supports of all the codewords with weight* k *in this code hold a 2-design, and in particular a 3-design if* $n \equiv 3 \pmod 4$.

Proof. It was proved in Section 3.8.2 that the group $\mathrm{PSL}_2(\mathrm{GF}(n))$ is a subgroup of the permutation automorphism group of $\overline{\mathrm{QRC}}_0^{(n,q)}$. It was proved in Section 1.8.10 that $\mathrm{PSL}_2(\mathrm{GF}(n))$ is doubly transitive on $\{0, 1, \ldots, n-1, \infty\}$ and 3-homogeneous on $\{0, 1, \ldots, n-1, \infty\}$ if $n \equiv 3 \pmod 4$. The desired conclusions then follow from Theorem 4.30. $\qquad\square$

Theorem 11.13 describes an infinite family of 2-designs for primes $n \equiv 1 \pmod 4$ and an infinite family of 3-designs for primes $n \equiv 3 \pmod 4$.

11.2.2 *Sporadic 5-Designs from Self-Dual Codes*

In this section, we document sporadic 5-designs from certain self-dual codes, which are extended irreducible cyclic codes. Some of the codes are the extended perfect Golay codes. The weight enumerators of these codes are computed with

Magma. Their design property can be proved with the Assmus-Mattson Theorem. An alternative proof of their design property is via their automorphism groups [Assmus and Mattson (1969)]. The automorphism groups of some of the codes presented in this section are called Mathieu groups [MacWilliams and Sloane (1977)][Chapter 20].

Example 11.14. The binary code $\overline{\mathrm{QRC}}_0^{(23,2)}$ has parameters $[24,12,8]$ and weight enumerator

$$1 + 759z^8 + 2576z^{12} + 759z^{16} + z^{24}.$$

The code is self-dual. By the Assmus-Mattson Theorem, it holds 5-designs. The parameters (v,k,λ) are

$$(24,8,1), \ (24,12,48), \ (24,16,78).$$

Example 11.15. The binary code $\overline{\mathrm{QRC}}_0^{(47,2)}$ has parameters $[48,24,12]$ and weight enumerator

$$1 + 17296z^{12} + 535095z^{16} + 3995376z^{20} + 7681680z^{24} +$$
$$3995376z^{28} + 535095z^{32} + 17296z^{36} + z^{48}.$$

The code is self-dual. By the Assmus-Mattson Theorem, it holds 5-designs. The parameters (v,k,λ) are

$$(48,12,8), \ (48,16,1365), \ (48,20,36176), \ (48,24,190680),$$
$$(48,28,229320), \ (48,32,62930), \ (48,36,3808).$$

Example 11.16. The ternary code $\overline{\mathrm{QRC}}_0^{(11,3)}$ has parameters $[12,6,6]$ and weight enumerator $1 + 264z^6 + 440z^9 + 24z^{12}$. The code is self-dual, and holds only one nontrivial 5-design, i.e., the Steiner system $S(5,6,12)$.

Example 11.17. Recall the BCH code $\mathcal{C}_{(q,n,\delta,b)}$ over $\mathrm{GF}(q)$ defined in Section 3.7, where n is the length with $\gcd(n,q)=1$, δ is the designed distance, and b is a nonnegative integer. In this example, we consider the code $\mathcal{C}_{(9,11,2,1)}$ over $\mathrm{GF}(9)$ and its extended code $\overline{\mathcal{C}_{(9,11,2,1)}}$.

The code $\mathcal{C}_{(9,11,2,1)}$ has parameters $[11,6,5]$ and weight enumerator

$$1 + 528z^5 + 528z^6 + 15840z^7 + 40920z^8 + 129800z^9 + 198000z^{10} + 145824z^{11}.$$

Its dual $\mathcal{C}_{(9,11,2,1)}^{\perp}$ has parameters $[11,5,6]$ and weight enumerator

$$1 + 528z^6 + 7920z^8 + 11000z^9 + 23760z^{10} + 15840z^{11}.$$

Notice that the code $\mathcal{C}_{(9,11,2,1)}$ over $\mathrm{GF}(9)$ has generator polynomial $x^5 + x^4 + 2x^3 + x^2 + 2$, which is over the subfield $\mathrm{GF}(3)$ and is irreducible over $\mathrm{GF}(9)$.

The subfield subcode $C_{(9,11,2,1)}|_{GF(3)}$ is the $[11,6,5]$ Golay ternary code treated in Section 10.5.3. The codes $C_{(9,11,2,1)}$ over GF(9) and its dual support the same set of 4-designs as the $[11,6,5]$ Golay ternary code and its dual documented in Section 10.5.3, including the Steiner system $S(4,5,11)$.

The extended code $\overline{C_{(9,11,2,1)}}$ over GF(9) has parameters $[12,6,6]$ and weight enumerator

$$1 + 1056z^6 + 23760z^8 + 44000z^9 + 142560z^{10} + 190080z^{11} + 129984z^{12}.$$

It is self-dual. Its subfield subcode $\overline{C_{(9,11,2,1)}}|_{GF(3)}$ is the code of Example 11.16, i.e., the extended Golay ternary code. The minimum weight codewords in $\overline{C_{(9,11,2,1)}}$ hold a Steiner system $S(5,6,12)$.

Example 11.18. The ternary code $\overline{\text{QRC}}_0^{(23,3)}$ has parameters $[24,12,9]$ and weight enumerator

$$1 + 4048z^9 + 61824z^{12} + 242880z^{15} + 198352z^{18} + 24288z^{21} + 48z^{24}.$$

The code is self-dual, and holds three nontrivial 5-designs. The parameters (v,k,λ) are

$$(24,9,6), \ (24,12,576), \ (24,15,8580).$$

Example 11.19. The ternary code $\overline{\text{QRC}}_0^{(47,3)}$ has parameters $[48,24,15]$ and weight enumerator

$$1 + 415104z^{15} + 20167136z^{18} + 497709696z^{21} + 5745355200z^{24} +$$
$$31815369344z^{27} + 83368657152z^{30} + 99755406432z^{33} + 50852523072z^{36} +$$
$$9794378880z^{39} + 573051072z^{42} + 6503296z^{45} + 96z^{48}$$

The code is self-dual, and holds 5-designs. The parameters (v,k,λ) of two known ones are

$$(48,15,364), \ (48,18,50456).$$

Example 11.20. The ternary code $\overline{\text{QRC}}_0^{(59,3)}$ has parameters $[60,30,18]$. It is self-dual, and holds 5-designs. The parameters (v,k,λ) of the design held by the minimum-weight codewords are

$$(60,18,3060).$$

Example 11.21. The code $\overline{\text{QRC}}_0^{(23,4)}$ over GF(4) has parameters $[24,12,8]$ and weight enumerator

$$1 + 2277z^8 + 220248z^{12} + 1020096z^{14} + 3895947z^{16} +$$
$$6120576z^{18} + 4462920z^{20} + 1020096z^{22} + 35055z^{24}.$$

The code is self-dual, and holds 5-designs. The parameters (v,k,λ) are

$$(24,8,1), \quad (24,12,708), \quad (24,14,8008), \quad (24,16,65598).$$

It holds three complete 5-designs with parameters

$$(24,18,27132), \quad (24,20,3876), \quad (24,22,171).$$

Note that $\overline{\mathrm{QRC}}_0^{(23,4)}$ holds one more 5-design than the binary code $\overline{\mathrm{QRC}}_0^{(23,2)}$ in Example 11.14.

Example 11.22. The code $\overline{\mathrm{QRC}}_0^{(29,4)}$ over GF(4) has parameters $[30,15,12]$ and weight enumerator

$$1 + 118755z^{12} + 1151010z^{14} + 12038625z^{16} +$$
$$61752600z^{18} + 195945750z^{20} + 341403660z^{22} +$$
$$312800670z^{24} + 129570840z^{26} + 18581895z^{28} + 378018z^{30}.$$

The code is formally self-dual, and holds 5-designs. The parameters (v,k,λ) are

$$(30,12,220), \quad (30,14,5390), \quad (30,16,123000).$$

The support set of the codewords of weight 18 in this code has cardinality 19716375. Then

$$19716375\binom{18}{5} \bmod \binom{30}{5} = 10962.$$

Hence, the codewords of weight 18 in this code do not support a 5-design. It is open if the codewords of weight k for $k \in \{20,22,24\}$ hold a 5-design or not. For other $k \in \{26,28,30\}$, the 5-designs must be trivial (as $5+k > 30$), if the codewords of weight k indeed support 5-designs.

We remark that all these $\mathrm{QRC}_0^{(n,q)}$ for these pairs (n,q) covered in this section hold 4-designs. A theoretical treatment of the 5-designs in the forgoing examples was given in Assmus and Mattson (1969).

11.3 Pless Symmetry Codes and Their Designs

The objective of this section is to introduce the Pless symmetry codes and their designs. We start with double circulant codes. A $k \times k$ matrix is said to be *circulant* if each row is obtained from the previous one by a cyclic shift over one position to the right. Hence, a circulant matrix is of the form

$$A = \begin{bmatrix} a_0 & a_1 & \cdots & a_{k-2} & a_{k-1} \\ a_{k-1} & a_0 & \cdots & a_{k-3} & a_{k-2} \\ \vdots & \vdots & \ddots & \vdots \\ a_1 & a_2 & \cdots & a_{k-1} & a_0 \end{bmatrix}. \tag{11.3}$$

Consider now the algebra of $k \times k$ circulant matrices over $GF(q)$. We associate each circulant matrix A in (11.3) with the polynomial

$$a(x) = a_0 + a_1 x + \cdots + a_{k-1} x^{k-1} \in GF(q)[x]. \qquad (11.4)$$

It is easily seen that the mapping $A \mapsto a(x)$ is an isomorphism from the algebra of $k \times k$ circulant matrices over $GF(q)$ to the algebra of polynomials in the ring $GF(q)[x]/(x^k - 1)$. Consequently, we have the following:

(a) The sum and product of two circulant matrices are circulant matrices. More specifically, $C = AB$ if and only if $c(x) = a(x)b(x) \bmod x^k - 1$.
(b) A is invertible if and only if $\gcd(a(x), x^k - 1) = 1$. If A is invertible, the inverse B is given by $a(x)b(x) = 1 \pmod{x^k - 1}$, where $b(x)$ can be computed with the extended Euclidean algorithm.
(c) The transpose A^T is a circulant matrix associated with the polynomial $a^T(x) = a_0 + a_{k-1} x + \cdots + a_1 x^{k-1}$.

A $[2k, k]$ code over $GF(q)$ is said to be *double circulant* if it has a generator matrix of one of the forms

$$G = [I_k \, A] \qquad (11.5)$$

and

$$G = \begin{bmatrix} a & 0 \cdots\cdots 0 & c & 1 \cdots\cdots 1 \\ b & & d & \\ \vdots & I_{k-1} & \vdots & H \\ b & & d & \end{bmatrix}. \qquad (11.6)$$

where I_m is the $m \times m$ identity matrix, A and H are $(k-1) \times (k-1)$ circulant matrices over $GF(q)$, and a and b and c are elements of $GF(q)$.

Double circulant codes are interesting partly because they are easy to encode. Our interest in these codes comes from the fact that some double circulant codes hold designs. A number of interesting classes of double circulant codes are known in the literature [Beenker (1980)].

We are now ready to introduce the Pless symmetry codes and their designs. The original codes were published in Pless (1972). Here we introduce their generalised version documented in Beenker (1980). Let q be a power of an odd prime with $q \equiv -1 \pmod 6$. Define the following $(q+1) \times (q+1)$ matrix over $GF(q)$

$$M_{q+1} = \begin{bmatrix} 0 & 1 \cdots\cdots 1 \\ \varepsilon & \\ \vdots & Q \\ \varepsilon & \end{bmatrix}, \qquad (11.7)$$

where $\varepsilon = 1$ if $q \equiv 1 \pmod 4$, $\varepsilon = -1$ if $q \equiv 3 \pmod 4$, Q is a $q \times q$ circulant matrix defined by $Q_{a,a} = 0$ and

$$Q_{a,b} = \begin{cases} 1 & \text{if } a - b \text{ is a square in GF}(q), \\ -1 & \text{if } a - b \text{ is not a square in GF}(q) \end{cases}$$

for all $a, b \in \text{GF}(q)$, $a \neq b$. The Pless symmetry code Pless_{2q+2} is the $[2q+2, q+1]$ code over $\text{GF}(3)$ with generator matrix

$$G_{2q+2} = [I_{q+1} \, M_{q+1}]. \tag{11.8}$$

It is clearly a double circulant code by definition.

Properties of the code Pless_{2q+2} are summarized in next theorem. A proof of these properties could found in Pless (1972) or Beenker (1980).

Theorem 11.23. *Let notation be as before. Then the following holds.*

(1) Pless_{2q+2} is self-dual and all weights are divisible by 3.
(2) The automorphism group $\text{Aut}(\text{Pless}_{2q+2})$ contains a subgroup isomorphic to $\text{PSL}_2(\text{GF}(q))$.
(3) Let d be the minimum weight of Pless_{2q+2}. Then

$$(d-1)^2 - (d-1) + 1 \geq 2q + 1 \text{ if } q \equiv -1 \pmod{12},$$

and

$$(d-1)^2 \geq 2q - 1 \text{ if } q \equiv 5 \pmod{12}.$$

When $q \equiv 1 \pmod 6$, the code Pless_{2q+2} could be defined in the same way. However, in this case the code is not self-dual. Experimental data indicates that the code Pless_{2q+2} is formally self-dual when $q \equiv 1 \pmod 6$. Hence, we propose the following problem.

Problem 11.24. Prove or disprove that Pless_{2q+2} is formally self-dual when $q \equiv 1 \pmod 6$.

Example 11.25. Let $q = 7$. Then the code Pless_{16} has parameters $[16, 8, 6]$ and weight enumerator

$$1 + 112z^6 + 224z^7 + 592z^8 + 672z^9 + 1456z^{10} +$$
$$1120z^{11} + 1456z^{12} + 448z^{13} + 448z^{14} + 32z^{16}.$$

The code is formally self-dual and has the following generator matrix

$$
\begin{bmatrix}
1 & 0 & 0 & 0 & 0 & 0 & 0 & 0 & 0 & 1 & 1 & 1 & 1 & 1 & 1 \\
0 & 1 & 0 & 0 & 0 & 0 & 0 & 0 & 2 & 0 & 1 & 1 & 2 & 1 & 2 & 2 \\
0 & 0 & 1 & 0 & 0 & 0 & 0 & 0 & 2 & 2 & 0 & 1 & 1 & 2 & 1 & 2 \\
0 & 0 & 0 & 1 & 0 & 0 & 0 & 0 & 2 & 2 & 2 & 0 & 1 & 1 & 2 & 1 \\
0 & 0 & 0 & 0 & 1 & 0 & 0 & 0 & 2 & 1 & 2 & 2 & 0 & 1 & 1 & 2 \\
0 & 0 & 0 & 0 & 0 & 1 & 0 & 0 & 2 & 2 & 1 & 2 & 2 & 0 & 1 & 1 \\
0 & 0 & 0 & 0 & 0 & 0 & 1 & 0 & 2 & 1 & 2 & 1 & 2 & 2 & 0 & 1 \\
0 & 0 & 0 & 0 & 0 & 0 & 0 & 1 & 2 & 1 & 1 & 2 & 1 & 2 & 2 & 0
\end{bmatrix}.
$$

The supports of the minimum weight codewords of this code do not form a 2-design.

The code Pless$_{2q+2}$ is interesting as it holds 5-designs in certain cases. We now introduce them. The smallest case is that $q = 5$, which is documented in the following example.

Example 11.26. Let $q = 5$. Then the code Pless$_{12}$ has parameters $[12,6,6]$ and weight enumerator

$$
1 + 264z^6 + 440z^9 + 24z^{12}.
$$

The code is self-dual and has the following generator matrix

$$
\begin{bmatrix}
1 & 0 & 0 & 0 & 0 & 0 & 0 & 1 & 1 & 1 & 1 & 1 \\
0 & 1 & 0 & 0 & 0 & 0 & 1 & 0 & 1 & 2 & 2 & 1 \\
0 & 0 & 1 & 0 & 0 & 0 & 1 & 1 & 0 & 1 & 2 & 2 \\
0 & 0 & 0 & 1 & 0 & 0 & 1 & 2 & 1 & 0 & 1 & 2 \\
0 & 0 & 0 & 0 & 1 & 0 & 1 & 2 & 2 & 1 & 0 & 1 \\
0 & 0 & 0 & 0 & 0 & 1 & 1 & 1 & 2 & 2 & 1 & 0
\end{bmatrix}.
$$

By the Assmus-Mattson theorem, this ternary code holds a 5-$(12,6,1)$ design. The supports of the codewords of weight 9 or 12 form trivial 5-designs.

The second set of designs held in the code Pless$_{2q+2}$ is given below.

Example 11.27. Let $q = 11$. Then the code Pless$_{24}$ has parameters $[24,12,9]$ and weight enumerator

$$
1 + 4048z^9 + 61824z^{12} + 242880z^{15} + 198352z^{18} + 24288z^{21} + 48z^{24}.
$$

The code is self-dual and has the following generator matrix

$$\begin{bmatrix}
1 & 0 & 0 & 0 & 0 & 0 & 0 & 0 & 0 & 0 & 0 & 0 & 1 & 1 & 1 & 1 & 1 & 1 & 1 & 1 & 1 & 1 \\
0 & 1 & 0 & 0 & 0 & 0 & 0 & 0 & 0 & 0 & 0 & 2 & 0 & 1 & 2 & 1 & 1 & 1 & 2 & 2 & 2 & 1 & 2 \\
0 & 0 & 1 & 0 & 0 & 0 & 0 & 0 & 0 & 0 & 0 & 2 & 2 & 0 & 1 & 2 & 1 & 1 & 1 & 2 & 2 & 2 & 1 \\
0 & 0 & 0 & 1 & 0 & 0 & 0 & 0 & 0 & 0 & 0 & 2 & 1 & 2 & 0 & 1 & 2 & 1 & 1 & 1 & 2 & 2 & 2 \\
0 & 0 & 0 & 0 & 1 & 0 & 0 & 0 & 0 & 0 & 0 & 2 & 2 & 1 & 2 & 0 & 1 & 2 & 1 & 1 & 1 & 2 & 2 \\
0 & 0 & 0 & 0 & 0 & 1 & 0 & 0 & 0 & 0 & 0 & 2 & 2 & 2 & 1 & 2 & 0 & 1 & 2 & 1 & 1 & 1 & 2 \\
0 & 0 & 0 & 0 & 0 & 0 & 1 & 0 & 0 & 0 & 0 & 2 & 2 & 2 & 2 & 1 & 2 & 0 & 1 & 2 & 1 & 1 & 1 \\
0 & 0 & 0 & 0 & 0 & 0 & 0 & 1 & 0 & 0 & 0 & 2 & 1 & 2 & 2 & 2 & 1 & 2 & 0 & 1 & 2 & 1 & 1 \\
0 & 0 & 0 & 0 & 0 & 0 & 0 & 0 & 1 & 0 & 0 & 0 & 2 & 1 & 1 & 2 & 2 & 2 & 1 & 2 & 0 & 1 & 2 & 1 \\
0 & 0 & 0 & 0 & 0 & 0 & 0 & 0 & 0 & 1 & 0 & 0 & 2 & 1 & 1 & 1 & 2 & 2 & 2 & 1 & 2 & 0 & 1 & 2 \\
0 & 0 & 0 & 0 & 0 & 0 & 0 & 0 & 0 & 0 & 1 & 0 & 2 & 2 & 1 & 1 & 1 & 2 & 2 & 2 & 1 & 2 & 0 & 1 \\
0 & 0 & 0 & 0 & 0 & 0 & 0 & 0 & 0 & 0 & 0 & 1 & 2 & 1 & 2 & 1 & 1 & 1 & 2 & 2 & 2 & 1 & 2 & 0
\end{bmatrix}.$$

By the Assmus-Mattson theorem, this ternary code holds designs with the following parameters:

$$5\text{-}(24, 9, 6), \quad 5\text{-}(24, 12, 576), \quad 5\text{-}(24, 15, 8580).$$

The supports of the codewords of weight 18 do not form a 4-design, but a 3-$(24, 18, 29784)$ design, which can be explained by the subgroup contained in the automorphism group of this code. The supports of the codewords of weight 21 or 24 form a trivial 5-design.

The third set of designs held in the code Pless_{2q+2} is documented below.

Example 11.28. Let $q = 17$. Then the code Pless_{36} has parameters $[36, 18, 12]$ and weight enumerator

$$1 + 42840z^{12} + 1400256z^{15} + 18452280z^{18} + 90370368z^{21} +$$
$$162663480z^{24} + 97808480z^{27} + 16210656z^{30} + 471240z^{33} + 888z^{36}.$$

It follows from the Assmus-Mattson theorem that this ternary code holds designs with the following parameters:

$$5\text{-}(36, 12, 45), \quad 5\text{-}(36, 15, 5577), \quad 5\text{-}(36, 18, 209685), \quad 5\text{-}(36, 21, 2438973).$$

The fourth set of designs held in the code Pless_{2q+2} is documented below.

Example 11.29. Let $q = 23$. Then the code Pless_{48} has parameters $[48, 24, 15]$ and weight enumerator

$$1 + 415104z^{15} + 20167136z^{18} + 497709696z^{21} + 5745355200z^{24} +$$
$$31815369344z^{27} + 83368657152z^{30} + 99755406432z^{33} + 50852523072z^{36} +$$
$$9794378880z^{39} + 573051072z^{42} + 6503296z^{45} + 96z^{48}.$$

By the Assmus-Mattson theorem, this ternary code holds 5-$(48, k, \lambda)$ designs with the following parameters (k, λ):

$(15, 364)$, $(18, 50456)$, $(21, 2957388)$, $(24, 71307600)$, $(27, 749999640)$.

The fifth set of designs held in the code Pless$_{2q+2}$ is introduced below.

Example 11.30. Let $q = 29$. Then the code Pless$_{60}$ has parameters $[60, 30, 18]$. The weight distribution of Pless$_{60}$ was given in Mallows, Pless and Sloane (1976). By the Assmus-Mattson theorem, this ternary code holds 5-$(60, k, \lambda)$ designs with the following values of k:

$$18, \ 21, \ 24, \ 27, \ 30, \ 33.$$

It is easily seen that the five codes Pless$_{12}$, Pless$_{24}$, Pless$_{36}$, Pless$_{48}$ and Pless$_{60}$ meet the following bound

$$d \leq 3 \left\lfloor \frac{n}{12} \right\rfloor + 3,$$

which was documented in Theorem 11.7. Hence, these five codes are extremal.

11.4 Other Self-Dual Codes Holding t-Designs

In Section 11.2.1, we described an infinite family of self-dual binary codes of prime length $n \equiv 7 \pmod{8}$ which hold 3-designs, but are not extremal in general. Another such infinite family is the Reed-Muller binary codes $\mathcal{R}_2((m-1)/2, m)$ for odd m, which were studied earlier. Hence, the study of non-extremal self-dual codes is interesting.

The number of self-dual codes over small finite fields is known ([Huffman and Pless (2003)], [Rains and Sloane (1998)]), and is huge. Some of them are not extremal, but may hold t-designs. There are hundreds of references on self-dual codes. The most comprehensive reference may be Rains and Sloane (1998).

Problem 11.31. Construct infinite families of self-dual codes (other than extended quadratic residue codes and Reed-Muller codes) that are not extremal but hold t-designs for some $t \geq 2$.

Chapter 12

Designs from Arc and MDS Codes

MDS codes do hold support t-designs for large t. But these designs are complete and not interesting. Nevertheless, certain MDS codes over $GF(2^m)$ yield hyperovals in $PG(2, GF(2^m))$, and such hyperovals give rise to two types of 2-designs and 3-designs, which are called hyperoval designs. This demonstrates that certain linear codes can be employed to construct designs in other ways. Maximal arcs are an interesting topic of study in finite geometries. They give interesting two-weight codes, which hold nice 2-designs. The objective of this chapter is to present these designs. Although all the designs treated in this chapter are from linear codes, some of them are support designs of linear codes, others are not support designs.

12.1 Arcs, Caps, Conics, Hyperovals and Ovals in $PG(2, GF(q))$

Recall the Desargusian projective plane $PG(2, GF(q))$ treated in Section 1.6.4. An *arc* in $PG(2, GF(q))$ is a set of at least three points in $PG(2, GF(q))$ such that no three of them are collinear. In general, an *arc* in $PG(r, GF(q))$ is a set of at least $r + 1$ points in $PG(r, GF(q))$ such that no $r + 1$ of them lie in a hyperplane. A *cap* in $PG(r, GF(q))$ is a set of points such that no three are collinear.

Theorem 12.1. *The set of points of* $PG(r, GF(q))$

$$\mathcal{A} = \{(t^r, t^{r-1}, \ldots, t^2, t, 1) : t \in GF(q)\} \cup \{(1, 0, \ldots, 0, 0, 0)\}$$

is an arc with $q + 1$ *points in* $PG(r, GF(q))$.

Given an arc $\mathcal{A}$ with n points in $PG(r, GF(q))$, the corresponding code $\mathcal{C}_{\mathcal{A}}$ defined in Section 2.15 is an $[n, r + 1, n - r]$ MDS code over $GF(q)$. This is a direct consequence of Theorem 2.43 and the definition of arcs. Conversely, the column vectors of a generator matrix of any $[n, r + 1, n - r]$ MDS code over $GF(q)$ form an arc $\mathcal{A}$ with n points in $PG(r, GF(q))$. We have then the following theorem.

Theorem 12.2. *Let $\mathcal{A}$ be an n-subset of the point set in $\mathrm{PG}(r, \mathrm{GF}(q))$ with $n \geq r+1$. Then $\mathcal{A}$ is an arc in $\mathrm{PG}(r, \mathrm{GF}(q))$ if and only if the corresponding code $\mathcal{C}_{\mathcal{A}}$ defined in Section 2.15 is an $[n, r+1, n-r]$ MDS code over $\mathrm{GF}(q)$.*

Hence, arcs in projective spaces over $\mathrm{GF}(q)$ and MDS codes over $\mathrm{GF}(q)$ are equivalent.

Theorem 12.3. *If $\mathcal{A}$ is an arc of $\mathrm{PG}(r, \mathrm{GF}(q))$, then $|\mathcal{A}| \leq q+r$.*

Proof. We take any subset S of $\mathcal{A}$ of size $r-1$. If the points of S do not span a subspace of dimension $r-2$ then we can find a hyperplane that contains $r+1$ points of $\mathcal{A}$, contradicting the definition of an arc. The space of dimension $r-2$ spanned by the points of S is contained in $q+1$ hyperplanes, each of which is incident with at most one point of $\mathcal{A} \setminus S$. Consequently.

$$|\mathcal{A}| \leq q+1+r-1 = q+r.$$

This completes the proof.   □

As a corollary of Theorem 12.3, we have $|\mathcal{A}| \leq q+2$ for an arc $\mathcal{A}$ in $\mathrm{PG}(2, \mathrm{GF}(q))$. This upper bound is achieved when q is even.

For odd q we have the following conclusion [MacWilliams and Sloane (1977)][p. 326].

Theorem 12.4. *If $\mathcal{A}$ is an arc of $\mathrm{PG}(r, \mathrm{GF}(q))$ and q is odd, then $|\mathcal{A}| \leq q+r-1$.*

Example 12.5. Let $q = 2^m$ with m odd. Then
$$\mathcal{A} = \{(t^6, t, 1) : t \in \mathrm{GF}(q)\} \cup \{(1, 0, 0)\}$$
is an arc with $q+1$ points in $\mathrm{PG}(2, q)$.

We now introduce ovals and hyperovals, which are our main subjects of study in this section. An *oval* O in $\mathrm{PG}(2, \mathrm{GF}(q))$ is a set of $q+1$ points such that no three of them are collinear, i.e., an arc with $q+1$ points. A *hyperoval* $\mathcal{H}$ in $\mathrm{PG}(2, \mathrm{GF}(q))$ is a set of $q+2$ points such that no three of them are collinear, i.e., an arc with $q+2$ points. Two ovals (resp. hyperovals) are said to be *equivalent* if there is a collineation (i.e., automorphism) of $\mathrm{PG}(2, \mathrm{GF}(q))$ that sends one to the other. The *automorphism group* of an oval (resp. hyperoval) is the set of all collineations of $\mathrm{PG}(2, \mathrm{GF}(q))$ that leave the oval (resp. hyperoval) invariant.

The arc in Example 12.5 is an oval by definition. Another example of ovals is the following.

Example 12.6. Let $q > 3$. Then
$$O = \{(t^2, t, 1) : t \in \mathrm{GF}(q)\} \cup \{(1, 0, 0)\}$$
is an oval in $\mathrm{PG}(2, \mathrm{GF}(q))$.

Theorem 12.7. *Let O be an oval in* $\mathrm{PG}(2,\mathrm{GF}(q))$. *Then through each point P of O, there is exactly one line whose intersection with O is just the point P. Such a line is called a* tangent *of O.*

Proof. Recall that $\mathrm{PG}(2,\mathrm{GF}(q))$ is a 2-$(q^2+q+1,q+1,1)$ design with q^2+q+1 lines. Each line has $q+1$ points and each point is on $q+1$ lines. By definition, O has $q+1$ points, say $P_0,P_1,\ldots,P_q$. Then $\overline{P_0P_i}$ are q pairwise distinct lines passing through P_0, where $1 \le i \le q$. Since P_0 is on $q+1$ lines, there is another line passing through P_0 which is different from the q lines mentioned above. This line must intersect O with only the point P_0, and is thus a tangent at P_0. Note that P_0 is an arbitrary point on O. The proof now is completed. □

By Theorem 12.7, there are $q+1$ tangents to O. Lines meeting an oval in two points are called *secants*. Figure 12.1 gives a pictorial illustration of tangents and secants. The total number of secants of O is clearly $q(q+1)/2$.

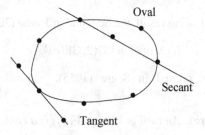

Oval

Secant

Tangent

Fig. 12.1 Tangents and secants of an oval O

Theorem 12.8. *Let O be an oval in* $\mathrm{PG}(2,\mathrm{GF}(q))$, *where* $q = 2^m$. *The* $q+1$ *tangents to O intersect a common point, called the* nucleus *or* knot *of O.*

Proof. Let P be any point of $\mathrm{PG}(2,\mathrm{GF}(q))$ outside O. Since the lines though P partition the points of O and $q+1$ is odd, P must be on at least one tangent to O. Now let ℓ be a secant to O with $\ell \cap O = \{Q,R\}$. The tangents of O at the points $O \setminus \{Q,R\}$ meet ℓ in distinct points. Thus, any point not on O that lies on a secant must lie on exactly one tangent. If we take the intersection of two tangents to O this point lies on two tangents and so cannot lie on any secants. Consequently, it lies on all the tangents to O. □

Let O be an oval in $\mathrm{PG}(2,\mathrm{GF}(q))$, where $q = 2^m$. Let K be the nucleus of O. The proof of Theorem 12.8 shows that $\mathcal{H} = O \cup \{K\}$ is a hyperoval. Hence, for even q an oval O can always be extended **uniquely** to a hyperoval $\mathcal{H}$.

Example 12.9. Let $q = 2^m$ with $m \geq 2$. Then the nucleus of the oval

$$O = \{(t^2, t, 1) : t \in \mathrm{GF}(q)\} \cup \{(1, 0, 0)\}$$

is $(0, 1, 0)$. Furthermore, $O \cup \{(0, 1, 0)\}$ is a hyperoval.

A *conic* in $\mathrm{PG}(2, \mathrm{GF}(q))$ is a set of points of $\mathrm{PG}(2, \mathrm{GF}(q))$ that are zeros of a nondegenerate homogeneous quadratic form $f(x, y, z)$ in three variables. It is known that every homogeneous quadratic equation in three variables over $\mathrm{GF}(q)$ has a solution [Payne (2007)][Section 4.2].

Example 12.10. Let $\mathcal{P}$ be the point set of $\mathrm{PG}(2, \mathrm{GF}(q))$, and let $f(x, y, z) = y^2 - xz$. Then the set

$$C = \{(x, y, z) \in \mathcal{P} : y^2 = xz\} = \{(t^2, t, 1) : t \in \mathrm{GF}(q)\} \cup \{(1, 0, 0)\}$$

is a conic in $\mathrm{PG}(2, \mathrm{GF}(q))$. The point $(1, 0, 0)$ is called the *point at infinity*, and denoted by P_∞.

A proof of the following result can be found in Payne (2007)[Chapter 4].

Theorem 12.11. *A conic is an oval in* $\mathrm{PG}(2, \mathrm{GF}(q))$.

The following is proved in Segre (1955), and also Assmus and Key (1992a)[Section 3.7].

Theorem 12.12 (Segre). *An oval in* $\mathrm{PG}(2, \mathrm{GF}(q))$ *is a conic if q is odd.*

Combining the two theorems above, we conclude that conics and ovals in $\mathrm{PG}(2, \mathrm{GF}(q))$ are the same when q is odd. A conic and its nucleus together form a hyperoval. Such hyperoval is called a *regular hyperoval*. The conic and its nucleus in Example 12.9 form a regular hyperoval.

The most important subject of study in this section is hyperovals. By Theorem 12.3, hyperovals are maximal arcs, as they have the maximal number of points as arcs. The next theorem shows that all hyperovals in $\mathrm{PG}(2, \mathrm{GF}(2^m))$ can be constructed with a special type of permutation polynomials on $\mathrm{GF}(2^m)$.

Theorem 12.13. *Let $q = 2^m$ with $m \geq 2$. Any hyperoval in* $\mathrm{PG}(2, \mathrm{GF}(q))$ *can be written in the form*

$$\mathcal{H}(f) = \{(f(c), c, 1) : c \in \mathrm{GF}(q)\} \cup \{(1, 0, 0)\} \cup \{(0, 1, 0)\},$$

where $f \in \mathrm{GF}(q)[x]$ is such that

(i) *f is a permutation polynomial of $\mathrm{GF}(q)$ with $\deg(f) < q$ and $f(0) = 0$, $f(1) = 1$;*

(ii) for each $a \in \mathrm{GF}(q)$, $g_a(x) = (f(x+a) + f(a))x^{q-2}$ is also a permutation polynomial of $\mathrm{GF}(q)$.

Conversely, every such set $\mathcal{H}(f)$ is a hyperoval.

Proof. See Lidl and Niederreiter (1997)[p. 504] for a proof. □

Polynomials satisfying Conditions (i) and (ii) of Theorem 12.13 are called *o-polynomials*, i.e., oval-polynomials. Two o-polynomials f and g are said to be *equivalent* if their hyperovals $\mathcal{H}(f)$ and $\mathcal{H}(g)$ are equivalent. In the next section, we will survey known o-polynomials on $\mathrm{GF}(2^m)$.

Example 12.14. $f(x) = x^2$ is an o-polynomial on $\mathrm{GF}(2^m)$ for all $m \geq 2$.

We now introduce properties of hyperovals in $\mathrm{PG}(2, \mathrm{GF}(2^m))$. The following theorem is essential for the construction of hyperoval designs later.

Theorem 12.15. *Any hyperoval O in $\mathrm{PG}(2, \mathrm{GF}(2^m))$ meets each line either in 0 or 2 points.*

Proof. Let O be a hyperoval in $\mathrm{PG}(2, \mathrm{GF}(2^m))$. By definition, O has $2^m + 2$ points. For any point P in O, the set $O \setminus \{P\}$ is an oval in $\mathrm{PG}(2, \mathrm{GF}(2^m))$. The proof of Theorem 12.8 shows that P is the nucleus of the oval $O \setminus \{P\}$. Hence, O has no tangents. By definition, any line intersects a hyperoval in at most two points. The desired conclusion then follows. □

Let O be a hyperoval in $\mathrm{PG}(2, \mathrm{GF}(2^m))$. A line ℓ in $\mathrm{PG}(2, \mathrm{GF}(2^m))$ is said to be *exterior* to O if ℓ meets O in zero point, and *interior* otherwise. Figure 12.2 is a pictorial illustration of interior and exterior lines to a hyperoval. Points on O are called *interior points* and those in $\mathrm{PG}(2, \mathrm{GF}(2^m)) \setminus O$ *exterior points* of O.

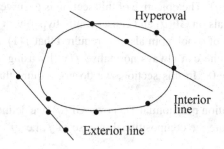

Fig. 12.2 Interior and exterior lines to a hyperoval O

12.2 Hyperovals in $\mathrm{PG}(2,\mathrm{GF}(q))$ and $[q+2,3,q]$ MDS Codes

Let $q = 2^m$. Given any hyperoval $\mathcal{H} = \{h_1, h_2, \ldots, h_{q+2}\}$ in $\mathrm{PG}(2,q)$, we construct a linear code $\mathcal{C}_{\mathcal{H}}$ of length $q+2$ over $\mathrm{GF}(q)$ with generator matrix $[h_1, h_2, \ldots, h_{q+2}]$, where each h_i is a column vector of $\mathrm{GF}(q)^3$ (see Section 2.15). It then follows from Theorems 12.15 and 2.43 that the code has only the nonzero weights q and $q+2$ and it is projective. Solving the first two Pless power moments, one obtains the following weight enumerator of the code:

$$1 + \frac{(q+2)(q^2-1)}{2}z^q + \frac{q(q-1)^2}{2}z^{q+2}.$$

Hence, $\mathcal{C}_{\mathcal{H}}$ is an MDS code over $\mathrm{GF}(q)$ with parameters $[q+2,3,q]$. The dual of $\mathcal{C}_{\mathcal{H}}$ is an MDS code over $\mathrm{GF}(q)$ with parameters $[q+2,q-1,4]$.

Conversely, given any MDS code $\mathcal{C}$ over $\mathrm{GF}(q)$ with parameters $[q+2,3,q]$, let $[h_1, h_2, \ldots, h_{q+2}]$ be a generator matrix of $\mathcal{C}$. Let $a_i \in \mathrm{GF}(q)^*$ such that $\bar{h}_i = a_i h_i$ is a point of $\mathrm{PG}(2,\mathrm{GF}(q))$. Then

$$\mathcal{H} = \{\bar{h}_1, \bar{h}_2, \ldots, \bar{h}_{q+2}\}$$

is a hyperoval in $\mathrm{PG}(2,\mathrm{GF}(q))$. The dual code $\mathcal{C}^{\perp}$ is an MDS code over $\mathrm{GF}(q)$ with parameters $[q+2,q-1,4]$.

Summarizing the discussions above, we conclude that constructing hyperovals in $\mathrm{PG}(2,\mathrm{GF}(q))$ is equivalent to constructing $[q+2,3,q]$ linear codes over $\mathrm{GF}(q)$.

12.3 Oval Polynomials on $\mathrm{GF}(2^m)$

Throughout this section, let $q = 2^m \geq 4$. To construct hyperovals in $\mathrm{PG}(2,\mathrm{GF}(q))$ with Theorem 12.13, and subsequently 2-designs and 3-designs, we need o-polynomials on $\mathrm{GF}(q)$. The objective of this section is to survey known constructions of o-polynomials on $\mathrm{GF}(q)$ and consequently hyperovals in $\mathrm{PG}(2,\mathrm{GF}(q))$.

In the definition of o-polynomials, it is required that $f(1) = 1$. However, this is not essential, as one can always normalise $f(x)$ by using $f(1)^{-1}f(x)$ due to the fact that $f(1) \neq 0$. In this section, we do not require that $f(1) = 1$ for o-polynomials.

For any permutation polynomial $f(x)$ over $\mathrm{GF}(q)$, we define $\overline{f}(x) = xf(x^{q-2})$, and use f^{-1} to denote the compositional inverse of f, i.e., $f^{-1}(f(x)) = x$ for all $x \in \mathrm{GF}(q)$.

12.3.1 Basic Properties of Oval Polynomials

The equivalence of o-monomials is settled and documented below [Xiang (1999)].

Lemma 12.16. *Let $q \geq 4$. Two monomial hyperovals $\mathcal{H}(x^j)$ and $\mathcal{H}(x^e)$ in* PG$(2,$GF$(q))$ *are equivalent if and only if $i \equiv e, 1/e, 1-e, 1/(1-e), e/(e-1)$ or $(e-1)/e$ (mod $q-1$).*

The following two theorems introduce basic properties of o-polynomials whose proofs can be found in Cherowitzo (1988).

Theorem 12.17. *Let f be an o-polynomial on* GF(q). *Then the following statements hold:*

(1) f^{-1} is also an o-polynomial;
(2) $f(x^{2^j})^{2^{m-j}}$ is also an o-polynomial for any $1 \leq j \leq m-1$;
(3) $\overline{f}$ is also an o-polynomial; and
(4) $f(x+1) + f(1)$ is also an o-polynomial.

Further, they are equivalent to f.

Theorem 12.18. *Let x^k be an o-polynomial on* GF(q). *Then every polynomial in*

$$\left\{ x^{\frac{1}{k}}, x^{1-k}, x^{\frac{1}{1-k}}, x^{\frac{k}{k-1}}, x^{\frac{k-1}{k}} \right\}$$

is also an o-polynomial, where $1/k$ denotes the multiplicative inverse of k modulo $q-1$. Further, they are all equivalent.

Theorem 12.19 (Maschietti (1998)). *A polynomial f from* GF(q) *to* GF(q) *with $f(0) = 0$ is an o-polynomial if and only if $f_u := f(x) + ux$ is 2-to-1 for every $u \in$ GF$(q)^*$.*

12.3.2 *Translation Oval Polynomials*

The translation o-polynomials are described in the following theorem [Segre (1957)].

Theorem 12.20. Trans$(x) = x^{2^h}$ *is an o-polynomial on* GF(q), *where* gcd$(h,m) = 1$.

The following is a list of known properties of translation o-polynomials.

(1) Trans$^{-1}(x) = x^{2^{m-h}}$ and
(2) $\overline{\text{Trans}}(x) = xf(x^{q-2}) = x^{q-2^{m-h}}$.

12.3.3 Segre and Glynn Oval Polynomials

The following theorem describes a class of o-polynomials, which are called Segre o-polynomials [Segre (1962, 1971)].

Theorem 12.21. *Let m be odd. Then* $\mathrm{Segre}(x) = x^6$ *is an o-polynomial over* GF(q).

For this o-monomial, we have the following.

(1) $\overline{\mathrm{Segre}}(x) = x^{q-6}$.

(2) $\mathrm{Segre}^{-1}(x) = x^{\frac{5 \times 2^{m-1}-2}{3}}$ [Ding and Yuan (2015)].

Glynn discovered two families of o-polynomials [Glynn (1983)]. The first is described as follows.

Theorem 12.22. *Let m be odd. Then* $\mathrm{Glynni}(x) = x^{3 \times 2^{(m+1)/2}+4}$ *is an o-polynomial.*

The second family of o-polynomials discovered by Glynn is documented in the following theorem.

Theorem 12.23. *Let m be odd. Then*

$$\mathrm{Glynnii}(x) = \begin{cases} x^{2^{(m+1)/2}+2^{(3m+1)/4}} & if\, m \equiv 1 \pmod 4, \\ x^{2^{(m+1)/2}+2^{(m+1)/4}} & if\, m \equiv 3 \pmod 4 \end{cases}$$

is an o-polynomial over GF(q).

12.3.4 Cherowitzo Oval Polynomials

The following theorem describes another class of o-polynomials discovered by Cherowitzo [Cherowitzo (1988, 1996)].

Theorem 12.24. *Let m be odd and $e = (m+1)/2$. Then*

$$\mathrm{Cherowitzo}(x) = x^{2^e} + x^{2^e+2} + x^{3 \times 2^e+4}$$

is an o-polynomial over GF(q).

For this o-trinomial, we have the following conclusions [Ding and Yuan (2015)].

(1) $\overline{\mathrm{Cherowitzo}}(x) = x^{q-2^e} + x^{q-2^e-2} + x^{q-3 \times 2^e-4}$.

(2) $\mathrm{Cherowitzo}^{-1}(x) = x(x^{2^e+1} + x^3 + x)^{2^{e-1}-1}$.

12.3.5 *Payne Oval Polynomials*

The following documents a family of o-trinomials [Ding and Yuan (2015)].

Theorem 12.25. *Let m be odd. Then* $\mathrm{Payne}_a(x) = x^{\frac{5}{6}} + ax^{\frac{3}{6}} + a^2 x^{\frac{1}{6}}$ *is an o-polynomial on* $\mathrm{GF}(q)$ *for every* $a \in \mathrm{GF}(q)$.

We have the following remarks on this family.

(1) $\mathrm{Payne}_1(x)$ is the original Payne o-polynomial [Payne (1985)]. So this is an extended family.
(2) $\mathrm{Payne}_a(x) = xD_5(x^{\frac{1}{6}}, a)$, where $D_5(x, a)$ is the Dickson polynomial of order 5.
(3) $\overline{\mathrm{Payne}}_a(x) = a^{q-3}\mathrm{Payne}_{a^{q-2}}(x)$.
(4) Note that

$$\frac{1}{6} = \frac{5 \times 2^{m-1} - 2}{3}.$$

We have then

$$\mathrm{Payne}_a(x) = x^{\frac{2^{m-1}+2}{3}} + ax^{2^{m-1}} + a^2 x^{\frac{5 \times 2^{m-1} - 2}{3}}.$$

Theorem 12.26 (Ding and Yuan (2015)). *Let m be odd. Then*

$$\mathrm{Payne}_1^{-1}(x) = \left(D_{\frac{3 \times 2^{2m}-2}{5}}(x, 1)\right)^6 \tag{12.1}$$

and $\overline{\mathrm{Payne}}_1^{-1}(x)$ *are o-polynomials.*

12.3.6 *Subiaco Oval Polynomials*

The Subiaco o-polynomials are given in the following theorem [Cherowitzo, Penttila, Pinneri and Royle (1996)].

Theorem 12.27. *Define*

$\mathrm{Subiaco}_a(x) = ((a^2(x^4 + x) + a^2(1 + a + a^2)(x^3 + x^2))(x^4 + a^2 x^2 + 1)^{2^{m-2}} + x^{2^{m-1}}$,

where $\mathrm{Tr}(1/a) = 1$ *and* $d \notin \mathrm{GF}(4)$ *if* $m \equiv 2 \bmod 4$. *Then* $\mathrm{Subiaco}_a(x)$ *is an o-polynomial on* $\mathrm{GF}(q)$.

As a corollary of Theorem 12.27, we have the following.

Corollary 12.28. *Let m be odd. Then*

$$\mathrm{Subiaco}_1(x) = (x + x^2 + x^3 + x^4)(x^4 + x^2 + 1)^{2^{m-2}} + x^{2^{m-1}} \tag{12.2}$$

is an o-polynomial over $\mathrm{GF}(q)$.

12.4   A Family of Hyperovals from Extended Cyclic Codes

In Section 12.2, it was proved that constructing hyperovals is equivalent to constructing $[q+2,3,q]$ MDS codes over $\mathrm{GF}(q)$, where $q = 2^m$. In this section, we present a family of extended cyclic codes, which are MDS codes over $\mathrm{GF}(q)$ with parameters $[q+2,q-1,4]$. Their dual codes have parameters $[q+2,3,q]$ and hence give a family of hyperovals.

Let $q = 2^m$ with $m \geq 2$. Let α be a generator of $\mathrm{GF}(q^2)^*$. Put $\beta = \alpha^{q-1}$. Then β is a $(q+1)$-th root of unity in $\mathrm{GF}(q^2)$. Let $\mathbb{M}_{\beta^i}(x)$ denote the minimal polynomial of β^i over $\mathrm{GF}(q)$, and C_q the cyclic code over $\mathrm{GF}(q)$ length $q+1$ with generator polynomial $\mathbb{M}_{\beta^{-1}}(x)$.

Theorem 12.29. *The cyclic code* C_q *has parameters* $[q+1,q-1,3]$ *and its dual* $C_q^{\perp}$ *has parameters* $[q+1,2,q]$, *where* $q \geq 4$.

Proof. Notice that $\beta^{-1} \in \mathrm{GF}(q^2) \setminus \mathrm{GF}(q)$. The degree of $\mathbb{M}_{\beta^{-1}}(x)$ is equal to 2. Consequently, the dimension of C_q is $q+1-2 = q-1$. It then follows from the Singleton bound that $d \leq 3$. By the Delsarte Theorem, $C_q^{\perp}$ is given by

$$C_q^{\perp} = \{(\mathrm{Tr}(\beta^i a)_{i=0}^q : a \in \mathrm{GF}(q^2))\}. \tag{12.3}$$

Obviously, $d \neq 1$. Suppose that $d = 2$. Then there are two integers i and j and some $u \in \mathrm{GF}(q)^*$ such that $0 \leq i < j \leq q$ and

$$\mathrm{Tr}(a\beta^i) = \mathrm{Tr}(ua\beta^j)$$

for all $a \in \mathrm{GF}(q^2)$. This implies that $\beta^{j-i} = \alpha^{(q-1)(j-i)} = u^{-1} \in \mathrm{GF}(q)^*$, which is impossible as $\gcd(q-1,q+1) = 1$ and $0 < j-i \leq q$. As a result, $d = 3$. Thus, C_q is an MDS code with parameters $[q+1,q-1,3]$. Since the dual of an MDS code is also an MDS code, $C_q^{\perp}$ has parameters $[q+1,2,q]$. $\square$

Note that the code $C_q^{\perp}$ in Theorem 12.29 is an irreducible cyclic code. Let $\overline{C_q}$ denote the extended code of C_q. We have then the following.

Theorem 12.30. *The code* $\overline{C_q}$ *has parameters* $[q+2,q-1,4]$ *and its dual* $\overline{C_q}^{\perp}$ *has parameters* $[q+2,3,q]$, *where* $q \geq 4$.

Proof. A proof based on the expression of (12.3) can be given. The details are left to the reader. $\square$

Any generator matrix of the code $\overline{C_q}^{\perp}$ in Theorem 12.30 gives a hyperoval. Therefore, the codes $\overline{C_q}^{\perp}$ define a family of hyperovals, which are not new due to the following result.

Theorem 12.31 (Abdukhalikov and Ho (2021)). *Any extended cyclic code over* GF(q) *with parameters* $[q+2,3,q]$ *is monomially-equivalent to an MDS code over* GF(q) *obtained from a regular hyperoval.*

It follows from Theorem 12.31 that not every MDS code over GF(q) with parameters $[q+2,3,q]$ is an extended cyclic code, as there are hyperovals not equivalent to the regular hyperovals.

12.5 Hyperoval Designs

Plugging all the o-polynomials described in Section 12.3 into Theorem 12.13, one obtains a number of classes of hyperovals in PG($2,$GF(2^m)). In this section, we show that these hyperovals can be employed to construct different classes of 2-$(2^{2m-1} - 2^{m-1}, 2^{m-1}, 1)$ Steiner systems. Throughout this section, we let $q = 2^m$ with $m \geq 2$.

Theorem 12.15 says that any hyperoval O in PG($2,$GF(q)) meets each line either in 0 or 2 points. Hence, a hyperoval partitions the lines of PG($2,$GF(q)) into two classes, i.e., interior and exterior lines (see Figure 12.2 for illustration). This property allows us to define the so-called hyperoval designs as follows.

Let O be a hyperoval in the Desarguesian projective plane PG($2,$GF(q)). The *hyperoval design* $\mathcal{W}(q,O)$ is the incidence structure with points the lines of PG($2,$GF(q)) exterior to O and blocks the points of PG($2,$GF(q)) not on the oval; incidence is given by the incidence in PG($2,$GF(q)). We have then the following conclusion on the incidence structure $\mathcal{W}(q,O)$.

Theorem 12.32. *The incidence structure* $\mathcal{W}(q,O)$ *defined by a hyperoval O in* PG($2,$GF(q)) *is a* 2-$((q-1)q/2,q/2,1)$ *design, i.e., a Steiner system.*

Proof. By definition, O has $q+2$ points and every pair of distinct points on O determines a unique line. Thus, the total number of exterior lines is

$$v := q^2 + q + 1 - \frac{(q+2)(q+1)}{2} = \frac{q(q-1)}{2},$$

which is the total number of points in the incidence structure $\mathcal{W}(q,O)$. In PG($2,$GF(q)), every point is on $q+1$ lines. Let p_1 be a point that is not on O. Between p_1 and every point p_2 on O there is an interior line, which intersects O on another point by Theorem 12.15. It then follows that any point that is not on O is on $(q+2)/2$ interior lines. Consequently, the point is on $q+1-(q+2)/2 = q/2$ exterior lines, i.e., the block size

$$k = \frac{q}{2}$$

for the incidence structure $\mathcal{W}(q, O)$. It is clear that every pair of distinct exterior lines meet on one unique point that is not on O. This completes the proof. ☐

Example 12.33. Let $q = 4$ and let w be a generator of $\mathrm{GF}(4)^*$ with minimal polynomial $w^2 + w + 1 = 0$. Then the point set of $\mathcal{W}(4, O)$ consist of

$$\{(w^2, 0, 1), (0, w^2, 1), (w, 1, 1), (1, 1, 0), (1, w, 1)\},$$
$$\{(w^2, 0, 1), (w, w, 1), (1, w^2, 1), (0, 1, 1), (w^2, 1, 0)\},$$
$$\{(1, 0, 1), (w^2, w^2, 1), (w, 1, 1), (w^2, 1, 0), (0, w, 1)\},$$
$$\{(w^2, w^2, 1), (w, 1, 0), (0, 1, 1), (w, 0, 1), (1, w, 1)\},$$
$$\{(0, w^2, 1), (1, 0, 1), (w, 1, 0), (w, w, 1), (w^2, 1, 1)\},$$
$$\{(1, w^2, 1), (w^2, 1, 1), (0, w, 1), (1, 1, 0), (w, 0, 1)\}.$$

The block set is composed of the following

$$(w^2, w^2, 1), (w, 0, 1), (0, w, 1), (w, w, 1), (1, 0, 1),$$
$$(w^2, 0, 1), (1, w, 1), (w, 1, 0), (0, 1, 1), (w, 1, 1),$$
$$(0, w^2, 1), (1, 1, 0), (w^2, 1, 0), (w^2, 1, 1), (1, w^2, 1).$$

Clearly, $\mathcal{W}(4, O)$ is a trivial 2-$(6, 2, 1)$ design.

The hyperoval design $\mathcal{W}(q, O)$ was first studied in Bose and Shrikhande (1973). Another derivation of these designs was given in Wertheimer (1990). The next theorem gives an upper bound on the 2-rank of the design $\mathcal{W}(q, O)$, i.e., the rank of the incidence matrix over $\mathrm{GF}(2)$ of the design, and is due to Mackenzie (1989).

Theorem 12.34. *Let O be a hyperoval in $\mathrm{PG}(2, \mathrm{GF}(q))$. Then*

$$\mathrm{rank}_2(\mathcal{W}(q, O)) \leq 3^m - 2^m. \tag{12.4}$$

It is conjectured that the equality in (12.4) holds in general. This conjecture is proved to be true in the special case specified below. The following result is due to Carpenter (1996).

Theorem 12.35. *Let O be a regular hyperoval in $\mathrm{PG}(2, \mathrm{GF}(q))$. Then*

$$\mathrm{rank}_2(\mathcal{W}(q, O)) = 3^m - 2^m.$$

Example 12.36. Let O be a translation hyperoval in $\mathrm{PG}(2, \mathrm{GF}(2^m))$, i.e., the hyperoval defined by the o-polynomial $f(x) = x^2$. When $m = 2$, the code $\mathcal{C}_{\mathrm{GF}(2)}(\mathcal{W}(q, O))$ has parameters $[6, 5, 2]$ and its dual has parameters $[6, 1, 6]$. When $m = 3$, the code $\mathcal{C}_{\mathrm{GF}(2)}(\mathcal{W}(q, O))$ has parameters $[28, 19, 4]$ and its dual has parameters $[28, 9, 10]$. When $m = 4$, the code $\mathcal{C}_{\mathrm{GF}(2)}(\mathcal{W}(q, O))$ has parameters $[120, 65, 8]$ and its dual has parameters $[120, 55, 18]$.

12.6 Hadamard Designs from Hyperovals

Throughout this section, let $q = 2^m \geq 4$. Let O be a hyperoval in $PG(2, GF(q))$. Let $\mathcal{P}$ be the set of $q^2 - 1$ exterior points to O, i.e., the set of points in $PG(2, GF(q)) \setminus O$. For each point $x \in \mathcal{P}$, define a block

$$B_x = \{y \in \mathcal{P} \setminus \{x\} : xy \text{ is a secant to } O\} \cup \{x\}.$$

Define further $\mathcal{B} = \{B_x : x \in \mathcal{P}\}$. We have then the following conclusion.

Theorem 12.37. *The incidence structure* $\mathcal{H}(q, O) := (\mathcal{P}, \mathcal{B})$ *is a symmetric 2-* $(q^2 - 1, \frac{1}{2}q^2 - 1, \frac{1}{4}q^2 - 1)$ *design.*

Proof. By definition, $|\mathcal{P}|$ is the number of exterior points to O and is $q^2 - 1$. Let x be any exterior point. There are altogether $(q+2)(q+1)/2$ secants. Out of them, $(q+2)/2$ secants pass through the exterior point x. Each secant passing through x has $q + 1 - 2 - 1 = q - 2$ exterior points other than x. Consequently,

$$|B_x| = \frac{q+2}{2}(q-2) + 1 = \frac{1}{2}q^2 - 1.$$

Since B_x consists of all the exterior points on the secants passing through x, B_x is different from B_y for any pair of distinct exterior points x and y. Hence, the total number of blocks is the same as the number of points. Let x and y be any pair of distinct exterior points. Clearly, the total number of blocks B_u containing x and y is independent of the choice of x and y, and is thus a constant λ. We have then

$$q^2 - 1 = \lambda \frac{\binom{q^2-1}{2}}{\binom{\frac{1}{2}q^2-1}{2}}.$$

It then follows that

$$\lambda = \frac{1}{4}q^2 - 1.$$

This completes the proof. □

Example 12.38. Let $q = 4$ and let w be a generator of $GF(4)^*$ with minimal polynomial $w^2 + w + 1 = 0$. Then the point set of $\mathcal{H}(4, O)$ consist of

$$(w^2, w^2, 1), (w, 0, 1), (0, w, 1), (w, w, 1), (1, 0, 1),$$
$$(w^2, 0, 1), (1, w, 1), (w, 1, 0), (0, 1, 1), (w, 1, 1),$$
$$(0, w^2, 1), (1, 1, 0), (w^2, 1, 0), (w^2, 1, 1), (1, w^2, 1).$$

The block set has the following blocks:

$$\{(0, w, 1), (w^2, w^2, 1), (w, 0, 1), (w, 1, 0), (w^2, 1, 1), (w^2, 0, 1), (1, 0, 1)\},$$

$\{(0, w^2, 1), (w, 1, 0), (w^2, 1, 0), (w^2, 1, 1), (1, 1, 0), (w, 0, 1), (1, w, 1)\},$

$\{(0, w^2, 1), (1, 0, 1), (w, 1, 1), (0, 1, 1), (0, w, 1), (w^2, 1, 1), (1, 1, 0)\},$

$\{(w^2, w^2, 1), (w, 1, 1), (w, w, 1), (0, w, 1), (1, 1, 0), (w, 0, 1), (1, w, 1)\},$

$\{(w^2, 0, 1), (0, w^2, 1), (w, 1, 0), (w, w, 1), (0, 1, 1), (0, w, 1), (1, w, 1)\},$

$\{(0, w^2, 1), (w^2, w^2, 1), (1, w^2, 1), (0, 1, 1), (w^2, 1, 0), (0, w, 1), (w, 0, 1)\},$

$\{(w^2, 0, 1), (0, w^2, 1), (1, 0, 1), (w, 1, 1), (w, w, 1), (w^2, 1, 0), (w, 0, 1)\},$

$\{(1, 1, 0), (w^2, w^2, 1), (0, 1, 1), (w, 1, 0), (1, 0, 1), (w^2, 1, 0), (w, w, 1)\},$

$\{(w^2, 0, 1), (1, 0, 1), (1, w^2, 1), (0, 1, 1), (1, 1, 0), (w, 0, 1), (1, w, 1)\},$

$\{(w, 1, 0), (w, 1, 1), (w, w, 1), (1, w^2, 1), (0, 1, 1), (w^2, 1, 1), (w, 0, 1)\},$

$\{(1, 0, 1), (w, w, 1), (1, w^2, 1), (w^2, 1, 0), (0, w, 1), (w^2, 1, 1), (1, w, 1)\},$

$\{(w^2, 0, 1), (0, w^2, 1), (w^2, w^2, 1), (w, w, 1), (1, w^2, 1), (w^2, 1, 1), (1, 1, 0)\},$

$\{(w^2, 0, 1), (w^2, w^2, 1), (w, 1, 1), (0, 1, 1), (w^2, 1, 0), (w^2, 1, 1), (1, w, 1)\},$

$\{(0, w^2, 1), (w^2, w^2, 1), (1, 0, 1), (w, 1, 0), (w, 1, 1), (1, w^2, 1), (1, w, 1)\},$

$\{(w^2, 0, 1), (w, 1, 0), (w, 1, 1), (1, w^2, 1), (w^2, 1, 0), (0, w, 1), (1, 1, 0)\}.$

$\mathcal{H}(4, O)$ is a 2-$(15, 7, 3)$ design.

The 2-rank of the Hadamard design $\mathcal{H}(q, O)$ is open. We have the following conjecture [Mackenzie (1989)].

Conjecture 12.39. *Let $m \geq 2$. Then*

$$\text{rank}_2(\mathcal{H}(q, O)) = 2^{m-1}m + 1.$$

Partial information on the binary code of the Hadamard design $\mathcal{H}(q, O)$ is summarised as follows [Carpenter (1996)].

Theorem 12.40. *Let O be a regular hyperoval in the Desargusian projective plane* $\text{PG}(2, \text{GF}(2^m))$. *Then the code* $\mathcal{C}_{\text{GF}(2)}(\mathcal{H}(q, O))$ *of the design* $\mathcal{H}(q, O)$ *contains a copy of the punctured first-order Reed-Muller code* $\mathcal{R}_2(1, 2m)^*$.

Example 12.41. Let O be a translation hyperoval in $PG(2, GF(2^m))$, i.e., the hyperoval defined by the o-polynomial $f(x) = x^2$. When $m = 2$, the code $C_{GF(2)}(\mathcal{H}(q, O))$ has parameters $[15, 5, 7]$ and its dual has parameters $[15, 10, 4]$. When $m = 3$, the code $C_{GF(2)}(\mathcal{H}(q, O))$ has parameters $[63, 13, 24]$ and its dual has parameters $[63, 50, 4]$. When $m = 4$, the code $C_{GF(2)}(\mathcal{H}(q, O))$ has parameters $[255, 33, 80]$ and its dual has parameters $[255, 222, 4]$.

Symmetric $2\text{-}(4n - 1, 2n - 1, n - 1)$ designs are traditionally called *Hadamard 2-designs* due to their association with Hadamard matrices (see Assmus and Key (1992a)[Sections 7.2 and 7.12] or Ionin and Shrikhande (2006)[Chapter 6] for detail). Any $3\text{-}(4n, 2n, n - 1)$ design is called a *Hadamard 3-design*. A Hadamard 2-design can be extended into a Hadamard 3-design as follows (see Theorem 4.14).

Theorem 12.42. *Let* $\mathbb{D} = (\mathcal{P}, \mathcal{B})$ *be a* $2\text{-}(2k - 1, k - 1, \lambda)$ *design with* $k > 2$. *Then* $\mathbb{D}$ *can be extended into a* $3\text{-}(2k, k, \lambda)$ *design* $\mathbb{D}^e$.

Proof. We now define a new structure $\mathbb{D}^e = (\mathcal{P}^e, \mathcal{B}^e)$, where $\mathcal{P}^e = \mathcal{P} \cup \{\infty\}$ and ∞ is a new symbol, and $\mathcal{B}^e$ is defined by

$$\mathcal{B}^e = \{\mathcal{P} \setminus B : B \in \mathcal{B}\} \cup \{B \cup \{\infty\} : B \in \mathcal{B}\}.$$

Note that the set $\{\mathcal{P} \setminus B : B \in \mathcal{B}\}$ consists of the complements of all the blocks in $\mathcal{B}$, and $\{B \cup \{\infty\} : B \in \mathcal{B}\}$ is composed of all the blocks adjoined by ∞ in $\mathcal{B}$. It is straightforward to verify that every 3-subset of $\mathcal{P}^e$ is contained in λ blocks of $\mathcal{B}^e$. $\qquad\square$

Let $\mathcal{H}(q, O)^e$ denote the extended design of $\mathcal{H}(q, O)$. Then $\mathcal{H}(q, O)^e$ is a $3\text{-}(q^2, \frac{1}{2}q^2, \frac{1}{4}q^2 - 1)$ design. Consequently, $[q + 2, 3, q]$ MDS codes over $GF(q)$ (equivalently, hyperovals in $PG(2, GF(q))$) give a number of classes of $3\text{-}(q^2, \frac{1}{2}q^2, \frac{1}{4}q^2 - 1)$ designs.

12.7 Maximal Arc Codes and Their Designs

A *maximal* (n, h)-*arc* $\mathcal{A}$ in the projective plane $PG(2, GF(q))$ is a subset of $n = hq + h - q$ points such that every line meets $\mathcal{A}$ in 0 or h points. A line is called a *secant* if it meets $\mathcal{A}$, and *external line* otherwise. A line in $PG(2, GF(q))$ is said to be external to a maximal arc $\mathcal{A}$ if it has no intersection with $\mathcal{A}$. The set of lines external to $\mathcal{A}$ is a maximal (n', h')-arc $\mathcal{A}'$ in the dual plane, where $n' = h'q + h' - q$ and $h' = q/h$. $\mathcal{A}'$ is called the *dual* of $\mathcal{A}$.

When $h = 2$, maximal arcs in $PG(2, GF(q))$ become hyperovals, which were treated in the forgoing section. Hence, in this section we are mainly interested in maximal (n, h)-arcs with $h > 2$.

Any point of $PG(2, GF(q))$ is a $(1,1)$-arc. The complement of any line is a maximal (q^2, q)-arc. These are called *trivial arcs*. It has been proved that only trivial maximal arcs exist in $PG(2, GF(q))$ for odd q [Ball, Blokhuis and Mazzocca (1997)]. For even q, we have the following conclusion [Hirschfeld (1998)].

Theorem 12.43. *Let $q > 2$ be even. A maximal (n,h)-arc $\mathcal{A}$ in $PG(2, GF(q))$ exists if and only if h divides q, where $2 \leq h < q$.*

In 1969 Denniston employed a special set of conics to construct maximal arcs in the Desarguessian planes $PG(2, GF(q))$ for even q [Denniston (1969)]. Below we introduce the Denniston arcs, and will assume that $q > 2$ is even.

Let $X^2 + \beta X + 1$ be an irreducible polynomial over $GF(q)$. It is known that the total number of such irreducible polynomials over $GF(q)$ is $q/2$ [Hirschfeld (1998)][Sec. 1.3]. Define

$$F_\lambda := \{(x,y,z) : \lambda x^2 + y^2 + \beta yz + z^2 = 0\}, \ \lambda \in GF(q) \cup \{\infty\}. \quad (12.5)$$

Since $X^2 + \beta X + 1$ is irreducible over $GF(q)$, F_0 is only the point $(1,0,0)$, and F_∞ is the line $x = 0$. Every other conic F_λ is non-degenerate and has nucleus F_0. Further, this pencil of conics

$$\{F_\lambda : \lambda \in GF(q) \cup \{\infty\}\}$$

is a partition of the projective plane.

Let $\lambda \in GF(q)^*$. Then $\lambda x^2 + y^2 + \beta yz + z^2 = 0$ if and only if

$$x = \lambda^{-\frac{q}{2}} \left(y + (\beta yz)^{\frac{q}{2}} + z \right).$$

It then follows that

$$F_\lambda := \left\{ \left(\lambda^{-\frac{q}{2}}, 1, 0 \right) \right\} \cup \left\{ \left(\lambda^{-\frac{q}{2}} \left(y + (\beta y)^{\frac{q}{2}} + 1 \right), y, 1 \right) : y \in GF(q) \right\}$$

for all $\lambda \in GF(q)^*$.

Example 12.44. Let $q = 2^2$. Let w be a generator of $GF(q)^*$ with $w^2 + w + 1 = 0$. Then $X^2 + wX + 1$ is irreducible over $GF(q)$. We haven then the following:

$$F_0 = \{(1,0,0)\},$$
$$F_1 = \{(1,0,1), (w^2, w^2, 1), (w^2, 1, 1), (1,1,0), (1,w,1)\},$$
$$F_w = \{(w,1,0), (1,w^2,1), (w,w,1), (1,1,1), (w,0,1)\},$$
$$F_{w^2} = \{(w,w^2,1), (w^2,0,1), (w,1,1), (w^2,1,0), (w^2,w,1)\},$$
$$F_\infty = \{(0,0,1), (0,w^2,1), (0,1,0), (0,1,1), (0,w,1)\}.$$

The following theorem documents *Denniston arcs* [Denniston (1969)]. The reader is encouraged to work out a proof of it.

Theorem 12.45. *Let A be an additive subgroup of* $\mathrm{GF}(q)$ *of order h. Then the set of points of all conics* F_λ *for* $\lambda \in A$ *form a maximal* (n,h)-*arc* $\mathcal{A}$, *where* $n = hq + h - q$.

More families of maximal arcs were discovered and reported in Thas (1974), Thas (1980) and Mathon (2002). Their relations with the Denniston arcs were discussed in Hamilton and Penttila (2001).

Given a maximal (n,h)-arc $\mathcal{A}$, the points in the arc define a $3 \times n$ matrix over $\mathrm{GF}(q)$, where each column vector is a point in the arc. We use $C(\mathcal{A})$ to denote the code spanned by the rows of this matrix, which is called a *maximal arc code* (see Section 2.15 for the general construction).

Theorem 12.46. *Let* $q = 2^m$ *for any* $m \geq 2$ *and* $h = 2^i$ *with* $1 \leq i < m$. *Let* $\mathcal{A}$ *be a maximal* (n,h)-*arc in* $\mathrm{PG}(2,\mathrm{GF}(q))$. *Then the arc code* $C(\mathcal{A})$ *has parameters* $[n, 3, n-h]$ *and weight enumerator*

$$1 + \frac{(q^2-1)n}{h} z^{n-h} + \frac{(q^3-1)h - (q^2-1)n}{h} z^n, \tag{12.6}$$

where $n = hq + h - q$.

Proof. By definition, $\mathcal{A}$ meets each line in either 0 or h points. Note that in $\mathrm{PG}(2,\mathrm{GF}(q))$ lines and hyperplanes are the same. Let $\mathbf{c} = \sum_{j=1}^{3} u_i \mathbf{g}_i$ be a nonzero codeword of $C(\mathcal{A})$, where $\mathbf{g}_i = (g_{i,1}, \ldots, g_{i,n})$ are the row vectors of the generator matrix of $C(\mathcal{A})$. Then

$$\mathbf{c} = \left(\sum_{j=1}^{3} g_{1,j} u_j, \sum_{j=1}^{3} g_{2,j} u_j, \ldots, \sum_{j=1}^{3} g_{n,j} u_j \right).$$

Note that $xu_1 + yu_2 + zu_3 = 0$ defines a hyperplane (also a line). It then follows that the Hamming weight of $\mathbf{c}$ is either n or $n - h$. Thus, $C(\mathcal{A})$ has only the two nonzero weights $n - h$ and n. Note that the dual code has minimum weight at least 2. Solving the first two Pless power moments yields the desired weight enumerator. Note that the conclusion can also be derived from Theorem 2.43. $\square$

Theorem 12.47. *Let* $q = 2^m$ *for any* $m \geq 2$ *and* $h = 2^i$ *with* $1 \leq i < m$. *Let* $\mathcal{A}$ *be a maximal* (n,h)-*arc in* $\mathrm{PG}(2,\mathrm{GF}(q))$. *Then the supports of the codewords of weight* $n - h$ *in the code* $C(\mathcal{A})$ *form a 2-design with parameters*

$$2 - \left(n, \, n-h, \, \frac{(n-h)(n-h-1)}{h(h-1)} \right),$$

where $n = hq + h - q$. *Its complementary design is a* 2-$(n,h,1)$ *Steiner system.*

Proof. It can be proved that $C(\mathcal{A})^{\perp}$ has parameters $[n, n-3, d^{\perp}]$ with the MacWilliams Identity and the weight enumerator in (12.6), where $d^{\perp} = 4$ if $h = 2$ and $d^{\perp} = 3$ otherwise. It then follows from the Assmus-Mattson Theorem that the supports of the codewords with weight $n - h$ in the code $C(\mathcal{A})$ form a 2-design. Since $n - h$ is the minimum distance of the code, the total number of blocks in the design is given by

$$\frac{(q^2 - 1)n}{(q-1)h} = \frac{(q+1)n}{h}.$$

As a result,

$$\lambda = \frac{(n-h)(n-1-h)}{h(h-1)}.$$

The desired conclusion on the complementary design is obvious. $\qquad\square$

The supports of the codewords of weight 3 in the dual code $C(\mathcal{A})^{\perp}$ also form a 2-design. The parameters of this 2-design can be worked out with the weight distribution formula given in (12.17).

The proof of Theorem 12.46 implies the following result.

Theorem 12.48. *Let $q = 2^m \geq 4$ and $h = 2^i$ with $1 \leq i < m$. Let C be an $[n, 3, n-h]$ code over $\mathrm{GF}(q)$ with weight enumerator*

$$1 + \frac{(q^2 - 1)n}{h} z^{n-h} + \frac{(q^3 - 1)h - (q^2 - 1)n}{h} z^n, \tag{12.7}$$

where $n = hq + h - q$. Let G be a generator matrix of C. Then the set of all column vectors of G is a maximal $(n.h)$-arc in $\mathrm{PG}(2, \mathrm{GF}(q))$.

Combining Theorems 12.46 and 12.48, we conclude that maximal (n, h)-arcs in $\mathrm{PG}(2, \mathrm{GF}(q))$ and $[n, 3, n-h]$ codes over $\mathrm{GF}(q)$ with the weight enumerator of (12.7) are the same, in the sense that one can be derived from the other. Notice that maximal $(n, 2)$-arcs in $\mathrm{PG}(2, \mathrm{GF}(q))$ become hyperovals.

12.8 A Family of Extended Cyclic Codes and Their Designs

In the preceding section, we introduced maximal arcs, their codes and designs. The objective of this section is to describe a family of extended cyclic codes and their designs, which yield maximal arcs by Theorem 12.48. The materials of this section come from De Winter, Ding and Tonchev (2019).

Let m and k be positive integers. Define

$$q = 2^{km}, \ h = 2^m, \ n' = (q+1)(h-1), \ N = (q-1)/(h-1), \ r = q^2.$$

By definition,

$$N = \frac{r-1}{n'} = \frac{q-1}{h-1} = (2^m)^{k-1} + (2^m)^{k-2} + \cdots + 2^m + 1.$$

It is straightforward to see that $\mathrm{ord}_{n'}(q) = 2$. Let α be a generator of $\mathrm{GF}(r)^*$. Put $\beta = \alpha^N$. Then the order of β is n'. Let $\mathrm{Tr}(\cdot)$ denote the trace function from $\mathrm{GF}(r)$ to $\mathrm{GF}(q)$.

The irreducible cyclic code of length n' over $\mathrm{GF}(q)$ is defined by

$$\mathcal{C}_{(q,2,n')} = \{\mathbf{c}_a : a \in \mathrm{GF}(r)\}, \tag{12.8}$$

where

$$\mathbf{c}_a = (\mathrm{Tr}(a\beta^0), \mathrm{Tr}(a\beta^1), \mathrm{Tr}(a\beta^2), \ldots, \mathrm{Tr}(a\beta^{n'-1})).$$

The complete weight distribution of some irreducible cyclic codes was determined in Baumert and McEliece (1972). However, the results in Baumert and McEliece (1972) do not apply to the cyclic code $\mathcal{C}_{(q,2,n')}$ of (12.8), as our q is not a prime. The weight distribution of $\mathcal{C}_{(q,2,n')}$ is given in the following theorem.

Theorem 12.49. *The code $\mathcal{C}_{(q,2,n')}$ of (12.8) has parameters $[n', 2, n'-h+1]$ and has weight enumerator*

$$1 + (q^2 - 1)z^{(h-1)q}.$$

Furthermore, the dual distance of $\mathcal{C}_{(q,2,n')}$ equals 3 if $m = 1$, and 2 if $m > 1$.

Proof. Since q is even, $\gcd(q+1, q-1) = 1$. It then follows that

$$\gcd\left(\frac{r-1}{q-1}, N\right) = \gcd\left(q+1, \frac{q-1}{h-1}\right) = 1.$$

The desired conclusions regarding the dimension and weight enumerator of $\mathcal{C}_{(q,2,n')}$ then follow from Theorem 15 in Ding and Yang (2013).

We now prove the conclusions on the minimum distance of the dual code of $\mathcal{C}_{(q,2,n')}$. To this end, we define a linear code of length $q+1$ over $\mathrm{GF}(q)$ by

$$\mathbb{E}_{(q,2,q+1)} = \{\mathbf{e}_a : a \in \mathrm{GF}(r)\}, \tag{12.9}$$

where

$$\mathbf{e}_a = (\mathrm{Tr}(a\beta^0), \mathrm{Tr}(a\beta^1), \mathrm{Tr}(a\beta^2), \ldots, \mathrm{Tr}(a\beta^q)).$$

Each codeword $\mathbf{c}_a$ in $\mathcal{C}_{(q,2,n')}$ is related to the codeword $\mathbf{e}_a$ in $\mathbb{E}_{(q,2,q+1)}$ as follows:

$$\mathbf{c}_a = \mathbf{e}_a || \beta^{(q+1)} \mathbf{e}_a || \beta^{(q+1)2} \mathbf{e}_a || \cdots || \beta^{(q+1)(h-2)} \mathbf{e}_a, \tag{12.10}$$

where $||$ denotes the concatenation of vectors. It is easy to prove

$$\{\beta^{(q+1)i} : i \in \{0, 1, \ldots, h-2\}\} = \mathrm{GF}(h)^* \subseteq \mathrm{GF}(q)^*.$$

It then follows that $\mathbb{E}_{(q,2,q+1)}$ has the same dimension as $\mathcal{C}_{(q,2,n')}$. Consequently, the dimension of $\mathbb{E}_{(q,2,q+1)}$ is 2, and the dual code $\mathbb{E}_{(q,2,q+1)}^{\perp}$ has dimension $q-1$. It then follows from the Singleton bound that the minimum distance $d_{\mathbb{E}}^{\perp}$ of $\mathbb{E}_{(q,2,q+1)}^{\perp}$ is at most 3. Obviously, $d_{\mathbb{E}}^{\perp} \neq 1$. Suppose that $d_{\mathbb{E}}^{\perp} = 2$. Then there are an element $u \in \mathrm{GF}(q)^*$ and two integers i,j with $0 \le i < j \le q$ such that $\mathrm{Tr}(a(\beta^i - u\beta^j)) = 0$ for all $a \in \mathrm{GF}(r)$. It then follows that $\beta^i(1 - u\beta^{j-i}) = 0$. As a result, $\beta^{j-i} = \alpha^{(q-1)(j-i)/(h-1)} = u^{-1} \in \mathrm{GF}(q)^*$, which is impossible, as $0 < j - i \le q$ and $\gcd(q+1,(q-1)/(h-1)) = 1$. Hence, $d_{\mathbb{E}}^{\perp} = 3$. Since $\mathbb{E}_{(q,2,q+1)}^{\perp}$ is a $[q+1,q-1,3]$ MDS code, $\mathbb{E}_{(q,2,q+1)}$ is a $[q+1,2,q]$ MDS code. When $m = 1$, we have $h = 2$ and hence $\mathcal{C}_{(q,2,n')} = \mathbb{E}_{(q,2,q+1)}$. Consequently, the dual distance of $\mathcal{C}_{(q,2,n')}$ is 3 when $m = 1$. When $m > 1$, we have $h - 1 > 1$. In this case, by (12.10) $\mathcal{C}_{(q,2,n')}^{\perp}$ has the following codeword

$$(\beta^{q+1}, \mathbf{0}, 1, 0, 0, \ldots, 0, 0),$$

which has Hamming weight 2, where $\mathbf{0}$ is the zero vector of length q. Hence, $\mathcal{C}_{(q,2,n')}^{\perp}$ has minimum distance 2 if $m > 1$. This completes the proof. $\quad\square$

The code $\mathcal{C}_{(q,2,n')}$ is a one-weight code over $\mathrm{GF}(q)$. We need to study the augmented code of $\mathcal{C}_{(q,2,n')}$. Let $Z(a,b)$ denote the number of solutions $x \in \mathrm{GF}(r)$ of the equation

$$\mathrm{Tr}_{r/q}(ax^N) = ax^N + a^q x^{Nq} = b, \tag{12.11}$$

where $a \in \mathrm{GF}(r)$ and $b \in \mathrm{GF}(q)$. A key result of this section is the following lemma whose proof can be found in De Winter, Ding and Tonchev (2019).

Lemma 12.50. *Let $a \in \mathrm{GF}(r)^*$ and $b \in \mathrm{GF}(q)$. Then*

$$Z(a,b) = \begin{cases} (h-1)N + 1 & \text{if } b = 0, \\ hN \text{ or } 0 & \text{if } b \in \mathrm{GF}(q)^*. \end{cases}$$

Define

$$\widetilde{\mathcal{C}}_{(q,2,n')} = \{\mathbf{c}_a + b\mathbf{1} : a \in \mathrm{GF}(r), b \in \mathrm{GF}(q)\}, \tag{12.12}$$

where $\mathbf{1}$ denotes the all-1 vector in $\mathrm{GF}(q)^{n'}$. By definition, $\widetilde{\mathcal{C}}_{(q,2,n')}$ is the augmented code of $\mathcal{C}_{(q,2,n')}$.

Theorem 12.51. *The cyclic code $\widetilde{\mathcal{C}}_{(q,2,n')}$ has length n', dimension 3 and only the following nonzero weights:*

$$n' - h, \ n' - h + 1, \ n'.$$

The dual distance of $\widetilde{\mathcal{C}}_{(q,2,n')}$ is 4 if $m = 1$, and 3 if $m > 1$.

Proof. By definition, every codeword in $\widetilde{C}_{(q,2,n')}$ is given by $\mathbf{c}_a + b\mathbf{1}$, where $a \in \mathrm{GF}(r)$ and $b \in \mathrm{GF}(q)$. By Theorem 12.49, the codeword $\mathbf{c}_a + b\mathbf{1}$ is the zero codeword if and only if $(a,b) = (0,0)$. Consequently, the dimension of $\widetilde{C}_{(q,2,n')}$ is 3.

When $a = 0$ and $b \neq 0$, the codeword $\mathbf{c}_a + b\mathbf{1}$ has weight n'. When $a \neq 0$ and $b = 0$, by Theorem 12.49, the codeword $\mathbf{c}_a + b\mathbf{1}$ has weight $n' - h + 1$. When $a \neq 0$ and $b \neq 0$, by Lemma 12.50, the weight of the codeword $\mathbf{c}_a + b\mathbf{1}$ is either n' or $n' - h$, depending on $Z(a,b) = 0$ or $Z(a,b) = hN$.

The proof of the conclusions on the dual distance of $\widetilde{C}_{(q,2,n')}$ is left to the reader. $\qquad\square$

Let $\widetilde{\overline{C}}_{(q,2,n')}$ denote the extended code of $\widetilde{C}_{(q,2,n')}$. The next theorem gives the parameters of this extended code.

Theorem 12.52. *Let* $mk \geq 1$, *and let* $\widetilde{\overline{C}}_{(q,2,n')}$ *be a linear code over* $\mathrm{GF}(q)$ *with parameters* $[n'+1, 3, n'+1-h]$ *and nonzero weights* $n'+1-h$ *and* $n'+1$. *Then the weight enumerator of* $\widetilde{\overline{C}}_{(q,2,n')}$ *is given by*

$$A(z) := 1 + \frac{(q^2-1)(n'+1)}{h} z^{n'+1-h} + \frac{(q^3-1)h - (q^2-1)(n'+1)}{h} z^{n'+1}.$$

Furthermore, the dual distance of the code is 3 when $m > 1$ *and 4 when* $m = 1$.

Proof. By definition, every codeword of $\widetilde{\overline{C}}_{(q,2,n')}$ is given by

$$(\mathbf{c}_a + b\mathbf{1}, \bar{c}),$$

where $\bar{c}$ denotes the extended coordinate of the codeword. Note that $\sum_{i=0}^{n'-1} \beta^i = 0$. We have

$$\bar{c} = n'b = b.$$

When $a \neq 0$ and $b = 0$, by Theorem 12.49,

$$\mathrm{wt}((\mathbf{c}_a + b\mathbf{1}, \bar{c})) = \mathrm{wt}(\mathbf{c}_a + b\mathbf{1}) = n' + 1 - h.$$

When $a \neq 0$ and $b \neq 0$, by the proof of Theorem 12.51,

$$\mathrm{wt}((\mathbf{c}_a + b\mathbf{1}, \bar{c})) = \begin{cases} n' + 1 - h & \text{if } Z(a,b) = hN, \\ n' + 1 & \text{if } Z(a,b) = 0. \end{cases}$$

When $a = 0$ and $b \neq 0$, it is obvious that $\mathrm{wt}((\mathbf{c}_a + b\mathbf{1}, \bar{c})) = n' + 1$. We then deduce that $\widetilde{\overline{C}}_{(q,2,n')}$ has only nonzero weights $n' + 1 - h$ and $n' + 1$. By Theorem 12.51, the minimum distance of $\widetilde{\overline{C}}_{(q,2,n')}^{\perp}$ is at least 3. The weight enumerator of $\widetilde{\overline{C}}_{(q,2,n')}$ is obtained by solving the first two Pless power moments.

We now prove the conclusions on the dual distance of $\overline{\overline{C}}_{(q,2,n')}$. For simplicity, we put

$$u = \frac{(q^2-1)(n'+1)}{h}, \quad v = \frac{(q^3-1)h - (q^2-1)(n'+1)}{h}.$$

By (12.13), the weight enumerator of $\overline{\overline{C}}_{(q,2,n')}$ is $A(z) = 1 + uz^{n'+1-h} + vz^{n'+1}$. It then follows from the MacWilliams Identity that the weight enumerator $A^{\perp}(z)$ of $\overline{\overline{C}}_{(q,2,n')}^{\perp}$ is given by

$$\begin{aligned}
q^3 A^{\perp}(z) &= (1+(q-1)z)^{n'+1} A\left(\frac{1-z}{1+(q-1)z}\right) \\
&= (1+(q-1)z)^{n'+1} + u(1-z)^{n'+1-h}(1+(q-1)z)^h + v(1-z)^{n'+1}.
\end{aligned}$$

$$(12.13)$$

We have

$$(1+(q-1)z)^{n'+1} = \sum_{i=0}^{n'+1} \binom{n'+1}{i}(q-1)^i z^i \qquad (12.14)$$

and

$$v(1-z)^{n'+1} = \sum_{i=0}^{n'+1} \binom{n'+1}{i}(-1)^i v z^i. \qquad (12.15)$$

It is straightforward to prove that

$$u(1-z)^{n'+1-h}(1+(q-1)z)^h = \sum_{\ell=0}^{n'+1}\left(\sum_{i+j=\ell} \binom{n'+1-h}{i}\binom{h}{j}(-1)^i(q-1)^j\right) u z^{\ell}. \qquad (12.16)$$

Combining (12.13), (12.14), (12.15) and (12.16), we obtain that

$$\begin{aligned}
q^3 A_1^{\perp} &= \binom{n'+1}{1}[(q-1)-v] + \\
&\quad \left[\binom{n'+1-h}{0}\binom{h}{1}(-1)^0(q-1)^1 + \binom{n'+1-h}{1}\binom{h}{0}(-1)^1(q-1)^0\right]u \\
&= (n'+1)[(q-1)-v] + [h(q-1) - (n'+1-h)]u \\
&= 0.
\end{aligned}$$

Combining (12.13), (12.14), (12.15) and (12.16) again, we get that

$$q^3 A_2^{\perp} = \binom{n'+1}{2}[(q-1)^2+v] + \binom{n'+1-h}{0}\binom{h}{2}(-1)^0(q-1)^2 u +$$
$$\binom{n'+1-h}{1}\binom{h}{1}(-1)^1(q-1)^1 u + \binom{n'+1-h}{2}\binom{h}{0}(-1)^2(q-1)^0 u$$
$$= \binom{n'+1}{2}[(q-1)^2+v] +$$
$$\left[\binom{h}{2}(q-1)^2 - (n'+1-h)h(q-1) + \binom{n'+1-h}{2}\right]u$$
$$= 0.$$

Combining (12.13), (12.14), (12.15) and (12.16) the third time, we arrive at

$$q^3 A_3^{\perp} = \binom{n'+1}{3}[(q-1)^3-v] +$$
$$\left[\binom{n'+1-h}{0}\binom{h}{3}(-1)^0(q-1)^3 + \binom{n'+1-h}{1}\binom{h}{2}(-1)^1(q-1)^2\right]u +$$
$$\left[\binom{n'+1-h}{2}\binom{h}{1}(-1)^2(q-1)^1 + \binom{n'+1-h}{3}\binom{h}{0}(-1)^3(q-1)^0\right]u$$
$$= \binom{n'+1}{3}[(q-1)^3-v] +$$
$$\left[\binom{h}{3}(q-1)^3 - \binom{n'+1-h}{1}\binom{h}{2}(q-1)^2\right]u +$$
$$\left[\binom{n'+1-h}{2}\binom{h}{1}(q-1) - \binom{n'+1-h}{3}\right]u.$$

It then follows that

$$6q^3 A_3^{\perp} = q^6 h^3 - 4q^6 h^2 + 5q^6 h - 2q^6 + q^5 h^3 - 3q^5 h^2 + 2q^5 h -$$
$$q^4 h^3 + 4q^4 h^2 - 5q^4 h + 2q^4 - q^3 h^3 + 3q^3 h^2 - 2q^3 h$$
$$= (h-2)(h-1)q^3(q^2-1)(qh-q+h).$$

Thus,

$$A_3^{\perp} = \frac{(h-2)(h-1)(q^2-1)(qh-q+h)}{6}. \tag{12.17}$$

When $m > 1$, we have $h > 3$. In this case, by (12.17) we have $A_3^{\perp} > 0$. When $m = 1$, by (12.17) we have $A_3^{\perp} = 0$. As a result, the dual distance is at least 4 when $m = 1$. On the other hand, the Singleton bound tells us that the dual distance is at most 4 when $m = 1$. Whence, the dual distance must be 4 when $m = 1$.

Thus, in all cases, the extended code $\widetilde{\overline{C}}_{(q,2,n')}$ is projective, hence is associated with a maximal $(n'+1,h)$-arc in $\mathrm{PG}(2,q)$. $\quad\square$

The designs held in $\overline{\overline{C}}_{(q,2,n')}$ are those documented in Theorem 12.47. Any generator matrix of $\overline{\overline{C}}_{(q,2,n')}$ yields a maximal arc, which must be equivalent to a Denniston arc [Abdukhalikov and Ho (2021); Hamilton and Penttila (2001)]. The extended cyclic code $\overline{\overline{C}}_{(q,2,n')}$ is monomially-equivalent to the Denniston code [Abdukhalikov and Ho (2021)]. The parameters of the designs held in $\overline{\overline{C}}_{(q,2,n')}$ and its dual were determined in Section 12.7.

Chapter 13

Designs from Oviod Codes

In the preceding chapter, we treated designs from some MDS codes and hyper-ovals, and observed a close connection between some MDS codes and hyperovals in $PG(2, GF(2^e))$. In this chapter we will deal with ovoids in $PG(3, GF(q))$, their codes and 3-designs held in these codes. We will see that ovoids in $PG(3, GF(q))$ are equivalent to $[q^2 + 1, 4, q^2 - q]$ codes over $GF(q)$.

13.1   Ovoids in $PG(3, GF(q))$ and Their Properties

Recall that a cap in $PG(3, GF(q))$ is a set of points in $PG(3, GF(q))$ such that no three are collinear. We first have the following result about caps in $PG(3, GF(q))$ whose proof can be found in Beutelspacher and Rosenbaum (1998) and Payne (2007)[Section 7.2], and whose development is documented in Bose (1947), Seiden (1950) and Qvist (1952).

Theorem 13.1. *Let $q > 2$. For any cap $\mathcal{V}$ in $PG(3, GF(q))$, we have $|\mathcal{V}| \leq q^2 + 1$.*

In the projective space $PG(3, GF(q))$ with $q > 2$, an *ovoid* $\mathcal{V}$ is a set of $q^2 + 1$ points such that no three of them are collinear (i.e., on the same line). In other words, an ovoid is a $(q^2 + 1)$-cap (a cap with $q^2 + 1$ points) in $PG(3, GF(q))$, and thus a maximal cap by Theorem 13.1. Two ovoids are said to be *equivalent* if there is a collineation (i.e., automorphism) of $PG(3, GF(q))$ that sends one to the other. The *automorphism group* of an ovoid is the set of all collineations of $PG(3, GF(q))$ that leave the ovoid invariant.

A *tangent line* to an ovoid $\mathcal{V}$ in $PG(3, GF(q))$ is a line which intersects $\mathcal{V}$ in one point. The following theorem shows the existence of such tangent lines and their properties [Payne (2007)][Section 7.2].

Theorem 13.2. *Let $\mathcal{V}$ be an oviod in $PG(3, GF(q))$, $q > 2$. Then for a point $P \in \mathcal{V}$, the union of all the tangent lines on P is a plane, which is called the* tangent plane *at P of* $\mathcal{V}$.

The theorem below says that every plane in $PG(3, GF(q))$ meets an oviod in some points ([Barlotti (1955)], [Barlotti (1965)], [Panella (1955)], [Payne (2007)][Section 7.2]).

Theorem 13.3. *Let* $\mathcal{V}$ *be an ovoid in* $PG(3, GF(q))$, $q > 2$. *Then exactly* $q^2 + 1$ *planes of* $PG(3, GF(q))$ *meet* $\mathcal{V}$ *in a unique point, and the other* $q^3 + q$ *planes meet* $\mathcal{V}$ *in an oval with* $q + 1$ *points.*

The $q^3 + q$ planes meeting $\mathcal{V}$ in an oval with $q + 1$ points are called *secant planes*. Below are two families of ovoids.

A *classical ovoid* $\mathcal{V}$ can be defined as the set of all points given by

$$\mathcal{V} = \{(0, 0, 1, 0)\} \cup \{(x, y, x^2 + xy + ay^2, 1) : x, y \in GF(q)\}, \qquad (13.1)$$

where $a \in GF(q)$ is such that the polynomial $x^2 + x + a$ has no root in $GF(q)$. Such ovoid is called an *elliptic quadric*, as the points come from a non-degenerate elliptic quadratic form.

For $q = 2^{2e+1}$ with $e \geq 1$, there is an ovoid which is not an elliptic quadric, and is called the *Tits oviod* [Tits (1960)]. It is defined by

$$\mathcal{T} = \{(0, 0, 1, 0)\} \cup \{(x, y, x^\sigma + xy + y^{\sigma+2}, 1) : x, y \in GF(q)\}, \qquad (13.2)$$

where $\sigma = 2^{e+1}$.

For odd q, any ovoid is an elliptic quadric (see Barlotti (1955) and Panella (1955)). For even q, Tits ovoids are the only known ones which are not elliptic quadratics. In the case that q is even, the elliptic quadrics and the Tits ovoid are not equivalent [Willems (1999)]. For further information about ovoids, the reader is referred to O'Keefe (1996), Hirschfeld and Storme (1998) and Payne (2007).

13.2   Ovoids in $PG(3, GF(q))$ and $[q^2 + 1, 4, q^2 - q]$ Codes

Let $\mathcal{V}$ be an ovoid in $PG(3, GF(q))$ with $q > 2$. Denote by

$$\mathcal{V} = \{\mathbf{v}_1, \mathbf{v}_2, \ldots, \mathbf{v}_{q^2+1}\},$$

where each $\mathbf{v}_i$ is a column vector in $GF(q)^4$. Let $\mathcal{C}_\mathcal{V}$ be the linear code over $GF(q)$ with generator matrix

$$G_\mathcal{V} = \begin{bmatrix} \mathbf{v}_1 \mathbf{v}_2 \cdots \mathbf{v}_{q^2+1} \end{bmatrix}. \qquad (13.3)$$

Note that $\mathcal{V}$ intersects each plane in either one point or $q + 1$ points. It then follows from Theorem 2.43 that $\mathcal{C}_\mathcal{V}$ has only the nonzero weights $q^2 - q$ and q^2. The code is clearly projective. Solving the first two Pless power moments, one obtains the following weight enumerator of the code:

$$1 + (q^2 - q)(q^2 + 1)z^{q^2 - q} + (q - 1)(q^2 + 1)z^{q^2}. \tag{13.4}$$

Hence, $C_{\mathcal{V}}$ is a $[q^2 + 1, 4, q^2 - q]$ code over GF(q). Its dual is a $[q^2 + 1, q^2 - 3, 4]$ code. It then follows from Theorem 4.24 (i.e., the Assmus-Mattson Theorem) that the minimum weight codewords in $C_{\mathcal{V}}$ hold a 3-design. The dual code also supports 3-designs. The parameters of the 3-designs will be described in Section 13.4.

Linear codes over GF(q) with parameters $[q^2 + 1, 4, q^2 - q]$ are special and attractive due to the following result [Bierbrauer (2017)][p. 192].

Lemma 13.4. *Any linear code over* GF(q) *with parameters* $[q^2 + 1, 4, q^2 - q]$ *must have the weight enumerator of (13.4).*

Combining Lemma 13.4 and the proof of Theorem 13.11, we then arrive at the following.

Theorem 13.5. *The dual of any linear code over* GF(q) *with parameters* $[q^2 + 1, 4, q^2 - q]$ *must have parameters* $[q^2 + 1, q^2 - 3, 4]$.

The following conclusion then follows from Theorem 13.5.

Theorem 13.6. *Let* C *be a* $[q^2 + 1, 4, q^2 - q]$ *code over* GF(q). *Let* G *be a generator matrix of* C. *Then the column vectors of* G *form an ovoid in* PG(3, GF(q)).

Due to Theorems 13.6 and 13.5, linear codes over GF(q) with parameters $[q^2 + 1, 4, q^2 - q]$ are called *ovoid codes*. Another special feature of ovoid codes is that they meet the Griesmer bound. Linear codes over GF(q) with parameters $[q^2 + 1, q^2 - 3, 4]$ are almost MDS codes. Note that the weight distribution of general almost MDS codes is not known, though that of MDS codes is determined.

Let $\lambda \in$ GF(q)*. A linear code C of length n over GF(q) is called a λ-*constacyclic code* if $(c_0, c_1, \ldots, c_{n-1}) \in C$ implies that $(\lambda c_{n-1}, c_0, \ldots, c_{n-2}) \in C$. By definition, 1-constacyclic codes are cyclic codes. Hence, constacyclic codes contain cyclic codes as a subclass. It is also known that the dual of a λ-constacyclic code is a λ^{-1}-constacyclic code. Elliptic quadric codes are characterized in terms of constacyclic codes as follows by Maruta (1995).

Theorem 13.7. *Let* $\mathcal{V}$ *be an ovoid in* PG(3, GF(q)). *Then* $\mathcal{V}$ *is an elliptic quadric if and only if* $C_{\mathcal{V}}$ *is monomially-equivalent to a* λ-*constacyclic code.*

When $\mathcal{V}$ *is an elliptic quadric and* q *is odd,* $C_{\mathcal{V}}$ *is monomially-equivalent to a* λ-*constacyclic code, where* λ *cannot be 1. When* $\mathcal{V}$ *is an elliptic quadric and* q *is even,* $C_{\mathcal{V}}$ *is monomially-equivalent to a cyclic code.*

The following theorem was also proved in Maruta (1995).

Theorem 13.8. *A constacyclic code over* GF(q) *with parameters* $[q^2+1, q^2-3, 4]$ *is unique up to monomial equivalence. Equivalently, a constacyclic code over* GF(q) *with parameters* $[q^2+1, 4, q^2-q]$ *is unique up to monomial equivalence.*

13.3 A Family of Cyclic Codes with Parameters $[q^2+1, 4, q^2-q]$

The objective of this section is to present a family of irreducible cyclic codes over GF(q) with parameters $[q^2+1, 4, q^2-q]$, which give a family of ovoids in PG$(3, \mathrm{GF}(q))$ by Theorem 13.6.

Let r be a power of q and q be a power of a prime p. Let $N > 1$ be an integer dividing $r-1$, and put $n = (r-1)/N$. Let α be a primitive element of GF(r) and let $\theta = \alpha^N$. The set

$$C(r, N) = \{(\mathrm{Tr}_{r/q}(\beta), \mathrm{Tr}_{r/q}(\beta\theta), ..., \mathrm{Tr}_{r/q}(\beta\theta^{n-1})) : \beta \in \mathrm{GF}(r)\} \quad (13.5)$$

is called an *irreducible cyclic* $[n, m_0]$ *code* over GF(q), where $\mathrm{Tr}_{r/q}$ is the trace function from GF(r) onto GF(q), m_0 is the multiplicative order of q modulo n and m_0 divides m.

Let $\zeta_p = e^{2\pi\sqrt{-1}/p}$, and $\chi(x) = \zeta_p^{\mathrm{Tr}_{r/p}(x)}$, where $\mathrm{Tr}_{r/p}$ is the trace function from GF(r) to GF(p). Then χ is an additive character of GF(r). Let α be a fixed primitive element of GF(r). Define $C_i^{(N,r)} = \alpha^i \langle \alpha^N \rangle$ for $i = 0, 1, ..., N-1$, where $\langle \alpha^N \rangle$ denotes the subgroup of GF$(r)^*$ generated by α^N. The cosets $C_i^{(N,r)}$ are called the *cyclotomic classes* of order N in GF(r). The *Gaussian periods* are defined by

$$\eta_i^{(N,r)} = \sum_{x \in C_i^{(N,r)}} \chi(x), \quad i = 0, 1, ..., N-1,$$

where χ is the canonical additive character of GF(r). Recall that cyclotomic classes and Gaussian periods were defined in Section 1.5.2.

To determine the weight distribution of some irreducible cyclic codes later, we need the following lemma [Ding and Yang (2013)].

Lemma 13.9. *Let e_1 be a positive divisor of $r-1$ and let i be any integer with $0 \le i < e_1$. We have the following multiset equality:*

$$\left\{\left\{xy : y \in \mathrm{GF}(q)^*, x \in C_i^{(e_1,r)}\right\}\right\} = \frac{(q-1)\gcd((r-1)/(q-1), e_1)}{e_1} * C_i^{(\gcd((r-1)/(q-1), e_1), r)},$$

where $\frac{(q-1)\gcd((r-1)/(q-1), e_1)}{e_1} * C_i^{(\gcd((r-1)/(q-1), e_1), r)}$ *denotes the multiset in which each element in the set* $C_i^{(\gcd((r-1)/(q-1), e_1), r)}$ *appears in the multiset with multiplicity exactly* $\frac{(q-1)\gcd((r-1)/(q-1), e_1)}{e_1}$.

Proof. We just prove the conclusion for $i = 0$. The proof is similar for $i \neq 0$ since

$$C_i^{(\gcd((r-1)/(q-1),e_1),r)} = \alpha^i C_0^{(\gcd((r-1)/(q-1),e_1),r)}.$$

Note that every $y \in \mathrm{GF}(q)^*$ can be expressed as $y = \alpha^{\frac{r-1}{q-1}\ell}$ for a unique ℓ with $0 \leq \ell < q-1$ and every $x \in C_0^{(e_1,r)}$ can be expressed as $x = \alpha^{e_1 j}$ for a unique j with $0 \leq j < (r-1)/e_1$. Then we have

$$xy = \alpha^{\frac{r-1}{q-1}\ell + e_1 j}.$$

It follows that

$$xy = \alpha^{\frac{r-1}{q-1}\ell + e_1 j} = \left(\alpha^{\gcd((r-1)/(q-1),e_1)}\right)^{\frac{r-1}{(q-1)\gcd((r-1)/(q-1),e_1)}\ell + \frac{e_1}{\gcd((r-1)/(q-1),e_1)}j}.$$

Note that

$$\gcd\left(\frac{r-1}{(q-1)\gcd((r-1)/(q-1),e_1)}, \frac{e_1}{\gcd((r-1)/(q-1),e_1)}\right) = 1.$$

When ℓ ranges over $0 \leq \ell < q-1$ and j ranges over $0 \leq j < (r-1)/e_1$, xy takes on the value 1 exactly $\frac{q-1}{e_1}\gcd((r-1)/(q-1),e_1)$ times.

Let $x_{i_1} \in C_0^{(e_1,r)}$ for $i_1 = 1$ and $i_1 = 2$, and let $y_{i_2} \in \mathrm{GF}(q)^*$ for $i_2 = 1$ and $i_2 = 2$. Then $\frac{x_1}{x_2} \in C_0^{(e_1,r)}$ and $\frac{y_1}{y_2} \in \mathrm{GF}(q)^*$. Note that $x_1 y_1 = x_2 y_2$ if and only if $\frac{x_1}{x_2}\frac{y_1}{y_2} = 1$. Then the conclusion of the lemma for the case $i = 0$ follows from the discussions above. $\qquad\square$

Let $N > 1$ be an integer dividing $r - 1$, and put $n = (r-1)/N$. Let α be a primitive element of $\mathrm{GF}(r)$ and let $\theta = \alpha^N$. Let $Z(r,a)$ denote the number of solutions $x \in \mathrm{GF}(r)$ of the equation $\mathrm{Tr}_{r/q}(ax^N) = 0$. We have then by Lemma 13.9

$$Z(r,a) = \frac{1}{q} \sum_{y \in \mathrm{GF}(q)} \sum_{x \in \mathrm{GF}(r)} \zeta_p^{\mathrm{Tr}_{q/p}(y\mathrm{Tr}_{r/q}(ax^N))}$$

$$= \frac{1}{q} \sum_{y \in \mathrm{GF}(q)} \sum_{x \in \mathrm{GF}(r)} \chi(yax^N)$$

$$= \frac{1}{q}\left[q + r - 1 + N \sum_{y \in \mathrm{GF}(q)^*} \sum_{x \in C_0^{(N,r)}} \chi(yax)\right]$$

$$= \frac{1}{q}\left[q + r - 1 + (q-1)\gcd(\frac{r-1}{q-1},N) \cdot \sum_{z \in C_0^{\left(\gcd\left(\frac{r-1}{q-1},N\right),r\right)}} \chi(az)\right].$$

Then the Hamming weight of the codeword

$$\mathbf{c}(\beta) = (\mathrm{Tr}_{r/q}(\beta), \mathrm{Tr}_{r/q}(\beta\theta), ..., \mathrm{Tr}_{r/q}(\beta\theta^{n-1})) \tag{13.6}$$

in the irreducible cyclic code of (13.5) is equal to

$$n - \frac{Z(r,\beta) - 1}{N} = \frac{(q-1)\left(r - 1 - \gcd\left(\frac{r-1}{q-1}, N\right) \eta_k^{\left(\gcd\left(\frac{r-1}{q-1}, N\right), r\right)}\right)}{qN}. \quad (13.7)$$

Below we present a family of two-weight cyclic codes which are in fact ovoid codes.

Theorem 13.10. *Let* $q = 2^s$, *where* $s \geq 2$. *Let* $m = 4$ *and* $N = q^2 - 1$. *Then the code* $C(r,N)$ *over* $GF(q)$ *of (13.5) has parameters* $[q^2 + 1, 4, q^2 - q]$ *and weight enumerator*

$$1 + (q^2 - q)(q^2 + 1)z^{q^2 - q} + (q-1)(q^2 + 1)z^{q^2}. \quad (13.8)$$

Proof. Let

$$N_1 = \gcd((r-1)/(q-1), N) = q + 1.$$

It then follows from Theorem 1.38 that

$$\eta_0^{(N_1,r)} = -(q^2 - q + 1), \quad \eta_i^{(N_1,r)} = q - 1 \text{ for } 1 \leq i \leq q.$$

Let $\beta \in C_i^{(N_1,r)}$, where $0 \leq i \leq q$. By (13.7), the Hamming weight of the codeword $\mathbf{c}(\beta)$ in (13.6) is given by

$$\begin{aligned}
\mathrm{wt}(\mathbf{c}(\beta)) &= \frac{(q-1)\left(r - 1 - \gcd\left(\frac{r-1}{q-1}, N\right) \eta_k^{\left(\gcd\left(\frac{r-1}{q-1}, N\right), r\right)}\right)}{qN} \\
&= \frac{(q-1)\left(r - 1 - (q+1)\eta_k^{(N_1,r)}\right)}{qN} \\
&= \begin{cases} q^2 & \text{if } i = 0, \\ q^2 - q & \text{if } 1 \leq i \leq q. \end{cases}
\end{aligned}$$

It is obvious that the dual code of $C(r,N)$ has minimum distance at least 2. Let $w_1 = q^2 - q$ and $w_2 = q^2$. Let A_{w_1} and A_{w_2} denote the number of codewords with weight w_1 and w_2 in $C(r,N)$, respectively. The first two Pless power moments then become

$$A_{w_1} + A_{w_2} = q^4 - 1 \text{ and } w_1 A_{w_1} + w_2 A_{w_2} = q^3(q-1)(q^2+1).$$

Solving this set of equations above yields

$$A_{w_1} = (q^2 - q)(q^2 + 1), \quad A_{w_2} = (q-1)(q^2 + 1).$$

This completes the proof. $\qquad\qquad\qquad\qquad\qquad\qquad\qquad\qquad\qquad\square$

The ovoid given by any generator matrix of the code $C(r,N)$ is equivalent to the elliptic quadrics (see Abdukhalikov and Ho (2021) for a proof). Hence, the elliptic quadric has a cyclic-code construction when q is even.

Recall the BCH code $C_{(q,n,\delta,b)}$ of length n over $GF(q)$ defined in Section 3.7. Let $q \geq 4$ be even. One can prove that the narrow-sense BCH code $C_{(q,q^2+1,2,1)}$ has parameters $[q^2+1, q^2-3, 4]$ and its dual $C_{(q,q^2+1,2,1)}^{\perp}$ has parameters $[q^2+1, 4, q^2-q]$. Hence, the code $C(r,N)$ is the code $C_{(q,q^2+1,2,1)}^{\perp}$ for a specific choice of the (q^2+1)-th root of unity in the extension field $GF(q^4)$.

13.4 Designs from Ovoid Codes over $GF(q)$

Let C be a $[q^2+1, 4, q^2-q]$ code over $GF(q)$, i.e., an ovoid code. The task of this section is to work out the designs held in C and its dual. We first determine the weight distribution of $C^{\perp}$.

Theorem 13.11. *Let $q \geq 4$, and let C be a $[q^2+1, 4, q^2-q]$ code over $GF(q)$. Then $C^{\perp}$ has parameters $[q^2+1, q^2-3, 4]$ and its weight distribution is given by*

$$q^4 A_{\ell}^{\perp} = \binom{q^2+1}{\ell}(q-1)^{\ell} + u \sum_{i+j=\ell} \binom{q^2-q}{i}(-1)^i \binom{q+1}{j}(q-1)^j +$$
$$v\left[(-1)^{\ell}\binom{q^2}{\ell} + (-1)^{\ell-1}(q-1)\binom{q^2}{\ell-1}\right] \tag{13.9}$$

for all $4 \leq \ell \leq q^2$, and

$$q^4 A_{q^2+1}^{\perp} = (q-1)^{q^2+1} + u(q-1)^{q+1} + v(q-1),$$

where

$$u = (q^2-q)(q^2+1), \quad v = (q-1)(q^2+1) \tag{13.10}$$

and $A_{\ell}^{\perp}$ denotes the number of codewords of weight ℓ in $C^{\perp}$.

Proof. By Theorem 13.10, the weight enumerator of C is

$$A(z) = 1 + uz^{q^2-q} + vz^{q^2}.$$

It then follows from the MacWilliams identity that

$$q^4 A^{\perp}(z) = (1+(q-1)z)^{q^2+1} A\left(\frac{1-z}{1+(q-1)z}\right)$$
$$= (1+(q-1)z)^{q^2+1}\left[1 + u\left(\frac{1-z}{1+(q-1)z}\right)^{q^2-q} + v\left(\frac{1-z}{1+(q-1)z}\right)^{q^2}\right]$$
$$= P_1(z) + P_2(z) + P_3(z),$$

where

$$P_1(z) = (1+(q-1)z)^{q^2+1} = \sum_{\ell=0}^{q^2+1} \binom{q^2+1}{\ell}(q-1)^{\ell},$$

$$P_2(z) = u(1-z)^{q^2-q}(1+(q-1)z)^{q+1}$$

$$= u \sum_{\ell=0}^{q^2+1} \left[\sum_{i+j=\ell} \binom{q^2-q}{i}(-1)^i \binom{q+1}{j}(q-1)^j \right] z^{\ell}$$

and

$$P_3(z) = v(1-z)^{q^2}(1+(q-1)z)$$

$$= v \left[1 + \sum_{\ell=1}^{q^2} \left[(-1)^{\ell} \binom{q^2}{\ell} + (-1)^{\ell-1}(q-1)\binom{q^2}{\ell-1} \right] z^{\ell} + (q-1)z^{q^2+1} \right].$$

For the easiness of description, let

$$P_i(z) = \sum_{\ell} P_{i,j} z^{\ell}$$

for all $1 \le i \le 3$. Obviously, the minimum distance $d^{\perp}$ of $C^{\perp}$ cannot be 1.

We first prove that $A_2^{\perp} = 0$. By definition,

$$P_{1,2} = \binom{q^2+1}{2}(q-1)^2$$

$$= \frac{1}{2}q^6 - q^5 + q^4 - q^3 + \frac{1}{2}q^2,$$

$$P_{2,2} = u \left[\sum_{i+j=2} \binom{q^2-q}{i}(-1)^i \binom{q+1}{j}(q-1)^j \right]$$

$$= -\frac{1}{2}q^7 + q^6 - q^5 + q^4 - \frac{1}{2}q^3$$

and

$$P_{3,2} = v \left[(-1)^2 \binom{q^2}{2} + (-1)^{2-1}(q-1)\binom{q^2}{2-1} \right]$$

$$= \frac{1}{2}q^7 - \frac{3}{2}q^6 + 2q^5 - 2q^4 + \frac{3}{2}q^3 - \frac{1}{2}q^2.$$

Consequently,

$$q^4 A_2^{\perp} = P_{1,2} + P_{2,2} + P_{3,2} = 0$$

and $A_2^{\perp} = 0$.

We then prove that $A_3^\perp = 0$. By definition,

$$P_{1,3} = \binom{q^2+1}{3}(q-1)^3$$

$$= \frac{1}{6}q^9 - \frac{1}{2}q^8 + \frac{1}{2}q^7 - \frac{1}{6}q^6 - \frac{1}{6}q^5 + \frac{1}{2}q^4 - \frac{1}{2}q^3 + \frac{1}{6}q^2,$$

$$P_{2,3} = u\left[\sum_{i+j=3}\binom{q^2-q}{i}(-1)^i\binom{q+1}{j}(q-1)^j\right]$$

$$= -\frac{1}{6}q^8 + \frac{1}{6}q^7 + \frac{1}{6}q^4 - \frac{1}{6}q^3$$

and

$$P_{3,3} = v\left[(-1)^3\binom{q^2}{3} + (-1)^{3-1}(q-1)\binom{q^2}{3-1}\right]$$

$$= -\frac{1}{6}q^9 + \frac{2}{3}q^8 - \frac{2}{3}q^7 + \frac{1}{6}q^6 + \frac{1}{6}q^5 - \frac{2}{3}q^4 + \frac{2}{3}q^3 - \frac{1}{6}q^2.$$

Consequently.

$$q^4 A_3^\perp = P_{1,3} + P_{2,3} + P_{3,3} = 0$$

and $A_3^\perp = 0$.

Finally, we compute $A_4^\perp$. By definition,

$$P_{1,4} = \binom{q^2+1}{4}(q-1)^4$$

$$= \frac{1}{24}q^{12} - \frac{1}{6}q^{11} + \frac{1}{6}q^{10} + \frac{1}{6}q^9 - \frac{1}{2}q^8 + \frac{1}{2}q^7 -$$
$$\frac{1}{4}q^6 - \frac{1}{6}q^5 + \frac{11}{24}q^4 - \frac{1}{3}q^3 + \frac{1}{12}q^2,$$

$$P_{2,4} = u\left[\sum_{i+j=4}\binom{q^2-q}{i}(-1)^i\binom{q+1}{j}(q-1)^j\right]$$

$$= \frac{1}{8}q^{10} - \frac{7}{24}q^9 + \frac{1}{12}q^8 + \frac{1}{12}q^7 - \frac{1}{8}q^6 + \frac{7}{24}q^5 - \frac{1}{12}q^4 - \frac{1}{12}q^3$$

and

$$P_{3,4} = v\left[(-1)^4\binom{q^2}{4} + (-1)^{4-1}(q-1)\binom{q^2}{4-1}\right]$$

$$= \frac{1}{24}q^{11} - \frac{5}{24}q^{10} + \frac{1}{8}q^9 + \frac{3}{8}q^8 - \frac{11}{24}q^7 + \frac{7}{24}q^6 - \frac{1}{8}q^5 - \frac{3}{8}q^4 + \frac{5}{12}q^3 - \frac{1}{12}q^2.$$

Consequently.

$$q^4 A_4^\perp = P_{1,4} + P_{2,4} + P_{3,4}$$
$$= \frac{1}{24}q^{12} - \frac{1}{8}q^{11} + \frac{1}{12}q^{10} - \frac{1}{24}q^8 + \frac{1}{8}q^7 - \frac{1}{12}q^6$$
$$= \frac{(q-2)(q-1)^2 q^6 (q+1)(q^2+1)}{24}.$$

We then deduce that

$$A_4^\perp = \frac{(q-2)(q-1)^2 q^2 (q+1)(q^2+1)}{24} > 0 \tag{13.11}$$

as $q \geq 4$. The desired general formula about $A_\ell^\perp$ follows from the fact that

$$q^4 A_\ell^\perp = P_{1,\ell} + P_{2,\ell} + P_{3,\ell}$$

and the formulas for $P_{i,\ell}$ derived above. $\square$

We are now ready to describe the 3-designs held in C and its dual. Our main result of this chapter is the following.

Theorem 13.12. *Let $q \geq 4$ and let C be a $[q^2 + 1, 4, q^2 - q]$ code over* GF(q). *Then the supports of the codewords of weight $q^2 - q$ in C form a design with parameters*

$$3\text{-}(q^2 + 1, \ q^2 - q, \ (q-2)(q^2 - q - 1)).$$

The complement of this design is a 3-$(q^2 + 1, q + 1, 1)$ Steiner system.

Furthermore, the supports of all the codewords of weight 4 in $C^\perp$ form a 3-$(q^2 + 1, 4, q - 2)$ design.

Proof. By Theorem 13.10, C is a two-weight code with the larger weight $q^2 > (q^2 + 1) - 2$. In addition, by Theorem 13.10, the minimum weight of $C^\perp$ is 4. It then follows from Theorem 4.24 (i.e., the Assmus-Mattson Theorem) that the supports of the codewords of weight $q^2 - q$ in the code C form a 3-design, and the supports of the codewords of weight 4 in the code $C^\perp$ form also a 3-design.

By Theorem 13.10, $A_{q^2-q} = q(q-1)(q^2+1)$. Since $q^2 - q$ is the minimum weight of C, the number of supports of the codewords of weight $q^2 - q$ is

$$b = \frac{A_{q^2-q}}{q-1} = q(q^2 + 1).$$

It then follows that

$$b = \lambda \frac{\binom{q^2+1}{3}}{\binom{q^2-q}{3}}.$$

Consequently, $\lambda = (q-2)(q^2 - q - 1)$.

Since 4 is the minimum weight of $C^{\perp}$, by (13.11) the number of supports of the codewords of weight 4 in $C^{\perp}$ is

$$b^{\perp} = \frac{A_4^{\perp}}{q-1} = \frac{(q-2)(q-1)q^2(q+1)(q^2+1)}{24}.$$

It then follows that

$$b^{\perp} = \lambda^{\perp} \frac{\binom{q^2+1}{3}}{\binom{4}{3}}.$$

Consequently, $\lambda^{\perp} = q - 2$. This completes the proof. $\qquad\square$

13.5 Ovoids, Codes, Designs and Inversive Planes

In the previous sections of this chapter, we established the following:

(1) Ovoids in $\mathrm{PG}(3, \mathrm{GF}(q))$ and $[q^2+1, 4, q^2-q]$ codes over $\mathrm{GF}(q)$ are the same, in the sense that one can be derived from the other.
(2) Every $[q^2+1, 4, q^2-q]$ code over $\mathrm{GF}(q)$ gives a $3\text{-}(q^2+1, q+1, 1]$ Steiner system.

The purpose of this section is to show that the $3\text{-}(q^2+1, q+1, 1]$ Steiner systems are in fact finite inversive planes (also called Möbius planes). Hence, ovoids and $[q^2+1, 4, q^2-q]$ codes over $\mathrm{GF}(q)$ can produce inversive planes.

An incidence structure $(\mathcal{P}, \mathcal{Z}, \in)$ with point set $\mathcal{P}$ and a set $\mathcal{Z}$ of circles (i.e., blocks) is called an *inversive plane* or *Möbius plane* if the following axioms hold:

A1: For any three pairwise distinct points A, B and C, there is exactly one circle that contains A, B, C.

A2: For any circle z, any point $P \in z$ and $Q \notin z$, there exists exactly one circle z' such that $P \in z'$, $Q \in z'$ and $z \cap z' = \{P\}$ (i.e., z and z' touch each other at point P).

A3: Every circle contains at least three points. There is at least one circle.

Four points A, B, C, D are said to be *concyclic* if there is a circle containing all of them.

Example 13.13. The smallest inversive plane is the incidence structure $(\mathcal{P}, \mathcal{Z}, \in)$ with $\mathcal{P} = \{A, B, C, D, \infty\}$ and

$$\mathcal{Z} = \{z : z \subset \mathcal{P}, \ |z| = 3\}.$$

The total number of circles is $\binom{5}{3} = 10$.

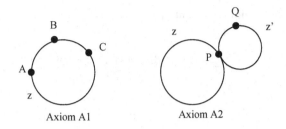

Axiom A1   Axiom A2

Example 13.14. Let $\mathbb{R}$ denote the set of real numbers. In the affine plane $AG(2,\mathbb{R})$ the *lines* are described by the equations $y = ax + b$ and $x = c$, and a *circle* is a set of points that fulfils an equation

$$(x - x_0)^2 + (y - y_0)^2 = r^2, \; r > 0.$$

The geometry of lines and circles of the affine (also called Euclidean) plane can be homogenized by embedding it into the incidence structure $(\mathcal{P}, \mathcal{Z}, \in)$ with

- $\mathcal{P} = \mathbb{R}^2 \cup \{\infty\}$, $\infty \notin \mathbb{R}$, *the point set*, and
- $\mathcal{Z} = \{\ell \cup \{\infty\} : \ell$ a line in $AG(2,\mathbb{R})\} \cup \{k : k$ a circle of $AG(2,\mathbb{R})\}$, the *set of circles*.

The incidence structure $(\mathcal{P}, \mathcal{Z}, \in)$ is called the *classical real Möbius plane*.

An inversive plane is *finite* if the point set $\mathcal{P}$ is a finite set. It is not hard to prove that in a finite inversive plane all circles have the same number of points. For a finite inversive plane $(\mathcal{P}, \mathcal{Z}, \in)$ and a circle $z \in \mathcal{Z}$, the integer $n := |z| - 1$ is called the *order of the plane*.

A proof of the next result could be found in Dembowski (1968)[Chapter 6].

Theorem 13.15. *Let* $(\mathcal{P}, \mathcal{Z}, \in)$ *be a finite inversive plane with order n. Then* $(\mathcal{P}, \mathcal{Z}, \in)$ *is a* 3-$(n^2 + 1, n + 1, 1)$ *design.*

Our main conclusion of this section is made in the following theorem.

Theorem 13.16. *Let* $(\mathcal{P}, \mathcal{Z}, \in)$ *be a* 3-$(n^2 + 1, n + 1, 1)$ *design with* $n \geq 4$. *If each block is viewed as a circle, then* $(\mathcal{P}, \mathcal{Z}, \in)$ *is a finite inversive plane with order n.*

Proof. Let $\mathbb{D} := (\mathcal{P}, \mathcal{Z}, \in)$ be a 3-$(n^2 + 1, n + 1, 1)$ design with $n \geq 4$. We now view each block in $\mathcal{Z}$ as a circle, and prove that the three axioms for inversive planes hold. By the definition of 3-$(n^2 + 1, n + 1, 1)$ designs, any three pairwise distinct points A, B, C in $\mathcal{Z}$ are incident with exactly one block in $\mathcal{Z}$. Hence, Axiom A1 holds.

Let $z := \{P_1, P_2, \ldots, P_n, P\}$ be a block in $\mathcal{Z}$ and let Q be a point outside z. We now consider the derived design $\mathbb{D}(P)$ with respect to the point P, which is defied by

$$\mathbb{D}(P) = (\mathcal{P} \setminus \{P\}, \{z \setminus \{P\} : P \in z\}, \in).$$

It is known that $\mathbb{D}(P)$ is 2-$(n^2, n, 1)$ design (see Section 4.1.6), i.e., an affine plane. In the affine plane $\mathbb{D}(P)$, $\{P_1, P_2, \ldots, P_n\}$ is a line (block), and Q is a point in $\mathbb{D}(P)$ but not on the line $\{P_1, P_2, \ldots, P_n\}$. Hence, there is a unique line ℓ (block) in $\mathbb{D}(P)$ containing Q that is parallel to $\{P_1, P_2, \ldots, P_n\}$. Thus,

$$\{P_1, P_2, \ldots, P_n\} \cap \ell = \emptyset.$$

Consequently, $\ell \cup \{P\}$ is the unique circle in $\mathbb{D}$ that touches on the circle $\{P_1, P_2, \ldots, P_n, P\}$ at the unique point P. Hence, Axiom A2 holds.

Axiom A3 clearly holds. The proof is then completed. $\qquad\square$

Let $q > 4$ be even. Then the irreducible cyclic code of Theorem 13.12 produces an inversive plane.

If an ovoid is classical, the ovoid and the corresponding inversive plane is *classical* or *Miquelian*. If $\mathcal{V}$ is an ovoid of $\mathrm{PG}(3, \mathrm{GF}(q))$, then the points of $\mathcal{V}$ together with the intersections of $\pi \cap \mathcal{V}$, with π a nontangent plane of $\mathcal{V}$ (i.e., π contains $q + 1$ points of $\mathcal{V}$), form an inversive plane of order q. Such an inversive plane is called *egglike*. Each inversive plane of even order is egglike [Dembowski (1963)].

13.6 Designs Held in Punctured and Shortened Ovoid Codes

In this section, we describe 2-designs held in some punctured and shortened codes of ovoid codes. We document the following results whose proofs can be found in [Liu, Ding and Tang (2021)].

Theorem 13.17. *Let $q > 3$ be a prime power, and let C be a $[q^2 + 1, 4, q^2 - q]$ code over $\mathrm{GF}(q)$. For any coordinate position i in C, let $C_{\{i\}}$ denote the code obtained by shortening C at coordinate position i. Then $C_{\{i\}}$ is a $[q^2, 3, q^2 - q]$ code over $\mathrm{GF}(q)$ with weight enumerator*

$$1 + (q^2 - q)(q + 1)z^{q^2 - q} + (q - 1)z^{q^2}.$$

The dual code $C_{\{i\}}^{\perp}$ has parameters $[q^2, q^2 - 3, 3]$.

The supports of all codewords of weight $q^2 - q$ in the shortened code $C_{\{i\}}$ form a 2-$(q^2, q^2 - q, q^2 - q - 1)$ design $\mathbb{D}_{\{i\}}$. The complement of $\mathbb{D}_{\{i\}}$ is a Steiner system with parameters 2-$(q^2, q, 1)$, i.e., an affine plane.

It would be interesting to compare the affine planes in Theorem 13.17 with those in the proof of Theorem 13.16. We now introduce 2-designs held in some punctured codes of ovoid codes.

Theorem 13.18. *Let $q > 3$ be a prime power, and let C be a $[q^2 + 1, 4, q^2 - q]$ code over $GF(q)$. For any coordinate position i in C, let $C^{\{i\}}$ denote the code obtained by puncturing C at coordinate position i. Then $C^{\{i\}}$ is a $[q^2, 4, q^2 - q - 1]$ code over $GF(q)$ with weight enumerator*

$$1 + (q^2 - q)^2 z^{q^2 - q - 1} + q(q^2 - 1)z^{q^2 - q} + q^2(q - 1)z^{q^2 - 1} + (q - 1)z^{q^2}.$$

The dual code $C_{\{i\}}^{\perp}$ has parameters $[q^2, q^2 - 4, 4]$.

The supports of all codewords of weight $q^2 - q - 1$ in the punctured code $C^{\{i\}}$ form a design with parameters

$$2\text{-}(q^2, q^2 - q - 1, (q - 2)(q^2 - q - 1)).$$

The complement of this design is a 2-$(q^2, q + 1, q)$ design.

The supports of all codewords of weight $q^2 - q$ in the punctured code $C^{\{i\}}$ form a 2-$(q^2, q^2 - q, q^2 - q - 1)$ design. The complement of this design is a Steiner system with parameters 2-$(q^2, q, 1)$, i.e., an affine plane.

Note that $C_{\{i\}}$ is a subcode of $C^{\{i\}}$. The weight enumerators of $C_{\{i\}}$ and $C^{\{i\}}$ tell us that the affine planes in Theorem 13.17 and those in Theorem 13.17 are the same set of affine planes.

At the end of this section, we present the following two theorems but skip their proofs.

Theorem 13.19. *Let $q = 2^m \geq 4$. Define*

$$D = \{x \in GF(q^4) : Tr_{q^4/q}(x^{q+1}) = 1 \text{ and } Tr_{q^4/q}(x) = 0\}$$

or

$$D = \{x \in GF(q^4) : Tr_{q^4/q}(x^{q+1} + x) = 1\}.$$

Let C_D denote the linear code over $GF(q)$ defined in (2.15) in Section 2.14. Then the code C_D has parameters $[q^2, 3, q^2 - q]$ and weight enumerator

$$1 + (q^2 - q)(q + 1)z^{q^2 - q} + (q - 1)z^{q^2}.$$

The dual code $C_D^{\perp}$ has parameters $[q^2, q^2 - 3, 3]$ and is AMDS.

The code C_D in Theorem 13.19 has the same parameters and the same weight enumerator as the code $C_{\{i\}}$ in Theorem 13.17. Hence, they support 2-designs with the same parameters.

Theorem 13.20. *Let $q = 2^m \geq 4$. Define*

$$D = \{x \in \mathrm{GF}(q^4) : \mathrm{Tr}_{q^4/q}(x^{q+1}) = 1 \text{ and } \mathrm{Tr}_{q^4/q}(x) \neq 0\}$$

Let C_D denote the linear code over $\mathrm{GF}(q)$ defined in (2.15) in Section 2.14. Then the code C_D has parameters $[q^3, 4, q^3 - q^2]$ and weight enumerator

$$1 + (q^4 - q)z^{q^3 - q^2} + (q-1)z^{q^3}.$$

The dual code $C_D^\perp$ has parameters $[q^3, q^3 - 4, 3]$. The minimum weight codewords in C_D support a $2\text{-}(q^3, q^3 - q^2, q^3 - q^2 - 1)$ design.

Chapter 14

Quasi-Symmetric Designs from Bent Codes

Designs are often associated with optimal codes. Symmetric designs with the symmetric difference property are a special type of symmetric designs and related to Hadamard difference sets and a type of linear codes. Their derived and residual designs are quasi-symmetric and have a close connection with a family of linear codes meeting the Grey-Rankin bound. The objectives of this chapter is to give a coding-theoretic construction of all quasi-symmetric SDP designs. It will be seen that the linear codes holding quasi-symmetric designs are optimal with respect to the Grey-Rankin bound (see Theorem 2.32).

14.1 Derived and Residual Designs of Symmetric Designs

The derived and residual designs with respect to a fixed point of a given design were defined in Section 4.1.6. In this section, we define the derived and residual designs of a symmetric design with respect to the complement of a fixed block, and state their basic properties.

Theorem 14.1. *Let* $\mathbb{D} = \{\mathcal{P}, \mathcal{B}\}$ *be a* 2-(v, k, λ) *symmetric design, where* $\mathcal{B} = \{B_1, B_2, \ldots, B_b\}$ *and* $b \geq 2$. *Then* $(B_1, \{B_2 \cap B_1, B_3 \cap B_1, \ldots, B_b \cap B_1\})$ *is a* 2-$(k, \lambda, \lambda - 1)$ *design.*

The proof of Theorem 14.1 is straightforward and left to the reader. The design of Theorem 14.1 is called the *derived design* of $\mathbb{D}$ with respect to B_1.

Theorem 14.2. *Let* $\mathbb{D} = \{\mathcal{P}, \mathcal{B}\}$ *be a* 2-(v, k, λ) *symmetric design, where* $\mathcal{B} = \{B_1, B_2, \ldots, B_b\}$ *and* $b \geq 2$. *Then* $(\bar{B}_1, \{B_2 \cap \bar{B}_1, B_3 \cap \bar{B}_1, \ldots, B_b \cap \bar{B}_1\})$ *is a* 2-$(v - k, k - \lambda, \lambda)$ *design, where* $\bar{B}_1 = \mathcal{P} \setminus B_1$.

The proof of Theorem 14.2 is also straightforward and left to the reader. The design of Theorem 14.2 is called the *residual design* of $\mathbb{D}$ with respect to B_1.

The b derived designs may be isomorphic or not. However, they have the same parameters. Consequently, we call them collectively the derived design. For the same reason, all the b residual designs are collectively called the residual design of $\mathbb{D}$. In this chapter, we use $\mathbb{D}^{de}$ and $\mathbb{D}^{re}$ to denote a derived and residual design of a symmetric design $\mathbb{D}$, respectively.

14.2   Symmetric and Quasi-Symmetric SDP Designs

If a symmetric design $\mathbb{D}$ has parameters

$$2 - (2^m, 2^{m-1} - 2^{(m-2)/2}, 2^{m-2} - 2^{(m-2)/2}), \tag{14.1}$$

its derived design has parameters

$$2 - (2^{m-1} - 2^{(m-2)/2}, 2^{m-2} - 2^{(m-2)/2}, 2^{m-2} - 2^{(m-2)/2} - 1), \tag{14.2}$$

and its residual design has parameters

$$2 - (2^{m-1} + 2^{(m-2)/2}, 2^{m-2}, 2^{m-2} - 2^{(m-2)/2}). \tag{14.3}$$

A symmetric 2-design is said to have the *symmetric difference property*, or to be a *symmetric SDP design*, if the symmetric difference of any *three* blocks is either a block or the complement of a block.

Theorem 4.9 says that the block intersection numbers of symmetric 2-designs are the same. This is a characterisation of such designs. A 2-design is *quasi-symmetric* with intersection numbers x and y if any two distinct blocks intersect in either x or y points for two fixed integers x and y with $0 \leq x < y$, and both intersection numbers x and y are realised.[1] A quasi-symmetric 2-design is said to have the *symmetric difference property*, or to be an *SDP design*, if the symmetric difference of any *two* blocks is either a block or the complement of a block.

14.3   The Roadmap of the Remaining Sections

Kantor constructed a very large number of symmetric SDP designs [Kantor (1975, 1983)]. Since then symmetric SDP designs and their codes, the derived and residual designs of symmetric SDP designs and their codes have been investigated in Assmus and Key (1992b); Dillon and Schatz (1987); Jungnickel and Tonchev (1991, 1992); Tonchev (1993).

---

[1]Here we require that $x \neq y$ so that symmetric designs cannot be a subclass of quasi-symmetric designs.

Dillon and Schatz (1987) characterised all symmetric SDP designs of parameters of (14.1) with its binary code which is generated by the first-order Reed-Muller code $\mathcal{R}(1,m)$ and the incidence vector of a Hadamard difference set with the following parameters

$$(2^m, 2^{m-1} \pm 2^{(m-2)/2}, 2^{m-2} \pm 2^{(m-2)/2}). \qquad (14.4)$$

This is the relation R.i depicted in Figure 14.1, which is documented in Theorem 14.6.

Jungnickel and Tonchev proved that the derived and residual designs of each symmetric SDP design with parameters of (14.1) are quasi-symmetric, and have the symmetric difference property and the parameters of (14.2) and (14.3), respectively (see Theorem 14.13 in Jungnickel and Tonchev (1991, 1992)). Tonchev showed that every quasi-symmetric SDP design with the parameters of (14.2) and (14.3) must be a derived or residual design of a symmetric SDP design with the parameters of (14.1). These are the relation R.ii depicted in Figure 14.1.

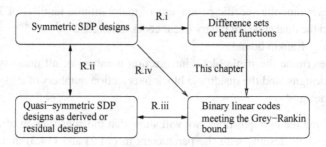

Fig. 14.1   Some connections among designs and codes.

Combining Relations R.i and R.ii, we conclude that every quasi-symmetric SDP design with the parameters of (14.2) or (14.3) comes from a Hadamard difference set with the parameters of (14.4). But we have the following question:

Problem 14.3. Given a Hadamard difference set in $(\mathrm{GF}(2^m), +)$ with the parameters of (14.4), how does one construct the corresponding quasi-symmetric SDP designs in a direct way?

Jungnickel and Tonchev observed that the binary code of the incidence matrix of a quasi-symmetric SDP design is a binary self-complementary code meeting the Grey-Rankin bound (see Theorem 2.32 in Jungnickel and Tonchev (1991)). McQuire noticed a one-to-one correspondence between quasi-symmetric SDP designs with the parameters of (14.2) and (14.3) with binary linear codes of certain parameters meeting the Grey-Rankin bound [McQuire (1997)]. Hence, each quasi-symmetric SDP design is generated by a binary linear code meeting the Grey-Rankin bound. As a result, every binary linear code of length $2^{m-1} \pm 2^{(m-1)/2}$ meeting the Grey-Rankin bound comes from a Hadamard difference set in $(\mathrm{GF}(2^m), +)$. The next question is as follows:

Problem 14.4. How does one construct binary linear codes of length $2^{m-1} \pm 2^{(m-2)/2}$ meeting the Grey-Rankin bound using Hadamard difference sets in $(\mathrm{GF}(2^m), +)$ with the parameters of (14.4)?

The two problems above are the motivations of this chapter. The objectives of this chapter are the following:

(a) We solve the two open questions above by presenting a general construction of binary linear codes of length $2^{m-1} \pm 2^{(m-2)/2}$ meeting the Grey-Rankin bound with Hadamard difference sets in $(\mathrm{GF}(2^m), +)$ having the parameters of (14.4).

(b) We determine the specific parameters of many infinite families of 2-designs held in the dual codes of binary linear codes of length $2^{m-1} \pm 2^{(m-2)/2}$ meeting the Grey-Rankin bound.

(c) We determine the triple block intersection numbers of all quasi-symmetric SDP designs, and the quadruple block intersection numbers of all symmetric SDP designs.

By answering the two questions, we will show that the construction of all quasi-symmetric SDP designs with the parameters in (14.2) and (14.3) and the construction of binary linear codes of length $2^{m-1} \pm 2^{(m-2)/2}$ meeting the Grey-Rankin bound become the problem of constructing Hadamard difference sets in $(\mathrm{GF}(2^m), +)$ with the parameters of (14.4), or equivalently, bent functions on $\mathrm{GF}(2^m)$.

Combining R.ii and R.iii properly, Tonchev proved that every self-complementary binary code of length $2^{m-1} \pm 2^{(m-2)/2}$ meeting the Grey-Rankin bound is the restriction of the code of a symmetric SDP design on the zero positions of a minimum codeword codeword or the complement of a minimum weight codeword [Tonchev (1993)][Theorem 6]. This is Relation R.iv in Figure 14.1.

14.4   Bent Functions

Let f be a Boolean function from $\mathrm{GF}(2^m)$ to $\mathrm{GF}(2)$. The *support* of f is defined to be

$$D_f = \{x \in \mathrm{GF}(2^m) : f(x) = 1\} \subseteq \mathrm{GF}(2^m).$$

Put $n_f = |D_f|$.

The *Walsh transform* of f is defined by

$$\hat{f}(w) = \sum_{x \in \mathrm{GF}(2^m)} (-1)^{f(x) + \mathrm{Tr}(wx)}, \tag{14.5}$$

where $w \in \mathrm{GF}(2^m)$.

A function from $\mathrm{GF}(2^m)$ to $\mathrm{GF}(2)$ is *bent* if $|\hat{f}(w)| = 2^{m/2}$ for every $w \in \mathrm{GF}(2^m)$. Bent functions exist only for even m. It is well known that a function f from $\mathrm{GF}(2^m)$ to $\mathrm{GF}(2)$ is bent if and only if D_f is a difference set in $(\mathrm{GF}(2^m), +)$ with the parameters of (14.4).

Let f be bent. Then by definition $\hat{f}(0) = \pm 2^{m/2}$. It then follows that

$$n_f = |D_f| = 2^{m-1} \pm 2^{(m-2)/2}. \tag{14.6}$$

There are many constructions of bent functions. The reader is referred to Carlet and Sihem (2016) for detailed information about bent functions.

14.5 Symmetric 2-$(2^m, 2^{m-1} - 2^{\frac{m-2}{2}}, 2^{m-2} - 2^{\frac{m-2}{2}})$ Designs and Their Codes

There are many symmetric designs with parameters of

$$2 - \left(2^m, \ 2^{m-1} \pm 2^{(m-2)/2}, \ 2^{m-2} \pm 2^{(m-2)/2} \right). \tag{14.7}$$

For example, the support of every bent function on $\mathrm{GF}(2^m)$ is a difference set with such parameters. If a design has one of the sets of parameters above, its complement design has the other set of parameters. Hence, we usually consider 2-(v, k, λ) designs with $k \le v/2$.

It is known that the 2-rank of any symmetric design with the parameters of (14.7) is at least $m + 2$. There are many such designs with the minimum rank $m + 2$, which will be briefly treated in the next subsection. There are much more symmetric designs with the parameters of (14.7) whose 2-ranks are larger than $m + 2$.

The following results are known ([Jungnickel and Tonchev (1991, 1992)], [McQuire and Ward (1998)]).

Theorem 14.5. *If $\mathbb{D}$ is a 2-$(2^m, 2^{m-1} - 2^{\frac{m-2}{2}}, 2^{m-2} - 2^{\frac{m-2}{2}})$ symmetric design, then its derived and residual designs have 2-rank at least $m + 1$.*

Many designs with the parameters of (14.2) and (14.3) have the minimum 2-rank $m + 1$. We will deal with some of them at due time.

14.6   Symmetric 2-$(2^m, 2^{m-1} - 2^{\frac{m-2}{2}}, 2^{m-2} - 2^{\frac{m-2}{2}})$ SDP Designs

Most symmetric designs with the parameters of (14.1) do not have the symmetric difference property. For example, most difference set designs from bent functions are not SDP designs. A lot of effort on characterising symmetric SDP designs with the parameters of (14.1) has been made. A nice characterisation is summarized as follows [Dillon and Schatz (1987); McQuire and Ward (1998)].

Theorem 14.6. *A symmetric design $\mathbb{D}$ with the parameters of (14.1) has the symmetric difference property if and only if* $\mathrm{rank}_2(\mathbb{D}) = m + 2$.

The binary code $C_2(\mathbb{D})$ of a symmetric SDP design $\mathbb{D}$ with the parameters of (14.1) is generated by the first order Reed-Muller code $\mathcal{R}(1, m)$ and the characteristic vector of a difference set with the parameters of (14.4). The code $C_2(D)$ has parameters $[2^m, m + 2, 2^{m-1} - 2^{(m-2)/2}]$ and weight enumerator

$$1 + 2^m z^{2^{m-1} - 2^{(m-2)/2}} + (2^{m+1} - 2) z^{2^{m-1}} + 2^m z^{2^{m-1} + 2^{(m-2)/2}} + z^{2^m}. \quad (14.8)$$

The 2^m codewords of weight $2^{m-1} - 2^{(m-2)/2}$ in the code correspond to the row vectors in the incidence matrix and the 2^m codewords of weight $2^{m-1} + 2^{(m-2)/2}$ correspond to the complements of the row vectors in the incidence matrix.

Theorem 14.6 says that every symmetric SDP design $\mathbb{D}$ with the parameters of (14.1) is a support design of a binary linear code with parameters $[2^m, m + 2, 2^{m-1} - 2^{(m-2)/2}]$ and is formed by the supports of codewords with minimum weight $2^{m-1} - 2^{(m-2)/2}$ in the code. Notice that the symmetric SDP design $\mathbb{D}$ with the parameters of (14.1) is not necessarily isomorphic to the development of the difference set specified in Theorem 14.6. This is because the 2-rank of the development of the difference set may be larger than $m + 2$. In fact, we have the following [Assmus and Key (1992b)].

Theorem 14.7. *Let $\mathbb{D}$ be a difference set design with the parameters of (14.1). Then the following holds:*

- *The code $C_2(\mathbb{D})$ contains the all-1 vector.*
- $\mathrm{rank}_2(\mathbb{D}) \leq 2^{m-1} + 1 - \frac{1}{2}\binom{m}{m/2}$. *Furthermore, any two such designs with 2-rank meeting this bound have equivalent binary codes.*

The next result follows from Theorems 14.6 and 14.7.

Theorem 14.8. *A difference set design $\mathbb{D}$ with the parameters of (14.1) has the symmetric difference property if and only if* $\mathrm{rank}_2(\mathbb{D}) = m + 2$.

Many symmetric 2-designs do not have the symmetric difference property. In order to better distinguish symmetric SDP designs from other symmetric designs, we shall prove new properties of symmetric SDP designs. In the rest of this subsection, we denote by $\mathbb{D}_m$ a symmetric SDP design with the parameters of (14.1), and by $C_2(\mathbb{D}_m)$ the binary code generated by the incidence matrix of $\mathbb{D}_m$. For simplicity, we let

$$v = 2^m, \quad k = 2^{m-1} - 2^{(m-2)/2}, \quad \lambda = 2^{m-2} - 2^{(m-2)/2}.$$

Lemma 14.9. *For any two distinct blocks A and B in $\mathbb{D}_m$, we have $|A \triangle B| = 2^{m-1}$ and $\sigma_A + \sigma_B$ is a codeword of weight 2^{m-1} in the binary code $C_2(\mathbb{D}_m)$, where $A \triangle B$ denotes the symmetric difference of A and B, and σ_A is the codeword in $C_2(\mathbb{D}_m)$ corresponding to the block A in $\mathbb{D}_m$.*

Proof. By definition,

$$|A \triangle B| = |A| + |B| - 2|A \cap B| = 2(k - \lambda) = 2^{m-1}.$$

Recall the binary code $C_2(\mathbb{D}_m)$ of $\mathbb{D}_m$ and the characterisation in Theorem 14.6. Let A and B be two distinct blocks in $\mathbb{D}_m$. Obviously, $\sigma_A + \sigma_B$ must be a codeword c in the code $C_2(\mathbb{D}_m)$. If c corresponds to a block C in $\mathbb{D}_m$, then $\sigma_A + \sigma_B = \sigma_C$. Consequently, $A \triangle B \triangle C$ is the empty set, which contradicts the symmetric difference property. If c corresponds to the complement $\overline{C}$ of a block C in $\mathbb{D}_m$, then $\sigma_A + \sigma_B = \sigma_C + \mathbf{1}$, where $\mathbf{1}$ stands for the all-1 vector. Consequently, $A \triangle B \triangle C$ is the point set of the design, which contradicts the symmetric difference property. Consequently, c must be a codeword of weight 2^{m-1}. $\square$

Lemma 14.10. *Let A, B and C be three pairwise distinct blocks in $\mathbb{D}_m$. Then*

$$4|A \cap B \cap C| = |A \triangle B \triangle C| + 6\lambda - 3k. \tag{14.9}$$

Proof. Recall that $\overline{A} = \mathcal{P} \setminus A$ is the complement of the block A in $\mathbb{D}_m$. It can be verified that

$$A \triangle B \triangle C = (A \cap \overline{B} \cap \overline{C}) \cup (\overline{A} \cap B \cap \overline{C}) \cup (\overline{A} \cap \overline{B} \cap C) \cup (A \cap B \cap C). \tag{14.10}$$

Note that the four sets inside the brackets in the right-hand side of (14.10) are pairwise disjoint. We then deduce that

$$|A \triangle B \triangle C| = |A \cap \overline{B} \cap \overline{C}| + |\overline{A} \cap B \cap \overline{C}| + |\overline{A} \cap \overline{B} \cap C)| + |A \cap B \cap C|. \tag{14.11}$$

It is not hard to see that

$$|A \cap \overline{B} \cap \overline{C}| = |A| - |A \cap C| - |A \cap B| + |A \cap B \cap C|. \tag{14.12}$$

By symmetry,

$$|\overline{A} \cap B \cap \overline{C}| = |B| - |B \cap C| - |A \cap B| + |A \cap B \cap C| \tag{14.13}$$

and

$$|\overline{A} \cap \overline{B} \cap C| = |C| - |B \cap C| - |A \cap C| + |A \cap B \cap C|. \tag{14.14}$$

Plugging (14.12), (14.13) and (14.14) into (14.11) yields

$$|A \triangle B \triangle C| = |A| + |B| + |C| - 2(|A \cap B| + |A \cap C| + |B \cap C|) + 4|A \cap B \cap C|. \tag{14.15}$$

The desired conclusion then follows from

$$|A| = |B| = |C| = k$$

and

$$|A \cap B| = |A \cap C| = |B \cap C| = \lambda.$$

$\square$

The following theorem follows from the symmetric difference property and Lemma 14.10.

Theorem 14.11. *Let A, B and C be three pairwise distinct blocks in* $\mathbb{D}_m$. *Then*

$$|A \cap B \cap C| = \begin{cases} 2^{m-3} - 2^{(m-2)/2} & \text{if } A \triangle B \triangle C \text{ is a block,} \\ 2^{m-3} - 2^{(m-4)/2} & \text{if } A \triangle B \triangle C \text{ is the complement of a block.} \end{cases}$$

The triple block intersection numbers were settled in Theorem 14.11. We now proceed to determine the quadruple block intersection numbers for the design $\mathbb{D}_m$. Our main result of this subsection is the following.

Theorem 14.12. *Let* $m \geq 6$ *be even. Let A, B, C and D be four pairwise distinct blocks in* $\mathbb{D}_m$. *Then* $|A \cap B \cap C \cap D|$ *takes on only numbers in the set*

$$\Big\{0, 2^{m-4} - 2^{\frac{m-2}{2}}, 2^{m-4} - 3 \times 2^{\frac{m-6}{2}}, 2^{m-4} - 2^{\frac{m-4}{2}},$$
$$2^{m-4} - 2^{\frac{m-6}{2}}, 2^{m-4}, 2^{m-3} - 2^{\frac{m-2}{2}}\Big\}. \tag{14.16}$$

Proof. Let A, B, C and D be four pairwise distinct blocks in $\mathbb{D}_m$. We first have

$$(A \triangle B \triangle C) \cap D = (A \cap D) \triangle (B \cap D) \triangle (C \cap D). \tag{14.17}$$

Applying (14.15) to the right-hand side of (14.17), we arrive at

$$|(A \triangle B \triangle C) \cap D| = |(A \cap D) \triangle (B \cap D) \triangle (C \cap D)|$$
$$= |A \cap D| + |B \cap D| + |C \cap D|$$
$$- 2(|A \cap B \cap D| + |B \cap C \cap D| + |A \cap C \cap D|)$$
$$+ 4|A \cap B \cap C \cap D|.$$

It then follows from Theorem 4.9 and Lemma 14.10 that

$$2|(A\triangle B\triangle C)\cap D|$$
$$= 9k - 12\lambda - 2(|A\triangle B\triangle D| + |B\triangle C\triangle D| + |A\triangle C\triangle D|)$$
$$+ 8|A\cap B\cap C\cap D|. \tag{14.18}$$

On the other hand, we have

$$2|(A\triangle B\triangle C)\cap D| = |A\triangle B\triangle C| + |D| - |A\triangle B\triangle C\triangle D|$$
$$= k + |A\triangle B\triangle C| - |A\triangle B\triangle C\triangle D|. \tag{14.19}$$

Combining (14.18) and (14.19) leads to

$$8|A\cap B\cap C\cap D| = (|A\triangle B\triangle C| + |A\triangle B\triangle D| + |A\triangle C\triangle D| + |B\triangle C\triangle D|)$$
$$- |A\triangle B\triangle C\triangle D| - 2^m - 4 \times 2^{\frac{m-2}{2}}, \tag{14.20}$$

which will be our key equation for proving the desired conclusion. We will continue our discussion by distinguishing the following cases.

Case I: We assume that $A\triangle B\triangle C\triangle D = \emptyset$. In this case, we have

$$A\triangle B\triangle C = D, \ A\triangle B\triangle D = C, \ A\triangle C\triangle D = B, \ B\triangle C\triangle D = A.$$

It then follows from (14.20) that

$$|A\cap B\cap C\cap D| = 2^{m-3} - 2^{\frac{m-2}{2}}.$$

Case II: We assume that $A\triangle B\triangle C\triangle D = \mathcal{P}$, which is the point set of $\mathbb{D}_m$. In this case, we have

$$A\triangle B\triangle C = \overline{D}, \ A\triangle B\triangle D = \overline{C}, \ A\triangle C\triangle D = \overline{B}, \ B\triangle C\triangle D = \overline{A}.$$

It then follows from (14.20) that

$$|A\cap B\cap C\cap D| = 0.$$

Case III: We assume that $A\triangle B\triangle C\triangle D \notin \{\mathcal{P}, \emptyset\}$. This case is further divided into the following five subcases.

Subcase III.1: We assume that all of the following four sets

$$A\triangle B\triangle C, \ A\triangle B\triangle D, \ A\triangle C\triangle D, \ B\triangle C\triangle D \tag{14.21}$$

are blocks in $\mathbb{D}_m$. By the symmetric difference property and Lemma 14.9,

$$|A\triangle B\triangle C\triangle D| = 2^{m-1}.$$

It then follows from (14.20) that

$$|A\cap B\cap C\cap D| = 2^{m-4} - 2^{\frac{m-2}{2}}.$$

Subcase III.2: We assume that all of the four sets of (14.21) are complements of blocks. By the symmetric difference property and Lemma 14.9,

$$|A \triangle B \triangle C \triangle D| = 2^{m-1}.$$

It then follows from (14.20) that

$$|A \cap B \cap C \cap D| = 2^{m-4}.$$

Subcase III.3: We assume that two of the four sets of (14.21) are blocks and the other two are complements of blocks in $\mathbb{D}_m$. By the symmetric difference property and Lemma 14.9,

$$|A \triangle B \triangle C \triangle D| = 2^{m-1}.$$

It then follows from (14.20) that

$$|A \cap B \cap C \cap D| = 2^{m-4} - 2^{\frac{m-4}{2}}.$$

Subcase III.4: We assume that one of the four sets of (14.21) is a block and the other three are complements of blocks in $\mathbb{D}_m$. By the symmetric difference property and Lemma 14.9,

$$|A \triangle B \triangle C \triangle D| = 2^{m-1}.$$

It then follows from (14.20) that

$$|A \cap B \cap C \cap D| = 2^{m-4} - 2^{\frac{m-6}{2}}.$$

Subcase III.5: We assume that three of the four sets of (14.21) are blocks and the other one is the complement of a block in $\mathbb{D}_m$. By the symmetric difference property and Lemma 14.9,

$$|A \triangle B \triangle C \triangle D| = 2^{m-1}.$$

It then follows from (14.20) that

$$|A \cap B \cap C \cap D| = 2^{m-4} - 3 \times 2^{\frac{m-6}{2}}.$$

Summarising the results in all the cases above proves the desired conclusion.
$\square$

It is observed that the quadruple block intersection number of a symmetric SDP design may take on all the numbers in the set of (14.16) or only values in the following subset

$$\left\{ 0,\ 2^{m-4} - 2^{\frac{m-2}{2}},\ 2^{m-4} - 2^{\frac{m-4}{2}},\ 2^{m-4},\ 2^{m-3} - 2^{\frac{m-2}{2}} \right\}. \tag{14.22}$$

Those with the quadruple block intersection numbers of (14.22) form a special subclass of symmetric SDP designs.

14.7 Derived and Residual Designs of Symmetric SDP Designs

As seen in Section 14.6, symmetric SDP designs are very special in the sense that they have the minimum 2-rank $m + 2$ and their binary codes are related to the first-order Reed-Muller codes. Naturally, their derived and residual designs must be also special. Below we summarize results on the derived and residual designs of symmetric SDP designs with the parameters:

$$2\text{-}(2^m, 2^{m-1} - 2^{(m-2)/2}, 2^{m-2} - 2^{(m-2)/2}).$$

The conclusions of the following theorem were established in Jungnickel and Tonchev (1992) and Tonchev (1993).

Theorem 14.13. *Let* $\mathbb{D}_m$ *be a symmetric SDP design with the parameters of (14.1). Then we have the following.*

- *The derived and residual designs of* $\mathbb{D}_m$ *are quasi-symmetric.*
- *The binary code* $C_2(\mathbb{D}_m^{de})$ *of the derived design* $\mathbb{D}_m^{de}$ *has parameters*

$$\left[2^{m-1} - 2^{(m-2)/2}, \ m+1, \ 2^{m-2} - 2^{(m-2)/2} \right]$$

and weight enumerator

$$1 + (2^m - 1)z^{2^{m-2} - 2^{(m-2)/2}} + (2^m - 1)z^{2^{m-2}} + z^{2^{m-1} - 2^{(m-2)/2}}.$$

The $2^m - 1$ *codewords of weight* $2^{m-2} - 2^{(m-2)/2}$ *in the code correspond to the row vectors in the incidence matrix and the* $2^m - 1$ *codewords of weight* 2^{m-2} *correspond to the complements of the row vectors in the incidence matrix. The dual code* $C_2(\mathbb{D}_m^{de})^{\perp}$ *has minimum weight 4. The supports of the minimum weight codewords in the code* $C_2(\mathbb{D}_m^{de})^{\perp}$ *form a 2-design with parameters*

$$2 - \left(2^{m-1} - 2^{(m-2)/2}, \ 4, \ (2^{(m-4)/2} - 1)(2^{(m-2)/2} + 1) \right).$$

- *The binary code* $C_2(\mathbb{D}_m^{re})$ *of the residual design* $\mathbb{D}_m^{re}$ *has parameters*

$$\left[2^{m-1} + 2^{(m-2)/2}, \ m+1, \ 2^{m-2} \right]$$

and weight enumerator

$$1 + (2^m - 1)z^{2^{m-2}} + (2^m - 1)z^{2^{m-2} + 2^{(m-2)/2}} + z^{2^{m-1} + 2^{(m-2)/2}}.$$

The $2^m - 1$ *codewords of weight* 2^{m-2} *in the code correspond to the row vectors in the incidence matrix and the* $2^m - 1$ *codewords of weight* $2^{m-2} + 2^{(m-2)/2}$ *correspond to the complements of the row vectors in the incidence matrix. The dual code* $C_2(\mathbb{D}_m^{re})^{\perp}$ *has minimum weight 4. The supports of the minimum weight codewords in the code* $C_2(\mathbb{D}_m^{re})^{\perp}$ *form a 2-design with parameters*

$$2 - \left(2^{m-1} + 2^{(m-2)/2}, \ 4, \ (2^{(m-4)/2} + 1)(2^{(m-2)/2} - 1) \right).$$

Theorem 14.13 summarises some known properties of the derived and residual designs of the symmetric SDP designs with the parameters of (14.1). There are many symmetric designs with the parameters of (14.1) which do not have the symmetric difference property but their residual and derived designs are not really studied.

Lemma 14.11 tells us that the block intersection numbers in the derived design of any symmetric SDP design with the parameters of (14.1) are $2^{m-3} - 2^{(m-2)/2}$ and $2^{m-3} - 2^{(m-4)/2}$. To classify derived and residual designs of symmetric SDP designs, we may use their triple intersection numbers.

Theorem 14.14. *Let $\mathbb{D}_m$ be a symmetric SDP design with the parameters of (14.1). Let $\mathbb{D}_m^{de}$ be a derived design of $\mathbb{D}_m$. Then the size of the intersection of any three pairwise distinct blocks in $\mathbb{D}_m^{de}$ takes on only numbers in the following set*

$$\left\{ 0,\, 2^{m-4} - 2^{\frac{m-2}{2}},\, 2^{m-4} - 3 \times 2^{\frac{m-6}{2}},\, 2^{m-4} - 2^{\frac{m-4}{2}}, \right.$$
$$\left. 2^{m-4} - 2^{\frac{m-6}{2}},\, 2^{m-4},\, 2^{m-3} - 2^{\frac{m-2}{2}} \right\}. \tag{14.23}$$

Proof. It follows from the definition of the derived designs and Theorem 14.11. $\qquad\square$

Example 14.24 shows that sometimes all the numbers in the set in (14.23) are taken, sometimes only a subset of these numbers is taken. This example also demonstrates that the triple block intersection numbers can be employed to prove the inequivalence of two designs with the same parameters.

By Theorem 14.11, the block intersection numbers of the residual design $\mathbb{D}_m^{re}$ of $\mathbb{D}_m$ are 2^{m-3} and $2^{m-3} - 2^{(m-4)/2}$. The next theorem gives the triple block intersection numbers.

Theorem 14.15. *Let $\mathbb{D}_m$ be a symmetric SDP design with the parameters of (14.1). Let $\mathbb{D}_m^{re}$ be a residual design of $\mathbb{D}_m$. Then the size of the intersection of any three pairwise distinct blocks in $\mathbb{D}_m^{re}$ takes on only numbers in the following set*

$$\left\{ 0,\, 2^{m-4} - 3 \times 2^{\frac{m-6}{2}},\, 2^{m-4} - 2^{\frac{m-4}{2}},\, 2^{m-4} - 2^{\frac{m-6}{2}}, \right.$$
$$\left. 2^{m-4},\, 2^{m-4} + 2^{\frac{m-6}{2}},\, 2^{m-3} - 2^{\frac{m-4}{2}} \right\}. \tag{14.24}$$

Proof. Let A, H, I and J be four pairwise distinct blocks in the design $\mathbb{D}_m$. Then $\bar{A} \cap H, \bar{A} \cap I$ and $\bar{A} \cap J$ are three pairwise distinct blocks in the residual design $\mathbb{D}_m^{re}$ with respect to A. Clearly,

$$|(\bar{A} \cap H) \cap (\bar{A} \cap I) \cap (\bar{A} \cap J)| = |\bar{A} \cap H \cap I \cap J| = |H \cap I \cap J| - |A \cap H \cap I \cap J|.$$

We consider the following cases.

When $H \triangle I \triangle J$ is a block in $\mathbb{D}_m$, by Theorem 14.11,

$$|H \cap I \cap J| = 2^{m-3} - 2^{(m-2)/2}.$$

In this case, only Cases I, III.1, III.3, III.4 and III.5 in the proof of Theorem 14.12 could happen. Hence, in this case $|(\bar{A} \cap H) \cap (\bar{A} \cap I) \cap (\bar{A} \cap J)|$ can take on only the following values:

$$0, \ 2^{m-4} - 3 \times 2^{\frac{m-6}{2}}, \ 2^{m-4} - 2^{\frac{m-4}{2}}, \ 2^{m-4} - 2^{\frac{m-6}{2}}, \ 2^{m-4}.$$

When $H \triangle I \triangle J$ is the complement of a block in $\mathbb{D}_m$, by Theorem 14.11,

$$|H \cap I \cap J| = 2^{m-3} - 2^{(m-4)/2}.$$

In this case, only Cases II, III.2, III.3, III.4 and III.5 in the proof of Theorem 14.12 could happen. Hence, in this case $|(\bar{A} \cap H) \cap (\bar{A} \cap I) \cap (\bar{A} \cap J)|$ can take on only the following values:

$$2^{m-4} - 2^{\frac{m-4}{2}}, \ 2^{m-4} - 2^{\frac{m-6}{2}}, \ 2^{m-4}, \ 2^{m-4} + 2^{\frac{m-6}{2}}, \ 2^{m-3} - 2^{\frac{m-4}{2}}.$$

Summarising the discussions in the two cases above proves the desired conclusion. $\qquad\square$

Example 14.25 shows that sometimes all the numbers in the set in (14.24) are taken, sometimes only a subset of these numbers is taken. This example also demonstrates that the triple block intersection numbers can be employed to prove the inequivalence of two designs with the same parameters.

At the end of this section, we present the following theorem but skip its proof.

Theorem 14.16. *Let $\ell \geq 7$ be odd. Define*

$$D = \{x \in \mathrm{GF}(2^\ell) : \mathrm{Tr}(x^3) = 1 \text{ and } \mathrm{Tr}(x) = 1\},$$

where $\mathrm{Tr}(x)$ denotes the absolute trace function on $\mathrm{GF}(2^\ell)$. Let C_D denote the binary code defined in (2.15) in Section 2.14.

If $\ell \equiv \pm 3 \pmod 8$, then C_D has parameters $[2^{\ell-2} - 2^{(\ell-3)/2}, \ell, 2^{\ell-3} - 2^{(\ell-3)/2}]$ and weight enumerator

$$1 + (2^{\ell-1} - 1)\left(z^{2^{\ell-3} - 2^{(\ell-3)/2}} + z^{2^{\ell-3}}\right) + z^{2^{\ell-2} - 2^{(\ell-3)/2}}.$$

The dual code $C_D^\perp$ has parameters $[2^{\ell-2} - 2^{(\ell-3)/2}, 2^{\ell-2} - 2^{(\ell-3)/2} - \ell, 4]$.

If $\ell \equiv \pm 1 \pmod 8$, then C_D has parameters $[2^{\ell-2} + 2^{(\ell-3)/2}, \ell, 2^{\ell-3}]$ and weight enumerator

$$1 + (2^{\ell-1} - 1)z^{2^{\ell-3}} + (2^{\ell-1} - 1)z^{2^{\ell-3} + 2^{(\ell-3)/2}} + z^{2^{\ell-2} + 2^{(\ell-3)/2}}.$$

The dual code $C_D^\perp$ has parameters $[2^{\ell-2} + 2^{(\ell-3)/2}, 2^{\ell-2} + 2^{(\ell-3)/2} - \ell, 4]$.

If $\ell \equiv \pm 3 \pmod 8$, then the 2-design supported by the minimum weight codewords in C_D has the same parameters as the design $\mathbb{D}^{de}_{\ell-1}$ and the code C_D has the same parameters and the weight distribution of $C_2(\mathbb{D}^{de}_{\ell-1})$ in Theorem 14.13. If $\ell \equiv \pm 1 \pmod 8$, then the 2-design supported by the minimum weight codewords in C_D has the same parameters as the design $\mathbb{D}^{re}_{\ell-1}$ and the code C_D has the same parameters and the weight distribution of $C_2(\mathbb{D}^{re}_{\ell-1})$ in Theorem 14.13. The code C_D in Theorem 14.16 should be related to the code C_{D_f} in Theorem 14.18.

14.8 A General Construction of Linear Codes with Bent Functions

Let f be a Boolean function from $\mathrm{GF}(2^m)$ to $\mathrm{GF}(2)$, and let D_f be the support of f. Denote $D_f = \{d_1, d_2, \ldots, d_{n_f}\} \subseteq \mathrm{GF}(2^m)$. Let Tr denote the trace function from $\mathrm{GF}(2^m)$ onto $\mathrm{GF}(2)$ throughout this section. We define a binary linear code of length n_f by

$$C_{D_f} = \{(\mathrm{Tr}(xd_1), \mathrm{Tr}(xd_2), \ldots, \mathrm{Tr}(xd_{n_f})) : x \in \mathrm{GF}(2^m)\}, \qquad (14.25)$$

and call D_f the *defining set* of this code C_{D_f}. This is a special case of a general construction of linear codes introduced in Section 2.14, which has been intensively and extensively investigated recently [Ding (2016)].

We have the following remarks on this general construction of linear codes with Boolean functions.

(1) It is known that every binary linear code can be expressed as C_{D_f} for a suitable Boolean function f from $\mathrm{GF}(2^m)$ to $\mathrm{GF}(2)$ for some m.
(2) The weight distribution of C_{D_f} is completely determined by by the Walsh spectrum of f [Ding (2016)].

The following was proved in Wolfmann (1999) and Ding (2015c).

Table 14.1 The weight distribution of the codes of Theorem 14.17

Weight w	Multiplicity A_w
0	1
$\frac{n_f}{2} - 2^{\frac{m-4}{2}}$	$\frac{2^m - 1 - n_f 2^{-\frac{m-2}{2}}}{2}$
$\frac{n_f}{2} + 2^{\frac{m-4}{2}}$	$\frac{2^m - 1 + n_f 2^{-\frac{m-2}{2}}}{2}$

Theorem 14.17. *Let f be a bent function from $\mathrm{GF}(2^m)$ to $\mathrm{GF}(2)$, where $m \geq 4$ and is even. Then C_{D_f} is an $[n_f, m, (n_f - 2^{(m-2)/2})/2]$ two-weight binary code with the weight distribution in Table 14.1, where n_f is defined in (14.6).*

It is straightforward to see that the dual code $C_{D_f}^{\perp}$ has minimum distance at least 3. Unfortunately, the code C_{D_f} and its dual $C_{D_f}^{\perp}$ do not hold 2-designs. However, we will show that their augmented codes hold infinite families of 2-designs.

Let f be a bent function from $\mathrm{GF}(2^m)$ to $\mathrm{GF}(2)$, and let D_f be the support of f. Denote $D_f = \{d_1, d_2, \ldots, d_{n_f}\} \subseteq \mathrm{GF}(2^m)$. We define a binary linear code of length n_f by

$$\tilde{C}_{D_f} = \{(\mathrm{Tr}(xd_1), \ldots, \mathrm{Tr}(xd_{n_f})) + y\mathbf{1} : x \in \mathrm{GF}(2^m), y \in \mathrm{GF}(2)\}, \quad (14.26)$$

where $\mathbf{1}$ denote the vector $(1, 1, \ldots, 1) \in \mathrm{GF}(2)^{n_f}$. This code $\tilde{C}_{D_f}$ is the augmented code of C_{D_f}.

We will prove the following, which gives an answer to Problem 14.4.

Table 14.2 The weight distribution of the codes of Theorem 14.18

Weight w	Multiplicity A_w
0	1
$\frac{n_f}{2} - 2^{\frac{m-4}{2}}$	$2^m - 1$
$\frac{n_f}{2} + 2^{\frac{m-4}{2}}$	$2^m - 1$
n_f	1

Theorem 14.18. *Let f be a bent function from $\mathrm{GF}(2^m)$ to $\mathrm{GF}(2)$, where $m \geq 6$ and is even. Then $\tilde{C}_{D_f}$ is an $[n_f, m+1, (n_f - 2^{(m-2)/2})/2]$ three-weight binary code with the weight distribution in Table 14.2, where n_f is defined in (14.6).*

Proof. Since the original code C_{D_f} does not contain the all-1 vector, the complement of any code in C_{D_f} is not a codeword of C_{D_f}. By definition, the augmented code $\tilde{C}_{D_f}$ is the union of C_{D_f} and its complement. The desired conclusions about $\tilde{C}_{D_f}$ then follow from Theorem 14.17. $\qquad\square$

Theorem 14.19. *Let f be a bent function from $\mathrm{GF}(2^m)$ to $\mathrm{GF}(2)$, where $m \geq 6$ and is even. When $n_f = 2^{m-1} - 2^{(m-2)/2}$, the dual code $\tilde{C}_{D_f}^{\perp}$ has parameters $[2^{m-1} - 2^{(m-2)/2}, 2^{m-1} - 2^{(m-2)/2} - m - 1, 4]$ and weight distribution*

$$A_{2\ell}^{\perp} = 2\binom{2^{m-1} - 2^{\frac{m-2}{2}}}{2\ell} +$$

$$(2^m - 1) \sum_{\substack{i+j=\ell \\ 0 \leq i \leq 2^{m-2} - 2^{\frac{m-4}{2}} \\ 0 \leq j \leq 2^{\frac{m-4}{2}}}} (-1)^i 2\binom{2^{m-2} - 2^{\frac{m-2}{2}}}{i}\binom{2^{\frac{m-2}{2}}}{2j} \quad (14.27)$$

for $2 \leq \ell \leq 2^{m-2} - 2^{(m-4)/2}$ and $A_i^{\perp} = 0$ for other i, where $A_i^{\perp}$ denotes the number of codewords of weight i in $\tilde{C}_{D_f}^{\perp}$.

When $n_f = 2^{m-1} + 2^{(m-2)/2}$, the dual code $\tilde{C}_{D_f}^{\perp}$ has parameters $[2^{m-1} + 2^{(m-2)/2}, 2^{m-1} + 2^{(m-2)/2} - m - 1, 4]$ and weight distribution

$$A_{2\ell}^{\perp} = 2 \binom{2^{m-1} + 2^{\frac{m-2}{2}}}{2\ell} +$$

$$(2^m - 1) \sum_{\substack{i+j=\ell \\ 0 \leq i \leq 2^{m-2} \\ 0 \leq j \leq 2^{\frac{m-4}{2}}}} (-1)^i 2 \binom{2^{m-2}}{i} \binom{2^{\frac{m-2}{2}}}{2j} \qquad (14.28)$$

for $2 \leq \ell \leq 2^{m-2} + 2^{(m-4)/2}$ and $A_i^{\perp} = 0$ for other i.

Proof. Assume that $n_f = 2^{m-1} - 2^{(m-2)/2}$. In this case, the code $\tilde{C}_{D_f}$ has parameters $[2^{m-1} - 2^{(m-2)/2}, m+1]$ and weight enumerator

$$A(z) = 1 + (2^m - 1)z^{2^{m-2} - 2^{\frac{m-2}{2}}} + (2^m - 1)z^{2^{m-2}} + z^{2^{m-1} - 2^{\frac{m-2}{2}}}. \qquad (14.29)$$

It then follows from Theorem 2.4 that

$$2^{m+1} A^{\perp}(z)$$

$$= (1+z)^{2^{m-1} - 2^{\frac{m-2}{2}}} A\left(\frac{1-z}{1+z}\right)$$

$$= (1+z)^{2^{m-1} - 2^{\frac{m-2}{2}}}$$

$$\times \left[1 + (2^m - 1) \left[\left(\frac{1-z}{1+z}\right)^{2^{m-2} - 2^{\frac{m-2}{2}}} + \left(\frac{1-z}{1+z}\right)^{2^{m-2}} \right] \right] +$$

$$(1+z)^{2^{m-1} - 2^{\frac{m-2}{2}}} \left(\frac{1-z}{1+z}\right)^{2^{m-1} - 2^{\frac{m-2}{2}}}$$

$$= (1+z)^{2^{m-1} - 2^{\frac{m-2}{2}}} + (1-z)^{2^{m-1} - 2^{\frac{m-2}{2}}}$$

$$+ (2^m - 1)(1 - z^2)^{2^{m-2} - 2^{\frac{m-2}{2}}} \left[(1+z)^{2^{\frac{m-2}{2}}} + (1-z)^{2^{\frac{m-2}{2}}} \right].$$

It is easily seen that

$$(1+z)^{2^{m-1} - 2^{\frac{m-2}{2}}} + (1-z)^{2^{m-1} - 2^{\frac{m-2}{2}}} = \sum_{\ell=0}^{2^{m-2} - 2^{\frac{m-4}{2}}} 2 \binom{2^{m-1} - 2^{\frac{m-2}{2}}}{2\ell} z^{2\ell}.$$

We have similarly

$$(1-z^2)^{2^{m-2}-2^{\frac{m-2}{2}}}\left[(1+z)^{2^{\frac{m-2}{2}}}+(1-z)^{2^{\frac{m-2}{2}}}\right]$$

$$=\left[\sum_{i=0}^{2^{m-2}-2^{\frac{m-2}{2}}}(-1)^i\binom{2^{m-2}-2^{\frac{m-2}{2}}}{i}z^{2i}\right]\left[\sum_{j=0}^{2^{\frac{m-4}{2}}}2\binom{2^{\frac{m-2}{2}}}{2j}z^{2j}\right]$$

$$=\sum_{\ell=0}^{2^{m-2}-2^{\frac{m-4}{2}}}\sum_{\substack{i+j=\ell\\0\le i\le 2^{m-2}-2^{\frac{m-4}{2}}\\0\le j\le 2^{\frac{m-4}{2}}}}(-1)^i2\binom{2^{m-2}-2^{\frac{m-2}{2}}}{i}\binom{2^{\frac{m-2}{2}}}{2j}z^{2\ell}.$$

Combining the three equations above yields the desired conclusion on the weight distribution of the dual code in this case. It can be checked that $A_2^{\perp}=0$ and

$$A_4^{\perp}=\frac{1}{3}2^{\frac{m-6}{2}}(2^{\frac{m-4}{2}}-1)(2^m-1)(2^{m-2}-1). \tag{14.30}$$

Therefore, the minimum distance of $\tilde{\mathcal{C}}_{D_f}^{\perp}$ is 4 as $m\ge 6$.

Assume that $n_f=2^{m-1}+2^{(m-2)/2}$. In this case, the code $\tilde{\mathcal{C}}_{D_f}$ has parameters $[2^{m-1}+2^{(m-2)/2},\,m+1]$ and weight enumerator

$$A(z)=1+(2^m-1)z^{2^{m-2}}+(2^m-1)z^{2^{m-2}+2^{(m-2)/2}}+z^{2^{m-1}+2^{(m-2)/2}}. \tag{14.31}$$

The desired conclusions for this case can be similarly proved. The details are omitted here.

□

Note that $\tilde{\mathcal{C}}_{D_f}$ contains $\mathcal{C}_{D_f}$ as a subcode. It will be shown in the next section that $\tilde{\mathcal{C}}_{D_f}$ and its dual hold exponentially many infinite families of 2-designs, though $\mathcal{C}_{D_f}$ and its dual do not hold 2-designs. In addition, the code $\tilde{\mathcal{C}}_{D_f}$ meets the Grey-Rankin bound.

Two bent functions f and g on $\mathrm{GF}(2^m)$ are said to be *equivalent* if $g(x)=f(\sigma(x)+b)$ for an automorphism $\sigma\in\mathrm{Aut}(\mathrm{GF}(2^m),+)$ and an element $b\in\mathrm{GF}(2^m)$. Equivalently, two difference sets D_1 and D_2 in $(\mathrm{GF}(2^m),+)$ are *equivalent* if $D_2=\sigma(D_1)+b$ for an automorphism $\sigma\in\mathrm{Aut}(\mathrm{GF}(2^m),+)$ and an element $b\in\mathrm{GF}(2^m)$. Two binary codes are *equivalent* if one can be obtained from the other by a coordinate permutation.

Problem 14.20. Let f and g be two bent functions on $\mathrm{GF}(2^m)$. What is the relationship between the equivalence of f and g and that of the two codes $\tilde{\mathcal{C}}_{D_f}$ and $\tilde{\mathcal{C}}_{D_g}$?

Even if Problem 14.20 is solved, we still face the equivalence problem of bent functions, which has been a hard problem for many years. Below we show that two inequivalent bent functions f may yield inequivalent binary codes $\tilde{C}_{D_f}$.

Example 14.21. Let w be a generator of $\mathrm{GF}(2^8)^*$ with $w^8 + w^4 + w^3 + w^2 + 1 = 0$. It is known that $f(x) = \mathrm{Tr}(wx^3)$ is a bent function on $\mathrm{GF}(2^8)$. The binary code $\tilde{C}_{D_f}$ has parameters $[120, 9, 56]$ and weight enumerator $1 + 255z^{56} + 255z^{64} + z^{120}$. The automorphism group of $\tilde{C}_{D_f}$ has size 47377612800.

The function $g(x) = \mathrm{Tr}(wx^{57})$ on $\mathrm{GF}(2^8)$ is bent and inequivalent to f. The binary code $\tilde{C}_{D_g}$ has the same parameters and weight enumerator as $\tilde{C}_{D_f}$. But, the size of the automorphism group of $\tilde{C}_{D_g}$ is only 12. Consequently, $\tilde{C}_{D_f}$ and $\tilde{C}_{D_g}$ are inequivalent.

The function $g_1(x) = \mathrm{Tr}(wx^{57} + wx)$ on $\mathrm{GF}(2^8)$ is also bent. The binary code $\tilde{C}_{D_{g_1}}$ has the same parameters and weight enumerator as $\tilde{C}_{D_f}$. But, the size of the automorphism group of $\tilde{C}_{D_{g_1}}$ is only 1. Consequently, $\tilde{C}_{D_f}$, $\tilde{C}_{D_g}$ and $\tilde{C}_{D_{g_1}}$ are pairwise inequivalent.

14.9 Infinite Families of 2-Designs from Bent Codes

It was known that binary codes with the weight distribution of Table 14.2 and their duals hold 2-designs [Tonchev (1993); McQuire (1997)]. Our objective of this section is to extend earlier results on the designs held in such linear codes by determining the specific parameters of these designs.

The next theorem gives an answer to Problem 14.3.

Theorem 14.22. *Let f be a bent function from* $\mathrm{GF}(2^m)$ *to* $\mathrm{GF}(2)$, *where $m \geq 6$ and is even. When*

$$n_f = 2^{m-1} - 2^{(m-2)/2},$$

the supports of codewords of weight $2^{m-2} - 2^{\frac{m-2}{2}}$ in the code $\tilde{C}_{D_f}$ of Theorem 14.18 form a quasi-symmetric SDP design with the following parameters:

$$2 - \left(2^{m-1} - 2^{\frac{m-2}{2}},\ 2^{m-2} - 2^{\frac{m-2}{2}},\ 2^{m-2} - 2^{\frac{m-2}{2}} - 1\right).$$

When

$$n_f = 2^{m-1} + 2^{(m-2)/2},$$

the supports of codewords of weight 2^{m-2} in the code $\tilde{C}_{D_f}$ of Theorem 14.18 form a quasi-symmetric SDP design with the following parameters:

$$2 - \left(2^{m-1} + 2^{\frac{m-2}{2}},\ 2^{m-2},\ 2^{m-2} - 2^{\frac{m-2}{2}}\right).$$

Proof. Combining Theorem 14.18 and Corollary 4.26 proves the 2-design property of the two support designs held in $\tilde{C}_{D_f}$. Let $\mathbb{D}$ be any of the two support designs. It is known that any design with parameters of (14.2) or (14.3) has minimum 2-rank $m + 1$. Hence, the code $\tilde{C}_{D_f}$ is also the code of the two support designs.

Let B_1 and B_2 be any two distinct blocks and c_1 and c_2 be their corresponding codewords in $\tilde{C}_{D_f}$, i.e., the supports of c_1 and c_2 are B_1 and B_2. It is clear now that

$$(B_1 \cup B_2) \setminus (B_1 \cap B_2) = \text{Suppt}(c_1 + c_2).$$

Note that c_1 and c_2 have the same weight and are distinct. Recall that both support designs have rank $m + 1$. As a result, $|\text{Suppt}(c_1 + c_2)|$ takes on both $\frac{n_f}{2} \pm 2^{\frac{m-4}{2}}$ with frequencies determined by the frequencies of the two weights when B_1 and B_2 range over all pairs of distinct blocks. It then follows that the design is quasi-symmetric. Note that the summer of the two weights is equal to the length n_f of the code and $c_1 + c_2$ is also a codeword with $0 < \text{wt}(c_1 + c_2) < n_f$. Consequently, the symmetric difference of B_1 and B_2 is either a block or the complement of a block. Thus, the design has the symmetric difference property. □

It would be good if the following problem could be solved.

Problem 14.23. Let f and g be two bent functions. What is the relationship between the equivalence of f and g and that of the designs with the same parameters held in the two codes $\tilde{C}_{D_f}$ and $\tilde{C}_{D_g}$?

In Example 14.21, we demonstrated that different bent functions f may give inequivalent codes $\tilde{C}_{D_f}$. Below we show that two inequivalent bent functions f may give non-isomorphic designs $\mathbb{D}(f, \pm 1)$, where ± 1 corresponds to the sign in $n_f = 2^{m-1} \pm 2^{(m-2)/2}$.

Example 14.24. Let w be a generator of $\text{GF}(2^8)^*$ with $w^8 + w^4 + w^3 + w^2 + 1 = 0$. It is known that $f(x) = \text{Tr}(wx^3)$ is a bent function on $\text{GF}(2^8)$. The triple block intersection numbers of the design $\mathbb{D}(f, -1)$ are

$$\{0, 8, 12, 16, 24\}.$$

The function $g(x) = \text{Tr}(wx^{57})$ on $\text{GF}(2^8)$ is bent and inequivalent to f. The triple block intersection numbers of the design $\mathbb{D}(g, -1)$ are

$$\{0, 8, 10, 12, 14, 16, 24\}.$$

Consequently, the two nonsymmetric designs $\mathbb{D}(f, -1)$ and $\mathbb{D}(g, -1)$ from the bent functions f and g are nonisomorphic.

Example 14.25. Let w be a generator of $GF(2^8)^*$ with $w^8 + w^4 + w^3 + w^2 + 1 = 0$. It is known that $f(x) = \mathrm{Tr}(wx^3) + 1$ is a bent function on $GF(2^8)$. The code $C_2(D_f)$ has parameters $[136, 9, 64]$ and weight enumerator $1 + 255z^{64} + 255z^{72} + z^{136}$. The triple block intersection numbers of the design $\mathbb{D}(f, +1)$ are

$$\{0, 12, 16, 28\}.$$

The function $g(x) = \mathrm{Tr}(wx^{57}) + 1$ on $GF(2^8)$ is also bent. The code $C_2(D_g)$ has parameters $[136, 9, 64]$ and weight enumerator $1 + 255z^{64} + 255z^{72} + z^{136}$. The 3-intersection numbers of the design $\mathbb{D}(g, +1)$ are

$$\{0, 10, 12, 14, 16, 18, 28\}.$$

Consequently, the two nonsymmetric designs from the bent functions f and g are not isomorphic.

Theorem 14.26. *Let f be a bent function from $GF(2^m)$ to $GF(2)$, where $m \geq 6$ and is even. When*

$$n_f = 2^{m-1} - 2^{(m-2)/2},$$

for each $2 \leq \ell \leq 2^{m-2} - 2^{(m-4)/2}$ with $A_{2\ell}^{\perp} \neq 0$, the supports of all codewords of weight 2ℓ in the code $\tilde{C}_{D_f}^{\perp}$ form a $2\text{-}(2^{m-1} - 2^{(m-2)/2}, 2\ell, \lambda^{\perp})$ design, where

$$\lambda^{\perp} = \frac{A_{2\ell}^{\perp}\binom{2\ell}{2}}{\binom{2^{m-1} - 2^{(m-2)/2}}{2}}$$

and $A_{2\ell}^{\perp}$ is given in (14.27).
    When

$$n_f = 2^{m-1} + 2^{(m-2)/2},$$

for each $2 \leq \ell \leq 2^{m-2} + 2^{(m-4)/2}$ with $A_{2\ell}^{\perp} \neq 0$, the supports of all codewords of weight 2ℓ in the code $\tilde{C}_{D_f}^{\perp}$ form a $2\text{-}(2^{m-1} + 2^{(m-2)/2}, 2\ell, \lambda^{\perp})$ design, where

$$\lambda^{\perp} = \frac{A_{2\ell}^{\perp}\binom{2\ell}{2}}{\binom{2^{m-1} + 2^{(m-2)/2}}{2}}$$

and $A_{2\ell}^{\perp}$ is given in (14.28).

Proof. As demonstrated in the proof of Theorem 14.22, the conditions in the Assmus-Mattson Theorem are met. Hence, the supports of codewords of each fixed nonzero weight form a 2-design. Since the code and its dual are binary, it is well known that the supports of every nonzero weight in the dual code also form a 2-design. □

The next result was presented in Tonchev (1993). For completeness, we present a proof.

Corollary 14.27. *Let f be a bent function from* $\mathrm{GF}(2^m)$ *to* $\mathrm{GF}(2)$*, where* $m \geq 6$ *and is even. When*

$$n_f = 2^{m-1} - 2^{(m-2)/2},$$

the supports of all codewords of weight 4 in the code $\tilde{C}_{D_f}^{\perp}$ *form a* 2-$(2^{m-1} - 2^{(m-2)/2}, 4, \lambda^{\perp})$ *design, where*

$$\lambda^{\perp} = (2^{(m-4)/2} - 1)(2^{(m-2)/2} + 1).$$

When

$$n_f = 2^{m-1} + 2^{(m-2)/2},$$

the supports of all codewords of weight 4 in the code $\tilde{C}_{D_f}^{\perp}$ *form a* 2-$(2^{m-1} + 2^{(m-2)/2}, 4, \lambda^{\perp})$ *design, where*

$$\lambda^{\perp} = (2^{(m-4)/2} + 1)(2^{(m-2)/2} - 1).$$

Proof. The conclusion of the first part follows from (14.30) and Theorem 14.26. When $n_f = 2^{m-1} + 2^{(m-2)/2}$, with the weight distribution formula in (14.28), one obtains that

$$A_4^{\perp} = \frac{1}{3} 2^{\frac{m-6}{2}} (2^{\frac{m-4}{2}} - 1)(2^m - 1)(2^{m-2} - 1). \tag{14.32}$$

The desired conclusion then follows from Theorem 14.26.

$\square$

Corollary 14.28. *Let f be a bent function from* $\mathrm{GF}(2^m)$ *to* $\mathrm{GF}(2)$*, where* $m \geq 6$ *and is even. When*

$$n_f = 2^{m-1} - 2^{(m-2)/2},$$

the supports of all codewords of weight 6 in the code $\tilde{C}_{D_f}^{\perp}$ *form a* 2-$(2^{m-1} - 2^{(m-2)/2}, 6, \lambda^{\perp})$ *design, where*

$$\lambda^{\perp} = \frac{1}{6}(2^{\frac{m-2}{2}} + 1)(2^{\frac{5m-10}{2}} - 3 \times 2^{2m-4} - 5 \times 2^{\frac{3m-8}{2}} + 25 \times 2^{m-3} + 2^{\frac{m}{2}} - 16).$$

When

$$n_f = 2^{m-1} + 2^{(m-2)/2},$$

the supports of all codewords of weight 6 in the code $\tilde{C}_{D_f}^{\perp}$ *form a* 2-$(2^{m-1} + 2^{(m-2)/2}, 6, \lambda^{\perp})$ *design, where*

$$\lambda^{\perp} = \frac{1}{6}(2^{\frac{m-2}{2}} - 1)(2^{\frac{5m-10}{2}} + 3 \times 2^{2m-4} - 5 \times 2^{\frac{3m-8}{2}} - 25 \times 2^{m-3} + 2^{\frac{m}{2}} + 16).$$

Proof. When

$$n_f = 2^{m-1} - 2^{(m-2)/2},$$

with the weight distribution formula in (14.27), one obtains that

$$A_6^{\perp} = \frac{1}{45} 2^{\frac{m-6}{2}} (2^m - 1)(2^{m-2} - 1)(2^{\frac{5m-10}{2}} - 3 \times 2^{2m-4} - 5 \times 2^{\frac{3m-8}{2}} + 25 \times 2^{m-3} + 2^{\frac{m}{2}} - 16).$$

The desired conclusion then follows from Theorem 14.26.

When

$$n_f = 2^{m-1} + 2^{(m-2)/2},$$

with the weight fotmula in (14.28), one obtains that

$$A_6^{\perp} = \frac{1}{45} 2^{\frac{m-6}{2}} (2^m - 1)(2^{m-2} - 1)(2^{\frac{5m-10}{2}} + 3 \times 2^{2m-4} - 5 \times 2^{\frac{3m-8}{2}} - 25 \times 2^{m-3} + 2^{\frac{m}{2}} + 16).$$

The desired conclusion then follows from Theorem 14.26. $\qquad\square$

14.10 Notes

The total number of bent functions on $GF(2^m)$ (equivalently, the total number of Hadamard difference sets in $(GF(2^m), +)$), denoted by N_m, has the following lower and upper bounds [Tokareva (2011)]:

$$2^{2^{(m/2)+\log_2(m-2)-1}} \leq N_m \leq 2^{2^{m-1}+\frac{1}{2}\binom{m}{m/2}}. \tag{14.33}$$

By now, the total number of bent functions constructed is the lower bound above, which is a huge number. They belong to many families (see Carlet and Sihem (2016)). Plugging them into the construction framework of Section 14.8, we can obtain

- $2^{2^{(m/2)+\log_2(m-2)-1}}$ binary linear codes of length $2^{m-1} \pm 2^{(m-2)/2}$ meeting the Grey-Rankin bound; and
- $2^{2^{(m/2)+\log_2(m-2)-1}}$ pairs of quasi-symmetric SDP designs with the parameters of (14.2) and (14.3).

It is open if the codes are equivalent and the designs are isomorphic. This problem is related to the classification of bent functions and Hadamard difference sets into equivalence classes, which is a very hard problem. Bent functions with different 2-ranks are inequivalent. Many families of bent functions have different 2-ranks, and are thus inequivalent [Weng, Feng, Qiu (2007); Weng, Feng, Qiu, Zheng (2008)].

Of course, the automorphism groups of the linear codes meeting the Grey-Rankin bound and quasi-symmetric SDP designs could be employed to distinguish among these codes and designs. Another way to do this is to use the triple block intersection numbers of quasi-symmetric designs determined earlier. A classification of quasi-symmetric 2-designs was done in Neumaier (1982).

In this chapter, we treated only quasi-symmetric 2-designs. In genera, a t-design is *quasi-symmetric* with intersection numbers x and y $(x < y)$ if any two distinct blocks intersect in either x or y points. Below we provide the reader with information on quasi-symmetric t-designs with $t \geq 3$, which is taken from Shrikhande (2007).

Theorem 14.29. *If* $\mathbb{D}$ *is a quasi-symmetric* 3-(v,k,λ) *design with* $x = 0$, *then* $y = \lambda + 1$ *and one of the following holds:*

(1) $v = 4(\lambda + 1)$, $k = 2(\lambda + 1)$;
(2) $v = (\lambda + 1)(\lambda^2 + 5\lambda + 5)$, $k = (\lambda + 1)(\lambda + 2)$; *or*
(3) $v = 496$, $k = 40$, $\lambda = 3$.

Theorem 14.30. *If* $\mathbb{D}$ *is a quasi-symmetric* 3-(v,k,λ) *design with* $x = 1$, *then* $\mathbb{D}$ *is the* 4-$(23,7,1)$ *design of Section 10.5.2 or its residual design, which is a* 3-$(22,7,4)$ *design.*

Theorem 14.31. *If* $\mathbb{D}$ *is a quasi-symmetric* 4-(v,k,λ), *then* $\mathbb{D}$ *is the* 4-$(23,7,1)$ *design of Section 10.5.2 or its complement.*

Theorem 14.32. *Quasi-symmetric t-designs do not exit for* $t \geq 5$.

An excellent reference on quasi-symmetric designs is Shrikhande and Sane (1991). Information on quasi-symmetric designs could also be found in Ionin and Shrikhande (2006).

Chapter 15

Almost MDS Codes and Their Designs

An $[n,k,n-k+1]$ code is said to be MDS. An $[n,k,n-k]$ code is said to be *almost MDS*. The support designs of MDS codes are complete (see Theorem 4.29), and thus not interesting. The task of this chapter is introduce almost MDS codes, their properties and their support designs. The most remarkable work of this chapter is an infinite family of near MDS codes supporting an infinite family of 4-designs. It shows the importance of almost MDS codes.

15.1 Almost MDS Codes

The *Singleton defect* of an $[n,k,d]$ code C is defined by $\text{def}(C) = n-k+1-d$. Thus, MDS codes are codes with defect 0. A code C is said to be *almost MDS* (AMDS for short) if it has defect 1. Hence, AMDS codes have parameters $[n,k,n-k]$. AMDS codes of dimension 1, $n-2$, $n-1$ and n are called *trivial*. Since it is easy to construct trivial AMDS codes of arbitrary lengths, we will consider only nontrivial AMDS codes.

The following theorem summarises some basic properties of AMDS codes (see Dodunekov and Landgev (1995) and Faldum and Willems (1997) for a proof).

Theorem 15.1. *Let C be an $[n,k,n-k]$ AMDS code over* $\text{GF}(q)$. *Then the following hold.*

(1) If $k \geq 2$, then $n \leq k+2q$.
(2) If $k \geq 2$ and $n-k > q$, then $k \leq 2q$.
(3) If $n-k > q$, then $C^\perp$ is also AMDS.
(4) If $k \geq 2$, then C is generated by its codewords of weight $n-k$ and $n-k+1$.
(5) If $k \geq 2$ and $n-k > q$, then C is generated by its minimum weight codewords.

Unlike MDS codes, the dual of an AMDS code may not be AMDS. Recall the generalised Hamming weights $d_r(C)$ introduced in Section 2.16. Then we

393

have the next result ([Dodunekov and Landgev (1995)] and [Faldum and Willems (1997)]).

Theorem 15.2. *Let C be an $[n,k,n-k]$ AMDS code over $GF(q)$. Then $C^{\perp}$ is AMDS if and only if $d_2(C) = n - k + 2$.*

The weight distributions of MDS codes over $GF(q)$ are given in Theorem 2.25 and are totally determined by their length, dimension and q. However, this is not true for AMDS codes. Partial information on the weight distribution of an AMDS code is given in the following theorem

Theorem 15.3 (Faldum and Willems (1997)). *Let C be an $[n,k,n-k]$ AMDS code and let $C^{\perp}$ be an $[n,n-k,d^{\perp}]$ code over $GF(q)$. Then the weight distribution $A_0, A_1, \ldots, A_n$ of C satisfies*

$$A_{n-d^{\perp}+r} = \sum_{j=d^{\perp}}^{k} \binom{j}{d^{\perp}-r} \left(\sum_{i=d^{\perp}}^{j} (-1)^{i-d^{\perp}+r} \binom{j-d^{\perp}+r}{j-i} \right) A_{n-j} +$$
$$\binom{n}{d^{\perp}-r} \sum_{i=0}^{r-1} (-1)^i \binom{n-d^{\perp}+r}{i} \left(q^{k-d^{\perp}+r-i} - 1 \right) \quad (15.1)$$

for $r = 1, 2, \ldots, d^{\perp}$.
In particular, $A_d, \ldots, A_{n-d^{\perp}}$ completely determine the weight distribution of C.

Theorem 15.3 indicates that two $[n,k,n-k]$ AMDS codes over $GF(q)$ may have different weight distributions. This will be demonstrated with an example in the next section.

15.2   Near MDS Codes

A code C is said to be *near MDS* (NMDS for short) if both C and $C^{\perp}$ are AMDS. By definition, C is near MDS if and only if $C^{\perp}$ is so. By definition and Theorem 15.2, we have the following.

Theorem 15.4. *An $[n,k,n-k]$ AMDS code is NMDS if and only if $d_2(C) = n - k + 2$.*

The next theorem follows from the definition of NMDS codes.

Theorem 15.5. *An $[n,k]$ code C over $GF(q)$ is NMDS if and only if $d(C) + d(C^{\perp}) = n$, where $d(C)$ denotes the minimum distance of C.*

The next theorem then follows from Theorem 2.50 [Dodunekov and Landgev (1995)].

Theorem 15.6. *An* $[n,k]$ *code* C *over* $GF(q)$ *is NMDS if and only if a parity-check matrix, say H, (and consequently every parity-check matrix of C) satisfies the following conditions:*

(a) any $n - k - 1$ *columns of H are linearly independent;*
(b) there exist $n - k$ *linearly dependent columns; and*
(c) any $n - k + 1$ *columns of H are of rank* $n - k$.

Theorem 15.6 is equivalent to the following.

Theorem 15.7. *An* $[n,k]$ *code* C *over* $GF(q)$ *is NMDS if and only if a generator matrix, say G, (and consequently every generator matrix of C) satisfies the following conditions:*

(a) any $k - 1$ *columns of G are linearly independent;*
(b) there exist k *linearly dependent columns; and*
(c) any $k + 1$ *columns of G are of rank* k.

As a corollary of Theorem 15.3, we have the following weight distribution formulas for AMDS codes.

Theorem 15.8 (Dodunekov and Landgev (1995)). *Let* C *be an* $[n,k,n-k]$ *NMDS code. Then the weight distributions of* C *and* $C^\perp$ *are given by*

$$A_{n-k+s} = \binom{n}{k-s} \sum_{j=0}^{s-1} (-1)^j \binom{n-k+s}{j}(q^{s-j}-1) + (-1)^s \binom{k}{s}A_{n-k} \quad (15.2)$$

for $s \in \{1,2,\ldots,k\}$, *and*

$$A_{k+s}^\perp = \binom{n}{k+s} \sum_{j=0}^{s-1} (-1)^j \binom{k+s}{j}(q^{s-j}-1) + (-1)^s \binom{n-k}{s}A_k^\perp \quad (15.3)$$

for $s \in \{1,2,\ldots,n-k\}$.

Note that $\sum_{i=0}^{n} A_i = q^k$ and $\sum_{i=0}^{n} A_i^\perp = q^{n-k}$. The A_{n-k} in (15.2) and $A_k^\perp$ in (15.3) cannot be determined by these two equations and Equations (15.2) and (15.3). It is possible that two $[n,k,n-k]$ NMDS codes over $GF(q)$ have different weight distributions. Thus, the weight distribution of an $[n,k,n-k]$ NMDS code over $GF(q)$ depends on not only n, k and q, but also some other parameters of the code. This is a major difference between MDS codes and NMDS codes.

Example 15.9. The $[11,6,5]$ ternary Golay code C_3 has weight enumerator

$$1 + 132z^5 + 132z^6 + 330z^8 + 110z^9 + 24z^{11}.$$

Take a generator matrix G_3 of the ternary Golay code C_3. When G_3 is viewed as a matrix over GF(9), it generates a linear code C_9 over GF(9) with parameters $[11,6,5]$ and weight enumerator

$$1 + 528z^5 + 528z^6 + 15840z^7 + 40920z^8 + 129800z^9 + 198000z^{10} + 145824z^{11}.$$

The dual code $C_9^\perp$ has parameters $[11,5,6]$. Hence, the code C_9 over GF(9) is NMDS.

The extended code $\overline{C_{(9,10,3,1)}}$ of the narrow-sense BCH code $C_{(9,10,3,1)}$ over GF(9) has parameters $[11,6,5]$ and weight enumerator

$$1 + 240z^5 + 2256z^6 + 11520z^7 + 46680z^8 + 125480z^9 + 199728z^{10} + 145536z^{11}.$$

Its dual has parameters $[11,5,6]$. Thus, $\overline{C_{(9,10,3,1)}}$ is an NMDS code over GF(9), which has the same parameters as C_9. However, the two codes have distinct weight enumerators.

It follows from Theorem 15.8 that $A_{n-k} = A_k^\perp$ for any $[n,k,n-k]$ NMDS code. Consequently, any $[2k,k,k]$ NMDS code C and its dual are formally self-dual.

The following results follow from Theorem 15.8 [Dodunekov and Landgev (1995)].

Corollary 15.10. *For an $[n,k,n-k]$ NMDS code over* GF(q), *it holds*

$$A_{n-k} \leq \binom{n}{k-1}\frac{q-1}{k}, \tag{15.4}$$

with equality if and only if $A_{n-k+1} = 0$. By duality,

$$A_k^\perp \leq \binom{n}{k+1}\frac{q-1}{n-k}, \tag{15.5}$$

with equality if and only if $A_{k+1}^\perp = 0$.

For an $[n,k,n-k]$ NMDS code over GF(q), we deduce from (15.4) that

$$\frac{A_{n-k}}{q-1} \leq \binom{n}{k-1}\frac{1}{k} = \binom{n}{n-k}\frac{n-k}{n-k+1} < \binom{n}{n-k}.$$

Therefore, if the minimum weight codewords of an $[n,k,n-k]$ NMDS code over GF(q) support a t-design, then the t-design cannot be the complete design.

It will be shown in Section 15.3 that an $[n,k,n-k]$ NMDS code C over GF(q) with $A_{n-k+1} = 0$ or $A_{k+1}^\perp = 0$ yields t-designs for some positive integer t, and are thus very attractive. One basic question is whether such code exists. We will look into this existence problem in Section 15.3.

The following result follows from Corollary 15.10 [Dodunekov and Landgev (1995)].

Corollary 15.11. *For any $[n, k, n-k]$ NMDS code over* GF(q) *with $A_{n-k+1} = 0$, we have $k \leq n/2$.*

NMDS codes have nice properties. In particular, up to a multiple, there is a natural correspondence between the minimum weight codewords of an NMDS code C and its dual $C^\perp$, which follows from the next result [Faldum and Willems (1997)].

Theorem 15.12. *Let C be an NMDS code. Then for every minimum weight codeword $\mathbf{c}$ in C, there exists, up to a multiple, a unique minimum weight codeword $\mathbf{c}^\perp$ in $C^\perp$ such that* Suppt$(\mathbf{c}) \cap$ Suppt$(\mathbf{c}^\perp) = \emptyset$. *In particular, C and $C^\perp$ have the same number of minimum weight codewords.*

The following result says that infinite families of NMDS codes do exist.

Theorem 15.13 (Tsfasman and Vladut (1991)). *Algebraic geometric $[n, k, n-k]$ NMDS codes over* GF(q), $q = p^m$, *do exist for every n with*

$$n \leq \begin{cases} q + \lceil 2\sqrt{q} \rceil & \text{if } p \text{ divides } \lceil 2\sqrt{q} \rceil \text{ and } m \text{ is odd,} \\ q + \lceil 2\sqrt{q} \rceil + 1 & \text{otherwise,} \end{cases}$$

and arbitrary $k \in \{2, 3, \ldots, n-2\}$.

While it is easy to construct NMDS codes, we are interested in only NMDS codes holding t-designs. We will treat such NMDS codes in Section 15.3.

We now deal with extremal NMDS codes. Let $n(k, q)$ denote the maximum possible length of an NMDS code of fixed dimension k over a fixed field GF(q). Then we have the following [Dodunekov and Landgev (1995)].

Lemma 15.14. *Let notation be the same as before. Then $n(k, q) \leq 2q + k$. For any $[2q + k, k, 2q]$ NMDS code over* GF(q), $A_{2q+1} = 0$.

Proof. The first part is the first conclusion of Theorem 15.1. We now prove it. It follows from (15.2) that

$$A_{n-k+2} = \binom{n}{k-2}(q-1)(q+k-n-1) + \binom{k}{2}A_{n-k}.$$

By Inequality (15.4), we have

$$\frac{q-1}{2}\binom{n}{k-2}(2q+k-n)$$

$$= \binom{n}{k-2}(q-1)(q+k-n-1) + \binom{k}{2}\binom{n}{k-1}\frac{q-1}{k}$$

$$\geq A_{n-k+2} \geq 0.$$

Whence, $n \leq 2q+k$.

If $n = 2q+k$, the above inequality implies that

$$A_{n-k} = \binom{n}{k-1}\frac{q-1}{k}.$$

It then follows from Corollary 15.10 that $A_{n-k+1} = 0$.   □

An NMDS code meeting the bound of Lemma 15.14 is said to be *extremal*, i.e., any $[2q+k,k,2q]$ NMDS code over GF(q) is *extremal*. The dual and the extended code of the $[11,6,5]$ ternary Golay code are extremal. NMDS codes over GF(q) with parameters $[2q+k,k+1,2q-1]$ are said to be *almost extremal*.

Theorem 15.15 (De Boer (1996)). *If C is a $[2q+k,k,2q]$ extremal NMDS code over* GF(q) *with $k > q$, then $C^\perp$ must be one of the following codes:*

(a) *the $[7,4,3]$ Hamming code over* GF(2);
(b) *the $[8,4,4]$ extended Hamming code over* GF(2) *(which is self-dual);*
(c) *a $[10,6,4]$ punctured Golay code over* GF(3);
(d) *the $[11,6,5]$ Golay code over* GF(3); *and*
(e) *the $[12,6,6]$ extended Golay code over* GF(3).

In spite of Theorem 15.15, $[2q+k,k,2q]$ extremal NMDS codes over GF(q) with $k \leq q$ may exist. It will be shown that extremal NMDS codes yield t-designs for some t. Thus, we are very much fond of extremal NMDS codes.

Theorem 15.16 (De Boer (1996)). *If C is a $[2q+k,k+1,2q-1]$ almost extremal NMDS code over* GF(q) *with $k \geq q$, then $C^\perp$ must be one of the following codes:*

(a) *a $[6,3,3]$ punctured Hamming code over* GF(2);
(b) *the $[7,3,4]$ Simplex code over* GF(2);
(c) *a $[9,5,4]$ shortened punctured Golay code over* GF(3);
(d) *a $[10,5,5]$ shortened Golay code over* GF(3); *and*
(e) *the $[11,5,6]$ dual code of the Golay $[11,6,5]$ code over* GF(3).

In spite of Theorem 15.16, $[2q+k,k+1,2q-1]$ almost extremal NMDS codes over GF(q) with $k < q$ may exist. It is open if almost extremal NMDS codes hold t-designs in general or not.

15.3 Designs from Near MDS Codes

Near MDS codes were discovered 70 years ago. The ternary $[11,6,5]$ Golay code and its extended code were discovered by Golay (1949). They hold a Steiner system $S(4,5,11)$ and $S(5,6,12)$, respectively. Sporadic NMDS codes holding t-designs for $t \geq 2$ were discovered in the past 70 years. On the other hand, many infinite families of NMDS codes were constructed in the literature. However, the question as to whether there is an infinite family of NMDS codes holding an infinite family of t-designs for $t \geq 2$ remained open for 70 years. This long-standing problem was finally settled by Ding and Tang (2020). A major task of this section is to introduce two infinite families of NMDS codes holding an infinite family of Steiner systems $S(3,4,3^s+1)$ and an infinite family of 2-designs discovered by Ding and Tang (2020). It had been a 71-year-old open problem whether there is an infinite family of linear codes holding an infinite family of 4-designs. This long-standing problem was also solved by Tang and Ding (2021). Another major task of this section is to introduce this breakthrough.

15.3.1 *A General Theorem about t-Designs from NMDS Codes*

First, we point out that some NMDS codes do not hold simple designs at all. Below is an example.

Example 15.17. The extended code $\overline{C_{(9,10,3,1)}}$ of the narrow-sense BCH code $C_{(9,10,3,1)}$ over GF(9) has parameters $[11,6,5]$. Its dual has parameters $[11,5,6]$. Both $\overline{C_{(9,10,3,1)}}$ and its dual $\overline{C_{(9,10,3,1)}}^{\perp}$ do not hold simple 1-designs according to our Magma computations.

Second, some NMDS codes may hold t-designs. The following theorem is very interesting, as it shows that some near MDS codes could hold t-designs.

Theorem 15.18 (Dodunekov and Landgev (1995)). *Let C be an $[n,k,n-k]$ NMDS code over GF(q). If there exists an integer $s \geq 1$ such that $A_{n-k+s} = 0$, then the supports of the codewords of weight k in $C^{\perp}$ form a $(k-s)$-design. In particular, the supports of all the minimum weight codewords in the dual of an extremal NMDS code form a Steiner system $S(k-1,k,2q+k)$.*

Proof. Set $t = k - s$. The desired first conclusion then follows from the Assmus-Mattson Theorem and Theorem 15.8. Note that in the design from the minimum weight codewords in the dual of an extremal NMDS code, each $(k-1)$-subset of the point set is contained in

$$\lambda = \frac{A_k^\perp}{q-1} \frac{\binom{k}{k-1}}{\binom{2q+k}{k-1}} = 1$$

block. This proves the second conclusion. $\qquad\square$

To apply Theorem 15.18, we have to find NMDS codes satisfying $A_{n-k+s} = 0$ for some $s < k$. The $[11, 6, 5]$ ternary Golay code and its duals as well as their extended codes are such NMDS codes. There are also several examples of such NMDS codes. But we are really interested in infinite families of such NMDS codes. In Section 15.3.2, we will present such infinite family of ternary codes.

15.3.2 *Infinite Families of NMDS Codes Holding Infinite Families of t-Designs*

Throughout this section, let $q = p^s$, where p is a prime and s is a positive integer. In this section, we consider the narrow-sense BCH code $C_{(q,q+1,3,1)}$ over $GF(q)$ and its dual, and prove that they hold 3-designs when $p = 3$ and 2-designs when $p = 2$ and s is even.

We will need the following lemma whose proof is straightforward.

Lemma 15.19. *Let $x, y, z \in GF(q^2)^*$. Then*

$$\begin{vmatrix} x^{-1} & y^{-1} & z^{-1} \\ x & y & z \\ x^2 & y^2 & z^2 \end{vmatrix} = \frac{(x-y)(y-z)(z-x)}{xyz}(xy+yz+zx).$$

We will also need the following lemma shortly.

Lemma 15.20. *Let U_{q+1} denote the set of all $(q+1)$-th roots of unity in $GF(q^2)$. Suppose that x, y, z are three pairwise distinct elements in U_{q+1} such that*

$$\begin{vmatrix} x^{-1} & y^{-1} & z^{-1} \\ x & y & z \\ x^2 & y^2 & z^2 \end{vmatrix} = 0. \tag{15.6}$$

Then $(x/y)^3 = 1$, which implies that 3 divides $q+1$.

Proof. It follows from Lemma 15.19 that

$$xy + yz + zx = 0. \tag{15.7}$$

Raising both sides of (15.6) to the q-th power yields

$$\begin{vmatrix} x^{-q} & y^{-q} & z^{-q} \\ x^q & y^q & z^q \\ x^{2q} & y^{2q} & z^{2q} \end{vmatrix} = 0. \tag{15.8}$$

Notice that $x, y, z \in U_{q+1}$. Equation (15.8) is the same as

$$\begin{vmatrix} x & y & z \\ x^{-1} & y^{-1} & z^{-1} \\ x^{-2} & y^{-2} & z^{-2} \end{vmatrix} = 0. \tag{15.9}$$

It then follows from Lemma 15.19 and (15.9) that

$$0 = \frac{1}{xy} + \frac{1}{yz} + \frac{1}{zx} = \frac{x+y+z}{xyz}.$$

Consequently,

$$x+y+z = 0. \tag{15.10}$$

Combining (15.7) and (15.10) gives that $x^2 + xy + y^2 = 0$. Thus $x^3 = y^3$ and $(x/y)^3 = 1$. Note that $(x/y)^{q+1} = 1$ and $x/y \neq 1$. We deduce that 3 divides $q+1$. This completes the proof. $\qquad\square$

We are now ready to prove the following result about the code $C_{(q,q+1,3,1)}$.

Theorem 15.21. *Let $q = p^s \geq 5$ with s being a positive integer. Then the narrow-sense BCH code $C_{(q,q+1,3,1)}$ over $\mathrm{GF}(q)$ has parameters $[q+1, q-3, d]$, where $d = 3$ if 3 divides $q+1$ and $d \geq 4$ if 3 does not divide $q+1$.*

Proof. Put $n = q + 1$. Let α be a generator of $\mathrm{GF}(q^2)^*$ and $\beta = \alpha^{q-1}$. Then β is an n-th root of unity in $\mathrm{GF}(q^2)$. Let $g_1(x)$ and $g_2(x)$ denote the minimal polynomial of β and β^2 over $\mathrm{GF}(q)$, respectively. Note that $g_1(x)$ has only roots β and β^q and $g_2(x)$ has roots β^2 and β^{q-1}. We deduce that $g_1(x)$ and $g_2(x)$ are distinct irreducible polynomials of degree 2. By definition, $g(x) := g_1(x)g_2(x)$ is the generator polynomial of $C_{(q,q+1,3,1)}$. Therefore, the dimension of $C_{(q,q+1,3,1)}$ is $q+1-4$. Note that $g(x)$ has only roots $\beta, \beta^2, \beta^{q-1}$ and β^q. By the BCH bound, the minimum weight of $C_{(q,q+1,3,1)}$ is at least 3. Put $\gamma = \beta^{-1}$. Then $\gamma^{q+1} = \beta^{-(q+1)} = 1$. It then follows from Delsarte's theorem that the trace expression of $C_{(q,q+1,3,1)}^{\perp}$ is given by

$$C_{(q,q+1,3,1)}^{\perp} = \{\mathbf{c}_{(a,b)} : a, b \in \mathrm{GF}(q^2)\}, \tag{15.11}$$

where $\mathbf{c}_{(a,b)} = (\mathrm{Tr}_{q^2/q}(a\gamma^i + b\gamma^{2i}))_{i=0}^q$.

Define

$$H = \begin{bmatrix} 1 & \gamma^1 & \gamma^2 & \cdots & \gamma^q \\ 1 & \gamma^2 & \gamma^4 & \cdots & \gamma^{2q} \end{bmatrix}. \tag{15.12}$$

It is easily seen that H is a parity-check matrix of $C_{(q,q+1,3,1)}$, i.e.,

$$C_{(q,q+1,3,1)} = \{\mathbf{c} \in \mathrm{GF}(q)^{q+1} : \mathbf{c}H^T = \mathbf{0}\}.$$

Assume that 3 divides $q + 1$. Notice that γ is a primitive $(q + 1)$-th root of unity. It then follows from $\gamma^{q+1} = 1$ that

$$1 + \gamma^{\frac{q+1}{3}} + \gamma^{\frac{q+1}{3}2} = 0.$$

Define a vector $\mathbf{c} = (c_0, c_1, \ldots, c_q) \in \mathrm{GF}(q)^{q+1}$, where

$$c_i = \begin{cases} 1 & \text{if } i \in \left\{0, \frac{q+1}{3}, \frac{2(q+1)}{3}\right\}, \\ 0 & \text{otherwise.} \end{cases}$$

Then $\mathbf{c} \in C_{(q,q+1,3,1)}$. Consequently, $d = 3$.

Assume now that 3 does not divide $q + 1$. We first prove that $d \neq 3$. On the contrary, suppose $d = 3$. Then there are three pairwise distinct elements x, y, z in U_{q+1} such that

$$a \begin{bmatrix} x \\ x^2 \end{bmatrix} + b \begin{bmatrix} y \\ y^2 \end{bmatrix} + c \begin{bmatrix} z \\ z^2 \end{bmatrix} = 0, \tag{15.13}$$

where $a, b, c \in \mathrm{GF}(q)^*$. Raising to the q-th power both sides of the equation $ax + by + cz = 0$ yields

$$ax^{-1} + by^{-1} + cz^{-1} = 0. \tag{15.14}$$

Combining (15.13) and (15.14) gives

$$a \begin{bmatrix} x^{-1} \\ x \\ x^2 \end{bmatrix} + b \begin{bmatrix} y^{-1} \\ y \\ y^2 \end{bmatrix} + c \begin{bmatrix} z^{-1} \\ z \\ z^2 \end{bmatrix} = 0.$$

It then follows that

$$\begin{vmatrix} x^{-1} & y^{-1} & z^{-1} \\ x & y & z \\ x^2 & y^2 & z^2 \end{vmatrix} = 0.$$

By Lemma 15.20, 3 divides $q + 1$. This is contrary to our assumption that 3 does not divide $q + 1$. This completes the proof. $\qquad\square$

The theorem below made a breakthrough in 70 years in the sense that it presents the first family of linear codes meeting the condition of Theorem 15.18 and holding an infinite family of 3-designs after the discovery of the first near MDS code (i.e., the $[11, 6, 5]$ ternary Golary code) by Golay (1949).

Theorem 15.22 (Ding and Tang (2020)). *Let $q = 3^s$ with $s \geq 2$. Then the narrow-sense BCH code $C_{(q,q+1,3,1)}$ over GF(q) has parameters $[q+1, q-3, 4]$, and its dual $C_{(q,q+1,3,1)}^{\perp}$ has parameters $[q+1, 4, q-3]$ and weight enumerator*

$$1 + \frac{(q-1)^2 q(q+1)}{24} z^{q-3} + \frac{(q-1)q(q+1)(q+3)}{4} z^{q-1} +$$
$$\frac{(q^2-1)(q^2-q+3)}{3} z^q + \frac{3(q-1)^2 q(q+1)}{8} z^{q+1}.$$

Further, the minimum weight codewords in $C_{(q,q+1,3,1)}^{\perp}$ support a 3-$(q+1, q-3, \lambda)$ design with

$$\lambda = \frac{(q-3)(q-4)(q-5)}{24},$$

and the minimum weight codewords in $C_{(q,q+1,3,1)}$ support a 3-$(q+1, 4, 1)$ design, i.e., a Steiner quadruple system $S(3, 4, 3^s + 1)$.

Proof. We follow the notation of the proof of Theorem 15.21. Since 3 does not divide $q + 1 = 3^s + 1$, by Theorem 15.21 the minimum distance d of $C_{(q,q+1,3,1)}$ is at least 4. We now prove that $d = 4$ and the codewords of weight 4 in $C_{(q,q+1,3,1)}$ support a 3-$(q+1, 4, 1)$ design.

Let x, y, z be three pairwise distinct elements in U_{q+1}. We conclude that $x + y + z \neq 0$. Suppose on the contrary that $x + y + z = 0$. We have then

$$0 = (x+y+z)^q = x^q + y^q + z^q = \frac{1}{x} + \frac{1}{y} + \frac{1}{z} = \frac{xy + yz + zx}{xyz}.$$

In summary, we have

$$\begin{cases} x+y+z = 0, \\ xy+yz+zx = 0, \end{cases}$$

which is the same as

$$\begin{bmatrix} x \\ x^2 \end{bmatrix} + \begin{bmatrix} y \\ y^2 \end{bmatrix} + \begin{bmatrix} z \\ z^2 \end{bmatrix} = \mathbf{0}.$$

This means that $C_{(q,q+1,3,1)}$ has a codeword of weight 3, which is contrary to Theorem 15.21.

We now prove that there is a unique $w \in U_{q+1} \setminus \{x, y, z\}$ such that

$$\begin{vmatrix} x^{-2} & y^{-2} & z^{-2} & w^{-2} \\ x^{-1} & y^{-1} & z^{-1} & w^{-1} \\ x & y & z & w \\ x^2 & y^2 & z^2 & w^2 \end{vmatrix}$$

$$= \frac{(z-w)(y-w)(y-z)(x-w)(x-z)(x-y)}{(xyzw)^2}(xy + xz + xw + yz + yw + zw)$$

$$= 0. \tag{15.15}$$

Note that $(z-w)(y-w)(y-z)(x-w)(x-z)(x-y) \neq 0$. It follows from (15.15) that

$$w = -\frac{xy+yz+zx}{x+y+z}. \tag{15.16}$$

We need to prove that $w \in U_{q+1}$. Note that

$$w = -xyz\frac{\frac{1}{x}+\frac{1}{y}+\frac{1}{z}}{x+y+z} = -xyz\frac{(x+y+z)^q}{x+y+z}.$$

We then have

$$w^{q+1} = (-xyz)^{q+1}(x+y+z)^{q^2-1} = 1.$$

By definition, $w \in U_{q+1}$.

We now prove that $w \neq x$. Suppose on the contrary that $w = x$, then

$$x = -\frac{xy+yz+zx}{x+y+z},$$

which yields

$$(x-z)(x-y) = 0.$$

Whence, $x = z$ or $x = z$, which is contrary to our assumption that x,y,z are three pairwise distinct elements in U_{q+1}. Due to symmetry, $w \neq y$ and $w \neq z$. The uniqueness of w is justified by (15.16).

Note that $U_{q+1} = \{1, \gamma, \gamma^2, \cdots, \gamma^q\}$. Let $\{x,y,z,w\}$ be any 4-subset of U_{q+1} such that (15.15) holds. Without loss of generality, assume that

$$x = \gamma^{i_1}, \ y = \gamma^{i_2}, \ z = \gamma^{i_3}, \ w = \gamma^{i_4},$$

where $0 \leq i_1 < i_2 < i_3 < i_4 \leq q$. Since $d \geq 4$, the rank of the matrix

$$\begin{bmatrix} x^{-2} & y^{-2} & z^{-2} & w^{-2} \\ x^{-1} & y^{-1} & z^{-1} & w^{-1} \\ x & y & z & w \\ x^2 & y^2 & z^2 & w^2 \end{bmatrix} \tag{15.17}$$

equals 3. Let $(u_{i_1}, u_{i_2}, u_{i_3}, u_{i_4})$ denote a nonzero solution of

$$\begin{bmatrix} x^{-2} & y^{-2} & z^{-2} & w^{-2} \\ x^{-1} & y^{-1} & z^{-1} & w^{-1} \\ x & y & z & w \\ x^2 & y^2 & z^2 & w^2 \end{bmatrix} \begin{bmatrix} u_{i_1} \\ u_{i_2} \\ u_{i_3} \\ u_{i_4} \end{bmatrix} = \mathbf{0}.$$

Since the rank of the matrix of (15.17) is 3, all these $u_{i_j} \neq 0$. Define a vector $\mathbf{c} = (c_0, c_1, \ldots, c_q) \in \mathrm{GF}(q)^{q+1}$, where $c_{i_j} = u_{i_j}$ for $j \in \{1,2,3,4\}$ and $c_h = 0$ for all $h \in \{0, 1, \ldots, q\} \setminus \{i_1, i_2, i_3, i_4\}$. It is easily seen that $\mathbf{c}$ is a codeword of weight

4 in $C_{(q,q+1,3,1)}$. The set $\{a\mathbf{c} : a \in \mathrm{GF}(q)^*\}$ consists of all such codewords of weight 4 with nonzero coordinates in $\{i_1, i_2, i_3, i_4\}$. Therefore, we have $d = 4$. Conversely, every codeword of weight 4 in $C_{(q,q+1,3,1)}$ with nonzero coordinates in $\{i_1, i_2, i_3, i_4\}$ must correspond to the set $\{x, y, z, w\}$. Hence, every codeword of weight 4 and its nonzero multiples in $C_{(q,q+1,3,1)}$ correspond to such set $\{x, y, z, w\}$ uniquely. We then deduce that the codewords of weight 4 in $C_{(q,q+1,3,1)}$ support a $3\text{-}(q+1, 4, 1)$ design. As a result,

$$A_4 = (q-1)\frac{\binom{q+1}{3}}{\binom{4}{3}} = \frac{(q-1)^2 q(q+1)}{24}.$$

Note that $C_{(q,q+1,3,1)}$ has parameters $[q+1, q-3, 4]$. We now prove that the minimum distance $d^\perp$ of $C_{(q,q+1,3,1)}^\perp$ is equal to $q - 3$. Recall that

$$C_{(q,q+1,3,1)}^\perp = \{\mathbf{c}_{(a,b)} : a, b \in \mathrm{GF}(q^2)\},$$

where $\mathbf{c}_{(a,b)} = (\mathrm{Tr}_{q^2/q}(a\gamma^i + b\gamma^{2i}))_{i=0}^q$. Let $u \in U_{q+1}$. Then

$$\mathrm{Tr}_{q^2/q}(au + bu^2) = au + bu^2 + a^q u^{-1} + b^q u^{-2} = u^{-2}(bu^4 + au^3 + a^q u + b^q).$$

Hence, there are at most four $u \in U_{q+1}$ such that $\mathrm{Tr}_{q^2/q}(au + bu^2) = 0$ if $(a,b) \neq (0,0)$. As a result, for $(a,b) \neq (0,0)$ we have

$$\mathrm{wt}(\mathbf{c}_{(a,b)}) \geq q + 1 - 4 = q - 3.$$

This means that $d^\perp \geq q - 3$. If $d = q - 2$, then $C_{(q,q+1,3,1)}^\perp$ would be an MDS code and $C_{(q,q+1,3,1)}$ would also be an MDS code, which leads to a contradiction. We then conclude that $d^\perp = q - 3$. Now both $C_{(q,q+1,3,1)}$ and its dual are AMDS. By definition, both $C_{(q,q+1,3,1)}$ and its dual are NMDS. It then follows from Theorem 15.12 that

$$A_{q-3}^\perp = A_4 = \frac{(q-1)^2 q(q+1)}{24}.$$

Applying Theorem 15.8, we obtain the desired weight enumerator of $C_{(q,q+1,3,1)}^\perp$. In particular, $A_{q-2}^\perp = 0$. It then follows from the Assmus-Mattson Theorem that the minimum weight codewords in $C_{(q,q+1,3,1)}^\perp$ support a $3\text{-}(q+1, q-3, \lambda)$ design with

$$\lambda = \frac{(q-3)(q-4)(q-5)}{24}.$$

$\square$

The proof of Theorem 15.22 also proved the following theorem.

Theorem 15.23. *Let $q = 3^s$ with $s \geq 2$. Let α be a generator of $GF(q^2)^*$, and put $\gamma = \alpha^{-(q-1)}$. Define $U_{q+1} = \{1, \gamma, \gamma^2, \ldots, \gamma^q\}$ and*

$$\mathcal{B} = \left\{ \{x, y, z, w\} \in \binom{U_{q+1}}{4} : xy + xz + xw + yz + yw + zw = 0 \right\}.$$

Then $(U_{q+1}, \mathcal{B})$ is a Steiner system $S(3, 4, 3^s + 1)$, and is isomorphic to the Steiner system supported by the minimum weight codewords of the code $C_{(q,q+1,3,1)}$.

It is known that a Steiner quadruple system $S(3, 4, v)$ exists if and only if $v \equiv 2, 4 \pmod 6$ [Hanani (1960)]. There are two different constructions of an infinite family of Steiner systems $S(3, q+1, q^s + 1)$ for q being a prime power and $s \geq 2$. The first produces the spherical geometry designs due to Witt (1937), which is based on the action of $PGL_2(GF(q^s))$ on the base block $GF(q) \cup \{\infty\}$ (see Section 4.7 for detail). The automorphism group of the spherical geometry design contains the group $P\Gamma L_2(GF(q^s))$. The second construction was proposed by Key and Wagner (1986), and is based on affine spaces. The Steiner systems $S(3, q+1, q^s + 1)$ from the two constructions are not isomorphic [Key and Wagner (1986)].

When $q = p^s$ for $p > 3$ and 3 does not divide $q + 1$, the code $C_{(q,q+1,3,1)}$ of Theorem 15.22 is still NMDS, but it does not hold 2-designs according to Magma experiments. The case $q = 3^s$ is really special. The reader is informed that the Steiner quadruple system $S(3, 4, 3^s + 1)$ of Theorem 15.22 is isomorphic to the spherical geometry design with the same parameters (see Section 15.5). The first contribution of Theorem 15.22 is a coding-theoretic construction of the spherical geometry design $S(3, 4, 3^s + 1)$. The second contribution is that the codes of Theorem 15.22 were the first infinite family of NMDS codes holding an infinite family of 3-designs since the first NMDS ternary code discovered 70 years ago by Golay (1949).

It was shown that the total number of nonisomorphic cyclic Steiner quadruple systems $S(3, 4, 28)$ is 1028387 [Chang, Fan, Feng, Holt and Östergård (2017)], which is a big number. This number indicates that it is a hard problem to classify Steiner quadruple systems.

A family of NMDS codes may not satisfy the condition of Theorem 15.18 (i.e., the conditions in the Assmus-Mattson theorem), but could still hold 2-designs. The next theorem introduces a family of such NMDS codes and their designs.

Theorem 15.24 (Ding and Tang (2020)). *Let $q = 2^s$ with $s \geq 4$ being even. Then the narrow-sense BCH code $C_{(q,q+1,3,1)}$ over $GF(q)$ has parameters $[q+1, q-3, 4]$, and its dual code $C_{(q,q+1,3,1)}^{\perp}$ has parameters $[q+1, 4, q-3]$ and weight* *enumerator*

$$1 + \frac{(q-4)(q-1)q(q+1)}{24}z^{q-3} + \frac{(q-1)q(q+1)}{2}z^{q-2} + \frac{(q+1)q^2(q-1)}{4}z^{q-1}$$
$$+ \frac{(q-1)(q+1)(2q^2+q+6)}{6}z^q + \frac{3q^4 - 4q^3 - 3q^2 + 4q}{8}z^{q+1}.$$

Further, the codewords of weight 4 in $C_{(q,q+1,3,1)}$ support a 2-$(q+1,4,(q-4)/2)$ design, and the codewords of weight $q-3$ in the dual code $C^{\perp}_{(q,q+1,3,1)}$ support a 2-$(q+1,q-3,\lambda^{\perp})$ design with

$$\lambda^{\perp} = \frac{(q-4)^2(q-3)}{24}.$$

Proof. Recall that $q = 2^s$ with $s \geq 4$. We follow the notation of the proof of Theorem 15.22. Let x, y, z, w be four pairwise distinct elements in U_{q+1}. It can be verified that

$$\begin{vmatrix} x^{-2} & y^{-2} & z^{-2} & w^{-2} \\ x^{-1} & y^{-1} & z^{-1} & w^{-1} \\ x & y & z & w \\ x^2 & y^2 & z^2 & w^2 \end{vmatrix}$$
$$= \frac{(z-w)(y-w)(y-z)(x-w)(x-z)(x-y)}{(xyzw)^2}(xy+xz+xw+yz+yw+zw).$$
$$(15.18)$$

Notice that 3 does not divide $2^s + 1$, as s is even. It can be similarly proved that $C_{(q,q+1,3,1)}$ over GF(q) has parameters $[q+1, q-3, 4]$, and its dual code $C^{\perp}_{(q,q+1,3,1)}$ has parameters $[q+1, 4, q-3]$. Thus, they are NMDS.

With arguments similar to the proof of Theorem 15.22, we can prove that every codeword of weight 4 in $C_{(q,q+1,3,1)}$ and its nonzero multiples correspond uniquely to a set $\{x, y, z, w\}$ of four pairwise distinct elements x, y, z, w in U_{q+1} such that the matrix

$$M(x,y,z,w) := \begin{bmatrix} x^{-2} & y^{-2} & z^{-2} & w^{-2} \\ x^{-1} & y^{-1} & z^{-1} & w^{-1} \\ x & y & z & w \\ x^2 & y^2 & z^2 & w^2 \end{bmatrix}$$

has rank 3.

Let x, y be two distinct elements in U_{q+1}. We now consider the total number of choices of z and w in U_{q+1} such the matrix $M(x,y,z,w)$ has rank 3. Using (15.18) we can verify that $M(x,y,z,w)$ has rank 3 if and only if

$$z \notin \left\{ x, y, x^2y^{-1}, y^2x^{-1}, (xy)^{2^{2s-1}} \right\}$$

and

$$w = \frac{xy + yz + zx}{x + y + z}. \tag{15.19}$$

Note that the elements in

$$\left\{ x, y, x^2 y^{-1}, y^2 x^{-1}, (xy)^{2^{2s-1}} \right\}$$

are pairwise distinct. It can be verified that if (z, w) is a choice, so is (w, z). Thus, the total number of choices of x and z such the matrix $M(x, y, z, w)$ has rank 3 is equal to

$$\frac{q + 1 - 5}{2} = \frac{q - 4}{2}.$$

Since this number is independent of the elements x and y, the codewords of weight 4 in $C_{(q,q+1,3,1)}$ support a 2-$(q+1, 4, (q-4)/2)$ design. Consequently,

$$A_4 = \frac{(q-4)(q-1)q(q+1)}{24}.$$

It then follows from Theorem 15.12 that

$$A_{q-3}^{\perp} = A_4 = \frac{(q-4)(q-1)q(q+1)}{24}.$$

Applying Theorem 15.8, we obtain the desired weight enumerator of $C_{(q,q+1,3,1)}^{\perp}$.

By Theorem 15.12, the minimum weight codewords in $C_{(q,q+1,3,1)}^{\perp}$ support a 2-design which is the complementary design of the design supported by all the minimum weight codewords in $C_{(q,q+1,3,1)}$. This completes the proof. □

With Theorem 15.8 and the expression of A_4, we can verify that $A_i > 0$ for all i with $4 \le i \le q+1$. Notice that $A_i^{\perp} > 0$ for all i with $q-3 \le i \le q+1$. The conditions in the Assmus-Mattson Theorem and the condition of Theorem 15.18 are not satisfied. But the codes still hold simple 2-designs.

We remark the code $C_{(q,q+1,3,1)}$ supports simple t-designs for $t \ge 2$ only when $p = 3$ or $p = 2$ and s is even. This makes this class of codes very special.

The proof of Theorem 15.24 also proved the following theorem.

Theorem 15.25. *Let $q = 2^s$ with $s \ge 4$ being even. Let α be a generator of $\mathrm{GF}(q^2)^*$, and put $\gamma = \alpha^{-(q-1)}$. Define $U_{q+1} = \{1, \gamma, \gamma^2, \ldots, \gamma^q\}$ and*

$$\mathcal{B} = \left\{ \{x, y, z, w\} \in \binom{U_{q+1}}{4} : xy + xz + xw + yz + yw + zw = 0 \right\}.$$

Then $(U_{q+1}, \mathcal{B})$ is a 2-$(q+1, 4, (q-4)/2)$ design, and is isomorphic to the 2-design supported by the minimum weight codewords of the code $C_{(q,q+1,3,1)}$.

Below we provide information on the subfield subcodes of the two families of near MDS codes documented in Theorems 15.22 and 15.24.

Let $q = p^s$, where p is a prime. We now consider the narrow-sense BCH code $C_{(q,q+1,3,1)}$ and its subfield subcode $C_{(q,q+1,3,1)}|_{GF(p)}$. We follow the notation in the proof of Theorem 15.21. By the Delsarte Theorem, we have

$$C_{(q,q+1,3,1)}|_{GF(p)} = \left(\text{Tr}_{q/p} \left(C_{(q,q+1,3,1)}^{\perp} \right) \right)^{\perp}. \tag{15.20}$$

By the proof of Theorem 15.21,

$$C_{(q,q+1,3,1)}^{\perp} = \{ (\text{Tr}_{q^2/q}(a\gamma^i + b\gamma^{2i}))_{i=0}^q : a, b \in GF(q^2) \}. \tag{15.21}$$

Combining (15.20) and (15.21) yields

$$C_{(q,q+1,3,1)}|_{GF(p)} = \left(\{ (\text{Tr}_{q^2/p}(a\gamma^i + b\gamma^{2i}))_{i=0}^q : a, b \in GF(q^2) \} \right)^{\perp}.$$

Again by the Delsarte Theorem, we obtain

$$C_{(q,q+1,3,1)}|_{GF(p)} = C_{(p,q+1,3,1)}. \tag{15.22}$$

This equality will be useful for deriving the parameters of the subfield subcode.

Theorem 15.26. *Let $s \geq 4$ be an even integer. Then the binary subfield subcode $C_{(2^s,2^s+1,3,1)}|_{GF(2)}$ has parameters $[2^s + 1, 2^s + 1 - 2s, 5]$.*

Proof. Let $q = 2^s$ and $n = q + 1 = 2^s + 1$. We follow the notation in the proofs of Theorems 15.21 and 15.24. Note that the 2-cyclotomic coset C_1 modulo n is given by

$$C_1 = \{1, 2, \ldots, 2^{s-1}, -1, -2, \ldots, -2^{s-1}\} \bmod n.$$

By definition, the minimal polynomial $\mathbb{M}_\beta(x)$ of β over $GF(2)$ is given by

$$\mathbb{M}_\beta(x) = \sum_{i \in C_1} (x - \beta^i).$$

By the definition of BCH codes, $C_{(2,2^s+1,3,1)}$ has generator polynomial $\mathbb{M}_\beta(x)$ with degree $2s$, and is the Zetterberg code. It is known that this code has minimum distance 5 [Schoof and van der Vlugt (1991)]. $\square$

Using the sphere packing bound, we can verify that the subfield subcode $C_{(2^s,2^s+1,3,1)}|_{GF(2)}$ is dimension-optimal. In addition, this binary code is also distance-optimal when $s \in \{2,4,6,8\}$. This makes the original code $C_{(2^s,2^s+1,3,1)}$ very interesting.

We inform the reader that $d(C_{(2^s,2^s+1,3,1)}|_{GF(2)}) = 3$ if s is odd, which follows from the fact that

$$1 + \gamma^{(q+1)/3} + \gamma^{2(q+1)/3} = 0.$$

This is why we are not interested in this code for the case s being odd.

Theorem 15.27. *Let $s \geq 4$ be an even integer. Then the code $(C_{(2^s,2^s+1,3,1)}|_{GF(2)})^{\perp}$ has parameters $[2^s + 1, 2s, 2^{s-1} - 2^{s/2} + 2]$.*

Proof. $(C_{(2^s,2^s+1,3,1)}|\text{GF(2)})^{\perp}$ is the dual of the Zetterberg code whose parameters are from Lachaud and Wolfmann (1990)[Theorem 6.6]. $\qquad\qquad\square$

When $s = 2$, $(C_{(2^s,2^s+1,3,1)}|\text{GF(2)})^{\perp}$ has parameters $[5,4,2]$, and is MDS. When $s = 4$, the code has parameters $[17,8,6]$, and is distance-optimal. When $s = 4$, the code has parameters $[65,12,26]$, and has the best known parameters and is an optimal cyclic code [Ding (2015a)][Appendix]. Thus, the code $(C_{(2^s,2^s+1,3,1)}|\text{GF(2)})^{\perp}$ is very interesting.

Theorem 15.28. *Let $s \geq 2$. Then the code $C_{(3^s,3^s+1,3,1)}|\text{GF(3)}$ has parameters $[3^s + 1, 3^s + 1 - 4s, d \geq 4]$.*

Proof. Let $q = 3^s$ and $n = q + 1 = 3^s + 1$. We follow the notation in the proofs of Theorems 15.21 and 15.22. Note that the 3-cyclotomic coset C_1 modulo n is given by

$$C_1 = \{1,3,\ldots,3^{s-1},-1,-3,\ldots,-3^{s-1}\} \bmod n.$$

Similarly, the 3-cyclotomic coset C_2 modulo n is given by $C_2 = 2C_1 \bmod n$. It is easily verified that $C_1 \cap C_2 = \emptyset$ and $|C_1| = |C_2| = 2s$.

By definition, the minimal polynomial $\mathbb{M}_{\beta^j}(x)$ of β^j over GF(3) is given by

$$\mathbb{M}_{\beta^j}(x) = \sum_{i \in C_j} (x - \beta^i)$$

for $j \in \{1,2\}$. By the definition of BCH codes, $C_{(3,3^s+1,3,1)}$ has generator polynomial $\mathbb{M}_{\beta}(x)\mathbb{M}_{\beta^2}(x)$. Therefore, the dimension of the code $C_{(3,3^s+1,3,1)}$ is given by

$$\dim(C_{(3,3^s+1,3,1)}) = 3^s + 1 - 4s.$$

By (15.22), $C_{(3^s,3^s+1,3,1)}|\text{GF(3)}$ has the same dimension and generator polynomial as $C_{(3,3^s+1,3,1)}$.

By Theorem 15.22, the code $C_{(3^s,3^s+1,3,1)}$ has minimum distance 4. It then follows from the definition of subfield subcodes that the minimum distance $d(C_{(3^s,3^s+1,3,1)}|\text{GF(3)}) \geq 4$. This completes the proof. $\qquad\square$

The minimum distance of the code $C_{(3^s,3^s+1,3,1)}|\text{GF(3)})$ is indeed 4 when $s = 3$. We have the following examples of the code $C_{(3^s,3^s+1,3,1)}|\text{GF(3)}$:

s	$C_{(q,q+1,3,1)}|\text{GF(3)}$	$(C_{(q,q+1,3,1)}|\text{GF(3)})^{\perp}$
2	$[10,2,5]$	$[10,8,2]$
3	$[28,16,4]$	$[28,12,8]$
4	$[82,66,6]$	$[82,16,36]$

$C_{(q,q+1,3,1)}|_{\mathrm{GF}(3)}$ and $(C_{(q,q+1,3,1)}|_{\mathrm{GF}(3)})^{\perp}$ both are distance-optimal cyclic codes when $s = 2$ and $s = 3$ according to Ding (2015a)[Appendix]. The distance optimality of these subfield subcodes make the original codes $C_{(q,q+1,3,1)}$ and $C_{(q,q+1,3,1)}^{\perp}$ very interesting.

It would be worthy to settle the minimum distances of $C_{(q,q+1,3,1)}|_{\mathrm{GF}(3)}$ and $C_{(q,q+1,3,1)}|_{\mathrm{GF}(3)})^{\perp}$. The reader is invited to attack this open problem.

15.3.3 An Infinite Family of Near MDS Codes Holding 4-Designs

The ideas and techniques of this section are an extension of those of Section 15.3.2. The materials presented in this section are mainly from Tang and Ding (2021).

15.3.3.1 Combinatorial t-Designs Constructed with Some Elementary Symmetric Polynomials

The task of this section is to construct 3-designs and 4-designs with elementary symmetric polynomials. These results would play a crucial role in proving that the codes constructed in the next section support 3-designs or 4-designs.

We define $[k] := \{1, 2, \cdots, k\}$. The *elementary symmetric polynomial (ESP)* of degree ℓ in k variables $u_1, u_2, \cdots, u_k$, written $\sigma_{k,\ell}$, is defined by

$$\sigma_{k,\ell}(u_1, \cdots, u_k) = \sum_{I \subseteq [k], |I| = \ell} \prod_{j \in I} u_j. \tag{15.23}$$

The elementary symmetric polynomials are a type of basic building blocks for symmetric polynomials, as every symmetric polynomial can be expressed as a polynomial in elementary symmetric polynomials. Throughout this section, we use $\sigma_{k,\ell}$ to abbreviate $\sigma_{k,\ell}(u_1, \cdots, u_k)$ when $u_1, \ldots, u_k$ are clear from the context.

Let $q = 2^m$ throughout this section. Let U_{q+1} be the subgroup of $\mathrm{GF}(q^2)^*$ of order $q + 1$, that is, $U_{q+1} = \{u \in \mathrm{GF}(q^2)^* : u^{q+1} = 1\}$. For any integer k with $1 \le k \le q + 1$, let $\binom{U_{q+1}}{k}$ denote the set of all k-subsets of U_{q+1}. Define

$$\mathcal{B}_{\sigma_{k,\ell},q+1} = \left\{ \{u_1, \cdots, u_k\} \in \binom{U_{q+1}}{k} : \sigma_{k,\ell}(u_1, \cdots, u_k) = 0 \right\}. \tag{15.24}$$

Then the incidence structure $\mathbb{D}_{\sigma_{k,\ell},q+1} := (U_{q+1}, \mathcal{B}_{\sigma_{k,\ell},q+1})$ may be a t-$(q+1, k, \lambda)$ design for some λ, where U_{q+1} is the point set, and the incidence relation is the set membership. In this case, we say that the ESP $\sigma_{k,\ell}$ supports a t-$(q+1, k, \lambda)$ design. The ESP $\sigma_{k,\ell}$ always supports a 1-design, but may not support 2-designs.

Define the block sets $\mathcal{B}^0_{\sigma_{6,3},q+1}$ and $\mathcal{B}^1_{\sigma_{6,3},q+1}$ by

$$
\mathcal{B}^0_{\sigma_{6,3},q+1} = \left\{ \begin{array}{c} \{u_1,u_2,u_3,u_4,u_5,u_6\} \in \mathcal{B}_{\sigma_{6,3},q+1} : \\ \{u_{i_1},u_{i_2},u_{i_3},u_{i_4},u_{i_5}\} \in \mathcal{B}_{\sigma_{5,2},q+1} \\ \text{for some } \{i_1,i_2,\cdots,i_5\} \text{ with} \\ 1 \le i_1 < i_2 < i_3 < i_4 < i_5 \le 6 \end{array} \right\}, \tag{15.25}
$$

and

$$
\mathcal{B}^1_{\sigma_{6,3},q+1} = \mathcal{B}_{\sigma_{6,3},q+1} \setminus \mathcal{B}^0_{\sigma_{6,3},q+1}. \tag{15.26}
$$

The three theorems and corollary below are the main results of this section. They show an interesting application of ESPs in the theory of t-designs.

Theorem 15.29. *Let $m \ge 5$ be odd. Then the incidence structure $(U_{q+1}, \mathcal{B}_{\sigma_{6,3},q+1})$ is a 4-$\left(q+1, 6, \frac{q-8}{2}\right)$ design, where the block set $\mathcal{B}_{\sigma_{6,3},q+1}$ was given by (15.24).*

Theorem 15.30. *Let $m \ge 4$ be an even integer. Then the incidence structure $(U_{q+1}, \mathcal{B}_{\sigma_{5,2},q+1})$ is a Steiner system $S(3,5,q+1)$, where the block set $\mathcal{B}_{\sigma_{5,2},q+1}$ is given by (15.24).*

Theorem 15.31. *Let $m \ge 4$ be an even integer. Then the incidence structure $(U_{q+1}, \mathcal{B}^0_{\sigma_{6,3},q+1})$ is a 3-$(q+1, 6, 2(q-4))$ design, and the incidence structure $(U_{q+1}, \mathcal{B}_{\sigma_{6,3},q+1})$ is a 3-$\left(q+1, 6, \frac{(q-4)^2}{6}\right)$ design.*

The following corollary follows immediately from the previous theorem.

Corollary 15.32. *Let $m \ge 4$ be an even integer. Then the incidence structure $(U_{q+1}, \mathcal{B}^1_{\sigma_{6,3},q+1})$ is a 3-$\left(q+1, 6, \frac{(q-4)(q-16)}{6}\right)$ design.*

From Theorems 15.29, 15.30 and 15.31, we get

$$
\left| \mathcal{B}_{\sigma_{5,2},q+1} \right| = \begin{cases} \frac{1}{10}\binom{q+1}{3}, & \text{if } m \text{ is even,} \\ 0, & \text{if } m \text{ is odd,} \end{cases}
$$

and

$$
\left| \mathcal{B}_{\sigma_{6,3},q+1} \right| = \begin{cases} \frac{(q-4)^2}{120}\binom{q+1}{3}, & \text{if } m \text{ is even,} \\ \frac{q-8}{30}\binom{q+1}{4}, & \text{if } m \text{ is odd.} \end{cases}
$$

In general, it is difficult to determine $\left| \mathcal{B}_{\sigma_{k,\ell},q+1} \right|$. It would be interesting to settle the following problem.

Problem 15.33. *Let k, ℓ be two integers with $1 \le \ell \le \frac{k}{2}$. Determine the cardinality of the set $\mathcal{B}_{\sigma_{k,\ell},q+1}$ given by (15.24) for $(k,\ell) \neq (6,3)$ and $(5,2)$.*

To prove Theorems 15.29, 15.30, and 15.31, we need the following lemmas. The first one is on quadratic equations over finite fields of characteristic 2 [Lidl and Niederreiter (1997)], and is documented below.

Lemma 15.34. *Let* $f(T) = T^2 + aT + b \in \mathrm{GF}(q)[T]$ *be a polynomial of degree 2. Then*

(1) f *has exactly one root in* $\mathrm{GF}(q)$ *if and only if* $a = 0$;

(2) f *has exactly two roots in* $\mathrm{GF}(q)$ *if and only if* $a \neq 0$ *and* $\mathrm{Tr}_{q/2}\left(\frac{b}{a^2}\right) = 0$; *and*

(3) f *has exactly two roots in* $\mathrm{GF}(q^2) \setminus \mathrm{GF}(q)$ *if and only if* $a \neq 0$ *and* $\mathrm{Tr}_{q/2}\left(\frac{b}{a^2}\right) = 1$.

Lemma 15.35. *Let* $\{u_1, u_2\} \in \binom{U_{q+1}}{2}$. *Then* $\frac{u_1 u_2}{u_1^2 + u_2^2} \in \mathrm{GF}(q)$ *and* $\mathrm{Tr}_{q/2}\left(\frac{u_1 u_2}{u_1^2 + u_2^2}\right) = 1$.

Proof. Let $a = \frac{u_1 u_2}{u_1^2 + u_2^2}$. Then $a^q = \frac{u_1^{-1} u_2^{-1}}{u_1^{-2} + u_2^{-2}} = a$. Thus $a \in \mathrm{GF}(q)$. Note that $\frac{1}{a} = u + \frac{1}{u}$, where $u = \frac{u_1}{u_2} \in U_{q+1}$. We have

$$(au)^2 + (au) + a^2 = 0, \tag{15.27}$$

where $au \in \mathrm{GF}(q^2) \setminus \mathrm{GF}(q)$. Hence, the equation $T^2 + T + a^2 = 0$ has two roots in $\mathrm{GF}(q^2) \setminus \mathrm{GF}(q)$. It then follows from Lemma 15.34 that $\mathrm{Tr}_{q/2}(a) = \mathrm{Tr}_{q/2}(a^2) = 1$. This completes the proof. $\square$

Lemma 15.36. *Let* $\{u_1, u_2, u_3, u_4\} \in \binom{U_{q+1}}{4}$. *Then we have the following.*

(1) $u_1 + u_2 + u_3 + u_4 \neq 0$.

(2) *If* m *is even, then* $u_1 + u_2 + u_3 \neq 0$.

Proof. Suppose that $u_1 + u_2 + u_3 + u_4 = 0$. We have then

$$\frac{1}{u_1} + \frac{1}{u_2} + \frac{1}{u_3} + \frac{1}{u_4} = (u_1 + u_2 + u_3 + u_4)^q = 0.$$

It follows from $u_4 = u_1 + u_2 + u_3$ that

$$\frac{1}{u_1} + \frac{1}{u_2} + \frac{1}{u_3} + \frac{1}{u_1 + u_2 + u_3} = 0.$$

Multiplying both sides of the previous equation by $u_1 u_2 u_3 (u_1 + u_2 + u_3)$ yields

$$(u_1 + u_2 + u_3)(u_1 u_2 + u_2 u_3 + u_3 u_1) + u_1 u_2 u_3 = 0,$$

which is the same as

$$(u_1 + u_2)(u_2 + u_3)(u_3 + u_1) = 0,$$

which is contrary to our assumption that u_1, u_2, u_3 are pairwise distinct. Thus, $u_1 + u_2 + u_3 + u_4 \neq 0$.

Let m be even. Suppose that $u_1 + u_2 + u_3 = 0$. Then $\frac{1}{u_1 + u_2} = \frac{1}{u_3} = \frac{1}{u_1} + \frac{1}{u_2} = \frac{u_1 + u_2}{u_1 u_2}$. We then have $u_1^2 + u_1 u_2 + u_2^2 = 0$. Thus, $u_1^3 = u_2^3$. Since m is even, $\gcd(3, q + 1) = 1$. It then follows from $u_1^3 = u_2^3$ that $u_1 = u_2$, which is contrary to our assumption that $u_1 \neq u_2$. This completes the proof. $\square$

Lemma 15.37. Let $\sigma_{3,1}, \sigma_{3,2}, \sigma_{3,3}$ be the ESPs given by (15.23) with $\{u_1, u_2, u_3\} \in \binom{U_{q+1}}{3}$. Then the following hold.

(1) $\sigma_{3,1}\sigma_{3,2} + \sigma_{3,3} = (u_1 + u_2)(u_2 + u_3)(u_3 + u_1)$.
(2) $\sigma_{3,1}\sigma_{3,2} + \sigma_{3,3} \neq 0$.
(3) $\sigma_{3,2}^2 + \sigma_{3,1}\sigma_{3,3} = \sigma_{3,3}^2 \left(\sigma_{3,1}^2 + \sigma_{3,2} \right)^q$.

Proof. The proofs are straightforward and omitted. $\square$

Lemma 15.38. Let m be even. Let $\sigma_{3,1}, \sigma_{3,2}, \sigma_{3,3}$ be the ESPs given by (15.23) with $\{u_1, u_2, u_3\} \in \binom{U_{q+1}}{3}$. Then

(1) $\sigma_{3,1}^2 + \sigma_{3,2} \neq 0$; and
(2) $\sigma_{3,2}^2 + \sigma_{3,1}\sigma_{3,3} \neq 0$.

Proof. Suppose that $\sigma_{3,1}^2 + \sigma_{3,2} = 0$, that is

$$u_1^2 + u_2^2 + u_3^2 + u_1 u_2 + u_2 u_3 + u_3 u_1 = 0.$$

Multiplying both sides of the previous equation by $u_1 + u_2 + u_3$ yields

$$u_1^3 + u_2^3 + u_3^3 + u_1 u_2 u_3 = 0.$$

It then follows that $|\{u_1^3, u_2^3, u_3^3, u_1 u_2 u_3\}| = 3$ from Lemma 15.36, which is contrary to the assumption that m is even. Combining Part 1 and Lemma 15.37 gives Part 2. This completes the proof. $\square$

Lemma 15.39. Let $u_j \in U_{q+1}$ such that $\sigma_{5,2} = 0$, where $j \in \{1, 2, 3, 4, 5\}$. Then

$$\begin{cases} (\sigma_{3,1}^2 + \sigma_{3,2})(u_4 + u_5) = \sigma_{3,1}\sigma_{3,2} + \sigma_{3,3}, \\ (\sigma_{3,1}^2 + \sigma_{3,2})u_4 u_5 = \sigma_{3,2}^2 + \sigma_{3,1}\sigma_{3,3}, \end{cases}$$

where $\sigma_{3,1}, \sigma_{3,2}, \sigma_{3,3}$ and $\sigma_{5,2}$ are the ESPs given by (15.23).

Proof. Observe first that

$$u_4 u_5 + \sigma_{3,1}(u_4 + u_5) + \sigma_{3,2} = 0. \tag{15.28}$$

Raising to the q-th power both sides of Equation (15.28) yields

$$u_4^{-1}u_5^{-1} + \sigma_{3,1}^q(u_4^{-1} + u_5^{-1}) + \sigma_{3,2}^q = 0,$$

which is the same as

$$\sigma_{3,1}u_4u_5 + \sigma_{3,2}(u_4 + u_5) + \sigma_{3,3} = 0. \tag{15.29}$$

The desired conclusion then follows from Equations (15.28) and (15.29). This completes the proof. $\qquad\square$

Lemma 15.40. *Let m be even and $\{u_1, u_2, u_3, u_4, u_5, u_6\} \in \mathcal{B}_{\sigma_{6,3},q+1}^0$. Let A and A' be two 5-subsets of $\{u_1, u_2, u_3, u_4, u_5, u_6\}$ such that $A, A' \in \mathcal{B}_{\sigma_{5,2},q+1}$. Then $A = A'$.*

Proof. Suppose that $A \neq A'$. Due to symmetry, let $A = \{u_1, u_2, u_3, u_4, u_5\} \in \mathcal{B}_{\sigma_{5,2},q+1}$ and $A' = \{u_1, u_2, u_3, u_4, u_6\} \in \mathcal{B}_{\sigma_{5,2},q+1}$. It then follows from Lemma 15.39 that

$$(\sigma_{3,1}^2 + \sigma_{3,2})(u_4 + u_5) = \sigma_{3,1}\sigma_{3,2} + \sigma_{3,3} = (\sigma_{3,1}^2 + \sigma_{3,2})(u_4 + u_6),$$

which gives

$$(\sigma_{3,1}^2 + \sigma_{3,2})(u_5 + u_6) = 0.$$

It then follows from Lemma 15.38 that $u_5 + u_6 = 0$, which is contrary to the assumption that $u_5 \neq u_6$. $\qquad\square$

The following result is an immediate consequence of Lemmas 15.37, 15.38 and 15.39.

Lemma 15.41. *Let $\{u_1, u_2, u_3\} \in \binom{U_{q+1}}{3}$ and $u_4, u_5 \in U_{q+1}$ such that $\sigma_{5,2} = 0$. Then none of $\sigma_{3,1}^2 + \sigma_{3,2}, \sigma_{3,1}\sigma_{3,2} + \sigma_{3,3}$ and $\sigma_{3,2}^2 + \sigma_{3,1}\sigma_{3,3}$ equals zero, and $u_4 \neq u_5$.*

Lemma 15.42. *Let $\{u_1, u_2, u_3\} \in \binom{U_{q+1}}{3}$ such that $(\sigma_{3,1}^2 + \sigma_{3,2})(\sigma_{3,1}\sigma_{3,2} + \sigma_{3,3})(\sigma_{3,2}^2 + \sigma_{3,1}\sigma_{3,3}) \neq 0$. Put $a = \frac{\sigma_{3,1}\sigma_{3,2} + \sigma_{3,3}}{\sigma_{3,1}^2 + \sigma_{3,2}}$ and $b = \frac{\sigma_{3,2}^2 + \sigma_{3,1}\sigma_{3,3}}{\sigma_{3,1}^2 + \sigma_{3,2}}$. Then $b \in U_{q+1}, \frac{b}{a^2} \in GF(q)$ and $\mathrm{Tr}_{q/2}\left(\frac{b}{a^2}\right) \equiv 1 + m \pmod 2$.*

Proof. First, it follows from Part 3 of Lemma 15.37 that $b \in U_{q+1}$. Next, observe that

$$\frac{b}{a^2} = \frac{u_1u_2}{(u_1 + u_2)^2} + \frac{u_2u_3}{(u_2 + u_3)^2} + \frac{u_3u_1}{(u_3 + u_1)^2} + 1. \tag{15.30}$$

The desired conclusion then follows from Lemma 15.35 and Equation (15.30). This completes the proof. $\qquad\square$

Lemma 15.43. *Let the notation and assumption be the same as in Lemma 15.42. Let $f(u)$ be the quadratic polynomial $u^2 + au + b \in \mathrm{GF}(q)[u]$. Then we have the following.*

(1) If m is odd, then f has no root in $U_{q+1} \setminus \{\sqrt{b}\}$.
(2) If m is even, then f has exactly two roots in U_{q+1}.

Proof. Let m be odd. Suppose that there exists an $u \in U_{q+1} \setminus \{\sqrt{b}\}$ such that $f(u) = 0$. Then

$$\left(\frac{u}{\sqrt{b}}\right)^2 + \frac{a}{\sqrt{b}} \left(\frac{u}{\sqrt{b}}\right) + 1 = 0.$$

From Lemma 15.34 and $\frac{u}{\sqrt{b}} \in U_{q+1} \setminus \{1\} \subseteq \mathrm{GF}(q^2) \setminus \mathrm{GF}(q)$, we have that $\mathrm{Tr}_{q/2}\left(\frac{b}{a^2}\right) = 1$, which is contrary to the result of Lemma 15.42.

Let m be even. By Lemmas 15.34 and 15.42, there exists $u' \in \mathrm{GF}(q^2) \setminus \mathrm{GF}(q)$ such that u', u'^q are exactly the two solutions of the quadratic equation $T^2 + \frac{a}{\sqrt{b}}T + 1 = 0$. It is easily checked that $u_4 = \sqrt{b}u'$ and $u_5 = \sqrt{b}u'^q$ are the two roots of f. Then the result follows from $u'^{q+1} = 1$. This completes the proof. $\qquad\square$

Combining Lemmas 15.41, 15.39, and 15.43 gives the following.

Lemma 15.44. *Let m be odd and $\{u_1, u_2, u_3, u_4, u_5\} \in \binom{U_{q+1}}{5}$. Then $\sigma_{5,2} \neq 0$.*

Lemma 15.45. *Let m be even and $\{u_1, u_2, u_3\} \in \binom{U_{q+1}}{3}$. Let u_4, u_5 be the two solutions of the quadratic equation $u^2 + au + b = 0$, where $a = \frac{\sigma_{3,1}\sigma_{3,2} + \sigma_{3,3}}{\sigma_{3,1}^2 + \sigma_{3,2}}$ and $b = \frac{\sigma_{3,2}^2 + \sigma_{3,1}\sigma_{3,3}}{\sigma_{3,1}^2 + \sigma_{3,2}}$. Then*

$$\{u_1, u_2, u_3, u_4, u_5\} \in \mathcal{B}_{\sigma_{5,2}, q+1}.$$

Proof. First, employing Lemmas 15.37, 15.38, and 15.43, we have that $u_4, u_5 \in U_{q+1}$ and $u_4 \neq u_5$. Using $\sigma_{5,2} = u_4 u_5 + (u_4 + u_5)\sigma_{3,1} + \sigma_{3,2}$ and Vieta's formulas yields

$$\sigma_{5,2} = \frac{\sigma_{3,2}^2 + \sigma_{3,1}\sigma_{3,3}}{\sigma_{3,1}^2 + \sigma_{3,2}} + \frac{\sigma_{3,1}\sigma_{3,2} + \sigma_{3,3}}{\sigma_{3,1}^2 + \sigma_{3,2}} \sigma_{3,1} + \sigma_{3,2} = 0.$$

Suppose that $u_4 = u_i$ and $u_5 = u_j$ for some $i, j \in \{1, 2, 3\}$. By symmetry, let $(i, j) = (3, 2)$. Then

$$\sigma_{5,2} = u_3 u_4 + u_2 u_5 = u_2^2 + u_3^2 = 0,$$

which is contrary to $u_2 \neq u_3$. Thus, $|\{u_1, u_2, u_3\} \cap \{u_4, u_5\}| \neq 2$.

Suppose that $|\{u_1, u_2, u_3\} \cap \{u_4, u_5\}| = 1$. By the symmetry of u_1, u_2, u_3, let $u_5 = u_3$ and $u_4 \notin \{u_1, u_2, u_3\}$. Then $\sigma_{5,2}(u_1, u_2, u_4, u_5, u_3) = 0$. Note that $\{u_1, u_2, u_4\} \in \binom{U_{q+1}}{3}$ and $u_5 = u_3$, which is contrary to Lemma 15.41. Thus, $|\{u_1, u_2, u_3\} \cap \{u_4, u_5\}| \neq 1$. Hence, $\{u_1, u_2, u_3, u_4, u_5\} \in \binom{U_{q+1}}{5}$. This completes the proof. □

Lemma 15.46. *Let* $\{u_1, u_2, u_3, u_4\} \in \binom{U_{q+1}}{4}$. *Then* $\sigma_{4,3}\sigma_{4,1} \neq 0$ *and* $(\sigma_{4,3} + u_i\sigma_{4,2})(\sigma_{4,2} + u_i\sigma_{4,1}) \neq 0$, *where* $i \in \{1, 2, 3, 4\}$.

Proof. Note that

$$\sigma_{4,3}\sigma_{4,1} = \sigma_{4,4}\sigma_{4,1}^{q+1}.$$

By Part 1 of Lemma 15.36, we have $\sigma_{4,3}\sigma_{4,1} \neq 0$.

Note that $(\sigma_{4,3} + u_i\sigma_{4,2})(\sigma_{4,2} + u_i\sigma_{4,1}) = u_i\sigma_{4,4}(\sigma_{4,2} + u_i\sigma_{4,1})^{q+1}$. We only need to prove that $\sigma_{4,2} + u_i\sigma_{4,1} \neq 0$. On the contrary, suppose that $\sigma_{4,2} + u_i\sigma_{4,1} = 0$. Using the symmetry of u_1, u_2, u_3, u_4, choose $u_i = u_4$. Then $\sigma_{3,2} + u_4^2 = u_1u_2 + u_2u_3 + u_3u_1 + u_4^2 = 0$, which is contrary to Part 1 of Lemma 15.36 if $u_4^2 \notin \{u_1u_2, u_2u_3, u_3u_1\}$. If $u_4^2 \in \{u_1u_2, u_2u_3, u_3u_1\}$, due to symmetry suppose that $u_4^2 = u_1u_2$. It then follows from $u_1u_2 + u_2u_3 + u_3u_1 + u_4^2 = 0$ that $u_1 = u_2$, which contradicts the assumption that $u_1 \neq u_2$. This completes the proof. □

The following result is a direct consequence of Lemma 15.46.

Lemma 15.47. *Let* $\{u_1, u_2, u_3, u_4\} \in \binom{U_{q+1}}{4}$. *Then* $\sqrt{\frac{\sigma_{4,3}}{\sigma_{4,1}}}, \frac{\sigma_{4,3} + u_i\sigma_{4,2}}{\sigma_{4,2} + u_i\sigma_{4,1}} \in U_{q+1}$, *where* $i \in \{1, 2, 3, 4\}$.

Lemma 15.48. *Let* $\{u_1, u_2, u_3, u_4\} \in \binom{U_{q+1}}{4}$. *Then*

$$\sigma_{6,3}\left(u_1, u_2, u_3, u_4, \sqrt{\frac{\sigma_{4,3}}{\sigma_{4,1}}}, \sqrt{\frac{\sigma_{4,3}}{\sigma_{4,1}}}\right) = 0$$

and

$$\sigma_{6,3}\left(u_1, u_2, u_3, u_4, \frac{\sigma_{4,3} + u_i\sigma_{4,2}}{\sigma_{4,2} + u_i\sigma_{4,1}}, u_i\right) = 0,$$

where $i \in \{1, 2, 3, 4\}$.

Proof. Set $u_5 = u_6 = \sqrt{\frac{\sigma_{4,3}}{\sigma_{4,1}}}$. Then

$$\begin{aligned}
\sigma_{6,3}(u_1, u_2, u_3, u_4, u_5, u_6) &= \sigma_{4,3} + (u_5 + u_6)\sigma_{4,2} + u_5u_6\sigma_{4,1} \\
&= \sigma_{4,3} + u_5^2\sigma_{4,1} \\
&= 0.
\end{aligned}$$

Thus, $\sigma_{6,3}\left(u_1,u_2,u_3,u_4,\sqrt{\frac{\sigma_{4,3}}{\sigma_{4,1}}},\sqrt{\frac{\sigma_{4,3}}{\sigma_{4,1}}}\right)=0$.

Choose $\sigma_5=\frac{\sigma_{4,3}+u_i\sigma_{4,2}}{\sigma_{4,2}+u_i\sigma_{4,1}}$ and $\sigma_6=u_i$. Then

$$\sigma_{6,3}=\sigma_{4,3}+(u_5+u_6)\sigma_{4,2}+u_5u_6\sigma_{4,1}$$

$$=\sigma_{4,3}+\left(\frac{\sigma_{4,3}+u_i\sigma_{4,2}}{\sigma_{4,2}+u_i\sigma_{4,1}}+u_i\right)\sigma_{4,2}+\frac{\sigma_{4,3}+u_i\sigma_{4,2}}{\sigma_{4,2}+u_i\sigma_{4,1}}u_i\sigma_{4,1}$$

$$=0.$$

This completes the proof. $\qquad\square$

Lemma 15.49. *Let $\{u_1,u_2,u_3,u_4\}\in\binom{U_{q+1}}{4}$ such that $\sigma_{5,2}(u_1,u_2,u_3,u_4,u_5)\neq 0$ for any $u_5\in U_{q+1}\setminus\{u_1,u_2,u_3,u_4\}$. Let S be the subset of U_{q+1} given by*

$$\left\{\frac{\sigma_{4,3}+u_i\sigma_{4,2}}{\sigma_{4,2}+u_i\sigma_{4,1}}:i=1,2,3,4\right\}\cup\{u_i:i=1,2,3,4\}\cup\left\{\sqrt{\frac{\sigma_{4,3}}{\sigma_{4,1}}}\right\}.$$

Then $|S|=9$.

Proof. First, we prove that $\sqrt{\frac{\sigma_{4,3}}{\sigma_{4,1}}}\neq u_4$. On the contrary, suppose that $\sqrt{\frac{\sigma_{4,3}}{\sigma_{4,1}}}=u_4$. Then

$$\sigma_{4,1}u_4^2+\sigma_{4,3}=0,$$

which is the same as

$$u_4^3+\sigma_{3,1}u_4^2+\sigma_{3,2}u_4+\sigma_{3,3}=0.$$

Then,

$$(u_4+u_1)(u_4+u_2)(u_4+u_3)=0,$$

which is contrary to the assumption that $\{u_1,u_2,u_3,u_4\}\in\binom{U_{q+1}}{4}$. Thus $\sqrt{\frac{\sigma_{4,3}}{\sigma_{4,1}}}\neq u_4$. By the symmetry of u_1,u_2,u_3,u_4,

$$\sqrt{\frac{\sigma_{4,3}}{\sigma_{4,1}}}\neq u_i \text{ for all } i. \qquad (15.31)$$

Suppose that $\frac{\sigma_{4,3}+u_4\sigma_{4,2}}{\sigma_{4,2}+u_4\sigma_{4,1}}=u_4$. Then $u_4=\sqrt{\frac{\sigma_{4,3}}{\sigma_{4,1}}}$, which is contrary to Inequality (15.31). Thus, $\frac{\sigma_{4,3}+u_4\sigma_{4,2}}{\sigma_{4,2}+u_4\sigma_{4,1}}\neq u_4$. By the symmetry of u_1,u_2,u_3,u_4,

$$\frac{\sigma_{4,3}+u_i\sigma_{4,2}}{\sigma_{4,2}+u_i\sigma_{4,1}}\neq u_i \text{ for all } i. \qquad (15.32)$$

Suppose that $\frac{\sigma_{4,3}+u_4\sigma_{4,2}}{\sigma_{4,2}+u_4\sigma_{4,1}} = u_3$. Then $\sigma_{4,3} + u_4\sigma_{4,2} + u_3(\sigma_{4,2} + u_4\sigma_{4,1}) = 0$, which is the same as $(u_3 + u_4)^2(u_1 + u_2) = 0$. This is contrary to our assumption that $\{u_1,u_2,u_3,u_4\} \in \binom{U_{q+1}}{4}$. Thus, $\frac{\sigma_{4,3}+u_4\sigma_{4,2}}{\sigma_{4,2}+u_4\sigma_{4,1}} \neq u_3$. By the symmetry of u_1,u_2,u_3,u_4,

$$\frac{\sigma_{4,3}+u_i\sigma_{4,2}}{\sigma_{4,2}+u_i\sigma_{4,1}} \neq u_j \text{ for all } i \neq j. \tag{15.33}$$

Suppose that $\frac{\sigma_{4,3}+u_i\sigma_{4,2}}{\sigma_{4,2}+u_i\sigma_{4,1}} = \sqrt{\frac{\sigma_{4,3}}{\sigma_{4,1}}}$ for some $i \in \{1,2,3,4\}$. Put $u_5 = \sqrt{\frac{\sigma_{4,3}}{\sigma_{4,1}}}$. It follows from Inequality (15.31) that $u_5 \notin \{u_1,u_2,u_3,u_4\}$. By Lemma 15.48, we have

$$\begin{cases} \sigma_{6,3}\left(u_1,u_2,u_3,u_4,u_5,u_i\right) = 0, \\ \sigma_{6,3}\left(u_1,u_2,u_3,u_4,u_5,\sqrt{\frac{\sigma_{4,3}}{\sigma_{4,1}}}\right) = 0. \end{cases}$$

By the assumption of this lemma, $\sigma_{5,2}(u_1,u_2,u_3,u_4,u_5) \neq 0$. Thus,

$$\begin{cases} u_i = \frac{\sigma_{5,3}}{\sigma_{5,2}}, \\ \sqrt{\frac{\sigma_{4,3}}{\sigma_{4,1}}} = \frac{\sigma_{5,3}}{\sigma_{5,2}}, \end{cases}$$

which is contrary to Inequality (15.31). Hence,

$$\frac{\sigma_{4,3}+u_i\sigma_{4,2}}{\sigma_{4,2}+u_i\sigma_{4,1}} \neq \sqrt{\frac{\sigma_{4,3}}{\sigma_{4,1}}}. \tag{15.34}$$

Assume that $\frac{\sigma_{4,3}+u_i\sigma_{4,2}}{\sigma_{4,2}+u_i\sigma_{4,1}} = \frac{\sigma_{4,3}+u_j\sigma_{4,2}}{\sigma_{4,2}+u_j\sigma_{4,1}}$ for some $i,j \in \{1,2,3,4\}$. Put $u_5 = \frac{\sigma_{4,3}+u_i\sigma_{4,2}}{\sigma_{4,2}+u_i\sigma_{4,1}}$. It follows from Inequalities (15.32) and (15.33) that $u_5 \notin \{u_1,u_2,u_3,u_4\}$. By Lemma 15.48, we have

$$\begin{cases} \sigma_{6,3}\left(u_1,u_2,u_3,u_4,u_5,u_i\right) = 0, \\ \sigma_{6,3}\left(u_1,u_2,u_3,u_4,u_5,u_j\right) = 0. \end{cases}$$

By the assumption of this lemma, $\sigma_{5,2}(u_1,u_2,u_3,u_4,u_5) \neq 0$. Thus,

$$\begin{cases} u_i = \frac{\sigma_{5,3}}{\sigma_{5,2}}, \\ u_j = \frac{\sigma_{5,3}}{\sigma_{5,2}}. \end{cases}$$

Then $i = j$. Hence,

$$\frac{\sigma_{4,3}+u_i\sigma_{4,2}}{\sigma_{4,2}+u_i\sigma_{4,1}} \neq \frac{\sigma_{4,3}+u_j\sigma_{4,2}}{\sigma_{4,2}+u_j\sigma_{4,1}}, \text{ for } i \neq j. \tag{15.35}$$

The desired conclusion then follows from Inequalities (15.31), (15.32), (15.33), (15.34) and (15.35). This completes the proof.

$$\square$$

Lemma 15.50. *Let m be even, and let $\{u'_1, u'_2, u'_3, u'_4, u'_5\} \in \mathcal{B}_{\sigma_{5,2},q+1}$ and $u_5, u_6 \in U_{q+1}$ such that $\sigma_{6,3}(u'_1, u'_2, u'_3, u'_4, u_5, u_6) = 0$. Then $u'_5 \in \{u_5, u_6\}$.*

Proof. Suppose that $u'_5 \notin \{u_5, u_6\}$. From Lemmas 15.38 and 15.39, it follows that $\sigma_{5,2}(u'_1, u'_2, u'_3, u'_4, u_5) \neq 0$. We have

$$\begin{cases} \sigma_{6,3}\left(u'_1, u'_2, u'_3, u'_4, u_5, u'_5\right) = 0, \\ \sigma_{6,3}\left(u'_1, u'_2, u'_3, u'_4, u_5, u_6\right) = 0, \end{cases}$$

which is the same as

$$\begin{cases} u'_5 = \frac{\sigma_{5,3}(u'_1, u'_2, u'_3, u'_4, u_5)}{\sigma_{5,2}(u'_1, u'_2, u'_3, u'_4, u_5)}, \\ u_6 = \frac{\sigma_{5,3}(u'_1, u'_2, u'_3, u'_4, u_5)}{\sigma_{5,2}(u'_1, u'_2, u'_3, u'_4, u_5)}. \end{cases}$$

This is contrary to our assumption that $u'_5 \notin \{u_5, u_6\}$. This completes the proof. $\qquad\square$

Lemma 15.51. *Let $\{u_1, u_2, u_3, u_4\} \in \binom{U_{q+1}}{4}$ such that $\sigma_{5,2}(u_1, u_2, u_3, u_4, u_5) \neq 0$ for any $u_5 \in U_{q+1} \setminus \{u_1, u_2, u_3, u_4\}$. Then*

$$\frac{\sigma_{5,3}\left(u_1, u_2, u_3, u_4, \sqrt{\frac{\sigma_{4,3}}{\sigma_{4,1}}}\right)}{\sigma_{5,2}\left(u_1, u_2, u_3, u_4, \sqrt{\frac{\sigma_{4,3}}{\sigma_{4,1}}}\right)} = \sqrt{\frac{\sigma_{4,3}}{\sigma_{4,1}}},$$

and

$$\frac{\sigma_{5,3}\left(u_1, u_2, u_3, u_4, \frac{\sigma_{4,3}+u_i\sigma_{4,2}}{\sigma_{4,2}+u_i\sigma_{4,1}}\right)}{\sigma_{5,2}\left(u_1, u_2, u_3, u_4, \frac{\sigma_{4,3}+u_i\sigma_{4,2}}{\sigma_{4,2}+u_i\sigma_{4,1}}\right)} = u_i,$$

where $i \in \{1, 2, 3, 4\}$.

Proof. The claim follows from Lemma 15.48. $\qquad\square$

We will need the following lemma whose proof is straightforward.

Lemma 15.52. *Let the set $\{u_1, u_2, u_3, u_4\} \in \binom{U_{q+1}}{4}$ and $u_5 \in U_{q+1}$ such that $\sigma_{5,2}(u_1, u_2, u_3, u_4, u_5) \neq 0$. Let $u_6 = \frac{\sigma_{5,3}(u_1, u_2, u_3, u_4, u_5)}{\sigma_{5,2}(u_1, u_2, u_3, u_4, u_5)}$. Then we have the following.*

(1) If $u_6 = u_5$, then $u_5 = \sqrt{\frac{\sigma_{4,3}}{\sigma_{4,1}}}$.

(2) If $u_6 = u_i$, then $u_5 = \frac{\sigma_{4,3}+u_i\sigma_{4,2}}{\sigma_{4,2}+u_i\sigma_{4,1}}$, where $i \in \{1, 2, 3, 4\}$.

Lemma 15.53. *Let m be an even integer and $\{u_1, u_2, u_3, u_4\} \in \binom{U_{q+1}}{4}$ such that $\sigma_{5,2}(u_1, u_2, u_3, u_4, u_5) \neq 0$ for any $u_5 \in U_{q+1} \setminus \{u_1, u_2, u_3, u_4\}$. Let S be the subset of U_{q+1} given by*

$$\left\{ \frac{\sigma_{4,3} + u_i \sigma_{4,2}}{\sigma_{4,2} + u_i \sigma_{4,1}} : i = 1, 2, 3, 4 \right\} \cup \{u_i : i = 1, 2, 3, 4\} \cup \left\{ \sqrt{\frac{\sigma_{4,3}}{\sigma_{4,1}}} \right\}.$$

Let $\tilde{u}_4$ and $\tilde{u}_5$ be the two solutions of the quadratic equation $u^2 + au + b = 0$, where $a = \frac{\sigma_{3,1}\sigma_{3,2} + \sigma_{3,3}}{\sigma_{3,1}^2 + \sigma_{3,2}}$ and $b = \frac{\sigma_{3,2}^2 + \sigma_{3,1}\sigma_{3,3}}{\sigma_{3,1}^2 + \sigma_{3,2}}$. Then $\tilde{u}_4 \notin S$ and $\tilde{u}_5 \notin S$.

Proof. By the definition of $\tilde{u}_4, \tilde{u}_5$ and Lemma 15.39, $u_4 \notin \{\tilde{u}_4, \tilde{u}_5\}$. Suppose that $\tilde{u}_4 = \sqrt{\frac{\sigma_{4,3}}{\sigma_{4,1}}}$. From Lemma 15.48 or 15.51, we get

$$\sigma_{6,3}\left(u_1, u_2, u_3, u_4, \tilde{u}_4, \sqrt{\frac{\sigma_{4,3}}{\sigma_{4,1}}}\right) = 0.$$

From Lemma 15.50 and $\tilde{u}_5 \neq u_4$, it follows that $\tilde{u}_5 = \sqrt{\frac{\sigma_{4,3}}{\sigma_{4,1}}} = \tilde{u}_4$, which is contrary to $a \neq 0$. Thus, $\tilde{u}_4 \neq \sqrt{\frac{\sigma_{4,3}}{\sigma_{4,1}}}$. By the symmetry of $\tilde{u}_4$ and $\tilde{u}_5$, $\tilde{u}_5 \neq \sqrt{\frac{\sigma_{4,3}}{\sigma_{4,1}}}$.

Suppose that $\tilde{u}_4 = \frac{\sigma_{4,3} + u_i \sigma_{4,2}}{\sigma_{4,2} + u_i \sigma_{4,1}}$. From Lemma 15.48 or 15.51, we have

$$\sigma_{6,3}(u_1, u_2, u_3, u_4, u_i, \tilde{u}_4) = 0.$$

From Lemma 15.50 and $\tilde{u}_5 \neq u_4$, it follows that $\tilde{u}_5 = u_i$, which is contrary to the definition of $\tilde{u}_5$. Thus, $\tilde{u}_4 \neq \frac{\sigma_{4,3} + u_i \sigma_{4,2}}{\sigma_{4,2} + u_i \sigma_{4,1}}$. By the symmetry of $\tilde{u}_4$ and $\tilde{u}_5$, $\tilde{u}_5 \neq \frac{\sigma_{4,3} + u_i \sigma_{4,2}}{\sigma_{4,2} + u_i \sigma_{4,1}}$. This completes the proof. $\square$

Proof of Theorem 15.29. Recall Theorem 15.29 first. Let $\{u_1, u_2, u_3, u_4\}$ be a fixed 4-subset of U_{q+1}. Set

$$S = \left\{ \frac{\sigma_{4,3} + u_i \sigma_{4,2}}{\sigma_{4,2} + u_i \sigma_{4,1}} : i = 1, 2, 3, 4 \right\} \cup \{u_i : i = 1, 2, 3, 4\} \cup \left\{ \sqrt{\frac{\sigma_{4,3}}{\sigma_{4,1}}} \right\}.$$

For any $u_5 \notin \{u_i : i = 1, 2, 3, 4\}$, $\sigma_{5,2}(u_1, u_2, u_3, u_4, u_5) \neq 0$ from Lemma 15.44. Define

$$\mathcal{T} = \left\{ \left\{ u_5, \frac{\sigma_{5,3}(u_1, u_2, u_3, u_4, u_5)}{\sigma_{5,2}(u_1, u_2, u_3, u_4, u_5)} \right\} : u_5 \in U_{q+1} \setminus S \right\}.$$

From Lemmas 15.51 and 15.52, it follows that $\frac{\sigma_{5,3}(u_1, u_2, u_3, u_4, u_5)}{\sigma_{5,2}(u_1, u_2, u_3, u_4, u_5)} \notin S$ if $u_5 \notin S$. By Lemma 15.49, $|\mathcal{T}| = \frac{(q+1-9)}{2}$. From Lemma 15.52 and $\frac{\sigma_{5,3}(u_1, u_2, u_3, u_4, u_5)}{\sigma_{5,2}(u_1, u_2, u_3, u_4, u_5)} \in U_{q+1}$, we deduce that $\{u_1, u_2, u_3, u_4, u_5, u_6\} \in \mathcal{B}_{\sigma_{6,3}, q+1}$ for any $\{u_5, u_6\} \in \mathcal{T}$.

On the other hand, let $\{u_1, u_2, u_3, u_4, u_5, u_6\} \in \mathcal{B}_{\sigma_{6,3}, q+1}$. Employing Lemma 15.51, $\{u_5, u_6\} \in \mathcal{T}$. Thus, $\{u_1, u_2, u_3, u_4, u_5, u_6\} \in \mathcal{B}_{\sigma_{6,3}, q+1}$ if and only if $\{u_5, u_6\} \in \mathcal{T}$. Hence, $(U_{q+1}, \mathcal{B}_{\sigma_{6,3}, q+1})$ is a 4-$\left(q+1, 6, \frac{q-8}{2}\right)$ design. This completes the proof. $\square$

Proof of Theorem 15.30. Recall Theorem 15.30 first. Let $\{u_1, u_2, u_3\}$ be a fixed 3-subset of U_{q+1}. By Lemmas 15.39 and 15.45, $\{u_1, u_2, u_3, u_4, u_5\} \in \mathcal{B}_{\sigma_{6,3}, q+1}$ if and only if u_4 and u_5 are the two solutions of the quadratic equation $u^2 + au + b = 0$ in U_{q+1}, where $a = \frac{\sigma_{3,1}\sigma_{3,2} + \sigma_{3,3}}{\sigma_{3,1}^2 + \sigma_{3,2}}$ and $b = \frac{\sigma_{3,2}^2 + \sigma_{3,1}\sigma_{3,3}}{\sigma_{3,1}^2 + \sigma_{3,2}}$. Hence, $(U_{q+1}, \mathcal{B}_{\sigma_{5,2}, q+1})$ is a Steiner System $S(3, 5, q+1)$. This completes the proof. □

Proof of Theorem 15.31. Recall Theorem 15.31 first. For a 3-subset $\{u_1, u_2, u_3\}$ of U_{q+1}, let $Q(u_1, u_2, u_3)$ denote the 2-subset

$$\{u \in U_{q+1} : u^2 + au + b = 0\},$$

where $a = \frac{\sigma_{3,1}\sigma_{3,2} + \sigma_{3,3}}{\sigma_{3,1}^2 + \sigma_{3,2}}$ and $b = \frac{\sigma_{3,2}^2 + \sigma_{3,1}\sigma_{3,3}}{\sigma_{3,1}^2 + \sigma_{3,2}}$. Next, let $\{u_1, u_2, u_3\}$ be fixed. Set

$$\mathcal{T}_1^0 = \{S^0 \cup \{u_6\} : u_6 \in U_{q+1} \setminus S^0\},$$

and

$$\mathcal{T}_{i,j}^0 = \{\{u_1, u_2, u_3, u_4\} \cup Q(u_i, u_j, u_4) : u_4 \in U_{q+1} \setminus S^0\},$$

where $1 \leq i < j \leq 3$ and $S^0 = \{u_1, u_2, u_3\} \cup Q(u_1, u_2, u_3)$. Let $\mathcal{T}^0 = \mathcal{T}_1^0 \cup \mathcal{T}_{1,2}^0 \cup \mathcal{T}_{1,3}^0 \cup \mathcal{T}_{2,3}^0$. It is easily checked that $\{u_1, u_2, u_3, u_4, u_5, u_6\} \in \mathcal{B}_{\sigma_{6,3}, q+1}$ if and only if $\{u_1, u_2, u_3, u_4, u_5, u_6\} \in \mathcal{T}^0$. Note that $|\mathcal{T}_1^0| = q - 4$ and $|\mathcal{T}_{i,j}^0| = \frac{q-4}{3}$, where $1 \leq i < j \leq 3$. From Lemma 15.40, it follows that $\mathcal{T}_1^0$, $\mathcal{T}_{1,2}^0$, $\mathcal{T}_{1,3}^0$ and $\mathcal{T}_{2,3}^0$ are pairwise disjoint. Then $(U_{q+1}, \mathcal{B}_{\sigma_{6,3}, q+1})$ is a 3-$(q+1, 6, 2(q-4))$ design.

Let $\{u_1, u_2, u_3\}$ be a fixed 3-subset of U_{q+1}. Define

$$\mathcal{T}^1 = \{\{u_1, u_2, u_3, u_4, u_5, u_6\} : u_4 \in U_{q+1} \setminus S^0, u_5 \in U_{q+1} \setminus (S^0 \cup S^1)\},$$

where $S^0 = \{u_1, u_2, u_3\} \cup Q(u_1, u_2, u_3)$, $S^1 = \left\{\frac{\sigma_{4,3} + u_i \sigma_{4,2}}{\sigma_{4,2} + u_i \sigma_{4,1}} : 1 \leq i \leq 4\right\} \cup \left\{\sqrt{\frac{\sigma_{4,3}}{\sigma_{4,1}}}\right\}$, and

$$u_6 = \frac{\sigma_{5,3}(u_1, u_2, u_3, u_4, u_5)}{\sigma_{5,2}(u_1, u_2, u_3, u_4, u_5)}.$$

Let $\mathcal{T} = \mathcal{T}_1^0 \cup \mathcal{T}^1$. It is easily checked that $B \in \mathcal{B}_{\sigma_{6,3}, q+1}$ if and only if $B \in \mathcal{T}$. Note that $|\mathcal{T}_1^0| = q - 4$ and $|\mathcal{T}^1| = \frac{(q+1-|S^0|)(q+1-|S^0 \cup S^1|)}{6}$. By Lemmas 15.49 and 15.53, $|S^0 \cup S^1| = 11$. From Lemma 15.40, it follows that $\mathcal{T}_1^0$ and $\mathcal{T}^1$ are disjoint. Then $(U_{q+1}, \mathcal{B}_{\sigma_{6,3}, q+1})$ is a 3-$\left(q+1, 6, \frac{(q-4)^2}{6}\right)$ design. This completes the proof. □

15.3.3.2 *Infinite Families of BCH Codes Holding t-Designs for t ∈ {3,4}*

Throughout this section, let $q = 2^m$, where m is a positive integer. We consider the narrow-sense BCH code $C_{(q,q+1,4,1)}$ over $\mathrm{GF}(q)$ and its dual, and prove that they are almost MDS, and support 4-designs when $m \geq 5$ is odd and 3-designs when $m \geq 4$ is even.

For a positive integer ℓ, define a $6 \times \ell$ matrix M_ℓ by

$$\begin{bmatrix} u_1^{-3} & u_2^{-3} & \cdots & u_\ell^{-3} \\ u_1^{-2} & u_2^{-2} & \cdots & u_\ell^{-2} \\ u_1^{-1} & u_2^{-1} & \cdots & u_\ell^{-1} \\ u_1^{+1} & u_2^{+1} & \cdots & u_\ell^{+1} \\ u_1^{+2} & u_2^{+2} & \cdots & u_\ell^{+2} \\ u_1^{+3} & u_2^{+3} & \cdots & u_\ell^{+3} \end{bmatrix}, \tag{15.36}$$

where these $u_1, \cdots, u_\ell \in U_{q+1}$. For $r_1, \cdots, r_i \in \{\pm 1, \pm 2, \pm 3\}$, let $M_\ell[r_1, \cdots, r_i]$ denote the submatrix of M_ℓ obtained by deleting the rows $(u_1^{r_1}, u_2^{r_1}, \cdots, u_\ell^{r_1}), \cdots,$ $(u_1^{r_i}, u_2^{r_i}, \cdots, u_\ell^{r_i})$ of the matrix M_ℓ.

Lemma 15.54. *Let M_ℓ be the matrix given by (15.36) with $\{u_1, \cdots, u_\ell\} \in \binom{U_{q+1}}{\ell}$. Consider the system of homogeneous linear equations defined by*

$$M_\ell(x_1, \cdots, x_\ell)^T = 0. \tag{15.37}$$

Then Equation (15.37) has a nonzero solution $(x_1, \cdots, x_\ell)$ in $\mathrm{GF}(q)^\ell$ if and only if $\mathrm{rank}(M_\ell) < \ell$, where $\mathrm{rank}(M_\ell)$ denotes the rank of the matrix M_ℓ.

Proof. It is obvious that $\mathrm{rank}(M_\ell) < \ell$ if Equation (15.37) has a nonzero solution $(x_1, \cdots, x_\ell)$ in $\mathrm{GF}(q)^\ell$.

Conversely, assume that $\mathrm{rank}(M_\ell) < \ell$. Then there exists a nonzero vector $\mathbf{x}' = (x_1', \cdots, x_\ell') \in \mathrm{GF}(q^2)^\ell$ such that $M_\ell \mathbf{x}'^T = 0$. Choose an $i_0 \in \{1, \cdots, \ell\}$ such that $x_{i_0}' \neq 0$. Put

$$\mathbf{x} = (x_1'' + x_1''^q, \cdots, x_{i_0}'' + x_{i_0}''^q, \cdots, x_\ell'' + x_\ell''^q),$$

where $(x_1'', \cdots, x_\ell'') = \frac{\alpha}{x_{i_0}'} \mathbf{x}'$ and α is a primitive element of $\mathrm{GF}(q^2)$. It is easily checked that $M_\ell \mathbf{x}^T = 0$ and $\mathbf{x} \in \mathrm{GF}(q)^\ell \setminus \{\mathbf{0}\}$. This completes the proof. $\quad\square$

Lemma 15.55. *Let M_4 be the matrix given by (15.36) with $\{u_1, u_2, u_3, u_4\} \in \binom{U_{q+1}}{4}$. Then $\mathrm{rank}(M_4) = 4$.*

Proof. Suppose that $\mathrm{rank}(M_4) < 4$. Then $\det(M_4[2,3]) = \frac{\prod_{1 \leq i < j \leq 4}(u_i + u_j)}{\sigma_{4,4}^3}(u_1 + u_2 + u_3 + u_4) = 0$, which is contrary to Lemma 15.36. This completes the proof. $\quad\square$

Lemma 15.56. *Let M_5 be the matrix given by (15.36) with $\{u_1, \cdots, u_5\} \in \binom{U_{q+1}}{5}$. Then $\operatorname{rank}(M_5) = 4$ if and only if $\sigma_{5,2}(u_1, \cdots, u_5) = 0$.*

Proof. First, note that

$$
\begin{cases}
\det(M_5[3]) &= \frac{\prod_{1 \le i < j \le 5}(u_i + u_j)}{\sigma_{5,5}^3} \sigma_{5,2}, \\[2mm]
\det(M_5[2]) &= \frac{\prod_{1 \le i < j \le 5}(u_i + u_j)}{\sigma_{5,5}^3} \left(\sigma_{5,1}\sigma_{5,2} + \sigma_{5,5}\sigma_{5,2}^q \right), \\[2mm]
\det(M_5[1]) &= \frac{\prod_{1 \le i < j \le 5}(u_i + u_j)}{\sigma_{5,5}^3} \left(\sigma_{5,1}\sigma_{5,5}\sigma_{5,2}^q + \sigma_{5,2}^2 \right), \\[2mm]
\det(M_5[-3]) &= \frac{\prod_{1 \le i < j \le 5}(u_i + u_j)}{\sigma_{5,5}} \sigma_{5,2}^q, \\[2mm]
\det(M_5[-2]) &= \frac{\prod_{1 \le i < j \le 5}(u_i + u_j)}{\sigma_{5,5}} \left(\sigma_{5,1}^q \sigma_{5,2}^q + \sigma_{5,5}^q \sigma_{5,2} \right), \\[2mm]
\det(M_5[-1]) &= \frac{\prod_{1 \le i < j \le 5}(u_i + u_j)}{\sigma_{5,5}} \left(\sigma_{5,1}^q \sigma_{5,5}^q \sigma_{5,2} + \sigma_{5,2}^{2q} \right).
\end{cases}
$$

The desired conclusion then follows from Lemma 15.55. This completes the proof. $\qquad\square$

Lemma 15.57. *Let M_6 be the matrix given by (15.36) with $\{u_1, \cdots, u_6\} \in \binom{U_{q+1}}{6}$. Then $\operatorname{rank}(M_6) < 6$ if and only if $\sigma_{6,3}(u_1, \cdots, u_6) = 0$.*

Proof. Note that

$$
\det(M_6) = \frac{\prod_{1 \le i < j \le 6}(u_i + u_j)}{\sigma_{6,6}^3} \sigma_{6,3},
$$

which completes the proof. $\qquad\square$

Lemma 15.58. *Let m be even and M_6 be the matrix given by (15.36) with $\{u_1, \cdots, u_6\} \in \binom{U_{q+1}}{6}$. Let $\{u_1, \cdots, u_6\} \in \mathcal{B}_{\sigma_{6,3}, q+1}^1$, where $\mathcal{B}_{\sigma_{6,3}, q+1}^1$ was defined by (15.26). Then the set of all solutions of the system $M_6(x_1, \cdots, x_6)^T = 0$ over $\mathrm{GF}(q)^6$ is*

$$
\{(ax_1, \cdots, ax_6) : a \in \mathrm{GF}(q)\},
$$

where $(x_1, \cdots, x_6)$ is a vector in $(\mathrm{GF}(q)^*)^6$.

Proof. Let $\{u_1, \cdots, u_6\} \in \mathcal{B}_{\sigma_{6,3}, q+1}^1$. By Lemma 15.57, $\operatorname{rank}(M_6) < 6$. By Lemma 15.54, there exists a nonzero $(x_1, \cdots, x_6) \in \mathrm{GF}(q)^6$ such that $M_6(x_1, \cdots, x_6)^T = 0$. Suppose that there is an i ($1 \le i \le 6$) such that $x_i = 0$. Then the submatrix of the matrix M_6 obtained by deleting the i-th column has rank less than 5, which is contrary to Lemma 15.56 and the definition of $\mathcal{B}_{\sigma_{6,3}, q+1}^1$. Thus, for any nonzero solution $(x_1, \cdots, x_6) \in \mathrm{GF}(q)^6$, we have $x_i \ne 0$, where $1 \le i \le 6$. The desired conclusion then follows. This completes the proof.

$\qquad\square$

Lemma 15.59. *Let m be even and M_6 be the matrix given by (15.36) with $\{u_1, \cdots, u_6\} \in \binom{U_{q+1}}{6}$. If there exists a vector $(x_1, \cdots, x_6) \in (GF(q)^*)^6$ such that $M_6(x_1, \cdots, x_6)^T = 0$, then $\{u_1, \cdots, u_6\} \in \mathcal{B}^1_{\sigma_{6,3}, q+1}$, where $\mathcal{B}^1_{\sigma_{6,3}, q+1}$ was defined by (15.26).*

Proof. From Lemma 15.57, it follows that $\{u_1, \cdots, u_6\} \in \mathcal{B}_{\sigma_{6,3}, q+1}$. Suppose that $\{u_1, \cdots, u_6\} \in \mathcal{B}^0_{\sigma_{6,3}, q+1}$. Without loss of generality, let $\sigma_{5,2}(u_1, \cdots, u_5) = 0$. By Lemmas 15.54 and 15.56, there exists a nonzero $(x'_1, \cdots, x'_5) \in GF(q)^5$ such that $M_5(x'_1, \cdots, x'_5)^T = 0$, that is, $M_6(x'_1, \cdots, x'_5, 0)^T = 0$. Note that

$$M_6\left(x_1 + \frac{x_1}{x'_1}x'_1, \cdots, x_5 + \frac{x_1}{x'_1}x'_5, x_6 + \frac{x_1}{x'_1}0\right)^T = 0.$$

Applying Lemma 15.56, we have $\sigma_{5,2}(u_2, \cdots, u_6) = 0$, which is contrary to Lemma 15.40 and $\sigma_{5,2}(u_1, \cdots, u_5) = 0$. This completes the proof. $\square$

Lemma 15.60. *Let $f(u) = \mathrm{Tr}_{q^2/q}\left(au^3 + bu^2 + cu\right)$ where $(a, b, c) \in GF(q^2)^3 \setminus \{\mathbf{0}\}$. Define $\mathrm{zero}(f) = \{u \in U_{q+1} : f(u) = 0\}$. Then $|\mathrm{zero}(f)| \leq 6$. Moreover, $|\mathrm{zero}(f)| = 6$ if and only if $a = \frac{\tau}{\sqrt{\sigma_{6,6}}}$, $b = \frac{\tau\sigma_{6,1}}{\sqrt{\sigma_{6,6}}}$ and $c = \frac{\tau\sigma_{6,2}}{\sqrt{\sigma_{6,6}}}$, where $\{u_1, \cdots, u_6\} \in \mathcal{B}_{\sigma_{6,3}, q+1}$ and $\tau \in GF(q)^*$.*

Proof. When $u \in U_{q+1}$, we have

$$f(u) = \frac{1}{u^3}\left(au^6 + bu^5 + cu^4 + c^q u^2 + b^q u + a^q\right). \tag{15.38}$$

Thus, $|\mathrm{zero}(f)| \leq 6$.

Assume that $|\mathrm{zero}(f)| = 6$. From (15.38), there exists $\{u_1, \cdots, u_6\} \in U_{q+1}$ such that $f(u) = \frac{a\prod_{i=1}^6 (u+u_i)}{u^3}$. By Vieta's formula, $b = a\sigma_{6,1}$, $c = a\sigma_{6,2}$, $0 = \sigma_{6,3}$, $c^q = a\sigma_{6,6}\sigma_{6,2}^q$, $b^q = a\sigma_{6,6}\sigma_{6,1}^q$ and $a^q = a\sigma_{6,6}$. We obtain $a = \frac{\tau}{\sqrt{\sigma_{6,6}}}$ from $a^{q-1} = \sigma_{6,6}$, where $\tau \in GF(q)^*$. Then $b = \frac{\tau\sigma_{6,1}}{\sqrt{\sigma_{6,6}}}$ and $c = \frac{\tau\sigma_{6,2}}{\sqrt{\sigma_{6,6}}}$.

Conversely, assume that $a = \frac{\tau}{\sqrt{\sigma_{6,6}}}$, $b = \frac{\tau\sigma_{6,1}}{\sqrt{\sigma_{6,6}}}$ and $c = \frac{\tau\sigma_{6,2}}{\sqrt{\sigma_{6,6}}}$, where $\{u_1, \cdots, u_6\} \in \mathcal{B}_{\sigma_{6,3}, q+1}$ and $\tau \in GF(q)^*$. Then $f(u) = \frac{a\prod_{i=1}^6(u+u_i)}{u^3}$. Thus, $\mathrm{zero}(f) = \{u_1, \cdots, u_6\}$ and $|\mathrm{zero}(f)| = 6$. $\square$

We are now ready to prove the following result about the code $\mathcal{C}_{(q,q+1,4,1)}$.

Theorem 15.61. *Let $m \geq 4$ be an integer. Then the narrow-sense BCH code $\mathcal{C}_{(q,q+1,4,1)}$ over $GF(q)$ has parameters $[q+1, q-5, d]$, where $d = 6$ if m is odd and $d = 5$ if m is even.*

Proof. Put $n = q + 1$. Let α be a generator of $\mathrm{GF}(q^2)^*$ and $\beta = \alpha^{q-1}$. Then β is a primitive n-th root of unity in $\mathrm{GF}(q^2)$, that is, β is a generator of the cyclic group U_{q+1}. Let $g_i(x)$ denote the minimal polynomial of β^i over $\mathrm{GF}(q)$, where $i \in \{1, 2, 3\}$. Note that $g_i(x)$ has only the roots β^i and β^{-i}. We deduce that $g_1(x)$, $g_2(x)$ and $g_3(x)$ are pairwise distinct irreducible polynomials of degree 2. By definition, $g(x) := g_1(x)g_2(x)g_3(x)$ is the generator polynomial of $\mathcal{C}_{(q,q+1,4,1)}$. Therefore, the dimension of $\mathcal{C}_{(q,q+1,4,1)}$ is $q + 1 - 6$. Note that $g(x)$ has only the roots $\beta^{-3}, \beta^{-2}, \beta^{-1}, \beta, \beta^2$ and β^3. By the BCH bound, the minimum weight of $\mathcal{C}_{(q,q+1,4,1)}$ is at least 4. Put $\gamma = \beta^{-1}$. Then $\gamma^{q+1} = \beta^{-(q+1)} = 1$. It then follows from Delsarte's theorem that the trace expression of $\mathcal{C}_{(q,q+1,4,1)}^{\perp}$ is given by

$$\mathcal{C}_{(q,q+1,4,1)}^{\perp} = \{\mathbf{c}_{(a,b,c)} : a, b, c \in \mathrm{GF}(q^2)\}, \tag{15.39}$$

where $\mathbf{c}_{(a,b,c)} = (\mathrm{Tr}_{q^2/q}(a\gamma^i + b\gamma^{2i} + c\gamma^{3i}))_{i=0}^{q}$.
Define

$$H = \begin{bmatrix} 1 & \gamma^{-3} & \gamma^{-6} & \gamma^{-9} & \cdots & \gamma^{-3q} \\ 1 & \gamma^{-2} & \gamma^{-4} & \gamma^{-6} & \cdots & \gamma^{-2q} \\ 1 & \gamma^{-1} & \gamma^{-2} & \gamma^{-3} & \cdots & \gamma^{-q} \\ 1 & \gamma^{+1} & \gamma^{+2} & \gamma^{+3} & \cdots & \gamma^{+q} \\ 1 & \gamma^{+2} & \gamma^{+4} & \gamma^{+6} & \cdots & \gamma^{+2q} \\ 1 & \gamma^{+3} & \gamma^{+6} & \gamma^{+9} & \cdots & \gamma^{+3q} \end{bmatrix}. \tag{15.40}$$

It is easily seen that H is a parity-check matrix of $\mathcal{C}_{(q,q+1,4,1)}$, i.e.,

$$\mathcal{C}_{(q,q+1,4,1)} = \{\mathbf{c} \in \mathrm{GF}(q)^{q+1} : \mathbf{c}H^T = \mathbf{0}\}. \tag{15.41}$$

Let m be odd. Note that $d \geq 4$. Suppose that $d = 4$. Then there exist $\{u_1, \cdots, u_4\} \in \binom{U_{q+1}}{4}$ and $(x_1, \cdots, x_4) \in (\mathrm{GF}(q)^*)^4$ such that $M_4(x_1, \cdots, x_4)^T = 0$. Thus $\mathrm{rank}(M_4) < 4$, which is contrary to Lemma 15.55. Suppose that $d = 5$. Then there exist $\{u_1, \cdots, u_5\} \in \binom{U_{q+1}}{5}$ and $(x_1, \cdots, x_5) \in (\mathrm{GF}(q)^*)^5$ such that $M_5(x_1, \cdots, x_5)^T = 0$. By Lemma 15.56, $\mathrm{rank}(M_5) < 5$ and $\sigma_{5,2} = 0$, which is contrary to Lemma 15.44. Thus, $d \geq 6$. By Theorem 15.29, $\mathcal{B}_{\sigma_{6,3},q+1} \neq \emptyset$. Choose $\{u_1, \cdots, u_6\} \in \mathcal{B}_{\sigma_{6,3},q+1}$. By Lemma 15.54, there exists $(x_1, \cdots, x_6) \in (\mathrm{GF}(q)^*)^6$ such that $M_6(x_1, \cdots, x_6)^T = 0$. Set $\mathbf{c} = (c_1, \cdots, c_{q+1})$ where

$$c_i = \begin{cases} x_j, & \text{if } i = i_j, \\ 0, & \text{otherwise,} \end{cases} \tag{15.42}$$

where γ^{i_j} is given by $u_j = \gamma^{i_j}$ ($j \in \{1, \cdots, 6\}$). By (15.41), $\mathbf{c} \in \mathcal{C}_{(q,q+1,4,1)}$ and $\mathrm{wt}(\mathbf{c}) = 6$. Thus, $d = 6$.

The proof for the even m case is similar to that for the odd m case and the detail is omitted. This completes the proof. $\qquad\square$

Theorem 15.62. *Let* $m \geq 4$ *and* $C^{\perp}_{(q,q+1,4,1)}$ *be the dual of the narrow-sense BCH code* $C_{(q,q+1,4,1)}$ *over* GF(q). *Then* $C^{\perp}_{(q,q+1,4,1)}$ *has parameters* $[q+1,6,q-5]$. *In particular,* $C_{(q,q+1,4,1)}$ *is a near MDS code if* m *is odd.*

Proof. From Theorems 15.29 and 15.31, $\mathcal{B}_{\sigma_{6,3},q+1} \neq \emptyset$. The desired conclusion then follows from Lemma 15.60 and Equation (15.39). This completes the proof. $\square$

Theorem 15.63. *Let* $m \geq 5$ *be odd. Then the incidence structure*

$$\left(\mathcal{P}\left(C_{(q,q+1,4,1)} \right), \mathcal{B}_6\left(C_{(q,q+1,4,1)} \right) \right)$$

of the minimum weight codewords in $C_{(q,q+1,4,1)}$ *is isomorphic to* $(U_{q+1}, \mathcal{B}_{\sigma_{6,3},q+1})$.

Proof. With the help of Lemma 15.57, the desired conclusion then follows by a similar discussion as in the proof of Theorem 15.61. This completes the proof. $\square$

The theorem below made a breakthrough in 71 years, as it presented the first family of linear codes supporting an infinite family of 4-designs after the first linear code holding a 4-design discovered by Golay (1949).

Theorem 15.64 (Tang and Ding (2021)). *Let* $m \geq 5$ *be odd. Then the minimum weight codewords in* $C_{(q,q+1,4,1)}$ *support a* 4-$(q+1, 6, (q-8)/2)$ *design and the minimum weight codewords in* $C^{\perp}_{(q,q+1,4,1)}$ *support a* 4-$(q+1, q-5, \lambda)$ *design with*

$$\lambda = \frac{q-8}{30}\binom{q-5}{4}.$$

Proof. The desired conclusion follows from Theorems 15.63, 15.29 and 15.12. This completes the proof. $\square$

Example 15.65. Let $m = 5$. Then $C_{(q,q+1,4,1)}$ has parameters $[33, 27, 6]$. The dual $C^{\perp}_{(q,q+1,4,1)}$ has parameters $[33, 6, 27]$ and weight distribution

$$1 + 1014816z^{27} + 1268520z^{28} + 20296320z^{29} + 64609952z^{30} +$$
$$210132384z^{31} + 399584823z^{32} + 376835008z^{33}.$$

The codewords of weight 6 in $C_{(q,q+1,4,1)}$ supports a 4-$(33, 6, 12)$ design, and the codewords of weight 27 in $C^{\perp}_{(q,q+1,4,1)}$ support a 4-$(33, 27, 14040)$ design.

In Example 15.65, the code $C_{(q,q+1,4,1)}$ has a codeword of weight i for all i with $6 \leq i \leq 33$. Hence, the Assmus-Mattson Theorem cannot be used to prove that the codes in Theorem 15.64 support 4-designs. It is an open problem whether the generalised Assmus-Mattson theorem (i.e., Theorem 16.28) can be used to prove that the codes in Theorem 15.64 support 4-designs. It looks impossible to prove that the codes in Theorem 15.64 support 4-designs with the automorphism groups of the codes due to the following:

(1) Except the Mathieu groups M11, M12, M23, M24, the alternating group A_n and the symmetric group S_n, no finite permutation groups are more than 3-transitive.
(2) No infinite family of 4-homogeneous permutation groups is known.

It would be a very interesting problem to determine the automorphism groups of the codes in Theorem 15.64.

Theorem 15.66 (Yan and Zhou (2021)). *Let $m \geq 5$ be odd. Then the codewords of weight 7 in $C_{(q,q+1,4,1)}$ support a 4-$(q+1,7,\lambda)$ design with*

$$\lambda = \binom{q-3}{3} - \frac{7(q-5)(q-8)}{6}.$$

The codewords of weight $q-4$ in $C_{(q,q+1,4,1)}^{\perp}$ support a 4-$(q+1,q-4,\binom{q-4}{4})$ design whose complementary design has parameters 4-$(q+1,5,5)$.

To present an infinite class of linear codes supporting Steiner systems $S(3,5,4^m+1)$, we prove the following theorem.

Theorem 15.67. *Let $m \geq 4$ be even. Then the incidence structure*

$$\left(\mathcal{P}\left(C_{(q,q+1,4,1)}\right), \mathcal{B}_5\left(C_{(q,q+1,4,1)}\right)\right)$$

of the minimum weight codewords in $C_{(q,q+1,4,1)}$ is isomorphic to $(U_{q+1}, \mathcal{B}_{\sigma_{5,2},q+1})$, and the incidence structure

$$\left(\mathcal{P}\left(C_{(q,q+1,4,1)}\right), \mathcal{B}_6\left(C_{(q,q+1,4,1)}\right)\right)$$

is isomorphic to $(U_{q+1}, \mathcal{B}_{\sigma_{6,3},q+1}^1)$. Moreover, the incidence structure

$$\left(\mathcal{P}\left(C_{(q,q+1,4,1)}^{\perp}\right), \mathcal{B}_{q-5}\left(C_{(q,q+1,4,1)}^{\perp}\right)\right)$$

is isomorphic to the complementary incidence structure of $(U_{q+1}, \mathcal{B}_{\sigma_{6,3},q+1})$.

Proof. Using Lemma 15.56, by a similar discussion as in the proof of Theorem 15.61, we can prove that the incidence structure

$$\left(\mathcal{P}\left(C_{(q,q+1,4,1)}\right), \mathcal{B}_5\left(C_{(q,q+1,4,1)}\right)\right)$$

is isomorphic to $(U_{q+1}, \mathcal{B}_{\sigma_{5,2},q+1})$. Employing Lemma 15.59, we can prove that

$$\left(\mathcal{P}\left(C_{(q,q+1,4,1)}\right), \mathcal{B}_6\left(C_{(q,q+1,4,1)}\right)\right)$$

is isomorphic to $(U_{q+1}, \mathcal{B}_{\sigma_{6,3},q+1}^1)$. The last statement then follows from Equation (15.39) and Lemma 15.60. This completes the proof. $\square$

The following theorem documents an infinite class of linear codes supporting Steiner systems $S(3, 5, 4^m + 1)$.

Theorem 15.68 (Tang and Ding (2021)). *Let $m \geq 4$ be an even integer. Then the minimum weight codewords in $C_{(q,q+1,4,1)}$ support a 3-$(q+1,5,1)$ design, i.e., a Steiner system $S(3, 5, q+1)$, and the minimum weight codewords in $C_{(q,q+1,4,1)}^{\perp}$ support a 3-$(q+1, q-5, \lambda)$ design with*

$$\lambda = \frac{(q-4)^2}{120} \binom{q-5}{3}.$$

Furthermore, all the codewords of Hamming weight 6 in $C_{(q,q+1,4,1)}$ support a 3-$\left(q+1, 6, \frac{(q-4)(q-16)}{6}\right)$ *design if $m \geq 6$.*

Proof. The desired conclusion follows from Theorems 15.67, 15.30, 15.31 and Corollary 15.32. This completes the proof. □

The Steiner system $S(3, 5, 4^m + 1)$ documented in Theorem 15.68 is isomorphic to the spherical geometry design with the same parameters (see Section 15.5). The contribution of Theorem 15.68 is a coding-theoretic construction of the spherical geometry design $S(3, 5, 4^m + 1)$.

Example 15.69. Let $m = 4$. Then $C_{(q,q+1,4,1)}$ has parameters $[17, 11, 5]$ and weight distribution

$$1 + 1020z^5 + 224400z^7 + 3730650z^8 + 55370700z^9 + 669519840z^{10} +$$
$$6378704640z^{11} + 47857084200z^{12} + 276083558100z^{13} + 1183224112800z^{14} +$$
$$3549668972400z^{15} + 6655630071165z^{16} + 5872614694500z^{17}.$$

The codewords of weight 5 in $C_{(q,q+1,4,1)}$ support a Steiner system $S(3, 5, 17)$.
The dual $C_{(q,q+1,4,1)}^{\perp}$ has parameters $[17, 6, 11]$ and weight distribution

$$1 + 12240z^{11} + 35700z^{12} + 244800z^{13} + 1203600z^{14} +$$
$$3292560z^{15} + 6398715z^{16} + 5589600z^{17}.$$

The codewords of weight 11 in $C_{(q,q+1,4,1)}^{\perp}$ support a 3-$(17, 11, 198)$ design.

This example shows that the Assmus-Mattson Theorem cannot be used to prove that the codes $C_{(q,q+1,4,1)}$ and $C_{(q,q+1,4,1)}^{\perp}$ support 3-designs. It is an open question if the generalised Assmus-Mattson theorem (i.e., Theorem 16.28) can be used to prove that the codes in Theorem 15.68 support 4-designs.

Theorem 15.70 (Yan and Zhou (2021)). *Let $m \geq 4$ be even. Then the codewords of weight 7 in $C_{(q,q+1,4,1)}$ support a 3-$(q+1, 7, \lambda)$ design with*

$$\lambda = \binom{q-2}{4} - \frac{7(q-4)(q-5)(q-10)}{24}.$$

15.4   Sporadic Designs from Near MDS Codes

Below are two near MDS codes holding 3-designs and 4-designs. It is open if they belong to an infinite family of near MDS codes holding 3-designs and 4-designs, respectively.

Example 15.71. Let $q = 9$. The extended narrow-sense BCH code $\overline{C_{(9,19,2,1)}}$ has parameters $[20,10,10]$ and weight enumerator

$$1 + 10,98496z^{10} + 358720z^{11} + 2416800z^{12} + 12366720z^{13} +$$
$$49211520z^{14} + 155149440z^{15} + 393012720z^{16} + 734679840z^{17} +$$
$$982376000z^{18} + 826436160z^{19} + 330677984z^{20}.$$

The code is formally self-dual, but not self-dual. The code holds simple designs with the following parameters

$$3\text{-}(20,10,1296) \text{ and } 3\text{-}(20,11,6490).$$

Example 15.72. Let $q = 32$. The narrow-sense BCH code $C_{(q,q+1,4,1)}$ has parameters $[33,27,6]$. The dual code $C_{(q,q+1,4,1)}^{\perp}$ has parameters $[33,6,27]$ and weight enumerator

$$1 + 1014816z^{27} + 1268520z^{28} + 20296320z^{29} + 64609952z^{30} +$$
$$210132384z^{31} + 399584823z^{32} + 376835008z^{33}.$$

Hence, $C_{(q,q+1,4,1)}$ and $C_{(q,q+1,4,1)}^{\perp}$ are NMDS. Their minimum weight codewords support a 4-$(33,6,12)$ design and a 4-$(33,27,14040)$ design, respectively.

15.5   Designs from Almost MDS Codes

In this section, we summarise AMDS codes which are not NMDS but hold t-designs. We treat only infinite families of such codes. Unfortunately, for such AMDS codes we do not have a general theorem like Theorem 15.18 for NMDS codes. The following is a list of such families of AMDS codes holding t-designs:

(a) The Hamming code over GF(q) with parameters $[q^2 + q + 1, q^2 + q - 2, 3]$ whose dual is the $[q^2 + q + 1, 3, q^2]$ Simplex code, which is not AMDS for $q > 3$. The codes hold 2-designs (see Section 10.5.4).
(b) The dual of the $[q^2 + 1, 4, q^2 - q]$ ovoid code over GF(q) with parameters $[q^2 + 1, q^2 - 3, 4]$, where q is even. The codes hold 3-designs (see Section 13.4).

(c) The extended narrow-sense primitive BCH code $\overline{C_{(q,q^2-1,2,1)}}$ with parameters $[q^2, q^2-3, 3]$. The dual code $\overline{C_{(q,q^2-1,2,1)}}^{\perp}$ has parameters $[q^2, 3, q^2-q]$ and weight enumerator $1 + (q^3-q)z^{q^2-q} + (q-1)z^{q^2}$, and is not AMDS when $q > 3$. The dual code $\overline{C_{(q,q^2-1,2,1)}}^{\perp}$ is the generalised first-order Reed-Muller code. The codes hold 2-designs.

(d) A family of $[q^2, q^2-4, 4]$ AMDS codes over GF(q) supporting 2-designs. The dual codes have parameters $[q^2, 4, q^2-q-1]$ [Heng, Wang and Ding (2020)].

(e) The AMDS code $C_{(2^{2s}, 2^{2s}+1,4,1)}^{\perp}$ with parameters $[2^{2s}+1, 6, 2^{2s}-5]$ for $s \geq 2$ in Theorem 15.68. The minimum weight codewords of this code support a 3-$(2^{2s}+1, 2^{2s}-5, \lambda)$ design with

$$\lambda = \frac{(2^{2s}-4)^2}{120} \binom{2^{2s}-5}{3}.$$

The following theorem was developed by Ding, Tang and Tonchev (2020).

Theorem 15.73. *Let $q = 2^m$ and $m \geq 4$ be even. Then the following hold.*

(a) *The BCH code $C_{(q,q+1,3,(q-4)/2)}$ has parameters $[q+1, q-3, 4]$ (an AMDS code). Its minimum weight codewords support a 3-$(q+1, 4, 2)$ design.*

(b) *The dual code $C_{(q,q+1,3,(q-4)/2)}^{\perp}$ has parameters $[q+1, 4, q-4]$ (not AMDS). Its minimum weight codewords support a 3-$(q+1, q-4, \lambda)$ design, where*

$$\lambda = \frac{(q-4)(q-5)(q-6)}{60},$$

whose complement is a Steiner system $S(3, 5, q+1)$.

As a generalisation of Theorems 15.22 and 15.68, we have the following coding-theoretic construction of the spherical geometry designs.

Theorem 15.74 (Liu, Ding, Mesnager, Tang and Tonchev (2021)). *Let $r \geq 3$ be a power of a prime p and let $m \geq 2$ be an integer. Then the narrow-sense BCH code $C_{(r^m, r^m+1, r, 1)}$ has parameters $[r^m+1, r^m-2r+3, r+1]$ and the dual code $C_{(r^m, r^m+1, r, 1)}^{\perp}$ has parameters $[r^m+1, 2r-2, r^m-2r+3]$. Furthermore, the minimum weight codewords in $C_{(r^m, r^m+1, r, 1)}$ support a 3-$(r^m+1, r+1, 1)$ design which is isomorphic to the spherical geometry design with the same parameters and has p-rank r^m+1.*

Chapter 16

Beyond the Assmus-Mattson Theorem

The Assmus-Mattson theorem was developed in 1969 and has been one of the two major tools for constructing t-designs from linear codes. In Section 8.5, it was shown that some linear codes holding t-designs do not satisfy the conditions in the Assmus-Mattson theorem and their automorphism groups are not t-transitive or t-homogeneous. Another family of such codes was given by Ding, Munemasa and Tonchev (2019). To prove that these codes hold t-designs in a uniform way, Tang, Ding and Xiong (2019) generalized the old Assmus-Mattson theorem and demonstrated the usefulness of the generalized Assmus-Mattson theorem. The objective of this chapter is to introduce the work of Tang, Ding and Xiong (2019), which also gives a different proof of the Assmus-Mattson theorem. The reader is warned that t-designs in this chapter are **not simple** in general, but are simple under certain conditions. Notice that in other chapters only simple designs are treated.

16.1   Introduction of Notation and Notions for This Chapter

Let $\mathcal{P}$ be a set of v elements and $\mathcal{B}$ a **multiset** of b k-subsets of $\mathcal{P}$, where $v \geq 1$, $b \geq 0$ and $1 \leq k \leq v$. Let t be a positive integer satisfying $1 \leq t \leq v$. The pair $\mathbb{D} = (\mathcal{P}, \mathcal{B})$ is called a t-(v, k, λ) *design*, or simply t-*design*, if every t-subset of $\mathcal{P}$ is contained in exactly λ elements of $\mathcal{B}$. The elements of $\mathcal{P}$ are called *points*, and those of $\mathcal{B}$ are referred to as *blocks*.

When $\mathcal{B} = \emptyset$, i.e., $b = 0$, we put $\lambda = 0$ and call $(\mathcal{P}, \emptyset)$ a t-$(v, k, 0)$ design for any t and k with $1 \leq t \leq v$ and $0 \leq k \leq v$. A t-(v, k, λ) design with $t > k$ must have $\lambda = 0$ and must be the design $(\mathcal{P}, \emptyset)$. These designs are called trivial designs. We will use the following conventions for the ease of description in the sequel. A t-(v, k, λ) design $(\mathcal{P}, \mathcal{B})$ is also said to be trivial if every k-subset of $\mathcal{P}$ is a block. Notice that trivial designs of this chapter have more types and are broader.

A t-design is called *simple* if $\mathcal{B}$ does not contain repeated blocks. A t-(v,k,λ) design is called a *Steiner system* and denoted by $S(t,k,v)$ if $t \geq 2$ and $\lambda = 1$. The parameters of a t-(v,k,λ) design satisfy:

$$\binom{v}{t}\lambda = \binom{k}{t}b.$$

Let C be a $[v,k,d]$ linear code over $\mathrm{GF}(q)$. Let $A_i := A_i(C)$, which denotes the number of codewords with Hamming weight i in C, where $0 \leq i \leq v$. The sequence $(A_0, A_1, \cdots, A_v)$ is called the *weight distribution* of C, and $\sum_{i=0}^{v} A_i z^i$ is referred to as the *weight enumerator* of C. Then the q-ary linear code C may induce a t-design under certain conditions, which is formed by the supports of codewords of a fixed Hamming weight in C. Let $\mathcal{P}(C) = \{0, 1, \ldots, v-1\}$ be the set of the coordinate positions of C, where v is the length of C. For a codeword $\mathbf{c} = (c_0, \ldots, c_{v-1})$ in C, the *support* of $\mathbf{c}$ is defined by

$$\mathrm{Supp}(\mathbf{c}) = \{i : c_i \neq 0, i \in \mathcal{P}(C)\}.$$

Let $\mathcal{B}_w(C) = \frac{1}{q-1}\{\{\mathrm{Supp}(\mathbf{c}) : wt(\mathbf{c}) = w \text{ and } \mathbf{c} \in C\}\}$, here and hereafter $\{\{\}\}$ is the multiset notation and $\frac{1}{q-1}S$ denotes the multiset obtained after dividing the multiplicity of each element in the multiset S by $q-1$. For some special C, $(\mathcal{P}(C), \mathcal{B}_w(C))$ is a t-(v,w,λ) design with b blocks, where

$$b = \frac{1}{q-1}A_w,$$

$$\lambda = \frac{\binom{w}{t}}{(q-1)\binom{v}{t}}A_w, \tag{16.1}$$

which follow from the definition of the block set $\mathcal{B}_w(C)$.

If $(\mathcal{P}(C), \mathcal{B}_w(C))$ is a t-design for any $0 \leq w \leq v$, we say that the code C *supports t-designs*. This terminology has also a special meaning in this chapter. Notice that such a design $(\mathcal{P}(C), \mathcal{B}_w(C))$ may have repeated blocks or may be simple or trivial.

16.2   The Assmus-Mattson Theorem in the Languge of This Chapter

In the language of Section 16.1, the original Assmus-Mattson theorem becomes the following.

Theorem 16.1. *Let C be a linear code over $\mathrm{GF}(q)$ with length v and minimum weight d. Let $C^\perp$ with minimum weight $d^\perp$ denote the dual code of C. Let t $(1 \leq t < \min\{d, d^\perp\})$ be an integer such that there are at most $d^\perp - t$ weights of C in $\{1, 2, \ldots, v-t\}$. Then $(\mathcal{P}(C), \mathcal{B}_k(C))$ and $(\mathcal{P}(C^\perp), \mathcal{B}_k(C^\perp))$ are t-designs for all $k \in \{0, 1, \ldots, v\}$.*

Notice that some of the designs in Theorem 16.1 may have **repeated** blocks or may be **trivial** in the senses defined in Section 16.1. The following lemma provides a criterion for obtaining a simple block set $\mathcal{B}_k(C)$, and is a special case of Lemma 4.25.

Lemma 16.2. *Let C be a linear code over $GF(q)$ with length v and minimum weight d. Let w be the largest integer with $w \leq v$ satisfying*

$$w - \left\lfloor \frac{w+q-2}{q-1} \right\rfloor < d.$$

Then there are no repeated blocks in $\mathcal{B}_k(C)$ for any $d \leq k \leq w$. Such a block set is said to be simple.

Combining Theorem 16.1 and Lemma 16.2, we obtain the following Assmus-Mattson theorem for constructing **simple** t-designs [Assmus and Mattson (1969)].

Theorem 16.3. *Let C be a linear code over $GF(q)$ with length v and minimum weight d. Let $C^\perp$ with minimum weight $d^\perp$ denote the dual code of C. Let t $(1 \leq t < \min\{d, d^\perp\})$ be an integer such that there are at most $d^\perp - t$ weights of C in the range $\{1, 2, \ldots, v - t\}$. Then the following holds:*

- *$(\mathcal{P}(C), \mathcal{B}_k(C))$ is a simple t-design provided that $A_k \neq 0$ and $d \leq k \leq w$, where w is defined to be the largest integer satisfying $w \leq v$ and*

$$w - \left\lfloor \frac{w+q-2}{q-1} \right\rfloor < d. \tag{16.2}$$

- *$(\mathcal{P}(C^\perp), \mathcal{B}_k(C^\perp))$ is a simple t-design provided that $A_k^\perp \neq 0$ and $d^\perp \leq k \leq w^\perp$, where $w^\perp$ is defined to be the largest integer satisfying $w^\perp \leq v$ and*

$$w^\perp - \left\lfloor \frac{w^\perp + q - 2}{q-1} \right\rfloor < d^\perp. \tag{16.3}$$

Note that Theorem 16.3 is the same as Theorem 4.24, as $\mathcal{B}_k(C)$ and $\mathcal{B}_k(C^\perp)$ do not have repeated blocks under the conditions of (16.2) and (16.3), respectively.

16.3 New Notation of Intersection Numbers of Designs

The intersection numbers of designs were introduced in Section 4.1.5. For the convenience of this chapter, we introduce intersection sets and new symbols of intersection numbers of designs.

Let $\mathbb{D} = (\mathcal{P}, \mathcal{B})$ be a t-(v, k, λ) design. Let T_0 and T_1 be two disjoint subsets of $\mathcal{P}$ with $|T_0| = t_0$ and $|T_1| = t_1$. Denote by $\lambda_{T_1}^{T_0}$ the number of blocks in $\mathcal{B}$ that contain T_1 and are disjoint with T_0. These numbers $\lambda_{T_1}^{T_0}$ are called *intersection numbers*. For convenience, $\lambda_{T_1}^{\emptyset}$ and $\lambda_{\emptyset}^{T_0}$ are also written as λ_{T_1} and λ^{T_0} respectively.

With the new notation above, Theorem 4.11 becomes the following.

Theorem 16.4. *Let $(\mathcal{P}, \mathcal{B})$ be a t-(v, k, λ) design. Let $T_0, T_1 \subseteq \mathcal{P}$, where $T_0 \cap T_1 = \emptyset$, $|T_0| = t_0$, $|T_1| = t_1$, and $t_0 + t_1 \leq t$. Then the intersection numbers $\lambda_{T_1}^{T_0}$ are independent of the specific choice of the elements in T_0 and T_1, and depend only on t_0 and t_1. Specifically,*

$$\lambda_{T_1}^{T_0} = \lambda(t_0, t_1),$$

where $\lambda(t_0, t_1) = \dfrac{\binom{v - t_0 - t_1}{k - t_1}}{\binom{v - t}{k - t}} \lambda.$

16.4   Shortened and Punctured Codes of Linear Codes Supporting t-Designs

In general, linear codes that support t-designs should have a certain kind of regularity. Hence, we would expect that some of the punctured and shortened codes of such linear codes would also be attractive. By puncturing or shortening such a code, we might obtain linear codes with new and interesting parameters, and other possibly interesting properties as well. This is one of the motivations behind studying the punctured and shortened codes of linear codes that support t-designs. Another more important motivation is to develop a characterization for t-designs supported by linear codes, which will be done in Section 16.5.

In this section, we will first develop some general theory for some shortened and punctured codes of linear codes supporting t-designs, and will then use the general theory to determine the parameters and weight distributions of some shortened and punctured codes of two families of binary linear codes supporting 2-designs.

16.4.1   *General Results for Shortened and Punctured Codes of Linear Codes Supporting t-Designs*

In this subsection, we establish general results about shortened and punctured codes of linear codes supporting t-designs.

Recall that the binomial coefficient $\binom{a}{b}$ equals 0 when $a < b$ or $b < 0$. Let $\mathcal{W}_i(C)$ denote the set of codewords of weight i in a code C and $A_i(C)$ be the number of elements of $\mathcal{W}_i(C)$. We first give some results on the parameters and the weight distributions of shortened codes and punctured codes of linear codes supporting t-designs.

Lemma 16.5. *Let C be a linear code of length v and minimum distance d over* GF(q) *and $d^\perp$ the minimum distance of $C^\perp$. Let t and k be two positive integers with $0 < t < \min\{d, d^\perp\}$ and $1 \le k \le v - t$. Let T be a set of t coordinate positions in $\mathcal{P}(C)$. Suppose that $(\mathcal{P}(C), \mathcal{B}_i(C))$ is a t-design for all i with $k \le i \le k + t$. Then*

$$A_k(C^T) = \sum_{i=0}^{t} \frac{\binom{v-t}{k}\binom{k+i}{t}\binom{t}{i}}{\binom{v-t}{k-t+i}\binom{v}{t}} A_{k+i}(C).$$

Proof. Let π^T be the map from C to C^T defined as

$$\pi^T : C \longrightarrow C^T,$$

$$(c_i)_{i \in \mathcal{P}(C)} \longmapsto (c_i)_{i \in \mathcal{P}(C) \setminus T}.$$

By Theorem 2.8, π^T is a one-to-one linear transformation. Then

$$A_k(C^T) = \sum_{t_1=0}^{t} \sum_{T_1 \subseteq T, |T_1| = t_1} \mu_{T_1}(\mathcal{W}_{k+t_1}(C)),$$

where $\mu_{T_1}(\mathcal{W}_{k+t_1}(C))$ is equal to the number of codewords in $\mathcal{W}_{k+t_1}(C)$ that satisfy the conditions $c_i = 0$ if $i \in T \setminus T_1$ and $c_i \neq 0$ if $i \in T_1$. Note that $(\mathcal{P}(C), \mathcal{B}_{k+t_1}(C))$ is a t-$(v, k+t_1, \lambda)$ design with $\frac{1}{q-1} A_{k+t_1}(C)$ blocks, where $\lambda = \frac{\binom{k+t_1}{t}}{\binom{v}{t}} \frac{1}{q-1} A_{k+t_1}(C)$. Let $\lambda_{T_1}^{T \setminus T_1}$ be the intersection number of the t-design $(\mathcal{P}(C), \mathcal{B}_{k+t_1}(C))$. By Theorem 16.4, we have

$$\mu_{T_1}(\mathcal{W}_{k+t_1}(C)) = (q-1)\lambda_{T_1}^{T \setminus T_1}$$

$$= (q-1)\frac{\binom{v-t}{k+t_1-t_1}}{\binom{v-t}{k+t_1-t}}\lambda$$

$$= \frac{\binom{v-t}{k}\binom{k+t_1}{t}}{\binom{v-t}{k-t+t_1}\binom{v}{t}} A_{k+t_1}(C).$$

It then follows that

$$A_k(C^T) = \sum_{t_1=0}^{t} \binom{t}{t_1} \frac{\binom{v-t}{k}\binom{k+t_1}{t}}{\binom{v-t}{k-t+t_1}\binom{v}{t}} A_{k+t_1}(C).$$

$\square$

Theorem 16.6. *Let C be a $[v, m, d]$ linear code over* GF(q) *and $d^\perp$ the minimum distance of $C^\perp$. Let t be a positive integer with $0 < t < \min\{d, d^\perp\}$. Let T be a set of t coordinate positions in $\mathcal{P}(C)$. Suppose that $(\mathcal{P}(C), \mathcal{B}_i(C))$ is a t-design for any i with $d \le i \le v - t$. Then the shortened code C_T is a linear code of length $v - t$ and dimension $m - t$. The weight distribution $(A_k(C_T))_{k=0}^{v-t}$ of C_T is independent of the specific choice of the elements in T. Specifically,*

$$A_k(C_T) = \frac{\binom{k}{t}\binom{v-t}{k}}{\binom{v}{t}\binom{v-t}{k-t}} A_k(C).$$

Proof. Let $C(T) = \{(c_i)_{i \in \mathcal{P}(C)} \in C : c_i = 0 \text{ for each } i \in T\}$. Let π_T be the map from $C(T)$ to C_T defined as

$$\pi_T : C(T) \longrightarrow C_T,$$

$$(c_i)_{i \in \mathcal{P}(C)} \longmapsto (c_i)_{i \in \mathcal{P}(C) \setminus T}.$$

By the definition of $C(T)$ and C_T, the map π_T is a one-to-one linear transformation. Then

$$A_k(C_T) = \mu^T(\mathcal{W}_k(C)),$$

where $\mu^T(\mathcal{W}_k(C))$ is equal to the number of codewords in $\mathcal{W}_k(C)$ that satisfy the conditions $c_i = 0$ if $i \in T$. Note that $(\mathcal{P}(C), \mathcal{B}_k(C))$ is a t-(v, k, λ) design with $\frac{1}{q-1} A_k(C)$ blocks, where $\lambda = \frac{\binom{k}{t}}{\binom{v}{t}} \frac{1}{q-1} A_k(C)$. Let λ^T be the intersection number of the t-design $(\mathcal{P}(C), \mathcal{B}_k(C))$. By Theorem 16.4, we have

$$\mu^T(\mathcal{W}_k(C)) = (q-1)\lambda^T$$

$$= (q-1)\frac{\binom{v-t}{k}}{\binom{v-t}{k-t}}\lambda$$

$$= \frac{\binom{k}{t}\binom{v-t}{k}}{\binom{v}{t}\binom{v-t}{k-t}}A_k(C).$$

The desired conclusion then follows from $A_k(C_T) = \mu^T(\mathcal{W}_k(C))$ and Theorem 2.8. $\qquad\square$

Let $(\mathcal{P}(C), \mathcal{B}_k(C))$ be a t-(v, k, λ_k) design for some integer λ_k. From the proof of Theorem 16.6, we have the following

$$A_k(C_T) = \frac{\binom{v-t}{k}}{\binom{v-t}{k-t}}(q-1)\lambda_k, \tag{16.4}$$

where T is a set of t coordinate positions in $\mathcal{P}(C)$.

Theorem 16.7. *Let C be a $[v, m, d]$ linear code over $\mathrm{GF}(q)$ and $d^{\perp}$ the minimum distance of $C^{\perp}$. Let t be a positive integer with $0 < t < d^{\perp}$. Let T be a set of t coordinate positions in $\mathcal{P}(C)$. Suppose that $(\mathcal{P}(C), \mathcal{B}_i(C))$ is a t-design for any i with $d \leq i \leq v$. Then the punctured code C^T is a linear code of length $v - t$ and dimension m. The weight distribution $\left(A_k(C^T)\right)_{k=0}^{v-t}$ of C^T is independent of the specific choice of the elements in T. Specifically,*

$$A_k(C^T) = \sum_{i=0}^{t} \frac{\binom{v-t}{k}\binom{k+i}{i}\binom{t}{i}}{\binom{v-t}{k-t+i}\binom{v}{t}}A_{k+i}(C).$$

Proof. The desired results follow from Theorem 2.8 and Lemma 16.5. $\qquad\square$

Theorems 16.6 and 16.7 above settle the parameters and weight distribution of the shortened code C_T and punctured code C^T of a code C supporting t-designs, respectively. In general it could be very hard to determine the weight distribution of a shortened or punctured code of a linear code.

16.4.2 *Punctured and Shortened Codes of a Family of Binary Codes*

In this subsection, we determine the parameters and weight distributions of some punctured and shortened codes of a family of binary linear codes constructed from bent Boolean functions. As will be demonstrated shortly, the shortened and punctured codes are quite interesting.

Let n be even, f be a bent function from $\mathrm{GF}(2^n)$ to $\mathrm{GF}(2)$, and let $D_f = \{d_0, d_1, \ldots, d_{v_f-1}\} \subseteq \mathrm{GF}(2^n)$ be the support of f. Define a binary code of length v_f by

$$C(D_f) = \{(\mathrm{Tr}_{2^n/2}(xd_0) + y, \ldots, \mathrm{Tr}_{2^n/2}(xd_{v_f-1}) + y) : x \in \mathrm{GF}(2^n), y \in \mathrm{GF}(2)\}.$$

It is well-known that for a bent function f over $\mathrm{GF}(2^n)$ we have

$$v_f = |D_f| = 2^{n-1} \pm 2^{\frac{n-2}{2}}.$$

Let $\alpha \in \mathrm{GF}(2^n)$ be a non-cube. Then it is known in Mesnager (2016) that $f(x) = \mathrm{Tr}_{2^n/2}(\alpha x^3)$ is a bent function with v_f given by

$$v_f = 2^{n-1} + (-2)^{\frac{n-2}{2}}. \tag{16.5}$$

The following theorem was proved in Sections 14.8 and 14.9.

Theorem 16.8. *Let f be a bent function from $\mathrm{GF}(2^n)$ to $\mathrm{GF}(2)$, where $n \geq 6$ and is even. Then $C(D_f)$ is a $[v_f, n+1, (v_f - 2^{\frac{n-2}{2}})/2]$ three-weight binary code with the weight distribution in Table 16.1 and it holds 2-designs. The dual code $C(D_f)^\perp$ has minimum distance 4.*

Table 16.1 Weight distribution of $C(D_f)$ of Theorem 16.8

Weight	Multiplicity
0	1
$\frac{v_f}{2} - 2^{\frac{n-4}{2}}$	$2^n - 1$
$\frac{v_f}{2} + 2^{\frac{n-4}{2}}$	$2^n - 1$
v_f	1

Taking $T = \{t_1\}$, we have the parameters and the weight distribution of the shortened code $C(D_f)_{\{t_1\}}$ of $C(D_f)$ in the following theorem.

Theorem 16.9. *Let t_1 be an integer with $0 \leq t_1 < v_f$. Let f be a bent function from* $GF(2^n)$ *to* $GF(2)$, *where* $n \geq 6$ *and is even. Then, the shortened code* $C(D_f)_{\{t_1\}}$ *is a two-weight binary linear code of length* $v_f - 1$ *and dimension n, and has the weight distribution in Table 16.2.*

Table 16.2   Weight distribution of $C(D_f)_{\{t_1\}}$ of Theorem 16.9

Weight	Multiplicity
0	1
$\frac{v_f}{2} - 2^{\frac{n-4}{2}}$	$\frac{v_f + 2^{\frac{n-2}{2}}}{2v_f}(2^n - 1)$
$\frac{v_f}{2} + 2^{\frac{n-4}{2}}$	$\frac{v_f - 2^{\frac{n-2}{2}}}{2v_f}(2^n - 1)$

Proof. By Theorem 16.6 and the weight distribution of $C(D_f)$,

$$A_k(C(D_f)_{\{t_1\}}) = \frac{v_f - k}{v_f} A_k(C(D_f)).$$

The desired results follow from Theorem 16.8.   □

Taking $T = \{t_1, t_2\}$, we have the parameters and the weight distribution of the shortened code $C(D_f)_{\{t_1, t_2\}}$ of $C(D_f)$ in the following theorem.

Theorem 16.10. *Let t_1 and t_2 be integers with $0 \leq t_1 < t_2 < v_f$. Let f be a bent function from* $GF(2^n)$ *to* $GF(2)$, *where* $n \geq 6$ *and is even. Then, the shortened code* $C(D_f)_{\{t_1, t_2\}}$ *is a two-weight binary linear code of length* $v_f - 2$ *and dimension* $n - 1$, *and has the weight distribution in Table 16.3.*

Table 16.3   Weight distribution of $C(D_f)_{\{t_1, t_2\}}$ of Theorem 16.10

Weight	Multiplicity
0	1
$\frac{v_f}{2} - 2^{\frac{n-4}{2}}$	$\frac{\left(v_f + 2^{\frac{n-2}{2}}\right)\left(v_f + 2^{\frac{n-2}{2}} - 2\right)}{4v_f(v_f - 1)}(2^n - 1)$
$\frac{v_f}{2} + 2^{\frac{n-4}{2}}$	$\frac{\left(v_f - 2^{\frac{n-2}{2}}\right)\left(v_f - 2^{\frac{n-2}{2}} - 2\right)}{4v_f(v_f - 1)}(2^n - 1)$

Proof. By Theorem 16.6 and the weight distribution of $C(D_f)$,

$$A_k(C(D_f)_{\{t_1, t_2\}}) = \frac{(v_f - k)(v_f - k - 1)}{v_f(v_f - 1)} A_k(C(D_f)).$$

The desired results follow from Theorem 16.8.   □

Taking $T = \{t_1\}$, we have the parameters and the weight distribution of the punctured code $C(D_f)^{\{t_1\}}$ of $C(D_f)$ in the following theorem.

Theorem 16.11. *Let t_1 be an integer with $0 \le t_1 < v_f$. Let f be a bent function from $\mathrm{GF}(2^n)$ to $\mathrm{GF}(2)$, where $n \ge 6$ and is even. Then, the punctured code $C(D_f)^{\{t_1\}}$ is a five-weight binary linear code of length $v_f - 1$ and dimension $n+1$, and has the weight distribution in Table 16.4.*

Table 16.4 Weight distribution of $C(D_f)^{\{t_1\}}$ of Theorem 16.11

Weight	Multiplicity
0	1
$\frac{v_f}{2} - 2^{\frac{n-4}{2}} - 1$	$\frac{v_f - 2^{\frac{n-2}{2}}}{2v_f}(2^n - 1)$
$\frac{v_f}{2} - 2^{\frac{n-4}{2}}$	$\frac{v_f + 2^{\frac{n-2}{2}}}{2v_f}(2^n - 1)$
$\frac{v_f}{2} + 2^{\frac{n-4}{2}} - 1$	$\frac{v_f + 2^{\frac{n-2}{2}}}{2v_f}(2^n - 1)$
$\frac{v_f}{2} + 2^{\frac{n-4}{2}}$	$\frac{v_f - 2^{\frac{n-2}{2}}}{2v_f}(2^n - 1)$
$v_f - 1$	1

Proof. By Theorem 16.7 and the weight distribution of C_f, for $k = \frac{v_f}{2} \pm 2^{\frac{n-4}{2}}$, we have

$$A_k(C(D_f)^{\{t_1\}}) = \frac{v_f - k}{v_f} A_k(C(D_f)),$$

and

$$A_{k-1}(C(D_f)^{\{t_1\}}) = \frac{k}{v_f} A_k(C(D_f)).$$

The desired results follow from Theorem 16.8. □

Taking $T = \{t_1, t_2\}$, we have the parameters and the weight distribution of the punctured code $C(D_f)^{\{t_1,t_2\}}$ of $C(D_f)$ in the following theorem.

Theorem 16.12. *Let t_1, t_2 be integers with $0 \le t_1 < t_2 < v_f$. Let f be a bent function from $\mathrm{GF}(2^n)$ to $\mathrm{GF}(2)$, where $n \ge 6$ and is even. Then, the punctured code $C(D_f)^{\{t_1,t_2\}}$ is a seven-weight binary linear code of length $v_f - 2$ and dimension $n+1$, and has the weight distribution in Table 16.5.*

Proof. By Theorem 16.7 and the weight distribution of $C(D_f)$, for $k = \frac{v_f}{2} \pm 2^{\frac{n-4}{2}}$, we have

$$A_k(C(D_f)^{\{t_1,t_2\}}) = A_k\left(C(D_f)_{\{t_1,t_2\}}\right),$$

Table 16.5   The weight distribution of $C(D_f)^{\{t_1,t_2\}}$ of Theorem 16.12

Weight	Multiplicity
0	1
$\frac{v_f}{2} - 2^{\frac{n-4}{2}} - 2$	$\frac{\left(v_f - 2^{\frac{n-2}{2}}\right)\left(v_f - 2^{\frac{n-2}{2}} - 2\right)}{4v_f(v_f-1)}(2^n-1)$
$\frac{v_f}{2} - 2^{\frac{n-4}{2}} - 1$	$\frac{v_f^2 - 2^{n-2}}{2v_f(v_f-1)}(2^n-1)$
$\frac{v_f}{2} - 2^{\frac{n-4}{2}}$	$\frac{\left(v_f + 2^{\frac{n-2}{2}}\right)\left(v_f + 2^{\frac{n-2}{2}} - 2\right)}{4v_f(v_f-1)}(2^n-1)$
$\frac{v_f}{2} + 2^{\frac{n-4}{2}} - 2$	$\frac{\left(v_f + 2^{\frac{n-2}{2}}\right)\left(v_f + 2^{\frac{n-2}{2}} - 2\right)}{4v_f(v_f-1)}(2^n-1)$
$\frac{v_f}{2} + 2^{\frac{n-4}{2}} - 1$	$\frac{v_f^2 - 2^{n-2}}{2v_f(v_f-1)}(2^n-1)$
$\frac{v_f}{2} + 2^{\frac{n-4}{2}}$	$\frac{\left(v_f - 2^{\frac{n-2}{2}}\right)\left(v_f - 2^{\frac{n-2}{2}} - 2\right)}{4v_f(v_f-1)}(2^n-1)$
$v_f - 2$	1

$$A_{k-1}(C(D_f)^{\{t_1,t_2\}}) = \frac{2k(v_f-k)}{v_f(v_f-1)}A_k(C(D_f))$$

and

$$A_{k-2}(C(D_f)^{\{t_1,t_2\}}) = \frac{k(k-1)}{v_f(v_f-1)}A_k(C(D_f)).$$

The desired results follow from Theorem 16.8 and Theorem 16.10.   □

Example 16.13. Let $GF(2^6) = GF(2)[u]/\left(u^6 + u^4 + u^3 + u + 1\right)$ and $\alpha \in GF(2^6)$ such that $\alpha^6 + \alpha^4 + \alpha^3 + \alpha + 1 = 0$. Then α is a primitive element of $GF(2^6)$ and $f(x) = \text{Tr}_{2^6/2}(\alpha x^3)$ is a bent function on $GF(2^6)$ with $v_f = |D_f| = 36$, which is consistent with Equation (16.5). $C(D_f)$ is a $[36,7,16]$ linear code with weight enumerator $1 + 63z^{16} + 63z^{20} + z^{36}$.

Let t_1 be an integer with $0 \leq t_1 \leq 35$. Then the shortened code $C(D_f)_{\{t_1\}}$ has parameters $[35,6,16]$ and weight enumerator $1 + 35z^{16} + 28z^{20}$. The punctured code $C(D_f)^{\{t_1\}}$ has parameters $[35,7,15]$ and weight enumerator $1 + 28z^{15} + 35z^{16} + 35z^{19} + 28z^{20} + z^{35}$. The code $C(D_f)_{\{t_1\}}$ is optimal and the code $C(D_f)^{\{t_1\}}$ is almost optimal with respect to the Griesmer bound.

Let t_1 and t_2 be two integers with $0 \leq t_1 < t_2 \leq 35$. Then the shortened code $C(D_f)_{\{t_1,t_2\}}$ has parameters $[34,5,16]$ and weight enumerator $1 + 19z^{16} + 12z^{20}$. The punctured code $C(D_f)^{\{t_1,t_2\}}$ has parameters $[34,7,14]$ and weight enumerator $1 + 12z^{14} + 32z^{15} + 19z^{16} + 19z^{18} + 32z^{19} + 12z^{20} + z^{34}$. The code $C(D_f)_{\{t_1,t_2\}}$ is optimal and the code $C(D_f)^{\{t_1,t_2\}}$ is almost optimal with respect to the Griesmer bound.

16.4.3 Punctured and Shortened Codes of Another Family of Binary Codes

In this subsection, we document the parameters and weight distributions of some punctured and shortened codes of another family of binary linear codes constructed from bent vectorial Boolean functions. It will be shown that the shortened and punctured codes are interesting.

Let ℓ be a positive integer, and let $f_1(x), \cdots, f_\ell(x)$ be Boolean functions from $\mathrm{GF}(2^{2m})$ to $\mathrm{GF}(2)$. The function $F(x) = (f_1(x), \cdots, f_\ell(x))$ from $\mathrm{GF}(2^{2m})$ to $\mathrm{GF}(2)^\ell$ is called a $(2m, \ell)$ *vectorial* Boolean function.

A $(2m, \ell)$ vectorial Boolean function $F(x) = (f_1(x), \cdots, f_\ell(x))$ is called a *bent vectorial function* if $\sum_{j=1}^{\ell} a_j f_j(x)$ is a bent function for each nonzero $(a_1, \cdots, a_\ell) \in \mathrm{GF}(2)^\ell$. For another equivalent definition of bent vectorial functions, the reader is referred to Mesnager (2016)[Chapter 12].

Example 16.14. Let $m \geq 1$ be an odd integer, $\beta_1, \beta_2, \cdots, \beta_m$ be a basis of $\mathrm{GF}(2^m)$ over $\mathrm{GF}(2)$, and let $u \in \mathrm{GF}(2^{2m}) \setminus \mathrm{GF}(2^m)$. Let i be a positive integer with $\gcd(2m, i) = 1$. Then

$$\left(\mathrm{Tr}_{2m/1}(\beta_1 u x^{2^i+1}), \mathrm{Tr}_{2m/1}(\beta_2 u x^{2^i+1}), \cdots, \mathrm{Tr}_{2m/1}(\beta_m u x^{2^i+1}) \right)$$

is a $(2m, m)$ bent vectorial function.

Let $F(x)$ be a vectorial function from $\mathrm{GF}(2^{2m})$ to $\mathrm{GF}(2^\ell)$. Let $C(F)$ be the binary code of length 2^{2m} defined by

$$C(F) = \left\{ (c_{a,b,c}(x))_{x \in \mathrm{GF}(2^{2m})} : (a,b,c) \in \mathrm{GF}(2^l) \times \mathrm{GF}(2^{2m}) \times \mathrm{GF}(2) \right\}, \quad (16.6)$$

where $c_{a,b,c}(x) = \mathrm{Tr}_{2^\ell/2}(aF(x)) + \mathrm{Tr}_{2^{2m}/2}(bx) + c$.

The following was proved by Ding, Munemasa and Tonchev (2019).

Theorem 16.15. *Let F be a bent vectorial function from $\mathrm{GF}(2^{2m})$ to $\mathrm{GF}(2^\ell)$, where $m \geq 3$. Then the set $C(F)$ is a $[2^{2m}, 2m + \ell + 1, 2^{2m-1} - 2^{m-1}]$ four-weight binary code with the weight distribution in Table 16.6. The dual code $C(F)^\perp$ has minimum distance 4.*

Taking $T = \{t_1\}$, we have the parameters and the weight distribution of the shortened code $C(F)_{\{t_1\}}$ of $C(F)$ in the following theorem.

Theorem 16.16. *Let t_1, m be integers with $0 \leq t_1 < 2^{2m}$ and $m \geq 3$. Let F be a bent vectorial function from $\mathrm{GF}(2^{2m})$ to $\mathrm{GF}(2^\ell)$. Then, the shortened code $C(F)_{\{t_1\}}$ is a binary linear code of length $2^{2m} - 1$ and dimension $2m + \ell$, and has the weight distribution in Table 16.7.*

Table 16.6 The weight distribution of the code $C(F)$ of Theorem 16.15

Weight	Multiplicity
0	1
$2^{2m-1} - 2^{m-1}$	$(2^l - 1)2^{2m}$
2^{2m-1}	$2(2^{2m} - 1)$
$2^{2m-1} + 2^{m-1}$	$(2^l - 1)2^{2m}$
2^{2m}	1

Table 16.7 The weight distribution of the code $C(F)_{\{t_1\}}$ of Theorem 16.16

Weight	Multiplicity
0	1
$2^{2m-1} - 2^{m-1}$	$(2^l - 1)\left(2^{2m-1} + 2^{m-1}\right)$
2^{2m-1}	$2^{2m} - 1$
$2^{2m-1} + 2^{m-1}$	$(2^l - 1)\left(2^{2m-1} - 2^{m-1}\right)$

Proof. By Theorem 16.6 and the weight distribution of $C(F)$,

$$A_k(C(F)_{\{t_1\}}) = \frac{2^{2m} - k}{2^{2m}} A_k(C(F)).$$

The desired results follow from Theorem 16.15. $\qquad\square$

Taking $T = \{t_1, t_2\}$, we have the parameters and the weight distribution of the shortened code $C(F)_{\{t_1, t_2\}}$ of $C(F)$ in the following theorem.

Theorem 16.17. *Let t_1, t_2 and m be integers with $0 \le t_1 < t_2 < 2^{2m}$ and $m \ge 3$. Let F be a bent vectorial function from $\mathrm{GF}(2^{2m})$ to $\mathrm{GF}(2^\ell)$. Then, the shortened code $C(F)_{\{t_1, t_2\}}$ is a binary linear code of length $2^{2m} - 2$ and dimension $2m + \ell - 1$, and has the weight distribution in Table 16.8.*

Table 16.8 The weight distribution of the code $C(F)_{\{t_1, t_2\}}$ of Theorem 16.17

Weight	Multiplicity
0	1
$2^{2m-1} - 2^{m-1}$	$(2^l - 1)2^{m-2}(2^m + 2)$
2^{2m-1}	$2^{2m-1} - 1$
$2^{2m-1} + 2^{m-1}$	$(2^l - 1)2^{m-2}(2^m - 2)$

Proof. By Theorem 16.6 and the weight distribution of $C(F)$,

$$A_k(C(F)_{\{t_1, t_2\}}) = \frac{(2^{2m} - k)(2^{2m} - k - 1)}{2^{2m}(2^{2m} - 1)} A_k(C(F)).$$

The desired results follow from Theorem 16.15. $\qquad\square$

Taking $T = \{t_1\}$, we have the parameters and the weight distribution of the punctured code $C(F)^{\{t_1\}}$ of $C(F)$ in the following theorem.

Theorem 16.18. *Let t_1 and m be integers with $0 \leq t_1 < 2^{2m}$ and $m \geq 3$. Let F be a bent vectorial function from $\mathrm{GF}(2^{2m})$ to $\mathrm{GF}(2^{\ell})$. Then, the punctured code $C(F)^{\{t_1\}}$ is a binary linear code of length $2^{2m} - 1$ and dimension $2m + \ell + 1$, and has the weight distribution in Table 16.9.*

Table 16.9   The weight distribution of the code $C(F)^{\{t_1\}}$ of Theorem 16.18

Weight	Multiplicity
0	1
$2^{2m-1} - 2^{m-1} - 1$	$(2^{\ell} - 1)\left(2^{2m-1} - 2^{m-1}\right)$
$2^{2m-1} - 2^{m-1}$	$(2^{\ell} - 1)\left(2^{2m-1} + 2^{m-1}\right)$
$2^{2m-1} - 1$	$2^{2m} - 1$
2^{2m-1}	$2^{2m} - 1$
$2^{2m-1} + 2^{m-1} - 1$	$(2^{\ell} - 1)\left(2^{2m-1} + 2^{m-1}\right)$
$2^{2m-1} + 2^{m-1}$	$(2^{\ell} - 1)\left(2^{2m-1} - 2^{m-1}\right)$
$2^m - 1$	1

Proof. By Theorem 16.7 and the weight distribution of $C(F)$, for $k \in \{2^{2m-1} - 2^{m-1}, 2^{2m-1}, 2^{2m-1} + 2^{m-1}\}$, we have

$$A_k(C(F)^{\{t_1\}}) = \frac{2^{2m} - k}{2^{2m}} A_k(C(F)),$$

and

$$A_{k-1}(C(F)^{\{t_1\}}) = \frac{k}{2^{2m}} A_k(C(F)).$$

The desired results follow from Theorem 16.15.   □

Taking $T = \{t_1, t_2\}$, we have the parameters and the weight distribution of the punctured code $C(F)^{\{t_1, t_2\}}$ of $C(F)$ in the following theorem.

Theorem 16.19. *Let t_1, t_2 and m be integers with $0 \leq t_1 < t_2 < 2^{2m}$ and $m \geq 3$. Let F be a bent vectorial function from $\mathrm{GF}(2^{2m})$ to $\mathrm{GF}(2^{\ell})$. Then, the punctured code $C(F)^{\{t_1, t_2\}}$ is a binary linear code of length $2^{2m} - 2$ and dimension $2m + \ell + 1$, and has the weight distribution in Table 16.10.*

Proof. By Theorem 16.7 and the weight distribution of $C(F)$, for $k \in \{2^{2m-1} - 2^{m-1}, 2^{2m-1}, 2^{2m-1} + 2^{m-1}\}$, we have

$$A_k(C(F)^{\{t_1, t_2\}}) = A_k\left(C(F)_{\{t_1, t_2\}}\right),$$

Table 16.10   The weight distribution of the code $C(F)^{\{t_1,t_2\}}$ of Theorem 16.19

Weight	Multiplicity
0	1
$2^{2m-1} - 2^{m-1} - 2$	$2^{m-2}(2^l - 1)(2^m - 2)$
$2^{2m-1} - 2^{m-1} - 1$	$2^{2m-1}(2^l - 1)$
$2^{2m-1} - 2^{m-1}$	$(2^l - 1)2^{m-2}(2^m + 2)$
$2^{2m-1} - 2$	$2^{2m-1} - 1$
$2^{2m-1} - 1$	2^{2m}
2^{2m-1}	$2^{2m-1} - 1$
$2^{2m-1} + 2^{m-1} - 2$	$2^{m-2}(2^l - 1)(2^m + 2)$
$2^{2m-1} + 2^{m-1} - 1$	$2^{2m-1}(2^l - 1)$
$2^{2m-1} + 2^{m-1}$	$(2^l - 1)2^{m-2}(2^m - 2)$
$2^m - 2$	1

$$A_{k-1}\left(C(F)^{\{t_1,t_2\}}\right) = \frac{2k(2^{2m} - k)}{2^{2m}(2^{2m} - 1)} A_k\left(C(F)\right)$$

and

$$A_{k-2}\left(C(F)^{\{t_1,t_2\}}\right) = \frac{k(k-1)}{2^{2m}(2^{2m} - 1)} A_k\left(C(F)\right).$$

The desired results follow from Theorem 16.15 and Theorem 16.17. $\square$

Example 16.20. Let $GF(2^6) = GF(2)[u]/\left(u^6 + u^4 + u^3 + u + 1\right)$ and $\alpha \in GF(2^6)$ such that $\alpha^6 + \alpha^4 + \alpha^3 + \alpha + 1 = 0$. Then $F(x) = \mathrm{Tr}_{2^6/2^3}(\alpha x^3)$ is a bent vectorial function from $GF(2^6)$ to $GF(2^3)$. The code $C(F)$ is a $[64, 10, 28]$ linear code with weight enumerator $1 + 448z^{28} + 126z^{32} + 448z^{36} + z^{64}$.

Let t_1 be an integer with $0 \le t_1 \le 63$. Then the shortened code $C(F)_{\{t_1\}}$ has parameters $[63, 9, 28]$ and weight enumerator $1 + 252z^{28} + 63z^{32} + 196z^{36}$. The punctured code $C(F)^{\{t_1\}}$ has parameters $[63, 10, 27]$ and weight enumerator $1 + 196z^{27} + 252z^{28} + 63z^{31} + 63z^{32} + 252z^{35} + 196z^{36} + z^{63}$. The code $C(F)_{\{t_1\}}$ is optimal with respect to a one-step Griesmer bound, and $C(F)^{\{t_1\}}$ has the same parameters as the best binary linear code known in the database maintained by Markus Grassl.

Let t_1 and t_2 be two integers with $0 \le t_1 < t_2 \le 63$. Then the shortened code $C(F)_{\{t_1,t_2\}}$ has parameters $[62, 8, 28]$ and weight enumerator $1 + 140z^{28} + 31z^{32} + 84z^{36}$. The punctured code $C(F)^{\{t_1,t_2\}}$ has parameters $[62, 10, 26]$ and weight enumerator $1 + 84z^{26} + 224z^{27} + 140z^{28} + 31z^{30} + 64z^{31} + 31z^{32} + 140z^{34} + 224z^{35} + 84z^{36} + z^{62}$. The code $C(F)_{\{t_1,t_2\}}$ is optimal with respect to a one-step Griesmer bound, and $C(F)^{\{t_1,t_2\}}$ has the same parameters as the best binary linear code known in the database maintained by Markus Grassl.

16.5 Characterizations of Linear Codes Supporting t-Designs via Shortened and Punctured Codes

In this section, we shall give a characterization of codes supporting t-designs in terms of their shortened and punctured codes. Let $\mathcal{P}$ be a set of v elements and $\mathcal{B}$ a **multiset** of k-subsets of $\mathcal{P}$, where $1 \leq k \leq v$. Let $\overline{\mathcal{B}} = \{\{P \setminus B : B \in \mathcal{B}\}\}$.

Lemma 16.21. *Let $(\mathcal{P}, \mathcal{B})$ be a $(v-k)$-(v, k, λ) design and t an integer with $1 \leq v-k \leq t \leq k$. Then $(\mathcal{P}, \mathcal{B})$ is also a t-$(v, k, \binom{v-t}{v-k}\lambda/\binom{v-t}{k-t}))$ design.*

Proof. Let T be any t-subset of $\mathcal{P}$. It is observed that

$$\{\{B \in \mathcal{B} : T \subseteq B\}\} = \cup_{T' \subseteq \mathcal{P} \setminus T, |T'| = v-k}\{\{B \in \mathcal{B} : B \cup T' = \mathcal{P}\}\}.$$

Then

$$\lambda_T = \sum_{T' \subseteq \mathcal{P} \setminus T, |T'| = v-k} \lambda^{T'},$$

where λ_T and $\lambda^{T'}$ are the intersection numbers of the design $(\mathcal{P}, \mathcal{B})$. By Theorem 16.4, we get

$$\lambda_T = \binom{v-t}{v-k}\lambda^{T'}$$

$$= \binom{v-t}{v-k}\frac{\binom{v-(v-k)}{k}}{\binom{v-t}{k-t}}\lambda$$

$$= \frac{\binom{v-t}{v-k}}{\binom{v-t}{k-t}}\lambda.$$

This completes the proof. $\qquad\square$

In the case of simple designs, Lemma 16.21 is known in the literature. The conclusion of Lemma 16.21 implies that a $(v-k)$-(v, k, λ) design must be a trivial design, as every k-subset of the point set is a block of the design.

Lemma 16.22. *Let $\mathbb{D} = (\mathcal{P}, \mathcal{B})$ be a t-(v, k, λ) design with $t \leq k \leq v-t$. Then $\overline{\mathbb{D}} = (\mathcal{P}, \overline{\mathcal{B}})$ is a t-$(v, v-k, \overline{\lambda})$ design, where $\overline{\lambda} = \frac{\binom{v-t}{k}}{\binom{v-t}{k-t}}\lambda$.*

Proof. The desired results follow from Theorem 16.4. $\qquad\square$

Lemma 16.23. *Let C be a $[v, m, d]$ linear code over $\mathrm{GF}(q)$. Let k and t be two positive integers with $t \leq k \leq v-t$. Suppose that $A_k(C_T)$ is independent of the specific choice of the elements in T, where T is any set of t coordinate positions in $\mathcal{P}(C)$. Let $\overline{\mathcal{B}}_k(C) = \frac{1}{q-1}\{\{\mathcal{P}(C) \setminus \mathrm{Supp}(\mathbf{c}) : \mathbf{c} \in C, \mathrm{wt}(\mathbf{c}) = k\}\}$. Then $\left(\mathcal{P}(C), \overline{\mathcal{B}}_k(C)\right)$ is* a t-$(\mathsf{v},\mathsf{v}-k,\overline{\lambda})$ design, where $\overline{\lambda} = A_k(C_T)/(q-1)$. Further, $(\mathcal{P}(C),\mathcal{B}_k(C))$ is a t-(v,k,λ) design, where

$$\lambda = \frac{\binom{\mathsf{v}-t}{\mathsf{v}-k}A_k(C_T)}{\binom{\mathsf{v}-t}{\mathsf{v}-t-k}(q-1)}.$$

Proof. Let $T = \{i_1,\ldots,i_t\}$ be a subset of $\mathcal{P}(C)$. Note that

$$T \subseteq \mathcal{P}(C) \setminus \mathrm{Supp}(\mathbf{c}) \text{ and } \mathtt{wt}(\mathbf{c}) = k$$

if and only if

$$T \cap \mathrm{Supp}(\mathbf{c}) = \emptyset \text{ and } \mathtt{wt}(\mathbf{c}) = k$$

if and only if

$$\mathbf{c} \in C_T \text{ and } \mathtt{wt}(\mathbf{c}) = k.$$

By assumption, T is contained in $A_k(C_T)/(q-1)$ blocks of $\overline{\mathcal{B}_k}(C)$, which is independent of the choices of the elements in T. This completes the proof of the first conclusion. The conclusion of the second part then follows from Lemma 16.22. □

The following theorem gives a characterization of codes supporting t-designs via the weight distributions of their shortened and punctured codes.

Theorem 16.24 (Tang, Ding and Xiong (2019)). *Let C be a $[\mathsf{v},m,d]$ linear code over $\mathrm{GF}(q)$ and $d^{\perp}$ the minimum distance of $C^{\perp}$. Let t be a positive integer with $0 < t < \min\{d,d^{\perp}\}$. Then the following statements are equivalent.*

(1) $(\mathcal{P}(C),\mathcal{B}_k(C))$ is a t-design for any $0 \le k \le \mathsf{v}$.

(2) $(\mathcal{P}(C^{\perp}),\mathcal{B}_k(C^{\perp}))$ is a t-design for any $0 \le k \le \mathsf{v}$.

(3) For any $1 \le t' \le t$, the weight distribution $(A_k(C_T))_{k=0}^{\mathsf{v}-t'}$ of the shortened code C_T is independent of the specific choice of the elements in T, where T is any set of t' coordinate positions in $\mathcal{P}(C)$.

(4) For any $1 \le t' \le t$, the weight distribution $\left(A_k(C^T)\right)_{k=0}^{\mathsf{v}-t'}$ of the punctured code C^T is independent of the specific choice of the elements in T, where T is any set of t' coordinate positions in $\mathcal{P}(C)$.

Proof. (3) $\implies$ (1): Suppose that the weight distribution $(A_k(C_T))_{k=0}^{\mathsf{v}-t'}$ of the shortened code C_T is independent of the specific choice of the elements in T, where $1 \le t' \le t$. By Lemmas 16.22 and 16.23, the pair $(\mathcal{P}(C),\mathcal{B}_k(C))$ is a t'-design for any $0 \le k \le \mathsf{v}-t'$. In particular, the pair $(\mathcal{P}(C),\mathcal{B}_k(C))$ is a t-design for any $0 \le k \le \mathsf{v}-t$ and $(\mathcal{P}(C),\mathcal{B}_k(C))$ is a $(\mathsf{v}-k)$-design for any $\mathsf{v}-t+1 \le k \le \mathsf{v}-1$. By Lemma 16.21, the pair $(\mathcal{P}(C),\mathcal{B}_k(C))$ is also a t-design for any $v - t + 1 \le k \le v - 1$. Since $(\mathcal{P}(C), \mathcal{B}_v(C))$ is always a t-design, the pair $(\mathcal{P}(C), \mathcal{B}_k(C))$ is a t-design for any $0 \le k \le v$.

(1) $\Longrightarrow$ (4): Recall that if $(\mathcal{P}(C), \mathcal{B}_v(C))$ is a t-design, the pair $(\mathcal{P}(C), \mathcal{B}_v(C))$ is also a t'-design for $1 \le t' \le t$. The desired results follow from Theorem 16.7.

(4) $\Longrightarrow$ (2): By the condition in (4), Lemma 2.8 and the Pless power moments in (2.6), the weight distribution $\left(A_k((C^\perp)_T)\right)_{k=0}^{v-t'}$ of the shortened code $(C^\perp)_T$ is independent of the specific choice of the elements in T. Since Statement (3) implies Statement (1), the desired conclusion then follows.

(2) $\Longrightarrow$ (3): By the condition in (2) and Theorem 16.7, the weight distribution $\left(A_k((C^\perp)^T)\right)_{k=0}^{v-t'}$ of the punctured code $(C^\perp)^T$ is independent of the specific choice of the elements in T, where T is any set of t' coordinate positions in $C^\perp$. The desired conclusion follows from Theorem 2.8 and the Pless power moments in (2.6). $\qquad\square$

Notice that some of the t-designs $(\mathcal{P}(C), \mathcal{B}_k(C))$ mentioned in Theorem 16.24 are trivial and some may not be simple.

Theorem 16.24 gives necessary and sufficient conditions for a code to support t-designs with $0 < t < \min\{d, d^\perp\}$. It demonstrates the importance of the weight distribution of linear codes in the theory of t-designs, and will be used to develop a generalization of the original Assmus-Mattson theorem in the next section.

The following well-known result is clearly a corollary of Theorem 16.24, and was also documented in Theorem 4.27. This demonstrates another usefulness of Theorem 16.24.

Corollary 16.25. *Let C be a $[v, m, d]$ binary linear code with $m > 1$, such that for each $w > 0$ the supports of the codewords of weight w form a t-design, where $t < d$. Then the supports of the codewords of each nonzero weight in $C^\perp$ also form a t-design.*

16.6 A Generalization of the Assmus-Mattson Theorem

The Assmus-Mattson theorem for matroids developed by Britz, Royle and Shiromoto (2009) does contain the original Assmus-Mattson theorem as a special case. But no one has shown that it can outperform the original Assmus-Mattson theorem when it is applied to linear codes. The objective of this section is to present a different generalization of the Assmus-Mattson theorem (Theorem 4.24) and demonstrate its advantages over the original version.

16.6.1   *The Generalization of the Assmus-Mattson Theorem*

To develop the generalization of the Assmus-Mattson theorem, we will need the following lemmas.

Lemma 16.26. *Let C be a linear code of length v over $GF(q)$ and $d^{\perp}$ the minimum distance of $C^{\perp}$. Let s and t be two positive integers with $0 < t < \min\{d, d^{\perp}\}$. Let T be a set of t coordinate positions in $\mathcal{P}(C)$. Suppose that $\left(\mathcal{P}(C^{\perp}), \mathcal{B}_i(C^{\perp})\right)$ are t-$(v, i, \lambda_i^{\perp})$ designs for all i with $0 \leq i \leq s+t-1$. Then*

$$A_k\left((C^{\perp})^T\right) = (q-1) \sum_{i=0}^{t} \binom{t}{i} \lambda_{k+i}^{\perp}(t-i, i),$$

where $0 \leq k \leq s-1$ and $\lambda_{k+i}^{\perp}(t-i,i) = \dfrac{\binom{v-t}{k}}{\binom{v-t}{k-t+i}} \lambda_{k+i}^{\perp}$.

Proof. The desired results follow from Lemma 16.5 and the fact that $A_{k+i}(C^{\perp}) = (q-1)\dfrac{\binom{v}{i}}{\binom{k+i}{i}} \lambda_{k+i}^{\perp}$. □

Lemma 16.27. *Let C be a $[v, m, d]$ code over $GF(q)$ and $d^{\perp}$ the minimum distance of $C^{\perp}$. Let $i_1, \ldots, i_s$ be s positive integers and T a set of t coordinate positions of C, where $0 \leq i_1 < \cdots < i_s \leq v - t$ and $1 \leq t < \min\{d, d^{\perp}\}$. Suppose that $A_i(C_T)$ ($i \notin \{i_1, \ldots, i_s\}$) and $A_1((C^{\perp})^T), \ldots, A_{s-1}((C^{\perp})^T)$ are independent of the elements of T. Then, the weight distribution of C_T is independent of the elements of T and can be determined from the first s equations in (2.6).*

Proof. By Theorem 2.8, C_T has dimension $m - t$, and $(C_T)^{\perp} = (C^{\perp})^T$. Then the desired conclusions of this lemma follow from Theorem 2.6. □

The next theorem documents the newly generalized Assmus-Mattson theorem.

Theorem 16.28 (Tang, Ding and Xiong (2019)). *Let C be a linear code over $GF(q)$ with length v and minimum weight d. Let $C^{\perp}$ denote the dual code of C with minimum weight $d^{\perp}$. Let s and t be two positive integers with $t < \min\{d, d^{\perp}\}$. Let S be an s-subset of $\{d, d+1, \ldots, v-t\}$. Suppose that $(\mathcal{P}(C), \mathcal{B}_{\ell}(C))$ and $\left(\mathcal{P}(C^{\perp}), \mathcal{B}_{\ell^{\perp}}(C^{\perp})\right)$ are t-designs for $\ell \in \{d, d+1, \ldots, v-t\} \setminus S$ and $0 \leq \ell^{\perp} \leq s + t - 1$. Then $(\mathcal{P}(C), \mathcal{B}_k(C))$ and $\left(\mathcal{P}(C^{\perp}), \mathcal{B}_k(C^{\perp})\right)$ are t-designs for any $t \leq k \leq v$, and in particular,*

- *$(\mathcal{P}(C), \mathcal{B}_k(C))$ is a **simple** t-design for all k with $d \leq k \leq w$, where w is defined to be the largest integer satisfying $w \leq v$ and*

$$w - \left\lfloor \frac{w+q-2}{q-1} \right\rfloor < d;$$

- *and* $\left(\mathcal{P}(C^{\perp}), \mathcal{B}_k(C^{\perp})\right)$ *is a* **simple** *t-design for all k with* $d \leq k \leq w^{\perp}$, *where* $w^{\perp}$ *is defined to be the largest integer satisfying* $w^{\perp} \leq v$ *and*

$$w^{\perp} - \left\lfloor \frac{w^{\perp} + q - 2}{q - 1} \right\rfloor < d^{\perp}.$$

Proof. For any $1 \leq t' \leq t$, let $S_{t'} = S \cup \{i : v - t + 1 \leq i \leq v - t'\}$ and $s' = |S_{t'}|$. Then, $s' = s + t - t'$. Then, the pair $(\mathcal{P}(C), \mathcal{B}_{\ell}(C))$ is t'-design for any $\ell \in \{0, 1, \ldots, v - t'\} \setminus S_{t'}$. By Equation (16.4), $A_i(C_T)$ $(i \in \{0, 1, \ldots, v - t'\} \setminus S_{t'})$ are independent of the elements of T, where T is any set of t' coordinate positions of C.

By the assumption of this theorem, the pair $\left(\mathcal{P}(C^{\perp}), \mathcal{B}_{\ell^{\perp}}(C^{\perp})\right)$ is a t'-design for $0 \leq \ell^{\perp} \leq s' + t' - 1 = s + t - 1$. By Lemma 16.26, $A_1\left((C^{\perp})^T\right)$, ..., $A_{s'-1}\left((C^{\perp})^T\right)$ are independent of the elements of T, where T is any set of t' coordinate positions of C.

By Lemma 16.27, the weight distribution of C_T is independent of the choice of the elements of T. It then follows from Theorem 16.24 that $(\mathcal{P}(C), \mathcal{B}_k(C))$ and $\left(\mathcal{P}(C^{\perp}), \mathcal{B}_k(C^{\perp})\right)$ are t-designs for any $t \leq k \leq v$. The last conclusions on the simplicity of the designs $(\mathcal{P}(C), \mathcal{B}_k(C))$ and $\left(\mathcal{P}(C^{\perp}), \mathcal{B}_k(C^{\perp})\right)$ follow from Lemma 16.2. □

Notice that some of the t-designs from Theorem 16.28 are trivial, and some may not be simple. However, many of them are simple and nontrivial, and thus interesting.

We are now ready to show that Theorem 4.24 (i.e., the original Assmus-Mattson theorem) is a corollary of Theorem 16.28. To this end, we use Theorem 16.28 to derive Theorem 4.24.

Proof of Theorem 4.24 using Theorem 16.28. Let $w_1, w_2, \ldots, w_s$ be the nonzero weights of C in $\{d, d + 1, \ldots, v - t\}$, where $s \leq d^{\perp} - t$. Put $S = \{w_1, w_2, \ldots, w_s\}$. Then $(\mathcal{P}(C), \mathcal{B}_{\ell}(C))$ is the trivial t-design $(\mathcal{P}(C), \emptyset)$ for all $\ell \in \{d, d + 1, \ldots, v - t\} \setminus S$. Note that $s + t - 1 \leq d^{\perp} - 1$. Clearly, $\left(\mathcal{P}(C^{\perp}), \mathcal{B}_{\ell^{\perp}}(C^{\perp})\right)$ are the trivial t-design $\left(\mathcal{P}(C^{\perp}), \emptyset\right)$ for all $0 \leq \ell^{\perp} \leq s + t - 1$. It then follows from Theorem 16.28 that $(\mathcal{P}(C), \mathcal{B}_k(C))$ and $\left(\mathcal{P}(C^{\perp}), \mathcal{B}_k(C^{\perp})\right)$ are t-designs for any $t \leq k \leq v$. Both $(\mathcal{P}(C), \mathcal{B}_k(C))$ and $\left(\mathcal{P}(C^{\perp}), \mathcal{B}_k(C^{\perp})\right)$ are clearly the trivial design $(\mathcal{P}(C), \emptyset)$ for $0 \leq k \leq t - 1$, as we assumed that $t < \min\{d, d^{\perp}\}$. The desired conclusions of Theorem 4.24 then follow. □

One would naturally ask if Theorem 16.28 is more powerful than Theorems 4.24 and 16.3. The answer is yes, and this will be justified in the next subsection.

16.6.2 *The Generalized Assmus-Mattson Theorem versus the Original*

The objective of this section is to show that Theorem 16.28 is more powerful than Theorems 4.24 and 16.3, and is indeed useful. To this end, we consider the linear codes investigated in Ding, Munemasa and Tonchev (2019) and Tang, Ding and Xiong (2019) in the two examples below.

Example 16.29. Let F be a bent vectorial function from $\mathrm{GF}(2^{2m})$ to $\mathrm{GF}(2^{\ell})$, where $m \geq 3$. Let $C(F)$ be the code given in (16.6). By the weight distribution of $C(F)$ in Table 16.6, for $k \notin \{2^{2m-1}, 2^{2m-1} \pm 2^{m-1}\}$, the pair $(\mathcal{P}(C(F)), \mathcal{B}_k(C(F)))$ is a trivial 2-design. By the definition of $C(F)$, we have $\mathcal{B}_{2^{2m-1}}(C(F)) = \mathcal{B}_{2^{m-1}}(\mathrm{RM}_2(1, 2m))$, where $\mathrm{RM}_2(1, 2m)$ is the first order Reed-Muller code given by

$$\mathrm{RM}_2(1, 2m) = \left\{ (\mathrm{Tr}(bx) + c)_{x \in \mathrm{GF}(2^{2m})} : b \in \mathrm{GF}(2^{2m}), c \in \mathrm{GF}(2) \right\}.$$

It is well known that $\mathcal{B}_{2^{m-1}}(\mathrm{RM}_2(1, 2m))$ holds 2-design. Let $S = \{2^{2m-1} + 2^{m-1}, 2^{2m-1} - 2^{m-1}\}$. Then, the pair $(\mathcal{P}(C(F)), \mathcal{B}_k(C(F)))$ is a 2-design for any $k \in \{0, 1, \ldots, 2^{2m} - 2\} \setminus S$. Since $d(((C(F))^{\perp}) = 4$, the pair $(\mathcal{P}(C(F)^{\perp}), \mathcal{B}_k(C(F)^{\perp}))$ is a trivial 2-design for $0 \leq k \leq 3 = |S| + 2 - 1$. Hence, by Theorem 16.28, the codes $C(F)$ and $C(F)^{\perp}$ support 2-designs [Ding, Munemasa and Tonchev (2019)]. The weight distribution of the code $C(F)$ and Lemma 16.2 tell us that the 2-designs supported by $C(F)$ are simple.

Example 16.30. Let m be an odd positive integer. Let C be the linear code defined by

$$C = \left\{ \left(\mathrm{Tr}_{3^m/3} \left(a\alpha^{4i} + b\alpha^{2i} \right) \right)_{i=0}^{\frac{3^m-1}{2}-1} : a, b \in \mathrm{GF}(3^m) \right\},$$

where $\mathrm{Tr}_{3^m/3}(\cdot)$ is the trace function from $\mathrm{GF}(3^m)$ to $\mathrm{GF}(3)$ and α is a generator of $\mathrm{GF}(3^m)^*$. Then the code C has parameters $[\frac{3^m-1}{2}, 2m, 3^{m-1} - 3^{\frac{m-1}{2}}]$. Let $S = \left\{ 3^{m-1}, 3^{m-1} \pm 3^{\frac{m-1}{2}} \right\}$. Then, $A_k(C) = 0$ if $k \notin S \cup \{0\}$. Thus, the pair $(\mathcal{P}(C), \mathcal{B}_k(C))$ is a trivial 2-design for any $k \in \{0, 1, \ldots, \frac{3^m-1}{2} - 2\} \setminus S$. According to Theorem 8.53, $(\mathcal{P}(C^{\perp}), \mathcal{B}_4(C^{\perp}))$ is a Steiner system $S(2, 4, \frac{3^m-1}{2})$ and is simple. It was known that $d(C^{\perp}) = 4$ [Tang, Ding and Xiong (2019)]. Thus the pair $(\mathcal{P}(C^{\perp}), \mathcal{B}_4(C^{\perp}))$ is a 2-design for $0 \leq k \leq 4 = |S| + 2 - 1$. Hence, by Theorem 16.28, the codes C and $C^{\perp}$ support 2-designs [Tang, Ding and Xiong (2019)]. The weight distribution of the code C and Lemma 16.2 tell us that the 2-designs supported by $C(F)$ are simple. Recall that it was proved in Section 8.5 with a direct approach that the code C supports 2-designs.

The weight distributions of the codes in Examples 16.29 and 16.30 and the minimum distances of their duals are known. They tell us that the original Assmus-Mattson theorems (i.e, Theorems 4.24 and 16.3) cannot be used to prove that the codes in Examples 16.29 and 16.30 support 2-designs. It is also known that the automorphism groups of these codes are not 2-transitive in general [Ding, Munemasa and Tonchev (2019); Tang, Ding and Xiong (2019)]. However, Theorem 16.28 can do it. Therefore, Theorem 16.28 is more powerful than Theorems 4.24 and 16.3. The reader is informed that Theorem 15.24 can also be proved with Theorem 16.28, but cannot be settled with the original Assmus-Mattson theorem. Another application of Theorem 16.28 will be given in the next section.

In order for Theorem 16.28 to outperform the Assmus-Mattson theorem, we have to choose two positive integers s and t with $t < \min\{d, d^\perp\}$ and an s-subset S of $\{d, d+1, \ldots, v-t\}$, and then prove that $(\mathcal{P}(C), \mathcal{B}_\ell(C))$ and $(\mathcal{P}(C^\perp), \mathcal{B}_{\ell^\perp}(C^\perp))$ are t-designs for $\ell \in \{d, d+1, \ldots, v-t\} \setminus S$ and $0 \le \ell^\perp \le s+t-1$ with some other approach. Hence, extra work is needed when applying Theorem 16.28. This intuitively explains why Theorem 16.28 can outperform the original Assmus-Mattson theorem. For example, in Example 16.29 the extra work beyond the original Assmus-Mattson theorem is to prove that the incidence structure $(\mathcal{P}(C(F)), \mathcal{B}_{2^{m-1}}(C(F)))$ is a 2-design, and in Example 16.30 the extra work is to prove that the pair $(\mathcal{P}(C^\perp), \mathcal{B}_4(C^\perp))$ is a 2-design.

16.7 Some 2-Designs and Differentially δ-Uniform Functions

Let F be a vectorial Boolean function from $\mathrm{GF}(2^n)$ to $\mathrm{GF}(2^m)$. If such F is used in an S-box of some cryptosystem, the efficiency of differential cryptanalysis is measured by the maximum of the cardinality of the set of elements x in $\mathrm{GF}(2^n)$ such that

$$F(x+a) + F(x) = b,$$

where $a \in \mathrm{GF}(2^n)^*$ and $b \in \mathrm{GF}(2^m)$. The function F is called a *differentially δ-uniform function* if

$$\max_{a \in \mathrm{GF}(2^n)^*, b \in \mathrm{GF}(2^m)} \delta(a, b) = \delta,$$

where $\delta(a, b) = |\{x \in \mathrm{GF}(2^n) : F(x+a) + F(x) = b\}|$. The function F is said to be *differentially two-valued* if $|\{\delta(a, b) : a \in \mathrm{GF}(2^n)^*, b \in \mathrm{GF}(2^m)\}| = 2$. The following result can be found in Blondeau, Canteaut and Charpin (2010).

Proposition 16.31. *Let F be a differentially δ-uniform function from $\mathrm{GF}(2^n)$ to itself. Assume that F is differentially two-valued. Then $\delta = 2^s$ for some s, where $1 \le s \le n$.*

Due to Proposition 16.31, we say that F is *differentially two-valued* with $\{0, 2^s\}$ if

$$\{\delta(a,b) : a \in \mathrm{GF}(2^n)^*, b \in \mathrm{GF}(2^m)\} = \{0, 2^s\}.$$

Results about differentially two-valued functions can be found in Charpin and Peng (2019a) and Charpin and Peng (2019b). When $n = m$, differentially 2-uniform functions are also called *almost perfect nonlinear* (APN) functions.

For any function F from $\mathrm{GF}(2^n)$ to itself, the *extended Walsh transform* of F at $(\lambda, \mu) \in \mathrm{GF}(2^n)^* \times \mathrm{GF}(2^n)$ is defined as

$$\mathcal{W}_F(\lambda, \mu) = \sum_{x \in \mathrm{GF}(2^n)} (-1)^{\mathrm{Tr}_{2^n/2}(\lambda F(x) + \mu x)},$$

where $\mathrm{Tr}_{2^n/2}(\cdot)$ is the absolute trace function from $\mathrm{GF}(2^n)$ to $\mathrm{GF}(2)$. $\mathcal{W}_F(\lambda, \mu)$ are also called the *extended Walsh coefficients* of F. The *component functions* of F are the Boolean functions $\mathrm{Tr}(\lambda F(x))$, where $\lambda \in \mathrm{GF}(2^n)^*$. A component function $\mathrm{Tr}(\lambda F(x))$ is said to be *bent* if $\mathcal{W}_F(\lambda, \mu) = \pm 2^{\frac{n}{2}}$, for all $\mu \in \mathrm{GF}(2^n)$. In this case, $\mathrm{Tr}(\lambda F(x))$ is also called a *bent component* of F. A component function $\mathrm{Tr}(\lambda F(x))$ of $F(x)$ is called *s-plateaued* if $\mathcal{W}_F(\lambda, \mu) = 0$, or $\pm 2^{\frac{n+s}{2}}$, for all $\mu \in \mathrm{GF}(2^n)$, where s and n always have the same parity. $F(x)$ is referred to as a *s-plateaued vectorial function* if $\mathrm{Tr}(\lambda F(x))$ is s-plateaued for all $\lambda \in \mathrm{GF}(2^n)^*$.

After the preparations above, we are ready to give a connection between differentially δ-uniform functions and 2-designs, and present some new 2-designs from some special differentially two-valued functions.

Let F be a differentially δ-uniform function over $\mathrm{GF}(2^n)$. Define the following linear code

$$C(F) = \left\{ (\mathrm{Tr}(aF(x) + bx) + c)_{x \in \mathrm{GF}(2^n)} : a, b \in \mathrm{GF}(2^n), c \in \mathrm{GF}(2) \right\}.$$

It follows from Delsarte's theorem that the dual code $C(F)^\perp$ of $C(F)$ can be given by

$$C(F)^\perp = \left\{ (c_x)_{x \in \mathrm{GF}(2^n)} \in \mathrm{GF}(2)^n : \sum_{x \in \mathrm{GF}(2^n)} c_x \mathbf{u}_x = 0 \right\},$$

where $\mathbf{u}_x = (F(x), x, 1)$. For any $x_1, x_2 \in \mathrm{GF}(2^n)$ with $x_1 \neq x_2$, denote by $\lambda_{\{x_1, x_2\}}$ the cardinality of the set

$$W_{\{x_1, x_2\}} = \left\{ \mathbf{c} = (c_x)_{x \in \mathrm{GF}(2^n)} \in C(F)^\perp : \mathrm{wt}(\mathbf{c}) = 4, c_{x_1} = c_{x_2} = 1 \right\}.$$

Let $a = x_1 + x_2$ and $b = F(x_1) + F(x_2)$. Denote

$$E_{\{x_1, x_2\}} = \{x \in \mathrm{GF}(2^n) : F(x + a) + F(x) = b\}.$$

Then, $\delta(a,b) = |E_{\{x_1,x_2\}}|$ and

$$E_{\{x_1,x_2\}} = \{x_1,x_2\} \cup \left(\cup_{i=1}^{\delta(a,b)/2-1} \{x_i', x_i' + a\} \right),$$

where $x_i' \in GF(2^n)$. Moreover, it is easily observed that

$$W_{\{x_1,x_2\}} = \{\mathbf{c}_i : 1 \le i \le \delta(a,b)/2 - 1\},$$

where $\mathbf{c}_i = (c_x)_{x \in GF(2^n)}$ with

$$c_x = \begin{cases} 1, & x \in \{x_i', x_i' + a, x_1, x_2\}; \\ 0, & \text{otherwise.} \end{cases}$$

Consequently, we have

$$\lambda_{\{x_1,x_2\}} = \frac{\delta(x_1 + x_2, F(x_1) + F(x_2)) - 2}{2}.$$

So, we have proved the following theorem, which establishes a link between some 2-designs and differentially two-valued functions.

Theorem 16.32. *Let $F(x)$ be a function over $GF(2^n)$. Then the incidence structure $\left(\mathcal{P}(C(F)^\perp), \mathcal{B}_4(C(F)^\perp) \right)$ is a 2-design if and only if F is differentially two-valued. Furthermore, if F is differentially two-valued with $\{0, 2^s\}$, then $\left(\mathcal{P}(C(F)^\perp), \mathcal{B}_4(C(F)^\perp) \right)$ is a 2-$(2^n, 4, 2^{s-1} - 1)$ design.*

Corollary 16.33. *Let $F(x)$ be a function over $GF(2^n)$. Then the incidence structure $\left(\mathcal{P}(C(F)^\perp), \mathcal{B}_4(C(F)^\perp) \right)$ is a Steiner system $S(2, 4, 2^n)$ if and only if F is differentially two-valued with $\{0, 4\}$.*

Magma test shows that the Steiner system $S(2, 4, 2^n)$ from the differentially two-valued $\{0, 4\}$ function $F(x) = x^{2^{2i} - 2^i + 1}$ [Blondeau, Canteaut and Charpin (2010); Hertel and Pott (2008)] or $F(x) = \alpha x^{2^i + 1} + \alpha^{2^m} x^{2^{2m} + 2^{m+i}}$ [Bracken, Tan and Tan (2012)] is equivalent to the incidence structure from points and lines of the affine geometry $AG(2^{\frac{n}{2}}, GF(4))$. It is still open whether there is a differentially two-valued $\{0, 4\}$ function $F(x)$ such that $\left(\mathcal{P}(C(F)^\perp), \mathcal{B}_4(C(F)^\perp) \right)$ is not equivalent to the Steiner system from affine geometry.

With Theorem 16.32, we can directly use results of the differentially two-valued functions to study the incidence structure $\left(\mathcal{P}(C(F)^\perp), \mathcal{B}_4(C(F)^\perp) \right)$. By Lemma 1 in Charpin and Peng (2019b) and Theorem 16.32, we have the following.

Corollary 16.34. *Let $F(x)$ be a differentially δ-uniform function over $GF(2^n)$. Then $\left(\mathcal{P}(C(F)^\perp), \mathcal{B}_4(C(F)^\perp) \right)$ forms a 2-design if and only if*

$$\sum_{(a,b) \in GF(2^n)^* \times GF(2^n)} \mathcal{W}_F(a,b)^4 = 2^{2n}(2^n - 1)\delta.$$

Theorem 16.35. *Let $F(x)$ over $GF(2^n)$ be a differentially two-valued s-plateaued vectorial function. Then, the code $C(F)$ and its dual $C(F)^{\perp}$ support 2-designs.*

Proof. Let $S = \left\{ 2^{n-1}, 2^{n-1} \pm 2^{\frac{n+s-2}{2}} \right\}$. Since $\mathcal{W}_F(\lambda, \mu) \in \{0, 2^{\frac{n+s}{2}}, -2^{\frac{n+s}{2}}\}$, the incidence structure $(\mathcal{P}(C(F)), \mathcal{B}_k(C(F)))$ forms a trivial 2-design for any $k \notin S$. It follows from Theorem 16.32 and $d(C(E)^{\perp}) \geq 4$ ([Carlet, Charpin and Zinoviev (1998)][Theorem 9]) that the incidence structure $(\mathcal{P}(C(F)^{\perp}), \mathcal{B}_k(C(F)^{\perp}))$ forms a 2-design for $0 \leq k \leq 4 = |S| + 2 - 1$. The desired conclusions then follow from Theorem 16.28. $\square$

Corollary 16.36. *Let q be a power of 2 and m be a positive integer. Let $F(x)$ be a quadratic permutation over $GF(q^m)$ of the form*

$$F(x) = \sum_{0 \leq i \leq j \leq m-1} c_{ij} x^{q^i + q^j}, \quad \forall c_{ij} \in GF(q^m).$$

Suppose that $F(x)$ is differentially q-uniform. Then, the code $C(F)$ and its dual $C(F)^{\perp}$ support 2-designs.

Proof. By Theorems 5 and 6 in Mesnager, Tang and Xiong (2020), the function $F(x)$ is differentially two-valued with $\{0, q\}$ and has extended Walsh coefficients in $\{0, \pm q^{\frac{m+1}{2}}\}$. The desired conclusion then follows from Theorem 16.35. $\square$

To determine the parameters of the 2-designs from the code $C(F)$ and its dual $C(F)^{\perp}$, we need the following lemma.

Lemma 16.37. *Let $F(x)$ be a s-plateaued vectorial function over $GF(2^n)$, where $1 \leq s \leq n - 1$. Then the code $C(F)$ has parameters $[2^n, 2n + 1, 2^{n-1} - 2^{\frac{n+s-2}{2}}]$ and its dual code $C(F)^{\perp}$ has minimum distance*

$$d^{\perp} = \begin{cases} 4, & s \geq 2, \\ 6, & s = 1. \end{cases}$$

Furthermore, the weight distribution of $C(F)$ is given by

$$A_{2^{n-1} - 2^{\frac{n+s-2}{2}}} = 2^{n-s}(2^n - 1),$$
$$A_{2^{n-1}} = (2^n - 1)(2^{n+1} - 2^{n-s+1} + 2),$$
$$A_{2^{n-1} + 2^{\frac{n+s-2}{2}}} = 2^{n-s}(2^n - 1),$$
$$A_{2^n} = 1,$$

and $A_i = 0$ for all other i. The number $A_4^{\perp}$ of the codewords of weight 4 in $C(F)^{\perp}$ is given by $\frac{2^{n-2}(2^n-1)(2^{s-1}-1)}{3}$.

Proof. Let $\mathbf{c}(a,b,c) = (\mathrm{Tr}\,(aF(x)+bx)+c)_{x\in\mathrm{GF}(2^n)}$, where $a,b \in \mathrm{GF}(2^n)$ and $c \in \mathrm{GF}(2)$. Then

$$\mathrm{wt}(\mathbf{c}(a,b,c)) = \frac{1}{2}\sum_{x\in\mathrm{GF}(2^n)}\left(1-(-1)^{\mathrm{Tr}(aF(x)+bx)+c}\right)$$

$$= 2^{n-1} - \frac{(-1)^c}{2}\sum_{x\in\mathrm{GF}(2^n)}(-1)^{\mathrm{Tr}(aF(x)+bx)}$$

$$= \begin{cases} 2^{n-1} - \frac{1}{2}\mathcal{W}_F(a,b), & a\neq 0, \\ 2^{n-1}, & a=0, b\neq 0, \\ 2^n, & a=b=0, c=1, \\ 0, & a=b=0. \end{cases}$$

Then, $\mathrm{wt}(\mathbf{c}(a,b,c)) \in \{0, 2^n, 2^{n-1}, 2^{n-1}\pm 2^{\frac{n+s-2}{2}}\}$, and $\mathrm{wt}(\mathbf{c}(a,b,c)) = 0$ if and only if $a=b=c=0$. Thus, the dimension of $C(F)$ is equal to $2n+1$. By Theorem 9 in Carlet, Charpin and Zinoviev (1998), the minimal distance $d^{\perp} = 4$ or 6. Let $i_1 = 2^{n-1}-2^{\frac{n+s-2}{2}}$, $i_2 = 2^{n-1}$, and $i_3 = 2^{n-1}+2^{\frac{n+s-2}{2}}$. Note that $A_{2^n} = 1$. The first three Pless power moments in (2.6) give

$$\begin{cases} A_{i_1}+A_{i_2}+A_{i_3} = 2^{2n+1}-2, \\ i_1 A_{i_1}+i_2 A_{i_2}+i_3 A_{i_3} = 2^{2n+1-1}\cdot 2^n - 2^n, \\ i_1^2 A_{i_1}+i_2^2 A_{i_2}+i_3^2 A_{i_3} = 2^{2n+1-2}\cdot 2^n(2^n+1) - 2^{2n}. \end{cases}$$

Solving this system of equations, we obtain

$$A_{2^{n-1}-2^{\frac{n+s-2}{2}}} = 2^{n-s}(2^n-1),$$

$$A_{2^{n-1}} = (2^n-1)(2^{n+1}-2^{n-s+1}+2),$$

$$A_{2^{n-1}+2^{\frac{n+s-2}{2}}} = 2^{n-s}(2^n-1).$$

Using the fourth Pless power moment in (2.6), we have

$$A_4^{\perp} = \frac{2^{n-2}(2^n-1)(2^{s-1}-1)}{3}.$$

Since $d^{\perp} = 4$ or 6, we obtain

$$d^{\perp} = \begin{cases} 4, & s\geq 2, \\ 6, & s=1. \end{cases}$$

This completes the proof. $\qquad\square$

Combining Equation (16.1), Theorem 16.35 and Lemma 16.37, we deduce the following.

Theorem 16.38. *Let $F(x)$ over $\mathrm{GF}(2^n)$ be a differentially two-valued s-plateaued vectorial function. Then, $C(F)$ holds a 2-$(2^n, k, \lambda)$ design for the following pair* (k,λ):

- $(k,\lambda) = \left(2^{n-1} \pm 2^{\frac{n+s-2}{2}}, \left(2^{n-s-1} \pm 2^{\frac{n-s-2}{2}}\right)\left(2^{n-1} \pm 2^{\frac{n+s-2}{2}} - 1\right)\right)$, *and*
- $(k,\lambda) = \left(2^{n-1}, (2^{n-1} - 1)(2^n - 2^{n-s} + 1)\right)$.

To show the existence of the 2-designs in Theorem 16.35, we describe some functions over $GF(2^n)$ which are differentially two-valued and have extended Walsh coefficients in $\{0, \pm 2^{\frac{n+s}{2}}\}$.

(1) The first family of differentially two-valued monomials with Kasami exponents: $F(x) = x^{2^{2i} - 2^i + 1}$, where n and i are positive integers, $n \neq 3i$, $s = \gcd(n,i)$, and $\frac{n}{s}$ is odd. Then $F(x)$ over $GF(2^n)$ is differentially two-valued with $\{0, 2^s\}$, and has extended Walsh coefficients in $\{0, \pm 2^{\frac{n+s}{2}}\}$ [Blondeau, Canteaut and Charpin (2010); Hertel and Pott (2008)].

(2) The second family of differentially two-valued functions was discovered by Bracken, Tan and Tan (2012): $F(x) = \alpha x^{2^i + 1} + \alpha^{2^m} x^{2^{2m} + 2^{m+i}}$, where $n = 3m$, m and i are two positive integers, $3 \nmid m$, $3 | (m+i)$, $s = \gcd(m,i)$, $2 \nmid \frac{m}{s}$, and α is a primitive element of $GF(2^n)$. Then $F(x)$ is over $GF(2^n)$ and differentially two-valued with $\{0, 2^s\}$, and has extended Walsh coefficients in $\{0, \pm 2^{\frac{3m+s}{2}}\}$.

When $s \geq 2$, the original Assmus-Mattson theorem says that the codes $C(F)$ and $C(F)^{\perp}$ for $F(x) = x^{2^{2i} - 2^i + 1}$ and $F(x) = \alpha x^{2^i + 1} + \alpha^{2^m} x^{2^{2m} + 2^{m+i}}$ support only 1-designs. Magma computation shows that, in general, the codes $C(F)$ and $C(F)^{\perp}$ are not 2-transitive or 2-homogeneous. However, with the generalized Assmus-Mattson theorem, we have proved that these codes support 2-designs. This is the third example showing that Theorem 16.28 is more powerful than the original Assmus-Mattson theorems (i.e., Theorems 4.24 and 16.3).

16.8   Notes

Recall that the block set $\mathcal{B}_k(C)$ may have repeated blocks or may be simple by definition. Even for a fixed linear code C, the block set $\mathcal{B}_k(C)$ may have repeated blocks or may be simple or empty, depending on the specific value of k. Thus, in this chapter we dealt with trivial designs and non-simple designs. However, our real objective of this chapter was to obtain simple designs. Theorem 16.28 does give simple t-designs.

The conditions in the original Assmus-Mattson theorem do use the parameters and limited information about the weight distributions of a linear code and its dual. Comparatively, Theorem 16.24 makes use of the information of the weight distributions of many punctured and shortened codes of a linear code and its dual.

It gives us a better understanding of the importance of the weight distributions of codes supporting t-designs.

So far, the generalized Assmus-Mattson theorem (Theorem 16.28) has been used to obtain t-designs from only several families of linear codes documented in this chapter and Theorem 9.29 [Xiang (2021)]. It should give more infinite families of t-designs. This would be a promising research direction.

Finally, the reader is encouraged to compare the work of Section 8.5 and the work of this chapter. This would be useful for understanding the technical details of this chapter.

Appendix A

Sporadic Designs from Linear Codes

In some preceding chapters, we introduced some sporadic designs held in some linear codes over finite fields. In this appendix, we document more sporadic t-designs from certain linear codes for $t \geq 3$. We are mainly interested in t-designs with $t \geq 4$. Some interesting 3-$(v, k, 1)$ designs are also included here. All the computation in this appendix was done with Magma.

A.1 Designs from Cyclic Codes of Length 17 over GF(4)

Let w be a generator of $GF(4)^*$ with $w^2 + w + 1 = 0$. The canonical factorisation of $x^{17} - 1$ over $GF(4)$ is given by

$$x^{17} - 1 = f_1(x)f_2(x)f_3(x)f_4(x)f_5(x),$$

where

$$
\begin{aligned}
f_1(x) &= x + 1, \\
f_2(x) &= x^4 + x^3 + wx^2 + x + 1, \\
f_3(x) &= x^4 + x^3 + w^2x^2 + x + 1, \\
f_4(x) &= x^4 + wx^3 + x^2 + wx + 1, \\
f_5(x) &= x^4 + w^2x^3 + x^2 + w^2x + 1.
\end{aligned}
$$

Below we introduce some 4-designs and 5-designs from some cyclic codes of length 17 over GF(4) and their extended codes.

Proposition A.1. *Let* $g(x) = f_i(x)f_j(x)$ *and let* C_g *denote the cyclic code of length 17 over* GF(4) *with generator polynomial* $g(x)$. *When*

$$\{i, j\} \in \{\{2, 4\}, \{2, 5\}, \{3, 4\}, \{3, 5\}\},$$

the code C_g *has parameters* $[17, 9, 7]$ *and weight enumerator*

$$
\begin{aligned}
A(z) = {}&1 + 1224z^7 + 1530z^8 + 10200z^9 + 8160z^{10} + 51408z^{11} + 25704z^{12} + \\
&85680z^{13} + 24480z^{14} + 45288z^{15} + 5661z^{16} + 2808z^{17}.
\end{aligned}
$$

461

The dual code $C_g^\perp$ has parameters $[17, 8, 8]$ and weight enumerator

$$A^\perp(z) = 1 + 1530z^8 + 8160z^{10} + 25704z^{12} + 24480z^{14} + 5661z^{16}.$$

The minimum weight codewords of C_g support a 4-$(17, 7, 6)$ design, and those of $C_g^\perp$ support a 4-$(17, 8, 15)$ design.

Further, the extended code $\overline{C_g}$ has parameters $[18, 9, 8]$ and weight enumerator

$$A(z) = 1 + 2754z^8 + 18360z^{10} + 77112z^{12} + 110160z^{14} + 50949z^{16} + 2808z^{18}.$$

The code $\overline{C_g}$ is formally self-dual, but not self-dual. The codewords of weight 8 in $\overline{C_g}$ or $\overline{C_g}^\perp$ support a 5-$(18, 8, 6)$ design.

Proof. The weight distributions of the four codes were obtained by Magma. The design property of the incidence structures in Proposition A.1 then follows from the Assmus-Mattson theorem and the weight distributions of the codes and their duals. □

A.2   Steiner Systems from Cyclic Codes of Length 17 over GF(16)

Let w be a generator of $GF(16)^*$ with $w^4 + w + 1 = 0$. Below we describe some 3-$(17, 5, 1)$ designs supported by some cyclic codes of length 17 over $GF(16)$.

Proposition A.2. *Let $g(x)$ be one of the following polynomials:*

$$x^6 + w^6 x^5 + w^{12} x^3 + w^6 x + 1,$$
$$x^6 + w^5 x^5 + w^4 x^4 + w^{10} x^3 + w^4 x^2 + w^5 x + 1,$$
$$x^6 + w^3 x^5 + w^6 x^3 + w^3 x + 1,$$
$$x^6 + w^{12} x^5 + w^9 x^3 + w^{12} x + 1,$$
$$x^6 + w^{10} x^5 + w^8 x^4 + w^5 x^3 + w^8 x^2 + w^{10} x + 1,$$
$$x^6 + w^{10} x^5 + w^2 x^4 + w^5 x^3 + w^2 x^2 + w^{10} x + 1,$$
$$x^6 + w^9 x^5 + w^3 x^3 + w^9 x + 1,$$
$$x^6 + w^5 x^5 + w x^4 + w^{10} x^3 + w x^2 + w^5 x + 1.$$

Let C_g denote the cyclic code of length 17 over $GF(16)$ with generator polynomial $g(x)$. Then C_g has parameters $[17, 11, 5]$ and weight enumerator

$$\begin{aligned}
A(z) = {}& 1 + 1020z^5 + 224400z^7 + 3730650z^8 + 55370700z^9 + 669519840z^{10} + \\
& 6378704640z^{11} + 47857084200z^{12} + 276083558100z^{13} + \\
& 1183224112800z^{14} + 3549668972400z^{15} + 6655630071165z^{16} + \\
& 5872614694500z^{17}.
\end{aligned}$$

The dual code $C_g^\perp$ has parameters $[17,6,11]$ and weight enumerator

$$A^\perp(z) = 1 + 12240z^{11} + 35700z^{12} + 244800z^{13} + 1203600z^{14} +$$
$$3292560z^{15} + 6398715z^{16} + 5589600z^{17}.$$

The codewords of weight 5 in C_g support a 3-$(17,5,1)$ design.

The Steiner systems in Proposition A.2 are likely isomorphic to the spherical geometry design or one of the known inversive planes.

The correctness of the conclusions of Proposition A.2 was verified by Magma. But the design property of the incidence structures in Proposition A.2 cannot be proved by the Assmus-Mattson theorem or the transitivity of the automorphism groups of the codes. However, with computational assistance the design property can be explained by the generalised AM theorem documented in Theorem 16.28.

A.3 Designs from Cyclic Codes of Length 23 over GF(3)

The binary quadratic code $\mathrm{QRC}_0^{(23,2)}$ is perfect. The code and its dual support 4-designs, which were documented in Section 10.5.2. The extended code $\overline{\mathrm{QRC}_0^{(23,2)}}$ is self-dual, and supports 5-designs, which were introduced in Section 11.2.2. In this section, we present 4-designs and 5-designs supported by cyclic codes of length 23 over GF(3).

The canonical factorization of $x^{23} - 1$ over GF(3) is

$$x^{23} - 1 = (x^{11} + 2x^8 + 2x^6 + x^4 + x^3 + 2x^2 + 2x + 2) \times$$
$$(x^{11} + x^{10} + x^9 + 2x^8 + 2x^7 + x^5 + x^3 + 2) \times (x - 1).$$

Let $f(x) = x^{11} + 2x^8 + 2x^6 + x^4 + x^3 + 2x^2 + 2x + 2$, and let C_f denote the cyclic code of length 23 over GF(3) with generator polynomial $f(x)$. Since 3 is a quadratic residue modulo 23, the code C_f and its dual $C_f^\perp$ are actually quadratic residue codes.

Proposition A.3. *The code C_f has parameters $[23,12,8]$ and weight enumerator*

$$A(z) = 1 + 1518z^8 + 2530z^9 + 30912z^{11} + 30912z^{12} + 151800z^{14} +$$
$$91080z^{15} + 148764z^{17} + 49588z^{18} + 21252z^{20} + 3036z^{21} + 48z^{23}.$$

The dual code $C_f^\perp$ has parameters $[23,11,9]$ and weight enumerator

$$A^\perp(z) = 1 + 2530z^9 + 30912z^{12} + 91080z^{15} + 49588z^{18} + 3036z^{21}.$$

The code C_f supports designs with the following parameters

$$4\text{-}(23,8,6),\ 4\text{-}(23,9,18),\ 4\text{-}(23,11,576),$$
$$4\text{-}(23,12,864),\ 4\text{-}(23,14,8580),\ 4\text{-}(23,15,7020).$$

The code $C_f^\perp$ supports designs with the following parameters

$$4\text{–}(23,9,18),\ 4\text{–}(23,12,864),\ 4\text{–}(23,15,7020).$$

Proof. The parameters and the weight distributions of C_f and $C_f^\perp$ are computed by Magma. The design property of the incidence structures follows from the Assmus-Mattson theorem. $\qquad\Box$

Proposition A.4. *The extended code $\overline{C_f}$ has parameters $[24,12,9]$ and weight enumerator*

$$A(z) = 1 + 4048z^9 + 61824z^{12} + 242880z^{15} + 198352z^{18} + 24288z^{21} + 48z^{24}.$$

The code $\overline{C_f}$ is self-dual, and supports designs with the following parameters

$$5\text{–}(24,9,6),\ 5\text{–}(24,12,576),\ 5\text{–}(24,15,8580).$$

Proof. The parameters and the weight distributions of C_f and $C_f^\perp$ are computed by Magma. The design property of the incidence structures follows from the Assmus-Mattson theorem. $\qquad\Box$

We remark that all the conclusions regarding the code C_f are true for the ternary code of length 23 with generator polynomial $x^{11} + x^{10} + x^9 + 2x^8 + 2x^7 + x^5 + x^3 + 2$.

A.4 Designs from Cyclic Codes of Length 29 over GF(4)

We consider the cyclic codes of length 29 over GF(4). The canonical factorization of $x^{29} - 1$ over GF(4) is

$$\begin{aligned}
x^{29} - 1 = &\ (x^{14} + wx^{13} + wx^{11} + w^2x^{10} + x^9 + w^2x^8 + \\
&\ wx^7 + w^2x^6 + x^5 + w^2x^4 + wx^3 + wx + 1) \times \\
&\ (x^{14} + w^2x^{13} + w^2x^{11} + wx^{10} + x^9 + wx^8 + \\
&\ w^2x^7 + wx^6 + x^5 + wx^4 + w^2x^3 + w^2x + 1) \times \\
&\ (x - 1),
\end{aligned}$$

where w is a generator of GF(4)* with $w^2 + w + 1 = 0$.

Let $f(x) = x^{14} + wx^{13} + wx^{11} + w^2x^{10} + x^9 + w^2x^8 + wx^7 + w^2x^6 + x^5 + w^2x^4 + wx^3 + wx + 1$, and let C_f denote the cyclic code of length 29 over GF(4) with generator polynomial $f(x)$. Since 4 is a quadratic residue modulo 29, the code C_f and its dual $C_f^\perp$ are actually quadratic residue codes.

Proposition A.5. *The code* C_f *has parameters* $[29, 15, 11]$ *and weight enumerator*

$$A(z) = 1 + 47502z^{11} + 71253z^{12} + 537138z^{13} + 613872z^{14} + 6420600z^{15} +$$
$$5618025z^{16} + 37051560z^{17} + 24701040z^{18} + 130630500z^{19} +$$
$$65315250z^{20} + 250362684z^{21} + 91040976z^{22} + 250240536z^{23} +$$
$$62560134z^{24} + 112294728z^{25} + 17276112z^{26} + 17343102z^{27} +$$
$$1238793z^{28} + 378018z^{29}.$$

The dual code $C_f^{\perp}$ *has parameters* $[29, 14, 12]$ *and weight enumerator*

$$A^{\perp}(z) = 1 + 71253z^{12} + 613872z^{14} + 5618025z^{16} +$$
$$24701040z^{18} + 65315250z^{20} + 91040976z^{22} +$$
$$62560134z^{24} + 17276112z^{26} + 1238793z^{28}.$$

The code C_f *supports designs with the following parameters*

$$4\text{--}(29, 11, 220), \ 4\text{--}(29, 12, 495), \ 4\text{--}(29, 13, 5390), \ 4\text{--}(29, 14, 8624).$$

The code $C_f^{\perp}$ *supports designs with the following parameters*

$$4\text{--}(29, 12, 495), \ 4\text{--}(29, 14, 8624).$$

Proof. The parameters and the weight distributions of C_f and $C_f^{\perp}$ are computed by Magma. The design property of the incidence structures follows from the Assmus-Mattson theorem. $\qquad\square$

Proposition A.6. *The extended code* $\overline{C_f}$ *has parameters* $[30, 15, 12]$ *and weight enumerator*

$$A(z) = 1 + 118755z^{12} + 1151010z^{14} + 12038625z^{16} +$$
$$61752600z^{18} + 195945750z^{20} + 341403660z^{22} +$$
$$312800670z^{24} + 129570840z^{26} + 18581895z^{28} + 378018z^{30}.$$

The code $\overline{C_f}$ *is formally self-dual, but not self-dual. It supports designs with the following parameters*

$$5\text{--}(30, 12, 220), \ 5\text{--}(30, 14, 5390).$$

Proof. The parameters and the weight distributions of C_f and $C_f^{\perp}$ are computed by Magma. The design property of the incidence structures follows from the Assmus-Mattson theorem. $\qquad\square$

We remark that all the conclusions regarding the code C_f are true for the cyclic code of length 29 over GF(4) with generator polynomial

$$x^{14} + w^2 x^{13} + w^2 x^{11} + w x^{10} + x^9 + w x^8 + w^2 x^7 + w x^6 + x^5 + w x^4 + w^2 x^3 + w^2 x + 1.$$

Appendix B

Designs from Binary Codes with Regularities

In some preceding chapters, we considered designs held in linear codes over finite fields. In this appendix, we consider support designs held in codes which may be linear or nonlinear. Most of the results presented in this appendix were developed in Delsarte (1973a), and results for binary codes were extended and strengthened in MacWilliams and Sloane (1977)[Chapter 6, Section 3]. We will summarize the major results without giving a proof. The reader is referred to Delsarte (1973a) and MacWilliams and Sloane (1977)[Chapter 6, Section 3] for a detailed proof. All codes mentioned in this appendix are binary.

B.1 Four Fundamental Parameters of Codes

An (n, M, d) code C over GF(2) is a subset of $GF(2)^n$ with cardinality M and minimum Hamming distance d. The code C may be linear or nonlinear. Our objective in this section is introduce basic terminologies and four fundamental parameters of codes studied by Delsarte.

Let C be an (n, M, d) code. The *distance distribution* of C is a sequence $(B_0, B_1, \ldots, B_n)$, where

$$B_i = \frac{1}{M} \sum_{c \in C} |\{c' \in C : \texttt{dist}(c, c') = i\}|, \tag{B.1}$$

where $\texttt{dist}(c, c')$ denotes the Hamming distance between c and c'. By definition, $B_0 = 1$ and

$$\sum_{i=0}^{n} B_i = |C| = M. \tag{B.2}$$

A code C is called *distance invariant* if the weight distribution of the translate $c + C$ is the same when c runs over all codewords in C. By definition, a linear code is always distance invariant. It is possible that a nonlinear code is distance invariant.

Example B.1. The following nonlinear code is distance invariant:

$$C = \{(1000), (0100), (0010), (0001)\}.$$

Its distance distribution is $(B_0, B_1, B_2, B_3, B_4) = (1, 0, 2, 0, 0)$ and its weight distribution is $(A_0, A_1, A_2, A_3, A_4) = (0, 4, 0, 0, 0)$.

If C is distance invariant and contains the zero codeword, then its distance distribution $(B_i)_{i=0}^n$ is identical with its Hamming weight distribution $(A_i)_{i=0}^n$. Let $\tau_0, \tau_1, \ldots, \tau_s$ be the indices i such that $B_i \neq 0$, where

$$0 = \tau_0 < \tau_1 < \cdots < \tau_s \leq n. \tag{B.3}$$

Then τ_1 is the minimum distance d of the code C. Both the minimum distance d (i.e., τ_1) and s here will play an important role in deciding whether C can hold t-designs or not, and are two of the four parameters of a code investigated in Delsarte (1973a) for the construction of t-design with codes.

We now introduce the other two parameters, which are defined by the MacWilliams transform of the distance distribution $(B_i)_{i=0}^n$ of a code C, which contains the zero vector. Define

$$B'_k = \frac{1}{|C|} \sum_{i=0}^n B_i P_k(2, n; i), \quad k = 0, 1, \ldots, n, \tag{B.4}$$

where

$$P_k(2, n; x) = \sum_{j=0}^k (-1)^j \binom{x}{j} \binom{n-x}{k-j}, \quad k = 0, 1, \ldots, n \tag{B.5}$$

which are the *Krawtchouk polynomials* treated in Section 1.4.3.

Note that $P_0(2, n; x) = 1$ for any x and $B_0 = 1$ for any code C. It then follows from (B.2) that $B'_0 = 1$. Let $\sigma_0, \sigma_1, \ldots, \sigma_s$ be the indices i such that $B'_i \neq 0$, where

$$0 = \sigma_0 < \sigma_1 < \cdots < \sigma_{s'} \leq n. \tag{B.6}$$

The parameter σ_1 is called the *dual distance* of C and is denoted by d'. If C is linear, then its dual distance d' is indeed equal to the minimum distance of the dual code $C^\perp$ (see Section 2.2 for explanations). The parameter s' is referred to as the *external distance* of C.

We summarize the four fundamental parameters below:

- d: the minimum distance of C.
- s: the number of distances in C.
- d': the dual distance.
- s': the external distance.

To facilitate understanding the situation, we draw the following diagram:

(A_i) the weight distribution $\longleftrightarrow$

$\updownarrow$ $\qquad\qquad$ $\updownarrow$ $\qquad\qquad\qquad\qquad\qquad$ $\updownarrow$

(B_i) the distance distribution $\longleftrightarrow$ (B_i') the MacWilliams transform of (B_i)

$0 = \tau_0 < \tau_1 < \cdots < \tau_s \leq n$ $\longleftrightarrow$ $\qquad$ $0 = \sigma_0 < \sigma_1 < \cdots < \sigma_{s'} \leq n$

$d = \tau_1$, the minimal distance $\longleftrightarrow$ $\qquad$ $d' = \sigma_1$, the dual distance

s, the number of distances $\longleftrightarrow$ $\qquad$ s', the external distance

B.2 Designs from Codes with Regularity

By now we have introduced the four parameters d, s, d' and s', and are ready to present the main results of this section. Throughout this section, let C be an (n, M, d) binary code containing the zero codeword, let (A_i) denote the weight distribution of C, and let (A_i') be MacWilliams transform of (A_i).

Proposition B.2. *The number of nonzero A_i is at most s, and the number of nonzero A_i' is at most s'.*

In Example B.1, the number of nonzero A_i is 1, while the number of nonzero B_i is 2. If C is linear, Proposition B.2 is straightforward, as the weight distribution and distance distribution are the same.

Proposition B.3. *If $s \leq d'$, then an explicit formula for the distance distribution (B_i) is*

$$B_{\tau_i} = -\prod_{\substack{j=1 \\ j \neq i}}^{s} \frac{\tau_j}{\tau_j - \tau_i} + \frac{M}{2^n} \sum_{t=0}^{n} \binom{n}{t} \prod_{\substack{j=1 \\ j \neq i}}^{s} \frac{\tau_j - t}{\tau_j - \tau_i}, \quad 1 \leq i \leq s,$$

where an empty product is equal to 1 by convention.

Proposition B.3 says that the distance distribution of C is totally determined by its distances, provided that the number of distances s in C is no more than the dual distance d'. In the case that C is linear, this proposition says that the weight distribution of C is determined by its nonzero weights, provided that the number of nonzero weights is no more than the dual distance. This is a kind of regularity in such binary codes.

Proposition B.4. *If $s \leq d'$ or $s' \leq d$, then $A_i = B_i$ for all i.*

In the linear case, the weight distribution and distance distribution are always the same. Hence, neither of the two conditions in Proposition B.4 is necessary. Proposition B.4 describes a kind of regularity in certain nonlinear binary codes.

Proposition B.5. *Suppose $s' \leq d$. Then $A_i' = B_i'$ for all i, and*

$$A_{\sigma_i}' = B_{\sigma_i}' = -\prod_{\substack{j=1 \\ j \neq i}}^{s'} \frac{\sigma_j}{\sigma_j - \sigma_i} + \frac{1}{M} \sum_{t=0}^{n} \binom{n}{t} \prod_{\substack{j=1 \\ j \neq i}}^{s'} \frac{\sigma_j - t}{\sigma_j - \sigma_i}, \quad 1 \leq i \leq s'.$$

In the linear case, the condition $s' \leq d$ in Proposition B.5 is unnecessary for the conclusion in the first part. However, it is still needed to prove the conclusion of the second part. In the linear case, if the external distance s' of C is no more than the minimum distance d, then the frequencies of first s' nonzero weights in the dual code $C^{\perp}$ are determined by the first s' weights in $C^{\perp}$. This is also a kind of regularity.

Proposition B.6. *If $s \leq d'$ or $s' \leq d$, then C is distance invariant.*

Although the condition $s \leq d'$ or $s' \leq d$ is sufficient for $A_i = B_i$. They are not necessary. Proposition B.6 documents a kind of regularity in certain nonlinear binary codes. All linear codes have naturally this kind of regularity.

B.2.1 Designs from Codes When $s \leq d'$

We assume that $s \leq d'$. Then $(A_i) = (B_i)$ and $A_n = B_n = 0$ or 1. We also assume that A_n is known, so the unknowns are $A_{\tau_1}, A_{\tau_2}, \ldots, A_{\tau_s}$. Define

$$\bar{s} = \begin{cases} s & \text{if } A_n = 0, \\ s - 1 & \text{if } A_n = 1. \end{cases} \tag{B.7}$$

Note that $\bar{s}$ is just a modification of the number of distances in C. Define a polynomial

$$S(x) = \prod_{j=1}^{\bar{s}} (\tau_j - x). \tag{B.8}$$

Proposition B.7. *If $\bar{s} \leq d'$, then for $1 \leq i \leq \bar{s}$,*

$$A_{\tau_i} = -\prod_{\substack{j=1 \\ j \neq i}}^{\bar{s}} \frac{\tau_j}{\tau_j - \tau_i} + \frac{M}{2^n} \sum_{t=0}^{n} \binom{n}{t} \prod_{\substack{j=1 \\ j \neq i}}^{\bar{s}} \frac{\tau_j - t}{\tau_j - \tau_i} - A_n \prod_{\substack{j=1 \\ j \neq i}}^{\bar{s}} \frac{\tau_j - n}{\tau_j - \tau_i}.$$

Proposition B.7 says that the frequencies of the first $\bar{s}$ nonzero weights in C can be computed from the first $\bar{s}$ nonzero dsiatnces. This is of course a kind of regularity. We are now ready to state the following theorem, which applies to both linear and nonlinear codes.

Theorem B.8. *If $\bar{s} < d'$, then the supports of the codewords of weight τ_i in C form a t-$(n, \tau_i, \lambda_{\tau_i})$ design, provided that $\tau_i \geq d' - \bar{s}$, where $t = d' - \bar{s}$ and λ_{τ_i} is given by*

$$\lambda_{\tau_i} \times \prod_{\substack{j=1 \\ j \neq i}}^{\bar{s}} (\tau_j - \tau_i) = \frac{A_n S(n)}{n - \tau_i} + \frac{M}{2^n} \sum_{r=t}^{n} \binom{n-t}{r-t} \frac{S(r)}{\tau_i - r}. \tag{B.9}$$

In the linear case, this theorem is a slightly strengthened version of the Assmus-Mattson theorem in the binary case (i.e., Corollary 4.26). Theorem B.8 gives a formula for computing the λ value in the deign, but it may not be easy to use it.

Theorem B.9. *Let C be a linear code with parameters d, s, d', s'. Let $\bar{s}$ be as above and*

$$\bar{s'} = \begin{cases} s' & \text{if } A'_n = 0, \\ s' - 1 & \text{if } A'_n = 1. \end{cases} \tag{B.10}$$

If either $\bar{s} < d'$ or $\bar{s'} < d$, then the codewords of weight w in C form a t-design, where

$$t = \max\{d' - \bar{s}, d - \bar{s'}\},$$

provided that $t < d$.

B.2.2 Designs from Nonlinear Codes When $s' \leq d$

In Section B.2.1, we described the designs held in C in the case $s \leq d'$. In this section, we document designs held in C in the case $s' \leq d$. Due to symmetry, we will not explain the results below.

The *annihilator polynomial* of C is defined to be

$$\Theta(x) = \frac{2^n}{M} \prod_{j=1}^{s'} \left(1 - \frac{x}{\sigma_j} \right), \tag{B.11}$$

where $0, \sigma_1, \ldots, \sigma_{s'}$ are the subscripts i for which $B'_i \neq 0$. Note that for $0 \leq i \leq n$ either $\Theta(i) = 0$ or $B'_i = 0$. The expansion of $\Theta(x)$ in terms of Krawchouk polynomials,

$$\Theta(x) = \sum_{i=0}^{s'} \Theta_i P_i(2, n; x), \tag{B.12}$$

is called the *Krawtchouk expansion* of $\Theta(x)$, and the Θ_i are called the *Krawtchouk coefficients*.

Theorem B.10. *If $d - s' \leq s' < d$, then the codewords of weight d in C form a $(d - s')$-$(n, d, (1 - \Theta_{d-s'})/\Theta_{s'})$ design.*

Theorem B.11. *If $d - s' \le s' < d$, then the codewords of any fixed weight w in C form a $(d - s')$-design.*

Although the λ values of the designs documented in Theorems B.10 and B.11 are given, it may be very difficult to compute them using these formulas.

Appendix C

Exercises on Mathematical Foundations

A number of mathematical foundations were briefly introduced in Chapter 1. The purpose of this appendix is to help advanced undergraduates and postgraduates master some of the mathematical foundations intuitively and quickly. This is achieved by providing further information and exercises on elementary number theory, finite fields, groups, rings and polynomials.

C.1 Modular Arithmetic

This section introduces the modulo-n arithmetic, where $n > 1$ is a positive integer. We start with the introduction of two special functions.

The *floor function* $\lfloor x \rfloor$ is defined to be the largest integer no more than a real number x. By definition, $\lfloor 3.99 \rfloor = 3$, $\lfloor 5/2 \rfloor = 2$, and $\lfloor 3 \rfloor = 3$. The *ceiling function* $\lceil x \rceil$ is defined to be the smallest integer no less than a real number x. By definition, $\lceil 3.99 \rceil = 4$, $\lceil 5/2 \rceil = 3$, and $\lceil 3 \rceil = 3$.

The first exercise is to prove the following theorem.

Theorem C.1 (Division Algorithm). *Let $b \neq 0$ be an integer and let a be any integer. Then there are two unique integers q and $0 \leq r < |b|$ such that $a = qb + r$.*

You are advised to give a constructive proof by giving a formula for q and r in terms of a and b, respectively. To this end, you may use the floor function defined above.

The q and r in Theorem C.1 are called the *quotient* and *remainder* when a is divided by b. We write $r = a \bmod b$. If $a \bmod b = 0$, b is called a *divisor* or *factor* of a. In this case, we say that a is divisible by b or b divides a.

Example C.2. 73 mod 7 = 3 and −11 mod 7 = 3.

A *prime* is a positive integer $n > 1$ with only two positive divisors 1 and n. A *common divisor* of two integers a and b is a divisor of both a and b. The *greatest common divisor* (GCD) of two integers a and b, denoted by $\gcd(a,b)$, is the largest among all the common divisors of a and b.

Example C.3. 60 and 24 have the positive common divisors $1,2,3,4,6,12$. In addition, $\gcd(60,24) = 12$.

The next exercise is to prove the following proposition.

Proposition C.4. *Let a and b be two integers such that $(a,b) \neq (0,0)$. Then*

- $\gcd(b,a)$ *must exist; and*
- $\gcd(b,a) = \gcd(-b,a) = \gcd(b,-a) = \gcd(-b,-a) = \gcd(a,b)$.

Because of this proposition, we will consider only the case that $a \geq 0$ and $b \geq 0$ in the sequel when we deal with $\gcd(a,b)$. Proposition C.4 shows that $\gcd(a,b)$ must exist. Our concern now is whether there is an efficient algorithm for computing $\gcd(a,b)$. To answer this question, we need the following lemma whose proof is left as an easy exercise.

Lemma C.5. *Let $b \neq 0$. Then $\gcd(a,b) = \gcd(b,a \bmod b)$.*

A recursive application of Lemma C.5 and the division algorithm in Theorem C.1 gives an efficient algorithm for computing the $\gcd(a,b)$, which is called the *Euclidean algorithm*. The following example clearly demonstrates the procedure of the algorithm.

Example C.6. The problem is to computer $\gcd(66,35)$. The Euclidean algorithm stops when the remainder becomes 0:

$$
\begin{aligned}
66 &= 1 \times 35 + 31 & \gcd(35,31), \\
35 &= 1 \times 31 + 4 & \gcd(31,4), \\
31 &= 7 \times 4 + 3 & \gcd(4,3), \\
4 &= 1 \times 3 + 1 & \gcd(3,1), \\
3 &= 3 \times 1 + 0 & \gcd(1,0).
\end{aligned}
$$

Hence by Lemma C.5 ,

$$\gcd(66,35) = \gcd(35,31) = \gcd(31,4) = \gcd(4,3) = \gcd(3,1) = \gcd(1,0) = 1.$$

We are now ready to introduce some modulo-n operations on integers. Let $n > 1$ be an integer. We define

$$
\begin{aligned}
x \oplus_n y &= (x+y) \bmod n, \text{ e.g., } [12 \oplus_5 7 = (12+7) \bmod 5 = 4], \\
x \ominus_n y &= (x-y) \bmod n, \text{ e.g., } [12 \ominus_5 7 = (12-7) \bmod 5 = 0], \\
x \otimes_n y &= (x \times y) \bmod n, \text{ e.g., } [12 \otimes_5 7 = (12 \times 7) \bmod 5 = 4],
\end{aligned}
$$

where $+$, $-$ and $\times$ are the school integer operations. The operations $\oplus_n$, $\ominus_n$ and $\otimes_n$ are called the modulo-n addition, modulo-n subtraction, and modulo-n multiplication. The integer n is called the *modulus*.

Proposition C.7. *Let $n > 1$ be the modulus, and $\mathbb{Z}_n = \{0, 1, \cdots, (n-1)\}$. Then the following hold.*

- *Commutative laws:*

$$x \oplus_n y = y \oplus_n x, \quad x \otimes_n y = y \otimes_n x.$$

- *Associative laws:*

$$(x \oplus_n y) \oplus_n z = x \oplus_n (y \oplus_n z),$$
$$(x \otimes_n y) \otimes_n z = x \otimes_n (y \otimes_n z).$$

- *Distribution law:*

$$z \otimes_n (x \oplus_n y) = (z \otimes_n x) \oplus_n (z \otimes_n y).$$

Proposition C.7 summarises basic properties of the modulo-n operations, which are derived from the same properties of the school operations on integers.

Let $x \in \mathbb{Z}_n = \{0, 1, \cdots, n-1\}$. If there is an integer $y \in \mathbb{Z}_n$ such that

$$x \otimes_n y =: (x \times y) \bmod n = 1,$$

x is said to be invertible, and the integer y is called the *multiplicative inverse* of x, usually denoted x^{-1} (it is unique if it exists, as we require that $y \in \mathbb{Z}_n$).

Example C.8. Let $n = 15$. Then 2 has the multiplicative inverse 8. But 3 is not invertible.

We have then the following questions:

- Which elements of $\mathbb{Z}_n$ have a multiplicative inverse?
- If x has a multiplicative inverse, is there any efficient algorithm for computing the inverse?

To answer these questions, we need a few lemmas below.

Lemma C.9. *For any two integers a and b with $(a, b) \neq (0, 0)$, there are two integers u and v such that $\gcd(a, b) = ua + vb$.*

Proof. Assume that $b \neq 0$. Set $a_0 = a$ and $a_1 = b$. Carrying out the Euclidean algorithm, we have

$$
\begin{aligned}
a_0 &= q_1 \times a_1 + a_2, \\
a_1 &= q_2 \times a_2 + a_3, \\
&\vdots \\
a_{t-2} &= q_{t-1} \times a_{t-1} + a_t, \\
a_{t-1} &= q_t \times a_t + 0,
\end{aligned}
$$

where $a_i \neq 0$ for $i \leq t$. Hence $\gcd(a,b) = a_t$. Reversing back step by step, we can express a_t as a linear combination of a_0 and a_1. This process is called the *extended Euclidean algorithm*.   □

To clearly demonstrate the extended Euclidean algorithm above, we present the following example.

Example C.10. To find integers u and v such that $\gcd(66, 35) = u66 + v35$, the extended Euclidean algorithm works as follows:

	Euclidean part ↓	Backtracking part ↑	
Step 1	$66 = 1 \times 35 + 31.$	$1 = -9 \times 66 + 17 \times 35.$	Step 9
Step 2	$35 = 1 \times 31 + 4.$	$1 = 8 \times 35 - 9 \times 31.$	Step 8
Step 3	$31 = 7 \times 4 + 3.$	$1 = -1 \times 31 + 8 \times 4.$	Step 7
Step 4	$4 = 1 \times 3 + 1.$	$1 = 4 - 1 \times 3.$	Step 6
Step 5	$3 = 3 \times 1 + 0.$		

Hence $u = -9$ and $v = 17$. Note that the left-hand part downwards (Steps 1–5) is the Euclidean algorithm part, and the right-hand part upwards (Steps 6–9) is the backtracking part and called the extended part.

The answer to one of the earlier questions is the following.

Theorem C.11. *Let $n > 1$ be an integer. Then any $a \in \mathbb{Z}_n$ has the multiplicative inverse modulo n if and only if $\gcd(a, n) = 1$.*

Proof. The proof is left as an exercise. One may use Lemma C.9 to prove the sufficiency.   □

Assume that $\gcd(a, n) = 1$. Applying the extended Euclidean algorithm to a and n, one can compute integers u and v such that $1 = ua + bn$. Then the multiplicative inverse of a modulo n is $u \mod n$. Hence, the extended Euclidean algorithm is an efficient algorithm for computing the multiplicative inverse of an integer modulo n. The answer to the other question raised earlier is now clear.

Problem C.12. Use Example C.10 to compute 35^{-1} mod 66, i.e., the multiplicative inverse of 35 modulo 66.

The following is a corollary of Theorem C.11.

Corollary C.13. *Let p be a prime. Then every nonzero element in $\mathbb{Z}_p$ has the multiplicative inverse modulo p.*

Let p be a prime. Then the triple $(\mathbb{Z}_p, \oplus_p, \otimes_p)$ is called a *finite field* with p elements. It is also denoted by $GF(p)$. General finite fields was abstractly introduced in Section 1.2. An intuitive introduction of general finite fields will be done in Section C.5.

C.2 Elementary Number Theory

To objective of this section is to introduce some basic elementary number theory. The proofs of most results in this section are left as an exercise.

Theorem C.14 (Fundamental Theorem of Arithmetic). *Every natural number $n > 1$ can be written as a product of primes uniquely up to order.*

Proof. We prove this theorem by strong mathematical induction. Suppose that the conclusion is true for all natural numbers m with $2 \leq m < n$. If n is a prime, the conclusion is obviously true. If n is composite, Then $n = n_1 n_2$ for some n_1 and n_2, where $1 < n_1 < n$ and $1 < n_2 < n$. By the induction hypothesis, n_1 and n_2 both are the product of prime numbers, so is $n = n_1 n_2$. $\qquad \square$

The following follows from Theorem C.14.

Theorem C.15 (Canonical Form). *Every natural number $n \geq 2$ can be factorized into*

$$n = p_1^{e_1} p_2^{e_2} \cdots p_t^{e_t},$$

where $p_1, p_2, \ldots, p_t$ are pairwise distinct primes, $e_1, e_2, \ldots, e_t$ are natural numbers, and t is also a natural number.

Example C.16. $n = 120 = 2^3 \times 3 \times 5$.

Theorem C.17 (Euclid). *There are infinitely many primes.*

Proof. It is left as an exercise. There is a very simple proof. $\qquad \square$

The following result is only for information. Its proof can be found in many textbooks about number theory.

Theorem C.18 (Dirichlet). *Let a and b be integers with $a \neq 0$ and $\gcd(a, b) = 1$. Then there are infinitely many primes of the form $ax + b$.*

Let $a, b \in \mathbb{Z}$ and n be a positive integer. We say that a is congruent to b modulo n if $n \mid (a - b)$ (i.e., n divides $(a - b)$), and write $a \equiv b \pmod{n}$. By definition, $30 \equiv -2 \pmod{2}$ and $16 \equiv 6 \pmod{5}$.

For any positive integer n, the *Euler totient function* $\phi(n)$ is defined by

$$\phi(n) = |\{1 \leq i < n \mid \gcd(i, n) = 1\}|.$$

Let $n = 15$. Then

$$\{1 \leq i < 15 \mid \gcd(i, 15) = 1\} = \{1, 2, 4, 7, 8, 11, 13, 14\}.$$

Hence, $\phi(15) = 8$.

Theorem C.19. *Let $n = \prod_{i=1}^{t} p_i^{e_i}$ be the canonical factorization of n. Then*

$$\phi(n) = \prod_{i=1}^{t} (p_i - 1) p_i^{e_i - 1}.$$

Sketch of proof. The first step is to prove that $\phi(nm) = \phi(n)\phi(m)$ if $\gcd(m, n) = 1$. The second step is to prove the conclusion of the theorem is true for $t = 1$. The detailed proof is left as an exercise. $\qquad\square$

The following theorem is due to Euler, and has different proofs. When n is a prime, Euler's Theorem is called Fermat's Theorem.

Theorem C.20. *Let n be a positive integer and $a \in \mathbb{Z}$. If $\gcd(a, n) = 1$, then $a^{\phi(n)} \equiv 1 \pmod{n}$.*

Proof. It is left as an exercise. $\qquad\square$

Let $a \in \mathbb{Z}$ and let n be a positive integer. If $\gcd(a, n) = 1$, the least $\ell \in \mathbb{N}$ such that $a^{\ell} \equiv 1 \pmod{n}$ is called the *order of a modulo n*, and is denoted by $\mathrm{ord}_n(a)$. The following result says that $\mathrm{ord}_n(a)$ exists if $\gcd(a, n) = 1$.

Proposition C.21. *Let $a \in \mathbb{Z}$ and $n > 1$ be a positive integer with $\gcd(a, n) = 1$. Then $\mathrm{ord}_n(a)$ exists and divides $\phi(n)$.*

Proof. It is left as an exercise. $\qquad\square$

The following two propositions are quite useful.

Proposition C.22. *Let $a \in \mathbb{Z}$ and $n > 1$ be a positive integer. Let $\gcd(a,n) = 1$. If $a^k \equiv 1 \pmod{n}$ for some integer $k > 1$, then $\text{ord}_n(a) \mid k$.*

Proof. It is left as an exercise. □

Proposition C.23. *Let $a \in \mathbb{Z}$ and let n be a positive integer with $\gcd(a,n) = 1$. Then $\text{ord}_n(a^k) = \frac{\text{ord}_n(a)}{\gcd(k, \text{ord}_n(a))}$, where $k > 1$ is an integer.*

Proof. It is left as an exercise. □

Let $n > 1$ be an integer. If there is an integer $a > 1$ such that $\gcd(a,n) = 1$ and $\text{ord}_n(a) = \phi(n)$, then a is called a *primitive root of n or modulo n*. By definition, 3 is a primitive root modulo 7. A proof of the following theorem can be found in most books on number theory. It is presented here for information only.

Theorem C.24. *There is a primitive root modulo n if and only if $n = 1, 2, 4, p^e$, or $2p^e$, where p is an odd prime.*

The reader is encouraged to work out a proof of the next theorem.

Theorem C.25. *If there is a primitive root modulo n, then the total number of primitive roots modulo n is $\phi(\phi(n))$.*

Most primes p have a small primitive root. For example, for the primes less than 100000, approximately 37.5% have 2 as a primitive root, and approximately 87.4% have a primitive root of value 7 or less.

In the rest of this section, we will introduce the Chinese remainder problem and the Chinese remainder theorem. To this end, we need to deal with linear congruence equations.

Proposition C.26. *If $\gcd(a,n) = 1$, then the equation $ax \equiv b \pmod{n}$ has a solution, and the solution is unique modulo n.*

Proof. It is left as an exercise. A solution of this equation can be expressed in terms of b and the multiplicative inverse of a modulo n. It is straightforward to prove the uniqueness of the solution modulo n. □

Proposition C.27. *The equation $ax \equiv b \pmod{n}$ has a solution if and only if $\gcd(a,n)$ divides b.*

Proof. It is left as an exercise. □

Let $m_1, m_2, \cdots, m_n$ be n positive integers that are pairwise relatively prime. The Chinese remainder problem is to find an integer x such that

$$x \equiv r_i \pmod{m_i}, \quad i = 1, 2, \cdots, n, \tag{C.1}$$

where $r_1, r_2, \cdots, r_n$ are any set of integers with $0 \leq r_i < m_i$.

The following questions then appear:

- Does the set of congruences in (C.1) have a solution?
- Is the solution unique?
- How does one find a specific solution x efficiently?

These questions are addressed by the following Chinese remainder theorem.

Theorem C.28. *Let $m_1, \cdots, m_n$ be n positive integers that are pairwise relatively prime. For any set of integers $r_1, \cdots, r_n$ with $0 \leq r_i < m_i$, there is an unique integer $0 \leq x < M$ such that*

$$x \equiv r_i \pmod{m_i}, \quad i = 1, 2, \cdots, n. \tag{C.2}$$

Furthermore,

$$x = \left(\sum_{i=1}^{n} r_i u_i M_i \right) \bmod M, \quad M = \prod_{i=1}^{n} m_i, \quad M_i = \frac{M}{m_i}$$

and u_i is the multiplicative inverse of $M_i \bmod m_i$, i.e., $u_i M_i \equiv 1 \pmod{m_i}$.

Proof. It is left as an exercise.   □

This is the Chinese remainder theorem in the original form. The Chinese remainder theorem has more general forms and applications in computing, coding theory and cryptography. The reader is referred to Ding, Pei and Salomaa (1996) for details.

C.3   Groups, Rings and Fields

A *group* is a set G together with a binary operation $*$ on G such that the following three properties hold:

(1) $a * b \in G$ for all $a \in G$ and $b \in G$ (i.e., G is closed under "$*$").
(2) $*$ is associative; that is, for any $a, b, c \in G$, $a * (b * c) = (a * b) * c$.
(3) There is an *identity* (or *unity*) element e in G such that for all $a \in G$, $a * e = e * a = a$.
(4) For each $a \in G$, there exists an inverse element $a^{-1} \in G$ such that $a * a^{-1} = a^{-1} * a = e$.

If $a*b = b*a$ for all $a, b \in G$, then G is called *abelian* (or *commutative*). For simplicity, we frequently use the notation of ordinary multiplication to designate the operation in the group, writing simply ab instead of $a*b$. But by doing so we do not assume that the operation actually is the ordinary multiplication.

Let $(G, *)$ be a group with identity e. Due to the associativity of $*$, we define

$$a^n = \underbrace{a*a*\cdots*a}_{n \text{ copies of } a}$$

for any positive integer n. The least positive integer n such that $a^n = e$, if it exits, is called the *order* of $a \in G$, and denoted by $\text{ord}(a)$.

If every element a of G can be expressed as g^k for some integer $k \geq 0$, then $g \in G$ is called a *generator* of G. In this case, $(G, *)$ is called a *cyclic group*. A group is called a *finite group* if it has finitely many elements. The number of elements in a finite group G is called its *order*, denoted by $|G|$.

A subset H of a group G is called a *subgroup* of G if H is itself a group with respect to the operation of G. Subgroups of G other than the trivial subgroups $\{e\}$ and G itself are called *nontrivial subgroups* of G.

Example C.29. Let $(G, *)$ be any group. Define $\langle a \rangle = \{a^i \mid i = 0, 1, 2, \cdots, \}$. Then it is easy to verify that $\langle a \rangle$ is a subgroup of G and $|\langle a \rangle| = \text{ord}(a)$.

Proof. It is left as an exercise. $\qquad\qquad\square$

Example C.30. Let $n > 1$ be an integer. Then $(\mathbb{Z}_n, \oplus_n)$ is an abelian group with n elements.

- The identity element of this group is 0.
- The inverse of any $a \in \mathbb{Z}_n$ is $n - a$.
- $\text{ord}(1) = n$.
- $(\mathbb{Z}_n, \oplus_n)$ is cyclic and 1 is a generator.
- If $n = n_1 n_2$, then $\langle n_1 \rangle = \{0, n_1, 2n_1, \cdots, (n_2 - 1)n_1\}$ is a subgroup of $(\mathbb{Z}_n, \oplus_n)$.

Proof. It is left as an exercise. $\qquad\qquad\square$

Example C.31. Let p be a prime. Then $(\mathbb{Z}_p^*, \otimes_p)$ is an abelian group with $p - 1$ elements, where $\mathbb{Z}_p^* = \{1, 2, 3, \ldots, p - 1\}$.

- The identity element of this group is 1.
- The inverse of any $a \in \mathbb{Z}_p^*$ is the multiplicative inverse of a modulo p.
- The group is cyclic, and has $\phi(p - 1)$ generators. Each generator is called a *primitive root* of p or modulo p, where $\phi(n)$ is the Euler totient function.

Proof. It is left as an exercise. □

Theorem C.32 (Lagrange). *The order of every subgroup H of a finite group G divides the order of G.*

Proof. Define a binary relation R_H on G by $(a,b) \in R_H$ if and only if $a = bh$ for some $h \in H$. Since H is a subgroup, it is easily verified that R_H is an equivalence relation. Hence, the equivalence classes, $\{aH \mid a \in G\}$, called *left cosets* of H, form a partition of G.

Now we define a map $f : aH \to bH$ by $f(x) = ba^{-1}x$. Then f is bijective as its inverse is given by $f^{-1}(y) = ab^{-1}y$. Hence, all the left cosets have the same number of elements, i.e., $|H|$. If we use $[G:H]$ to denote the number of distinct left cosets, we have then $|G| = [G:H]|H|$. The desired conclusion then follows. □

The following is a corollary of Theorem C.32.

Corollary C.33. *Let G be a finite group. Then $\mathrm{ord}(a)$ divides $|G|$ for every $a \in G$.*

Problem C.34. In the group $(\mathbb{Z}_{19}^*, \otimes_{19})$, determine $\mathrm{ord}(3)$.

A *ring* $(R, +, \cdot)$ is a set R, together with two binary operations, denoted by $+$ and $\cdot$, such that:

(1) $(R, +)$ is an abelian group.
(2) $\cdot$ is associative, i.e., $(a \cdot b) \cdot c = a \cdot (b \cdot c)$ for all $a, b, c \in R$.
(3) The distributive laws hold; that is, for all $a, b, c \in R$ we have

$$a \cdot (b + c) = a \cdot b + a \cdot c \text{ and } (b + c) \cdot a = b \cdot a + c \cdot a.$$

For a given ring $(R, +, \cdot)$, we do the following:

- We use 0 (called the *zero element*) to denote the identity of the group $(R, +)$.
- $-a$ denotes the inverse of a with respect to $+$.
- By $a - b$ we mean $a + (-b)$.
- Instead of $a \cdot b$, we write ab.
- $a0 = 0a = 0$.
  - Note $a(0 + 0) = a0 + a0$ by the distribution law. But $0 + 0 = 0$. Hence $a0 = a0 + a0$ and $a0 = 0$.
- We shall use R as a designation for the ring $(R, +, \cdot)$, and stress that the operations $+$ and $\cdot$ are not necessarily the ordinary operations with numbers.

We have the following definitions:

(1) A ring is called a *ring with identity* if the ring has a multiplicative identity, i.e., if there is an element e such that $ae = ea = a$ for all $a \in R$.

(2) A ring is *commutative* if $\cdot$ is commutative.

(3) A ring is called an *integral domain* if it is a commutative ring with identity $e \neq 0$ in which $ab = 0$ implies $a = 0$ or $b = 0$.

(4) A ring is called a *division ring* (or *skew field*) if the nonzero elements of R form a group under "$\cdot$".

(5) A commutative division ring is called a *field*.

Example C.35. $(\mathbb{Z}, +, \times)$ is a commutative ring with identify 1 and an integral domain, but not a division ring, not a field.

Proof. It is left as an exercise. $\qquad\qquad\square$

Example C.36. Let $n > 1$ be an integer. Then $(\mathbb{Z}_n, \oplus_n, \otimes_n)$ is a commutative ring with identity 1. In particular, $(\mathbb{Z}_n, \oplus_n, \otimes_n)$ is a field if and only if n is a prime.

Proof. It is left as an exercise. $\qquad\qquad\square$

Let p be any prime. We use GF(p) to denote the field $(\mathbb{Z}_p, \oplus_p, \otimes_p)$, which is called a *prime field* and was treated at the end of Section C.1. GF(p) is called a *finite field*, as it has finitely many elements.

Example C.37. Let $\mathbb{Q}$ denote the set of all rational numbers. Then $(\mathbb{Q}, +, \times)$ is a field.

Proof. It is left as an exercise. $\qquad\qquad\square$

Example C.38. Let $\mathbb{R}$ denote the set of all real numbers. Then $(\mathbb{R}, +, \times)$ is a field.

Proof. It is left as an exercise. $\qquad\qquad\square$

Example C.39. Let $\mathbb{C}$ denote the set of all complex numbers. Then $(\mathbb{C}, +, \times)$ is a field.

Proof. It is left as an exercise. $\qquad\qquad\square$

A *Euclidean domain* is an integral domain $(R, +, \cdot)$ associated with a function g from R to the set of nonnegative integers such that

C1: $g(a) \leq g(ab)$ if $b \neq 0$; and

C2: for all $a, b \neq 0$, there exist q and r ("quotient" and "remainder") such that $a = qb + r$, with $r = 0$ or $g(r) < g(b)$.

Proposition C.40. $(\mathbb{Z},+,\cdot,g)$ *is a Euclidean domain, where* $g(a) = |a|$ *and* $\mathbb{Z}$ *is the set of all integers.*

Proof. It is left as an exercise. □

Example C.41. Let $R = \{a+b\sqrt{-1} \mid a,b \text{ integers }\}$. Define $g(a+b\sqrt{-1}) = a^2 + b^2$. Then $(R,+,\cdot,g)$ is an Euclidean domain.

Proof. It is left as an exercise. □

C.4 Polynomials over a Field $\mathbb{F}$

In the preceding sections of this appendix, we have learnt the following fields:

- The prime fields $(\mathbb{Z}_p, \oplus_p, \otimes_p)$, denoted by $\mathrm{GF}(p)$, where p is any prime.
- The field $(\mathbb{Q},+,\cdot)$ of rational numbers.
- The field $(\mathbb{R},+,\cdot)$ of real numbers.
- The field $(\mathbb{C},+,\cdot)$ of complex numbers.

Throughout this section, let $\mathbb{F}$ denote any field. We then define and study polynomials over $\mathbb{F}$.

A *polynomial* over $\mathbb{F}$ is an expression of the form

$$f(x) = \sum_{i=0}^{n} a_i x^i = a_0 + a_1 x + \cdots + a_n x^n,$$

where n is a nonnegative integer, the coefficients a_i, $0 \le i \le n$, are elements of the field $\mathbb{F}$, and x is a symbol not belonging to $\mathbb{F}$, called an *indeterminate* over $\mathbb{F}$.

For any positive integer h, the polynomial $f(x)$ above may be given in the equivalent form

$$f(x) = \sum_{i=0}^{n} a_i x^i = a_0 + a_1 x + \cdots + a_n x^n + 0 x^{n+1} + \cdots + 0 x^{n+h}.$$

By convention, we usually do not write terms with 0 coefficients. Let $\mathbb{F}[x]$ denote the set of all polynomials in indeterminate x over $\mathbb{F}$.

Let $f(x) = \sum_{i=0}^{n} a_i x^i \in \mathbb{F}[x]$ and $g(x) = \sum_{i=0}^{n} b_i x^i \in \mathbb{F}[x]$. The two polynomials $f(x)$ and $g(x)$ are considered *equal* if and only if their coefficients are equal, i.e., $a_i = b_i$ for all $0 \le i \le n$. The *sum* (or *addition*) of $f(x)$ and $g(x)$ is defined by

$$f(x) + g(x) = \sum_{i=0}^{n} (a_i + b_i) x^i \in \mathbb{F}[x].$$

Proposition C.42. $(\mathbb{F}[x],+)$ *is an abelian group with identity* 0, *called the* zero *polynomial, whose all coefficients are zero.*

Proof. It is left as an exercise. □

Let $f(x) = \sum_{i=0}^{n} a_i x^i \in \mathbb{F}[x]$ and $g(x) = \sum_{i=0}^{m} b_i x^i \in \mathbb{F}[x]$. The *product* (or *multiplication*) of $f(x)$ and $g(x)$ is defined by

$$f(x) \cdot g(x) = \sum_{i=0}^{n+m} c_k x^k \in \mathbb{F}[x],$$

where

$$c_k = \sum_{\substack{i+j=k \\ 0 \le i \le n, 0 \le j \le m}} a_i b_j.$$

This is the polynomial multiplication we learnt in school, except that the computation of each c_k is over $\mathbb{F}$.

Proposition C.43. $(\mathbb{F}[x], +, \cdot)$ *is a commutative ring with identity* 1.

Proof. We have the following:

- The binary operation $\cdot$ is associative, as the multiplication $\cdot$ in $\mathbb{F}$ is so.
- The distribution laws hold as $\mathbb{F}$ is a field.
- The binary operation $\cdot$ for polynomials is commutative, as $\mathbb{F}$ is commutative.
- $1 \cdot f = f \cdot 1 = f$ for all $f \in \mathbb{F}[x]$. Hence, 1 is the identity.

The desired conclusion then follows from Proposition C.42. □

Let $f(x) = \sum_{i=0}^{n} a_i x^i \in \mathbb{F}[x]$ and $f \ne 0$. Suppose that $a_n \ne 0$. Then a_n is called the *leading coefficient* of $f(x)$ and a_0 the *constant term*, while n is called the *degree* of $f(x)$, and denoted by $\deg(f)$. We define $\deg(0) = -\infty$. Polynomials of degree ≤ 0 are called *constant* polynomials. A polynomial over $\mathbb{F}$ is called *monic* if its leading coefficient is 1.

Proposition C.44. *Let* $f, g \in \mathbb{F}[x]$. *Then*

$$\deg(f+g) \le \max(\deg(f), \deg(g)),$$
$$\deg(fg) = \deg(f) + \deg(g).$$

Proof. The proof is trivial and left as an exercise. □

Proposition C.45. $(\mathbb{F}[x], +, \cdot)$ *is an integral domain.*

Proof. Let $f \in \mathbb{F}[x]$ and $g \in \mathbb{F}[x]$ be any two nonzero polynomials. Then

$$f(x) = \sum_{i=0}^{m} a_i x^i \text{ and } g(x) = \sum_{j=0}^{n} b_j x^j$$

where m and n are nonnegative integers such that $a_m \neq 0$ and $b_n \neq 0$. Then

$$f(x) \cdot g(x) \neq 0$$

as the leading coefficient of $f(x) \cdot g(x)$ is equal to $a_m b_n \neq 0$. The desired conclusion then follows from Proposition C.43. $\qquad\square$

Proposition C.46 (Division Algorithm for Polynomials). *Let $g \neq 0$ be a polynomial in $\mathbb{F}[x]$. Then for any $f \in \mathbb{F}[x]$ there exist unique polynomials $q, r \in \mathbb{F}[x]$ such that*

$$f = qg + r,$$

where either $r = 0$ or $\deg(r) < \deg(g)$.

Proof. One can give a proof by induction. This is left as an exercise. $\qquad\square$

In the Division Algorithm above, the polynomial q is called the *quotient* and r the *remainder*, in symbol we write $r = f \bmod g$.

Problem C.47. Let $f = x^3 + x^2 - 1 \in \mathbb{R}[x]$ and $g(x) = x - 1 \in \mathbb{R}[x]$. Find the quotient $q(x)$ and remainder $r(x)$ such that

$$f = qg + r,$$

where either $r = 0$ or $\deg(r) < \deg(g)$.

Theorem C.48. $(\mathbb{F}[x], +, \cdot, \deg)$ *is a Euclidean domain.*

Proof. It follows from Propositions C.45 and C.46. $\qquad\square$

Let $f, g \neq 0$ be two polynomials in $\mathbb{F}[x]$. In the Division Algorithm, if the remainder $r = 0$, then g is called a *divisor* or *factor* of f. In this case, we say that g divides f and f is divisible by g.

Example C.49. $x + 2 \in \mathrm{GF}(3)[x]$ is a divisor of $x^2 - 1 \in \mathrm{GF}(3)[x]$.

Proof. It is left as an exercise. $\qquad\square$

A *common divisor* $h(x) \in \mathbb{F}[x]$ of $f \in \mathbb{F}[x]$ and $g \in \mathbb{F}[x]$ is a divisor of both f and g. The *greatest common divisor*, denoted by $\gcd(f, g)$, of $f \in \mathbb{F}[x]$ and $g \in \mathbb{F}[x]$ is the common divisor of f and g with leading coefficient 1 and the largest degree. By definition, $\gcd(f, g)$ is unique, and can be computed with the Euclidean Algorithm for polynomials, which is similar to that for integers. The *least common multiple*, denoted by $\mathrm{LCM}(f, g)$, of f and g is the monic polynomial with the least degree that is a multiple of both f and g.

Problem C.50. Let $f(x) = 2x^6 + x^3 + x^2 + 2 \in \mathrm{GF}(3)[x]$ and $g(x) = x^4 + x^2 + 2x \in \mathrm{GF}(3)[x]$. Use the Euclidean algorithm to prove that $\gcd(f, g) = 1$.

Two polynomials $f, g \in \mathbb{F}[x]$ are said to be *coprime* or *relatively prime*, if $\gcd(f, g) = 1$.

Example C.51. Let $f(x) = x^2 + 1 \in \text{GF}(2)[x]$ and $g(x) = x^2 + x + 1 \in \text{GF}(2)[x]$. Then $\gcd(x^2 + 1, x^2 + x + 1) = 1$. Hence, they are coprime.

Theorem C.52. *Let $f \in \mathbb{F}[x]$ and $g \in \mathbb{F}[x]$, which are not zero at the same time. Then there exist two polynomials $u \in \mathbb{F}[x]$ and $v \in \mathbb{F}[x]$ such that*

$$\gcd(f, g) = uf + vg.$$

Proof. The Extended Euclidean Algorithm for polynomials, which is similar to that for integers, gives a constructive proof of this conclusion. □

Problem C.53. Let $f(x) = 2x^6 + x^3 + x^2 + 2 \in \text{GF}(3)[x]$ and $g(x) = x^4 + x^2 + 2x \in \text{GF}(3)[x]$. Use the Extended Euclidean Algorithm to find two polynomials u and v such that $\gcd(f, g) = uf + vg$.

Let $f \in \mathbb{F}[x]$. An element $a \in \mathbb{F}$ is called a *zero* or *root* of f if $f(a) = 0$.

Example C.54. The polynomial $f(x) = x^2 + x + 2 \in \text{GF}(3)[x]$ has no zero in $\text{GF}(3)$, while $g = x^2 + x + 1$ has the zero 1.

An important connection between roots and divisibility is given by the following theorem.

Theorem C.55. *An element $b \in \mathbb{F}$ is a root of $f \in \mathbb{F}[x]$ if and only if $x - b$ divides $f(x)$, i.e., $x - b$ is a divisor of $f(x)$.*

Proof. By the Division Algorithm, we find $q \in \mathbb{F}[x]$ and $c \in \mathbb{F}$ such that $f(x) = q(x)(x - b) + c$. Substituting b for x, we obtain that $c = f(b)$. Hence, $f(x) = q(x)(x - b) + f(b)$. The desired conclusion then follows. □

A polynomial $f \in \mathbb{F}[x]$ is called *irreducible* over $\mathbb{F}$ (or in $\mathbb{F}[x]$) if f has positive degree and only divisors $a \in \mathbb{F}$ and af, where a is a nonzero element of $\mathbb{F}$. Irreducible polynomials in $\mathbb{F}[x]$ are similar as primes in $\mathbb{Z}$.

Example C.56. $f(x) = x^2 + x + 2 \in \text{GF}(3)[x]$ is irreducible over $\text{GF}(3)$.

Proof. Since $f(a) \neq 0$ for all $a \in \text{GF}(3)$, $f(x)$ cannot have a divisor of degree one in $\text{GF}(3)[x]$. □

Theorem C.57 (Canonical factorization). *Any polynomials $f \in \mathbb{F}[x]$ with positive degree can be written in the form*

$$f = a p_1^{e_1} p_2^{e_2} \cdots p_k^{e_k},$$

where $a \in \mathbb{F}$, $p_1, p_2, \ldots, p_k$ *are distinct monic irreducible polynomials in* $\mathbb{F}[x]$, $e_1, e_2, \ldots, e_k$ *are positive integers. Moreover, this factorization is unique apart from the order in which the factors occur.*

Proof. An inductive proof on the degree of f is easily worked out and left as an exercise. □

Example C.58. The canonical factorization of $f(x) = x^9 + x^8 + 2x^7 + x^5 + 2x^4 + x^3 + 2x^2 + x + 1 \in \mathrm{GF}(3)[x]$ is

$$f(x) = (x^2 + x + 2)^3 (x + 2)(x + 1)^2.$$

Proof. The equality is easily verified. It is left as an exercise to prove that $x^2 + x + 2$ is irreducible over $\mathrm{GF}(3)$. □

Let $f(x), g(x)$, and $m(x)$ be polynomials in $\mathbb{F}[x]$. We say that $f(x)$ is congruent to $g(x)$ modulo $m(x)$, written as $f(x) \equiv g(x) \pmod{m(x)}$, if $f(x) - g(x)$ is divisible by $m(x)$.

Example C.59. Let $f(x) = x^4 + x^2 + x \in \mathrm{GF}(2)[x]$, $g(x) = x^2 + x + 1 \in \mathrm{GF}(2)[x]$ and $m(x) = x^2 + 1 \in \mathrm{GF}(2)[x]$. Then $f(x) \equiv g(x) \pmod{m(x)}$.

Solving polynomial congruence equations is similar to solving integer congruence equations. The reader is encouraged to solve the following problem.

Problem C.60. Work out the Chinese remainder problem and Chinese remainder theorem for polynomials in $\mathbb{F}[x]$.

C.5 A Constructive Introduction to Finite Fields

The prime fields $\mathrm{GF}(p) := (\mathbb{Z}_p, \oplus_p, \otimes_p)$ were treated in Sections C.1 and C.3 in detail. In this section, we will use $+$ and $\cdot$ to mean $\oplus_p$ and $\otimes_p$, respectively, and define $\mathrm{GF}(p)^* = \mathrm{GF}(p) \setminus \{0\}$. Our objective in this section is to treat finite fields $\mathrm{GF}(p^m)$ with p^m elements. Our approach will be *constructive*, so that it will be easy to understand finite fields. To this end, we need to employ irreducible polynomials over $\mathrm{GF}(p)$. Recall that polynomials over general fields were treated in detail in Section C.4.

Recall that a polynomial $f \in \mathrm{GF}(p)[x]$ with positive degree is *irreducible* over $\mathrm{GF}(p)$ if f has only constant divisors a and divisors of the form af, where $a \in \mathrm{GF}(p)^*$. We have then the following questions:

- Is there any irreducible polynomial over $\mathrm{GF}(p)$ of degree d for any given positive integer m and prime p?

- What is the total number of irreducible polynomials over $GF(p)$ of degree m?
- How to find out an irreducible polynomial over $GF(p)$ of degree m, if it exists?

Below we will answer these questions.

The *Möbius function* μ is the function on $\mathbb{N}$ (i.e., the set of natural numbers) defined by

$$\mu(n) = \begin{cases} 1 & \text{if } n = 1, \\ (-1)^k & \text{if } n \text{ is the product of } k \text{ distinct primes}, \\ 0 & \text{if } n \text{ is divisible by the square of a prime}. \end{cases}$$

Example C.61. Some initial terms of the Möbius sequence $(\mu(i))_{i=1}^{\infty}$ is given by

$$(1, -1, -1, 0, -1, 1, -1, 0, 0, 1, \dots,).$$

Theorem C.62. *The number $N_p(m)$ of monic irreducible polynomials in $GF(p)[x]$ of degree m is given by*

$$N_p(m) = \frac{1}{m} \sum_{d|m} \mu(m/d) p^d = \frac{1}{m} \sum_{d|m} \mu(d) p^{m/d}.$$

The reader is informed of the following.

- For a proof of Theorem C.62, see Lidl and Niederreiter (1997)[Chapter 3].
- $N_p(m) \geq \frac{1}{m}(p^m - p^{m-1} - p^{m-2} - \cdots - p) = \frac{1}{m}\left(p^m - \frac{p^m - p}{p - 1}\right) > 0$.
- For the construction of irreducible polynomials in $GF(p)[x]$ of any degree, see Lidl and Niederreiter (1997)[Section 3.3].
- Tables of monic irreducible polynomials of certain degrees in $GF(p)[x]$ are given in the Appendix in Lidl and Niederreiter (1997).

Example C.63. All monic irreducible polynomials of degree 4 in $GF(2)[x]$ are given by

$$x^4 + x^3 + 1, \ x^4 + x^3 + x^2 + x + 1, \ x^4 + x + 1.$$

Example C.64. All monic irreducible polynomials of degree 3 in $GF(3)[x]$ are given by

$$x^3 + 2x + 1, \ x^3 + 2x^2 + 2x + 2, \ x^3 + x^2 + x + 2, \ x^3 + 2x + 2,$$
$$x^3 + x^2 + 2, \ x^3 + 2x^2 + x + 1, \ x^3 + x^2 + 2x + 1, \ x^3 + 2x^2 + 1$$

For any prime p and positive integer m, we are now ready to construct the finite field $GF(p^m)$ with p^m elements. To do so, we need a monic irreducible polynomial $\pi(x)$ of degree m over $GF(p)$. By Theorem C.62, the number $N_p(m)$ of irreducible polynomials of degree m over $GF(p)$ is at least one.

Let $GF(p^m)$ be the set of all polynomials of degree at most $m-1$ over $GF(p)$. By definition, $|GF(p^m)| = p^m$.

Example C.65. Let $p = 2$ and $m = 3$. Then the set $GF(2^3)$ is composed of the following 8 polynomials:

$$f_0 = 0, \; f_1 = 1, \quad f_2 = x, \quad f_3 = 1+x,$$
$$f_4 = x^2, \; f_5 = 1+x^2, \; f_6 = x+x^2, \; f_7 = 1+x+x^2.$$

Let

$$f(x) = \sum_{i=0}^{m-1} a_i x^i \in GF(p)[x] \text{ and } g(x) = \sum_{i=0}^{m-1} b_i x^i \in GF(p)[x].$$

Then the addition of f and g is defined by

$$f(x) + g(x) = \sum_{i=0}^{m-1} (a_i + b_i) x^i \in GF(p)[x].$$

Theorem C.66. $(GF(p^m), +)$ *is a finite abelian group with the identity* 0, *i.e., the zero polynomial.*

Proof. It is straightforward and left as an exercise. $\square$

Let $\pi(x) \in GF(p)[x]$ be a monic irreducible polynomial of degree m over $GF(p)$, and let

$$f(x) = \sum_{i=0}^{m-1} a_i x^i \in GF(p)[x] \text{ and } g(x) = \sum_{i=0}^{m-1} b_i x^i \in GF(p)[x].$$

Then the multiplication of f and g is defined by

$$f(x) \cdot g(x) = f(x)g(x) \bmod \pi(x),$$

where $f(x)g(x)$ is the ordinary multiplication of two polynomials.

Example C.67. Let $p = 2$ and $m = 3$, and let the monic irreducible polynomial $\pi(x) = x^3 + x + 1 \in GF(2)[x]$. Then the set $GF(2^3)$ is composed of the following 8 polynomials:

$$f_0 = 0, \; f_1 = 1, \quad f_2 = x, \quad f_3 = 1+x,$$
$$f_4 = x^2, \; f_5 = 1+x^2, \; f_6 = x+x^2, \; f_7 = 1+x+x^2.$$

By definition

$$f_6 \cdot f_7 = f_6 f_7 \bmod \pi(x) = (x^4 + x) \bmod (x^3 + x + 1) = x^2,$$
$$f_7 \cdot f_7 = f_7 f_7 \bmod \pi(x) = (x^4 + x + 1) \bmod (x^3 + x + 1) = 1 + x.$$

Proposition C.68. *Let* $\pi(x)$ *be a monic irreducible polynomial over* GF(p) *of degree m. Let* $f \in$ GF(p^m) *and* $f \neq 0$. *Then there is an element* $g \in$ GF(p^m) *such that* $f \cdot g = 1$. *This polynomial g is called the* multiplicative inverse *of f modulo* π.

Proof. Since $\pi(x)$ is irreducible and $f \neq 0$ with degree at most $m - 1$, $\gcd(f, \pi) = 1$. By Theorem C.52 and with the Extended Eulidean Algorithm, one can find two polynomials $u(x) \in$ GF(p)[x] and $v(x) \in$ GF(p)[x] such that

$$1 = \gcd(f, \pi) = uf + v\pi.$$

It then follows that uf mod $\pi = 1$. Hence, $g = u$ mod π is the desired polynomial. □

Theorem C.69. *Let* GF(p^m)* = GF(p^m) \ \{0\}. *Then* (GF(p^m)*, $\cdot$) *is a finite abelian group with identity* 1.

Proof. Since $\pi(x)$ is irreducible, GF(p^m)* is closed under the binary operation "$\cdot$". It is obvious that 1 is the identity. By Proposition C.68, every element $f \in$ GF(p^m)* has its inverse. The binary operation "$\cdot$" is commutative, as the ordinary multiplication for polynomials over GF(p) is so. The desired conclusion then follows. □

Theorem C.70. *Let* $\pi(x) \in$ GF(p)[x] *be any irreducible polynomial over* GF(p) *with degree m. Then* (GF(p^m), $+$, $\cdot$) *is a finite field with* p^m *elements.*

Proof. By the definitions of the binary operations "$+$" and "$\cdot$", the distribution laws hold. It then follows from Theorems C.66 and C.69 that (GF(p^m), $+$, $\cdot$) is a finite field with p^m elements. □

Let $\mathbb{F}$ be a field. If there exists a positive integer n such that $na = 0$ for all $a \in \mathbb{F}$, such least n is called the *characteristic* of $\mathbb{F}$. If there is no such n, we say that $\mathbb{F}$ has characteristic 0.

Example C.71.

- The field $(\mathbb{Q}, +, \cdot)$ of rational numbers has characteristic 0.
- The field $(\mathbb{R}, +, \cdot)$ of real numbers has characteristic 0.
- The field $(\mathbb{C}, +, \cdot)$ of complex numbers has characteristic 0.

Theorem C.72. *The finite field* GF(p^m) *has characteristic p.*

Proof. It is left as an exercise. □

Theorem C.73. *Let $\mathbb{F}$ be any field with characteristic p. Then $(a+b)^{p^n} = a^{p^n} + b^{p^n}$ for all $a, b \in \mathbb{F}$ and $n \in \mathbb{N}$.*

Proof. For all integers i with $1 \leq i \leq p-1$, we have

$$\binom{p}{i} = \frac{p(p-1)\cdots(p-i+1)}{1 \cdot 2 \cdots i} \equiv 0 \pmod{p}.$$

Then by the binomial theorem,

$$(a+b)^p = a^p + \binom{p}{1}a^{p-1}b + \cdots + \binom{p}{p-1}ab^{p-1} + b^p = a^p + b^p.$$

The desired conclusion follows the induction on n. □

We now study the group $(\mathrm{GF}(p^m)^*, \cdot)$ of the finite field $\mathrm{GF}(p^m)$. Our task now is to prove that the group $(\mathrm{GF}(q)^*, \cdot)$ is cyclic. To this end, we need to prove a number of auxiliary results.

Proposition C.74. *For any $a \in \mathrm{GF}(q)^*$, there exists a positive integer ℓ such that $a^\ell = 1$.*

Proof. Consider the following sequence of elements in $\mathrm{GF}(q)^*$:

$$a^0, a^1, a^2, \cdots.$$

Since the group $\mathrm{GF}(q)^*$ has order $q-1$, there exist two distinct $0 \leq h < k$ such that $a^h = a^k$. Hence, $a^h(a^{k-h} - 1) = 0$ and $a^{k-h} = 1$. The desired conclusion then follows. □

The *order* of $a \in \mathrm{GF}(q)^*$, denoted by $\mathrm{ord}(a)$, is the least positive integer ℓ such that $a^\ell = 1$. The following is a corollary of Theorem C.32.

Proposition C.75 (Lagrange's Theorem). *For any $a \in \mathrm{GF}(q)^*$, $\mathrm{ord}(a)$ divides $q-1$.*

The following conclusion follows from Proposition C.75.

Proposition C.76. *Every $a \in \mathrm{GF}(q)$ satisfies $a^q = a$.*

The proof of the following proposition is left as an exercise.

Proposition C.77. *For any $a \in \mathrm{GF}(q)^*$, we have $\mathrm{ord}(a^i) = \mathrm{ord}(a)/\gcd(\mathrm{ord}(a), i)$.*

Proposition C.78. *For any $a \in \mathrm{GF}(q)^*$ and $b \in \mathrm{GF}(q)^*$, we have $\mathrm{ord}(ab) = \mathrm{ord}(a)\mathrm{ord}(b)$ if $\gcd(\mathrm{ord}(a), \mathrm{ord}(b)) = 1$.*

Proof. Let ℓ be a positive integer such that $(ab)^\ell = 1$. Then $a^\ell = b^{-\ell}$. Hence, $a^{\ell \operatorname{ord}(b)} = (b^{\operatorname{ord}(b)})^{-\ell} = 1$. It then follows that $\operatorname{ord}(a) \mid \ell \operatorname{ord}(b)$. Since $\gcd(\operatorname{ord}(a), \operatorname{ord}(b)) = 1$, $\operatorname{ord}(a)$ divides ℓ. By symmetry, $\operatorname{ord}(b)$ divides ℓ. Consequently, $\operatorname{LCM}(\operatorname{ord}(a), \operatorname{ord}(b))$ must divide ℓ. But $\operatorname{LCM}(\operatorname{ord}(a), \operatorname{ord}(b)) = \operatorname{ord}(a)\operatorname{ord}(b)$, as $\gcd(\operatorname{ord}(a), \operatorname{ord}(b)) = 1$.

On the other hand, it is obvious that $(ab)^{\operatorname{ord}(a)\operatorname{ord}(b)} = 1$. The desired conclusion then follows. $\square$

Proposition C.79. *If $g(x) \in \mathbb{F}[x]$ has degree n, then the equation $g(x) = 0$ has at most n solutions in $\mathbb{F}$, where $\mathbb{F}$ is any field.*

Proof. The proof is by induction on n. If $n = 1$, the equation is of the form $ax + b = 0$, which obviously has only the solution $x = -b/a$. If $n \geq 2$ and $g(x) = 0$ has no solution, then we are done. Otherwise, $g(\alpha) = 0$ for some $\alpha \in \mathbb{F}$, and apply the Division Algorithm to divide $g(x)$ by $x - \alpha$. Then we have

$$g(x) = q(x)(x - \alpha) + g(\alpha) = q(x)(x - \alpha).$$

Now $\deg(q(x)) = n - 1$. By induction, $q(x) = 0$ has at most $n - 1$ solutions. Whence, $g(x) = 0$ has at most n solutions. $\square$

Theorem C.80. *The multiplicative group $\operatorname{GF}(q)^*$ is cyclic.*

Proof. We assume that $q \geq 3$. Let $h := q - 1 = p_1^{r_1} p_2^{r_2} \cdots p_n^{r_n}$ be the canonical factorization of $q - 1$. For every i with $1 \leq i \leq n$, by Proposition C.79, the polynomial $x^{h/p_i} - 1$ has at most h/p_i roots in $\operatorname{GF}(q)$. Since $h/p_i < h$, it follows that there are nonzero elements in $\operatorname{GF}(q)$ that are not roots of this polynomial. Let a_i be such an element, and set $b_i = a_i^{h/p_i^{r_i}}$.

By Proposition C.75, $b_i^{p_i^{r_i}} = a_i^h = a_i^{q-1} = 1$. Hence, $\operatorname{ord}(b_i) = p_i^{s_i}$, where $0 \leq s_i \leq r_i$. On the other hand, $b_i^{p_i^{r_i-1}} = a_i^{h/p_i} \neq 1$. It follows that $\operatorname{ord}(b_i) = p_i^{r_i}$.

By Proposition C.78, we have

$$\operatorname{ord}(b_1 b_2 \cdots b_n) = \operatorname{ord}(b_1)\operatorname{ord}(b_2) \cdots \operatorname{ord}(b_n) = h = q - 1.$$

$\square$

Any element in $\operatorname{GF}(q)^*$ with order $q - 1$ is called a *generator* of $\operatorname{GF}(q)^*$ and a *primitive element* of $\operatorname{GF}(q)$.

Theorem C.81. $\operatorname{GF}(q)$ *has $\phi(q - 1)$ primitive elements.*

Proof. By Theorem C.80, GF(q) has a primitive element α. Hence, every element $\beta \in \mathrm{GF}(q)^*$ can be expressed as $\beta = \alpha^k$ for some k. By Proposition C.77, β is a primitive element if and only if $\gcd(k, q-1) = 1$. The desired conclusion then follows. $\qquad\square$

Two fields $\mathbb{F}_1$ and $\mathbb{F}_2$ are said to be *isomorphic* if there is a bijection σ from $\mathbb{F}_1$ to $\mathbb{F}_2$ satisfying the following:

(1) $\sigma(a+b) = \sigma(a) + \sigma(b)$ for all $a, b \in \mathbb{F}_1$.
(2) $\sigma(ab) = \sigma(a)\sigma(b)$ for all $a, b \in \mathbb{F}_1$.
(3) $\sigma(1_{\mathbb{F}_1}) = 1_{\mathbb{F}_2}$, where $1_{\mathbb{F}_1}$ and $1_{\mathbb{F}_2}$ are the identities of $\mathbb{F}_1$ and $\mathbb{F}_2$, respectively.

Two isomorphic fields have the same properties, and thus can be viewed as identical. The following theorem is proved in Lidl and Niederreiter (1997)[Chapter 2].

Theorem C.82. *Any finite field with p^m elements is isomorphic to* GF(p^m), *which is constructed with a fixed monic irreducible polynomial* $\pi(x) \in \mathrm{GF}(p)[x]$ *with degree m.*

Due to this theorem, we do not need to specify the monic irreducible polynomial $\pi(x)$ over GF(p) with degree m when we mention GF(p^m).

Let $\mathbb{F}$ be a field. A subset $\mathbb{K}$ of $\mathbb{F}$ that is itself a field under the operations of $\mathbb{F}$ will be called a *subfield* of $\mathbb{F}$. In this context, $\mathbb{F}$ is called an *extension field* of $\mathbb{K}$. If $\mathbb{K} \neq \mathbb{F}$, we say that $\mathbb{K}$ is a *proper subfield* of $\mathbb{F}$. A field containing no proper subfields is called a *prime field*. Examples of prime fields are GF(p), where p is any prime.

Example C.83. GF(p^m) is an extension field of GF(p), and GF(p) is a subfield of GF(p^m).

Theorem C.84. *If* GF(p^k) *is a subfield of* GF(p^m), *then* $k \mid m$.

Proof. Every $b \in \mathrm{GF}(p^m)$ must be a root of $x^{p^m} = x$. Every $a \in \mathrm{GF}(p^k)$ must be a root of $x^{p^k} = x$. Since GF(p^k) $\subseteq$ GF(p^m), every $a \in \mathrm{GF}(p^k)$ is also a root of $x^{p^m} = x$. Thus, $(x^{p^k} - x) \mid (x^{p^m} - x)$, and $(x^{p^k-1} - 1) \mid (x^{p^m-1} - 1)$. It then follows that

$$x^{p^k-1} - 1 = \gcd(x^{p^k-1} - 1, x^{p^m-1} - 1).$$

But, we have

$$\gcd(x^{p^k-1} - 1, x^{p^m-1} - 1) = x^{\gcd(p^k-1, p^m-1)} - 1 = x^{p^{\gcd(k,m)}-1} - 1. \tag{C.3}$$

Hence, $k \mid m$. $\qquad\square$

Theorem C.85. *Let* $k \mid m$. *Then* $\mathrm{GF}(p^m)$ *has a subfield with* p^k *elements.*

Proof. Since $k \mid m$, it follows from (C.3) that $(x^{p^k} - x) \mid (x^{p^m} - x)$. Note that all the elements of $\mathrm{GF}(p^m)$ are the roots of $x^{p^m} - x = 0$. It then follows that the set

$$\mathbb{K} = \{a \in \mathrm{GF}(p^m) \mid a^{p^k} = a\}$$

has cardinality p^k. Let $a, b \in \mathbb{K}$. Then

$$(a+b)^{p^k} = a^{p^k} + b^{p^k} = a + b, \ (ab)^{p^k} = a^{p^k} b^{p^k} = ab, \ (a^{-1})^{p^k} = (a^{p^k})^{-1} = a^{-1}.$$

Hence, $\mathbb{K}$ is a subfield with p^k elements. $\qquad\square$

Theorem C.86. *Let* $k \mid m$ *and let* $\mathrm{GF}(p^k)$ *denote the subfield of* $\mathrm{GF}(p^m)$. *Let* α *be a generator of* $\mathrm{GF}(p^m)^*$, *and let* $\beta = \alpha^{(p^m-1)/(p^k-1)}$. *Then* β *is a generator of* $\mathrm{GF}(p^k)^*$.

Proof. By definition, $\beta^{p^k} = \beta$. It then follows from the proof of heorem C.85 that $\beta \in \mathrm{GF}(p^k)$. By Proposition C.77,

$$\mathrm{ord}(\beta) = \frac{\mathrm{ord}(\alpha)}{\gcd\left(\mathrm{ord}(\alpha), \frac{p^m-1}{p^k-1}\right)} = \frac{p^m-1}{\gcd\left(p^m-1, \frac{p^m-1}{p^k-1}\right)} = p^k - 1.$$

The desired conclusion then follows. $\qquad\square$

Let r be a power of p below. Let $\ell \geq 1$ be an integer. For any $a \in \mathrm{GF}(r^\ell)^*$, the monic polynomial $P_a(x) \in \mathrm{GF}(r)[x]$ with the least degree such that $P_a(a) = 0$ is called the *minimal polynomial* over $\mathrm{GF}(r)$ of a. We have the following remarks.

- The existence of the minimal polynomial is guaranteed by Proposition C.76 (i.e., $a^{r^\ell-1} - 1 = 0$).
- By definition, $P_a(x)$ is irreducible over $\mathrm{GF}(r)$.
- It follows from Proposition C.76 that $P_a(x)$ divides $x^{r^\ell-1} - 1$.

Proposition C.87. *Let* $a \in \mathrm{GF}(r^\ell)^*$. *Then the minimal polynomial* $P_a(x)$ *of a over* $\mathrm{GF}(r)$ *has degree at most* ℓ.

Proof. Note that $a^{r^\ell} = a$ for any $a \in \mathrm{GF}(r^\ell)^*$. The set $\{a^{r^i} : i = 0, 1, 2, \ell - 1\}$ has at most ℓ elements. Let e be the smallest positive integer such that $a^{r^e} = a$. Then $e \leq \ell$. Define

$$g(x) = \prod_{i=0}^{e-1} (x - a^{r^i}).$$

Since $g(x)^r = g(x^r)$, g is a polynomial over $\mathrm{GF}(r)$. On the other hand, $g(a) = 0$ and $\deg(g) = e$. The desired conclusion then follows. $\qquad\square$

Proposition C.88. *If* α *is a generator of* $\mathrm{GF}(r^\ell)^*$, *the minimal polynomial* $P_\alpha(x)$ *has degree* ℓ.

Proof. Let α be a generator of $\mathrm{GF}(r^\ell)^*$. Suppose that the minimal polynomial $P_\alpha(x)$ has degree $e < \ell$. Let

$$P_\alpha(x) = x^e + a_{e-1}x^{e-1} + a_{e-2}x^{e-2} + \cdots + e_1 x + e_0.$$

Then each α^i can be expressed as $\sum_{k=0}^{e-1} b_k \alpha^k$, where all $b_i \in \mathrm{GF}(r)$. Then we have

$$|\{0, \alpha^0, \alpha^1, \alpha^2, \cdots, \alpha^{r^\ell - 2}\}| \leq r^e < r^\ell.$$

This is contrary to the assumption that α is a generator of $\mathrm{GF}(r^\ell)^*$. The desired conclusion then follows from Proposition C.87. $\qquad\square$

Example C.89. Let α be a generator of $\mathrm{GF}(2^3)^*$ with minimal polynomial $P_\alpha(x) = x^3 + x + 1$. Then the minimal polynomials over $\mathrm{GF}(2)$ of all the elements of $\mathrm{GF}(2^3)$ are:

$a \in \mathrm{GF}(2^3)$	Minimal polynomial of a
0	$x,$
α^0	$x - 1,$
α^1	$x^3 + x + 1,$
α^2	$x^3 + x + 1,$
α^3	$x^3 + x^2 + 1,$
α^4	$x^3 + x + 1,$
α^5	$x^3 + x^2 + 1,$
α^6	$x^3 + x^2 + 1.$

Note that the canonical factorization of $x^{2^3 - 1} - 1$ over $\mathrm{GF}(2)$ is given by

$$x^7 - 1 = (x - 1)(x^3 + x + 1)(x^3 + x^2 + 1).$$

Proof. It is left as an exercise. $\qquad\square$

We now show that $\mathrm{GF}(q^n)$ can be viewed as an n-dimensional vector space over $\mathrm{GF}(q)$. To this end, we first recall vector spaces over a field $\mathbb{F}$.

A *vector space V over* $\mathbb{F}$ has a binary operation "$+$" on V and a *scalar multiplication* on $\mathbb{F} \times V$ such that

(1) $(V, +)$ is an abelian group with identity 0;
(2) $av \in V$ for all $a \in \mathbb{F}$ and all $v \in V$;
(3) $a(bv) = (ab)v$ for all $a, b \in \mathbb{F}$ and all $v \in V$;
(4) $(a + b)v = av + bv$ for all $a, b \in \mathbb{F}$ and all $v \in V$;
(5) $a(v_1 + v_2) = av_1 + av_2 \in V$ for all $a \in \mathbb{F}$ and all $v_1, v_2 \in V$; and

(6) $1v = v$ for all $v \in V$.

Let V be a vector space over a field $\mathbb{F}$. A set $\{v_1, v_2, \cdots, v_n\}$ of elements in V is called a *basis* of V over $\mathbb{F}$ if

- $v_1, v_2, \cdots, v_n$ are *linearly independent* over $\mathbb{F}$, i.e., $\sum_{i=1}^{n} a_i v_i = 0$, where all $a_i \in \mathbb{F}$, if and only if all $a_i = 0$; and
- every element $v \in V$ can be expressed as $v = \sum_{i=1}^{n} a_i v_i$, where all $a_i \in \mathbb{F}$.

In this case, we say that V has dimension n or V is an n-dimensional vector space over $\mathbb{F}$.

Example C.90. $\mathbb{Q}^n = \mathbb{Q} \times \mathbb{Q} \times \cdots \times \mathbb{Q}$ is an n-dimensional vector space over the field $\mathbb{Q}$ of rational numbers.

Theorem C.91. $\mathrm{GF}(q^n)$ *is an n-dimensional vector space over* $\mathrm{GF}(q)$ *with respect to the addition and multiplication of the finite field* $\mathrm{GF}(q^n)$.

Proof. $\mathrm{GF}(q^n)$ is a vector space over $\mathrm{GF}(q)$ due to the following:

(1) $(\mathrm{GF}(q^n), +)$ is an abelian group with identity 0;
(2) $av \in \mathrm{GF}(q^n)$ for all $a \in \mathrm{GF}(q)$ and all $v \in \mathrm{GF}(q^n)$;
(3) $a(bv) = (ab)v$ for all $a, b \in \mathrm{GF}(q)$ and all $v \in \mathrm{GF}(q^n)$;
(4) $(a+b)v = av + bv$ for all $a, b \in \mathrm{GF}(q)$ and all $v \in \mathrm{GF}(q^n)$;
(5) $a(v_1 + v_2) = av_1 + av_2 \in \mathrm{GF}(q^n)$ for all $a \in \mathrm{GF}(q)$ and all $v_1, v_2 \in \mathrm{GF}(q^n)$; and
(6) $1v = v$ for all $v \in \mathrm{GF}(q^n)$.

We now prove that the dimension of $\mathrm{GF}(q^n)$ over $\mathrm{GF}(q)$ is n. Let α be a generator of $\mathrm{GF}(q^n)^*$. By Proposition C.87, the minimal polynomial $P_\alpha(x)$ over $\mathrm{GF}(q)$ of α has degree n. We now claim that $\{1, \alpha, \alpha^2, \cdots, \alpha^{n-1}\}$ is a basis of $\mathrm{GF}(q^n)$ over $\mathrm{GF}(q)$.

First of all, $1, \alpha, \alpha^2, \cdots, \alpha^{n-1}$ are linearly independent over $\mathrm{GF}(q)$, otherwise, the minimal polynomial of α over $\mathrm{GF}(q)$ would have degree less than n.

Secondly, the set $\{\sum_{i=0}^{n-1} a_i \alpha^i \mid a_i \in \mathrm{GF}(q)\}$ has cardinality q^n, as the elements $1, \alpha, \alpha^2, \cdots, \alpha^{n-1}$ are linearly independent over $\mathrm{GF}(q)$.

Hence $\{1, \alpha, \alpha^2, \cdots, \alpha^{n-1}\}$ is a basis of $\mathrm{GF}(q^n)$ over $\mathrm{GF}(q)$, and is referred to as a *polynomial basis*. $\square$

Let $\mathbb{K}$ be a subfield of $\mathbb{F}$. We use $[\mathbb{F} : \mathbb{K}]$ to denote the dimension of $\mathbb{F}$ when $\mathbb{F}$ is viewed as a vector space over $\mathbb{K}$. By Theorem C.91, $[\mathrm{GF}(q^n) : \mathrm{GF}(q)] = n$. A basis of $\mathrm{GF}(q^n)$ over $\mathrm{GF}(q)$ of the form $\{\alpha, \alpha^q, \cdots, \alpha^{q^{n-1}}\}$ is called a *normal basis* of $GF(q^n)$ over $GF(q)$, where $\alpha \in GF(q^n)$. Normal bases are sometimes more convenient to use than polynomial bases.

Example C.92. Let α be a generator of $GF(2^3)^*$ with minimal polynomial $x^3 + x^2 + 1$ over $GF(2)$. Then $\{\alpha, \alpha^2, \alpha^4\}$ is a normal basis of $GF(2^3)$ over $GF(2)$. Note that $\alpha^4 = 1 + \alpha + \alpha^2$.

Proof. It is left as an exercise. $\qquad\square$

The existence of a normal basis is guaranteed by the following theorem whose proof can be found in Lidl and Niederreiter (1997)[p. 60].

Theorem C.93 (Normal Basis Theorem). *For any finite field $\mathbb{K}$ and any finite extension $\mathbb{F}$ of $\mathbb{K}$, there exists a normal basis of $\mathbb{F}$ over $\mathbb{K}$.*

We now define and study two special functions from $GF(q^n)$ to $GF(q)$. They play an extremely important role in many applications. The first one is the trace function defined below.

For $a \in \mathbb{F} = GF(q^n)$ and $\mathbb{K} = GF(q)$, the *trace* $\mathrm{Tr}_{\mathbb{F}/\mathbb{K}}(a)$ of a over $\mathbb{K}$ is defined by

$$\mathrm{Tr}_{\mathbb{F}/\mathbb{K}}(a) = a + a^q + \cdots + a^{q^{n-1}}.$$

If $\mathbb{K}$ is the prime subfield of $\mathbb{F}$, then $\mathrm{Tr}_{\mathbb{F}/\mathbb{K}}(a)$ is called the *absolute trace* of a and simply denoted by $\mathrm{Tr}_{\mathbb{F}}(a)$. The following theorem describes important properties of the trace function $\mathrm{Tr}_{\mathbb{F}/\mathbb{K}}(x)$ from $\mathbb{F}$ to $\mathbb{K}$.

Theorem C.94. *Let $\mathbb{F} = GF(q^n)$ and $\mathbb{K} = GF(q)$. Then the trace function $\mathrm{Tr}_{\mathbb{F}/\mathbb{K}}(x)$ from $\mathbb{F}$ to $\mathbb{K}$ has the following properties:*

(1) $\mathrm{Tr}_{\mathbb{F}/\mathbb{K}}(a+b) = \mathrm{Tr}_{\mathbb{F}/\mathbb{K}}(a) + \mathrm{Tr}_{\mathbb{F}/\mathbb{K}}(b)$ for all $a, b \in \mathbb{F}$.
(2) $\mathrm{Tr}_{\mathbb{F}/\mathbb{K}}(ca) = c\mathrm{Tr}_{\mathbb{F}/\mathbb{K}}(a)$ for all $a \in \mathbb{F}$ and $c \in \mathbb{K}$.
(3) $\mathrm{Tr}_{\mathbb{F}/\mathbb{K}}(c) = n\mathrm{Tr}_{\mathbb{F}/\mathbb{K}}(c)$ for all $c \in \mathbb{K}$.
(4) $\mathrm{Tr}_{\mathbb{F}/\mathbb{K}}(a^q) = \mathrm{Tr}_{\mathbb{F}/\mathbb{K}}(a)$.

Proof. It is left as an exercise. $\qquad\square$

Another important property of the trace function is its transitivity, which is depicted in the next theorem.

Theorem C.95. *Let $\mathbb{K}$ be a finite field, let $\mathbb{F}$ be a finite extension of $\mathbb{K}$, and $\mathbb{E}$ a finite extension of $\mathbb{F}$. Then*

$$\mathrm{Tr}_{\mathbb{E}/\mathbb{K}}(a) = \mathrm{Tr}_{\mathbb{F}/\mathbb{K}}(\mathrm{Tr}_{\mathbb{E}/\mathbb{F}}(a))$$

for all $a \in \mathbb{E}$.

Proof. Let $\mathbb{K} = \mathrm{GF}(q)$, let $[\mathbb{F} : \mathbb{K}] = \ell$ and $[\mathbb{E} : \mathbb{F}] = n$. Then $[\mathbb{E} : \mathbb{K}] = n\ell$ and

$$|\mathbb{F}| = q^{\ell}, \quad |\mathbb{E}| = q^{\ell n}.$$

Then for any $a \in \mathbb{E}$ we have

$$
\begin{aligned}
\mathrm{Tr}_{\mathbb{F}/\mathbb{K}}(\mathrm{Tr}_{\mathbb{E}/\mathbb{F}}(a)) &= \sum_{i=0}^{\ell-1} \mathrm{Tr}_{\mathbb{E}/\mathbb{F}}(a)^{q^i} = \sum_{i=0}^{\ell-1} \left(\sum_{j=0}^{n-1} a^{q^{\ell j}} \right)^{q^i} \\
&= \sum_{i=0}^{\ell-1} \sum_{j=0}^{n-1} a^{q^{\ell j + i}} = \sum_{k=0}^{n\ell-1} a^{q^k} \\
&= \mathrm{Tr}_{\mathbb{E}/\mathbb{K}}(a).
\end{aligned}
$$

$\square$

The second important function from $\mathbb{F}$ to its subfield $\mathbb{K}$ is the norm function defined below. For $a \in \mathbb{F} = \mathrm{GF}(q^n)$ and $\mathbb{K} = \mathrm{GF}(q)$, the *norm* $\mathrm{N}_{\mathbb{F}/\mathbb{K}}(a)$ of a over $\mathbb{K}$ is defined by

$$\mathrm{N}_{\mathbb{F}/\mathbb{K}}(a) = a \cdot a^q \cdots a^{q^{n-1}} = a^{\frac{q^n-1}{q-1}}.$$

Note that $\mathrm{N}_{\mathbb{F}/\mathbb{K}}(a)^q = \mathrm{N}_{\mathbb{F}/\mathbb{K}}(a)$ for all $a \in \mathbb{F}$. we have $\mathrm{N}_{\mathbb{F}/\mathbb{K}}(a) \in \mathbb{K}$ for all $a \in \mathbb{F}$.

The following theorem describes basic properties of the norm function whose proofs are straightforward and left as exercises.

Theorem C.96. *Let $\mathbb{K} = \mathrm{GF}(q)$ and $\mathbb{F} = \mathrm{GF}(q^n)$. Then the norm function $\mathrm{N}_{\mathbb{F}/\mathbb{K}}(x)$ has the following properties:*

(1) $\mathrm{N}_{\mathbb{F}/\mathbb{K}}(ab) = \mathrm{N}_{\mathbb{F}/\mathbb{K}}(a)\mathrm{N}_{\mathbb{F}/\mathbb{K}}(b)$ *for all $a, b \in \mathbb{F}$.*
(2) $\mathrm{N}_{\mathbb{F}/\mathbb{K}}$ *maps $\mathbb{F}$ onto $\mathbb{K}$ and $\mathbb{F}^*$ onto $\mathbb{K}^*$.*
(3) $\mathrm{N}_{\mathbb{F}/\mathbb{K}}(a) = a^n$ *for all $a \in \mathbb{K}$.*
(4) $\mathrm{N}_{\mathbb{F}/\mathbb{K}}(a^q) = \mathrm{N}_{\mathbb{F}/\mathbb{K}}(a)$ *for all $a \in \mathbb{F}$.*

The norm function has also the following transitivity.

Theorem C.97. *Let $\mathbb{K}$ be a finite field, let $\mathbb{F}$ be a finite extension of $\mathbb{K}$, and $\mathbb{E}$ a finite extension of $\mathbb{F}$. Then*

$$\mathrm{N}_{\mathbb{E}/\mathbb{K}}(a) = \mathrm{N}_{\mathbb{F}/\mathbb{K}}(\mathrm{N}_{\mathbb{E}/\mathbb{F}}(a))$$

for all $a \in \mathbb{E}$.

Proof. It is straightforward and left as an exercise. $\square$

Finite fields have a lot of applications in science and engineering. Below is a list of some applications.

- Mathematics (finite geometry, combinatorial designs, algebraic geometry, number theory).
- Computer science (cryptography and coding theory, computer algorithms, data storage systems, simulation, software testing).
- Electrical engineering (CDMA communications, error detection and correction, signal processing, signal designs).

Bibliography

Abdukhalikov, K. and Ho, D. (2021). Extended cyclic codes, maximal arcs and ovoids, *Des. Codes Cryptogr.* **89**, pp. 2283–2294.

Alltop, W. O. (1975). Extending t-designs, *J. Combin. Theory A* **18**, pp. 177–186.

Antweiler, M. and Bomer, L. (1992). Complex sequences over $GF(p^M)$ with a two-level autocorrelation function and a large linear span, *IEEE Trans. Inform. Theory* **8**, pp. 120–130.

Artin, E. (1957). *Geometric Algebra* (Wiley Interscience, New York).

Aschbacher, M. (2000). *Finite Group Theory* (Cambridge University Press, Cambridge).

Assmus, Jr., E. F. (1995). On 2-ranks of Steiner triple systems, *Electron. J. Comb.* **2**, #R9.

Assmus, Jr. E. F. and Key, J. D. (1986). On an infinite class of Steiner systems with $t = 3$ and $k = 6$, *J. Combin. Theory Ser. A* **42**, pp. 55–60.

Assmus, Jr. E. F. and Key, J. D. (1992). *Designs and Their Codes, Cambridge Tracts in Mathematics*, Vol. 103 (Cambridge University Press, Cambridge).

Assmus, Jr. E. F. and Key, J. D. (1992). Hadamard matrices and their designs: a coding-theoretic approach, *Transactions of the American Mathematical Society* **330**, pp. 269–293.

Assmus, Jr. E. F. and Key, J. D. (1998). Polynomial codes and finite geometries, in *Handbook of Coding Theory*, Eds., Pless, V. S., Huffman, W. C. (Elsevier, Amsterdam), pp. 1269–1440.

Assmus, Jr. E. F. and Mattson, H. F. (1969). New 5-designs, *J. Combin. Theory* **6**, pp. 122–151.

Assmus, Jr. E. F. and Mattson, H. F. (1974). Coding and combinatorics, *SIAM Rev.* **16**, pp. 349–388.

Ball, S. (2012). On sets of vectors of a finite vector space in which every subset of basis size is a basis, *J. Eur. Math. Soc.* **14**, pp. 733–748.

Ball, S., Blokhuis, A. and Mazzocca, F. (1997). Maximal arcs in Desarguesian planes of odd order do not exist, *Combinatorica* **17**, pp. 31–41.

Barlotti, A. (1955). Unéstensione del teorema di Segre-Kustaanheimo, *Boll. Un. Mat. Ital. Ser. III* **10**, pp. 498–506.

Barlotti, A. (1965). Some topics in finite geometrical structures, Institute of Statistics Mimeo Series No. 439 (University of North Carolina, California).

Baumert, L. D. and McEliece, R. J. (1972). Weights of irreducible cyclic codes, *Inform.*

and Control **20**, 2, pp. 158–175.

Baumert, L. D., Mills, W. H. and Ward, R. L. (1982). Uniform cyclotomy, *J. Number Theory* **14**, pp. 67–82.

Beenker, G. J. M. (1980). On double circulant codes, EUT report. WSK, Vol. 80-WSK-04, Eindhoven University of Technology, Eindhoven.

Berger, T. P. (1994). The automorphism group of double-error correcting codes, *IEEE Trans. Inform. Theory* **40**, 2, pp. 538–542.

Berger, T. P. and Charpin, P. (1996). The permutation group of affine-invariant extended cyclic codes, *IEEE Trans. Inform. Theory* **42**, pp. 2194–2209.

Berger, T. P. and Charpin, P. (1999). The automorphism groups of BCH codes and of some affine-invariant codes over extension fields, *Des. Codes Cryptogr.* **18**, pp. 29–53.

Beth, T., Jungnickel, D. and Lenz, H (1999). *Design Theory*, Vol. I, 2nd edition, *Encyclopedia of Mathematics and its Applications*, Vol. 69 (Cambridge University Press, Cambridge).

Beutelspacher, A. and Rosenbaum, U. (1998). *Projective Geometry: from Foundations to Applications* (Cambridge University Press, Cambridge).

Bierbrauer, J. (2010). New semifields, PN and APN functions, *Des. Codes Cryptogr.* **54**, pp. 189–200.

Bierbrauer, J. (2017). *Introduction to Coding Theory*, Second Edition (CRC Press, New York).

Blahut, R. E. (1991). The Gleason-Prange Theorem, *IEEE Trans. Inform. Theory* **37**, 5, pp. 1269–1273.

Blondeau, C., Canteaut, A. and Charpin, P. (2010). Differential properties of power functions, in *Proceedings of the 2010 IEEE International Symposium on Information Theory* (IEEE Press, USA), pp. 2478–2482.

Bonisoli, A. (1984). Every equidistant linear code is a sequence of dual Hamming codes, *Ars Combinatoria* **18**, pp. 181–186.

Bose, R. C. (1947). Mathematical theory of the symmetrical factorial design, *Sankhya* **8**, pp. 107–166.

Bose, R. C. (1961). On some connections between the design of experiments and information theory, *Bull. Intern. Statist.* **38**, pp. 257–271.

Bose, R. C. and Ray-Chaudhuri, D. K. (1960). On a class of error correcting binary group codes, *Inform. and Control* **3**, pp. 68–79.

Bose, R. C. and Shrikhande, S. S. (1973). Embedding the complement of an oval in a projective plane of even order, *Disc. Math.* **6**, pp. 305–312.

Bracken, C., Tan, C. H. and Tan, Y. (2012). Binomial differentially 4-uniform permutations with high nonlinearity, *Finite Fields Appl.* **18**, 3, pp. 537–546.

Bridges, W. G., Hall Jr., M. and Hayden, J. L. (1981). Codes and designs, *J. Combin. Theory Ser. A* **31**, pp. 155–174.

Britz, T., Royle, G. and Shiromoto, K. (2009). Designs from matroids, *SIAM Discrete Math.* **23**, pp. 1082–1099.

Budaghyan, L. and Helleseth, T. (2008). New perfect nonlinear multinomials over $F_{p^{2k}}$ for any odd prime p, in *Proc. of SETA 2008*, LNCS 5203 (Springer-Verlag, Heidelberg), pp. 403–414.

Byrne, E. and Ravagnani, A. (2019). An Assmus-Mattson theorem for rank metric codes, *SIAM J. Discrete Math.* **33**, pp. 1242–1260.

Calderbank, A. R. (1982). On uniformly packed $[n, n - k, 4]$ codes over $GF(q)$ with a class of caps in $PG(k - 1, q)$, *J. London Math. Soc.* **2**, pp. 365–384.

Calderbank, A. R., Delsarte, P. and Sloane, N. J. A. (1991). A strengthening of the Assmus-Mattson theorem, *IEEE Trans. Inform. Theory* **37**, 5, pp. 1261–1268.

Calderbank, A. R. and Goethals, J. M. (1984). Three-weight codes and association schemes, *Philips J. Res.* **39**, pp. 143–152.

Calderbank, A. R. and Kantor, W. M. (1985). The geometry of two-weight codes, *Bull. London Math. Soc.* **18**, pp. 97–122.

Cameron, P. J. and van Lint, J. H. (1991). Designs, Graphs, Codes and Their Links (Cambridge University Press, Cambridge).

Carlet, C., Charpin, P. and Zinoviev, V. (1998). Codes, bent functions and permutations suitable for DES-like cryptosystems, *Des. Codes Cryptogr.* **15**, 2, pp. 125–156.

Carlet, C. and Ding, C. (2004). Highly nonlinear mappings, *J. Complexity* **20**, 2, pp. 205–244.

Carlet, C., Ding, C. and Yuan, J. (2005). Linear codes from highly nonlinear functions and their secret sharing schemes, *IEEE Trans. Inform. Theory* **51**, 6, pp. 2089–2102.

Carlet, C. and Mesnager, S. (2011). On Dillion's class H of bent functions, Niho bent functions and o-polynomials, *J. Combin. Theory Ser. A* **118**, pp. 2392–2410.

Carlet, C. and Mesnager, S. (2016). Four decades of research on bent functions, *Des. Codes Cryptogr.* **78**, pp. 5–50.

Carpenter, L. L. (1996). Oval designs on Desarguesian projective planes, *Des. Codes Cryptogr.* **9**, pp. 51–59.

Chang, Y., Fan, B., Feng, T., Holt, D. F. and Östergård, R. J. (2017). Classification of cyclic Steiner quadruple systems, *J. Comb. Designs* **25**, pp. 103–121.

Charpin, P. (1990). Codes cycliques étendus affines-invariants et antichaînes d'un ensemble partiellement ordonné, *Discrete Math.* **80**, 229–247.

Charpin, P. and Peng, J. (2019). Differential uniformity and the associated codes of cryptographic functions, *Advances in Mathematics of Communications* **13**, 4, pp. 579–600.

Charpin, P. and Peng, J. (2019). New links between nonlinearity and differential uniformity, *Finite Fields Appl.* **56**, pp. 188–208.

Chen, Y. Q. and Polhill, J. (2011). Paley type group schemes and planar Dembowski-Ostrom polynomials, *Disc. Math.* **311**, 14, pp. 1349–1364.

Cherowitzo, W. (1988). Hyperovals in Desarguesian planes of even order, *Annals of Discrete Math.* **37**, pp. 87–94.

Cherowitzo, W. (1996). Hyperovals in Desarguesian planes: an update, *Disc. Math.* **155**, pp. 31–38.

Cherowitzo, W., Penttila, T., Pinneri, I. and Royle, G. F. (1996). Flocks and ovals, *Geometriae Dedicata* **60**, pp. 17–37.

Cho, E.-K., Ding, C. and Hyun, J. Y. (2019). A spectral characterisation of t-designs and its applications, *Advances in Mathematics of Communications* **13**, pp. 477–503.

Cohen, G., Honkala, I., Litsyn, S. and Lobstein, A. (1997). *Covering Codes*, North-Holland Mathematics Library, Vol. 54 (North-Holland, Amsterdam).

Colbourn, C. J. and Mathon, R. (2007). Steiner systems, in *Handbook of Combinatorial Designs* (CRC Press, New York), Eds., Colbourn, C. J. and Dinitz, J., pp. 102–110.

Coulter, R. (2002). The number of rational points of a class of Artin-Schreier curves, *Finite Fields and Their Applications* **8**, pp. 397–413.

Coulter, R. and Matthews, R. W. (1997). Planar functions and planes of Lenz-Barlotti class II, *Des. Codes Cryptogr.* **10**, pp. 167–184.

Danev, D. and Dodunekov, S. (1973). A family of ternary quasi-perfect BCH codes, *Des. Codes Cryptogr.* **49**, pp. 265–271.

De Boer, M. A. (1996). Almost MDS codes, *Des. Codes Cryptogr.* **9**, pp. 143–155.

Delsarte, P. (1970). On cyclic codes that are invariant under the general linear group, *IEEE Trans. Inform. Theory* **16**, pp. 760–769.

Delsarte, P. (1973a). Four fundamental parameters of a code and their combinatorial significance, *Inform. and Control* **23**, pp. 1–79.

Delsarte, P. (1973b). An algebraic approach to the association schemes of coding theory, *Philips Res. Rep. Suppl.* **10**, pp. 407–438.

Delsarte, P. (1975). On subfield subcodes of modified Reed-Solomon codes, *IEEE Trans. Inform. Theory* **21**, 5, pp. 575–576.

Delsarte, P., Goethals, J. M. and MacWilliams, F. J. (1970). On generalized Reed-Muller codes and their relatives, *Inform. and Control* **18**, pp. 403–442.

Dembowski, P. (1963). Inversive planes of even order, *Bull. Amer. Math. Soc.* **69**, pp. 850–854.

Dembowski, P. (1968). *Finite Geometries* (Springer-Verlag, Heidelberg).

Dembowski, P. and Ostrom, T. G. (1968). Planes of order n with collineation groups of order n^2, *Math. Z.* **193**, pp. 239–258.

Denniston, R. H. F. (1969). Some maximal arcs in finite projective planes, *J. Combin. Theory Ser. A* **6**, pp. 317–319.

De Winter, S., Ding, C. and Tonchev, V. D. (2019). Maximal arcs and extended cyclic codes, *Des. Codes Cryptogr.* **87**, pp. 807–816.

Dianwu, Y. and Zhengming, H. (1996). On the dimension and minimum distance of BCH codes over $GF(q)$, *J. of Electronics (in Chinese)* **13**, 3, pp. 216–221.

Dickson, L. E. (1896). The analytic representation of substitutions on a power of a prime number of letters with a discussion of the linear group, *Ann. of Math.* **11**, pp. 65–120, pp. 161–183.

Dillon, J. F. and Schatz, J. R. (1987). Block designs with the symmetric difference property, in *Proc. of the NSA Mathematical Sciences Meetings*, Ed., Ward R. L., pp. 159–164.

Ding, C. (2009). A class of three-weight and four-weight codes, in *Proceedings of International Conference on Coding and Cryptography*, Lecture Notes in Computer Science 5557 (Springer Verlag, Heidelberg), pp. 34–42.

Ding, C. (2015a). *Codes from Difference Sets* (World Scientific, Singapore).

Ding, C. (2015b). Parameters of several classes of BCH codes, *IEEE Trans. Inform. Theory* **61**, 10, pp. 5322–5330.

Ding, C. (2015c). Linear codes from some 2-designs, *IEEE Trans. Inform. Theory* **60**, pp. 3265–3275.

Ding, C. (2016). A construction of binary linear codes from Boolean functions, *Disc. Math.* **339**, pp. 2288–2303.

Ding, C. (2018a). An infinite family of Steiner systems $S(2,4,2^m)$ from cyclic codes, *J. Combinatorial Designs* **26**, 3, pp. 127–144.

Ding, C. (2018b). A sequence construction of cyclic codes over finite fields, *Cryptogr. and Commun.* **10**, pp. 319–341.

Ding, C. (2018c). Infinite families of 3-designs from a type of five-weight code, *Des. Codes*

Cryptogr. **86**, 3, pp. 703–719.

Ding, C., Du, X. and Zhou, Z. (2015). The Bose and minimum distance of a class of BCH codes, *IEEE Trans. Inform. Theory* **61**, 5, pp. 2351–2356.

Ding, C., Fan, C. and Zhou, Z. (2017). The dimension and minimum distance of two classes of primitive BCH codes, *Finite Fields Appl.* **45**, pp. 237–263.

Ding, C., Helleseth, T., Kløve, T. and Wang, X. (2007). A generic construction of Cartesian authentication codes, *IEEE Trans. Inform. Theory* **53**, 6, pp. 2229–2235.

Ding, C., Kohel, D. and Ling, S. (2000). Elementary 2-group character codes, *IEEE Trans. Inform. Theory* **46**, pp. 280–284.

Ding, C., Lam, K. Y. and Xing, C. (1999). Enumeration and construction of all duadic codes of length p^m, *Fundamenta Informaticae* **38**, 1, pp. 149–161.

Ding, C. and Li, C. (2017). Infinite families of 2-designs and 3-designs from linear codes, *Disc. Math.* **340**, pp. 2415–2431.

Ding, C., Li, C., Li, N. and Zhou, Z. (2016). Three-weight cyclic codes and their weight distributions, *Disc. Math.* **339**, 2, pp. 415–427.

Ding, C., Li, C. and Xia, Y. (2018). Another generalization of the Reed-Muller codes, *Finite Fields and Their Applications* **53**, pp. 147–174.

Ding, C. and Lin, S. (2013). A q-polynomial approach to cyclic codes, *Finite Fields and Their Applications* **20**, pp. 1–14.

Ding, C., Luo, J. and Niederreiter, H. (2008). Two weight codes punctured from irreducible cyclic codes, in *Proc. of the First International Workshop on Coding Theory and Cryptography*, Eds., Li, Y., Ling, S., Niederreiter, H., Wang, H., Xing, C., Zhang, S. (Singapore, World Scientific), pp. 119–124 .

Ding, C., Munemasa, A. and Tonchev, V. D. (2019). Bent vectorial functions, codes and designs. *IEEE Trans. Inform. Theory* **65**, 11, pp. 7533–7541.

Ding, C. and Niederreiter, H. (2007). Cyclotomic linear codes of order 3. *IEEE Trans. Inform. Theory* **53**, 6, pp. 2274–2277.

Ding, C., Pei, D. and Salomaa, A. (1996). *Chinese Remainder Theorem: Applications in Computing, Coding and Cryptography* (World Scientific, Singapore).

Ding, C. and Pless, V. (1999). Cyclotomy and duadic codes of prime lengths, *IEEE Trans. Inform. Theory* **45**, 2, pp. 453–466.

Ding, C. and Tang, C. (2020). Infinite families of near MDS codes holding t-designs, *IEEE Trans. Inform. Theory* **66**, 9, pp. 5419–5428.

Ding, C. and Tang, C. (2020). Combinatorial t-designs from special functions, *Cryptography and Communications* **12**, 5, pp. 1011–1033.

Ding, C., Tang, C. and Tonchev, V. D. (2020). The projective general linear groups $PGL(2, 2^m)$ and linear codes of length $2^m + 1$, *Des. Codes Cryptogr.* **89**, 7, pp. 1713–1734.

Ding, C. and Wang, X. (2005). A coding theory construction of new systematic authentication codes, *Theoretical Computer Science* **330**, 1, pp. 81–99.

Ding, C., Xiao, G. and Shan, W. (1991). *The Stability Theory of Stream Ciphers*, Lecture Notes in Computer Science, Vol. 561 (Springer-Verlag, Heidelberg).

Ding, C. and Yang, J. (2013). Hamming weights in irreducible cyclic codes, *Disc. Math.* **313**, 4, pp. 434–446.

Ding, C., Yang, Y. and Tang, X. (2010). Optimal sets of frequency hopping sequences from linear cyclic codes, *IEEE Trans. Inform. Theory* **56**, 7, pp. 3605–3512.

Designs from Linear Codes

Ding, C. and Yin, J. (2008). Sets of optimal frequency hopping sequences, *IEEE Trans. Inform. Theory* **54**, 8, pp. 3741–3745.

Ding, C. and Yuan, J. (2006). A family of skew Hadamard difference sets, *J. Combin. Theory Ser. A* **113**, pp. 1526–1535.

Ding, C. and Yuan, P. (2015). Five constructions of permutation polynomials over $GF(q^2)$, http://arxiv.org/abs/1511.00322.

Ding, C. and Zhou, Z. (2017). Parameters of 2-designs from some BCH codes, in *Codes, Cryptography and Information Security*, Lecture Notes in Computer Science, Vol. 10194, Eds., El Hajji, S., Nitaj, A. and Souidi, E. M. (Springer Verlag, Heidelberg), pp. 110–127.

Dixon, J. D. and Mortimer B. (1996). *Permutation Groups*, Graduate Texts in Mathematics, Vol. 163 (Springer Verlag, New York).

Dodunekov, S. and Landgev, I. (1995). On near-MDS codes, *J. Geometry* **54**, pp. 30–43.

Draper, S. and Hou, X. D. (2008). Explicit evaluation of certain exponential sums of quadratic functions over F_{p^n}, p odd, *arXiv:0708.3619v1*.

Du, X., Wang, R. and Fan, C. (2020). Infinite families of 2-designs from a class of cyclic codes, *J. Comb. Designs* **28**, 3, pp. 157–170.

Du, X., Wang, R., Tang, C. and Wang, Q. (2020a). Infinite families of 2-designs from linear codes, *Applicable Algebra in Engineering, Communication and Computing*, https://doi.org/10.1007/s00200-020-00438-8.

Du, X., Wang, R., Tang, C. and Wang, Q. (2020b). Infinite families of 2-designs from two classes of binary cyclic codes with three nonzeros, Advances in Mathematics of Communications, DOI:10.3934/amc.2020106.

Faldum, A. and Willems, W. (1997). Codes of small defect, *Des. Codes Cryptogr.* **10**, pp. 341–350.

Gauss, C. F. (1801). *Disquisitiones Arithmeticae* (Leipzig) (English translation, Yale, New Haven, 1966; Reprint by Springer Verlag, Berlin, Heidelberg, and New York, 1986).

Gilbert, E. N. (1952). A comparison of signaling alphabets, *Bell System Tech. J.* **31**, pp. 504–522.

Gleason, A. M. (1971). Weight polynomials of self-dual codes and the MacWilliams identities, in *Actes du Congrés International des Mathématiciens* (Nice, 1970 Tome 3) (Gauthier-Villars, Paris), pp. 211–215.

Glynn, D. G. (1983). Two new sequences of ovals in finite Desarguesian planes of even order, in *Combinatorial Mathematics X*, Lecture Notes in Mathematics 1036, Ed., Casse, L. R. A. (Springer Verlag, Heidelberg), pp. 217–229.

Glynn, D. G. (1989). A condition for the existence of ovals in $PG(2,q)$, q even, *Geometriae Dedicata* **32**, pp. 247–252.

Goethals, J.-M. (1979). Association schemes, in *Algebraic Coding Theory and Applications, CISM Courses and Lectures No. 258*, Ed., Longo (Springer Verlag, New York), pp. 243–283.

Goethals, J.-M., van Tilborg, H. C. A. (1975). Uniformly packed codes, *Philips Res. Reports* **30**, pp. 9–36.

Golay, M. J. E. (1949). Notes on digital coding, *Proceedings of the I.R.E.* **37**, p. 657.

Gold, R. (1968). Maximal recursive sequences with 3-valued recursive crosscorrelation functions, *IEEE Trans. Inform. Theory* **14**, pp. 154–156.

Gorenstein, D. C., Peterson, W. W. and Zieler N. (1960). Two-error correcting Bose-

Chaudhuri codes are quasi-perfect, *Inform. and Control* **3**, pp. 291–294.

Griesmer, J. H. (1960). A bound for error-correcting codes, *IBM J. Research Develop.* **4**, pp. 532–542.

Gurak, S. J. (2004). Period polynomials for $\mathbb{F}_q$ of fixed small degree, *Centre de Recherches Mathématiques CRM Proceedings and Lecture Notes* **36**, pp. 127–145.

Hall, Jr., M. (1959). *The Theory of Groups* (Macmillan Company).

Hall, Jr., M. (1986). *Combinatorial Theory*, Second Edition (Wiley).

Hamada, N. (1973). On the p-rank of the incidence matrix of a balanced or partially balanced incomplete block design and its applications to error correcting codes, *Hiroshima Math. J.* **3**, 153–226.

Hamilton, N. and Penttila, T. (2001). Groups of maximal arcs, *J. Combin. Theory Ser. A* **94**, pp. 63–86.

Hanani, H. (1960). On quadruple systems, *Canad. J. Math.* **12**, pp. 145–157.

Hanani, H. (1961). The existence and construction of balanced incomplete block designs, *Ann. Math. Stat.* **32**, pp. 361–386.

Hanani, H. (1975). Balanced incomplete block designs and related designs, *Discrete Math.* **11**, pp. 255–369.

Hartmann, C. R. P. and Tzeng, K. K. (1972). Generalizations of the BCH bound, *Inform. and Control* **20**, pp. 489–498.

Helleseth, T., Rong, C. and Yang, K. (2001). On t-designs from codes over $\mathbb{Z}_4$, *Disc. Math.* **238**, pp. 67–80.

Heng, Z. and Ding, C. (2019). A construction of q-ary linear codes with irreducible cyclic codes, *Des. Codes Cryptogr.* **87**, 5, pp. 1087–1108.

Heng, Z., Wang, Q. and Ding, C. (2020). Two families of optimal linear codes and their subfield codes, *IEEE Trans. Inform. Theory* **66**, 11, pp. 6872–6883.

Heng, Z., Wang, W. and Wang, Y. (2021). Projective binary linear codes from special Boolean functions, *Applicable Algebra in Engineering, Communication and Computing* **32**, 4, pp. 521–552.

Herbert, V. and Sarkar, S. (2011). On the triple-error-correcting codes with zero set $\{1, 2^i + 1, 2^j + 1\}$, in *Cryptography and Coding*, Lecture Notes in Computer Science 7089, Ed. Chen, L. (Springer-Verlag, Berlin), pp. 79–96.

Hertel, D. and Pott, A. (2008). Two results on maximum nonlinear functions, *Des. Codes Cryptogr.* **47**, 1–3, pp. 225–235.

Hirschfeld, J. W. P. (1998). *Projective Geometries over Finite Fields*, Second Edition (Oxford Univ. Press, Oxford).

Hirschfeld, J. W. P. and Storme, L. (1998). The packing problems in statistics, coding theory and finite projective spaces, *J. Statist. Plann. Inference* **72**, pp. 355–380.

Hocquenghem, A. (1959). Codes correcteurs d'erreurs, *Chiffres (Paris)* **2**, pp. 147–156.

Hoshi, A. (2006). Explicit lifts of quintic Jacobi sums and period polynomials for F_q, *Proc. Japan Acad. Ser. A* **82**, pp. 87–92.

Hou, X.-D. (2005). Enumeration of certain affine invariant extended cyclic codes, *J. Combin. Theory Ser. A* **110**, pp. 71–95.

Huffman, W. C. (1998). Codes and groups, in *Handbook of Coding Theory*, Eds., Pless, V. S. and Huffman, W. C. (Elsevier, Amsterdam), pp. 1345–1440.

Huffman, W. C. and Pless, V. (2003). *Fundamentals of Error-Correcting Codes* (Cambridge University Press, Cambridge).

Humphreys, J. F. and Prest, M. Y. (2004). *Numbers, Groups and Codes* (Cambridge University Press, Cambridge).

Ionin, Y. J. and Shrikhande, M. S. (2006). *Combinatorics of Symmetric Designs* (Cambridge University Press, Cambridge).

Janusz, G. J. (2000). Overlap and covering polynomials with applications to designs and self-dual codes, *SIAM J. Discrete Math.* **13**, pp. 154–178.

Jungnickel, D., Magliveras, S. S., Tonchev, V. D. and Wassermann, A. (2017). On classifying Steiner triple systems by their 3-rank, In *MACIS 2017, LNCS 10693*, Eds., Blömer, J. et al. (Springer, Heidelberg), pp. 295–305.

Jungnickel, D. and Pott, A. (1999a). Difference sets: an introduction, in *Difference sets, sequences and their correlation properties*, Eds., Pott, A., Kumar, P. V., Helleseth, T. and Jungnickel, D. (Klumer, Amsterdam), pp. 259–296.

Jungnickel, D. and Pott, A. (1999b). Perfect and almost perfect sequences, *Discrete Applied Math.* **95**, pp. 331–359.

Jungnickel, D. and Tonchev, V. D. (1991). Exponential number of quasi-symmetric SDP designs and codes meeting the Grey-Rankin bound, *Des. Codes Cryptogr.* **1**, pp. 247–253.

Jungnickel, D. and Tonchev, V. D. (1992). On symmetric and quasi-symmetric designs with the symmetric difference property and their codes, *J. Combin. Theory Ser. A* **59**, pp. 40–50.

Jungnickel, D. and Tonchev, V. D. (2018). On Bonisoli's theorem and the block codes of Steiner triple systems, *Des. Codes Cryptogr.* **86**, pp. 449–462.

Jungnickel, D. and Tonchev, V. D. (2019). Counting Steiner triple systems with classical parameters and prescribed rank, *J. Comb. Theory Ser. A* **162**, pp. 10–33.

Kantor, W. M. (1972). k-homogeneous groups, *M. Z.* **124**, pp. 261–265.

Kantor, W. M. (1975). Symplectic groups, symmetric designs, and line ovals, *J. Algebra* **33**, pp. 43–58.

Kantor, W. M. (1983). Exponential number of two-weight codes, difference sets and symmetric designs, *Disc. Math.* **46**, pp. 95–98.

Kantor, W. M. (2003). Commutative semifields and symplectic spreads, *J. Algebra* **270**, pp. 96–114.

Kasami, T. (1969). Weight distributions of Bose-Chaudhuri-Hocquenghem codes, in *Combinatorial Mathematics and Applications*, Eds., Bose, R. C. and Dowlings, T. A. (Univ. North Carolina Press, Chapel Hill, NC), ch. 29.

Kasami, T., Lin, S. and Peterson, W. (1968). Some results on cyclic codes which are invariant under the affine group and their applications, *Inform. and Control* **11**, pp. 475–496.

Kasami, T., Lin, S. and Peterson, W. (1968). Generalized Reed-Muller codes, *Electron. Commun. Japan* **51-C3**, pp. 96–104.

Kasami, T., Lin, S. and Peterson, W. (1968). New generalizations of the Reed-Muller codes, Part I: primitive codes, *IEEE Trans. Inform. Theory* **14**, pp. 189–199.

Kasami, T. and Tokura, N. (1970). On the weight structure of Reed-Muller codes, *IEEE Trans. Inform. Theory* **16**, pp. 752–759.

Kasami, T., Tokura, N. and Azumi, S. (1974). On the weight enumeration of weights less than $2.5d$ of Redd-Muller codes (Faculty of Engineering Science, Osaka University, Osaka, Japan).

Key, J. D. and Wagner, A. (1986). On an infinite class of Steiner systems constructed from affine spaces, *Arch. Math.* **47**, pp. 376–378.

Klemm, M. (1986). Über den *p*-Ranken von Inzidenzmatrizen, *J. Combin. Theory Ser. A* **43**, pp. 138–139.

Kolesnik, V. D. and Mironchikov, E. T. (1968). Cyclic Reed-Muller codes and their decoding, *Prpblem of Info. Trans.* **4**, pp. 15–19.

Lachaud, G. and Wolfmann, J. (1990). The weights of the orthogonals of the extended quadratic binary Goppa codes, *IEEE Trans. Inform. Theory* **36**, pp. 686–692.

Leon, J. S., Masley, J. M. and Pless, V. (1984). Duadic codes, *IEEE Trans. Inform. Theory* **30**, pp. 709–714.

Li, C., Ding, C. and Li, S. (2017). LCD cyclic codes over finite fields, *IEEE Trans. Inform. Theory* **63**, 7, pp. 4344–4356.

Li, C., Wu, P. and Liu, F. (2019). On two classes of primitive BCH codes and some related codes, *IEEE Trans. Inform. Theory* **65**, 6, pp. 3830–3840.

Li, S. (2017). The minimum distance of some narrow-sense primitive BCH codes, *SIAM J. Discrete Math.* **31**, 4, pp. 2530–2569.

Li, S. (2019). On the weight distribution of second order Reed-Muller codes and their relatives, *Des. Codes Cryptogr.* **87**, pp. 2447–2460.

Li, S., Ding, C., Xiong, M. and Ge, G. (2017). Narrow-sense BCH codes over GF(q) with length $n = (q^m - 1)/(q - 1)$, *IEEE Trans. Inform. Theory* **63**, 11, pp. 7219–7236.

Lidl, R., Mullen, G. L. and Turnwald, G. (1993). *Dickson Polynomials* (Longman, England).

Lidl, R. and Niederreiter, H. (1997). *Finite Fields*, 2nd Edition (Cambridge University Press, Cambridge).

Liu, H., Ding, C. and Li, C. (2017). Dimensions of three types of BCH codes over GF(q), *Disc. Math.* **340**, pp. 1910–1927.

Liu, Q., Ding, C., Mesnager, S., Tang, C. and Tonchev, V. D. (2021). On infinite families of narrow-sense antiprimitive BCH codes admitting 3-transitive automorphism groups and their consequences, arXiv:2109.09051 [cs.IT].

Liu, Y., Ding, C. and Tang, C. (2021). Shortened linear codes over finite fields, *IEEE Trans. Inform. Theory* **67**, 8, pp. 5119–5132.

Lucas, E. (1878). Sur les congruences des nombres euleriennes et des coefficients différentiels des fonctions trigonomètriques, suivant un module premier, *Bull. Soc. Math. (France)* **6**, pp. 49–54.

Mackenzie, K. (1989). Codes of designs, Ph.D. Thesis (University of Birmingham).

MacWilliams, F. J., Mallows, C. L. and Sloane, N. J. A. (1972). Generalizations of Gleason's theorem on weight enumerators of self-dual codes, *IEEE Trans. Inform. Theory* **18**, pp. 794–805.

MacWilliams, F. J., Odlyzko, A. M., Sloane, N. J. A, and Ward, H. N. (1978). Self-dual codes over GF(4), *J. Combin. Theory Ser. A* **25**, 3, pp. 288–318.

MacWilliams, F. J. and Sloane, N. J. A. (1977). *The Theory of Error-Correcting Codes* (North-Holland, Amsterdam).

MacWilliams, F. J., Sloane, N. J. A. and Goethals J. M. (1972). The MacWilliams identities for nonlinear codes, *Bell Syst. Tech. J.* **51**, pp. 803–819.

Malevich, A. (2012). *Extremal self-dual codes*, Ph.D. Thesis (Otto-von-Guericke-University Magdeburg, Magdeburg).

Mallows, C. L., Pless, V. and Sloane, N. J. A. (1976). Self-dual codes over GF(3), *SIAM J. Applied Math.* **31**, 4, pp. 649–666.

Mallows, C. L. and Sloane, N. J. A. (1973). An upper bound for self-dual codes, *Inform. and Control* **22**, pp. 188–200.

Maruta, T. (1995). Optimal pseudo-cyclic codes and caps in PG$(3, q)$, *Geometriae Dedicata* **54**, pp. 263–266.

Maschietti, A. (1998). Difference sets and hyperovals, *Des. Codes Cryptogr.* **14**, pp. 89–98.

Mathon, R. (2002). New maximal arcs in Desarguesian planes, *J. Combin. Theory Ser. A* **97**, pp. 353–368.

McEliece, R. J. (1969). Quadratic forms over finite fields and second-order Reed-Muller codes, *JPL Space Program Summary* **37-58-III**, pp. 28–33.

McEliece, R. J. (1978). A public-key cryptosystem based on algebraic coding theory, *DSN Progress Report* **44**, pp. 114–116.

McFarland, R. L. and Rice, B. F. (1978). Translates and multipliers of abelian difference sets, *Proc. Amer. Math. Soc.* **68**, pp. 375–379.

McQuire, G. (1997). Quasi-symmetric designs and codes meeting the Grey-Rankin bound, *J. Combin. Theory Ser. A* **78**, pp. 280–291.

McQuire, G. and Ward, H. N. (1998). Characterisation of certain minimal rank designs, *J. Combin. Theory Ser. A* **83**, pp. 42–56.

Mesnager, S. (2016). *Bent functions: fundamentals and results* (Springer, Switzerland).

Mesnager, S., Tang, C. and Xiong, M. (2020). On the boomerang uniformity of quadratic permutations over $\mathbb{F}_{2^n}$, *Des. Codes Cryptogr.* **88**, pp. 2233–2246.

Morales, J. V. S. and Tanaka, H. (2018). An Assmus-Mattson theorem for codes over commutative association schemes, *Des. Codes Cryptogr.* **86**, pp. 1039–1062.

Muller, D. E. (1954). Application of boolean algebra to switching circuit design and to error detection, *IEEE Trans. Computers* **3**, pp. 6–12.

Myerson, G. (1981). Period polynomials and Gauss sums for finite fields, *Acta Arith.* **39**, pp. 251–264.

Neumaier, A. (1982). Regular sets and quasi-symmetric 2-designs, in *Combinatorial Theory*, Eds., Jungnickel, D. and Vedder, K. (Springer, Berlin), pp. 258–275.

Newhart, D. W. (1988). On minimum weight codewords in QR codes, *J. Combin. Theory Ser. A* **48**, pp. 104–119.

Niederreiter, H. and Xing, C. (2009). *Algebraic Geometry in Coding Theory and Cryptography* (Princeton University Press, New Jersey).

O'Keefe, C. M. (1996). Ovoids in PG$(3, q)$: a survey, *Disc. Math.* **151**, pp. 175–188.

Paige, L. J. (1956). A note on the Mathieu groups, *Canad. J. Math.* **9**, pp. 15–18.

Panella, G. (1955). Caratterizzazione delle quadriche di uno spazio (tridimensionale) lineare sopra un corpo finito, *Boll. Un. Mat. Ital. Ser. III* **10**, pp. 507–513.

Payne, S. E. (1985). A new infinite family of generalized quadrangles, *Congressus Numerantium* **49**, pp. 115–128.

Payne, S. E. (2007). *Topics in Finite Geometry: Ovals, Ovoids and Generalized Quadrangles* (University of Colorado, Denver).

Pless, V. (1968). On the uniqueness of the Golay code, *J. Combin. Theory Ser. A* **5**, pp. 213–228.

Pless, V. (1972). Symmetry codes over GF(3) and new 5-designs, *J. Combin. Theory Ser. A* **12**, pp. 119–142.

Pless, V. (1986). Q-codes, *J. Combin. Theory Ser. A* **43**, pp. 258–276.

Pless, V. (1993). Duadic codes and generalizations, in *Proc. of Eurocode 1992*, CISM Courses and Lectures No. 339, Eds., Camion, P., Charpin, P. and Harari, S. V. (Springer, Berlin), pp. 3–16.

Plotkin, M. (1960). Binary codes with specified minimum distances, *IRE Trans. Inform. Theory* **6**, pp. 445–450.

Pollack, P. (2009). *Not Always Buried Deep: A Second Course in Elementary Number Theory* (AMS Press, Providence).

Pott, A. (2016). Almost perfect and planar functions, *Des. Codes Cryptogr.* **78**, pp. 141–195.

Qvist, B. (1952). Some remarks concerning curves of the 2nd degree in a finite plane, *Ann. Acad. Sci. Fennica Ser. A* **134**, pp. 5–27.

Rains, E. M. (1998). Shadow bounds for self-dual codes, *IEEE Trans. Inform. Theory* **44**, 1, pp. 134–139.

Rains, E. M. (2003). New asymptotic bounds for self-dual codes and lattices, *IEEE Trans. Inform. Theory* **49**, 5, pp. 1261–1274.

Rains, E. M. and Sloane, N. J. A. (1998). Self-dual codes, in *Handbook of coding theory*, Eds., Pless, V. S. and Huffman, W. C. (North-Holland, Amsterdam), pp. 177–294 .

Reed, I. S. (1954). A class of multiple-error-correcting codes and the decoding scheme, *IRE Trans. Inform. Theory* **4**, pp. 38–49.

Reed, I. S. and Solomon, G. (1960). Polynomial codes over certain finite fields, *J. SIAM* **8**, pp. 300–304.

Reid, C. and Rosa, A. (2010). Steiner systems $S(2,4)$ – a survey, *The Electronic Journal of Combinatorics*, #DS18.

Rifà, J. and Zinoviev V. A. (2010). New completely regular q-ary codes based on Kronecker products, *IEEE Trans. Inform. Theory* **56**, pp. 266–272.

Roos, C. (1982). A generalization of the BCH bound for cyclic codes, including the Hartmann-Tzeng bound, *J. Combin. Theory Ser. A* **33**, pp. 229–232.

Roos, C. (1982). A new lower bound on the minimum distance of a cyclic code, *IEEE Trans. Inform. Theory* **29**, pp. 330–332.

Rothshild, B. L. and van Lint, J. H. (1974). Characterizing finite subspaces, *J. Combin. Theory Ser. A* **16**, pp. 97–110.

Rushanan, J. J. (1986). Generalized Q-codes, Ph.D. Thesis, California Institute of Technology, USA.

Schoof, R. (1995). Families of curves and weight distributions of codes, *Bull. Amer. Math. Soc.* **32**, pp. 171–183.

Schoof, R. and van der Vlugt, M. (1991). Hecke operators and the weight distribution of certain codes, *J. Comb. Theory Ser. A* **57**, pp. 163–186.

Segre, B. (1955). Ovals in a finite projective plane, *Canad. J. Math.* **7**, pp. 414–416.

Segre, B. (1957). Sui k-archi nei piani finiti di caratteristica 2, *Revue de Math. Pures Appl.* **2**, pp. 289–300.

Segre, B. (1962). Ovali e curvenei piani di Galois di caratteristica due, *Atti Accad. Naz. Lincei Rend.* **32**, pp. 785–790.

Segre, B. and Bartocci, U. (1971). Ovali ed alte curve nei piani di Galois di caratteristica due, *Acta Arith.* **18**, pp. 423–449.

Seiden, E. (1950). A theorem in finite projective geometry and an application to statistics,

Proc. Amer. Math. Soc. **1**, pp. 282–286.

Semakov, N. V., Zinovjev, V. A. and Zaitzev, G. V. (1973). Uniformly packed codes, *Problemy Peredachi Informatsii* **7**, pp. 38–50.

Shrikhande, M. S. (2007). Quasi-symmetric designs, in *Handbook of Combinatorial Designs, 2nd Edition* Eds., Colbourn, C. J. and Dinitz, J. H. (CRC Press, New York), pp. 578–582.

Shrikhande, M. S. and Sane, S. S. (1991). *Quasi-symmetric Designs* (Cambridge University Press, Cambridge).

Shult, E. and Surowski, D. (2015). *Algebra: A Teaching and Source Book* (Springer, Heidelberg).

Singleton, R. C. (1964). Maximum distance q-ary codes, *IEEE Trans. Inform. Theory* **10**, pp. 116–118.

Sloane, N. J. A. and Berlekamp, E. R. (1970). Weight enumerator for second-order Reed-Muller codes, *IEEE Trans. Inform. Theory* **16**, pp. 745–751.

Stichtenoth, H. (1993). *Algebraic Function Fields and Codes* (Springer, New York).

Storer, T. (1967). *Cyclotomy and Difference Sets* (Markham, Chicago).

Tanabe, K. (2000). An Assmus-Mattson theorem for $\mathbb{Z}_4$-codes, *IEEE Trans. Inform. Theory* **46**, pp. 48–53.

Tang, C. and Ding, C. (2021). C. An infinite family of linear codes supporting 4-designs, *IEEE Trans. Inform. Theory* **67**, 1, pp. 244–254.

Tang, C., Ding, C. and Xiong, M. (2019). Steiner systems $S(2,4,\frac{3^m-1}{2})$ and 2-designs from ternary linear codes of length $\frac{3^m-1}{2}$, *Des. Codes Cryptog.* **87**, pp. 2793–-2811.

Tang, C., Ding, C. and Xiong, M. (2020). Codes, differentially δ-uniform functions and *t*-designs, *IEEE Trans. Inform. Theory* **66**, pp. 3691–3703.

Thas, J. A. (1974). Construction of maximal arcs and partial geometries, *Geom. Dedicata* **3**, pp. 61–64.

Thas, J. A. (1980). Construction of maximal arcs and dual ovals in translation planes, *European J. Combin.* **1**, pp. 189–192.

Tits, J. (1960). Les groupes simples de Suzuki et de Ree, *Sém. Bourbaki* **210**, pp. 1–18.

Tokareva, N. (2011). On the number of bent functions from iterative constructions: lower bounds and hypotheses, *Advances in Mathematics of Communications* **5**, pp. 609–621.

Tonchev, V. D. (1993). Quasi-symmetric designs, codes, quadrics, and hyperplane sections, *Geometriae Dedicata* **48**, pp. 295–308.

Tonchev, V. D. (1996). The uniformly packed binary $[27,21,3]$ and $[35,29,3]$ codes. *Disc. Math.* **149**, pp. 283–288.

Tonchev, V. D. (1999). Linear perfect codes and a characterization of the classical designs, *Des. Codes Cryptogr.* **17**, pp. 121–128.

Tonchev, V. D. (2007). Codes, in *Handbook of Combinatorial Designs, 2nd Edition* Eds., Colbourn, C. J. and Dinitz, J. H. (CRC Press, New York), pp. 677–701.

Tsfasman, M. A. and Vladut, S. G. (1991). *Algebraic-geometric Codes* (Kluwer, Dordrecht).

Tze, T. W., Chanson, S., Ding, C., Helleseth, T. and Parker, M. (2003). Logarithm authentication codes, *Information and Computation* **184**, 1, pp. 93–108.

Van Lint, J. H. (1971). *Coding Theory*, Lecture Notes in Mathematics, Vol. 201, Chapter 5

(Springer-Verlag, Berlin).

Van Lint, J. H. (1973). A survey of perfect codes, *Rocky Mountain J. of Mathematics* **5**, 2, pp. 199–224.

Van Lint, J. H. (1992). *Introduction to Coding Theory, 2nd Edition* (Springer-Verlag, Heidelberg).

Van Lint, J. H. and Wilson, R. W. (1986). On the minimum distance of cyclic codes, *IEEE Trans. Inform. Theory* **32**, pp. 23–40.

Van Tilborg, H. C. A. (1976). Uniformly packed codes, Ph.D. Thesis.

Van Tilborg, H. C. A. (1980). On the uniqueness resp. nonexistence of certain codes meeting the Griesmer bound, *Inform. and Control* **44**, pp. 16–35.

Varshamov, R. R. (1957). Estimate of the number of signals in error correcting codes, *Dokl. Akad. Nauk SSSR* **117**, pp. 739–741.

Wang, Q. (2019). Steiner systems $S(2, 4, 2^m)$ for $m \equiv 2$ (mod 4) supported by a family of extended cyclic codes, arXiv:1904.02310.

Wang, R., Du, X. and Fan, C. (2021). Infinite families of 2-designs from a class of nonbinary Kasami cyclic codes, *Advances in Mathematics of Communications* **15**, 4, pp. 663–676.

Wang, R., Du, X., Fan, C. and Niu, Z. (2021). Infinite families of 2-designs from a class of linear codes related to Dembowski, *International Journal of Foundations of Computer Science* **32**, 3, pp. 253–267.

Ward, H. N. (1981). Divisible codes, *Archiv Math.* **36**, pp. 485–494.

Ward, H. N. (1998). Quadratic residue codes and divisibility, in *Handbook of Coding Theory*, Eds., Pless, V. S., Huffman, W. C. (Elsevier, Amsterdam), pp. 827–870.

Ward, H. N. (1999). An introduction to divisible codes, *Des. Codes Cryptogr.* **17**, pp. 73–79.

Wei, V. K. (1991). Generalized Hamming weights for linear codes, *IEEE Trans. Inform. Theory* **37**, pp. 1412–1418.

Weng, G., Feng, R., Qiu, W. (2007). On the ranks of bent functions, *Finite Fields Appl.* **13**, pp. 1096–1116.

Weng, G., Feng, R., Qiu, W., Zheng Z. (2008). The ranks of Maiorana-McFarland bent functions, *Sci. China Ser. A* **51**, pp. 1726–1731.

Wertheimer, M. A. (1990). Oval designs in quadrics, *Contemporary Mathematics* **111**, pp. 287–297.

Willems, W. (1999). *Codierungstheorie* (deGruyter, Berlin).

Witt, E. (1937). Über Steinersche Systeme, *Abh. Math. Sem. Hamburg* **12**, pp. 265–275.

Wolfmann, J. (1975). Codes projectifs à deux ou trois poids associés aux hyperquadriques d'une géométrie finie, *Discrete Math.* **13**, 2, pp. 185–211.

Wolfmann, J. (1989). New bounds on cyclic codes from algebraic curves, in *Proceedings of the third international colloquium on coding theory and applications*, Lecture Notes in Computer Science, Vol. 388, (Springer Verlag, Heidelberg), pp. 47–62.

Wolfmann, J. (1999). Bent functions and coding theory, in *Difference Sets, Sequences and their Correlation Properties*, Eds., Pott, A., Kumar, P. V., Helleseth, T., Jungnickel, D. (Kluwer, Amsterdam), pp. 393–417.

Xiang, C. (2016). It is indeed a fundamental construction of all linear codes, arXiv:1610.06355.

Xiang, C. (2021). Infinite families of t-designs from BCH codes, *Advances in Mathematics of Communications*, to appear.

Xiang, Q. (1999). Recent results on difference sets with classical parameters, in *Difference Sets, Sequences and their Correlation Properties*, Eds., A. Pott et al. (Kluwer), pp. 419–437.

Yan, H. (2018). A class of primitive BCH codes and their weight distribution, *Applicable Algebra in Engineering, Communication and Computing* **29**, 1, pp. 1–11.

Yan, Q. and Zhou, J. (2021). Infinite families of linear codes supporting more t-designs, arXiv:2106.10903v2 [cs.IT].

Yuan, J., Carlet, C. and Ding, C. (2006). The weight distribution of a class of linear codes from perfect nonlinear functions, *IEEE Trans. Inform. Theory* **52**, 2, pp. 712–717.

Yuan, J. and Ding, C. (2006). Secret sharing schemes from three classes of linear codes, *IEEE Trans. Inform. Theory* **52**, 1, pp. 206–212.

Zeng, X., Hu, L., Jiang, W., Yue, Q. and Cao, X. W. (2010). The weight distribution of a class of p-ary cyclic codes, *Finite Fields Appl.* **16**, 1, pp. 56–73.

Zeng, X., Li, N. and Hu, L. (2008). A class of nonbinary codes and sequence families, in *Sequences and Their Applications – SETA 2008, LNCS 5203*, Eds., Golomb, S. et al. (Springer Verlag, Berlin), pp. 81–94.

Zha, Z., Kyureghyan, G. and Wang, X. (2009). Perfect nonlinear binomials and their semi-fields, *Finite Fields Appl.* **15**, pp. 125–133.

Zha, Z. and Wang, X. (2009). New families of perfect nonlinear polynomial functions, *J. Algebra* **322**, 1, pp. 3912–3918.

Zha, Z. and Wang, X. (2011). Almost perfect nonlinear power functions in odd characteristic, *IEEE Trans. Inform. Theory* **57**, 7, pp. 4826–4832.

Zhang, S. (1999). On the nonexistence of extremal self-dual codes, *Discrete Appl. Math.* **91**, 1-3, pp. 277–286.

Zhou, Z. and Tang, X. (2011). Generalized modified Gold sequences, *Des. Codes Cryptogr.* **60**, 3, pp. 241–253.

Notation and Symbols

$AG(m, GF(q))$ — the affine space or affine geometry of dimension m.

A_i and $A_i^\perp$ — the number of codewords of Hamming weight i in a code C and its dual $C^\perp$, respectively.

$A_i(C)$ — the number of codewords in a code C.

$\mathrm{Aut}(C)$ — the automorphism group of a linear code C.

$\mathrm{Aut}(\mathbb{D})$ — the automorphism group of a design $\mathbb{D}$.

$\mathcal{B}_i(C)$ — the set of the supports of all codewords of Hamming weight i in a code C, which is a multiset in Chapter 16 and a simple set in other chapters.

C and $C^\perp$ — a linear code C and its dual code $C^\perp$.

$\overline{C}$ — the extended code of C.

$\tilde{C}$ — the augmented code of C.

C^T — the punctured code of a code C at the set T of coordinate positions.

C_T — the shortened code of a code C at the set T of coordinate positions.

$C|_{GF(q)}$ — the subfield subcode over $GF(q)$ of a code C over an extension field of $GF(q)$.

$C_{GF(q)}(\mathbb{D})$ — the linear code over $GF(q)$ spanned by the rows of the incidence matrix of an incidence structure $\mathbb{D}$.

$C_{(q,n,\delta,b)}$ — a BCH code over $GF(q)$ with length n and designed distance δ.

$\mathbf{c}^T$ — the transpose of the vector $\mathbf{c}$.

$d(C)$ — the minimum distance of a linear code C.

$\dim(C)$ — the dimension of a linear code or a linear subspace C.

$D_h(x, a)$ — the Dickson polynomial of the first kind.

$e(C)$ — the error-correcting capability of a code C, i.e., $\lfloor (d(C) - 1)/2 \rfloor$.

$E_h(x, a)$ — the Dickson polynomial of the second kind.

$\mathrm{GF}(q)$ — the finite field with q elements.

$\mathrm{GF}(q)^n$ — the set of all n-tuples over $\mathrm{GF}(q)$ or a vector space of dimension n over $\mathrm{GF}(q)$.

$\mathrm{GA}_m(\mathrm{GF}(q))$ — the general affine group.

$\mathrm{GL}_m(\mathrm{GF}(q))$ — the general linear group.

$\Gamma\mathrm{A}_m(\mathrm{GF}(q))$ — the semilinear affine group.

$\Gamma\mathrm{L}_m(\mathrm{GF}(q))$ — the general semilinear group.

$\mathcal{H}_{q,m}$ — the Hamming code.

$\mathbb{M}_\lambda(x)$ — the minimal polynomial over $\mathrm{GF}(q)$ of $\lambda \in \mathrm{GF}(q^m)$ for some q and m.

$\mathrm{MAut}(C)$ — the monomial automorphism group of a linear code C.

$\mathrm{N}_{q^m/q}$ — the norm function from $\mathrm{GF}(q^m)$ to $\mathrm{GF}(q)$.

$\mathcal{P}(C)$ — the set of all coordinate positions in a code C.

$\mathrm{PAut}(C)$ — the permutation automorphism group of a linear code C.

$\mathrm{PG}(m, \mathrm{GF}(q))$ — the projective space or projective geometry of dimension m.

$\mathrm{PGL}_m(\mathrm{GF}(q))$ — the projective general linear group.

$P_k(q, n; x)$ — the Krawtchouk polynomial.

$\mathrm{PSL}_m(\mathrm{GF}(q))$ — the projective special linear group.

$\mathrm{P}\Gamma\mathrm{L}_m(\mathrm{GF}(q))$ — the projective semilinear group.

$\mathrm{QRC}_i^{(n,q)}$ — a quadratic residue code over $\mathrm{GF}(q)$ with length n.

$\mathrm{rank}_p(\mathbb{D})$ — the p-rank of an incidence structure $\mathbb{D}$.

$\mathcal{R}_2(r, m)$ — the binary Reed-Muller code of length 2^m and order r.

$\mathcal{R}_q(r, m)$ — the generalised Reed-Muller code of length q^m and order r over $\mathrm{GF}(q)$.

$\mathcal{R}_q(r, m)^*$ — the punctured generalised Reed-Muller code of length $q^m - 1$ and order r over $\mathrm{GF}(q)$.

$\mathrm{SA}_m(\mathrm{GF}(q))$ — the special affine group.

$\mathrm{SL}_m(\mathrm{GF}(q))$ — the special linear group.

S_n or Sym_n — the symmetric group on a set of n symbols.

$\mathrm{Tr}_{q^m/q}$ — the trace function from $\mathrm{GF}(q^m)$ to $\mathrm{GF}(q)$.

$\mathrm{wt}(\mathbf{c})$ — the Hamming weight of a vector or codeword $\mathbf{c}$.

$\mathbb{Z}_n$ — the ring of integers modulo n.

$\Omega(q, m, h)$ — The Dilix code.

$\rho(C)$ — the covering radius of a code C.

$(\mathcal{P}, \mathcal{B}, \mathcal{R})$ — an incidence structure with point set $\mathcal{P}$, block set $\mathcal{B}$ and incidence relation $\mathcal{R}$.

$\binom{S}{t}$ — the set of all t-subsets of S.

$\sum_{i=0}^n A_i z^i$ — the weight enumerator of a linear code of length n.

$\sum_{i=0}^n A_i(C) z^i$ — the weight enumerator of a linear code C of length n.

Index

Printed in the United States
by Baker & Taylor Publisher Services

Printed in the United States
by Baker & Taylor Publisher Services